Tax Implications of Brexit

Tax Implications of Brexit

General Editor

Nicola Saccardo LLM

Partner, Maisto e Associati

With contributions by

Peter Adriaansen
Partner, Loyens & Loeff

Paolo Arginelli PhD, LLM
Of counsel, Maisto e Associati

Maria Inês Assis
Associated Partner, Abreu Advogados

Piotr Augustyniak LLM, MBA, TEP
Partner, PATH LLP

Nuno Cunha Barnabé
Partner, Abreu Advogados

Barbara Belgrano
Barrister, Pump Court Tax Chambers

Gabriele Colombaioni LLM
Associate, Maisto e Associati

Roderick Cordara QC
Essex Court Chambers, New Chambers, Sydney

Julian Ghosh QC
One Essex Court, Peterhouse, Cambridge and King's College, London

Bruno Gibert
Partner, CMS Francis Lefebvre Avocats

Amit Havenaar
Associate, Loyens & Loeff

Pál Jalsovszky LLM
Managing Partner, Jalsovszky

Erik Kastrop
Associate, Loyens & Loeff

Dr Christoph Klein
Tax Adviser, Flick Gocke Schaumburg

Marc Klerks
Partner, Loyens & Loeff

Pierre-Antoine Klethi
Senior Associate, Loyens & Loeff

Stephan Kraan
Associate, Loyens & Loeff

Timothy Lyons QC, BL
39 Essex Chambers

Jonas Lynghøj Madsen
Senior Attorney, Kromann Reumert

Dr Marcus Mick LLM
Partner, Flick Gocke Schaumburg

Helena Navrátilová
Tax Partner, Kocián Šolc Balaštík

Hannelore Niesten
Associate, Stibbe

Darragh Noone
Tax Associate, A&L Goodbody

Arne Møllin Ottosen
Partner, Kromann Reumert

Conor Quigley QC
Serle Court

Martin Segerström
Tax Adviser, EY

James Somerville
Tax Partner, A&L Goodbody

Kelly Stricklin-Coutinho
Barrister, 39 Essex Chambers

Ramón Tejada Fernández
Partner, Garrigues

Mario Tenore PhD, LLM
Associate, Maisto e Associati

Henk Verstraete LLM
Partner, Stibbe

Manuela Wenger MSc
Associate, Binder Grösswang

Lawrence Williams
Doctoral Candidate, Stockholm University and Tax Adviser, EY

Christian Wimpissinger LLM
Partner, Binder Grösswang

Bloomsbury Professional

LONDON • DUBLIN • EDINBURGH • NEW YORK • NEW DELHI • SYDNEY

BLOOMSBURY PROFESSIONAL
Bloomsbury Publishing Plc
50 Bedford Square, London, WC1B 3DP, UK
1385 Broadway, New York, NY 10018, USA
29 Earlsfort Terrace, Dublin 2, Ireland

BLOOMSBURY and the Diana logo are trademarks of Bloomsbury Publishing Plc

First published in Great Britain 2021

British Library Cataloguing-in-Publication Data

A catalogue record for this book is available from the British Library.

ISBN:	PB:	978-1-52651-680-0
ISBN:	Epub:	978-1-52651-681-7
ISBN:	Epdf:	978-1-52651-682-4

Typeset by Evolution Design & Digital Ltd (Kent)
Printed and bound by CPI Group (UK) Ltd, Croydon, CR0 4YY

MIX
Paper from responsible sources
FSC® C013604

To find out more about our authors and books visit www.bloomsburyprofessional.com. Here you will find extracts, author information, details of forthcoming events and the option to sign up for our newsletters

Preface

I am delighted to present this book, which deals with the tax ramifications from such a ground-breaking event: Brexit. I wish to express my deepest gratitude to all the authors that contributed to this book (particularly to those that took up the challenge to write on previously unexplored matters). It was my privilege to coordinate such an outstanding team of more than 30 leading experts, from both the UK and EU countries.

In particular, this book is meant to address the tax implications of Brexit, both in the UK and in the EU, following the end of the transition period. It is divided into two parts.

Part One includes four subject-specific chapters. In particular, the first chapter addresses the UK statutory regime, so far as it relates to EU law, after the exit of the UK from the European Union on 31 January 2020 and the expiry of the transition period. The second chapter focuses on the implications of Brexit on VAT, whilst the third chapter focuses on the implications of Brexit on customs and excise duties. Finally, chapter four provides for an analysis of the impact of state aid legislation on tax matters and of the related ramifications from Brexit.

Part Two comprises 16 country chapters dealing with the UK and 15 EU countries. Except for the UK, the chapters follow the same structure. They deal with UK-EU cross-border investments (both inbound and outbound), cross-border tax consolidation, as well as cross-border mergers, other reorganisations and transfers of residence. The structure of the UK country chapter is adapted to the peculiar position of the UK. Indeed, the first section of the UK chapter contains the topics addressed by the other country chapters in this book, by stating in brief terms the law as it currently is and, where possible, indications as to the likely future legislative changes. In the subsequent sections, the UK chapter deals with the UK position as a third country and with the impact of Brexit on tax disputes.

This book is available in both hard copy and online versions. Both the hard copy and online versions will be periodically updated to reflect future developments.

I am indebted to the team at Bloomsbury Professional, particularly Claire McDermott, for her continued brilliant assistance, Dave Wright and Jessica D'Alvarez, and to Claire Banyard for her support with the editing process.

Nicola Saccardo
London
13 March 2021

Authors

Nicola Saccardo is a partner of the Italian tax law firm Maisto e Associati and heads the London office of the firm. He graduated from Bocconi University in Milan and holds a LL.M. in international taxation from Leiden University (The Netherlands). He is an Italian lawyer (and chartered accountant) specialised in Italian tax law. Most of his practice has a cross-border nature, with a significant focus on inbound investments into Italy. He leads the EU tax law course of the Master of Laws (LL.M.) of the King's College in London. He has extensively written and spoken on Italian tax law matters.

Peter Adriaansen is partner in the international tax practice at Loyens & Loeff. He has a broad Luxembourg tax practice that includes advising fund managers, family offices and wealthy individuals, as well as financial institutions and other corporate clients. His work involves advising on complex cross-border restructurings, and regularly includes work with UK-based clients.

Paolo Arginelli (PhD and LLM at Leiden University) is Professor of EU Tax Law and Corporate Tax Law at Università Cattolica del Sacro Cuore in Italy. He is Adjunct Post-Doc Research Fellow at the IBFD (Amsterdam), as well as a member of the International Fiscal Association and a faculty member of the LLM programmes (International Taxation) of the Universities of Vienna, Leiden, Amsterdam and Lausanne. His main areas of expertise are international tax law, EU tax law, corporate and group taxation, financial and estate tax planning. He is the author of several articles in Italian and foreign tax journals and books, as well as of a monograph on tax treaty interpretation (published by IBFD). He usually participates as speaker to tax conferences both in Italy and abroad.

Maria Inês Assis is an Associate Partner in the tax team at Abreu Advogados. After concluding an LLM in international taxation from ITC, Leiden University, she specialised in international tax matters. Maria has considerable experience in cross-border investment taxation, M&A corporate taxation and family business restructures. She has been recognised as a rising star since 2019 as a subject matter expert on tax matters related to foreign investments in Portugal (taxation of non-resident companies and individuals) as well as Portuguese investments abroad.

Piotr Augustyniak is one of Poland's foremost internationally recognised private wealth law specialists. He is a founding partner of PATH LLP in

Warsaw and is also responsible for the day-to-day operations of PATH Family Office in Geneva. He holds an MA degree from the University of Warsaw (summa cum laude), an LLM degree from WU Vienna and an MBA degree from NYU, LSE and HEC Paris. His international expertise, combined with corporate and tax experience, makes him a market leader in cross-border matters, particularly those with a taxation and asset protection angle. He has been constantly recognised as a tier one private wealth lawyer by Chambers and Partners and Legal 500.

Nuno Barnabé is a senior partner at ABREU Advogados, at Portugal, where he co-heads the firm's tax practice. He is also a founding judge of the Portuguese tax arbitration court and in the beginning of his career was a lecturer at the economic legal sciences department of the Law Faculty of the University of Lisbon. He has 20 years' experience on international tax law and specialises in wealth taxation, advising HNWI's individuals, family offices, private banking and asset manager businesses in Portugal, Portuguese speaking countries and Switzerland (cross-border). Nuno is a member of the Society of Trust and Estate Practitioners (Central London branch) and of The International Academy of Estate and Trust Law.

Barbara Belgrano is a barrister specialising in all areas of revenue law at Pump Court Tax Chambers. She graduated with a BA in English and French Law from the University of Cambridge, Downing College (including a *Maîtrise en Droit* from University of Paris 2 Panthéon-Assas).

Barbara has a wide-ranging practice and regularly appears in the tax tribunals and higher courts.

Significant recent cases include: *Prudential Assurance Company Ltd v HMRC* [2019] AC 929 (Supreme Court; case concerning corporation tax, EU law and restitution); *RFC 2012 Plc (In Liquidation) (formerly Rangers Football Club Plc) v Advocate General for Scotland* [2017] 1 W.L.R. 2767 (Supreme Court; case concerning diversion of earnings, employee benefit trusts, PAYE and national insurance contributions); *R (on the application of Aozora GMAC Investment Ltd) v HMRC* [2019] EWCA Civ 1643 (Court of Appeal; case concerning judicial review and reliance on HMRC's published guidance); *Fisher v HMRC* [2020] UKUT 62 (TCC) (Upper Tribunal; case concerning the Transfer of Assets Abroad regime and EU law); *Centrica Overseas Holdings Ltd v Revenue and Customs Commissioners* [2020] UKFTT 197 (TC) (First-tier Tribunal; case concerning corporation tax deductions for expenses of management); *Hastings Insurance Services Ltd v HMRC* [2018] UKFTT 27 (TC) (First-tier Tribunal; case concerning VAT and the 'place of supply' rules).

Gabriele Colombaioni (LLM at Vienna Wirtschaftsuniversität) is senior associate at Maisto e Associati. His main areas of expertise are international tax law, EU tax law, estate and tax planning for high net worth individuals and corporate tax law. He has authored several articles in Italian and foreign tax journals.

Roderick Cordara, QC, SC is a leading indirect practitioner in the UK and Australia. He has chambers in London and Sydney, and has appeared in leading cases at the highest level in both jurisdictions, as well as the Court of Justice of the European Union. He has a particular interest in the relationship between indirect tax and financial services. Another focus of his is on tax restitution, where states ought to return overpaid tax. He also acts in the growing area of tax and investor state arbitration.

Tamás Fehér is a partner at Jalsovszky, a boutique law firm established in 2005, primarily focused on taxation. Tamás is an attorney and tax adviser and holds an LLM degree in International Tax Law from the WU in Vienna. Besides advising on tax matters, he regularly represents clients in court and he has also acted before the Court of Justice of the European Union on several occasions.

Julian Ghosh QC is a practising Barrister at One Essex Court, a Judge of the First-Tier Tribunal (Tax Chamber) and a Deputy Judge of the Upper Tribunal. He is a Bye-Fellow at Peterhouse, Cambridge (teaching Tax Law, Constitutional Law, Administrative Law and Contract).

Bruno Gibert is an attorney at law and a partner in CMS Francis Lefebvre Avocats since 2001. Before this, he worked with the French Tax Authorities for 16 years, in particular as Director of the International Division in charge of treaty negotiations and competent authority. He was, since its creation in 2002 and until 2019, Chair of the EU Joint Transfer Pricing Forum. He has been appointed by the French Authorities as an independent person of standing for the EU Arbitration Convention and for the Directive on Tax Dispute Resolution and has already been a member of consultative commissions. He chairs the IFA French Branch.

Amit Havenaar, tax adviser at Loyens & Loeff in London, is a member of the International Tax Services practice group and the M&A tax team. Amit specialises in cross-border transactions, reorganisations, private equity, and share based (real estate) acquisitions. He advises both Dutch and international clients, investment funds and corporate clients.

Pál Jalsovszky is managing partner at Jalsovszky, a medium-sized Hungarian law firm with key focus on taxation. Pál is a permanent contributor to *Világgazdaság*, the leading Hungarian business daily newspaper. Besides advising on tax matters, he is regularly involved in mergers and acquisitions and capital market matters as well.

Erik Kastrop, tax adviser at Loyens & Loeff in London, is a member of the Investment Management practice group. Erik specialises in European cross-border transactions and reorganisations, with a focus on the Benelux countries, Italy and the UK. He advises both Dutch and international clients, including investment funds, corporate clients and sovereign wealth funds.

Christoph Klein is an associate with Flick Gocke Schaumburg in Frankfurt, Germany. He is a certified tax adviser and holds a diploma in business administration. He specialises in domestic and international taxation and corporate tax law. His main activities focus on cross-border corporate structuring and financing transactions. He advises on a wide range of tax matters including financing, M&A transactions, the reorganisation process of companies and financial products. He can be contacted at christoph.klein@fgs.de.

Marc Klerks is a partner in Loyens & Loeff's International Tax Services practice group and heads the practice in their London office. From 1995 through to 1998, Marc worked at Loyens & Loeff's New York office and headed the London office from 2000 to 2006.

Marc practices in the area of tax law and has extensive experience advising clients on a broad range of complex corporate and commercial tax matters, with particular emphasis on private equity transactions, including investments, private and public company takeovers, public and private fund formation and restructurings, as well as other funds issues. He also assists clients on complex finance transactions and management incentive arrangements.

Pierre-Antoine Klethi is a senior tax associate at Loyens & Loeff Luxembourg. He advises predominantly fund managers in the alternative fund sector during the various stages of the lifecycle of their funds, and international corporate groups on a range of Luxembourg and EU tax matters. He was seconded to the London office of Loyens & Loeff in 2017–2018.

Stephan Kraan, tax adviser at Loyens & Loeff in Amsterdam, is a member of the Transfer Pricing & Economics Team and the International Tax Services practice group. Stephan advises a wide range of multinationals and private equity funds. His advice mainly focuses on matters of international (corporation) tax, the transfer pricing aspects of financial transactions, the allocation of risk between associated companies, and tax decision making and modelling.

Timothy Lyons QC 39 Essex Chambers, is a member of the Bars of England and Wales, Ireland and Brussels. His varied practice in EU and UK law has an emphasis on customs, tax, trade law and WTO matters. His clients include multi-national enterprises, high net wealth individuals and governments. He appears in a wide variety of courts and tribunals, including the CJEU. He is a regular lecturer throughout the EU, has written *EU Customs Law* (2018, 3rd edn, OUP) and is an assistant editor of the British Tax Review. He is an honorary visiting professor at City, University of London.

Jonas Lynghøj Madsen is an attorney and a senior member of Kromann Reumert's tax law group. He specialises in corporate and international tax matters. Jonas is the author of several articles on EU tax law and international taxation. He holds a law degree, University of Copenhagen (cand.jur. 2008) and a LL.M. in international tax, International Tax Center in Leiden, the Netherlands (2011).

Marcus Mick is a partner with Flick Gocke Schaumburg in Frankfurt, Germany. He is an attorney at law, certified tax advisor and received an LL.M. at Fordham University, New York City. He specialises in domestic and international taxation and corporate tax law. His main activities focus on cross-border corporate structuring and financing transactions. He advises on a wide range of tax matters, including financing, M&A transactions, the reorganisation process of companies and financial products. Marcus is a lecturer at the University of Frankfurt am Main; Who's Who in 2014–2020 for 'Corporate Tax in Germany'; 'Best Lawyers in Germany (Tax) 2019'. He can be contacted at marcus.mick@fgs.de.

Helena Navrátilová is a tax partner at Kocián Šolc Balaštík, advokátní kancelář, s.r.o. in Prague. She is a graduate of the University of Economics in Prague and has been a qualified tax consultant for more than 25 years. Helena advises on all corporate tax aspects of business transactions, including cross-border taxation and tax planning, personal income taxation, and tax procedures and controversy proceedings. She has been published widely in a range of foreign and domestic professional tax publications, as well as in domestic business magazines, and is an active member of the Czech Chamber of Tax Advisors' corporate taxation and cross-border taxation committees. Helena has been repeatedly recognised by Chambers & Partners as a Notable Practitioner for tax services and as a leading tax specialist for the Czech Republic by The International Who's Who of Corporate Tax Lawyers.

Hannelore Niesten is a tax associate at Stibbe. She assists clients in the corporate and private sector with regard to various tax matters with a focus on international and European tax law. Prior to joining Stibbe, she was a researcher at Hasselt University and Maastricht University and was awarded a PhD on 'Tax Benefits of Cross-Border Persons'. Hannelore was a Fulbright post-doctoral scholar at Georgetown Law School and Levin College of Law at the University of Florida. In parallel, she was a consultant in the poverty and equity global practice department of the World Bank in Washington DC.

Darragh Noone is an Associate in the Tax Department of A&L Goodbody Solicitors in Dublin. He is a solicitor and graduate of University College Dublin. He has previously participated on various industry association subcommittees of Irish Funds and IDSA. He currently sits on the Irish Funds FATCA and CRS working group.

Arne Møllin Ottosen is head of Kromann Reumert's tax law group and specialises in business taxation advisory work and tax litigation. He is widely recognised as one of the most outstanding tax lawyers in Denmark and internationally and is top-rated in Chambers and Legal 500 and inducted into the Legal 500 Hall of Fame. Arne is a member of the Danish Supreme Court Bar and has conducted numerous landmark tax law cases. He holds a

Law degree, Aarhus University (cand.jur. 1993) and a LL.M., King's College, University of London (1999).

Conor Quigley QC specialises in EU law, in particular state aid law, with a noted interest in the interaction of state aid and taxation which now forms the subject matter of the major part of his professional practice. He is the author of the leading textbook, *EU State Aid Law and Policy*, 3rd edn (Hart/Bloomsbury, 2015), and has written and lectured widely on fiscal state aid issues. For several years, he has been a Visiting Research Fellow at the Institute for European and Comparative Law, University of Oxford.

Martin Segerström is a tax lawyer at Ernst & Young AB. He focuses on tax controversy, in particular within the international tax area. He represents clients at all levels of the Swedish administrative courts, including the Supreme Administrative Court. He also regularly assists multinational enterprises during tax audits and in relation to Mutual Agreement Procedures and Advance Pricing Agreements. Prior to joining EY in 2011, Martin clerked at the Administrative Court in Stockholm. He has published a number of articles in Swedish tax journals commenting on procedural matters and international tax law. He has a Master of Law from Stockholm University.

James Somerville is a tax partner in A&L Goodbody Solicitors in Dublin. He is a solicitor and chartered tax adviser and a graduate of Trinity College Dublin. He has previously chaired the Irish Law Society's tax committee, and the Foreign Lawyers Forum of the ABA Tax Section. He currently sits on TALC, the main liaison body between practitioners and the Irish Revenue Commissioners.

Kelly Stricklin-Coutinho is a practicing Barrister at 39 Essex Chambers and is qualified in England and Wales (2006), and in Ireland (2020). Her practice includes tax disputes and advice in respect of EU and International Tax Law, and domestic tax matters in the UK. She is a Visiting Lecturer at the Centre for European Law at King's College London. She is ranked in the Legal 500 and in Chambers and Partners.

Ramón Tejada Fernández is a partner in the Tax Department of Garrigues and is head of one of the tax practice groups in Madrid. He has been a member of Madrid Bar Association since 1993. He is joint nationwide head of Garrigues' 'Banks and Savings Banks' multidisciplinary group.

He is an expert in, inter alia, the taxation of financial institutions and insurance companies, as well as in all tax aspects relating to capital markets and financial products. He has been named as one of Spain's standout tax lawyers in various national and international directories such as Chambers, Legal 500, Martindale, International Who's Who of Corporate Tax Lawyers and Best Lawyers.

Mario Tenore is senior associate at Maisto e Associati. He holds a PHD in tax law and obtained an LL.M. degree in International Tax Law from the University of Leiden, The Netherlands. His main areas of expertise are corporate taxation, European and international tax law, state aids as well as taxation of artists and sportspersons. He is a member of the International Fiscal Association and a faculty member of the LL.M. programmes (International Taxation) of the Universities of Amsterdam and Lausanne. He is also the author of several publications in the field of international and European tax law and is regularly invited as speaker at international tax conferences.

Henk Verstraete is a tax partner at Stibbe. He has over 20 years of experience in tax matters, including tax litigation. He assists clients in various sectors on a range of tax matters, including international tax, corporate mergers and acquisitions, fund structuring, and financing transactions. In addition, Henk is a part-time professor in tax law at the University of Leuven (KU Leuven) and at the Fiscale Hogeschool Brussel (Brussels Tax School). He is also a member of the Tax Practice Council of the International Tax Program at NYU School of Law. He regularly publishes on tax matters, speaks at various tax seminars and is the editor of Tijdschrift Beleggingsfiscaliteit/Revue Fiscalité des Placements. Henk is ranked in Legal 500, Who's Who Legal 100, Chambers Europe and Expert Guides.

Manuela Wenger is an associate of Binder Grösswang focusing on corporate income tax law, international tax law, tax procedures, and tax criminal law. Manuela studied Business Law as well as Management and Economics at the University of Innsbruck. She received her master's degree in Accounting, Auditing and Taxation and did an exchange semester at the Stockholm University.

Lawrence Williams is an Assistant Manager within the International Tax and Transaction Services department at EY Stockholm, focusing mainly on transfer pricing matters. In combination with working at EY, he is a PhD research candidate situated at Stockholm University through funding from the Torsten Söderbergs Foundation. His research focuses on the areas of transfer pricing and international trade law, specifically the World Trade Organization Agreement. Lawrence also teaches Swedish tax law and international tax law at Stockholm University. Lawrence studied Law with European Legal Systems (LLB) at the University of East Anglia and holds a Masters in International Tax Law and European Tax Law from Uppsala University in Sweden.

Christian Wimpissinger is a partner of Binder Grösswang with a focus on international taxation, corporate income tax law, and accounting law. Christian is an adjunct faculty member of the Graduate Tax Program at the University of Miami Law School and an officer of the IBA's Taxes Committee.

Contents

Table of Statutes

[All references are to paragraph number.]

Table of Statutory Instruments

[All references are to paragraph number.]

Table of EU legislation and other guidance

[All references are to paragraph number.]

Table of Cases

[All references are to paragraph number.]

F

M

N

O

P

R

U

V

W

Part 1

General

Chapter 1

EU Law in the United Kingdom Post-31 December 2020: The Statutory Regime

Julian Ghosh QC[1]

1.1 This chapter sets out the statutory regime (there are in fact three: see below), relating to EU law, after the exit of the United Kingdom from the European Union (EU) on 31 January 2020[2] and the expiry of the 'implementation period' provided in the *European Union (Withdrawal Agreement) Act 2020* (*EUWAA 2020*), as enacted in the *European Union (Withdrawal) Act 2018* (*EUWA 2018*), *ss 1A* and *1B*. The observations made here raise points of general principle and will be revisited in the context of specific areas in the chapters which follow.[3]

1 I am indebted to Professor Michel Dougan, University of Liverpool for his helpful comments on a draft of this chapter and to Laura Ruxandu, Barrister, for having read the draft. I am also very grateful to Professor Catherine Barnard, of Trinity College, Cambridge for extremely valuable discussions on the issue of continuing supremacy of retained EU law (see below), following a talk I delivered at the Centre of European Law Studies, University of Cambridge, on 3 February 2021. I am further privileged to have discussed aspects of this paper with Professor Marise Cremona, Professor of European Law, European University Institute, Florence and Professor Paul Craig, Professor of English Law, St John's College, Oxford. Inevitably, there are issues on which we agreed and other issues on which we disagreed. Errors are unintended and would be mine.

2 'Brexit'.

3 The United Kingdom is also leaving the European Atomic Energy Community (Euratom) and the European Economic Area (EEA). Furthermore, the United Kingdom's leaving the EU terminates the United Kingdom's participation in the Agreement on the Free Movement of Persons (AFMP) between the EU and Switzerland. In addition to the EU-United Kingdom Withdrawal Agreement, discussed below, the United Kingdom has also concluded the EEA-EFTA Agreement and the Switzerland Citizens' Rights Agreement to accommodate reciprocal rights and obligations upon the United Kingdom's exit from the EU. The Withdrawal Agreement, the EEA-EFTA Agreement and the Switzerland Citizens' Rights Agreement are, collectively, known in the *EUWA 2018* as 'relevant separation agreement law': *s 7C(3)*. The United Kingdom statutory regime discussed below, to apply upon the expiry of the 'implementation period' which eases the United Kingdom's EU exit, adopts provisions analogous to those discussed here in relation to the regime for EU law to reflect both the EEA-EFTA Agreement and the Switzerland Citizens' Rights Agreement. This chapter deals only with the relevant EU provisions in the statutory provisions which implement the Withdrawal Agreement and establish a regime to assimilate EU law into United Kingdom domestic law,

1.1 *EU Law in the UK Post-31 December 2020: The Statutory Regime*

There are three distinct post-Brexit regimes: (1) the Withdrawal Agreement, (2) 'retained EU law', and (3) the free trade agreement comprised in the EU-United Kingdom Trade and Cooperation Agreement (TCA).

The Withdrawal Agreement (enacted into United Kingdom domestic law by a combination of the *EUWAA 2020* and the *EUWA 2018*) deals with the rights of EU nationals in the United Kingdom and United Kingdom nationals in EU Member States; the framework of 'retained EU law' (also enacted by the *EUWA 2018*[4]) aspires to establish a static framework of law which allows EU law to continue to apply in the United Kingdom, post-31 December 2020,[5] in the state and manner that EU law stood as at 11.00 on that date (subject to certain important modifications) and the TCA, introduced into United Kingdom law by the *European Union (Future Relationship) Act 2020* (*FRA 2020*), establishes a free trade regime which applies[6] from 1 January 2021 (which is of a very different nature to both EU law, as it applied re-Brexit and retained EU law).

It is as well to note at the outset that both the *EUWA 2018*, at least as regards retained EU law and the TCA (and indeed the *FRA 2020*), are highly problematic, in relation to certain fundamental issues. Perhaps this is inevitable in the context of a highly charged political and legal context of a Member State leaving the EU but the result is that the United Kingdom courts and tribunals will have to grapple with major points of uncertainty on the application of *EUWA 2018*, the TCA and the *FRA 2020* as from 1 January 2021. It equally follows that many of the points raised below and any tentative conclusions offered, will be necessarily overtaken by subsequent legislative clarification and United Kingdom case law. The limited ambition of this chapter is to offer a framework for that subsequent clarification to take place. Devolution issues (of which there are many) are not dealt with in this chapter at all.

This chapter has the following structure: Part 1 deals with the Withdrawal Agreement and retained EU law (both are encompassed in the *EUWA 2018*). Part 2 deals with the TCA and the *FRA 2020*.

---

with only brief passing reference to the EEA-EFTA Agreement and the Swiss Citizens' Rights Agreement. Further, provisions in the statutory regime specific to the devolved Parliaments and Assemblies are not dealt with here.

4 Inevitably, there are other Brexit-related statutes, with specific application, which are not relevant here: see, for example, the *Taxation (Post-Transition Period) Act 2020*, which relates to VAT and duties in Northern Ireland and the application of the Northern Ireland Protocol, overseas online sales and VAT, Insurance Premium Tax and specific provisions permitting HMRC to recover corporation tax from beneficiaries of illegal state aid in relation to controlled foreign companies.

5 'IP completion day': *EUWA 2018, s 1A(6)*. This latter term and the date of 31 December 2020 shall be used interchangeably in this chapter.

6 Provisionally, subject to ratification by the EU Member States: see below.

PART 1: THE WITHDRAWAL AGREEMENT AND RETAINED EU LAW

1.2

- Section I deals with the United Kingdom's membership of the EU and the sources of EU law. The *EUWA 2018* (and indeed the *EUWAA 2020*) is impossible to understand without a complete knowledge of EU law. Thus a summary of EU law is necessary to understand how and to what extent EU law is retained in United Kingdom law after the United Kingdom's exit on 31 January 2020 and the expiry of the 'implementation period' on 31 December 2020, particularly as different types of 'retained EU law' are treated in different ways.
- Section II sets out the mechanism by which EU law was incorporated into United Kingdom domestic law. Again, the dualist character of the United Kingdom's constitution as regards international law is critical background to understand the legislative regime put in place once United Kingdom EU membership ended.
- Section III sets out the terms of the EU-United Kingdom Withdrawal Agreement, which explains the substantive terms of category of EU rights protected after the United Kingdom's exit from the EU.
- Section IV sets out the United Kingdom's domestic implementation of the Withdrawal Agreement.
- Section V analyses the United Kingdom's preservation of EU law after the United Kingdom's exit from the EU on 31 January 2020 and the expiry of the implementation period on 31 December 2020. It is this analysis which must be set against the background of Sections I–IV. Put short, this legislative regime seeks to 'freeze' EU law as it stands at 31 December 2020 ('retained EU law') and apply this 'frozen' EU law as United Kingdom domestic law (in diluted form, especially in relation to supremacy and the application of general principles of EU law). The regime is highly problematic in principle and will, it is feared, lead to enormous uncertainty in practice.
- Section VI is a brief conclusion on retained EU law.

I. The United Kingdom's membership of the European Union: EU law in the United Kingdom 1 January 1973–31 January 2020

1.3 It is both an instructive and salutary observation that neither the statutory regime which applies in the United Kingdom, as from 31 January 2020 during the 'implementation period', nor the regime which applies (subject to subsequent modification by Parliament) indefinitely from 31 December

2020, can be understood without a prior knowledge of EU law. Instructive because it shows the depth to which EU law had become embedded into the domestic law of the United Kingdom. Salutary because it demonstrates the virtual impossibility of drafting a statutory regime which can function intelligibly in all of the areas previously occupied by EU law, without recourse to EU law itself. Thus the analysis of the United Kingdom regime which accommodates EU law, post-31 January 2020, must be necessarily preceded with a (brief) summary of the substantive nature of EU law, as it applied to the United Kingdom prior to its leaving the EU.

The United Kingdom became a member of the European Economic Community (EEC), which became the EU, on 1 January 1973. Following a referendum on 23 June 2016, in which 52% of the United Kingdom's population voted to leave the EU, the *EU (Notification of Withdrawal) Act 2017* (*EUNWA 2017*) was passed,[7] under which Theresa May, the United Kingdom Prime Minister, notified the EU of the United Kingdom's decision to leave, under Article 50 of the Consolidated Version of the Treaty on European Union (TEU).

After three extensions to the two-year period specified in Article 50 for a Member State to leave the EU,[8] the United Kingdom left the EU on 31 January

7 The decision of the majority of the United Kingdom Supreme Court in *R (Miller) v Secretary of State for Exiting the European Union, In Re McCord (Lord Advocate and others intervening), In Re Agnew (Lord Advocate and others intervening)* [2017] UKSC 5 (*Miller*) held that the Royal Prerogative could not be used to effect a notification under Article 50 TEU. The prerogative cannot be used, either to frustrate the objectives of an act of Parliament, or to defeat domestic rights [51], [56]. The Prerogative to engage on the international plane and conclude treaties could not be used to make a notification under Article 50 TEU, for two reasons. First, EU law conferred domestic rights and obligations, so far as the United Kingdom is concerned, which meant that the Prerogative could not be used by the Executive to make an Article 50 notification, which would have a fundamental effect on these domestic rights and obligations: [86]. This was a sufficient reason (although not expressly recognised as such by the Supreme Court) to prevent the use of the Prerogative under Article 50: see further below. Secondly, and, seemingly, separately, the Supreme Court held, effectively as a matter of statutory construction of the *ECA 1972*, that the fundamental constitutional effect of the *ECA 1972* (giving the *ECA 1972* the status of a 'constitutional Act' [67]) of the United Kingdom becoming a member of the EU (and leaving the EU) meant that Parliament must have intended that the United Kingdom could only be committed to leaving the EU with Parliamentary approval [81], [85]–[93]. A contrary view would have the startling result that the Executive could commit to the United Kingdom leaving the EU, in the absence of any referendum at all: [91]. *Miller* was decided on the basis that notification under Article 50 TEU was irrevocable [26], which basis turned out to be mistaken (*Wightman v Secretary of State for Exiting the European Union* (Case C-621/18), [37]–[75]) but this mistake played no part in either the reasoning or conclusions of the United Kingdom Supreme Court.

8 The first extension was agreed between the United Kingdom and the EU on 21 March 2019. The second extension deferred the United Kingdom's exit from the EU until 1 June 2019, if the United Kingdom failed to hold EU Parliament elections, or 31 October 2019 if such elections were held. The third and final extension deferred exit until 31 January 2020. The *EU (Withdrawal) Act 2019* (the so-called '*Cooper Act*') and the *EU (Withdrawal) (No 2) Act 2019* (the so-called '*Benn Act*') required the United Kingdom government to seek the second and third extensions (the former was passed after the then Prime Minister, Theresa May,

2020 (exit day),[9] subject to an 'implementation period', which expired on 31 December 2020,[10] during which 'implementation period' EU law applied to the United Kingdom in, broadly, its full pre-31 January 2020 form. The United Kingdom and the EU concluded a 'Withdrawal Agreement', summarised below, under Article 50 TEU, giving rise to reciprocal binding legal obligations, implemented in the United Kingdom by a combination of the *EUWA 2018* and the *EUWAA 2020.*

Sources of EU law

1.4 Member States of the EU, by the time of the United Kingdom's exit, were signatories to two treaties, the TEU and the Consolidated Version of the Treaty for the Functioning of the European Union (TFEU).[11] Article 1 TEU had an express objective of '... creating an ever closer union among the peoples of Europe ...'. The objectives of the EU ranged from general objectives (for example, the promotion of 'peace, [the EU's] values and the well-being of [the EU's] peoples' (Article 3.1 TEU) and the principle of 'the equality of ... citizens' (Article 9 TEU), to specific economic objectives, in

had already requested the second extension). Both were repealed by the *EU (Withdrawal Agreement) Act 2020, s 36(e), (f).*

9 *EUWA 2018, s 20(1).*

10 'IP completion day', (that is, the date on which the 'implementation period' to ease the consequences of the United Kingdom's leaving the EU expired).

11 This is a simplistic account. According to J-C Piris's account, there were three basic Treaties (EC, TEU and Euratom) with a total of 36 Protocols (of the same legal value as the Treaties to which they are attached), nine amending or supplementary Treaties and six accession Treaties (18 treaties not counting Protocols) all with provisions in force: Jean-Claude Piris, *The Constitution for Europe: A Legal Analysis* (Cambridge University Press, 2006) 57. Anything approaching a full description of the EU institutions responsible for the governance of the EU is outside the scope of this chapter. Put short, the EU institutions comprise the European Parliament, the European Council (comprising the heads of state of each Member State), the Council (which, jointly with the European Parliament, exercises legislative and budgetary functions), the European Commission (which comprises the executive arm of the EU but also has legislative responsibilities, in that EU legislative acts may only be adopted on the basis of a proposal by the European Commission), the Court of Justice of the European Union (CJEU), the European Central Bank and the Court of Auditors: Articles 13–19 TEU, Title I TFEU. The EU had 'exclusive competence' in relation to the customs union, internal market competition rules, Euro-Member State monetary policy, the common fisheries policy, the common commercial policy and importantly, for the conclusion of international agreements where the TEU/TFEU provides for such in a legislative act of the EU, or, where this is necessary to 'enable the EU to exercise its internal competence', or where an international agreement would materially affect the 'common rules': Article 3.1, 3.2 TFEU; the EU and Member States had 'shared competence' on the internal market, social policy, economic, social and territorial cohesion, agricultural and fisheries, environment, consumer protection, transport, trans-European networks, energy, areas of freedom, security and justice, common safety concerns and public health matters: Article 4.1, 4.2 TFEU. All other areas remained within the exclusive competence of Member States: Article 4.1 TEU.

particular, the establishment of an 'internal market' (Article 3.3 TEU[12]), which provided for the free movement, within the EU, without restriction, of the factors of production (goods,[13] workers [employees],[14] natural and legal [self-employed] persons ('the freedom of establishment'),[15] the provision of services[16] and capital and payments[17]). The internal market provisions have had a fundamental impact on United Kingdom domestic law, including such matters as immigration and border control,[18] direct taxation[19] and pensions law.[20] Specific taxation measures established a common customs union and prohibited the imposition of customs duties on imports and exports (or charges with equivalent effect) amongst Member States[21] and prohibited discriminatory internal product taxation.[22] And established the regime for Value Added Tax. It is also convenient to note, at this stage, Article 4.3 TEU, which tasks both the EU and each Member State to '... assist each other in carrying out tasks which flow from the [TEU/TFEU]' (the 'loyalty clause', imposing the reflexive 'duty of sincere cooperation' between the EU and Member States).

All of the provisions mentioned here are important in understanding the statutory regime put in place by the United Kingdom to accommodate the United Kingdom leaving the EU.

Specific types of EU law

1.5 The rights and obligations of Member States (and their respective citizens), arose under EU law by way of:

---

12 These provisions applied in a very particular way, namely: (1) the establishment of a breach of one or more of these internal market provisions by a Member State, (2) the Member State seeking to establish a justification for any breach, either by reference to express provisions in the TFEU, or by an appeal to an open-ended category of 'implied' justifications, (mandatory requirements) established by the CJEU in *Rewe v Bundesmonopolverwaltung fur Branntwein* ('*Cassis de Dijon*') (Case 120/78) [8] and (3) even if a Member State could establish a prima facie justification, whether the Member State action which breached the relevant internal market provision was proportionate (that is, only went up to what was necessary to achieve the justified objective and no further): see eg *Futura Participations SA and Singer v Administration des contributions* (Case C-250/95), [24]–[43] of the CJEU judgment.

13 Articles 34–37 TFEU.

14 Articles 45–48 TFEU.

15 Articles 49–55 TFEU.

16 Articles 56–62 TFEU.

17 Articles 63–66 TFEU.

18 *Carpenter v Secretary of State for the Home Department* (Case C-60/00).

19 *Cadbury Schweppes plc v IRC* (Case C-196/04).

20 *Marshall v Southampton and South West Hampshire Area Health Authority* (Case 152/84).

21 Articles 30–33 TFEU.

22 Article 110 TFEU.

The TEU and TFEU themselves ('principle of direct effect')

1.6 Those provisions not only conferred legislative and budgetary functions and powers on EU institutions (and jurisdiction on judicial bodies) and rights and obligations on Member States, but in so far as these Treaty provisions revealed an intention to confer rights of individuals which were clear, unconditional and precise ('self-executing') had a substantive legal effect, both for EU institutions and within Member States, whether or not a Member State had correctly implemented these provisions, or, indeed, implemented them at all.[23] Critically, directly applicable provisions of the TEU/TFEU locate rights not only in Member States, as against institutions of the EU, or vice versa, or in Member States' citizens as against their own or other Member States ('vertical effect') but also locate rights in Member States' citizens as against each other (''horizontal effect'). So a Latvian company successfully pleaded its rights under Article 56 TFEU (right to provide cross-border services, from Latvia to Sweden) as overriding the right to take collective action by a Swedish trade union.[24]

The Charter of Fundamental Rights

1.7 By the time the United Kingdom had left the EU, Article 6.1 TEU incorporated the EU Charter of Fundamental Rights[25] and expressly gave the Charter the same legal value as the TEU and TFEU. The description of the Charter of Fundamental Rights as a mere codification of existing general principles of EU law in the Explanatory Notes to *EUWA 2018*[26] is controversial.[27] The relationship of the Charter to general principles of EU law is important, since, as discussed below, the Charter of Fundamental Rights

23 *Van Gend en Loos v Nederlandse Administratie der Belastingen* (Case 26/62) ('*Van Gend en Loos*').

24 *Laval* (Case C-341/05); see also *Viking* (Case C-438/05).

25 The Charter incorporates, in six 'titles', six fundamental values: dignity, freedom, equality, solidarity, citizens' rights and justice; the Charter itself contains provisions which set out the scope of the Charter and articulate legitimate grounds of qualifications to Charter rights (as well as the Charter's perception of its relationship with other national and international instruments).

26 [106], [107].

27 The substantive scope and application of the six 'titles' is founded upon and 'explained' by reference to the case law of the CJEU which acknowledged the embedding of fundamental rights in the case law of the general EU principles (see Explanations relating to the Charter of Fundamental Rights OJ [2007] C303/02), to which the CJEU must give 'due regard': Article 6(2) TEU) but the Charter also incorporates rights from elsewhere, such as the TEU/TFEU and the European Convention of Human Rights, which are to inform the interpretation of Charter rights: See Article 52(2), (3) of the Charter. Thus, it is not the case that the exclusion of the Charter has no substantive effect at all in relation to the retention of the EU's protection of fundamental rights (indeed if this were so, it is to be wondered what the point of the exclusion is). Even though the United Kingdom continues, after exit from the EU, to be a signatory to the Council if Europe and a signatory to the ECHR, the interpretation of Charter rights informed by the ECHR is, of course, a different juristic exercise to the application of ECHR rights (whether simpliciter or via the *Human Rights Act 1998*).

has no application to United Kingdom domestic law after 31 December 2020 (subject to transitional provisions), whereas general principles (which include fundamental rights guaranteed by the ECHR) continue to apply, albeit in diluted form (see below).

Regulations

1.8 Article 288 TFEU provides that a regulation has general application, binding in its entirety and directly applicable in all Member States.

Directives

1.9 Article 288 TFEU provides that a Directive is binding 'as to the result to be achieved' upon Member States but is to be implemented (by way of domestic legislation) by Member States. So, for example, the Principal VAT Directive is implemented by the *Value Added Tax Act 1994*. However, particular provisions of Directives are also subject to the principle of direct effect, even if unimplemented or misimplemented, if the provisions are 'clear, precise and unconditional',[28] but only with a vertical effect.[29]

Decisions

1.10 Article 288 TFEU provides that decisions by the European Commission, broadly on state aid and competition law matters), are binding on addressees (whether specific persons, or Member States).

General principles of EU law

1.11 These are substantive principles, which are members of an open-ended class. General principles have been gleaned from the TEU/TFEU by the CJEU and articulated as principles of law which are inherent in the TEU/TFEU and apply independently and irrespective of the particular text of any provision of the TEU/TFEU/a Regulation/a Directive. General principles may apply both vertically, against a Member State[30] or an EU institution[31]

28 *Van Duyn v Home Office* (Case 41/74) [12]; Member States cannot rely on direct effect to cure failure to implement a Directive, or misimplementation: *Pubblico Ministero v Tullio Ratti* (Case 148/78) [23].

29 *Faccini Dori v Recreb Srl* (Case C-91/92).

30 *R v Secretary of State for transport, ex p Factortame* (Case C-213/89) (the general principle of effectiveness, requiring that EU rights must not be impossible or excessively difficult to enforce, requires domestic provisions of a national legal system which impedes the application of that general principle to be set aside, here permitting, for the first time, the possibility of an injunction against the Crown).

31 So a Regulation which compelled the purchase of skimmed milk, in order to alleviate the overproduction of skimmed milk was held to be disproportionate and void *Bela Muhle* (Case 114/76).

and horizontally, for example, by an employee against an employer.[32] The methodology by which a general principle may be identified were set out by the Advocate General in *Dominguez*,[33] namely that the putative general principle must have: (1) found expression in many rules of primary law and in secondary EU law, and (2) found such expression in an unconditional and precise manner. Certain general principles have been codified. So the principle of 'conferral' (no EU institution may legislate beyond its express powers) is articulated in Article 5.1, 5.2 TEU. The principle of subsidiarity (the EU should only legislate if and insofar as the objectives of the proposed action cannot be sufficiently achieved by Member States) is set out at Article 5.3 TEU and the principle of proportionality (EU action should not exceed what is necessary to achieve TEU/TFEU objectives) is set out at Article 5.4 TEU.[34] Other general principles acknowledged in the CJEU case law include the principle of non-discrimination (which is now included in a more general principle of a right to equal treatment[35]), the principle of effectiveness (so that EU rights should not be made impossible or excessively difficult to enforce),[36] the principle of equivalence (EU rights to be given equal protection to domestic rights, within Member States),[37] legitimate expectation and legal certainty.[38] Certain principles have an uncertain status. For example, the principle of 'mutual recognition' (something lawful in one Member State is presumptively lawful in another, particularly in the context of the internal market provisions)[39] is seemingly distinct from the principle of non-discrimination and has, on more than one occasion, been described as a 'general principle' by the CJEU but not always acknowledged as such.[40] Furthermore, general principles do not always locate or protect rights in the hands of Member State citizens, against either EU institutions, or Member States but rather vice versa. So, for example, the general principle of 'abuse of law' (or 'abuse of right') permits the redefinition of actions, and transactions, of persons where those actions/transactions manipulate the provisions of EU law (of whatever description), so as to give

32 *Mangold v Rudiger Helm* (Case C-144/04); *Kucukdeveci v Swedex GmBh & Co* (Case C-555/07): in both cases the employee successfully pleaded the application of the general principle of equal treatment, prohibiting age discrimination against their respective employers.

33 Case C-282/10, [99] and [135], which was not quarrelled with by the CJEU.

34 Article 5.4 TEU codifies previous case law. The principle of proportionality also applies, as observed above, to control Member States' justification of a breach of the internal market provisions.

35 So persons in similar circumstances should not be treated differently, to the disadvantage of one, or treated the same, to the disadvantage of one, if in different circumstances, which prohibition extends to nationality discrimination, discrimination on grounds of gender and on grounds of age: the principle was thus expressed early on in the CJEU case law: *Ruckdeschel v Hauptzollamt Hamburg-St Annen* (Cases 117/76 and 16/77).

36 See above.

37 *San Giorgio* (Case 199/82), [12]; *Edis* (Case 231/98), [36] and [37].

38 See K Lenaerts and T Corthaut, 'Judicial Review and a Contribution to the Development of European Constitutionalism' (2002) 22 *YBEL* 1.

39 *Cassis de Dijon*, supra n 12.

40 See J Ghosh, 'Tax Law and the Internal Market: A Critique of the Principle of Mutual Recognition'(2014) *CYELS* 189.

rise to an unintended consequence. So to locate a subsidiary company in a low tax Member State, without truly exercising the rights of establishment by way of having relevant staff, premises and sufficient economic resources to truly locate any profit in that low tax Member State is to 'abuse' the right of establishment in Article 49 TFEU, which would permit a Member State to impose its own (higher) taxes on that subsidiary.[41] The treatment of general principles in the post-31 January 2020/31 December 2020 statutory regime in the United Kingdom is a particularly vexed question, as discussed below.

EU institutions may also adopt *recommendations and opinions*, which have no binding force.

The jurisdiction of the CJEU: direct effect and supremacy combined

1.12 The CJEU (which includes the General Court[42] and certain specialist courts) has final jurisdiction over the interpretation of provisions of EU law and exclusive jurisdiction over their validity.[43] The validity of any provisions of EU law (other than those of the TEU/TFEU, the validity of which cannot be questioned) may be reviewed directly under Article 263 TFEU,[44] or as part of proceedings referred by Member State national courts to the CJEU, where a Member State court seeks, in the course of a domestic hearing, a 'preliminary ruling' from the CJEU as to the meaning of a particular provision of EU law.[45]

Direct effect

1.13 The direct application of the provisions in TEU/TFEU (both vertical and horizontal) and of Directives (vertical only), even in the absence of Member State domestic implementation (or misimplementation) has been discussed above.

Supremacy

1.14 Direct effect was combined in the CJEU case law with the principle of supremacy of EU law. In any conflict between EU law and Member State domestic law, EU law (of whatever description) had primacy. The legitimacy of the CJEU's approach was rooted in the explanation of the EU as a 'new legal order', with legal personality, with a new legal system, governed by specifically created institutions, all of which, in the light of some textual support from

41 *Cadbury Schweppes plc v IRC*, supra n 19.
42 To which certain actions go initially, eg, direct actions on the validity of EU instruments under Article 263 TFEU and certain actions concerning state aid and competition law.
43 *Foto-Frost v Hauptzollamt Lubeck-Ost* (Case 314/85).
44 Different applicants have different rules as to standing.
45 Article 267 TFEU.

various provisions in the predecessor Treaty[46] to TEU/TFEU, meant that Member States are properly viewed as having yielded sovereignty to the EU in the capacity of signatory Member States:[47] 'By creating a Community of unlimited duration, having its own institutions, its own personality, its own legal capacity and capacity of representation on the international plane and, more particularly, real power stemming from a limitation of sovereignty or the transfer of powers from the states to the Community, the member states have limited their sovereign rights, albeit within limited fields ... the executive force of Community law cannot vary from one state to another in deference to subsequent domestic laws ... It follows from all these observations that the law stemming from [TEU/TFEU], **an independent source of law**, could not, because of its special and original nature, be overridden by domestic legal provisions ... The transfer by the states from their domestic legal systems to the Community legal system of the rights and obligations arising under [TEU/TFEU] carries with it a permanent limitation of their sovereign rights, against which a subsequent unilateral act incompatible with the concept of the Community cannot prevail.' The approach of the CJEU is thus very firmly monist. The TEU/TFEU are 'independent' sources of substantive legal rights and obligations, that is, 'independent' from the legal systems, or domestic constitutional principle, of the respective Member States. Critically, supremacy, *as interpreted and applied by the CJEU*, extends to all Member State laws, even constitutional laws[48] and even where the resolution of any conflict between a provision of EU law and domestic constitutional law is, as a matter of a Member State's constitutional law, exclusively within the jurisdiction of that Member State's constitutional court.[49]

Protection of EU rights and remedies for breach

Sympathetic construction

1.15 The principle of 'sympathetic construction' is a function of the duty of sincere cooperation in Article 4.3 TEU and supremacy, both individually and in combination and not just of supremacy.[50] All Member State domestic law provisions should be construed and applied, as far as judicial interpretative techniques permit, to be compliant with EU law (that is TEU/TFEU,

46 The Treaty of Rome.
47 *Costa v ENEL* (Case 6/64), emphasis added. Supremacy of EU law had been presaged in *Van Gend en Loos* (supra n 23).
48 *International Handelsgesellschaft mbH v Einfuhr-und Vorrastelle fur Getreide und Futtermittel* (Case 11/70).
49 *Simmenthal* (Case 106/77).
50 The Explanatory Notes, [104], treat the doctrine as one exclusively of supremacy, which is wrong: see C Barnard and J Ghosh, 'Judicial Techniques in relation to Remedies for Overpaid Tax' in *Restitution of Overpaid Tax* (Oxford, Hart Publishing, 2013), p 169.

Regulations, Directives and Decisions).[51] However, Member State domestic laws cannot be construed *contra legem*.[52] The principle of 'sympathetic construction' as applied by the English courts goes far beyond the techniques of 'construction' applied in a purely domestic context. Words may be read in and particular provisions may be partially 'disapplied', so as to give the provision a different (EU compliant) meaning, all in a manner wholly different to the exercise of 'construction' in a purely domestic context.[53] Sympathetic construction is not a general principle of EU law, albeit that the duty of Member State domestic courts to this doctrine is absolute. The CJEU has never, to the writer's knowledge, described this doctrine as amongst the general principles of EU law as a *source* of EU law (as opposed to a technique of application of EU law) discussed above. The survival of sympathetic construction as part of 'retained EU law' is a difficult issue, discussed below.

Disapplication

1.16 If sympathetic construction is not possible, the offending, non-EU compliant, domestic Member State provision is disapplied, that is, it is set aside so as not to interfere with established EU rights.[54] Disapplication is a remedy specific to EU law; *ultra vires* subordinate legislation, or administrative acts are, as a matter of United Kingdom public law, void.[55]

Damages

1.17 It may be that a particular person's complaint is the absence of equal favourable treatment to, say, a commercial competitor, in breach of that person's EU rights. In this case dis-application of the Member State's domestic provisions which confer that favourable treatment will not cure the complaint, since the complainant may not be interested in equal misery for all. The complainant wants to be made whole for the breach of its EU rights. The principle of effectiveness requires, said the CJEU, the prospect of damages

51 *Marleasing* (Case 106/89), *Pfeiffer* (Case C-397/01).

52 *Dominguez* (Case C-282/10), [27].

53 The *contra legem* limitation, expressed as requiring a court to 'go with the grain' of the text of the provision being 'construed', so that no fundamental feature is distorted (*Ghaidan v Godin-Mendoza* [2004] UKHL 30, [33] per Lord Nicholls, [121] per Lord Roger), appears to have been left well and truly behind. This technique has been acknowledged expressly to apply only to the moulding of United Kingdom domestic provisions into an EU compliant construct, so that the same provisions are construed (and therefore applied) in a perhaps very different way in either wholly internal situations, or in circumstances where EU law is not relevant (to 'third countries'): see Barnard and Ghosh op cit.

54 Disapplication is not invalidation: the offending provision is simply not to be applied so as to frustrate established EU rights but may be applied in circumstances where EU rights are not engaged: *IN.CO.GE* (Case C-10/97–C-22/97).

55 This proposition has been true since *Anisminic Ltd v FCC* [1969] 2 AC 147, 170 (Lord Reid). See below as to how an analogous United Kingdom (that is English, Scots and Northern Ireland) domestic remedy might be uncovered in relation to 'retained EU law'.

(non-contractual liability) in such a case: *Francovich and Bonifaci v Italy*,[56] albeit subject to particular conditions.[57] This particular remedy has been repealed in the United Kingdom, after exit from the EU, by the *EUWA 2018*, see below.

Restitution

1.18 Finally, restitutionary remedies, distinct from damages[58] lie where a breach of EU law results in a person holding monies which they should not have collected: see *San Giorgio*.[59]

Laying restitution to one side, the model for remedies, in EU law, of sympathetic construction, failing which disapplication, failing which damages[60] at least theoretically leaves the prospect of a complainant obtaining no remedy at all, despite a breach of EU law by a Member State.[61]

II. EU law in the United Kingdom 1 January 1973–31 January 2020

1.19 Constitutional orthodoxy in the United Kingdom secures and protects absolute continuing Parliamentary sovereignty. Parliament cannot bind herself, as regards future Parliaments and Parliament is not subject to any higher juristic body or principle.[62] A dualist juristic attitude to international obligations, whereby international obligations have no domestic effect until and unless enacted into domestic law by Parliament is a mere extension and application of Parliamentary sovereignty.

EU law was implemented in the United Kingdom by the *European Communities Act 1972* (*ECA 1972*). *Section 2(1)* provided that: 'All such rights, powers, liabilities, obligations and restrictions from time to time created or arising by or under [TEU/TFEU], and all such remedies and procedures from time

56 Joined Cases C-6/90, 9/90.

57 That the EU provision which the Member State breached was intended to create rights in the hands of the person making the particular complaint, there was a causal connection between the Member State's breach and damage to that person and the Member State's breach was 'sufficiently serious', showing a wanton disregard of that Member State's EU obligations: *Brasserie du Pecheur and Factortame Ltd* (Joined Cases C-46/93, C-48/93).

58 In particular, there is no need to establish 'sufficiently serious breach' in order to recover the wrongly-collected monies.

59 Case 199/82.

60 This is the model contemplated by the CJEU in *Faccini Dori*, supra n 29.

61 In fact, the prospect is not merely theoretical: in *BT* (Case C-392/98), the United Kingdom had misimplemented the relevant Directive but not in a manner which has shown a serious 'disregard' for the United Kingdom's EU obligations, so that while the United Kingdom was obliged to rectify the relevant domestic provisions, the complainant, BT, did not obtain any damages.

62 All affirmed in *Miller*.

to time provided for by or under [TEU/TFEU] as in accordance with [TEU/TFEU] are *without further enactment*[63] to be given legal effect or used in the United Kingdom shall be recognised and available in law, and be enforced, allowed and followed accordingly.' *Section 2(2)* established the power for the Executive to enact secondary legislation, to permit the United Kingdom to implement the United Kingdom's EU obligations. And *section 2(4)* provided that 'any enactment past ought to be passed, other than one contained in [ECA 1972], shall be construed and have effect subject to the foregoing provisions [of section 2]'.

Section 2(1) thus, according to the United Kingdom Supreme Court, provides a 'conduit pipe' through which EU law is not only conveyed to the repositories of United Kingdom law but also transmogrified into United Kingdom domestic law ('… without further enactment to be given legal effect …'). The United Kingdom Supreme Court in *Miller* described EU law as having a non-United Kingdom *source* (in that the substantive content of EU law, whether of legislative provisions, or the CJEU case law originates by acts of EU institutions, perhaps with no input at all from the United Kingdom[64]) albeit that EU law is domestically *applied* by the *ECA 1972* so as to give rise to a type of *United Kingdom* law, consistent with the dualist nature of the United Kingdom.[65] For all that the content of EU law arises from acts of EU institutions (and CJEU case law), EU law has substantive force in the United Kingdom by reason of the *ECA 1972* and no other principle of law at all.[66] It is the *ECA 1972* and the dualist nature of the United Kingdom's attitude to the incorporation of international obligations which establishes the domestic nature of EU rights and obligations (which means that the prerogative cannot be used to effect a fundamental change to the latter).[67]

---

63 Emphasis added.

64 The United Kingdom had transferred legislative powers to the EU, rather than delegated these powers: in no sense are the EU institutions 'delegates' of the United Kingdom Parliament: rather they are assignees of Parliament's legislative powers on the terms of the TEU/TFEU, at least for the duration of the *ECA 1972*: *Miller* [68].

65 *Miller*, [61], [65]. So although, in the view of the Supreme Court, *ECA 1972* is not 'itself the originating source [in the sense of giving EU law its content] of [EU law]' [65], the *ECA 1972 constituted*, according to the Supreme Court, EU law (that is, applied and introduced EU law), once EU institutions had formulated it, as 'an entirely new, independent and overriding source [that is, type] of domestic law …' [80].

66 Which makes the provisions of *EUWAA 2020, s 38* particularly futile. *Section 38(1)–(3)* provides 'It is recognised that the Parliament of the United Kingdom is sovereign' [notwithstanding the continued direct application of EU law during the implementation period and the implementation of the withdrawal agreement which has direct effect], so that 'accordingly, nothing in the [EUWAA 2020] derogates from the sovereignty of the Parliament of the United Kingdom'. The very notion of absolute continuing Parliamentary sovereignty is independent of the particular provisions in any statute, which is why *s 38* is an example of a pointless legislative slogan.

67 The location of rights in United Kingdom nationals and non-United Kingdom nationals, enforceable in the United Kingdom, makes the 'domestic' nature of EU law quite obvious. The direct horizontal effect of particular provisions of TEU/TFEU, in particular internal market provisions, although not mentioned in the Supreme Court's judgment in *Miller*, either

The dualist approach in the *ECA 1972* is clearly at odds with the monist approach of the CJEU in *Costa*. And indeed the United Kingdom Supreme Court has expressed the possibility that EU law will not be applied in circumstances which undermine Parliamentary sovereignty.[68] But it is the dualist nature of the United Kingdom's constitution which, in acknowledging the domestic nature of rights and obligations established by EU law, meant that the notification under Article 50 TEU could not be made under the Prerogative but required an Act of Parliament. The monist approach of the CJEU in *Costa*, which views EU law (and critically, EU rights and obligations) as emanating from the TEU/TFEU *alone* would, it is submitted, have meant that so far as the CJEU was concerned, the Executive could (and should) have used the Prerogative, without any endorsement from Parliament, in making a notification under Article 50 TEU. The *Costa* monist view excludes any contingency in the application of any of the provisions of TEU/TFEU (including Article 50), or any EU legislation, where that contingency takes the form of a Member State legislature's blessing to the application of any such provisions.[69] If and when any divergence of judicial opinion between the monist CJEU and dualist Member State domestic courts, including the United Kingdom courts becomes a collision, the jurisdictional tussle for the juristic nature of the supremacy of EU law will have to be resolved. For the reasons given below, this tussle may well yet be had between the CJEU and the UK courts, despite the United Kingdom leaving the EU.

---

by the majority or the minority, makes the 'domestic' nature of EU rights and obligations even more stark and highly visible. Consider a shareholder selling shares in a family company who prohibits, say, a purchaser with French parentage from offering to buy the shares. Such nationality discrimination is not compliant with the internal market provisions (whether it be Article 49 TFEU [freedom of establishment] or Article 63 TFEU [free movement of capital]) on any view. Thus private law contracts, governed by English law, between two private parties, are subject to EU law. It is a misuse of language to say that EU law does not, in such circumstances, give rise to 'domestic' rights and obligations.

68 *Assange v Swedish Prosecution Authority* [2012] UKSC 22; *R (HS2 Action Alliance Ltd) v Secretary of State for Transport* [2014] UKSC 3; *Pham v Secretary for Home Department* [2015] UKSC 19. And there are certainly instances where the United Kingdom Supreme Court has simply refused to follow the guidance given by the CJEU in a preliminary reference: *HMRC v Aima Coalition Loyalty UK Ltd (formerly known as Loyalty Management UK Ltd) (No2)* [2013] UKSC 42.

69 The reference to the 'constitutional requirements' of Member States as informing the withdrawal procedure under Article 50, in the light of *Simmenthal*, is to Member States' constitutional requirements as modified by EU membership (there is a contrary view, which is that withdrawal is a wholly internal decision and so outside the scope of *Simmenthal* but it is considered that this is not the better view, since Article 50 is a fundamental provision in the TEU and there is no reason why Article 50, which applies to current Member States (which have decided to leave), should be differently treated to the rest of TEU/TFEU). And the doctrine of subsidiarity would make no difference to this monist analysis, since it is the nature of substantive EU law, including TEU/TFEU which is at stake, not the level of application which is most appropriate.

III. The EU-United Kingdom Withdrawal Agreement

1.20 Article 50.2 TEU contemplated a withdrawing Member State and the EU concluding a 'Withdrawal Agreement' which set out the terms of withdrawal and a 'framework' for the 'future relations' between the EU and the Member State which has left. The EU and the United Kingdom concluded a Withdrawal Agreement on 24 January 2020.[70] Part IV of the Withdrawal Agreement provided for a 'transition period' (described, in the United Kingdom's domestic implementation as the 'Implementation Period': see below, which expired on 31 December 2020) during which, broadly, EU law continued to apply to the United Kingdom in exactly the same way[71] as it had done since 1 January 1973.[72]

The Withdrawal Agreement expressly has direct effect,[73] in accordance with 'methods and general principles'[74] of EU law. The 'methods and general principles' of EU law necessarily incorporate both the supremacy of EU law in any conflict with domestic Member State law (and thus, in relation to a conflict with a former Member State, the United Kingdom, a conflict would have to be resolved 'in accordance with' such supremacy) and the application of all of the substantive general principles recognised by the CJEU. This follows, not only from the text discussed above but also from the observation that the Withdrawal Agreement is between the EU and an extant Member State of the EU (the United Kingdom), albeit a Member State which is leaving the EU. The Withdrawal Agreement is concluded under Article 50.2 TEU, which brings the Withdrawal Agreement within the scope of *ECA 1972, s 2*, which applied until the United Kingdom left the EU and the *ECA 1972* has been repealed. To the extent that Article 50.2 is imprinted with the features of direct effect and supremacy, so must be any Withdrawal Agreement concluded under that TEU provision.[75] The CJEU has jurisdiction over the interpretation of the Withdrawal Agreement.[76] Disputes are resolved by a 'Joint Committee'

70 Agreement on the withdrawal of the United Kingdom of Great Britain and Northern Ireland from the European Union and the European Atomic Energy Community (2019/C 384 I/01), which replaced a previous Withdrawal Agreement, endorsed at a special meeting of the European Council on 25 November 2018, which 2018 Withdrawal Agreement failed to obtain United Kingdom Parliamentary approval.

71 So that provisions which did not apply to the United Kingdom during the United Kingdom's membership of the EU do not apply during the transition period: Article 127.1 Withdrawal Agreement.

72 Articles 126, 127.1, 127.3 Withdrawal Agreement. This also means that the United Kingdom is bound by any international agreements concluded by the EU during the transitional period: Article 129.1 Withdrawal Agreement.

73 Part I, Article 4.1, Article 4.4.

74 Article 4.3.

75 *EUWA 2018, s 5(7)* exempts the provisions of *EUWAA 2020, s 5(1)–(6)* which implement the Withdrawal Agreement from the qualification of the EU principle of supremacy, which reinforces this view.

76 Article 4.4. All language versions of the Withdrawal Agreement are equally authoritative: Article 183.

(comprised of both EU and United Kingdom appointees), which may refer matters to an arbitration panel which, in turn, may refer the matter to the CJEU.[77]

It is considered unlikely that the Withdrawal Agreement will have horizontal effect (and certainly not direct horizontal effect), unlike the TEU/TFEU. Direct vertical effect of the TEU/TFEU was a function, according to the CJEU, of the signatories to the Treaty of Rome including the 'peoples' of the Member States as well as the Member States themselves. Contrast Directives, for which the CJEU has consistently denied horizontal effect, on the basis that the addressee of a Directive is a Member State alone.[78] The Withdrawal Agreement is between the EU and the United Kingdom, not their respective 'peoples'. The purpose of the Withdrawal Agreement is to regulate reciprocal rights and obligations of the EU on the one hand and the United Kingdom on the other. While this includes the protection of citizens' rights, the Withdrawal Agreement protects such rights by (at least for eight years after the end of the 'transition period') a resolution by the Joint Committee, failing which the matter is put to an Arbitration Panel which may make a reference to the CJEU. There is no direct route for citizens' rights under the Withdrawal Agreement as a matter of domestic remedies or the *EUWAA 2020* to be protected in an action taken by the citizen themselves, although the direct effect of the Withdrawal Agreement means that the Withdrawal Agreement may be pleaded in an action before national courts against the EU, a Member State, or the United Kingdom. There is, therefore, no scope for the direct horizontal effect of the Withdrawal Agreement.[79]

Part II of the Withdrawal Agreement deals with citizens' rights (as to residence,[80] rights of family members, children's' rights, rights of frontier workers, social security rights, mutual recognition of professional qualifications, protection from discrimination,[81] a right to equal treatment[82] and specific rights for workers and self-employed persons[83]). The rights are dependent upon the timeous submission of applications for residence status[84] and are enforceable for the lifetime of the citizen concerned.[85] The CJEU has jurisdiction over the interpretation of the provisions of Part II for eight years from the end of the transition period; the CJEU's jurisdiction

77 Part VI, Articles 164, 166, 170–181 Withdrawal Agreement.

78 *Faccini Dori* (supra n 29).

79 It is true the CJEU has been prepared to interpret provisions of EU external agreements as granting *horizontally* directly effective rights (*Pokrzeptowicz-Meyer* (Case C-162/00); *Simutenkov* (Case C-265/03)) but these decisions concern intra-EU rights. The absence of the 'peoples' as signatories to the Withdrawal Agreement means that horizontal effect is not contemplated by the parties, despite the direct effect of the Withdrawal Agreement.

80 Article 20.

81 Article 12.

82 Article 23.

83 Article 24.

84 Article 18.

85 Article 39.

is the same as it had previously been for a preliminary reference under Article 267 TFEU.[86] A critical question is whether the notion of "citizen' in Part II includes legal persons, such as companies. On the assumption that the scope of the Withdrawal Agreement's protection of citizens' rights is congruent with citizens who were within the scope of Article 20 TFEU, the better answer is 'yes'. Article 4.1 expressly refers to 'natural and legal persons' and locates the rights it directly confers in such persons. Of course many of the specific rights conferred by the Withdrawal Agreement are irrelevant to legal persons. Article 39 (citizens' rights last for the lifetime of the citizen) makes no sense in the context of legal persons. Neither do attendant rights of family members. But rights, such as the protection against discriminatory treatment, are perfectly intelligibly located in legal persons. It may be that the extension of the Withdrawal Agreement to legal persons will be limited to those specific provisions which actually mention legal persons but not otherwise (which is probably the intention of the draftspersons of the Withdrawal Agreement and this, it is submitted, is the better view). However, the question remains textually open and authoritative interpretation will have to determine this issue.

Part III deals with 'other separation issues'.[87] Importantly, the United Kingdom remains subject to infraction proceedings by the European Commission for four years after the end of the 'transitional period'.[88] Disputes may be referred to the CJEU on a basis similar to a preliminary reference under Article 267 TFEU.[89] The United Kingdom also remains subject to Decisions of the European Commission on competition law and state aid, as well as to investigations relating to European Anti-Fraud Offences (OLAF), for four years after the end of the 'transitional period'.[90] A challenge to any act of the European Commission may be made on the same basis as Article 263 TFEU.[91]

Rights of audience before the CJEU are broadly protected for United Kingdom legal representatives for matters referred to the CJEU, involving the United Kingdom under the Withdrawal Agreement.[92]

86 Articles 4.4, 158.2. Special rules apply in relation to documentation required under applications made under Articles 18 and 19 (applications for recognition of citizens' rights).

87 Part V deals with financial provision. Part III concerns goods placed on the market, customs, intellectual property, police and judicial cooperation on criminal matters, public procurement, Euratom (nuclear safeguards, the transfer of United Kingdom equipment, Euratom international agreements, property in fissile material, responsibility for radioactive waste), ongoing judicial administration procedures, the functioning of EU institutions, agencies and bodies (including the treatment of classified information).

88 Article 87.

89 Article 188.

90 Article 92.

91 Article 95.3.

92 Articles 91.1 and 97.

IV. Domestic implementation of the Withdrawal Agreement in the United Kingdom

1.21 The Withdrawal Agreement is implemented by the United Kingdom by a combination of provisions in the *EUWA 2018* and the *EUWAA 2020*.[93]

The 'transition period' dealt with in Part IV of the Withdrawal Agreement is introduced as an 'implementation period' in *EUWA 2018, ss 1A* and *1B*, which, as observed above, broadly maintain the full effect of EU law in the United Kingdom until 31 December 2020 ('IP completion day'[94]).

The direct effect of the Withdrawal Agreement is secured by *EUWA 2018, s 7A*, which replicates the wording of *ECA 1972, s 2*: all 'rights, powers, liabilities, obligations and restrictions … created by or under the Withdrawal Agreement, and … all such remedies and procedures from time to time provided for by under the Withdrawal Agreement … As in accordance with the Withdrawal Agreement are without further enactment to be given legal effect when used in the United Kingdom … [so as to be] recognised and available in domestic law, and … enforced allowed and followed accordingly'.[95] Supremacy for the Withdrawal Agreement over conflicting domestic provisions is secured by *s 7A(3)* which provides that 'every enactment (including an enactment contained in [EUWA 2018] is to be read and has effect subject to [the rights and liabilities of the Withdrawal Agreement]'. There is a general power for Ministers to make regulations to 'supplement' Part III of the Withdrawal Agreement and *EUWA 2018, s 7A* in *EUWA 2018, s 8B*.[96]

The jurisdiction of the CJEU on matters allocated to the CJEU in the Withdrawal Agreement is dealt with opaquely and unsatisfactorily by *s 7C(1)*. 'Relevant separation agreement law' (broadly, United Kingdom domestic law which implements the Withdrawal Agreement, in particular citizens' rights, so, for example, *s 7A*[97]) is to be construed as to its 'validity, meaning or effect' in 'accordance' with the Withdrawal Agreement. *Section 7C(2)* mentions (not exhaustively) various provisions of the Withdrawal Agreement, including Articles 158 and 160, so *s 7C* clearly applies to require determination of 'any question' to be compliant with the Withdrawal Agreement, including the jurisdiction of the CJEU, in circumstances where the Withdrawal Agreement was given direct effect on supremacy by *s 7A*. *Section 7C* is silent as to any specific procedure to protect any rights conferred by the Withdrawal Agreement, however, which means, as observed above, there is no direct right of action on the part of any person who obtains rights under the Withdrawal

93 With wide powers conferred on ministers to enact laws to supplement these provisions which implement the Withdrawal Agreement: *EUWA 2018, ss 8A, 8B*.

94 *EUWA 2018, s 1A(6), EUWAA 2020, s 39(1)–(5)*.

95 *Section 7A(1), (2)*; *s 7B* reproduces this effect for the EEA-EFTA Agreement and the Swiss Citizens' Rights Agreement.

96 No regulations have been made at the time of writing.

97 *Section 7C(3)*.

Agreement to protect such rights. Either the complaints of a breach of rights conferred by the Withdrawal Agreement, as implemented by *s 7A*, are taken up by the Joint Committee, (howsoever conveyed to it) or a person who complains of such breach seeks remedy by way of judicial review (either directly or through a complaint to the Independent Monitoring Authority: see below), against any legislative or administrative act which offends against a Withdrawal Agreement right. Neither is there any provision of domestic law, at least in the *EUWA 2018*, which implements a procedure which permits the United Kingdom to complain to the CJEU about a decision of the European Commission under Articles 92 and 93 of the Withdrawal Agreement (competition law, state aid etc). The Withdrawal Agreement, in such cases, permits the United Kingdom to complain by way of a procedure analogous to Article 263 TFEU. But neither the *EUWA 2018*, nor the *EUWAA 2020*, nor any other legislative provision sets out, as a matter of United Kingdom law, how this is to be done as a matter of domestic legal procedure.

The *EUWAA 2020* deals with the implementation of the substantive rights and obligations of the Withdrawal Agreement. Citizens' rights which are the subject matter of Part II of the Withdrawal Agreement are dealt with in *Part 3* of *EUWAA 2020*, which specifies various powers for ministers to make regulations.[98] Citizens' rights will only be secured, in implementation of the Withdrawal Agreement, once regulations have been enacted. Importantly, *s 14* contemplates regulations to implement the non-discrimination provisions of the Withdrawal Agreement.[99] *Section 15* and *Schedule 2* establish the Independent Monitoring Authority (IMA), which has powers to establish an inquiry[100] and to raise an action for judicial review.[101]

At first sight, the terms of *EUWAA 2020* offer very little comfort to those seeking reassurance that citizens' rights will be adequately protected. The apparent paucity of remedies, at least in the face of the *EUWAA 2020*, for a breach of the citizens' rights guaranteed by Part II of the Withdrawal Agreement is self-evidently troubling, especially if general principles of EU law, such as the principle of effectiveness, to prevent EU rights are being impossible or excessively difficult to enforce form no part of the United Kingdom's domestic law after 31 December 2020, whether in the context of protecting rights conferred by the Withdrawal Agreement, or to protect those rights embedded in EU law, as it will continue to apply in the United Kingdom after that date ('retained EU law': see below). However, the better view is that EU general principles, including the general principle of

98 *Section 7* gives power to make regulations in relation to applications for residence status; *s 8* deals with frontier workers; *s 9* concerns powers to restrict entry; *s 10* amends the *Immigration Act 1971*, in relation to deportation; *s 12* deals with the recognition of professional qualifications; *s 13* deals with the coordination of social security systems.

99 Article 12 (prohibition against nationality discrimination) and Article 23 (right to equal treatment).

100 *EUWAAA 2020, Sch 2, para 25.*

101 *EUWAAA 2020, Sch 2, paras 29, 30.*

effectiveness, will apply in their full sense to protect Withdrawal Agreement rights which would require the United Kingdom (through the respective legal systems of each of England and Wales, Scotland and Northern Ireland) to provide (if necessary new) remedies to secure the enforcement of such rights (once implemented by regulations). This is on the basis that the Withdrawal Agreement, which has direct effect through *EUWA 2018, s 7A* operates, as observed above, in accordance with the 'methods and general principles' of EU law.[102] Thus, despite the emasculation of general principles of EU law described below, the combination of Article 4.3 of the Withdrawal Agreement and *EUWA 2018, s 7A* permit application of the general principles of EU law, of effectiveness in particular but also of equivalence (EU rights to be afforded no less protection than domestic rights), to afford citizens' rights, as implemented in *Part 3* of *EUWAA 2020*, greater protection than a right only of judicial review and a complaint to the Joint Committee.[103] This analysis is consistent with the text of the Withdrawal Agreement and *EUWA 2018, s 7A*. It is also consistent with *EUWA 2018, s 7A(1)* and *(3)* imprinting the dual features of direct effect and supremacy in the domestic implementation of the Withdrawal Agreement, by contrast to the disapplication of the EU principle of supremacy in relation to domestic law enacted post-31 December 2020 for 'retained EU law' (see below). This analysis is also consistent with *EUWA 2018, s 5(7)*, which provides that the qualification of the EU principle of supremacy in relation to the assimilation of EU law into United Kingdom domestic law ('retained EU law') after 31 December 2020 ('IP completion day')[104] does not apply to the domestic statutory provisions which implement the Withdrawal Agreement ('relevant separation agreement law'), which thus, in giving domestic direct effect to the Withdrawal Agreement, preserves supremacy of the provisions of the Withdrawal Agreement given domestic direct effect. All of which suggests that citizens' rights protected by the Withdrawal Agreement and implemented in *EUWAA 2020, Part 3* are 'ring fenced' and afforded the same protection as under EU law, as it applied in the United Kingdom up to 31 December 2020.

V. The continued application of EU law in the United Kingdom post-31 December 2020 ('IP completion date'): 'retained EU law'

1.22 As observed above, Part IV of the Withdrawal Agreement provided for a 'transitional period' from the time at which the United Kingdom left the EU (31 January 2020), which expired on 31 December 2020. The transitional

102 Article 4.3 Withdrawal Agreement

103 Indeed, there is no specific procedure by which a private person may complain to the Joint Committee.

104 See below.

period was implemented by the *EUWAA 2020*, which enacted two new sections inserted into the *EUWA 2018*, *ss 1A* and *1B*. Put short, EU law, including the Charter of Fundamental Rights, applied in full to the United Kingdom during an 'implementation period'[105] which expired on 31 December 2020 ('IP completion day').[106]

Turning to the application of EU law after IP completion day, the *EUWA 2018* uses terms of art of EU law (such as supremacy) without statutory explanation or definition, which means that the *EUWA 2018* cannot, on any view, be read or understood without a full knowledge of EU law. Importantly, there is no analogue to Article 4.3 of the Withdrawal Agreement, which applies the 'methods and principles' of EU law to the latter. Thus, the *EUWA 2018* must be construed and applied on its own specific terms, which gives rise to particular problems, discussed below. The *EUWA 2018* has a twofold objective: first, to ensure that the United Kingdom has a functioning statute book after 31 December 2020 by preserving continuity in the regulation of the very many aspects of private law and public law into which EU law is inextricably woven, and second to begin the process of branding United Kingdom laws enacted after 31 December 2020 as peculiarly British laws, subject neither to the EU principle of supremacy, nor to the substantive application of general principles of EU law. It is considered that the *EUWA 2018* does not achieve either objective particularly well. It is convenient to note here that the *EUWA 2018* does not, on any view, seek to preserve EU law as part of the United Kingdom's post-Brexit juristic heritage, within the repository of 'retained EU law'. Rather, 'retained EU law' reflects a legislative technique with the limited purpose of preserving the continuity of the United Kingdom's domestic law, which will be subject to a progressive dilution of its EU parentage.

Frozen nature of retained EU law

1.23 In relation to the objective of continuity, the *EUWA 2018* identifies EU law which United Kingdom will continue to apply, post-IP completion day: 'retained EU law' ('EU-derived domestic legislation' within *EUWA 2018, s 2(1)*, 'direct EU legislation' within *s 3(1)* and the EU rights 'recognised and available' within *s 4(1)*). All of these terms are examined below. 'Retained EU law' is EU law which is (subject to transitional provisions: see below) effectively

105 Importantly, the mechanism for this continued application of EU law in the United Kingdom is the continued application of *ECA 1972, s 2(1)* in its pre-exit day form (*s 1A(2)*); thus, each and every provision of EU law, including the Charter of Fundamental Rights, applies in the United Kingdom between exit day on 31 January 2020 and IP completion date on 31 December 2020.

106 *EUWA 2018, s 1A(6)*. *Section 1A* saves the application of *ECA 1972, s 2A* (which was repealed by *EUWA 2018, s 1* as from 31 January 2020 ('exit day')) for the implementation period.

'frozen' as at immediately before IP completion day.[107] Any reference in an enactment, to 'direct EU legislation' within *s 3*, or in any 'document' to legislative instruments which fall within the notion of 'direct EU legislation', or to instruments which confer rights under *s 4* (primarily the TEU/TFEU and Directives) is deemed to be a reference to those instruments in the form immediately before IP completion day.[108] The power to modify primary legislation conferred prior to the passing of *the EUWA 2018* extends to, 'direct EU legislation' within *EUWA 2018, s 3* and 'recognised and available rights' within *s 4*.[109]

The *EUWA 2018* seeks to ensure continuity by taking an effective snapshot of EU law as it stands at 31 December 2020 ('retained EU law'), as it applies in each and every area of United Kingdom law and giving that snapshot the force of law. 'Retained EU law' will thus apply in the United Kingdom indefinitely. However, 'retained EU law' is heavily modified in its application, as compared to the application of EU law in the United Kingdom during the United Kingdom's membership of the EU and during the 'implementation period'.[110]

---

107 'EU-derived domestic legislation' is retained 'as it has effect in domestic law immediately before IP completion date' (*s 2(1)*), 'direct EU legislation' is within *s 3(1)* on the 'so far as operative immediately before IP completion date' and rights etc within *s 4(1)* are those which are 'recognised and available' 'immediately before IP completion day'.

108 *EUWA 2018, Sch 8, paras 1, 2.* The reference to 'document' (not defined), may be problematic if it is a reference to all instruments, including private law contracts, may well be problematic, if the intention of the relevant parties was different to the *para 1* form of the relevant reference. Provisions implementing the Withdrawal Agreement are carved out of these 'freezer' provisions, in that the Withdrawal Agreement is not within *Sch 8, para 2(1)(a)*. Rather, *Sch 8, para 1A* (existing ambulatory references) and *para 2A* (existing non ambulatory references) make provision (very broadly) for all references to EU law for the purpose of the Withdrawal Agreement (and the EEA, EFTA and the Swiss citizens' rights agreement) to take the meaning under those respective agreements.

109 *The European Union (Withdrawal) Act 2018 (Consequential Modifications and Repeals and Revocations) (EU Exit) Regulations 2019, SI 2019/628, reg 3.* Special provision is made, for 'enactments' which refer to, broadly, particular 'direct EU legislation' as it has effect at a particular [pre-IP completion day] time: if that particular 'direct EU legislation' has been modified in an immaterial way before IP completion day, the reference is taken to be to the IP completion day form of the relevant 'direct EU legislation'. If, however, the relevant 'direct EU legislation' has been modified in a material way (so that the enactment in question would have had to change the way it referred to that particular 'direct EU legislation' to accommodate the modification, the modification is simply ignored and the reference is to the unmodified version of the 'direct EU legislation': *EUWA 2018, Sch 8, para 2.* Finally, if a United Kingdom enactment refers to 'direct EU legislation' which is 'modified' by United Kingdom law, post-IP completion date, none of the statutory restrictions in these regulations apply. Rather, the normal principles of statutory construction will apply to the United Kingdom enactment and any references it makes to 'direct EU legislation'.

110 Ministers have been given extremely wide powers to cure 'deficiencies' which arise by reason of the United Kingdom's withdrawal from the EU: *EUWA 2018, s 8*: see in particular discussion below of regulations excising the freedom of establishment and the freedom to provide services, from rights otherwise available under *EUWA 2018, s 4*, enacted under *s 8*.

'Retained EU law' comprises three separate categories of EU law:[111] 'EU derived domestic legislation' defined in *EUWA 2018, s 1B*,[112] 'direct EU legislation' defined in *s 3* and what, at least as a matter of rhetoric, is a residual category defined in *s 4*, being 'any rights, powers, liabilities, obligations, restrictions, remedies and procedures which, immediately before [IP completion day, 31 December 2020] ... are recognised[113] and available in domestic law by virtue of [ECA 1972, section 2(1))', which would encompass directly applicable Treaty rights (vertical and horizontal) and directly applicable rights arising under a Directive. *Section 4* also encompasses general principles of EU law but, as discussed below, the application of such general principles is heavily qualified. The 'domestication' of rights, obligations etc means that these may be subject to such other modification as Parliament considers fit and cannot be 'entrenched' or preserved in any way.[114]

Each category of 'retained EU law' merits separate consideration. It is critical to note that provisions of EU law which are outside all three categories of 'retained EU law' are not part of United Kingdom law at all, post-IP completion day.

EU-derived domestic legislation

1.24 'EU-derived domestic legislation' is given 'effect in domestic law' in the same manner (as it has 'effect') after 'IP completion day',[115] as it did before 'IP completion day'.[116] So the interpretation and application of 'EU derived domestic legislation' in essentially unaffected by its status as 'retained EU law' by reason of *s 1B*. This category of 'retained EU law' catches virtually all

111 *EUWA 2018, s 6(7)*; *Schedule 6* specifies 'exempt instruments' which are excluded from being 'retained EU law'. In fact, the notion of 'retained EU law' in *s 6(7)* includes not only the material contained in *EUWA 2018, ss 2–4*, which confine the EU law to be given domestic force in the form in which that material exists immediately before IP completion day (31 December 2020) but also certain future 'modifications' of that material made by United Kingdom domestic law. That 'modified' material falls, by reason of that 'modification', outside *ss 2–4* but keeps its character as 'retained EU law' which is subject to the rules of interpretation in *EUWA 2018, s 6*, discussed below.

112 Or, more precisely, *s 1B* by reference to *s 1B(7)*, which provides the definition of 'EU derived legislation' post-IP completion day, which the draftsperson incomprehensibly considered to be more efficient than simply retaining the original definition already in *s 1B(2)*.

113 See below for the difficulties arising from the term 'recognised'.

114 For an example of an EU Regulation which is prima facie within the notion of 'retained EU law' (being 'direct EU legislation': see below) which is excluded from being 'retained EU law' see the *Taxation (Cross-border Trade) Act 2018, s 42*, which excludes the VAT Implementing Regulation from being 'retained EU law' see further chapter 2 relating to VAT.

115 So a modification of 'EU-derived domestic legislation' after IP completion day will take it outside *s 1B*.

116 This category of domestic United Kingdom legislation was also saved (insofar as it needed saving: see below) for the implementation period by *EUWA 2018, s 1B*.

existing domestic United Kingdom legislation, primary or secondary, which is somehow connected to the EU.

Section 1B(7) defines 'EU-derived domestic legislation'[117] as 'any enactment' which is: (1) 'made under' *ECA 1972, s 2(2)*, that is, subordinate legislation which has the latter as its enabling power,[118] (2) 'passed or made, or operating, for a purpose mentioned' in *ECA 1972, s 2(2)(a), (b)* (so 'EU-derived domestic legislation' includes primary Acts of Parliament which do not need saving at all and which would have continued effect in any event, absent their being repealed; the *Value Added Tax Act 1994*, for example, is clearly 'EU-derived domestic legislation', 'relating', as it does, 'to the EU'),[119] or (3) 'relating otherwise to the EU …').[120] While United Kingdom primary or secondary legislation passed for an *ECA 1972* Act 'purpose' or which 'relates to' EU law is within *s 1B(7)/s 2* even if it is non-EU compliant, that is, it, for example, it misimplements a Directive, this has little legislative impact, for the reasons given below.[121]

Category (1) saves the validity of United Kingdom secondary legislation which had the *ECA 1972, s 2* as its enabling provision. This is self-evidently necessary. Categories (2) and (3) are, in fact, redundant but no worse than that. Primary legislation does not need saving at all. Secondary United Kingdom legislation which does not depend on *ECA 1972, s 2* for its validity does not need saving either (unless their particular enabling provision has been repealed by reason of Brexit). But given that their legislative attributes are unaffected by the *EUWA 2018*, no real problems arise by their inclusion in the notion of 'retained EU law'.

Direct EU legislation

1.25 'Direct EU legislation' encompasses[122] EU regulations, EU decisions and EU 'tertiary legislation'[123] (but not Directives, which are encompassed

117 By reference to *s 1B(7)*.

118 Which would need to be saved. EU-derived domestic law retains its status after its transmogrified occasion from primary or secondary legislation into 'EU-derived domestic legislation': *EUWA 2018, s 7(1), (1A)*.

119 *EUWA 2018, s 2(2)(a)–(d)*.

120 Or related to any of the previous categories, or indeed to other categories of 'retained EU law' defined in *ss 3* and *4* (see below).

121 Indeed, it is supposed that an enactment may 'relate' to EU without having been enacted or modified to enable the United Kingdom to comply with EU obligations. For example, the *Companies Act 2006* has never been amended to comply with EU shareholder Directives as it was understood to be EU compliant in any event. But the *Companies Act 2006* would certainly apply in circumstances where EU law was relevant and to that extent may be properly said to 'relate' to EU law. But as observed below, the status of EU derived domestic legislation (except where its validity is saved by *s 2*) is to a large extent an irrelevance.

122 *Section 3(2)*.

123 Provisions made under EU regulations, decisions, and Directives under Article 290, or Article 291(2) TEU: *EUWA 2018, s 20(1)*.

by *s 4*: see below) which are 'operative' (that is, in force[124]) on 'IP completion day'.[125] *Section 3(1)* provides that 'direct EU legislation' has continued effect, since it 'forms part of domestic law on an after exit day.'

Problematic questions arise as to the juristic quality of 'direct EU legislation'.[126] What does it mean for legal material which has lost its statutory authority (*ECA 1972, s 2*) to 'form part of domestic law'? Certainly, unlike primary Acts of Parliament which fall within the notion of 'EU-derived domestic legislation' in *s 1B*, 'direct EU legislation' would need saving after the repeal of *ECA 1972*, since there would be no domestic 'conduit pipe' to give regulations, decisions or 'EU tertiary legislation' the force of law in the United Kingdom. But in simply providing that 'direct EU legislation' has continued effect because it 'forms part of domestic law' raises fundamental questions as to status and quality of this category of 'retained EU law'. One question is whether 'direct EU legislation' displaces the exercise of the Prerogative in any particular area. The answer is that the Prerogative is indeed probably circumscribed by 'direct EU legislation', on the basis that the United Kingdom Supreme Court's analysis that such 'direct EU legislation' 'originated' upon an effective 'transfer'[127] (or 'assignment') of legislative functions by Parliament itself, so that 'direct EU legislation' has the same authority as a primary Act of Parliament. Incidentally, 'direct EU legislation' is to be treated as 'primary' legislation for the purposes of the *Human Rights Act 1998* (*HRA 1998*), *s 21(1)*.[128] But this is a tentative answer to a vexed (fundamental) question, which may well be subject to further legislative guidance, quite apart from decisions by the United Kingdom courts. The second objective of *EUWA 2018*, of distancing 'EU retained law' from its EU roots, is evident in *s 3(4)*, which treats only the English language version of 'direct EU legislation' as authoritative, with other language versions being relegated to an interpretative role only.

---

124 Enacted direct EU legislation which has effect on a date after enactment is only 'in force' from the date it has effect: *EUWA 2018, s 3(3)*.

125 *Section 3(1), (3)*; the condition of the provisions being 'operative' indicates the objective of 'freezing' EU law as IP completion day; so a modification of 'direct EU legislation' after IP completion day will take it outside *s 3*. On the face of *s 3*, 'direct EU legislation' will include any legislation repealed by the EU after post-IP completion day.

126 *EUWA 2018, s 7* provides, broadly, that 'direct EU legislation' may only be modified by a primary act of Parliament, other primary legislation, or subordinate legislation insofar as there is vires, or specified provisions under *EUWA 2018, Sch 8* (which distinguishes between EU regulations and other 'EU tertiary legislation' ['retained direct principle EU legislation' and 'retained direct minor EU legislation'], which does not really offer any further clues as to the juristic nature of 'direct EU legislation'.

127 *Miller* [68]; Such 'transfer' was clearly not complete, given the Supreme Court's express reservation as to the limits of EU law in the case law discussed above.

128 *EUWA 2018, Sch 8, para 30*: It is unlikely that 'retained EU law' and 'direct EU legislation' should be non-*HRA 1998* compliant, since EU law should, as a matter of principle, be compliant with both the ECHR and the Charter of Fundamental Rights but it is perfectly (realistically) possible that, 'direct EU legislation' may be disproportionate and offend one or more Convention rights under *HRA 1998*.

'*Section 4* rights'

1.26 *Section 4(1)* makes 'recognised and available in domestic law … to be enforced, allowed and followed accordingly …'[129] any 'rights, powers, liabilities, obligations, restrictions, remedies and procedures which … are recognised *and* available in domestic law immediately before IP completion day[130] by virtue of [ECA 1972, section 2(1)] but only insofar as not already incorporated into domestic law by virtue of being 'direct EU legislation' within *s 3*.[131]

It is difficult to understand why the draftsperson felt the need to define 'direct EU legislation' separately in *s 3*, when the latter clearly falls within the category of 'retained EU law' set out in *s 4*.

Crucially and most unsatisfactorily, rights emanating from the TEU/TFEU which relate to the freedom of establishment under Article 49 TFEU and the free movement of services under Article 56 TFEU are excluded from continuing rights available in United Kingdom domestic law (which would otherwise have been available under *s 4*), not on the face of *s 4* itself but rather under regulations made by Ministers.[132] Even more startlingly, the enabling power is cited as *EUWA 2018, s 8(1)*, which is a provision which entitles ministers to enact subordinate legislation to cure 'deficiencies' in 'retained EU law'.[133] The freedom of establishment and freedom to provide services are fundamental and far-reaching provisions of the TEU/TFEU (perhaps the most fundamental and far-reaching). If these regulations are indeed *intra vires*, quite apart from excising two of the most visible and jealously guarded rights which arise in EU law, the regulations demonstrate the enormous scope of the enabling provisions to enact subordinate legislation conferred by *EUWA 2018, s 8*.

Turning to the conditions in *s 4* that EU rights must be 'recognised' and 'available' in United Kingdom domestic law to fall within the scope of *s 4*.[134] The terms 'recognised' and 'available' are not themselves defined. On the basis that retained EU law has the limited function of ensuring the continuity of the United Kingdom's statute book and not to serve as a repository of EU law which might permit the emergence of new rights, it is submitted that

129 *Section 4(1)*.

130 The dual requirements of 'recognition' and 'availability' (the latter must mean 'available to be enforced') again reinforces the objective of 'freezing' EU law as at IP completion day. It follows that that any material modification of such rights after IP completion day will take the modified rights outside *s 4*. The need for a right to have been enforced prior to IP completion day is seemingly disapplied in relation to cases begun before IP completion day: *Sch 8, para 37*.

131 *Section 4(2)(a), (b)*.

132 *The Freedom of Establishment and Free Movement of Services (EU Exit) Regulations 2019, SI 2019/1401, paras 2, 3*.

133 And *even* more startlingly, the Explanatory Notes say that an impact study was not published because there was no significant impact on the private, public or voluntary sectors.

134 *Section 3* takes precedence over *s 4* for any provision of EU law which might fall into both *s 3* and *s 4*: *s 4(2)(a)*.

'recognised' means 'acknowledged as part of the ratio of a decision' (and not as obiter observations), while 'available' means 'enforceable' ('available to be deployed'). Thus rights which may have been 'recognised' but were never made visible because a particular issue was never litigated are outside the scope of these '*s 4* rights'.[135]

In relation to Directives, rights arising by reason of the direct effect of Directives are within *s 4* but such rights must have been '*recognised* by the European Court[136] or any court or tribunal in the United Kingdom in a case decided before exit day (whether or not as an essential part of the decision in the case)'.[137]

The stark nature and consequences of the 'freezing' exercise undertaken by the *EUWA 2018* is illustrated by the question of the tax treatment of cross-border losses, where the CJEU changed direction dramatically. Put short, losses incurred by an entity in one Member State could not, said the CJEU in *Futura Participations and Singer v Administration des contributions*,[138] be set against the profits obtained in another Member State, since that offended the principle of 'territoriality'. In subsequent case law, the CJEU held that such cross-border loss relief was indeed mandated by the internal market provisions.[139] It is inevitable that future changes of direction by the CJEU, subsequent to IP completion day must be ignored by the United Kingdom courts and tribunals, for better or worse.[140]

---

135 This conclusion is not arbitrary or unfair. Retained EU law has the function of retaining those aspects of EU law which were in the United Kingdom's domestic law as at 31 December 2020, not to serve as a separate source of EU legal rights and obligations after that date: hence the suggested meanings ascribed to 'recognised' and 'available' by reference to Parliamentary intention. A court or tribunal may have to grapple with the question of whether a particular Directive provision has been 'recognised' as directly applicable by considering conflicting decisions of different courts which disagree as to whether or not a particular director provision is directly applicable. Faced with such a conflict, it is submitted that a court should adopt a common sense approach and treat observations made by the higher courts as being more persuasive than those of lower courts and concrete observations as more persuasive than passing remarks (especially in the context of 'retained EU law', which is supposedly a term which encompasses *existing* EU-related rules and principles which the United Kingdom has chosen to *keep*, as opposed to inchoate rules or principles not as yet applied by the courts) but in the absence of any guidance, the jurist can do little more than wait and see how this question will be resolved. In any event, Directive provisions which have juristic features which suggest they should have direct application will not be part of 'retained EU law' and not give rise to domestic rights if that provision has been untested in the courts.

136 That term is given its meaning in the *Interpretation Act 1978, Sch 1*.

137 *EUWA 2018, s 4(2)(b)*: the absence of the term 'available' in *s 4(2)(b)* means that a right is 'recognised' by the CJEU/a domestic court or tribunal

138 Case C-250/95 [18]–[25], supra n 12.

139 *Marks & Spencer plc v Halsey* (Case C-446/03).

140 Indeed, a decision of the General Court, made pre-IP completion day, will be 'retained EU law', whereas a decision of the Court of Justice on Appeal, reversing the decision of the General Court, made post-IP completion day, will not be retained EU law at all.

Relationship of different categories of 'retained EU law' *inter se* and to United Kingdom domestic law

1.27 All three categories of 'retained EU' are treated as 'domestic law'. *Section 5(2)* provides for the continued supremacy of 'EU law' (importantly not 'retained EU law'), which confers supremacy on rights conferred by *s 3* and *s 4* over pre-31 December 2020 United Kingdom domestic legislation (the latter being subject to disapplication in the event of inconsistency with retained EU law within *s 3* or *s 4*). Post-31 December 2020 legislation is not subject to the EU principle of supremacy at all. *Section 5(2)* also means that *s 1B* 'EU derived domestic legislation', in so far as inconsistent with direct EU legislation in *s 3* or rights (in so far as 'recognised and available' as at IP completion day) within *s 4*,[141] yields to 'EU law' (as within *s 3* and *s 4*) and may be disapplied.

Application of the EU principle of supremacy to retained EU law[142]

1.28 At first sight, *s 5(2)* seems to attribute supremacy, over inconsistent pre-31 December 2020 United Kingdom domestic law, to all three categories of retained EU law, *s 1B* 'EU derived domestic legislation' (which, as observed above, may well include non-EU compliant domestic primary or secondary legislation), *s 3* 'direct EU legislation' and '*s 4* rights'.

An initial observation is that this attribution of supremacy is constitutionally odd. Supremacy of EU law makes perfect sense when hand-in-hand with the principle of direct effect and is indeed indispensable for the fructification of the EU project for the reasons given by the CJEU in *Van Gend en Loos*. Supremacy of EU law (*a fortiori* 'retained EU law') over inconsistent domestic law loses legitimacy when the relevant state (here, the United Kingdom, post-Brexit) has no international commitments founded on the duty of sincere cooperation in Article 4.3 TEU. Neither is supremacy needed for a continuing functioning statute book. The United Kingdom courts are perfectly capable of grappling with inconsistencies between retained EU law and other United Kingdom domestic provisions and reaching an answer based on Parliamentary intention. Nevertheless, supremacy for EU law, as 'frozen' in *s 3* and in *s 4*, remains a juristic attribute which must be applied by the courts (so that inconsistent pre-31 December 2020 United Kingdom domestic law must be disapplied[143]).

But what about *s 1B*? *Section 5(2)* does not, on its terms, exclude *s 1B* 'EU derived domestic legislation' from its scope. If *s 5(2)* indeed attributed supremacy to 'EU derived domestic legislation', this would give supremacy to

141 Because the EU derived domestic legislation in question is, in fact, non-EU compliant.

142 I am very grateful to Professor Barnard for valuable discussions on this issue.

143 Although see below for the diluted effect of EU general principles.

a very wide category of United Kingdom primary and secondary legislation indeed, whether or not this legislation was EU compliant. This reading of *s 5(2)* (which is certainly textually possible) would also give primary and secondary legislation within *s 1B* a different legislative effect to that which it had pre-IP completion day. In the case of a primary Act which implements a Directive (for example, the *VATA 1994*), an attribution would give the latter automatic primacy over all inconsistent pre-31 December 2020 domestic provisions, whether or not the Directive itself would have had direct effect as a matter of EU law. And take perfectly EU compliant secondary legislation, which implements, for example, a Directive. Say this secondary legislation is inconsistent with a pre-31 December 2020 primary Act. Supremacy would give the EU compliant *s 2–s 5(2)* supremacy-attributed secondary legislation primacy over the inconsistent pre-31 December primary Act, which stands the United Kingdom's legislative hierarchy on its head.[144]

This absurd result may be avoided by a careful application of *s 5(2)* and *s 2(1)*. *Section 5(2)* applies the principle of supremacy of 'EU law' (not, as already observed, 'retained EU law'). *Section 5(2)* does not attribute primacy to all categories of retained EU law. So the answer to the question '*to which provisions of the EUWA 2018 does section 5(2) apply supremacy*' must be answered by: (1) acknowledging that it is the EU principle of supremacy which is being applied, so one must look to EU law to identify the attributes of supremacy, and (2) *s 2(1)* expressly retains the same effect of EU derived domestic legislation as it had immediately before IP completion day.

Prior to IP completion day (and during the time of the United Kingdom's membership of the EU), if a primary Act or secondary legislation which implemented EU obligations[145] was inconsistent with United Kingdom domestic law, the inconsistency would be resolved thus: EU law was supreme over inconsistent domestic law; the primary Act or secondary legislation implementing EU law is not itself EU law; rather it is the TEU/TFEU obligation (or the obligation to, say, implement a Directive) which is the relevant EU law. So once a domestic court or the CJEU acknowledged that the offending United Kingdom domestic provision was indeed inconsistent with the United Kingdom's TEU/TFEU/Directive obligation, the offending inconsistent domestic law would be disapplied (if not able to be sympathetically construed to be EU compliant[146]). The primary Act or secondary legislation which implemented the United Kingdom's EU obligations were not, as such, given primacy over non-EU compliant United Kingdom legislation.

---

144 *A fortiori* if the *s 1B* secondary legislation is not EU compliant (or indeed non-EU compliant primary legislation within *s 1B*), although in both cases, this non-EU compliant legislation is subject to the filters of *s 3* and *s 4* and so may themselves be subject to disapplication by reason of *s 5(2)*.

145 Whether under the TEU/TFEU, or to implement a Directive.

146 See below for what is considered to be the exclusion of the exercise of sympathetic construction in the strong, EU sense by the new legislative post-Brexit architecture.

To apply this technique to *s 5(2)*, the 'EU principle of supremacy' simply does not apply to domestic legislation (even that within *s 2*) to give it primacy over inconsistent pre-31 December legislation. And this conclusion is reinforced by *s 2(1)* which, as observed above, preserves the pre-IP completion day legislative effect (and status) of EU derived domestic legislation. To be sure, the absence of any exclusion of *s 1B* EU derived domestic legislation from the application of *s 5(2)*[147] means that the contrary view is difficult to dismiss as unarguable. But this contrary view is most definitely absurd and the analysis and conclusion delivered here is the better view. *Section 5(2)* does not confer supremacy on *s 1B* EU derived domestic legislation. Rather, the EU principle of supremacy is confined to direct EU legislation (so long as this is 'operative' as at IP completion day) and 'recognised and available' *s 4* rights. It follows that the status of EU derived domestic legislation is of very little significance indeed (beyond the saving of that secondary legislation which had the *ECA 1972, s 2*, as its enabling provision).

Application of retained EU law

1.29 The *EUWA 2018* substantially alters the application of 'retained EU law' (of any specified category) from the way that EU law applied up to 31 December 2020 to the United Kingdom. These modifications relate to: (1) the substantive content of EU law, (2) the interpretation of EU law and (3) procedural protections and remedies, which the *EUWA 2018* applies to 'retained EU law'.

Modifications to the substantive content of EU law for 'retained EU law'

1.30 'Retained EU law' will apply in exactly the same manner as it did prior to the United Kingdom's exit from the EU during the implementation period, from the United Kingdom's exit from the EU on 31 January 2020, until IP completion day on 31 December 2020. Thus the principles of sympathetic construction and the remedy of disapplication shall continue to operate for pre-IP completion day United Kingdom law.[148]

However, any enactment or 'rule of law' passed or made on or after 31 December 2020 is not subject to the EU principle of supremacy.[149]

147 *Section 7(5)(a)* does not expressly exclude retained EU law within *s 1B* from having the attribute of *s 5* supremacy either.
148 *EUWA 2018, s 5(2)*: but not damages: see below.
149 *EUWA 2018, s 5(1)*.

Certain categories of EU law are excluded from being 'retained EU law' altogether: Charter of Fundamental Rights and General Principles

1.31 *Charter of Fundamental Rights*: The Charter of Fundamental Rights is expressly excluded from being 'part of domestic law'[150] on or after exit day (although *s 1A(2)* seemingly preserves its application during the implementation period, so that the exclusion only operates from 31 December 2020 onwards). The exclusion, in *s 5(4)*[151] does not extend to domestic legislation (EU-derived domestic legislation or otherwise) which either implements the Charter of Fundamental Rights, or is drafted to be compliant with it, which, therefore, continue in full force. This is not surprising, given that the United Kingdom, at least presently, remains a signatory to the European Convention of Human Rights and the *HRA 1998* remains in force, so that United Kingdom domestic legislation is enacted to be compliant with those instruments, notwithstanding the excision of the Charter of Fundamental Rights from United Kingdom domestic law. However, see below for observations on problematic provisions on the interpretation of CJEU case law which concerns Charter rights.

General principles: As observed above, general principles of EU law are substantive principles, which operate independently of the text of any particular provision of either the TEU/TFEU, or the provisions of any regulation, Directive or decision. It has also been observed above that general principles are gleaned by the CJEU from the specific provisions of TEU/TFEU and constitute an open-ended category. While the category of EU law comprised in notion of 'general principles' is not excluded in its entirety, *EUWA 2018, Sch 1, para 2* provides that 'no general principle of EU law is part of domestic law on or after exit day if it was not recognised as a general principle of EU law by the European court in a case decided before exit day (whether or not as an essential part of the decision in the case)'. The difficulties with the term 'recognised' have been discussed above and apply with equal force here. Take the general EU principle of effectiveness: the CJEU had pronounced, in *European Commission v Greece*,[152] that a right to a remedy was a 'general principle' of EU law. But this statement has been subsequently explained as an articulation of the general principle of effectiveness, exemplified in Article 19 TEU, in the context of which the compatibility of the *denial* of a remedy for the breach of EU rights, say, in particular, by the application of proportionate limitation periods has been readily endorsed by both the CJEU[153] and domestic courts in the United Kingdom.[154] Thus the moment in time at which a particular general principle of EU law must be 'recognised' may make all the difference as to the substantive content of that 'recognised' general principle as part of 'retained

150 But not for cases decided before IP completion day: *EUWA 2018, Sch 8, para 39(3)*.

151 See discussion of *s 5(5)*, which purports to preserve 'fundamental rights and principles', although not Charter rights, below.

152 Case 68/88, [23], [24].

153 See eg *Fantask* (Case C-188/95).

154 *Leeds City Council v HMRC* [2016] STC 2256.

EU law', quite apart from the difficulties of what constitutes 'recognition' in the first place.

Equally fundamentally, *Sch 1, para 3* provides '(1) there is no right of action in domestic law on or after exit day based on a failure to comply with any of the general principles of EU law [and] (2) no court or tribunal or other public authority may, on or after exit day (a) to disapply or quash any enactment or other rule of law, or (b) quash any conduct or otherwise decide that it is unlawful, because it is incompatible with any of the general principles of EU law.' *Schedule 1, para 3* does not operate merely to exclude *remedies* otherwise available on the application of EU general principles (disapplication or quashing of non-general principle-compliant enactments etc). *Paragraph 3(1)*, by excluding rights of action on the basis of a breach of an EU general principle, effectively *excludes* EU general principles from being substantive principles of law from United Kingdom domestic law and converts these general principles into interpretative principles only. There is no other juristic work for EU general principles to do, if they cannot ground a course of action, other than to supplement the interpretation of specific express legislative provisions of EU-derived domestic legislation comprised in *EUWA 2018, s 1B*, direct EU legislation comprised in *s 3*, or other legislation comprised in *s 4*.[155] Thus the provisions in *EUWA 2018, Sch 1, para 3* perform an exclusionary function in relation to the substantive content of EU law, in its adaptation into 'retained EU law'. There is an important caveat to the modified application of general principles of EU law: *EUWA 2018, Sch 8, para 39(6)* disapplies *Sch 1, para 3(2)* to any post-IP completion day decisions of courts or tribunals (or other public authority) which are a 'necessary consequence of any [pre-IP completion day] court/tribunal decision'. In other words, a pre-IP completion day decision which applies a general principle of EU law in the full sense, that is, non-modified *Sch 1* sense, binds a court, in a post-IP completion day case, to apply that general principle in the full sense. So, for example, in a post-IP completion day case, a court or tribunal may well say 'we are not entitled to apply the general principle of [say, effectiveness] in a substantive, free standing way, so as to disapply a particular provision of domestic United Kingdom law, by reason of EUWA 2018, schedule 1, paragraph 3 but we are bound, as a matter of stare decisis, to follow and apply [a particular, binding, pre-IP completion day decision] which reaches exactly that same result and we must do the same'. It is the binding nature of the pre-IP completion day case, which makes following that case a 'necessary consequence'.[156] *Paragraph 39(6)* effectively 'ring fences' pre-IP completion day case law (but not the general principle itself), insofar as they apply general principles of EU law in the full sense.

155 The *Taxation (Cross-border Trade) Act 2018* (*TCBTA 2018*), *s 42(4)* provides that the general principle of 'abuse' continues to apply, seemingly in its unrestricted, full sense but provides the *EUWA 2018* as the legislative foundation for this, which suggests that 'abuse', for the purpose of the *TCBTA 2018*, applies in its restricted *EUWA 2018* sense.

156 The same would be true of a 'public authority'.

Interpretation of 'retained EU law'

1.32 *Sympathetic construction:* As observed above, the principles of 'sympathetic construction' adopted by the domestic courts of the United Kingdom, so far as EU law is concerned, are a function of both the 'loyalty clause' in Article 4.3 TEU and the EU principle of supremacy. Certainly, it should follow that during the 'implementation period', until 31 December 2020, the principle of supremacy[157] should inform the construction of all United Kingdom domestic law in exactly the same manner as it does, prior to exit day on 31 January 2020, since EU law continued in full force and effect until that date by reason of *s 1A(2)*. It has also been observed that the United Kingdom courts' notion of 'sympathetic construction' in relation to EU law is peculiarly robust and sui generis, in that it is confined to securing the compliance of United Kingdom domestic law, in its *meaning*, with EU law.

The landscape of the principles of construction for retained EU law changes considerably after 31 December 2020.

An immediate and fundamental question of principle arises after the expiry of the implementation period. After this time, it is the *EUWA 2018 which must be construed and applied on its own terms*. It is considered that 'sympathetic construction', in the peculiar EU sense, as developed by the United Kingdom courts, does not survive post-IP completion day. There are four reasons: first, *EUWA 2018* does not, as observed above, apply all of the 'methods and principles' of EU law to 'retained EU law', contrary to Article 4.3 of the Withdrawal Agreement, as effected into United Kingdom domestic law by *EUWA 2018, s 7A*. Secondly, 'sympathetic construction' is not a general principle preserved in the *EUWA 2018*. Thirdly, the provisions of *EUWA 2018* itself, as to the interpretation of 'retained EU law', which heavily modifies how 'retained EU law' is to be interpreted and applied, show that on any view, 'sympathetic construction' is not, so far as the draftsperson of *EUWA 2018* is concerned, preserved in anything like pre-IP completion day form. Fourthly, the *EUWA 2018* is located within a post-Brexit constitutional architecture which comprises the Withdrawal Agreement (within the *EUWA 2018* itself), 'retained EU law', the *United Kingdom Internal Market Act 2020* which arrogates powers to the United Kingdom Government which cuts directly across the devolution settlement effected by the *Scotland Act 1998*, the *Government of Wales Act 1998* and the *Northern Ireland Act 1998* (themselves very firmly part of the constitutional architecture). Each of these constitutional statutes has its own (non-EU) legislative agenda. To ascribe 'retained EU law' a construction which relates exclusively to its EU roots (when 'retained EU law' is United Kingdom domestic law, which exists only because of Brexit) would be constitutionally improper. It is true that supremacy of 'retained EU law' survives, at least as against unmodified pre-IP completion day United

157 Assuming *s 1A* and *s 1B* take priority over the remainder of *EUWA 2018*, including *s 5* and *Sch 1*, as discussed above.

Kingdom domestic law. But sympathetic construction is not, it is submitted, exclusively a function of supremacy and even if it were, that preserved supremacy of 'retained EU law' must be applied in the legislative context of the *EUWA 2018*, when the United Kingdom has left the EU. So the unwelcome prospect of exactly the same provision of 'retained EU law' (say a provision of 'EU-derived domestic legislation', in a primary Act of Parliament) being interpreted in one way as against a pre-IP completion day United Kingdom statute but in a different way, using different principles of interpretation, as against a post-IP completion day statute, does not arise, although this does mean that 'retained EU law' (particularly 'EU-derived domestic law' will be interpreted differently after IP completion day than before that day (this latter proposition is not at all startling: the very notion of 'received law' which is subject to 'local circumstances exceptions' illustrates this latter approach: see below).[158]

1.33 Now the United Kingdom has left the EU, the interpretative exercise must start by asking: 'in applying sympathetic construction, what is the legislative archaeology of the relevant provision of "retained EU law" properly considered to be?' Put another way, in the light of the United Kingdom having left the EU, in applying principles of 'sympathetic interpretation', a court or tribunal must ask 'sympathetic to *what*?' Prior to the United Kingdom having left the EU, all domestic statutory provisions had to be construed sympathetically to the TEU/TFEU and *a fortiori* to any regulations, decisions or Directives which they implemented. But post-31 December 2020, 'retained EU law', whether 'EU-derived domestic legislation', 'direct EU legislation', or the 'residual' category of EU provisions in *EUWA 2018, s 4*, such as directly applicable TEU/TFEU provisions, or directly applicable Directive provisions, will necessarily have to be construed in the light of Parliament's intentions embodied in the *EUWA 2018* and the *EUWAA 2020*, which implement the United Kingdom's *withdrawal* from the EU and establish the application of 'retained EU law' in the light of that withdrawal. And given that the 'loyalty clause' in Article 4.3 TEU has no application post-31 December 2020, in the

158 It follows that the Explanatory Notes to the *EUWA 2018*, which suggest that sympathetic construction in its full EU sense continues in relation to retained EU law, are simply wrong. See Explanatory Notes for the *EUWA 2018* [104] (on *s 5(2)*), which suggest that sympathetic construction must continue as a function of the supremacy of retained EU law (as least so far as pre-31 December 2020 United Kingdom domestic legislation is concerned). But sympathetic construction is a function of both supremacy and the loyalty clause and the loyalty clause has ceased to have effect since 31 January 2021. See also Explanatory Notes [111] (relating to *s 6(3)* on general principles, which suggest that sympathetic construction, in the EU sense, continues for retained EU law by reason of the application of general principles). Sympathetic construction is not itself a general principle and thus is not engaged by *s 6(3)*. These observations are quite apart from the points made above as to the changed constitutional context of the United Kingdom's domestic law. It is trite law that an Explanatory Note cannot change the meaning of a statutory term. For a sceptical approach to the value of Explanatory Notes expressed in general terms, see *Astall and Anr v HMRC* [2010] STC 137 at [43], per Arden LJ.

absence of any express provision in either *EUWA 2018*, or *EUWAA 2020*, which preserves the principle of 'sympathetic construction' as developed by the United Kingdom courts specific to the implementation and application of EU law, during the United Kingdom's membership of the EU, there is no reason in principle why 'sympathetic construction', in the strong sense applied by United Kingdom courts and tribunals to secure compliance of United Kingdom legislation with EU law should be applied to construe 'retained EU law', after 31 December 2020. What principles of statutory construction should, post-IP completion day, apply to 'retained EU law'? So far as 'EU-derived domestic legislation' is concerned, this category of 'retained EU law' is subject to the conventional principles of statutory construction of all United Kingdom legislation, albeit subject to the specific statutory rules which apply to 'retained EU law' in *EUWA 2018* discussed below. 'Direct EU legislation' and the rights and obligations contained in *s 4* of the *EUWA 2018* are far more difficult. As observed above, the legal material comprised in each of these categories of 'retained EU law' is, in no sense, United Kingdom 'legislation': the only 'legislation' is *EUWA 2018, ss 3* and *4*, which introduce this latter legal material into United Kingdom domestic law. The legal material comprised in 'direct EU legislation' and in *EUWA 2018, s 4* is, it is considered, best interpreted by analogy to statutes enacted in colonial times, retained by former colonies, post-independence. As such, the default rule is that of the general 'reception of law doctrine': an enactment should be 'interpreted in the context of the common law in which it was enacted.'[159] Such 'received law' is properly construed, however, in the light of a 'local circumstances exception': the construction of 'received law' is modified and updated by reference to changes to the legal landscape of the relevant jurisdiction, so that the construction of particular legal material, put simply, changes over time, even though the legal material itself remains unchanged.[160] Adapted to 'retained EU law', this is properly construed in the light of its original purpose to implement the EU project but heavily acknowledging the United Kingdom's exit from the EU

159 *Pollock v Manitoba* [2004] 64 WIR 228.

160 *Re First Virginia Reinsurance Ltd* (2005) 66 WIR 133 (Bermuda Supreme Court); so retained extradition provisions in the *Fugitive Offenders Act 1881* which were incompatible with the post-independence Indian Constitution on the grounds that they were discriminatory and were repugnant to the independent status of India (in that they could not be applied by an Order in Council of the United Kingdom Parliament and other former British colonies could not be compelled to assist in extradition proceedings, as contemplated by the Act) were held by the Indian Supreme Court to be void: *State of Madras v MG Menon and Anr* (1955) 1 SCR 280. Indeed, in the context of revenue law, the Privy Council held that certain tax provisions concerning reorganisations enacted in Jamaican revenue law should not be interpreted in the same manner as the identically worded United Kingdom provisions, since the rationale of the relevant Jamaican tax regime was different to that which applied in the United Kingdom; Carrera is properly viewed as an application of the 'local circumstances exception': *Carreras Group Ltd v Stamp Commissioner* [2004] STC 1377 PC. See, generally, R-M Belle Antoine, *Commonwealth Caribbean Law and Legal Systems*, 2nd edn (Routledge-Cavendish, 2008), p 279 et seq, which draws attention to and very helpfully analyses this conceptual issue.

which, on a case by case basis, may of course change the rationale of the particular 'retained EU law' being construed.

Turning to the specific statutory rules enacted in the *EUWA 2018* which United Kingdom courts and tribunals must apply to interpret 'retained EU law', these specific rules make the process of interpretation of 'retained EU law' not only different to the process of interpretation of EU law, during the United Kingdom's membership of the EU but different to any process of interpretation of legislative provisions currently known and adopted by courts and tribunals in the United Kingdom hitherto. First, *EUWA 2018, s 6(1)(a), (b)* provides that a court or tribunal 'is not bound by any principles laid down, or any decisions made, on or after IP completion day by the European court and … cannot refer any matter to the European court order after IP completion date'. United Kingdom courts and tribunals may, however, 'have regard' to not only decisions of the CJEU but also 'anything done' by 'another EU entity or the EU [which includes the European Commission]', so far as it is 'relevant to any matter before the court or tribunal'.[161] Although one might quibble with the term 'bound', in that, although the CJEU is the ultimate guardian of the construction of any provision of EU law, it is the national court which is ultimately responsible for the application of any decision by the CJEU to the particular facts, the relegation of post-IP completion day decisions of the CJEU to, at most, persuasive status is unexceptionable. The United Kingdom courts would have no legal compulsion to cede the interpretation of 'retained EU law', which is part of United Kingdom domestic law, to any court outside the jurisdiction of the United Kingdom itself. *Section 6(4), (5)*, in providing that the Supreme Court and the High Court of Justiciary in Scotland[162] are not 'bound' by any CJEU decisions,[163] even if made before IP completion day, although any departure from 'retained EU case law' is subject to the same test as is applied in either court deciding to depart from its own case law[164] is also perfectly sensible, recognising Parliament's intention, reflected in the *EUWA 2018* and the *EUWAA 2020*, that the United Kingdom is legally separated from the EU.

1.34 However, the interpretation exercise itself of 'retained EU law' as to its 'validity, meaning or effect', as established in the *EUWA 2018*, is cumbersome and problematic.

'EU law' (not 'retained EU law' but 'EU law', which is not defined) is a question of law.[165] So the matter will be dealt with, in legal proceedings, as one of submissions and not as a question of fact, to be decided on the basis of evidence

161 *EUWA 2018, s 6(2)*, which is permissive, not mandatory: so a United Kingdom court or Tribunal cannot be criticised for failing to have regard to a post-IP completion day CJEU judgment, although its decision may of course, be poorer for any such disregard.

162 Scotland's highest criminal court, from which there is no appeal.

163 'Retained EU case law', which has effect prior to IP completion day: *EUWA 2018, s 6(7)*.

164 And may be subject to regulations enacted by a minister: *EUWA 2018, s 6(5A)(d)(i)*.

165 *EUWA 2018, Sch 5, para 3*.

given by an expert on foreign law. *Section 6(3), (7)* requires United Kingdom courts and tribunals to interpret 'retained EU law', so far as that 'retained EU law' is 'unmodified', in accordance with 'retained case law' (a combination of pre-IP completion day United Kingdom Court/tribunal decisions ['retained domestic case law'[166]] and pre-IP completion day CJEU decisions ['retained EU case law']) and 'retained general principles of EU law, being 'general principles of EU law, as they have effect in EU law immediately before IP completion date'.[167] As has already been observed, *Sch 1, para 3* transmogrifies EU general principles from substantive principles into interpretative principles, which means that their application will be very different to that in EU law. Indeed, this may hamper United Kingdom authorities. An interpretative provision is only relevant to construe the text of a particular provision. Thus, for example, the application of the principle of abuse of law in, say, the context of VAT may be very different if that principle only applies to interpret particular provisions, rather than, as it operates in the context of EU law, operating on particular transactions, independent of any specific provisions, albeit in the light of their purpose.[168] The principle of supremacy of EU law is conferred on 'retained EU law' only to the extent of its application to pre-IP completion day United Kingdom law.[169] As observed above, the Charter of Fundamental Rights is not part of United Kingdom domestic law after IP completion day and cannot form part of any interpretative exercise of 'retained EU law'.[170] While *EUWA 2018, s 5(5)* purports to retain 'fundamental rights are principles which exist irrespective of the Charter', insofar as these constitute 'general principles of EU law', they are emasculated in effect, while to the extent that the CJEU has recognised any such Charter-independent 'rights or principles', which are not general principles of EU law, the reader will be left to ascertain whether the CJEU consider these to be 'fundamental' (and whether these fall within *s 4(1)*, which is the only candidate provision to confer 'retained EU law' status on

166 This reference to 'retained domestic case law' is puzzling. Any court or tribunal in the United Kingdom is subject to the doctrine of *stare decisis*. A legislative direction to decide a matter 'in accordance' with 'retained domestic case law' seems wholly redundant, although the term assumes particular significance in relation to the application of *s 6(5A)–(5C)* and a potential legislative direction to depart from 'retained EU case law': see below.

167 *Section 6(3)(b)* requires courts and tribunals to have regard to 'EU competences', which presumably means that 'retained EU law' is to be construed the principle of conferral in mind, so that the scope of, say, a regulation or Directive which is part of 'retained EU law' should be interpreted as applying only so far as the relevant EU institution had power to enact it.

168 It may be said by, say, HMRC, that *Sch 1, para 3*, in precluding a 'right of action in domestic law' which is 'based on a failure to comply with [general principles]' does not encompass an 'action' raised by HMRC which is founded on 'abuse of law' and the prohibited 'quashing of conduct' in *para 3(2)(b)* on the grounds that the conduct is 'unlawful' by reference to the application of a 'general principle' does not encompass the re-categorisation of a transaction, so that abuse of law continues to apply in a substantive, not only interpretative sense. See the comments made above in relation to the *TCBTA 2018, s 42* and chapter 2 of this title. And of course, pre-IP completion day case law relating to EU general principles is preserved and ring fenced: see above.

169 *EUWA 2018, s 5(1), (2)*.

170 *EUWA 2018, s 5(4)*: see above.

such rights or principles, since these cannot, by definition, be contained in 'EU-derived domestic legislation', or legislated by means of 'direct EU legislation'). Furthermore, *s 5(5)* requires 'any case law … to be read as if … references to [the Charter] were references to [these] corresponding fundamental rights or principles'. The Charter of Fundamental Rights is, of course, more than a mere codification of a collection of pre-existing 'fundamental' rights (see above: otherwise it would be unintelligible to exclude the application of the Charter but retain the application of the latter) and identification of a 'corresponding' principle to substitute for a reference to a provision in the Charter, in a case report is an artificial (and therefore unsatisfactory) exercise.

The problems get worse. The provisions in *s 6(5A)–(5C)* merit the description of 'quite extraordinary'. These provisions permit a minister to make regulations for any court or tribunal (that is, not just the Supreme Court or the High Court of Justiciary) not to be 'bound by' (that is, ignore) 'retained EU case law' (that is, pre-IP completion day CJEU decisions)[171] and retained domestic case law in so far as the latter 'relates' to 'retained EU case law'[172] (so that, for example, regulations may specify that a particular tribunal, in the context of a particular area of law which is concerned with 'retained EU law', may ignore a Supreme Court decision which follows a particular CJEU decision), specify the test as to when that 'retained EU case law' may be ignored, specify the 'considerations' relevant to the application[173] of this test (which assumes that, somehow, 'considerations' which are relevant to the application of a test are distinct from the test itself, which is not readily intelligible), such regulations being made after a (non-binding) consultation with the senior judiciary.[174] Regulations have now been passed[175] which entitle the Court of Appeal (Civil

171 *EUWA 2018, s 6(5A)(a)–(d).*

172 *EUWA 2018, s 6(5B)(b).*

173 There is a puzzling provision in *s 6(5B)(c)* which permits regulations to be made on '… other (that is, other than United Kingdom courts and tribunals being "bound" by retained domestic case law) matters arising in relation to retained domestic case law which relates to retained EU case law …'. At face value, this is simply a wide enabling power to permit regulations to be made on any 'matter' which 'relates' to the subject matter of any decision of the CJEU which has been implemented or followed by domestic case law, which is available to the legislature in any event and, at least on its terms, a fantastically wide enabling power for a minister to make delegated legislation. Assuming that the intention is not to confer power on a minister to, effectively, make regulations on any 'matter' relating to the EU whatsoever, *s 6(5B)(c)* is best read as implicitly restricted to a power to specify particular circumstances in which particular pre-IP completion day decisions of United Kingdom courts or tribunals may be amended or reversed ('matters … In relation to retained domestic case law' being restricted to 'the effect of decisions'), on the basis that Parliament could not have intended to permit ministers to enact regulations on any EU matter whatsoever, in a provision dealing with the binding nature of 'retained case law'.

174 *EUWA 2018, s 6(5C).*

175 *The European Union (Withdrawal Act) 2018 (Relevant Court) (Retained EU Case Law) Regulations 2020, SI 2020/1525.* These Regulations clearly provide an additional basis for the Court of Appeal in England and Wales (and in Northern Ireland) and the Inner House in Scotland to depart from prior decisions but more fundamental questions arise: is the right to depart subject to *stare decisis*? May, for example, the English Court of Appeal abandon

and Criminal Divisions) in England and Wales, the Inner House of the Court of Session, the High Court of Justiciary in Scotland, the Court of Appeal in Northern Ireland, Court Martial Appeal Court, and the Lands Valuation Appeal Court all to depart from CJEU decisions, unless the particular court is bound by a post-31 December 2020 ruling by a higher court.[176]

These provisions are constitutionally troubling, unnecessary, productive of uncertainty and potentially wholly ineffective. Constitutionally troubling because in so far as the imposition of any 'test' as to when a court is entitled to ignore any particular decision carries with it an implicit direction to *in fact* ignore that decision constitutes an improper legislative and executive (particularly because the substantive provisions will be contained in regulations promulgated by a minister) interference in judicial decisions offends the separation of powers. Unnecessary because judicial decisions of any description may be reversed by legislation. Productive of uncertainty to the extent that CJEU decisions are made with regard to particular areas of law, it may, without adequate guidance, be unclear exactly what is being departed from. The CJEU decision on narrow terms? Or the principle it sets down?[177] And potentially wholly ineffective, in that a court or tribunal which is permitted to ignore a particular decision which it otherwise would have felt compelled to follow may come to the same decision as the 'ignored decision' in any event. It is not possible to find anything to commend *EUWA 2018, s 6(5A)–(5C)*.[178]

1.35 An additional layer of difficulty in construing 'retained EU law' is provided by *s 6(6)*. *Section 6(3)* provides rules for the exercise of determining the 'validity meaning or effect' of 'retained EU law', so far as it is 'unmodified' on or after IP completion day. To 'modify' means to 'amend, repeal or revoke'.[179] Thus *s 6(3)* will not apply to any 'retained EU law' insofar as there is any material legislative amendment. Such 'modified' 'retained EU law' may, according to *s 6(6)* still be decided upon, in relation to its 'validity, meaning or effect' if the legislative amendment ('modification') is 'consistent' with the *s 6(3)* rules continuing to apply. If the legislative amendment, the 'modification' is not consistent with the 'retained EU law' being interpreted and applied in

---

a particular CJEU decision despite the Supreme Court having followed and applied it? The better answer is 'no'. Nothing in the Regulations qualifies the principles of precedent and *Reg 4(2)* on 'post-transition case law' (see below) assumes the conventional principles of precedent continue to apply.

176 'Post-transition case law': *European Union (Withdrawal Act) 2018 (Relevant Court) (Retained EU Case Law) Regulations 2020, SI 2020/1525, Regs 2* and *4(2)*.

177 Here a Practice Note would be welcome from the relevant Courts as to how any departure from a CJEU decision should be expressed and conveyed.

178 Incidentally, *s 6(1)–(6)*, including *s 6(5A)–(5C)* are subject to 'relevant separation agreement law', that is the United Kingdom legislation implementing the Withdrawal Agreement, so that the implementation of the Withdrawal Agreement, in particular citizens' rights, continues to be subject to EU law, including the principles of supremacy and the application of EU general principles and being ring fenced against the application of *s 6*: *s 6(6A)*.

179 *EUWA 2018, s 20(1)*. The definition is inclusive. Related expressions are to be treated accordingly, which would include the term 'unmodified'.

accordance with 'retained case law' and 'retained general principles of EU law' (say a statute within the notion of 'EU-derived domestic legislation is heavily amended to exclude a retained general principle, such as proportionality),[180] the draftsperson's thought is presumably that purely domestic techniques of statutory construction would apply, on the basis that the 'modified' provision was no longer 'retained EU law' (because it is not in the form which 'had effect,' or was 'operative', or was 'recognised and available' immediately before IP completion day[181]). But the assumption that such an 'intention' can be readily divined from the nature of the 'modification' is, it is considered, optimistic. While there is, of course, nothing to prevent a 'modification' from expressly stating that a particular provision of 'retained EU law' is 'no longer intended to be 'retained EU law', in the absence of such a bald statement, such an intention may be difficult to establish, particularly in relation to a provision of 'retained EU law' which is only explicable as a measure to make United Kingdom law EU-compliant (such as the *VATA 1994*).

Procedural protections and remedies

1.36 A series of procedural safeguards and remedies have been simply excised by the *EUWA 2018*. Of course, references may no longer be made, post-IP completion day to the CJEU.[182] Challenges to the validity of EU instruments may no longer be made (under Article 263 TFEU) after IP completion day.[183] The right to damages 'in accordance with the rule in *Francovich*' is repealed,[184] although purely domestic rights to damages will remain. It is awaited as to how the principles for damages awarded on a breach of 'retained EU law' rights might be developed. The restitutionary *San Giorgio* right is not repealed. Incidentally, it was observed above that disapplication of non-EU law compliant Member State domestic provisions was a peculiarly EU remedy. To the extent that domestic United Kingdom law (certainly pre-IP completion day domestic law) does not comply with 'retained EU law', the United Kingdom Courts will have to apply either: (1) the doctrine of implied repeal to give 'retained EU law' force over the non-'retained EU law'-compliant provisions, or (2) develop principles of construction to give 'retained EU law' priority as a matter of necessary implication (as a function of supremacy), which should be (relatively) straightforward.

180 For example, imposing a disproportionate penalty in a primary Act.

181 Using the terminology in *ss 2–4*.

182 *EUWA 2018, s 6(1)*.

183 *EUWA 2018, Sch 1, para 1(1)*. *Paragraph 1(2)* preserves a right to challenge the validity of an EU instrument if the General Court/CJEU has held the instrument to be invalid, before IP completion day. Further, *The Challenges to Validity of EU Instruments (EU Exit) Regulations 2019, SI 2019/673* permit challenges to be made to the validity of EU instruments in respect of claims based on such invalidity in proceedings 'begun' before IP completion day (*EUWA 2018, Sch 1, para 3*). *Paragraph 4* gives jurisdiction to United Kingdom courts and tribunals to declare an EU instrument invalid (which is necessary, since preliminary references under Article 267 TFEU will no longer be possible after IP completion day).

184 *EUWA 2018, Sch 1, para 4*.

Critical 'transitional' provisions

1.37 It is an inevitable feature of the combination of the complex nature of the United Kingdom's withdrawal from the EU and the unsatisfactory approach and drafting of the *EUWA 2018* that some of the most important protections are contained in 'saving' or 'transitional' provisions in *Sch 8*, in relation to cases begun[185] but not yet decided before IP completion day.

First, in relation to the Charter of Fundamental Rights, the Charter continues to apply to such cases: *(EUWA 2018, Sch 8, para 39(3))*.

Secondly, the general principles of EU law have full effect (not the modified effect provided by *EUWA 2018, Sch 1, para 3*). In relation to general principles, proceedings 'begun' within three years of IP completion day are to be decided by reference to the full effect of EU general principles of law (that is, *Sch 1, para 3* is disapplied) but only insofar as their application challenges something which occurred before IP completion day and the challenge does not seek to disapply an act of Parliament, a rule of law, or subordinate legislation which owes its legal force to either) (*Sch 8, para 39(5)*). This caveat to the application of general principles of EU law is separate to the application of binding 'retained case law' discussed above.

Thirdly, *Francovich* damages are available for such cases (*para 39(3)*) and indeed *Francovich* damages are available in for cases relating to something 'done', pre-IP completion day, so long as the relevant proceedings are 'begun' two years from IP completion day (*para 39(7)*).

VI. Conclusion

1.38 To implement the United Kingdom's withdrawal from the EU was never going to be easy. However, the commentary and discussion above shows that the exercise to achieve predictability, consistency and continuity is imperfect. It is wholly unsatisfactory for fundamental questions such as those discussed above to remain open. It is difficult to be optimistic about the operation of this new regime, post-IP completion day (unless one is a lawyer instructed in the inevitable litigation to determine how this regime will apply).

A useful summary of the application of 'retained EU law' is as follows:

(1) Identify the category of 'retained EU law' which is to be interpreted and applied (if necessary, identify whether it has been 'recognised' pre-IP completion day).

185 The term 'begun' is not defined, so it is an open question as to the procedural stage which qualifies a case to have 'begun'. A sensible approach is the commencement of the formal state of litigation, say, the issue of a claim form, or a notice of appeal.

(2) Interpret that 'retained EU law' by reference to: (a) general principles as interpretative principles only (but subject to 'ring fenced' binding case law which have a 'necessary consequence' of the application of general principles in the full EU law sense); (b) *United Kingdom* principles of construction, recognising the United Kingdom's departure from the EU (not EU 'sympathetic construction'), whether against pre- or post-IP completion day United Kingdom statutes; (c) binding 'retained case law'; (d) any specific regulations which make otherwise binding case law not binding; (e) (of persuasive value only) post-IP completion day CJEU case law and CJEU legislative provisions which are not within 'retained EU law'; in so far as CJEU case law refers to the Charter of Fundamental Freedoms, read that case law as if references are to 'corresponding' general principles.

(3) Apply the 'retained EU law' as supreme over pre-IP completion day United Kingdom domestic law (or where any post-IP completion day 'modifications' are consistent with the continued application of supremacy) but with no attribute of supremacy over post-IP completion day United Kingdom statutes.

This is a deceptively neat package, beset with conceptual difficulties. Courts and tribunals deserve patience and forgiveness as they grapple with this new regime.

PART 2: THE EU-UK TRADE AND COOPERATION AGREEMENT[186]

1.39 Part 2 of this chapter deals with the Trade and Cooperation Agreement between the European Union, the European Atomic Energy Community (Euratom)[187] and the United Kingdom (the TCA). Put short, the TCA has no relevant substantive impact on retained EU law, although this paper takes a long time to say so.

186 For Part 2 of this chapter, I am extremely grateful to Dr Lorand Bartels, of Trinity Hall, Cambridge for his generous consideration and help on this topic and for sight of his draft (unpublished) paper on the Trade and Co-operation Agreement. Dr Bartels' observations on the draft of this paper have greatly improved it and I am grateful for the opportunity to acknowledge his help. Dr Andrew Sanger, of Corpus Christi, Cambridge also made valuable comments on the draft from the perspective of Pubic International Law. My indebtedness to Professor Cremona and to Professor Craig extends to receiving helpful comments on Part 2. And I am also very grateful to Ross Denton, Senior Consultant, Head of International Trade, Ashurst, LLP, for having read and commented on the draft. Errors (as in the case of Part 1 on retained EU law) are still mine.

187 Adopted by the EU by Council Decision on signature 2020/2252 29 December 2020 ('the Council Decision on Signature'). It is convenient to ignore Euratom for present purposes, since Euratom's status as a signatory to the TCA does not affect any of the principles discussed here.

The structure of Part 2 is as follows:

- Section I is a short introduction.
- Section II: (a) makes general observations on the structure of the TCA, (b) makes preliminary observations on the application[188] of the TCA as regards EU Member States, and (c) identifies structural and practical problems in the application of the TCA.
- Section III considers the juristic nature of the TCA.
- Section IV looks at three specific sections of the TCA, concerning goods, investment and services.
- Section V discusses the weak substantive nature of the trade rights conferred by the TCA, at least in relation to investment and services.
- Section VI discusses exceptions, that is, areas where the TCA does not apply.
- Section VII considers the dispute settlement procedure.
- Section VIII analyses the method of giving effect to the TCA, through the *FRA 2020, s 29.*
- Section IX gives a brief conclusion as to the TCA and the post-Brexit regime overall.

I. Introduction

1.40 The TCA was concluded on 24 December 2020 and provisionally applied[189] by both parties from 1 January 2021.[190] The TCA entered the EU legal order by way of the Council Decision on Signature and was introduced into United Kingdom domestic law by the *European Union (Future Relationship) Act 2020* (*FRA 2020*). The TCA is a free trade agreement wholly different to the TEU and TFEU.

A preliminary but vital feature of the TCA is that, unlike the TEU and TFEU, the TCA is clear that the Parties retain sovereignty and their respective 'domestic laws' (a term used in the TCA: see below, so one which assumed by the draftsperson to somehow have meaning in respect of the EU) have primacy over the TCA. Thus the dynamic and hierarchy of international law and domestic law is reversed for the Parties.

188 Or rather, the non-application: see below.

189 Reflecting the terminology of the Vienna Convention, Article 25.

190 Although see TCA, Part Seven, Article FINPROV 10: the TCA must be published in all of the languages of each EU Member State, which (in each of its linguistic forms) will take precedence, in the event of any inconsistency, over the text of the TCA concluded on 24 December 2020. The legal review of the TCA ('legal scrub') may also change the terminology.

Before embarking on a discussion of the TCA, it is as well to point out that the TCA is an unusual international treaty, from the perspective of both the EU and United Kingdom. It is the first international treaty concluded between the EU and a former EU Member State, where strong substantive EU internal market provisions for the latter are replaced by necessarily far weaker trade rights. It is different to recent Treaties concluded by the EU with other third countries, such as the Comprehensive Economic and Trade Agreement ('CETA') between the EU and Canada, or the Comprehensive Agreement on Investment ('CIA') with China.[191] These latter international agreements accommodate the prospect of dispute resolution mechanisms, in the form of investor-state dispute resolution (ISDS) investment courts. Indeed, the EU seeks to eventually establish a single Multilateral Investment Court, with jurisdiction over all international investment disputes involving the EU, currently covered by ISDS. By contrast, as discussed below, the TCA has an arbitration system which has little or no general legal impact.

The TCA is an international agreement which, moreover, will be quite alien to EU internal market lawyers, not only in its terminology (although some of the terminology of the TCA will be familiar to an EU lawyer, for no other reason than the TEU and TFEU replicated GATT terminology, albeit subject to what became a distinct evolutionary process, assisted by the CJEU) but also in its substantive effect. A strong and familiar legal regime comprised of the TEU and TFEU, supplemented by Regulations, Directives and Decisions, enforced by the CJEU, is replaced by a regime, comprised in the TCA, where the substantive obligations (certainly those imposed on the EU: see below) are difficult to identify and even more difficult to enforce. For this reason, the TCA requires careful analysis, even if many of the conclusions are self-evident to an international trade lawyer and even if that careful analysis concludes, as it does, that the TCA has, except, perhaps, in the field of goods and customs duties,[192] very little to say about the domestic law of the United Kingdom in general, retained EU law in particular, or the United Kingdom's tax law.

Both the text of the TCA and the manner of its introduction into United Kingdom domestic law under the *FRA 2020, s 20(1)* raise difficult questions of interpretation and application. These questions touch on fundamental principles of the United Kingdom's constitutional law. However, it is considered that, ultimately, the TCA has little direct substantive effect on United Kingdom domestic law (including retained EU law), although the process of reaching this short conclusion is necessarily long and, at times, turgid. In any event and on any view, the TCA is self-evidently critical to the terms of trade between the United Kingdom and the EU and must be considered separately

191 Agreed in principle.

192 From the perspective of an internal market EU law: there are (relatively) detailed provisions in TCA, Part Two, Heading Three (road transport) and Heading Four (social security coordination and visas for short-term visits), which latter Heading will have important interactions with the Withdrawal Agreement and Part Three, on law enforcement and judicial cooperation in criminal matters.

to the provisions of retained EU law. And the TCA's special treatment of tax provisions (both double tax conventions and the tax provisions in the domestic tax codes of the United Kingdom and individual EU Member States), discussed below, is of particular interest.

II. General observations on the TCA as to structure and the application of the TCA to EU Member States

The structure of the TCA

1.41 The TCA owes much of its terminology to the WTO Agreement. This is important in relation to the nature, interpretation and application of the TCA (and by contrast to the nature and application of the internal market provisions in the TEU and TFEU).

The TCA comprises seven 'Parts'. While the instrument comprising the TCA is vast (over 1,200 pages), compared to the TEU and TFEU, it is slim compared to the instrument comprising the WTO agreement (over 30,000 pages, although these do include schedules for 137 parties). Each Part is a self-contained collection of provisions, mutually exclusive from every other Part (albeit part of an instrument to be construed as a whole), apart from Part One ('common and institutional provisions'), Part Six ('dispute settlement and horizontal provisions')[193] and Part Seven ('final provisions'), which are (broadly) relevant to the interpretation of the entirety of the TCA. The other Parts of the TCA are: Part Two ('trade, transport fisheries and other arrangements'), Part Three ('law enforcement and judicial cooperation in criminal matters'), Part Four ('thematic cooperation, in the areas of health security and cyber security') and Part Five ('participation in union programs, sound financial management and financial provisions'). Each 'Part' is divided into 'Titles' (except for Part Two, where the volume of material is large; Part Two is divided into 'Headings' and each heading is divided into 'Titles'). There are a substantial number of Annexes to the TCA, which are expressly provided to be 'integral' to the TCA and three Protocols (on, first, administrative cooperation and combating fraud in relation to VAT and mutual assistance for the recovery of claims relating to taxes and duties, secondly, on mutual administrative assistance on customs matters and third on social security coordination[194]).

This chapter shall focus attention on Part One, Part Two and Part Six, as it is these parts which correspond most closely to any discussion of the EU internal market provisions, that applied while the United Kingdom was an EU Member State and to the discussion of retained EU law above.

---

193 Part Six is excluded for certain specific matters, which have their own dispute resolution procedure: see further below.

194 There are also certain Declarations, the status of which is still presently unclear.

Preliminary observations on the application of the TCA to individual EU Member States

1.42 The 'Parties' to the TCA are the EU, Euratom and the United Kingdom. So far as the United Kingdom is concerned, the TCA is an international treaty concluded (and potentially amended, or terminated) by an exercise of the prerogative. And so far as the EU, as a separate legal person,[195] is concerned, the TCA is the result of an exercise of exclusive competence under Articles 3(1)(e),[196] (2), 217[197] TFEU.[198]

There are three separate sets of issues arising from the TCA being a function of the exclusive competence of the EU to which EU Member States are not parties (and therefore do not assume primary obligations, at least under the TCA, in relation to the United Kingdom).

The first set of issues is structural: in the absence of any substantive obligations under the TCA for individual Member States, there are certain provisions of the TCA, particularly in relation to investment, services and capital payments, which have very little substantive content at all (and are of therefore very little value to the United Kingdom). The second set of issues is practical, in that an alleged breach by an individual EU Member State of a provision of the TCA, even if it could be visited on the EU, is very likely to become entangled in a dispute between that Member State and the EU, which latter dispute would have to be resolved by the CJEU as a matter of EU law.[199] The third set of issues, at first sight, concern seemingly sterile points of drafting of certain provisions in the TCA which make it difficult to identify exactly how these provisions apply. However, these 'drafting points' in fact reflect the structural and practical issues about to be discussed and therefore cannot simply be ignored.

Structural issues: no TCA primary obligations on individual EU Member States

1.43 The first set of (structural) issues arise precisely because the only primary (ie direct) obligations under the TCA, so far as the EU is concerned,

195 Article 47 TEU.

196 Common commercial policy.

197 Under the procedure in Article 218 TFEU and (subject to ratification by individual Member States) adopted by way of a decision under Article 288 TFEU. Whether the EU has vires to conclude all of the substantive provisions of the TCA is controversial, particularly as, as pointed out below, the obligations of individual EU Member States may be extended by the application of the 'most favoured nation' (MFN) principle: see further below.

198 Signed on the legal basis of Article 217 TFEU (association agreements); it is worth noting that while certain aspects of the TCA fall within exclusive competence (trade), others fall within shared competences (eg social security coordination).

199 Put another way, the TCA does not create international legal obligations for Member States as against the United Kingdom, albeit that the TCA clearly creates EU obligations for Member States as regards the EU (to comply with the TCA, or any EU agreement): *Kupferberg* (Case 104/81), paras 11–13.

lie with the EU, not individual EU Member States. The TCA forms part of the EU legal order by reason of the Council Decision on Signature, see Article 4.3 TEU and Articles 216 and 217 TFEU. The Council Decision on Signature is, of course, secondary EU legislation,[200] over which the TEU and the TFEU have primacy, although, of course the TCA requires the consent of the European Parliament. So while the United Kingdom may enforce TCA obligations on the EU, EU Member State compliance will be, on the one hand, a function of the standard public international law 'good faith' provisions in Part One, Article COMPROV.3 (whereby the United Kingdom will look to the EU to secure Member State compliance with the TCA) and the application of EU law as between the EU and Member States on the other. Individual EU Member States would be bound to respect the terms of the TCA only by a combination of the loyalty clause ('duty of sincere cooperation'), Articles 4.3 and 216 TEU.[201]

But a breach of the TCA is far more likely to occur because of the actions of an individual EU Member State, rather than the EU itself. The result is that any breach by individual EU Member States gives rise to a substantive complaint for the United Kingdom that the EU has breached its good-faith obligation to secure Member State compliance, rather than the breach of a primary obligation imposed on the EU as such, which potentially attracts the questions of: (1) the scope and extent of the good-faith obligation on the part of the EU to secure Member State compliance,[202] and (2) whether the EU has a legal basis to compel Member State compliance,[203] in relation to the specific TCA provision being disputed. It is this asymmetry which is structural: there are substantive TCA obligations imposed on the United Kingdom but the same substantive obligations imposed on the EU which have, by and large, a practical concern for the United Kingdom play out at EU Member State level; the latter have no substantive obligations under the TCA at all.

---

200 Although the TCA does have primacy over other secondary EU legislation (not over the EU Treaties nor EU constitutional principles/fundamental rights/Charter): See *Intertanko* (Case C308/06), para 42; *Kadi* (Case C-402/05 & C-415/05), paras 306–308.

201 Perhaps coloured by Article 21.3 TEU (EU external action should be consistent over different areas).

202 While Article 27 of the Vienna Convention on the Law of Treaties prohibits a party from relying on the provisions of 'internal law' in any dispute on alleged breach, it remains that if Member States cannot readily be brought into line in relation to any dispute regarding the TCA, the United Kingdom's capacity to obtain a satisfactory remedy (short of retaliation) is compromised.

203 Despite action taken under Article 217 requiring unanimity, hindsight may persuade a Member State that a particular provision of the TCA is non Article 217-compliant. And the prospect of disputes over the vires of an agreement concluded by the EU is neither theoretical nor negligible: see eg *France v Commission* (Case C-293/91), where the CJEU held a purported agreement between the Commission and the United States on the application of competition law to be void as the Commission had no *vires* to conclude any such agreement.

Practical issues: how does the United Kingdom complain about EU Member State breach?

1.44 The second set of (practical) issues concern the mechanism by which the United Kingdom may complain about any such breach of the TCA, which is seemingly clumsy. These issues flow directly from the structural asymmetry discussed above. Any complaint by the EU of a breach of the TCA by the United Kingdom would be resolved by an immediate engagement in the consultation process and, if necessary, arbitration as set out in Part Six of the TCA, discussed further below. But if an individual EU Member State breaches a provision in the TCA, the United Kingdom would complain to the EU about the failure of the EU to secure Member State compliance (see above). In addressing any complaint by the United Kingdom, the EU might well be faced with: (1) a battle as to whether the relevant provision was indeed within the exclusive competence of the EU, (2) any submission by the Member State in question as to whether the question of whether the 'loyalty clause' and/or Article 216 TFEU indeed prohibited such alleged breach of the TCA, and (3) a difference of opinion between a Member State and the EU as to whether that Member State's actions did indeed result in a breach of the EU's obligations under the TCA (all of these being internal EU disputes, within the EU legal order determined by the CJEU), which, issues, even if they did not delay the EU engaging with a complaint by the United Kingdom under the TCA, would inevitably become embroiled in and have an impact on the TCA proceedings. Furthermore, the jurisdiction of the CJEU informs the operation of the TCA in a material way. The obligation on the Parties to provide judicial oversight in certain, limited, circumstances is imposed, so far as the EU is concerned, on the EU (rather than any individual EU Member State, without any obligation on the part of the EU to accommodate any form of direct complaint against an individual EU Member State),[204] which means that the relevant court which provides judicial oversight, from the EU's perspective is the CJEU. All of which makes dispute resolution, from the perspective of the United Kingdom, highly sensitive to decisions of the CJEU.

These potential difficulties would not arise in a mixed agreement (of course, only to the extent that the disputed provisions were subject to the shared competence of the EU and EU Member States: the provisions of any mixed agreement which were subject to the exclusive competence of the EU would have the same problems as those expressed here in relation to the TCA) where the EU and Member States were both parties, such as CETA. Where a free trade agreement is a mixed agreement, the counterparty to the EU would have a direct right to enforce (shared competence) obligations against individual Member States.

---

204 See Part One, Title II, Article COMPROV.13; which makes it clear that it is the courts and 'domestic law' of the Parties (so the EU, not Member States, so far as EU obligations are concerned) and Part Two, Title II, Article SERVIN 5.12.

Drafting issues: not merely a question of legal language

1.45 The third set of issues, concerning the drafting of the TCA, also arises from the observation that the 'Parties' to the TCA are the EU (not Member States) and the United Kingdom. These drafting issues raise problems as to the TCA's interpretation and construction. The discussion below is peppered with observations (not to say complaints) that the TCA refers to, variously and non-exhaustively, the goods 'of' the EU, 'national treatment [of goods]' by the EU[205] and the domestic law 'of' the EU,[206] in setting out its substantive terms. These terms are not readily intelligible and the fact that individual Member States are, as a matter of EU law, obliged to respect the terms of the TCA do not help with the interpretation and application of these terms as between the EU and the United Kingdom.

It is true that in Part One, Title II, the obligation, so far as it relates to the EU, to afford unimpeded market access for cross-border investment and to afford non-discriminatory treatment as regards 'its' nationals for cross-border investors expressly extends to 'territorial sub-divisions' of the 'Parties', which would include individual EU Member States.[207] But there is no such reference to any individual Member State treatment as regards the application of the 'most-favoured-nation' principle (MFN), discussed further below. In relation to cross-border services, it is only the EU's obligation to afford unimpeded market access which extends to 'territorial sub-divisions'.[208] There is no such extension of the EU's obligation to ensure non-discriminatory 'national' treatment, or the application of MFN, in relation to cross-border services. The provisions relating to capital movements are linked to services and investment by Article CAP.3. Indeed, in relation to goods, cross-border investment, cross-border services and capital payments, other than provisions relating to the protection of certain existing measures from the application of the TCA altogether[209] and the provisions concerning legal services[210] there is no reference to the domestic legal regimes of individual EU Member States at all. These drafting questions may be (insofar as the remain unresolved after the 'legal scrub') resoluble, easily enough, by the WTO (although perhaps not with much juristic elegance). But what they reveal, on any view, is that an agreement between the EU on the one hand and a single, sovereign state on the

---

205 Part Two, Title I, Article GOODS.4.

206 See Part One, Title II, Article COMPROV.13.2 for a reference to the 'domestic law' of the Parties.

207 Part Two, Title II, Article SERVIN.2.2, SERVIN.2.3.2.

208 Part Two, Title II, Article SERVIN.3.2. It is true that Article SERVIN 2.3 does refer to Member States in the context of national treatment.

209 Which do refer to measures passed by central government or local government of individual EU Member States on the one hand and the United Kingdom on the other: see Part Two, Title II, Article SERVIN.2.7, Article SERVIN.3.6.

210 Part Two, Title II, Chapter 5 which does carefully define 'host-state jurisdiction' for both the United Kingdom and individual EU Member States.

other raises important questions as to the location of primary obligations and the practicalities of enforcement.

III. The juristic nature of the TCA

1.46 In no sense is the TCA the foundation of a 'new legal order'. The TCA, to the contrary, expressly preserves the 'autonomy and sovereignty' of its signatories, the 'Parties'.[211] On its express terms, as discussed below, the TCA does not confer rights on private persons[212] and thus there is no impediment which confronts the executive from exercising the prerogative without the need for Parliamentary consent, contrary to the circumstances of *Miller.* Importantly, the EU, as a 'Party', has concluded the TCA in the exercise of its exclusive external competence, as a distinct legal person. This makes the interpretation and application of certain fundamental provisions of the TCA problematic. For example, in relation to TCA, Part Two, Title I, Article GOODS.2, which provides that Chapter 1 (national treatment and market access for goods (including trade remedies)) applies to trade in goods 'of a Party', but what constitutes goods 'of' the EU (as opposed to the goods 'of' an EU Member State?).[213] This point is far more than a sterile, logical puzzle and gives rise to fundamental problems, which are discussed below.

The juristic nature and characteristics of the TCA: the TCA is a commercial free trade agreement and not a constitutional international instrument

1.47 The TCA is a free trade agreement.[214] As already observed, sovereignty and autonomy are expressly acknowledged and preserved for the

211 Part One, Title I, Article COMPROV 1.

212 Subject to Part One, Title II, Article COMPROV 16.1 which allows for the application of the TCA to private rights within Article MOBI.SSC.67 and Part Three (law enforcement and judicial cooperation in criminal matters, as regards the EU: this exception may be significant, as the prospect of individual rights being located within EU private persons by reason of Part Three may well affect criminal proceedings and makes the discussion of the effect of the *FRA 2020, s 29* below of real practical importance). A discussion of Part Three is, however, outside the scope of this Chapter.

213 Part Two, Title I, Chapter Two deals, relatively comprehensively, with the rules of origin, which are the foundation for the application of 'preferential tariff treatment' within Title I. The simple point is that the TCA does not equate with goods originating in a particular territory with goods being 'of' that territory (and therefore 'of' that Party). As already observed, it is not suggested that this question is impossible to resolve by the WTO, probably by equating the good 'of' the EU with goods 'originating in the territory of' the EU. It does highlight, however, the stark dichotomy between the assumption of primary obligations (by the EU) and the absence of statehood on the part of the EU, which cannot readily claim that goods or persons are 'of' the EU, rather than 'of' a particular Member State, without specific legislative direction.

214 Although made without prejudice to earlier EU-United Kingdom agreements, so that the Withdrawal Agreement prevails in any conflict with the TCA: Part Seven, Article FINPROV.2.

Parties. It is true that there is an obligation on both Parties to '... in full mutual respect and good faith, assist each other in carrying out tasks that flow from [the TCA and to take] ... all appropriate measures ... to ensure the fulfilment of the obligations arising from [the TCA] and [to] refrain from any measures which could jeopardise the attainment of the objectives of [the TCA]'.[215] But the very nature of the TCA is that of a free trade agreement, rather than a multilateral treaty which seeks to establish a 'new legal order'. So these provisions are not properly treated as analogous to the 'loyalty clause' and the duty of 'sincere cooperation' in Article 4.3 TEU. This is confirmed by Part One, Title II, Article COMPROV 13.2, which provides that the TCA should be interpreted in accordance with the customary rules of interpretation of public international law and need not be construed by either party 'in accordance with the domestic law' of either the EU or the United Kingdom.[216]

This latter provision is puzzling on a number of levels. First, as already observed, one relevant 'Party' is the EU. Article COMPROV.13 permits the United Kingdom to interpret the TCA in a manner which is not 'in accordance with' the domestic law of the United Kingdom (which means, it is supposed, that it may be interpreted in some autonomous, *sui generis* sense) but the reference to the 'domestic law' of the 'EU' (as a Party) is not readily intelligible. As already observed, EU Member States, as such, are not, in any sense, 'Parties' to the TCA. If it is a reference to 'EU law', Article COMPROV 13.2 permits the United Kingdom to interpret the TCA in a manner which is inconsistent with EU law (and therefore, inconsistent with the notion of sympathetic construction mandated in the CJEU case law[217]), which is not to say very much at all. If it is a reference to something else, it is not readily apparent what that something else might be. But on any view, Article COMPROV 13.2 reinforces the notion that the TCA is an agreement between two independent parties, which excludes the specific notion of sympathetic construction, as developed by the CJEU. Secondly, Article COMPROV 13.2 is redundant. A free trade agreement never requires one party to construe or be bound by a decision which interprets that agreement given by the courts of the other party.[218]

The free trade, non-constitutional nature of the TCA is made even clearer by Part One, Title II, Article COMPROV.16,[219] which provides that the TCA may neither confer rights or obligations on private persons, nor be 'directly

215 Part One, Title I, Article COMPROV 3: good faith.

216 Part One, Title II, Article COMPROV 13.2.

217 While the CJEU has held that it should endeavour to interpret EU secondary law consistently with the EU's international treaty obligations (*Commission v Germany* (Case C-61/94), para 52), there is no duty for the United Kingdom courts to do so, so the latter will simply apply a standard (rebuttable) assumption that the United Kingdom will fulfil its international obligations.

218 Which makes Part One, Title II, Article COMPROV 13.3, which provides that a decision by a court of one Party shall be binding on the courts of the other Party also wholly redundant. Again, it is unclear what is meant by a court 'of' the EU: the only candidate is the CJEU, but not the domestic courts of each and every EU Member State.

219 Private rights.

invoked in the domestic legal systems of the Parties'. This is, of course, in direct contrast to the internal market provisions of the TEU and TFEU. It also makes the way that the United Kingdom has given the TCA effect in domestic United Kingdom law a curiosity. The *FRA 2020, s 29* may be read (wrongly: see below) to do exactly that: that is, to give the TCA direct effect (seemingly in a strong sense) into United Kingdom domestic law, so as to change that domestic law. *Section 29* is discussed further below.

Decisions of the Partnership are enforceable by political institutions (the EU and the United Kingdom at governmental level) as a matter of public international law, nothing more. Not only is the TCA a free trade agreement and not the foundation for any sort of institutional pooling of sovereignty (quite the opposite), its mechanics are far more a function of political action, rather than the application of hard-edged legal principles.

The observation just made is founded on the governance structure of the TCA. Put short, the application of the TCA is in the hands of a 'Partnership Council' which comprises a member of the European Commission and a governmental minister of the United Kingdom at ministerial level.[220] It is this 'Partnership Council' which makes recommendations to the Parties regarding the implementation and application of the TCA and adopts decisions to amend the TCA, in certain permitted circumstances.[221] There is no judicial oversight of the Partnership Council in the TCA whatsoever.[222]

IV. Substantive provisions of the TCA: goods, investment and services

1.48 So far as the substantive provisions of the TCA are concerned, this chapter focuses attention on Part Two, Heading One (trade), Title I (trade in goods), Title II (services and investment) and Title IV (capital movements, payments, transfers and temporary safeguard measures), since these provisions are most closely analogous to the free movement internal market provisions of TEU and TFEU.[223]

---

220 Part One, Title III, Article INST.1.

221 Part One, Title III, Article INST.1.4. The partnership committee may delegate powers to 'trade partnership committees' or to 'specialised committees': see also Article INST.2 (Committees) and Article INST.3 (Working Groups).

222 This is not to say that decisions of the Partnership Council will not ever come under the scrutiny of the CJEU: *Sevince* (C-192/89), paras 8–10.

223 The scope of Part Two is: Heading One (trade), Title I (trade in goods), Title II (services and investment), Title III (digital trade), Title IV (capital movements etc), Title V (intellectual property, Title VI (public procurement), Title VII (small and medium-sized enterprises), Title VIII (energy), Title IX (transparency), Title X (good regulatory practices and regulatory cooperation), Title XI (level playing field for open and fair competition) and Title XII (exceptions (that is, dis-application of substantive provisions in Part Two in certain circumstances): see further below, particularly in relation to tax provisions).

The TCA provides for, broadly, a form of market access rights, a prohibition against discrimination which favours a host state, as compared to non-host state goods, services and capital payments and (for services, investment and capital movements) a 'most-favoured-nation' (MFN) prohibition[224] on discrimination as between two non-host state services, investments and capital payments (so that if a particular treatment is afforded by a Party, say, the United Kingdom, to any non-United Kingdom service provider, investor or the maker of a capital payment, that same treatment must be given to all other non-United Kingdom service providers, investors, or makers of capital payments). These substantive provisions mirror the WTO Agreement. Critically, the express prohibition against the creation of rights in private persons makes these TCA substantive rights a very heavily watered down version of the internal market provisions in the TEU and TFEU, quite apart from certain important textual qualifications to these rights in the TCA, Some of these differences between the TCA provisions and the EU internal market provisions are highlighted below.

Specific areas of the TCA considered: goods, services and investment

Goods

1.49 The TCA provides for an extensive regime for the trade in goods between the EU and the United Kingdom. For the effect of the TCA on customs duties, see chapter 3 of this title. In relation to the 'trade in goods', dealt with in Title I, the TCA deals with the goods 'of' both the EU and United Kingdom.[225] The now familiar point as to the difficulties of construction of the term 'goods *of* [the EU]' surfaces, therefore as to the scope of Title I. This issue is exacerbated by a critical substantive right provided by Title I:[226] the right to national treatment in relation to internal taxation and regulation. This right is afforded 'in accordance with Article III of GATT 1994 …'. The latter is couched in terms of a prohibition of 'internal taxes or other internal charges of any kind in excess of those applied, directly or indirectly, to like domestic products'.[227] Thus Part Two, Title I, Article GOODS.4 begs the question as to what is meant by 'national' treatment, in relation to the EU, while the incorporation of Article III of the General Agreement on Tariffs and Trade 1994 (GATT 1994) begs the question as to what is meant by 'like' treatment, in the context of an obligation imposed on the EU. This is simply not answered by the terms of the TCA. Part Two, Title I, Chapter 2 (Rules of origin) provides detailed rules as to when goods 'originated' in either the EU or United Kingdom and the rules of origin provide a foundation of many of the

224 With important carve outs: see below.
225 Part Two, Title 1, Article GOODS.2.
226 Part Two, Title I, Article GOODS.4.
227 GATT 1994, Article III.2.

substantive rights and obligations, in relation to goods in the TCA. But these rules do not help with the interpretation and application of the term 'national' treatment, in the context of the EU. As observed above, one may be confident that the WTO can resolve questions such as what are the goods 'of' the EU and what is meant by 'national' treatment, in relation to the EU (a tentative answer may be that goods which originate anywhere in the EU are goods 'of' the EU and nationality treatment of any EU Member State is 'nationality' treatment by the EU since the EU is a single, amorphous bloc, at least in its capacity as a counterparty to the TCA). But this important question will need authoritative resolution at some point.

Each Party's goods are afforded freedom of transit through the territory of the other;[228] customs duties are prohibited,[229] as are import and export restrictions (under GATT rules).[230] Unlike the internal market provisions, there is no extension of import and export restrictions to 'measures with equivalent effect'.

Services and investment

1.50 Cross-border investment and cross-border services are dealt with by Part Two, Heading One, Title II, Chapter 2 and Chapter 3 respectively. By contrast to its treatment of goods, the treatment of cross-border investment and cross-border services is relatively threadbare. Indeed, the TCA provisions read almost like the mere foundation for the conclusion of further, more detailed, EU-United Kingdom, or, state-by-state bilateral investment treaties[231] (BITs) between the United Kingdom and individual EU Member States.[232]

In relation to cross-border investors, Part Two, Title Two, Chapter 2 applies to investors 'of' the EU and United Kingdom. An investor 'of' the EU is defined as 'a natural or legal person of [the EU]', being a national of any EU Member State (in relation to natural persons[233]), or any legal person constituted or

228 Part Two, Title I, Article GOODS.4A.

229 Part Two, Title I, Article GOODS.5.

230 Part Two, Title I, Article GOODS.10.

231 Depending on where competence lies under TFEU, Article 207.

232 The United Kingdom had concluded BITs with 12 states, prior to their joining the EU: Bulgaria, Croatia, the Czech Republic, Estonia, Hungary, Latvia, Lithuania, Malta, Poland (Poland has reneged on its agreement on 22 November 2019 but there is a 15-year period before this BIT is terminated), Romania, Slovakia and Slovenia. The European Commission had issued a reasoned opinion to the United Kingdom, following the decision of the CJEU in *Achmea* (Case C-284/16), calling on the United Kingdom to terminate these BITs but they have not, to date, been terminated and are seemingly intact: see the decision of the Supreme Court in *Micula v Romania* [2020] UKSC 5, confirming that the United Kingdom had retained enforcement rights in relation to these BITs, since they were concluded prior to the counterparty-states acceding to the EU. Future BITs between individual EU Member States and the United Kingdom are, furthermore, seemingly perfectly competent.

233 Part Two, Heading Six, Article OTH.1(l): equally, a natural person is 'of' United Kingdom if that person is United Kingdom citizen, ibid.

organised under the laws of the EU,[234] or any Member State, engaged in 'substantive business operations', which excludes shell companies.[235]

Similarly, Chapter 3 applies to 'services' and 'services suppliers' of the EU and United Kingdom. A 'service supplier' 'of' the EU is a 'natural or legal person of [the EU],[236] where the terms 'natural person' and 'legal person' had the same meaning as they do in relation to cross-border investment (thus confining the scope of Chapter 3 to nationals of EU Member States, for natural persons and non-shell companies formed under the law of an EU Member State, for legal persons).[237] The term 'service' is very broad: it encompasses 'any service in any sector' (except services supplied in the exercise of governmental authority).[238] So, for example, financial services are included within the scope of any provisions which apply generally for the purpose of Title II.[239]

For present purposes, it is sufficient to note that both investors and service providers[240] of one Party are entitled to: (1) market access rights (in the form of a prohibition on any restrictions on the nature and extent of economic activities which they may undertake),[241] (2) a protection against nationality discrimination which confers more favourable treatment to investors or service providers of the other Party,[242] and (3) MFN treatment, so that if one Party gives a particular, favourable treatment to an investor or service supplier of a 'third country' (that is, a jurisdiction which is neither the EU, nor the United Kingdom), investors and service suppliers of the other Party are entitled to that same favourable treatment.[243]

---

234 Shipping companies established under third country laws are included if they are controlled by natural persons of an EU Member State and are registered in and fly the flag of an EU Member State. Part Two, Title II, Article SERVIN.1.2(l)(B).

235 Part Two, Title II, Article SERVIN.1.2(d), (h), (j), (k), (l); The investment provisions in Part Two, Title II also encompass 'covered enterprises', being a branch or company established cross-border in either the EU or the United Kingdom by an investor 'of' the other Party.

236 Part Two, Title II, Article SERVIN.1.2(q).

237 With the extension for shipping companies, referred to above.

238 Part Two, Title II, Article SERVIN.1.2(o).

239 It is true that certain special provisions in relation to the TCA regulation of each Party's regulatory framework which govern services and investment make special provision for 'financial services' which seem, at first sight, to exclude, for example, the provision of venture capital or private equity: see Part Two, Title II, Article SERVIN.5.38(a). But the general provisions of Title II will apply to all services, including financial services, unless expressly excluded. There are general exclusions to the application of Title II (see Part Two, Title II, Article SERVIN.1.1.5 and 1.1.6) but these exclusions do not extend to financial services.

240 See Part Two, Title II, Article SERVIN.2.1 to Article SERVIN.2.7 for cross-border investors and Part Two, Title II, Article SERVIN.3.1 to Article SERVIN.3.6 for cross-border service providers.

241 Article SERVIN.2.2 for cross-border investors and Article SERVIN.3.2 for cross-border service providers.

242 See Article SERVIN.2.3 for cross-border investors and Article SERVIN.3.4 for cross-border service providers.

243 See Article SERVIN.2.4 for cross-border investors and Article SERVIN.3.5 for cross-border service providers. Again, there are specific important carve outs and reservations

Capital payments etc

1.51 The free movement of capital payments between the EU and the United Kingdom are secured by Part Two, Heading One, Title IV. The free movement of payments and transfers on both the current account and capital account of the balance of payments of each Party (yet another provision which makes no sense in the context of a 'Party' being the EU) is secure, subject to certain permitted restrictions, so long as those restrictions are not applied in an arbitrary or discriminative manner, or in a way which constitutes a disguised restriction on capital movements.[244] However, the prohibition on the creation of private rights also applies in relation to capital movements in Title IV also.

V. Weak substantive strength of the TCA

1.52 However, what seem at first sight to be strong substantive measures, to secure impediment-free trade between the EU and the United Kingdom are revealed to be, in fact, relatively weak, to the point of being non-existent. A preliminary observation is that the Parties' commitment to a 'level playing field for open and fair competition and sustainable development' in Part Two, Title XI are expressly excluded from the TCA dispute settlement regime,[245] although there are dispute resolution provisions[246] relating specifically to 'non-regression' and 'rebalancing'.

More fundamentally, the absence of any substantive juristic strength of the TCA provisions is apparent from the TCA itself, certainly in relation to investment and services.

First, there is the recurrent theme that the primary obligation is on the EU and not on Member States and the consequent difficulty of identifying the substantive content of the EU's obligation, whether in relation to cross-border investment[247] or services.[248] So it is difficult to identify the substantive content of the obligation on the EU to afford 'national treatment' (that is, 'treatment no less favourable than that it accords, in like situations, to its own [investors or services and services suppliers]'[249]), when most of the operational rules apply at Member State level (so that, in ascertaining whether, say, cross-border investment or services from the United Kingdom into Germany is afforded 'national' treatment the comparator treatment, at least textually, is

244 Part Two, Heading One, Title IV, Article CAP.1–Article CAP.4.

245 Part Two, Title XI, Article 1.3.

246 Consultation and arbitration: Part Two, Title XI, Articles 9.1–9.4.

247 Part Two, Title II, Article SERVIN.2.3.

248 Part Two, Title II, Article SERVIN. 3.4.

249 Part Two, Title II, Article SERVIN.2.3 and Article SERVIN.3.4: similar observations may be made in relation to MFN treatment: see Part Two, Title II, Article SERVIN.2.4 and Article SERVIN.3.5.

that given 'by' the EU, not Germany, which is meaningless:[250] there is no provision, at least in the context of cross-border investment or services, which assimilates Member State acts to EU acts). The watery nature of the cross-border provisions on investment and services is confirmed by the provisions of ANNEX SERVIN-1,[251] which provides that 'for the [EU], the obligation to grant national treatment does not entail the requirement to extend to natural or legal persons of the United Kingdom the treatment granted in a Member State, pursuant to the TFEU …'.[252] This latter provision confirms not only that the TCA acknowledges that the primary obligations are those of the EU, not Member States but also makes it quite clear that the substantive provisions of the EU internal market regime have no part to play in interpreting or applying the TCA. The substantive provisions for 'national' treatment and MFN treatment would, of course, make perfect sense in any BITs concluded between the UK and individual Member States but make little sense within the TCA itself. Perhaps the most can be said is that their inclusion in the TCA will reassure the United Kingdom that any future EU-United Kingdom BIT will have such provisions as its foundations and also reassure EU Member States who wish to conclude BITs with the United Kingdom (with EU authorisation) that provisions as to unimpeded market access, national treatment and MFN should be included as a matter of orthodoxy.

Secondly, as already observed, the TCA measures are incapable of giving rise to rights and obligations in relation to private persons. As discussed below, these provisions cannot be enforced by private persons, in any meaningful sense, even if the EU or the United Kingdom failed to properly implement a particular TCA provision.

Thirdly, there are specific carve outs (even before the discussion progresses to the treatment of tax provisions: see further below), which exclude the market access, non-discrimination and MFN rules for 'any existing non-conforming measure', which 'non-conforming measure' may indeed be continued, renewed (albeit that the renewal must be 'prompt') or even modified, so long as the degree of non-conformity is not increased by any such 'modification'.[253] To be sure, the United Kingdom's domestic legal regime, including provisions which apply to investors and service providers, should most likely conform to the EU internal market provisions, at least at present. But those which, for one reason or another, are not internal market compliant (and not TCA compliant) are left

250 It is true that Opinion 2/15 seemingly considers that the comparator would be Germany (in its treatment of the EU-Singapore FTA). The complaint made here is that this (sensible) approach is not textually correct and that Germany is not a party to the TCA and thus has no direct obligations which would make Germany an appropriate comparator.

251 'Existing Measures'.

252 ANNEX SERVIN-1, Article 10.

253 See Article SERVIN.2.7.1 for cross-border investors and Article SERVIN.3.6.1 for cross-border service providers. They provide for non-conforming measures to be specifically listed in 'schedules'. New measures which do not meet the renewal conditions are prohibited.

untouched and protected by these 'non-conformity provisions'. Furthermore, the TCA itself provides for extensive specific reservations and derogations.[254]

Fourthly, tax provisions are effectively taken out of the scope of the TCA altogether: see further below.

VI. Exceptions to the application of Part Two of the TCA (especially tax provisions)

1.53 The substantive scope of the TCA is further confined by Part Two, Heading One, Title XII, which sets out 'exceptions' to the application of Part Two of the TCA. These applications include measures necessary to protect public security, public morals, human, animal or plant life or health[255] which would be familiar to an EU lawyer but which do not operate as 'justifications' for a 'breach' of any obligations. Instead these comprise carve outs from the application of Part Two of the TCA altogether. Thus there is no obvious reason to apply a presumption that such exceptions should be construed narrowly.[256] Taxation features prominently in these exceptions, for which see further below.

Tax provisions: excluded from the scope of the TCA

1.54 The TCA has very little indeed to say about tax, except to confirm that tax law will play virtually no part in the development of the jurisprudence of the TCA. Taxation is expressly mentioned in two Titles of Part Two.

First, Title XI, Chapter Five (taxation), commits both the EU and United Kingdom to pursuing an attack on harmful tax competition and tax avoidance. Chapter Five reiterates support for the OECD Base Erosion and Profit Shifting (BEPs) Action Plan and the mutual exchange of information. Second, far more fundamentally, Chapter Three of Title XI, in dealing with subsidies (state aid) gives the Parties seemingly enormous scope to confer state aid through tax measures ('fiscal subsidies'). Title XI, Chapter Three, Article 3.2 deems 'tax measures' as non-'specific' unless there is a discriminatory effect, which (very broadly) codifies the case law of the CJEU to date.[257]

Special treatment of tax provisions

1.55 It might be thought that principles of unimpeded market access, non-discrimination and MFN would have a significant impact on the tax laws of the

254 See Article SERVIN.2.7.2-4 for cross-border investors and Article SERVIN.3.6.2 for cross-border service providers.
255 Title XII, Article EXC.1.2(a), (b).
256 Indeed, they may be construed very broadly: WTO case law militates against any narrow reading.
257 This chapter will not consider state aid. See chapter 4 of this title in relation to state aid.

Parties (the United Kingdom and the EU/individual EU Member States). It is in this context that a long and careful analysis is needed to come to a very short proposition: quite apart from the weak substantive nature of the principles of unimpeded market access, non-discrimination and MFN, so far as the TCA is concerned, the domestic tax codes of the Parties are not affected by these principles. Indeed, the TCA has, it is considered, very little impact on the domestic legal regimes of either individual EU Member States, or the United Kingdom (and has little or no impact on 'retained EU law'). It is frustrating that this short proposition needs such a long analysis. Frustrating for the reader, who will have much to read to arrive at a short conclusion; frustrating for the writer (or anyone with an ambition that free-trade provisions have adequate legal protection), since the analysis reveals that much of the TCA has very little legal impact at all.

In relation to tax laws, a right to MFN treatment for cross-border investors, or service providers, is specifically curtailed in relation to any double tax international agreement, or any other 'international agreement or arrangement relating wholly or mainly to taxation'.[258]

The exclusion of tax provisions (indeed the provisions of TEU and TFEU generally) from the principle of MFN replicates the case law of the CJEU and therefore does not represent any change from the time during which the United Kingdom was a Member State of the EU.[259]

Turning to a broader discussion of the application of the TCA to tax provisions, the provisions concerning the exclusion of double tax treaty conventions from MFN treatment in Part Two, Title II, in relation to cross-border investors and cross-border service providers, if looked at in isolation, suggest: (a) that double tax conventions are subject to the TCA provisions regarding market access and non-discrimination as regards host-state national treatment, and (b) that provisions in the domestic tax code of the United Kingdom (and presumably individual EU Member States: see below), as opposed to the provisions of a double tax convention, do, indeed, attract the application of MFN treatment (not to say market access treatment and non-discrimination protection as regards host state nationals).

However, express treatment of taxation provisions much later in the TCA, at Part Two, Title XII (exceptions) excludes double tax conventions from the scope of the TCA altogether, certainly in the context of cross-border investment, the provision of cross-border services and capital payments: in the event of any

258 See Part Two, Title II, Article SERVIN.2.4.3 for cross-border investors and Article SERVIN.3.5.2 for cross-border service providers. The exclusion of MFN in relation to double tax conventions which apply to cross-border investors is repeated (in a wholly redundant manner) in Part Two, Title XII (exceptions), Article EXC.2.4(b).

259 See *D* (Case C-376/03).

inconsistency between the TCA and any double tax convention, the latter is to prevail.[260]

As for provisions in the domestic tax code of the United Kingdom and individual EU Member States, Title XII, Article EXC.2.3 provides that domestic tax provisions may ensure the equitable or effective imposition or collection of direct taxes (being taxes on income or capital) and may distinguish between taxpayers, who are not in the same situation, in particular with regard to the place of (tax) residents or with regard to the place where their capital is invested. This is subject to a prohibition of any 'arbitrary or unjustifiable discrimination between countries were like conditions prevail', or a 'disguised restriction on trade and investment'.[261] This caveat is discussed below.

Thus double tax conventions are, quite simply, left untouched by the TCA. For example, the United Kingdom may freely give a more favourable treatment to cross-border investment, or cross-border services from one particular jurisdiction (including an EU Member State jurisdiction) than to analogous investment or services from another jurisdiction.

What of the United Kingdom's domestic tax code? Does Article EXC.2.3 entitled the United Kingdom to practise tax discrimination in a manner prohibited by the internal market provisions? The short answer is, it is considered, 'yes'. As already observed above, the TCA is a free-trade agreement, not the foundation of a 'new legal order'. An international trade lawyer would perhaps consider Article EXC.2 is simply acknowledging that international tax matters are dealt with under double tax conventions and the latter is the exclusive mechanism for dealing with cross-border tax matters, whereas the effect of exclusion of the Parties' domestic tax regimes is an equally unremarkable acknowledgement of tax sovereignty for the United Kingdom on the one hand, and individual EU Member States on the other. An EU lawyer would, no doubt, point to the case law of the CJEU, which demands that legislative sovereignty, whether in relation to a domestic tax code, or in relation to the conclusion of double tax conventions, must comply with the internal market provisions (and therefore be non-discriminatory and allow unimpeded market access).[262]

---

260 The treatment of double tax conventions, and their exception from the application of the TCA, applies in relation to, *inter alia*, Part Two, Heading One, Titles I to VII (which would include Title II on services and investment and Title IV on capital payments): see Part Two, Title XII (exceptions), Article EXC.2.1. In a seemingly redundant provision, Article EXC2.2 expressly excludes the right to MFN treatment, as regards cross-border investment and the right to host-state national treatment as regards cross-border services.

261 See further L Bartels, 'The Chapeau of the General Exceptions in the WTO GATT and GATS Agreements: A Reconstruction' (2015) *American Journal of International Law* 95.

262 For selected highlights, see *EC v France* (Case 270/83) ('*Avoir fiscal*': discriminatory to confer tax credits for dividend payments by a French-tax resident subsidiary to a French-resident parent company but to withhold such credits for the repatriation of profits by a French branch of a non-French president company to its head office outside France: see further below), *Marks & Spencer v Halsey* (Case C-446/03) (discriminatory to permit the group relief of losses by one company to another within a group where both the surrendering company and the claimant company are established in one jurisdiction but to prohibit such group

The application of the TCA to the domestic tax codes of individual EU Member States and the United Kingdom will depend, critically, on what is meant by 'arbitrary or unjustifiable discrimination' in circumstances where 'like conditions' prevail in the two jurisdictions being compared, in the application of Article EXC.2.3. Article EXC.2.3 replicates the text of Article 65.1 TFEU, which provides that the free movement of capital provisions in Article 63 TFEU are without prejudice to the right Member States to 'apply … [their domestic tax law provisions] which distinguish between taxpayers who are not in the same situation with regard to their place of residence or with regard to the place whether capital is invested …'. Article 65.1 TFEU is also subject to Article 65.3, which prohibits 'arbitrary discrimination or a disguised restriction on the free movement of capital and payments'. Article 65.1 TFEU has never prevented the CJEU from applying the free movement of capital provisions in a manner which permitted a non-tax resident to obtain the same tax treatment as a host state tax-resident. Put another way, so far as the CJEU internal market case law is concerned, a resident and non-resident are, generally, in 'similar circumstances' for the purpose of applying a non-discrimination principle. So, in *Avoir Fiscal*, the comparison was made between a hypothetical non-French tax resident company which had established itself in France through a branch and its French-resident corporate competitor, which had a French-resident subsidiary. The proper comparison, said the CJEU, was between the non-French tax resident company and its French-tax resident corporate competitor, which meant that they were in 'similar circumstances'. The fact that the hypothetical non-French resident company had established itself through a branch, whereas its French-resident competitor had established a subsidiary was neither here nor there.

It is considered that, so far as the TCA is concerned, Part Two, Title XII, Article EXC.2.3 would operate quite differently to the internal market provisions and permit substantial differentiation, based on tax residence, of domestic and foreign persons by the EU (and individual EU Member States) on the one hand and the United Kingdom on the other.

First, it has already been observed that the TCA is a free-trade agreement, quite different to the TEU and the TFEU. Secondly, the principles of unimpeded market access, non-discrimination and MFN have all been expressly qualified, as has been observed above, in relation to double tax conventions. Thirdly, contrary to the TEU and TFEU, (again as observed above) the 'autonomy and sovereignty' of the Parties are expressly preserved. Fourthly, the scrutiny of the economic actors who might complain of discrimination or a market access impediment with an appeal to Article EXC.2.3 seems to be focused on the particular juristic attributes of the particular economic actors; for

---

relief cross-border), *Cadbury Schweppes plc v IRC* (Case C-196/04) (discriminatory and a prohibited restriction on market access to apply anti-avoidance provisions to a subsidiary company established in a low-tax EU Member State by reason of the latter's low tax rate alone).

example, Part Two, Title II, Article SERVIN.3.4.4 expressly permits national treatment to be withheld if a competitive disadvantage results from the 'foreign character of the relevant services or service suppliers'. [263] So different juristic attributes may give rise, of themselves, to economic actors not being located in 'like conditions'. *A fortiori* if the respective tax codes of the two jurisdictions being compared are very different. In terminology familiar to an EU lawyer, compensating advantages which arise from the juristic character of an economic actor, or the terms of the application of a home state or host-state tax code (which would have been irrelevant in the CJEU case law) may result in, contrary to CJEU internal market case law, an economic actor finding themselves not to be in 'like conditions' with its host-state competitor. And fifthly, the express absence of private rights means that the assessment of 'like conditions' is made by reference to the intentions of the Parties at governmental level, who have clearly gone to great lengths to preserve fiscal legislative autonomy.

It is for these reasons that the TCA cannot be said to have any substantive impact on the domestic tax codes of the individual EU Member States or the United Kingdom. For the reasons given below, this conclusion is unaffected by the *FRA 2020, s 29*.[264]

VII. The TCA dispute settlement procedure: a case-by-case disposition of a specific dispute

1.56 The TCA dispute settlement procedure firmly reinforces the primacy of domestic law (whatever this means in the context of the EU) of the Parties over the TCA.

In any dispute[265] involving a 'complaining party', which alleges that the other, 'respondent party'[266] is in breach of its obligations under the TCA, the TCA Part Six general provisions[267] have, for all intents and purposes, the express objective of resolving a particular dispute in favour of one or other

263 It may be the case that this provision is restricted to services (and does not apply to investment) since it reflects the General Agreement on Trade in Services (GATS), Article XVII:1, fn 10; see also Panel Report *Canada-Autos* (2000) where the limited scope of this provision was stressed.

264 It is certainly possible, although this observation is best relegated to a footnote, that the relatively light impact of the TCA on tax treaties and domestic tax codes will lead to increased visibility and litigation on the terms of double tax treaties themselves, in particular the non-discrimination clause: see eg *UBS AG v HMRC* [2007] STC 588, *FCE Bank plc v HMRC* [2013] STC 14, although, of course, EU Member State double tax treaties must be TEU/TFEU compliant.

265 The European Commission represents the EU in any arbitration proceedings (see below): see Council Decision on Signature, Recital 11.

266 Part Six, Title I, Chapter 2, Article INST.13.1.

267 Part Six, Title I, Chapter 1, Article INST.10.2(a)-(j) and 10.5 sets out those provisions of the TCA which are not subject to the Part Six dispute settlement procedure.

Party, without laying down any general principles of law.[268] Rather, a Party who successfully maintains that the other Party has breached the TCA, by (ultimately) securing a favourable decision from an arbitration tribunal (see below), obtains access to the remedies of requiring the offending party to cure the breach within 'a reasonable time', failing which the offending party may have to pay 'temporary compensation' and ultimately be subject to retaliatory measures.[269]

Part Six imposes an initial obligation on the Parties to enter into consultations, although this consultation obligation may be abandoned.[270] Consultations are effected through inter-Party communication[271] (so, so far as the United Kingdom is concerned, the consultation is undertaken by the United Kingdom government, in the exercise of the prerogative). It is only if, one way or another, a dispute is not resolved by consultation that a dispute is settled in a juristic setting, that is, an arbitration. The parties to the arbitration are, of course, the Parties to the TCA, being the EU and the United Kingdom. There is scope for an arbitration tribunal to receive 'unsolicited written submissions (limited to 15 pages, double spaced) from natural persons of a Party or legal persons established in the territory of a Party that are independent from the governments of the Parties'[272] but the arbitration tribunal need not take such submissions into account[273] and there seems to be no scope for such private persons making oral submissions.[274] Thus any breach of the TCA by one party may be simply accepted by the other party through the 'consultation' process and even if the matter proceeds to arbitration, private persons affected by the decision of the arbitration panel have very limited rights to make written representations and no rights at all to appear in the arbitration hearing itself.

268 From the perspective of the EU, the TCA dispute settlement procedure must not permit any dispute settlement body from construing EU law in any definitive way, in interpreting the TCA. The interpretation of EU law must, as a matter of the TEU and TFEU, be left to the CJEU alone (see Opinion 1/10 [78], [89]; Opinion 2/13 [170]–[200]; Opinion 1/17 [106]–[161]).

269 Part Six, Title I, Chapter 3, Articles INST.23, INST.24.

270 Part Six, Title I, Chapter 2, Article INST.13, 14.1(c).

271 Part Six, Title I, Chapter 2, INST.13.2: Pre-arbitration consultation for certain disputes may take place within the framework of a Specialised Committee, being the delegatee of Partnership Council powers, or the Partnership Council itself (but disputes subject to such a framework exclude, *inter alia*, disputes in the context of Part Two, Heading One, Titles II–VII, including trade in goods (Title I), services and investment (Title II) and capital movements and payments (Title IV), which latter disputes are, therefore, subject to the looser form of consultation-through-communication process envisaged by Article INST.13.2).

272 ANNEX INST: RULES OF PROCEDURE FOR DISPUTE SETTLEMENT, Article XII (p 1057).

273 Ibid.

274 Indeed, even the heading of Article XII of ANNEX INST on p 1057 is odd: 'Amicus curiae submissions', which suggests that any private person, non-Party, submissions are impartial as between the Parties to the TCA and concern only the integrity of a proper interpretation and application of the relevant TCA provisions, whereas submissions made by private persons may well, of course, have an agenda which is intensely supportive of one or other TCA Party.

Furthermore, consistent with the provisions of Article COMPROV.16.1 in Part One, Title II, which precludes the TCA from conferring rights or obligations on private persons, Part Six, Title I, Chapter 4, Article INST.29.2 provides that an arbitration panel's decision or ruling 'shall not create any rights or obligations with respect to natural or legal persons'. Indeed, Article INST.29.3 provides that decisions and rulings of the arbitration tribunal 'cannot add to or diminish the rights and obligations of the parties under the [TCA] …'.[275] So if, as a respondent party, the United Kingdom decides not to insist upon the fulfilment of one or other obligation which the EU was found to have breached under the TCA, perhaps as a matter of political expediency, whether in a 'consultation process' with the EU or even after a favourable arbitration tribunal decision, affected private persons have no remedy (or even avenue of complaint) to cure either that breach or, indeed, any continuing breach. Article INST.29.3 insulates the terms of the TCA from the effect of any arbitration tribunal decision,[276] although perhaps the Parties may perhaps found 'legitimate expectations' on the basis of a consistent line of Arbitration tribunal decisions.

What also follows from the above discussion is that there is no remedy for any private person who complains that one or other party has misimplemented the TCA. So a private person has no judicial mechanism to complain about any provision of domestic law which infringes the TCA (whatever that may mean in the EU). Any complaint is a matter for the EU and the United Kingdom, the latter at governmental level, alone.

Neither can the interpretation and application of the TCA be (at least with any ease) shoehorned into any other form of litigation. Article INST.11 secures an undertaking from both the EU and the United Kingdom not to submit any dispute regarding the interpretation or application of the TCA to

275 Underscored by Article INST.29.4, which prohibits an Arbitration Tribunal from assessing the legality of a measure alleged to constitute a breach of the TCA. The latter is consistent with both: (1) the exclusive jurisdiction of the CJEU in determining the scope and effect of EU law, including the legality of a measure of EU law or, perhaps, EU Member State law (and its relationship to Article 4.3 TEU and Article 216 TFEU), which allegedly breaches the TCA (see Opinion 1/10 [78], [89]; Opinion 2/13 [170]–[200]; Opinion 1/17 [106]–[161]), and (2) the primacy of domestic law over the TCA asserted by both Parties.

276 It follows that there is no reason whatsoever why arbitration tribunals cannot come to directly contradictory conclusions, on the interpretation and application of any particular TCA provision. The wording replicates 'the Understanding on Rules and Procedures Governing the Settlement of Disputes or Dispute Settlement Understanding' (DSU) signed by WTO members in 1994, Article 19.2 (on which see L Bartels, 'The Applicable Law in WTO Dispute Settlement Proceedings' (2001) 35(3) *Journal of World Trade Law* 499). The position is made even clearer by Article INST.29.4, which provides that an arbitration tribunal has no jurisdiction to determine the legality of any measure alleged to constitute a breach of the TCA. 'Legality' is clearly a reference to 'legality' under the law of the respective Parties (so EU law, as regards the EU). The provision was approved by the CJEU in Opinion 1/19.

any mechanism outside the TCA itself.[277] And the courts of both the EU and the United Kingdom are also excluded from having any jurisdiction over the resolution of any dispute between the parties under the TCA.[278] This latter provision does not prohibit any domestic court, whether in the UK or within the EU from construing the TCA (in the light of the *FRA 2020, s 29*, this is in any event impossible) but any exercise in interpreting the TCA may not, of course: (a) locate rights or obligations in private persons, or (b) settle any dispute between the EU and the United Kingdom as to what their respective obligations under the TCA might be. There are specific provisions which do afford access to judicial remedies but only in very specific circumstances: for example, in relation to customs duties, Article CUSTMS.14 in Part Two, Heading One, Title I, Chapter 5 requires both the EU and the United Kingdom to provide 'effective prompt, non-discriminatory and easily accessible procedures' which guarantee a right of appeal against administrative actions but only against rulings and decisions which affect import or export of goods, or goods in transit. There is an analogous provision in Title II, Chapter 5, Section 2, Article SERVIN.5.12 for cross-border investment and cross-border services. Whilst Title XI, Chapter Three, Article 3.10 (courts and tribunals) obliges the Parties to maintain judicial oversight of 'subsidy decisions' to ensure that subsidies are not granted so as to distort trade or investment 'between the Parties'.[279] There is also a general provision in Title IX, Article TRNSY.7.1 which requires both the EU and United Kingdom to establish or maintain 'judicial arbitral or administrative tribunals and procedures' for the purpose of the review and correction of 'administrative decisions'. But these provisions do not qualify the observation that there is no scope for private persons to raise a legal complaint that one or other of the EU or the United Kingdom has misimplemented particular provisions of the TCA. Tellingly, even the provisions as to judicial oversight of 'subsidy decisions' in Title XI, Chapter Three, Article 3.10 make it clear that the latter does not '[require] either Party to create rights of action, remedies procedures, or the scope or grounds of review … [and does not require] either Party to widen the scope or grounds of review by its courts and tribunals …', making it quite clear that

277 Where the breach of a TCA provision also breaches an equivalent obligation under a different international agreement, to which both the EU and the United Kingdom are a party, Article INST.12 permits a complaining party to select the forum to settle the dispute. This means that ISDS mechanisms in other international agreements concluded by the United Kingdom are unlikely to be available, certainly in relation to disputes on cross-border investment or cross-border services, since, for the reasons given above, the EU is unlikely to breach an analogous provision to the investment and services provisions in the TCA, under some other international agreement to which both the EU and United Kingdom are parties. And of course, private persons cannot rely on any ISDS mechanism for TCA purposes, since the TCA does not (subject to specific exceptions referred to in Part One, Title II, COMPROV 16) confer private rights.

278 Part Six, Title I, Chapter 4, Article INST.29.4A (although, once again, the phrase the courts 'of' [the EU] needs intelligent amplification).

279 And that the grant of 'subsidies' comply with the 'principles' set out in Title XI, Chapter Three, Article 3.4.

Article 3.10 is very firmly confined as to its scope and does not generally assume the location of private rights by reason of the TCA.

VIII. FRA 2020, section 29

1.57 The TCA is implemented into United Kingdom domestic law by *FRA 2020, s 29(1)* which provides: 'existing[280] domestic law has effect … with such modifications as are required for the purposes of implementing in that law the [TCA] … so far as … not otherwise so implemented and so far as such implementation is necessary for the purposes of complying with international obligations of the United Kingdom under the [TCA]'.

Section 29(1), like many of the substantive provisions of the TCA itself, appears to deliver a far more fundamental effect than it actually does. At first sight, the text of *s 29(1)* amalgamates both supremacy and direct effect by, on its terms, 'modifying' existing domestic United Kingdom law, to secure compliance with the TCA. *Section 29(1)*, in other words, seemingly does not simply give the TCA direct effect in the United Kingdom but goes further and subjects each and every statutory provision and the common law (including retained EU law) to the TCA ('modifies' these) to make them TCA-compliant.

This would be a quite remarkable result. As observed above, the TCA is a free-trade agreement. There is an express intention, on the face of the TCA, to ensure that no rights or obligations are located in private persons. So, in other words, no domestic rights or obligations are supposed to be created by the TCA. Its terms and conditions were negotiated by the government, that is, the executive, as an exercise of the prerogative. The TCA may be amended by the Partnership Council, where the United Kingdom's representation is again comprised by government ministers, exercising prerogative powers.[281] Indeed, if the TCA had direct effect so as to locate rights in private persons by 'modifying' domestic law (contrary to the TCA's specific terms), there would at the very least be a question as to whether the United Kingdom government, exercising the prerogative in the Partnership Council, could amend the TCA and undermine this new right. So *s 29* would fetter the extent to which the United Kingdom might agree to any amendment of the TCA, which is another nonsensical result. Nothing in the TCA suggest that the Parties consider that the TCA is to have 'direct effect' in the same manner as EU law.[282] It is the United Kingdom executive, not Parliament, which would exercise any option to

280 See below for further consideration of the term 'existing'.

281 And for a specific example of the subjection of the substantive principles to the political consensus established under the Partnership Council, see Title XI, Chapter Three, Article 3.5, which makes it clear that the 'principles' articulated in Article 3.4 are subject to 'updating' by the Partnership Council.

282 For example, the 'principles' set out in Title XI, Chapter Three, Article 3.4 expressly acknowledge that it is 'for each party to determine how its obligations … are implemented … in its own domestic law …' (Article 3.4.3).

terminate under Part Seven, Article FINPROV.9. All of which takes the TCA outside the scope of *Miller*, since no domestic rights or obligations can ever be at stake.[283] This is, of course, true despite the self-evident requirement that the TCA be introduced into domestic law by a primary Act of Parliament (here the *FRA 2020*). But if *s 29(1)* did indeed 'modify' all United Kingdom 'domestic' law, the TCA would have effect to create legal rights and obligations (such as the right to unimpeded market access, a protection against discrimination as regards host-state nationals and MFN treatment) automatically. The absence of remedies for any misimplementation would have become irrelevant, since all domestic laws would be automatically 'modified', which is self-evidently inconsistent with the express provisions of the TCA which prohibit the location of TCA-sourced rights in private persons. Any strong view of the effect of the 'modification' of United Kingdom domestic law by *s 29* would create a vicious circularity: the TCA prohibits the creation of private rights; the direct effect of the TCA by a *s 29* 'modification' of domestic law would create new rights in private persons, the creation of which is expressly and with great precision prohibited by the TCA (but which needs, on a strong view of the effect of *s 29*, to be given direct effect by 'modifying' domestic law and so on). And any amendment of the TCA by the Partnership Council would have the effect of amending the United Kingdom's 'domestic' law, through the surrogate of *s 29(1)*. All in the light of the observation, made above, that any 'modification' to United Kingdom domestic law would be the subject of a consultation process and ultimately a decision made by an arbitration tribunal, which may vary from case to case, which makes the prospective identification of any 'modification' very uncertain indeed. In other words, any TCA 'modification' is a wholly contingent event, which cannot be anticipated in a manner which changes the substantive application of domestic law. Furthermore, on a strong interpretation of the 'modifying' effect of *s 29(1)*, which locates TCA-sourced rights in private persons, the option to terminate (as opposed to any amendment of the TCA) would have to be sanctioned by Parliament, since the TCA-modified rights in domestic law would be necessarily changed on any termination of the TCA.

All of the above consequences are highly implausible. It is considered that the better view (and given the terms of the TCA the only plausible view) is that the 'modification' of United Kingdom domestic law effected by *s 29(1)* is that: (1) all United Kingdom domestic law (both statute and common law) without exception is subject to scrutiny as to whether it is TCA-compliant (displacing the weaker presumption that statute enacted by Parliament was not intended to breach international law obligations assumed by the United Kingdom[284]),

283 A significant exception would be a private right which arises within the EU under Part Three, which would at least give rise to the question as to whether the United Kingdom had assumed international law (TCA) obligations by reason of *s 29* to protect such EU-TCA-Part Three rights. This question is self-evidently of great importance but a discussion of Part Three is outside the scope of this Chapter.

284 See eg *Post Office v Estuary Radio* [1968] 2 QB 740.

and (2) all United Kingdom domestic law shall be applied in a manner, in relation to a particular case, consistent with the result of a consultation process or, ultimately, an arbitration decision. This view converts *s 29(1)* from being the fountainhead of a juristic revolution into nothing more than a statutory acknowledgement that the TCA imposes obligations on the United Kingdom in international law and the result is that all of the United Kingdom's domestic law is subject to the TCA's application (which may resolve in a consultation process and arbitration under Part Six, at its highest).

This view also means that there is no prospect of an 'indirect' location of TCA-sourced rights in private persons, in a manner analogous to the indirect horizontal application of unimplemented EU Directives into EU Member State domestic law. In the case of an EU unimplemented Directive, in a horizontal, exclusively private-person action, a private person is unable to plead the direct effect of an EU Directive to have horizontal effect against the other private person in the action (a shield, rather than a sword). However, where that Directive has direct vertical effect, so as to render a domestic law, on which their opponent relies, non-Directive compliant, a private person may rely on that direct effect of the Directive to prevent their opponent from relying on domestic legal provisions which offend the Directive.[285] It might be thought that, although the TCA forbids the location of rights in private persons, a private person may nevertheless rely on the application of the TCA to a particular non-TCA compliant domestic provision, which is 'modified' by *s 29(1)*, to escape the application of the domestic non-TCA compliant domestic provision. But if the 'modification' effected by *s 29(1)* is simply a contingent 'wait and see' direction, on a case-by-case basis, to await the result of a consultation or arbitration process, such an 'indirect' location of private rights by the TCA cannot occur.

All of the observations just made apply equally whether in relation to the United Kingdom generally or to retained EU law in particular.[286]

IX. Conclusion in relation to the TCA

1.58 The TCA is one more international treaty in a collection of international trade treaties concluded by the United Kingdom. The TCA does not have any fundamental impact on United Kingdom domestic law (in

285 *CIA Security International v Signalson SA* (Case C-194/94).

286 To return to the term 'existing' [United Kingdom domestic law] in *s 29*, the objections to some sort of 'direct' effect of the TCA are strengthened, if this term is respected as having a strong substantive effect. If 'existing' means 'United Kingdom law existing at the time of Royal Assent of the FRA', we have the absurd conclusion that domestic law enacted after that date is not 'modified' by the terms of the TCA, via *s 29*. If the term 'existing' is not a temporal limitation but rather a mere linguistic device to contra-distinguish United Kingdom law from the TCA, the term 'modify' may also be given a similarly weak meaning, quite apart from the textual and interpretative points made above.

particular retained EU law). The TCA especially has little relevant impact on the United Kingdom's tax code. There is little left to say, other than to sympathise with those who derived much intellectual joy from addressing the issues raised by the application of the EU internal market to the domestic legal (in particular tax) regimes of the United Kingdom. Those days have gone.

The post-Brexit regime: overall conclusion

1.59 Both in relation to retained EU law and the TCA, the regimes established by the *EUWA 2018* and the TCA/*FRA 2020* are problematic, unnecessarily so. And the thorny legal issues which they raise may bring excitement and succour to both academics and practitioners, including the judiciary. But this is at the expense of certainty for those who are subject to these regimes. Academics and practitioners would make a valuable contribution to a post-Brexit world (at least within the United Kingdom) by airing all of the issues discussed here (and other issues, not dealt with here) to make reasoned and sensible conclusions arrive sooner rather than later.

Chapter 2

Brexit Implications for VAT

Roderick Cordara QC
Barbara Belgrano

INTRODUCTION

2.1 Value Added Tax was introduced into the UK on 1 January 1973, by means of the *Finance Act 1972*. As is well known, the introduction was part of the UK's process of joining the European Economic Community (the predecessor of the EU[1]). The UK was obliged to give up its Purchase Tax (on goods), and to introduce VAT, by reason of the First and Sixth EU VAT Directives. These Directives set out the aspiration of the European legislators for a harmonised single system of consumption taxation throughout the Community. This ambition was driven less by mere tax raising than by the need to have a uniform pan-EU consumption tax to remove fiscal temptations to locate transactions where tax was most favourable, thereby distorting the operation of the single market. This overarching ambition was set out in the preambles to the Sixth Directive, including 'Whereas the taxable base must be harmonised so that the application of the Community rate to taxable transactions leads to comparable results in all the Member States.'.

Harmonisation and neutrality are paramount expressions of the same politico-economic ambition – as the preambles also show; so also is the principle of the strict construction of exemptions (given that exemptions cause potential distortion by treating exempt traders as if they were final consumers, with the resultant distorting build-up of irrecoverable VAT in the supply chain, rather than simply at the point of final consumption).

All these avowed objectives played their part in supporting the overarching/wider ambition of establishing a single market. Every VAT case which has involved the application of concepts of distortion or arguments about harmonisation or neutrality (in either sense, see below) or the strict interpretation

1 At the risk of anachronism, but for simplicity, 'EU' will be used to refer both to the EEC and its later manifestations.

of an exemption is, in truth, a particular expression of the progress towards this overriding political/economic ambition of a harmonised single market.

Thus, European VAT is a tax with a uniquely sophisticated political and economic agenda – a 'tax with attitude'.

The agenda of building a single market, which all these principles serve, is still ongoing, of course. But that agenda no longer includes the UK. The EU-wide aspiration towards a single market notoriously failed in the case of the UK. It is therefore leaving the single market and reverts to being a single market of its own (or at least Great Britain does – time will stand still, to some extent, in Northern Ireland, at least in VAT terms, as further discussed below).[2]

The question immediately arises as to what, if any, role is to be attributed to the single market policy objectives in the future; the UK is already a single market – what need of these policies? They are largely the reason for the long-standing acceptance that VAT legislation is to be interpreted purposively – they *are* its purpose, even more fundamentally than money raising.[3] Are they so embedded in VAT law and practice that they will outlive their source?

This is no idle question. One can contrast the more widespread, VAT-in-one-country systems, that do not have any concept of final consumer, consumption, distortion, nor (obviously) harmonisation. There is no agenda of building a single market, because it is already there. One example is Australia (which has probably the most complex VAT system of any country): the *A New Tax System (Goods and Services Tax) Act 1999,* which brought in a VAT-style goods and services tax has no preambles,[4] nor any concepts of the sort mentioned above. It is a 'black letter' VAT system. The Judges interpret it with reference to what is on the page of the statute, no more or less. Nothing conceptual intrudes. It is seen merely as a 'practical business tax'.[5]

However, as hinted at above, for reasons embedded in recent Anglo-Irish history, the single market aspiration has remained in place for Northern Ireland. As such, it will remain significantly within the EU VAT net, albeit as part of the UK VAT system (see below).

For the rest of the UK (ie, Great Britain) that aspiration for a single market has emphatically gone, leaving the UK free to strike ambitious trade deals around

2 We refer throughout to the UK, rather than GB, but it should be borne in mind NI will to a significant degree remain within the EU market for goods, at least.

3 After all, no pure Anglo-Saxon/'common law' tax would ever countenance the existence of 'repayment traders', but that is because UK taxes are traditionally just about money raising, rather than shaping economic market practice.

4 It does have the nearest equivalent in the common law world: Explanatory Memorandum. However, the only conceptual comments it makes is: 'GST is effectively a tax on final private consumption in Australia'.

5 *Sterling Guardian Pty Limited v Commissioner of Taxation* [2005] FCA 1166 at [39] per Stone J. See also: *ATS Pacific Pty Ltd v Commissioner of Taxation* [2014] FCAFC 33 at [71] per Pagone J.

the world. That ambition, in the eyes of the British, outweighs the attractions of the single market on the doorstep which the EU offered.

One such trade deal has been made with the EU itself: on 24 December 2020, the UK, EU and European Atomic Energy Community entered into a free trade agreement, the 'Trade and Cooperation Agreement' ('TCA').[6] The implications of that agreement are addressed in Chapter 1. As explained by Julian Ghosh QC in Chapter 1, the TCA does not affect the central concept of 'retained EU law', which we discuss in the context of VAT, below. At this point, two observations fall to be made. First, we are considering UK legislation which has its own political agenda, just as the EU legislation mentioned above. However, the economic agenda of the EU legislation was at least clear – closer union. Such an agenda has a comprehensible economic destination – that is, a single market. That cannot be said of the UK legislation: it has the agenda of separation ('taking back control'), but no more than that can be discerned in terms of the destination, particularly in economic terms. VAT therefore will fall back into the main stream of money raising taxes, pure and simple.

The suite of principal statutes and statutory instruments where the building blocks of our analysis are to be found are summarised in Chapter 1, where they have been analysed by Julian Ghosh QC. We gratefully build on this excellent foundation. On the basis of that background, and the VAT-specific exceptions and variations to it, we comment on Brexit's implications for the UK VAT system. It necessarily will lead us into the complex thicket of rules and exceptions that may shape the VAT system after the end of the implementation period (ie, 31 December 2020).

We share with the reader, at this point, a challenge which has faced us in organising this chapter: there is a tension between taking VAT issues one at a time (eg, supply, consideration, etc), and organising matters in order of complexity: that is, those things which change in a simple and obvious way (eg, the end of acquisition supplies), or those which do not appear to change at all (eg, the concept of supply), in contrast with matters which may change in complex and nuanced ways (eg, the role of the Implementing Regulation[7]).

Behind all these specifics are the grinding 'continental plates' of a changed legislative and political landscape to note, and many specific issues, such as the impact on pending or proposed litigation of the new regime, (including the new power of the UK executive to change the law on certain matters at will), overriding both Parliamentary and judicial decision-making. In the face of

6 Which includes a 'Protocol on Administrative Cooperation and Combating Fraud in the Field of Value Added Tax and on Mutual Assistance for the Recovery of Claims Relating to Taxes and Duties', providing for the exchange of information and other forms of cooperation to ensure compliance with VAT legislation and to combat VAT fraud. It is notable that 'value added tax' is defined as meaning, 'value added tax pursuant to Council Directive 2006/112/EC on the common system of value added tax for the Union and … value added tax pursuant to the Value Added Tax Act 1994 for the United Kingdom' (Article 3(t) of the Protocol).

7 *Council Implementing Regulation (EU) No 282/2011.*

this challenge, we have compromised, dealing with specifics and more general points in the best order we can envisage.

THE STATUTORY PILLARS OF THE VAT SYSTEM

2.2 First, we consider the legislative pillars of the EU/UK VAT system as they stood at the moment of departure: the Directives, the Regulations, the VAT Act, the statutory instruments, and the Public Notices with the force of law. We start with the European law pillars, and then pass to the UK pillars. In conducting this assessment, it is worth keeping an eye out for the three main elements of the VAT system, namely supply, consideration, and input tax recovery.

The EU Directives

2.3 The VAT Directives are currently binding as to the result to be achieved but generally (like all Directives) need to be implemented by the UK in order to have effect in domestic law (see also Chapter 1 at **1.9**). Following 'IP completion day' (31 December 2020 at 11pm), the UK's obligations to implement EU Directives ceased.

However, the historic principle of direct effect (considered below) will continue to apply as regards certain provisions that are contained in Directives and that have been historically recognised as being directly effective, see **2.12** below.

The EU Regulations

2.4 *Section 3* of the *European Union (Withdrawal) Act 2018* (*EUWA 2018*), converts directly applicable[8] EU legislation, in particular Regulations, as well as Decisions, Tertiary legislation and Annexes and Protocols to the EEA Agreement, so far as operative immediately before IP completion day, into domestic law on and after IP completion day.

Notably, in relation to VAT, 'direct EU legislation' would logically be expected to include the all-important Implementing Regulation (Council Implementing Regulation (EU) No 282/2011) which, under *EUWA 2018, s 3* would thus be imported into the domestic VAT code.

However, such legislation was a particularly clear erosion of Parliamentary sovereignty, so the *Taxation (Cross-border Trade) Act 2018* (*TCBTA 2018*),

8 That is EU legislation that did not need to be specifically enacted in UK law to have effect in domestic law.

which makes specific provision relating to VAT in *Part 3* and in *Schedule 8*, provides that the Implementing Regulation ceases to have effect:[9]

> '(1) Any EU regulation so far as applying in relation to value added tax, and any direct EU legislation so far as relevant to any such regulation, that form part of the law of the United Kingdom as a result of section 3 of the European Union (Withdrawal) Act 2018 **cease to have effect (but, in the case of the implementing VAT regulation, see also subsection (5)).'** [emphasis added]

TCBTA 2018, s 42(5) provides that:

> 'Where the principal VAT directive remains relevant for determining the meaning and effect of the law relating to value added tax, that **directive is to be read for that purpose in the light of the provision made by the implementing VAT regulation** but ignoring such of its provisions as are excluded by regulations made by the Treasury by statutory instrument.'

Accordingly, in relation to VAT, although *EUWA 2018, s 3* would, in principle, apply to convert the text of the Implementing VAT Regulation that applies in relation to VAT immediately before IP completion day into domestic legislation, such legislation ceases to have effect (*TCBTA 2018, s 42(1)*).

But that is not the end of the story, since it lives on in a parasitic way attached to the Principal VAT Directive (PVD), if (as is likely to be the usual case) it throws light on it. Thus, *TCBTA 2018, s 42(5)* sets out a special rule relating to the application of the Implementing Regulation: it will be relevant '[w]here the … [PVD] remains relevant for determining the meaning and effect of the law relating to value added tax' (considered below) because, in those circumstances, the PVD is to be read 'in the light of' the Implementing Regulation, shorn of any provisions that are excluded by regulations made by the Treasury by statutory instrument. Such regulations can only be made before 1 April 2023.

The questions that naturally arise, particularly in the light of *TCBTA 2018, s 42(5)*, are: (i) 'when will the PVD remain relevant' for the purpose of determining the meaning and effect of UK VAT; and (ii) how is the phrase 'in the light of' to be construed?

As explained below, the PVD (Council Directive 2006/112/EC on the common system of value added tax) will remain relevant, *inter alia,* on the basis that:

---

9 The provisions of the *TCBTA 2018* took effect at different times, although subject to transitional provisions (see *The Taxation (Cross-border Trade) Act 2018 (Value Added Tax Transitional Provisions) (EU Exit) Regulations 2019, SI 2019/105*). Although the detail of when each provision took effect may be significant in certain contexts, it is sufficient for present purposes to note that *Part 3* of the *TCTBA 2018* was brought into force (so far as not already in force) on IP completion day, see *The Finance Act 2016, Section 126 (Appointed Day), the Taxation (Cross-border Trade) Act 2018 (Appointed Day No. 8, Transition and Saving Provisions) and the Taxation (Post-transition Period) Act 2020 (Appointed Day No. 1) (EU Exit) Regulations 2020, SI 2020/1642, reg 4.*

- 'retained EU law' (which, as explained below, includes the *Value Added Tax Act 1994* (*VATA 1994*) must be interpreted in accordance with pre-IP completion day domestic and CJEU case law (ie, cases decided at a time when the provisions of the PVD had to be given effect to in domestic law) under *EUWA 2018, s 6(3)*;
- retained EU law must be interpreted in accordance with retained general principles of EU law (notably the abuse principle, the principles of equivalence, effectiveness and fiscal neutrality); and
- provisions of the PVD that have been held by Courts in the past to be directly effective will confer rights that are preserved pursuant to *EUWA 2018, s 4*.

The mere fact that a specific statutory reference to the PVD has been deleted is not to be taken as meaning that it does not remain relevant.[10]

The VAT Act and statutory instruments

2.5 We turn to the UK statutory pillars. The *VATA 1994*, and the subordinate legislation made under that Act, is not repealed by *EUWA 2018*.

Accordingly, in principle, the building blocks of VAT (as a matter of domestic law) might have been relatively unaffected by the *EUWA 2018* and might not have needed to specifically be 'preserved'.

Nonetheless, *VATA 1994* (and subordinate legislation) falls within the scope of *EUWA 2018, s 2*, which provides that 'EU-derived domestic legislation' continues to have effect in domestic law on and after IP completion day 'as it has effect in domestic law immediately before' that day.

'EU-derived domestic legislation' is defined in *EUWA 2018, s 1B(7)* as follows:

> 'In this Act "EU-derived domestic legislation" means any enactment so far as—
>
> (a) made under section 2(2) of, or paragraph 1A of Schedule 2 to, the European Communities Act 1972,
>
> (b) passed or made, or operating, for a purpose mentioned in section 2(2) (a) or (b) of that Act,
>
> (c) relating to—
>
> (i) anything which falls within paragraph (a) or (b), or
>
> (ii) any rights, powers, liabilities, obligations, restrictions, remedies or procedures which are recognised and available in domestic

10 See *TCBTA 2018, Sch 8, Pt 1, para 99*, headed, 'Effect of amendments made by this Part of this Schedule'.

law by virtue of section 2(1) of the European Communities Act 1972, or

(d) relating otherwise to the EU or the EEA,

but does not include any enactment contained in the European Communities Act 1972 or any enactment contained in this Act or the European Union (Withdrawal Agreement) Act 2020 or in regulations made under this Act or the Act of 2020.'

Notably, *EUWA 2018, s 1B(7)(b)* provides that EU-derived domestic legislation includes any enactment 'passed or made, or operating' **for the purpose of** (broadly) implementing EU obligations of the UK, enabling any rights enjoyed or to be enjoyed by the UK under or by virtue of the Treaties to be exercised or dealing with matters related to any rights, powers, liabilities, obligations, restrictions, remedies or procedures which are recognised and available in domestic law by virtue of the *European Communities Act 1972 (ECA 1972), s 2(1).*

VATA 1994 (and subordinate legislation) has hitherto been intended to discharge the UK's obligation to implement EU VAT, which has predominantly been given effect through successive VAT Directives.

Accordingly, *VATA 1994* would fall within the scope of *s 1B(7)(b)* (and, as noted in Chapter 1 at **1.24**, on any view falls within *s 1B(7)(d)* as relating to the EU). Under *EUWA 2018, s 2* it would continue to have effect in domestic law on and after IP completion day 'as it has effect in domestic law immediately before IP completion day'.[11]

Although a 'saving' may not have been strictly necessary because *VATA 1994*, as an Act of Parliament, would not have ceased to have effect as a result of *EUWA 2018* (and because subordinate legislation has been made under that Act rather than pursuant to, for example *ECA 1972, s 2(2)*), the saving nonetheless has important consequences because the effect of the application of *EUWA 2018, ss 1B and 2* is that *VATA 1994* and subordinate legislation made under it constitutes 'retained EU law', which is defined in *EUWA 2018, s 6(7)* as:

'… anything which, on or after IP completion day, continues to be, or forms part of, domestic law by virtue of section 2, 3 or 4 or [section 6] subsection (3) or (6) above (as that body of law is added to or otherwise modified by or under this Act or by other domestic law from time to time)'.

The *EUWA 2018* sets out specific provisions for the 'interpretation' of retained EU law, which are considered at **2.8** to **2.18** below. Thus, although *VATA 1994* and SIs made under it continue to have effect as 'EU-derived

11 Perhaps unsurprisingly, *VATA 1994* and the regulations made under it continue to be treated as 'enactment[s] of the same kind' ie as legislation of the same type (primary legislation and subordinate legislation respectively) (*EUWA 2018, s 7(1)(a)*).

domestic legislation' in domestic law on and after IP completion day 'as it has effect in domestic law immediately before IP completion day', they will fall to be construed by reference to those principles rather than by virtue of only domestic canons of construction applicable to (ordinary) domestic law.

Public notices with the force of law

2.6 We expect HMRC's public notices which have the force of law to continue in force (subject to amendments)[12] on the basis that the enabling legislation for the notices is contained in the *VATA 1994* and statutory instruments made under that Act. Accordingly, the repeal of *ECA 1972, s 2(1)* that is, the 'conduit pipe' of EU law (*R(on the application of Miller and another) v Secretary of State for Exiting the European Union* [2017] UKSC 5; [2018] A.C. 61 at [65]) will not automatically cause those notices to cease to have effect.

Supply, consideration, input tax recovery

2.7 From the above, it will be seen that the three main elements of the VAT system are intact, namely supply, consideration, and input tax recovery. Nor do we detect any political will to interfere with these three basic concepts in the future. They will be reshaped around the edges (eg, 'imports' will expand to include what were intra-EU acquisitions) but are unlikely to be significantly different on a day to day level. In particular, we can see no changes in consideration, nor input tax *nexus* (even though the Eighth Directive will no longer figure).

The same is true of the vast majority of the 'nuts and bolts' provisions in the legislation at all levels – with some notable but inevitable statutory disappearances, discussed below.

We turn next to the general principles of EU law, before considering how they interact with the statutory pillars.

12 Moreover, the *Cross-border Trade (Public Notices) (EU Exit) Regulations 2019, SI 2019/1307*, which have effect from IP completion day, provide HM Treasury (on recommendation from HMRC) with a power to make provisions varying the rules for VAT (albeit not VAT rates) through public notices. The effect of the notices is, however, restricted: the notices can only be effective for 60 days and the regulations (together with current notices) will cease to have effect six months after IP completion day. At least two such notices have already been issued, see: www.gov.uk/government/publications/notice-made-under-the-value-added-tax-northern-ireland-eu-exit-regulations-2020 and www.gov.uk/government/publications/notice-made-under-the-value-added-tax-regulations-1995-as-amended-by-the-value-added-tax-miscellaneous-amendments-northern-ireland-protocol-and-savi.

THE GENERAL PRINCIPLES

2.8 Having considered above the impact of Brexit on the statutory pillars of the system as they currently stand, let us return to the general principles with which we began.

Dealing first with the basic principles: even though some of them may have lost their wider politico-economic purpose, the UK has clearly decided that it would assist no one to ditch the baggage of nearly 50 years of VAT law and interpretative practice that attaches to the EU VAT system as applied in the UK (even if rooted in a failed political enterprise). Too many wheels would have to be reinvented for almost every part of the domestic VAT system.[13] As will be seen, many, but not all, of the single market orientated principles will survive, albeit frozen as they looked at the end of the implementation period (subject to modification or erasure in the future).[14]

Accordingly, certain general principles have been retained as aids to construction of VAT.[15] Broadly, *EUWA 2018, s 6(3)* will require 'retained EU law' be interpreted 'in accordance with' those general principles:

> '(3) Any question as to the validity, meaning or effect of any retained EU law is to be decided, so far as that law is unmodified on or after IP completion day and so far as they are relevant to it—
>
> in accordance with any retained case law and any retained general principles of EU law, and
>
> …'

'Retained general principles of EU law' is a reference to general principles of EU law (so far as they relate to *VATA 1994*) that have been 'recognised'[16] as general principles of EU law by the CJEU in a case decided before IP completion day (*EUWA 2018, Sch 1, para 2*).[17] As explained above, 'retained EU law' (not co-terminus with 'retained general principles of EU law') is likely to include *VATA 1994* as at 31 December 2020.

Importantly, the content and operation of those general principles is frozen by reference to their effect in EU law immediately before IP completion day. Moreover, as considered below, those principles are subject to subsequent

13 Except for the content of many of the zero-rates, which have evolved without reference to EU law (save in terms of the cut-off date of 1 January 1991 for any expansion of Zero rates (Article 28(2) Sixth Directive) or (in the case of food, at least) without reference to logic of any kind.

14 31 December 2020.

15 The nature of general principles and their continued relevance outside the specific context of VAT is considered in Chapter 1.

16 As noted in Chapter 1 at **1.26**, 'recognition' is not itself defined and it will be left to the courts to identify how that expression falls to be applied.

17 This does not affect any decision of a court or tribunal made before IP completion day (*EUWA 2018, Sch 8, para 39(2)*).

modifications by or under *EUWA 2018* or by other domestic law. There is no conceptual limit to the form or effect of such potential modifications – it is a very clear example of the UK 'taking back control'. Unfortunately, given the lack of any more specific political or economic agenda, on the part of the UK (as noted above), it is difficult to divine where the future trends will point.

As further evidence of the unshackling of the UK government from the norms and obligations of EU membership in the VAT sphere, the effect of retained general principles of EU law is severely restricted; thus, the general rule is that even if a general principle has been 'recognised' as such before IP completion day (eg, legal certainty – for example, as a bar to retrospective abolition of accrued claims for VAT repayment), there is (subject to transitional provisions): (i) no right of action in domestic law, based on a failure to comply with general principles of EU law on or after IP completion day, (*EUWA 2018, Sch 1, para 3(1)*), and (ii) Courts will not be able to disapply domestic law, on the basis that it is incompatible with general principles of EU law on or after IP completion day, (*EUWA 2018, Sch 1, para 3(2)*).[18]

Historically, the courts have sometimes treated partial disapplication and conforming construction as two ways of achieving the same result (ie, one can either call it disapplication or conforming construction) and they have considered there to be little practical effect in the distinction (see eg, *Prudential Assurance Company Limited v HMRC* [2013] EWHC 3249 (Ch) at [100]) but this will now change and there may be much more debate over whether disapplication is truly the only way of giving effect to a general principle (eg, as the Court of Appeal[19] had held was the case in *Littlewoods Retail Limited and Others v The Commissioners for Her Majesty's Revenue & Customs* where it decided, but were reversed by the Supreme Court, that the claimants' entitlement to interest under EU law was not satisfied by the payment of simple interest under *VATA 1994, s 78* and that, in accordance with the EU principle of effectiveness, the claimants' entitlement to interest was to be given effect in English law by disapplying *VATA 1994, ss 78(1) and 80(7)*).

However, as VAT practitioners will be well aware, it is frequently the case that the statutes consist only of broad brush strokes, leaving all the critical detail unspecified. This is the very situation that pertains here. Accordingly, all the work required in:

(1) identifying which general principles have been 'recognised' as such immediately before 31 December 2020;

(2) determining what their 'effect' in EU law was immediately before 31 December 2020;

(3) policing the restriction on actions based on a breach of general principles; and

18 Ibid.
19 [2015] EWCA Civ 515.

(4) deciding whether the validity, meaning or effect of VATA 1994 can be decided 'in accordance with' the relevant general principle(s) or whether the application of the general principle(s) would require (or, but for Brexit, would have required) the now forbidden, process of disapplication,

has, in principle, been left to the Courts. One can readily imagine the complex and long running issues that could arise in this context. We would anticipate an underlying wish on the part of the judiciary in most cases, to change things as little as possible – if only in the interests of legal stability. However, the UK government may have other ideas, and indeed other means of frustrating any such judicial conservatism, as we will see.

Moreover, there could be another way in which general principles may continue to affect UK VAT.

As set out above, *EUWA 2018, s 6(3)(a)* requires the validity, meaning, or effect of any retained *VATA 1994* to be decided in accordance with 'retained case law', which is defined as the pre-IP completion day principles and decisions of domestic courts or the CJEU – so far as they relate to retained EU law (and are not excluded by *s 5* or *Sch 1*, or subsequently modified by or under *EUWA 2018* or by other domestic law). This bristles with potential points of debate.

Imagine, for example, that a pre-IP completion day Supreme Court or CJEU decision disapplies a provision of *VATA 1994* on the basis that it is contrary to a (retained) general principle of EU law. Could a litigant argue, in a lower court, *post-IP completion day*, that the court is bound to also disapply that provision of the *VATA 1994* because, although general principles can only be used to interpret rather than disapply retained EU law, the lower court is bound to apply the Supreme Court/CJEU decision?

In the writers' view, the answer is likely to be 'yes' because the prohibition on general principles' being used, post-IP day, to disapply any enactment by the Courts, does not apply in relation to any decision of a court or tribunal (or other public authority) on or after IP completion day which is a 'necessary consequence of' any decision of a court or tribunal: (i) made before IP completion day, or (ii) made on or after that day by virtue of *para 39* (*EUWA 2018, Sch 8, para 39(6)*). The explanatory notes to *EUWA 2018, Sch 8, para 39(6)* explain that,

> '… This saves **the effect of case law** decided before exit day or during the transitional period in which the courts have disapplied a provision of pre-exit legislation on the grounds that it is incompatible with one of the general principles of EU law.' (Emphasis added.)

There is no definition of 'necessary consequence' but the writers consider that the doctrine of precedent, for example, is part of the 'effect of case law', and therefore ought sensibly to mean that in the example above, the lower court's disapplication of the *VATA 1994* provision is a 'necessary consequence of' the binding pre-IP completion day CJEU or Supreme Court decision. We would add that logic ought also to play a significant part in applying the concept of 'necessary consequence'.

However, the Supreme Court will not be bound by any principles laid down by, and any decisions of, the CJEU (as they had effect in EU law immediately before 11 pm on 31 December 2020). Nor, in certain circumstances, will a number of other appellate courts: the *EU (Withdrawal Agreement) Act 2020* modified the *EUWA 2018* in a significant way by inserting *EUWA 2018, s 6(5A)* which allows a Minister to make regulations setting out the extent to which courts and tribunals will be bound by pre-IP completion day CJEU decisions and retained domestic case law in so far as the latter 'relates' to 'retained EU case law'.

Following a consultation process, the Secretary of State made Regulations 'in exercise of the powers conferred by section 6(5A)(a), (b) and (c) and (5B)(a)' of the *EUWA 2018*.

The *European Union (Withdrawal) Act 2018 (Relevant Court) (Retained EU Case Law) Regulations 2020, SI 2020/1525*, which came into force on IP completion day, provide that the following courts are only bound by retained EU case law 'so far as there is post-transition case law [meaning any principles laid down by, and any decisions of, a court or tribunal in the United Kingdom, as they have effect on or after IP completion day] which modifies or applies that retained EU case law and which is binding on the relevant court':

(a) the Court Martial Appeal Court,

(b) the Court of Appeal in England and Wales,

(c) the Inner House of the Court of Session,

(d) the High Court of Justiciary when sitting as a court of appeal in relation to a compatibility issue (within the meaning given by section 288ZA(2) of the Criminal Procedure (Scotland) Act 1995(3)) or a devolution issue (within the meaning given by paragraph 1 of Schedule 6 to the Scotland Act 1998(4)),

(e) the court for hearing appeals under section 57(1)(b) of the Representation of the People Act 1983(5),

(f) the Lands Valuation Appeal Court, and

(g) the Court of Appeal in Northern Ireland.

In short, those Courts will only be bound by principles laid down by, and any decisions of, the CJEU (including the General Court), as they have effect in EU law immediately before IP completion day, subject to any post-IP day decision of a UK court or tribunal that 'modifies or applies' the CJEU decision and is binding on the above relevant courts.

In deciding whether to depart from any retained EU case law the Supreme Court and the above courts must apply the same test as the Supreme Court would apply in deciding whether to depart from the case law of the Supreme Court, namely whether it appears right to do so.

We turn now to consider some of the principles that are likely to be 'retained general principles' that will continue to have effect 'as they have effect in EU law immediately before IP completion day' (*EUWA 1994, s 6(7)*), generally as interpretative principles.

Equivalence and effectiveness

2.9 As explained in Chapter 1 at **1.11**, the principles of equivalence and effectiveness constitute important general principles of EU law. Those principles require the detailed procedural rules governing actions for safeguarding a taxpayer's rights under EU law to be no less favourable than those governing similar domestic actions (principle of equivalence) and those rules must not be framed in such a way as to render impossible in practice or excessively difficult the exercise of rights conferred by EU law (principle of effectiveness) (see *Test Claimants in the FII Group Litigation v Inland Revenue Commissioners* (Case C-362/12) [2014] AC 1161 at [32]).

Fiscal neutrality

2.10 The position with fiscal neutrality is more nuanced. Clearly, it is fundamental to EU VAT in two broad ways:

- EU VAT is a general tax on consumption and is exactly proportional to the price of the goods and services, however many transactions take place in the production and distribution process before the stage at which the tax is charged (Article 1(2) PVD). Neutrality requires the rate of VAT should be such as to enable, as a general rule, deduction of the VAT applied at the preceding stage and that VAT should be assessed on no more than the amount of consideration actually paid (recital 30 PVD) ('**transaction neutrality**') (see, eg, *Elida Gibbs Ltd v C & E Commrs* (Case C-317/94) [1997] BVC 80); and
- neutrality in that VAT should result in neutrality in competition, such that within the territory of each Member State similar goods and services bear the same tax burden, whatever the length of the production and distribution chain (recital 7 PVD) ('**competition neutrality**') (see, eg, *HMRC v The Rank Group plc* (Joined Cases C-259/10 and C-260/10) [2012] STC 23).

Both aspects of fiscal neutrality[20] have been described by the CJEU as 'fundamental' to the EU VAT system.

20 For similar terminology, see A van Doesum and H van Kesteren, *Fundamentals of EU VAT Law* (Kluwer Law International, 2016), para 1.12.1, who refer to 'system neutrality' and the 'legal' aspect of fiscal neutrality (broadly analogous to 'transaction neutrality' and 'competition neutrality' as referred to above).

In relation to transaction neutrality, the CJEU held, in *Zita Modes Sàrl v Administration de l'enregistrement et des domaines* (Case C-497/01) at [37], that:

> 'As for the purpose of the Sixth Directive, it should be borne in mind that, on the one hand, according to the fundamental principle which underlies the common VAT system and which follows from Article 2 of First Council Directive 67/227/EEC of 11 April 1967 on the harmonisation of legislation of Member States concerning turnover taxes (OJ, English Special Edition 1967, p. 14), and from the Sixth Directive, VAT applies to each transaction by way of production or distribution after deduction of the VAT directly borne by the various cost components (Case C-98/98 Midland Bank [2000] ECR I-4177, paragraph 29, and Abbey National, cited above, paragraph 27).'

As regards competition neutrality, which ensures that: (a) 'similar' goods, and (b) transactions or supplies with a similar 'economic' effect are treated equally for the purposes of VAT in order to avoid distorting competition, the CJEU explained, in *Ampliscientifica Srl v Ministero dell'Economia e delle Finanze* (Case C-162/07) at [25], that:

> '... the principle of fiscal neutrality is a fundamental principle of the common system of VAT ... which precludes, on the one hand, treating similar goods, which are thus in competition with each other, differently for VAT purposes ... and, on the other hand, treating similar economic transactions, which are therefore in competition with each other, differently for VAT purposes ...'.

This aspect of fiscal neutrality also reflects the EU law general principle of equal treatment, (see *Fiscale eenheid Koninklijke Ahold NV v Staatssecretaris van Financiën* (Case C-484/06) at [36]) and it has been described *in terms* by the CJEU as a 'general principle' of Community law applicable to fiscal matters (*The Commissioners of Her Majesty's Revenue & Customs v Isle of Wight Council and Others* (Case C-288/07) at [41]).

However, it appears that the principle of fiscal neutrality is not a 'general principle' of EU law that applies to all areas of EU law (unlike, for example, the principle of equality or the principle of effectiveness), see for example *NCC Construction Danmark A/S v Skatteministeriet* (Case C-174/08), where the CJEU explained (at [42]):

> 'However, while that latter principle [equal treatment], like the other general principles of Community law, has constitutional status, the principle of fiscal neutrality requires legislation to be drafted and enacted, which requires a measure of secondary Community law (see, by analogy, with regard to the protection of minority shareholders, Case C-101/08 Audiolux and Others [2009] ECR I-0000, paragraph 63).'

In the writers' view, although fiscal neutrality emerges as a principle only in the context of specific legislation (as opposed to being a self-standing principle, such as effectiveness, which pervades EU law even in the absence of legislation), the better view is that it should fall within the concept of 'retained general principles' because it is inherent in the VAT 'retained EU law' (principally, *VATA 1994*). In that 'imported' context, it is a fundamental principle of EU law (see above). However, taxpayers who may have the principle deployed against them in future cases, might wish to apply the approach of the Advocate General in *Dominguez* (Case C-282/10) (see Chapter 1 at **1.11**), arguing that fiscal neutrality has not: (a) found expression in many rules of **primary law** and in secondary EU law, and (b) found such expression in an **unconditional and precise** manner or, put another way, that context specific principles cannot be 'general' principles.

Indeed, because fiscal neutrality arises out of the context of the EU VAT legislation, it is perhaps more susceptible than other retained principles to being *impliedly* removed by reason of subsequent legislation that is inconsistent with it. For example, if the UK system of VAT is modified to the extent that it no longer acts as a tax on consumption, it may be difficult to justify any continued reference to fiscal neutrality as a general principle.

A further complexity is that fiscal neutrality currently has 'effect in EU law' as more than merely an interpretative principle. Currently, the EU VAT regime must be applied (and VAT must be levied) in a manner that is consistent with the principle of fiscal neutrality.

Therefore, this could mean that as long as the principle of neutrality requires the court to recharacterise a transaction, without disapplying a provision of *VATA 1994*, the principle can apply but that if fiscal neutrality means that a charge to VAT should not be applied, the principle cannot be given effect to disapply that provision (since disapplication is forbidden, see above).

Moreover, the 'evolution' of the principle of fiscal neutrality in the CJEU's future case law will not be directly relevant: although courts will be allowed to have 'regard' to post-IP completion day cases, it is clear that they should not consider themselves to be bound by them (see below). For example, imagine that the CJEU releases a judgment, after IP completion day in a case that restricts the currently understood meaning of 'fiscal neutrality'. What is the effect of that decision in a case before the domestic courts which concerns the retained *VATA 1994* and the application of that principle?

The writers consider that, on any view, a court or tribunal in the UK would not be bound by the post-IP completion day CJEU decision (*EUWA 2018, s 6(1)*), albeit that they could have 'regard' to it. The difficulty is, however, that the new decision would be likely to shed light on how the principle of fiscal neutrality was operating in EU law immediately before IP day: we are told (by *EUWA 2018, s 6(7)*) that the courts must apply general principles of EU law when interpreting the retained *VATA 1994* as those principles had 'effect in EU law' immediately before IP completion day.

Readers will know that, even where the CJEU restates principles of EU law, it very rarely (expressly) departs from its previous decisions. Accordingly, the post-IP completion day case may, on its terms, simply explain/clarify how the principle of fiscal neutrality was already operating in EU law before that day and it might therefore be argued that domestic courts must apply that case in identifying how to interpret the retained *VATA 1994* (*EUWA 2018, s 6(3)*).

In the writers' view, the likely success of such an argument would turn on the outcome of a battle in the judicial bosom, between the innate conservatism mentioned above, and the clear intention, as set out in *EUWA 2018, s 6(1)* that courts and tribunals should not be bound by CJEU cases decided on or after IP completion day. In this circumstance, one should not underestimate the potential for judicial creativity.

Abuse

2.11 The concept of 'abuse of law' has been described by the Supreme Court as a 'general principle of central importance to the operation of the VAT scheme' (see the judgment of Lord Carnwath in *Pendragon Plc and others v Revenue and Customs Commissioners* [2015] UKSC 37, [2015] STC 1825 (*Pendragon*) at [50]).

The principle, which was first recognised by the Grand Chamber of the CJEU as applying to VAT in *Halifax Plc and others v Customs and Excise Commissioners* (Case C-255/02) [2006] ECR I-1609, [2006] Ch 387, [2006] STC 919, operates to disallow the claimed VAT consequences where: (a) application of the legislative provisions which are *prima facie* applicable result in the accrual of a tax advantage which would be contrary to the purpose of those provisions, and (b) it is objectively apparent that the essential aim of the transactions is to obtain a tax advantage.

As explained by Lord Sumption in *Pendragon*, the concept of 'abuse of law' derives from civil law jurisprudence and has been applied in the UK as a result of the application of European law:

> '4. … Value Added Tax is an EU tax imposed pursuant to successive Directives of the European Union, at the relevant time the Sixth Directive. The Directives are subject to the principle of abuse of law. By virtue of section 2(1) of the European Communities Act 1972 the same principle must apply to domestic legislation implementing the Directives.
>
> 5. Abuse of law is a concept derived from civil law jurisprudence, which is unknown to English common law but has been adopted by the law of the European Union. In its simplest form, it confines the exercise of legal rights to the purpose for which they exist, and precludes their use for a collateral purpose. For present purposes, the expression

> détournement de droit adopted by some French writers is probably a better description of its content …'

Where the *Halifax* principle is engaged and it is necessary to counter an abuse of law, the transactions have to be redefined in order to entitle HMRC to treat them (for VAT purposes) as shorn of their abusive elements, as explained by Lord Sumption at [41] of *Pendragon*:

> '… so as to re-establish the situation that would have prevailed in the absence of the transactions constituting that abusive practice': Halifax , para 98. The redefinition is purely notional. Its effect is not to alter retrospectively the terms of the transactions, but simply to entitle the Commissioners, as between themselves and the taxpayer, to treat them for the purpose of assessing VAT as if their abusive features had not been present: see Revenue and Customs Commissioners v Newey (Case C-653/11) [2013] STC 2432, paras 50–51 …'

Moreover, a further significant application of the abuse principle was recognised by the CJEU in Joined Cases C-439/04 *Axel Kittel v Belgian State* and C-440/04 *Belgian State v Recolta Recycling SPRL* (*Kittel*), where the CJEU extended the abuse principle in *Halifax* to persons who knew or should have known that they were taking part in a fraudulent chain of transactions. As Moses LJ explained in *Mobilx Ltd (in Administration) v HMRC* [2010] EWCA Civ 517:

> 'fraudulent tax evasion falls outwith the scope of VAT and thus the scope of the right to deduct input tax'.

Accordingly, the effect of *Kittel* and *Halifax* is that fraudulent evasion of tax (including by persons who knew or should have known that they were taking part in a fraudulent chain of transactions) does not meet the objective criteria (such as whether the activity is 'economic activity' or a taxable person is 'acting as such') by which the scope of VAT and the right to deduct are identified and therefore lose the right to deduct.

The 'abuse' principle, that is the principle that abuse of rights is prohibited, has been described by the CJEU as a 'general' principle of EU law (see the judgment of the CJEU in *Hans Markus Kofoed v Skatteministeriet* (Case C-321/05) at [38]).

Accordingly, the abuse principle will continue to be relevant to the interpretation of retained EU law (albeit that, post-IP day, courts will not be able to disapply enactments on the grounds that they breach the abuse principle). Indeed, that is made plain by *TCBTA 2018, s 42(3)–(4)* that expressly provides that the abuse principle 'continues to be relevant':

> '(3) Further provision relevant to the law relating to value added tax is made by the European Union (Withdrawal) Act 2018: see, for example, section 6 of that Act (interpretation of retained EU law).

(4) One of the consequences of the provision made by that Act is that the principle of EU law preventing the abuse of the VAT system (see, for example, the cases of Halifax and Kittel) continues to be relevant, in accordance with that Act, for the purposes of the law relating to value added tax.'

The difficulties, identified above, in restricting the application of general principles to principles of interpretation only (and which cannot lead to disapplication) may have less effect on the abuse principle than they do as regards fiscal neutrality.

That is because, as discussed above, the abuse principle in *Halifax* and *Kittel* generally applies to amend the nature of transactions (for example, by recharacterising the parties to a supply or by identifying the transaction as one that was carried out for fraudulent ends and which does not therefore fall within the concept of an economic activity for VAT purposes) rather than by requiring the VAT legislation itself to be read in a modified way. That said, there may be a fine line between amending a transaction (permitted) and disapplying (say) a tax relief, which fits the facts, but which would offend the abuse principle if granted (arguably, not permitted), see also the discussion in Chapter 1 at **1.34**.

DIRECT EFFECT

2.12 The doctrine of direct effect has been of central importance in the context of EU VAT because the contents of EU VAT are principally set out in EU Directives, which are not directly applicable in domestic UK law. Taxpayers are therefore generally reliant on the UK taking steps to properly implement the Directives in a timely manner. It is the very kind of political subordination that Brexit is designed to bring to an end.

However, the doctrine of direct effect means that, where the UK has failed to implement an EU Directive (or has misimplemented it) a taxpayer (but not HMRC) may rely directly on provisions in the EU Directive that are (broadly) unconditional and sufficiently precise.

The consequences of the doctrine of direct effect were summarised by the CJEU in Case 8/81 *Becker v Finanzamt Münster-Innenstadt* [1982] ECR 53 as follows (at [25]):

> '… wherever the provisions of a directive appear, as far as their subject matter is concerned, to be unconditional and sufficiently precise, **those provisions may, in the absence of implementing measures adopted within the prescribed period, be relied upon as against any national provision which is incompatible with the directive or in so far as the provisions define rights which individuals are able to assert against the State**.' (Emphasis added.)

Certain rights which had their origin in the doctrine of direct effect will continue to be available to taxpayers even after IP completion day but only as proffered by the now Supreme UK Parliament. Thus, *EUWA 2018, s 4* is headed, 'saving for rights etc under section 2(1) of the ECA' and provides that:

> '(1) Any rights, powers, liabilities, obligations, restrictions, remedies and procedures which, immediately before IP completion day—
>
> (a) are recognised and available in domestic law by virtue of section 2(1) of the European Communities Act 1972, and
>
> (b) are enforced, allowed and followed accordingly,
>
> continue on and after IP completion day to be recognised and available in domestic law (and to be enforced, allowed and followed accordingly).
>
> (2) Subsection (1) does not apply to any rights, powers, liabilities, obligations, restrictions, remedies or procedures so far as they—
>
> ...
>
> (b) arise under an EU directive (including as applied by the EEA agreement) and are not of a kind recognised by the European Court or any court or tribunal in the United Kingdom in a case decided before IP completion day (whether or not as an essential part of the decision in the case).
>
> (3) This section is subject to section 5 and Schedule 1 (exceptions to savings and incorporation) and section 5A (savings and incorporation: supplementary).'

In the context of VAT, significant 'rights' available to taxpayers have historically arisen under the EU VAT Directives. Prior to IP completion day, where a Directive that confers rights on taxpayers has (wrongly) not been implemented or implemented correctly by the UK, a taxpayer will (as noted above) be entitled to rely directly on the Directive in order to enforce its EU rights where the relevant provisions are sufficiently clear, precise and unconditional.

There is no definition of rights which, immediately before IP completion day are 'recognised and available' in domestic law 'by virtue of section 2(1) of the European Communities Act 1972', and that are 'enforced, allowed and followed'. The difficulties of pinning down the meaning of 'recognised' have been considered in Chapter 1, see especially at **1.26**.

However, the writers consider that directly effective rights that have been historically recognised as arising under Directives would plainly be recognised and available in domestic law 'by virtue of section 2(1) of the European Communities Act 1972' (see, eg, *R (on the application of Miller and another) v Secretary of State for Exiting the European Union* [2017] UKSC 5 [2018] A.C. 61 at [190]) and would be 'enforced' accordingly by courts, within the meaning of *EUWA 1972, s 4(1)*.

But, as ever, for every ladder in the board game of Brexit legislation, there is a snake – here in the form of the 'saving' under *EUWA 2018, s 4(1)* which applies, in relation to VAT, 'subject to any exclusions or other modifications made by regulations made by the Treasury by statutory instrument' (*TCBTA 2018, s 42(2)*). Such regulations can only be made up to 31 March 2023 (*TCBTA 2018, s 42(6)*).

Moreover, there is an important restriction to the saving, namely that it does not apply to directly effective rights which arise under a Directive (including as applied by the EEA agreement) 'and are not of a kind recognised by the European Court or any court or tribunal in the United Kingdom in a case decided before IP completion day (whether or not as an essential part of the decision in the case)'.

This is very significant for VAT, because directly effective rights arising under a Directive are excluded unless they have been historically recognised by a UK court or the CJEU (defined as 'European Court', see *EUWA 2018, Sch 8, Pt 2, para 22*) in a case 'decided' before IP completion day (*EUWA 2018, s 4(2)(b)*, above). (It is not required that the case be finally decided, merely decided.) It is to be hoped that after nearly 50 years of VAT litigation in the UK and the EU, all the directly effective rights that needed to be judicially recognised, have been.

A further possible question that arises, in relation to directly effective rights arising under the PVD that are preserved, is whether those rights are saved both for the benefit of the taxpayer and HMRC or only for the benefit of the taxpayer.

The writers consider that the saving would apply only for the taxpayer's benefit: the saved rights are ones that are 'recognised' by the CJEU or a domestic court before IP-completion day which (as noted above) are rights that could only be enforced by the taxpayer and could not be relied on by HMRC against the taxpayer. (This is presumably why the doctrine of abuse gets a special treatment, as noted above: it is not a statutory concept, nor does it confer rights on taxpayers.)

CONFORMING INTERPRETATION

2.13 National courts and tribunals were, until 31 December 2020, obliged to construe domestic legislation in a manner that gives effect to EU law. Of particular relevance to VAT is the courts' obligation to interpret domestic legislation designed to give effect to the PVD so as to make it (so far as possible) compatible with the Directive. As with much of what has been discussed above, this represents a loss of sovereignty, which Brexit aims to reverse.

In *Marleasing SA v La Comercial Internacional de Alimentacion SA* (Case C-106/89), the CJEU described the obligation of the national courts of the

Member States to interpret domestic law in conformity with EU law as follows (see [8] of the CJEU's judgment):

> '... in applying national law, whether the provisions in question were adopted before or after the directive, the national court called upon to interpret it is required to do so, as far as possible, **in the light of the wording and the purpose of the directive in order to achieve the result pursued by the latter** and thereby comply with the third paragraph of Article 189 of the Treaty.' (Emphasis added.)

The obligation to construe domestic VAT law in a manner that gives effect to EU VAT is a strong one. In particular, the Court's approach in identifying whether a conforming construction is possible is not constrained by conventional (domestic) rules of construction (*The Commissioners for her Majesty's Revenue and Customs v IDT Card Services Ireland Ltd* [2006] EWCA Civ 29 (*IDT*) at [82]), does not require ambiguity in the legislative language (*Ghaidan v Godin-Mendoza* [2004] 2 AC 557 (*Ghaidan*) at [32]), permits departure from the strict and literal application of the legislation (*Ghaidan* at [31]), permits the implication of words necessary to comply with EU law obligations, whether by reading in, or reading down or disapplying a provision (*IDT* at [89] and *Vidal-Hall v Google Inc* [2015] EWCA Civ 311 at [90]).

A conforming construction is only constrained to the extent that it must not go against the grain of the legislation or lead to an interpretation which is inconsistent with a fundamental or cardinal feature of the legislation (*Ghaidan* at [33], *IDT* at [82] and [113]) and cannot require the courts to make decisions for which they are not equipped or give rise to important practical repercussions which the court is not equipped to evaluate (*IDT* at [113]).

The issue whether 'conforming construction' has been retained, post-IP completion day, is a difficult one (see also Chapter 1 at **1.32** to **1.33**). Certainly, *EUWA 2018* (and the VAT 'retained EU law') does not preserve the obligation in terms.

However, the principle lives on in two forms:

(1) as noted above, *EUWA 2018, s 6(3)* requires courts to construe retained EU law (including *VATA 1994*) in a manner that is consistent with relevant case law (including CJEU decisions) and general principles as they are immediately before IP completion day; and

(2) the principle of supremacy of EU law continues to apply to retained EU law (to the extent that it is not subsequently modified or is modified in a way that is consistent with the application of the principle of supremacy). It is noteworthy that the Explanatory Notes to *EUWA 2018, s 5(2)* treat the principle of conforming construction as an adjunct of the principle of (historic) EU law supremacy:[21]

21 Albeit that this is at its lowest controversial, see Chapter 1 at **1.32**.

> 'The principle of supremacy also means that domestic law must be interpreted, as far as possible, in accordance with EU law. So, for example, domestic law must be interpreted, as far as possible, in light of the wording and purpose of relevant directives. Whilst this duty will not apply to domestic legislation passed or made on or after exit day, subsection (2) preserves this duty in relation to domestic legislation passed or made before exit.'

Although the principle of supremacy of EU law will not apply to any enactment or rule of law passed or made on or after IP completion day, it will continue to apply on or after IP completion day so far as relevant to the interpretation, disapplication or quashing of an enactment or rule of law passed or made before that day (*EUWA 2018, s 5(1)–(2)*).

An immediate question is, therefore, whether the principle of supremacy will apply to *VATA 1994* once it is modified to take account of Brexit. For example, as described at **2.15** below, the *TCBTA 2018* amends *VATA 1994* to remove the concept of 'acquisition VAT' and replaces it with 'import VAT' in the light of the UK's exit from the EU and the Single Market in a 'no deal' situation). This in turn is one of a long list of nearly 100 specific amendments made to the VAT system. This will be likely to generate a compartmentalised approach whereby certain 'areas' of VAT are treated as sufficiently untouched by future amendments still to attract the full application of the principles being discussed.

Would supremacy therefore cease to apply to *VATA 1994* as a whole? We consider the answer to be 'not completely'. Supremacy may apply to a 'modification' made on or after IP completion day of any enactment or rule of law passed or made before IP completion day if the application of the principle is 'consistent with the intention of the modification' (*EUWA 2018, s 5(3)*).

'Modify' is widely defined in *EUWA 2018, s 20* as including amending, repealing or revoking (and related expressions are to be read accordingly).

Therefore, (returning to the acquisition VAT example) whilst we would not expect the principle of supremacy to continue to apply by reference to any of the sections of *VATA 1994* that concern acquisition VAT, it could continue to apply to other parts of *VATA 1994* that have not themselves been modified and that do not rely on the concept of acquisition VAT.

GENERAL PRINCIPLES INTERACTING WITH STATUTORY PILLARS

2.14 We turn next to the symbiotic relationship between the general principles and the statutory pillars, having discussed each of them separately above. As is usual with the drafting of indirect tax legislation worldwide, only relatively broad concepts are set out by the legislators, leaving it to the judges to work out the vast detail that is required in practice. Accordingly, for example, supply is very lightly defined in the PVD (Articles 14–29) and the *VATA* (*ss 4–5*, and *Sch 4*), but has spawned an endless line of cases, above all about single v multiple analysis[22] or the definition of economic activity.[23] The same can be said of consideration and input tax *nexus*. These multiple glosses of judge-made law, establish or deploy many of the general principles covered by the prior section, demonstrating the importance of the general principles to bringing life and force to the letter of statutory VAT law. Further, we note that the general principles include the need for purposive (teleologicial) interpretation. So, any interference with the general principles, will inevitably impact on the statutory pillars.

INEVITABLE DISAPPEARANCES

2.15 Brexit is about disengagement, and we note now the unavoidable aspects of change in the VAT system.

First, anything expressly dependant on the UK's being within the territory of the EU will cease to apply – at least in Great Britain. Thus between Great Britain and the Member States remaining in the EU: (i) the concept of intra-EU acquisition[24] is necessarily at an end, since the UK is no longer *intra,* 'import VAT' will apply to all cross-border supplies of goods into the UK,[25] (ii) Eighth Directive input tax claims are also gone except in relation to businesses in Northern Ireland in relation to EU VAT paid on goods used for the purposes of intra-EU transactions, while all UK businesses otherwise pass to the more choppy waters of the Thirteenth Directive,[26] (iii) the place of supply rules will not change, but they no longer will address the issue of possible intra-EU conflict between Member States, so much discussed in the CJEU case

22 *Card Protection Plan Ltd v C & E Commrs*; *Dr Beynon* (Case C-349/96) [2004] UKHL 53; *Levob Verzekeringen BV and OV Bank NV v Staatssecretaris van Financiën* (Case C-41/04); *College of Estate Management* [2005] UKHL 62; *Weight Watchers (UK) Ltd* [2008] EWCA Civ 715; BGZ Leasing sp z.o.o (Case C-224/11); *Město Žamberk v Finanční ředitelství* (Case C-18/12).

23 *EC Commission v Finland* (Case C-246/08); *Gemeente Borsele v Staatssecretaris van Financiën* (Case C-520/14); *Longridge on the Thames v HMRC* [2016] EWCA Civ 930; *Wakefield College v Revenue and Customs Commissioners* [2018] EWCA Civ 952.

24 *TCBTA 2018, s 41* (abolition of acquisition VAT and extension of import VAT).

25 So, goods entering Great Britain from the EU will be imports subject to import VAT (albeit that businesses may be able to use postponed import VAT accounting to account for import VAT on their VAT returns, see *SI 2019/60*); goods entering Northern Ireland from the EU will be treated as intra-EU acquisitions. There are special rules for imported goods of a low value and for supplies of goods by persons outside the UK that are facilitated by online marketplaces, see *Schedule 3* to the *Taxation (Post-transition Period) Act 2020*.

26 With the consequence that EU traders incurring UK VAT are treated as third country claimants going forward. See *TCBTA 2018, Sch 8, para 41* amending *VATA 1994, s 39(1)* and *(2)*.

law,[27] and (iv) the objective of harmonising the taxable base and VAT rates between EU Member States (subject to any ongoing requirements as to state aid/competition law that could restrict the UK's freedom to undercut EU VAT rates).

A number of prohibitions on national legislative sovereignty will also cease to apply, along with the supervisory jurisdiction of the European Commission and the CJEU in the area of infringement. Thus, the UK will be free to enact new zero-rates[28] (something that it has not done (officially) since January 1991), and will have complete autonomy as to its standard and reduced rates. It can adjust its exemptions as it pleases.

Above, all the UK can also enact fresh VAT legislation on any subject without restraint and without fear of infringement proceedings initiated by the EU Commission. By the same token, nor can taxpayers any longer lodge complaints at the Commission in the hope of stirring up such actions.

Secondly, there will be no right in domestic law on or after IP completion day to claim *Francovich* damages (although this will not apply in relation to any proceedings begun within two years beginning with IP completion day so far as they relate to anything which occurred before that day, see *EUWA 2018, Sch 1, para 4* and *Sch 8, para 39(7)*).

Finally, the CJEU has no further role in receiving references from the Courts of Great Britain (*EUWA 2018, s 6(1)(b)*). This has been a politically charged issue. It is also a logical consequence of Brexit. We consider it next in more detail.

The UK's new status as a third country has in some cases led to a better VAT position for businesses: for example, businesses who supply insurance intermediary services or finance intermediary services (ie, intermediary services which fall within the *Value Added Tax (Input Tax) (Specified Supplies) Order 1999, SI 1999/3121*) would previously only have been able to recover input tax where the supplies were made to a person who belonged outside the EU. Following IP completion day, input tax can be recovered in respect of such supplies made to a person who belongs outside the UK (see *VATA 1994, s 26*, the *Value Added Tax (Input Tax) (Specified Supplies) Order 1999, SI 1999/3121, Article 3*, and the *Value Added Tax (Miscellaneous Amendments, Northern Ireland Protocol and Savings and Transitional Provisions) (EU Exit) Regulations 2020, SI 2020/1545, reg 91*).

---

27 See *Kollektivavtalsstiftelsen TRR Trygghetsrådet* (Case C-291/07) at [30], where the Court explained that the objective of Article 9 of the Sixth Directive (supply of services) was to lay down a conflict of laws rule.

28 And has done so, in relation to women's sanitary products: see *Finance Act 2016, s 126* and *SI 2020/1642, reg 3*. Cf Article 110 PVD (which permits the preservation in each Member State (so far as zero-rating is concerned) of the treatment under that Member State's domestic law for zero-rating of items, which existed as at 1 January 1991).

CURRENT AND FUTURE ROLE OF THE CJEU

2.16 Although *EUWA 2018, s 1* repealed the *ECA 1972* on 'exit day', being 31 January 2020 at 11.00 pm (*EUWA 2018, s 20*), the 'pre-Brexit' EU VAT rules continued to apply until 11pm on 31 December 2020.

That was of course due to the UK and EU's 'Withdrawal Agreement', which provided that the UK's exit from the European Union should be followed by an 'implementation period' until 11pm on 31 December 2020, during which the status of the CJEU's case law remained the same as prior to Brexit.

After IP completion day, any question as to the validity, meaning or effect of any retained EU law is to be decided (so far as that law is unmodified) in accordance with *inter alia* any retained case law, being:

- decisions of domestic courts and tribunals; and
- decisions of the CJEU,

both as modified by or under *EUWA 2018* and to the extent that those decisions are not 'excluded' by *s 5* (supremacy, see **2.13** above) or *Sch 1* (notably, the restriction that the only principles who will be treated as general principles are ones that have been recognised as a general principle of EU law by the CJEU in a case decided before IP completion day, see **2.8** above).

However, the status of the CJEU's case law changed dramatically on IP completion day.

First, domestic courts will not be bound by and CJEU decisions made on or after IP completion day and will not be able to refer any case to the CJEU (*EUWA 2018, s 6(1)*), although the CJEU continues to have jurisdiction to give preliminary rulings on requests from UK courts and tribunals made before the end of the transition period: Article 86 of the '*Agreement on the withdrawal of the United Kingdom of Great Britain and Northern Ireland from the European Union and the European Atomic Energy Community*'. (This is subject to exceptions – the CJEU will retain jurisdiction in respect of certain parts of the Withdrawal Agreement but not VAT: see the discussion of the EU-United Kingdom Withdrawal Agreement in Chapter 1.)

Second, pre-IP completion day case law will not bind the Supreme Court or the High Court of Justiciary (albeit that in deciding whether to depart from the CJEU's case law, those Courts must apply the same test as they would apply in deciding whether to depart from their own case law namely whether it appears right to do so (*Austin v Mayor and Burgesses of the London Borough of Southwark* [2011] 1 AC 355 at [24]–[25]), *EUWA 2018, ss 6(4) and (5)*.

Third, as explained above at **2.8** regulations designate certain 'relevant courts' including the Court of Appeal in England and Wales and the Inner House of the Court of Session that will only be bound by principles laid down by, and any decisions of, the CJEU so far as a post-IP day decision of a UK court or tribunal 'modifies or applies' the CJEU decision and is binding on the relevant courts. Those courts are otherwise not bound, under the general rule, by pre-IP completion day CJEU case law when determining the validity or interpretation of unmodified retained EU law.

PAST UK CASE LAW – STATUS

2.17 As set out above, questions as to the validity, meaning or effect of the *VATA 1994*, in the form it has been saved by *EUWA 2018, s 2* on IP completion day, fall to be decided in accordance with relevant principles laid down by and decisions of the domestic courts or tribunals (as they have effect in EU law immediately before IP completion day, subject to any modification under *EUWA 2018* or domestic law and subject to the exclusions set out in *EUWA 2018, s 5* and *Sch 1*).

Accordingly, domestic case law, so far as relevant to the validity or interpretation of retained EU law, will remain relevant and binding in accordance with the normal rules of precedent (see *s 6(4)(c)*, which provides that no court or tribunal is bound by any such case law that it 'would not otherwise be bound by').

PENDING OR PROPOSED LITIGATION IN THE UK – STATUS

2.18 Many will be asking whether proposed litigation in the UK on some outstanding issue should be accelerated to try to get a decision (an unlikely possibility in current circumstances).

There are significant transitional savings in *EUWA 2018, Sch 8*. The writers suggest that the following are likely to be most relevant to VAT.

First, the rule in *EUWA 2018, s 4(2)(b)* which allows only rights arising under a Directive that have been recognised by the CJEU or a domestic court before IP completion day to be saved does not apply to circumstances where a domestic court has recognised the right in a case which, although decided after IP completion day, was begun before it (*EUWA 2018, Sch 8, para 38*). Put another way, directly effective rights must have been recognised by either the CJEU or domestic courts in cases decided before IP completion day, or recognised by domestic courts in cases begun before IP completion day (even if they are decided after IP completion day).

There is no definition of when proceedings will have 'begun' but the writers would expect this to relate to the relevant formal step necessary to commencing proceedings, for example, filing a notice of appeal or issuing a claim.

The effect of the transitional provision is strengthened by the fact that, even after IP completion day, questions as to the meaning or effect of EU law in legal proceedings are to be treated as questions of law (*EUWA 2018, Sch 5, para 3*). Had it been otherwise and had EU law been treated as foreign law that would need to be proved as a matter of fact, the necessary evidence may not have been presented in cases begun before IP completion day.

However, the transitional provision is restricted to decisions by domestic courts recognising directly effective rights. The surprising result may be that, if a domestic court had referred a question relating to the direct effect of a provision to the CJEU and the CJEU had not 'decided' the case before IP completion day but subsequently held that the provision had direct effect, the taxpayer would not be able to rely on their directly effective rights. By contrast, had the domestic Court not referred the issue and had simply decided the point itself, the taxpayer would be entitled to rely on the right. In practice, the domestic court would itself need to 'recognise' the direct effect, having received the CJEU's judgment.

Second, *EUWA 2018, Sch 1, para 3*, which prevents general principles from being used to disapply enactments post-IP completion day, will not apply in relation to:

- any proceedings 'begun, but not finally decided' before a court or tribunal in the UK before IP completion day (*EUWA 2018, Sch 8, para 39(3)*); or
- proceedings begun within three years of IP completion day so far as the proceedings involve a challenge to 'anything' which occurred prior to IP completion day and the challenge is not for the disapplication or quashing of an Act of Parliament or rule of law (or anything which gives effect to or enforces an Act or rule of law or could not have been different as a result of an Act or a rule of law), *EUWA 2018, Sch 8, para 39(4)*).

Third, *EUWA 2018, Sch 1, para 3*, which prevents general principles from being used to disapply enactments post-IP completion day, will also not apply in relation to a decision of a domestic court or tribunal or other public authority (including, therefore, HMRC) which is made on or after IP completion day but is a 'necessary consequence of': (i) a pre-IP day decision of a court or tribunal, or (ii) a decision made on or after IP day by virtue of the transitional provisions in *EUWA 2018, Sch 8, para 39*.

Fourth, the rule that removes the right to *Francovich* damages from IP completion day (see **2.15** above) does not apply in relation to proceedings begun within two years from IP completion day, albeit only in so far as the proceedings relate to 'anything' which occurred before IP completion day.

THE NEW FRAMEWORK

2.19 What, then, can VAT practitioners tentatively conclude on the basis of the above? We take an example which points out the steps that will be necessary in the new world of VAT that we are entering.

Imagine that *VATA 1994* provides that supplies by 'artists' are subject to a special place of supply rule, whilst the PVD provides that the rule applies to 'professionals'.

What could an adviser consider, post-IP completion day, to assist a doctor who seeks to rely on the rule, assuming (for the purposes of this example) that the two rules are inconsistent and lead to different results?

First, consider whether the provision of the PVD was recognised as being directly effective before IP completion day (and consider the transitional rules). If it was, the argument would be that the directly effective right is saved by *EUWA 2018, s 4*.

However, second, the adviser also knows that *VATA 1994* is 'retained EU law', being 'EU-derived domestic legislation'. Will the *section 4* right prevail?

The writers consider that it will, by virtue of the principle of supremacy, which will continue to apply to legislation passed or made before IP completion day (*EUWA 2018, s 5(2)*) on the basis that the *section 4* right should trump domestic legislation which was inconsistent, pre-IP completion day, with the PVD (see also the discussion on the application of the EU principle of supremacy to retained EU law in Chapter 1, at **1.28**).

Third, what if the provision of the PVD does not have direct effect?

The adviser should then consider whether there is any binding 'retained case law' (either domestic or CJEU) that a court or tribunal would need to apply in the doctor's case (*EUWA 2018, s 6(3)*). If there is, although the doctor cannot rely on the PVD itself, the binding case law may give him/her the result they seek.

Fourth, in the absence of any binding retained case law, the adviser will need to identify whether any retained general principles of EU law (including fiscal neutrality) may assist the doctor.

Fifth, if such a principle is found, the adviser must then go on to ask whether the *VATA 1994* place of supply rule can be construed 'in accordance' with the general principle or whether disapplication would be required in order to render the *VATA 1994* compatible with the principle, the latter being impermissible (*EUWA 2018, Sch 1, para 3*).

Sixth, what rules of construction could the adviser use? Ordinary domestic canons or the 'highly muscular' approach adopted in relation to pre-IP completion day conforming construction (see *Test Claimants in the FII Group Litigation v Revenue and Customs Commissioners* [2012] UKSC 19, [2012] 2 AC 337 at [176])?

Seventh, as observed in Chapter 1 at **1.33**, the 'loyalty' clause will no longer apply post-IP completion day and the UK – particularly the UK courts – will no longer be obliged as a matter of EU law to take all appropriate measures, whether general or particular, to ensure the fulfilment of EU law obligations. It may, therefore, be that the adviser must ask whether, applying only domestic canons of construction, the rule in the *VATA 1994* can be read 'in accordance with' the general principle. However, it is highly unsatisfactory that the *EUWA 2018* itself does not provide a clear answer. Indeed, the Explanatory Notes suggest that the Act was intended to apply a strong approach to interpretation that 'renders' retained EU law compatible with pre-IP completion day general principles:

> '[Explanatory note to section 5 EUWA 2018]
>
> 104 The principle of supremacy also means that domestic law must be interpreted, as far as possible, in accordance with EU law. **So, for example, domestic law must be interpreted, as far as possible, in light of the wording and purpose of relevant directives**. Whilst this duty will not apply to domestic legislation passed or made on or after exit day, subsection (2) preserves this duty in relation to domestic legislation passed or made before exit. [Explanatory note to section 6 EUWA 2018]
>
> 111 Subsection (3) provides that any question as to the meaning of unmodified retained EU law will be determined in UK courts in accordance with relevant pre-exit CJEU case law and general principles. This means, for example, **taking a purposive approach to interpretation where the meaning of the measure is unclear (i.e. considering the purpose of the law from looking at other relevant materials such as the treaty legal base for a measure, its recitals and preambles, and the travaux preparatoires (working papers) leading to the adoption of the measure). It also means applying an interpretation that renders the provision of EU law compatible with the treaties and general principles of EU law**. Non-binding instruments, such as recommendations and opinions, would still be available to a court to assist with interpretation of retained EU law after exit.' (Emphasis added.)

The writers consider that there must be limits to the principles of 'interpretation' (were it otherwise, the prohibition in relation to the 'disapplication' of enactments would have no effect) but that, again, the identification and delineation of those limits has been left to the Courts.

SPECIAL ARRANGEMENTS: NORTHERN IRELAND

2.20 We have already noted that Northern Ireland was intended to remain for certain purposes inside the EU.[29] One of those was VAT.

29 In Tudor-Jacobean times, the first 'plantations' of protestant settlers were imposed on the indigenous Catholic Irish, and led to the existence of Ulster, which was not permitted to gain independence from the UK, in 1922, leading to the 'Troubles' which intensified from the 1970s. These were ended by the Belfast (or Good Friday) Agreement of 1998, which has been implemented so as to allow daily commercial life to function on the island of Ireland, as if it were a single political unit, or, at least, a single market.

Under the Northern Ireland Protocol (contained in the Withdrawal Agreement), Northern Ireland is part of the UK's VAT system but remains aligned to EU VAT as regards supplies of goods (albeit that there is a specific provision in the Protocol which allows the government to apply in Northern Ireland VAT exemptions and reductions, including zero rating, corresponding to those applicable in Ireland). CJEU case law will continue to apply. By contrast, UK VAT rules will apply to transactions in services.

In general terms, the position of the UK is that '[a]t the heart of our proposals is a consensual, pragmatic approach: one that will best protect the Belfast (Good Friday) Agreement; support businesses and the economy; protect the EU's Single Market; and ensure Northern Ireland benefits most fully from its access to the GB and EU markets and our trade deals across the world.' The UK's approach to the Protocol is that it was, '... designed as a practical solution to avoiding a hard border on the island of Ireland, whilst ensuring that the UK, including Northern Ireland, could leave the EU as a whole.' (UK Command paper as at 27 May 2020.)

Turning to specifics, Article 8 of the Protocol provides that the following provisions of Union law concerning goods shall apply to and in the UK in respect of Northern Ireland:

> '1. Value Added Tax
>
> – Council Directive 2006/112/EC of 28 November 2006 on the common system of value added tax
>
> – Council Directive 2008/9/EC of 12 February 2008 laying down detailed rules for the refund of value added tax, provided for in Directive 2006/112/EC, to taxable persons not established in the Member State of refund but established in another Member State
>
> – Council Regulation (EU) No 904/2010 of 7 October 2010 on administrative cooperation and combating fraud in the field of value added tax
>
> – Council Directive 2010/24/EU of 16 March 2010 concerning mutual assistance for the recovery of claims relating to taxes, duties and other measures
>
> – Thirteenth Council Directive 86/560/EEC of 17 November 1986 on the harmonization of the laws of the Member States relating to turnover taxes – Arrangements for the refund of value added tax to taxable persons not established in Community territory
>
> – Council Directive 2007/74/EC of 20 December 2007 on the exemption from value added tax and excise duty of goods imported by persons travelling from third countries
>
> – Council Directive 2009/132/EC of 19 October 2009 determining the scope of Article 143(b) and (c) of Directive 2006/112/EC as regards

exemption from value added tax on the final importation of certain goods

– Council Directive 2006/79/EC of 5 October 2006 on the exemption from taxes of imports of small consignments of goods of a non-commercial character from third countries

– Obligations stemming from the Agreement between the European Union and the Kingdom of Norway on administrative cooperation, combating fraud and recovery of claims in the field of value added tax

– Obligations stemming from the Cooperation agreement between the European Community and its Member States, of the one part, and the Swiss Confederation, of the other part, to combat fraud and any other illegal activity to the detriment of their financial interests'.

The *Taxation (Post-transition Period) Act 2020 (TPPA 2020), s 3(1)* inserts *s 40A* into *VATA 1994*, which gives effect to three new schedules[30] that implement the Protocol, the most important of which for present purposes are:[31]

- *VATA 1994, Sch 9ZA* (which provides for a charge to VAT on acquisitions of goods in Northern Ireland from a Member State, and contains modifications of the other provisions of *VATA 1994* in connection with the movement of goods between Northern Ireland and Member States); and
- *VATA 1994, Sch 9ZB* (which concerns VAT charged on goods imported into the United Kingdom as a result of their entry into Northern Ireland, the VAT treatment of goods that are removed from Northern Ireland to Great Britain and goods that are removed from Great Britain to Northern Ireland).

Schedule 9ZA makes provision for the continued application of EU VAT rules on goods in relation to NI and introduces 'NI acquisition VAT', being VAT charged on the acquisition of goods in Northern Ireland from a Member State. The person liable for the VAT, which becomes due at the time of acquisition (subject to provisions about accounting and payment) is the person who acquires the goods (*VATA 1994, Sch 9ZA, para 1*).

The charge applies to 'taxable acquisitions' of goods (broadly, supplies or removals of goods, see *para 3*) from taxable persons in Member States, where the acquisition is not in pursuant of a taxable supply made in the UK (or where

30 As amended by the *Value Added Tax (Miscellaneous Amendments to the Value Added Tax Act 1994 and Revocation) (EU Exit) Regulations 2020. The Value Added Tax (Miscellaneous Amendments, Northern Ireland Protocol and Savings and Transitional Provisions) (EU Exit) Regulations 2020* make consequential amendments to secondary legislation in consequence of provisions made in the *TPPA 2020.*

31 *VATA 1994, Sch 9ZC* concerns sales that are facilitated by online marketplaces and the importation of goods of low value, relating to the Northern Ireland Protocol.

the goods acquired are subject to a duty of excise or consist in a new means of transport) (*VATA 1994, Sch 9ZA, para 2*). There are specific provisions setting out the time and place of acquisition (*paras 4, 5*), acquisitions involving intermediary suppliers (*para 6*), how to value acquisitions (*part 2*), the rules relating to payment of NI acquisition VAT (*part 3*), reliefs (including reduced rates and zero-rating) (*part 4*), the rules relating to grouping and other specific case (*part 5*), procedures for administration, collection, enforcement and appeals (*parts 6* and *7*), registrations (*parts 8* and *9*), call-off stock arrangements (where goods are transported by the supplier from their state of origin to the state of destination at a time when the supplier already knows the identity of the customer) (*part 10*), consequential modifications to other enactments (*parts 11* and *12*) and the interpretation of the schedule (*part 13*).

Schedule 9ZB, part 1, modifies the charge to import VAT: the charge does not apply to 'Union goods' (broadly, goods wholly obtained or produced in the EU or in free circulation in the EU) imported into the UK from the EU as a result of their entry into Northern Ireland. By contrast, VAT is chargeable on the importation of any other goods imported into the UK as a result of their entry into Northern Ireland.

Part 2 of *Schedule 9ZB* introduces a charge on goods removed from NI to GB and vice versa. *Paragraph 3* imposes a VAT charge on removals between Northern Ireland and Great Britain: VAT is charged on the entry of those goods into Great Britain 'as if those goods had been imported into the United Kingdom' but supplies of goods that involve the removal of goods from Northern Ireland to Great Britain or vice versa is zero-rated, subject to conditions set out by HMRC or in regulations (*para 3*) and *paragraph 4* identifies the person liable to the VAT payable.

Thus, import VAT will be due on goods that enter Northern Ireland from Great Britain (except in relation to qualifying Northern Ireland goods that are not removed in the course of a supply, *para 6*). The Government has endeavoured to minimise the impact to businesses:[32]

> '… Under the Protocol, transactions in goods between Northern Ireland and EU businesses and consumers will continue as they do today. The same processes and reporting requirements will apply and Northern Ireland businesses intending to make transactions under the Protocol should ensure they are able to continue to operate in this way.
>
> The only change is related to the use of the 'XI' prefix when trading under the Northern Ireland protocol …'

If goods are transported from Great Britain to Northern Ireland and then sold from Northern Ireland to the EU, HMRC's guidance (Policy paper, 'Accounting

32 See www.gov.uk/government/publications/accounting-for-vat-on-goods-moving-between-great-britain-and-northern-ireland-from-1-january-2021/accounting-for-vat-on-goods-moving-between-great-britain-and-northern-ireland-from-1-january-2021.

for VAT on goods moving between Great Britain and Northern Ireland from 1 January 2021') explains that there will be two distinct movements:

(1) a movement of the seller's own goods from Great Britain to Northern Ireland (triggering a VAT liability for the seller, see *Sch 9ZB, para 30*). HMRC's policy paper suggest that a business making taxable supplies would usually be able to recover the VAT but that businesses that make some exempt supplies may suffer irrecoverable VAT twice in respect of the same goods. HMRC explain that, '[t]o prevent this, businesses will be able to reattribute the previously unrecovered input VAT on the original purchase in Great Britain as if the goods had been used for a taxable purchase' but that anti-avoidance rules will also be introduced);[33] and

(2) an intra-Community sale (it should be noted that *VATA 1994, s 30(6)* (zero-rating of exports by supplier) has effect as if reference to the export of goods did not include the export of goods from Northern Ireland to a place in the Member States, see *VATA 1994, Sch 9ZB, para 9* and Item 3 of Group 13 of Schedule 8 (zero-rating) has effect as if the reference to goods for export did not include goods for export from Northern Ireland to a place in the Member States, see *VATA 1994, Sch 9ZB, para 14*).

CONCLUSION

2.21 There is an immensely complex new landscape in the VAT field. Nor has that landscape yet stopped moving. For traders who operate within the UK market, making no acquisitions from the EU, little will change. However, for everyone else, change is potentially very significant. The retention of much of the substance of EU law as at IP completion day, will act as something of a short-term brake on aggressive change by the Commissioners. The great discretion given to the judiciary will also have the same effect, given judicial conservatism.

33 See also the *Value Added Tax (Northern Ireland) (EU Exit) Regulations 2020* in relation to the application of an offset in certain circumstances, where VAT has already been paid on the goods.

Chapter 3

Customs and Excise and Brexit

Timothy Lyons QC

3.1 The content of this book, generally, is up to date as of the end of the transition period. Due to significant subsequent developments in relation to customs and excise after that time some, but not all, material relevant to customs and excise has been referenced up to 13 March 2021.

During the course of the debates over Brexit, customs and excise issues regularly became matters of public debate. The technicalities of these areas, however, have frequently been neglected. Many commercial operators appear understandably bemused by the level of bureaucracy which has resulted from the UK leaving the EU customs union and internal market and replacing it with a free trade area. The high level of bureaucracy associated with free trade areas is, however, widely acknowledged. Indeed, in one recent paper some researchers considered that, viewed globally, free trade agreements may be seen as stepping stones to customs unions and noted that, Brexit apart, once in a customs union, countries rarely left.[1]

Clearly, customs and excise matters are bound to be of crucial importance for any state. They are frequently the most visible expression of a country's trade policy. They are certainly important for the EU which, the Union Customs Code (UCC) says 'is based upon a customs union'.[2]

Customs law, though, is not just about the levying of customs duty and the levels of tariffs. The mission statement of customs authorities in the UCC makes clear the breadth of modern customs activity.[3] The task of protecting legitimate trade and countering illegitimate trade results in the enforcement of sanitary and phytosanitary requirements, regulations governing the movement of animals and farm products and those concerned with environmental protection, for example, in relation to timber and fishery products. Also requiring enforcement are rules concerned with product safety and the

1 H Gnutzmann and A Gnutzmann-Mkrtchyan, 'The silent success of customs unions' (2019) 52(1) *Canadian Journal of Economics/Revue canadienne d'économique* 178 at 179 and 182f: '2. Silent success: FTAs upgrade to customs unions'.

2 Regulation (EU) No 952/2013 of the European Parliament and of the Council of 9 October 2013 laying down the Union Customs Code (recast) OJ L 269/1. 10.10.2013, recital (9).

3 See Article 3 UCC.

protection of intellectual property rights as well as those addressing illicit trade in drug precursors, in endangered species, and in products which have a dual civilian and military use.

The wide range of activity in relation to customs means that customs law can give rise to non-tariff barriers. The creation of such barriers by the operation of customs regimes has always been a danger. In one famous case in 1982, the French managed dramatically to reduce imports of Japanese video cassette recorders simply by requiring them to pass through a customs office in Poitiers.[4] In the EU the creation of the single market reduced the impact of customs bureaucracy significantly by removing customs borders. As the Court of Justice has noted:

> 'The abolition of customs and tax frontiers, …, is a direct result of Article 13 of the Single Act, which became Article 7a of the EC Treaty, which provides that "the internal market shall comprise an area without internal frontiers". It is thus a direct and necessary consequence of that provision.'[5]

That observation makes clear that when one assesses customs matters in the context of the relationship between the UK and the EU, the regulation of the EU's single market, and the effects of leaving it, will continue to be important.

The single market is also the proper EU context in which to consider some excise duties. The excise duty legislation passed to create the single market included Council Directive 92/12/EEC on the general arrangements for products subject to excise duty and on the hold, movement and monitoring of such products. It was applicable to alcoholic liquors, hydrocarbon oil and tobacco products. Its fourth recital notes that:

> '… in order to ensure the establishment and functioning of the internal market, chargeability of excise duties should be identical in all the Member States.'[6]

Customs unions and single markets have profound impacts on a nation state's legislative, judicial and administrative functions. That was recognised by the UK Government which has noted:

> 'On 31 December 2020, at the end of the transition period provided for in that agreement, the UK will fully recover its economic and political

4 See further The World Development Report 1987, 'The Poitiers Effect' World Bank, p 141, Box 8.5 available at: http://documents.worldbank.org/curated/en/458211468158384680/pdf/105960REPLACEMENT0WDR01987.pdf.

5 *Edouard Dubois et Fils SA v Council and Commission* (Case T-113/96) [1998] ECR II-125, 29 January 1998, para 46. The case was dismissed on appeal. See *Edouard Dubois and Fils* (Case C-95/98 P) ECR [1999] I-4835.

6 Council Directive 92/12/EEC of 25 Feb 1992 OJ L76/1, 23.3.1992, repealed by Council Directive 2008/118/EC, of 16 December 2008, OJ 9/12, 14.1.2009. The directive of 2008 has been repealed, as from 13 February 2023 by Council Directive (EU) 2020/262 of 19 December 2019 laying down general arrangements for excise duty (recast).

independence. The UK will no longer be a part of the EU Single Market or the EU Customs Union.'[7]

The state of affairs which that paper anticipated is now a reality. In the period between 31 January 2020 and 31 December 2020 the Withdrawal Agreement (WA) ensured that the UK was in an implementation or transitional period when it had left the EU but remained subject to EU law.[8] The Withdrawal Agreement was brought into domestic law by the *European Union (Withdrawal Agreement) Act 2020 (EUWAA 2020)* which amended the *European Union (Withdrawal) Act 2018 (EUWA 2018)* where necessary and made other appropriate provisions.

Although the implementation period has now ended and the relationship between the EU and the UK is governed by the Trade and Cooperation Agreement between them,[9] it may still be necessary on occasions to be clear as to what happened during the implementation period. In some respects, leaving aside the Protocol on Ireland/Northern Ireland, the WA provisions on customs apply for a number of years after the end of the implementation period. Consequently, customs and excise during the implementation period is considered briefly below.

CUSTOMS AND EXCISE IN THE IMPLEMENTATION PERIOD

3.2 The WA provided that during the implementation period: 'Unless otherwise provided in this Agreement, Union law shall be applicable to and in the United Kingdom …'.[10] The period starts on 'Exit day' which is defined as 31 January at 11pm.[11] It ends on 'IP completion day'.[12]

Section 1 of the *2018 Act* provides that the *European Communities Act 1972* is repealed on exit day. *Section 2* of the *1972 Act* contains well-known provisions permitting effect to be given to rights and obligations and so on created by, or arising by or under, the relevant treaties. *Section 5* of the *1972 Act* contains a particular provision permitting the levying of EU customs duty.

7 'The Future Relationship with the EU: The UK's Approach to Negotiations', CPP 211, February 2020, Introduction, para 2.

8 The Agreement on the withdrawal of the United Kingdom of Great Britain and Northern Ireland from the European Union and the European Atomic Energy Community, OJ 31.1.2020, L29/7. The transition period is defined in Article 126 WA. The *European Union (Withdrawal Agreement) Act 2020* defines 'IP completion day' as 31 December 2020 at 11pm: see *s 39(1)* and *(2)*. Provision was made for the amendment of IP completion day in *s 39(4)*. The implementation period could have been extended but was not: see Article 164 WA.

9 Discussed below at **3.15** onwards.

10 Article 127.1.

11 See the *EUWA 2018, s 20.*

12 The *EUWAA 2020* defines 'IP completion day' as 31 December 2020 at 11pm: see *s 39(1)* and *(2)*.

Despite the repeal of the *1972 Act* on exit day, there are two provisions which ensured that customs and excise law in the UK was unchanged during the implementation period. The first is in the *EUWA 2018, s 1A*. This provides that the *1972 Act* continues to have effect as provided in that section and that the WA Part Four (Articles 126 to 132) headed 'Transition') is to be one of the treaties to which *s 2(1)* of the *1972 Act* refers.[13] The second provision is in *EUWA 2018, s 1B*. This provides that EU-derived domestic legislation, which will cover some excise duty legislation, has effect in domestic law. The provisions of *s 1A*, and the relevant provisions of *s 1B*, are repealed on IP completion day.[14]

During the implementation period and in preparation for the time when EU law would not apply in relation to the UK, a number of official statements were issued to assist traders. The EU issued both Brexit Preparedness Notices in anticipation of the UK's departure as an EU Member State[15] and Stakeholder Preparedness Notices in preparation for the end of the implementation period.[16]

Separation provisions in the WA

3.3 The WA Part Three is headed 'Separation Provisions'. It deals with 'Goods placed on the market' in Title I, 'Ongoing customs procedures' in Title II and 'Ongoing Value Added Tax and Excise Duty Matters' in Title III.

So far as Title I is concerned its substantive provisions start with Article 41. It makes clear that a good lawfully placed on the market during the implementation period may 'be further made available on the market of the Union or of the United Kingdom and circulate between these two markets until it reaches its end-user'.[17]

The first provision in Title II, Article 47, deals with movements of goods which started before and end after the termination of the implementation period.[18] Where the goods move either from the UK customs territory to that of the EU or vice versa Article 5(23) UCC[19] applies, that is, the goods shall be considered 'Union goods'. In some circumstances the status of such goods is to be presumed pursuant to Article 153 UCC and in other situations proof of status must be provided.[20] By virtue of Article 48 WA, entry summary

13 See *EUWA 2018, s 1A(3)*. Note also the specific reference to customs duties in *s 1A(3)(e)*.
14 See *EUWA 2018, ss 1A(5)* and *1A(6)*.
15 Available at https://ec.europa.eu/info/brexit/brexit-preparedness/preparedness-notices_en.
16 Available at https://ec.europa.eu/info/european-union-and-united-kingdom-forging-new-partnership/future-partnership/getting-ready-end-transition-period_en. See now https://ec.europa.eu/info/relations-united-kingdom_en.
17 Article 41.1 WA.
18 Article 47.1 WA.
19 Regulation (EU) No 2013/952 of the European Parliament and of the Council of 9 October 2013 laying down the Union Customs Code (recast) OJ L269/1, 10 October 2013, as amended.
20 Article 47.1 WA.

declarations and pre-departure declarations, lodged as specified before the end of the implementation period, have the same effects in the EU and the UK after the end of the implementation period.

Provision is also made in Article 49 WA in respect of non-Union goods that were in temporary storage, or subject to special customs procedures, within the UK's customs territory at the end of the implementation period. The UCC is to apply to them until the temporary storage ends, the special customs procedure ends, the goods are released for free circulation, or the goods are taken out of the EU's customs territory, provided that the event occurs after the end of the implementation period and before the time limits specified in Annex III of the Withdrawal Agreement. The Article also contains provisions on matters such as customs debts and tariff quotas.

Customs databases and cooperation

3.4 One inevitable consequence of the EU customs union is that the national customs authorities of Member States act as one and cooperate fully with the Commission which administers the customs union.[21] The requirement to cooperate requires participation in EU databases. There is now a Work Programme relating to the development and deployment of electronic systems provided for in the UCC.[22] It is intended that the required computer systems will all be operating by 2025 at the latest. A good few are already in operation.

During the implementation period the UK continued to have access to EU customs networks. Article 8 WA says:

> 'Unless otherwise provided in this Agreement, at the end of the transition period the United Kingdom shall cease to be entitled to access any network, any information system and any database established on the basis of Union law. The United Kingdom shall take appropriate measures to ensure that it does not access a network, information system or database which it is no longer entitled to access.'

By way of derogation from the terms of this article, Article 50 provides that the UK shall have access to certain systems and databases so that it can comply with the provisions of the WA concerning ongoing customs procedures.[23] The derogation is time limited as set out in Annex IV WA. Access to most systems ends at some point in 2021, though access to a few systems continues for considerably longer.

21 See further Communication from the Commission to the European Parliament, the Council and the European Economic and Social Committee 'Developing the EU Customs Union and its Governance' COM(2016) 813 final, Brussels, 21.12.2016, at p 7.

22 Commission Implementing Decision (EU) 2019/2151 of 13 December 2019 establishing the Work Programme relating to the development and deployment of the electronic systems provided for in the Union Customs Code [2019] OJ L325/168.

23 Article 50 WA.

The WA also contains provisions on cooperation between customs authorities more generally. Article 63.1(b) specifically addresses issues arising under the Convention on mutual assistance and cooperation between customs administrations drawn up on the basis of Article K.3 of the Treaty on European Union (the so-called 'Naples II Convention' of 18 December 1997).[24] It is one of a number of important bases for cooperation. Others are Council Regulation 515/97 as amended[25] and Council Decision 2009/917/JHA.[26]

Broadly speaking, the effect of Article 63.1(b) is that the Convention is to apply in respect of requests for information, surveillance and so on, made before the end of the implementation period. A similar approach is taken in respect of requests made under another instrument of cooperation, namely Council Decision 2009/917/JHA.[27]

Other provisions in the WA concerning administrative cooperation for customs are contained in Article 98 WA. In short, procedures between the UK and another Member State launched before the end of the implementation period are to be completed in accordance with EU law. Those procedures launched within three years of the end of the implementation period but which relate to facts occurring before the end of the period are also to be concluded in accordance with EU law.

According to Article 100 WA, Council Directive 2010/24/EU on mutual assistance for the recovery of claims relating to taxes, duties and other measures[28] is to apply until five years after the end of the implementation period. It concerns claims relating to amounts that became due before the end of the implementation period, claims relating to transactions that took place before the end of the implementation period but where amounts became due after that period, and claims relating to certain transactions within Article 51 WA (which concerns VAT) and movements of excise goods covered by Article 52 WA. Article 100 also contains a derogation from Article 8 in relation to access to databases and computer systems, time limited as set out in Annex IV.

Trade and customs agreements

3.5 The customs law of the EU is governed not only by primary and secondary legislation but also to a very significant extent by agreements

24 OJ [1998] C24/1. See also the explanatory memorandum at OJ [1998] C189/1. The Convention is broader than Council Regulation 515/97 as amended because it covers national as well as EU customs matters.

25 Council Regulation (EC) 515/97 of 13 March 1997 concerning mutual assistance between Member States OJ [1997] L82/1 as amended.

26 Council Decision 2009/917/JHA of 30 November 2009 on the use of information technology for customs purposes OJ [2009] L323/20.

27 See ibid and Article 63.1(d) WA.

28 Council Directive 2010/24/EU of 16 March 2010; OJ [2010] L84/1.

with third countries. The nature of these depends upon the quality of the relationship established. There are, for example, Association Agreements, one of which now governs the EU/UK relationship, Free Trade Agreements such as those with Singapore and Vietnam, Deep and Comprehensive Free Trade Agreements such as exists with Canada and Economic Partnership Agreements such as exist with certain African partners. There are also customs cooperation agreements.

As customs law depends so heavily upon agreements with non-EU countries the WA has to address the significance of those agreements during the implementation period. Accordingly, Article 129.1 WA provides that:

> '… during the transition period the United Kingdom shall be bound by the obligations stemming from the international agreements concluded by the Union, by Member States acting on its behalf, or by the Union and its Member States acting jointly …'[29]

One of the results of the UK leaving the EU is the UK's ability to develop its own trade policy and establish its own trade agreements. This is clearly an important matter for the UK both politically and commercially.[30] The UK's position in relation to such agreements is referred to in Article 129.4 WA. This states that:

> '… during the transition period, the United Kingdom may negotiate, sign and ratify international agreements entered into in its own capacity in the areas of exclusive competence of the Union, provided those agreements do not enter into force or apply during the transition period, unless so authorised by the Union.'

Excise goods

3.6 Article 52 WA concerns excise goods. It provides that EU law in the form of Council Directive 2008/118/EC referred to above[31] is to apply in respect of movements of excise goods from the territory of the UK to the territory of a Member State, or vice versa, under a duty suspension arrangement and after release for consumption, provided that the movement started before and ended after the end of the implementation period. Article 53 WA contains a derogation from Article 8 WA in respect of access to computer networks, databases and so on comparable to that made in respect of customs matters noted above. The derogation is time limited as set out in Annex IV WA. As a result, for example, control reports issued by the UK authorities in relation to movements of goods ongoing at the end of

29 The provision goes on to refer to the definition of Union law in Article 2(a)(iv) which refers to international agreements.

30 See generally www.gov.uk/guidance/uk-trade-agreements-with-non-eu-countries.

31 See n 6 above.

the transition period are valid where the report is issued before 31 May 2021. Movements of goods not ended on 31 May 2021 will become movements to and from a third country.[32]

Article 99 WA contains particular provisions concerning administrative cooperation between authorities responsible for the application of excise duty legislation. Certain EU law applies up to four years after the end of the implementation period in respect of movements of goods which occurred before the end of the implementation period or which are covered by EU law under Article 52. Excise duty also falls within the scope of Article 100 WA which deals with mutual assistance for the recovery of claims and has already been considered in relation to customs duty.

CUSTOMS AND EXCISE AFTER THE IMPLEMENTATION PERIOD

3.7 One of the aims of the *EUWA 2018* was that notwithstanding the repeal of the *European Communities Act 1972*:[33] 'As a general rule, the same rules and laws will apply on the day after exit as on the day before'.[34] Consequently, broadly speaking, after the implementation period, EU-derived legislation continues to have effect in domestic law.[35] That means that customs legislation such as may be contained in the *Customs and Excise Management Act 1979* is unaffected by Brexit. Direct EU legislation becomes part of domestic law.[36] Rights, powers, liabilities, obligations, restrictions, remedies and procedures which were available prior to exit day by virtue of the *European Communities Act 1972, s 2(1)* continue to be available.[37] The provisions of the *EUWA 2018* in relation to the supremacy of EU law and the principles it establishes for the interpretation and status of EU retained law are applicable.[38] These matters are discussed more generally in Chapter 1.

The general approach adopted in relation to EU direct legislation could not be followed in relation to EU customs law otherwise the UCC would have been part of UK domestic law and it would have been impossible for the UK to set up its own customs system. Accordingly, it was necessary to remove from UK law much of the law of the EU customs system including much of the UCC which had been retained in UK domestic law by virtue of being EU retained

32 See further Notice to Stakeholders Withdrawal of the United Kingdom and EU rules in the field of excise, REV 1 which replaces the Notice of 11 March 2019 at p 5.

33 By the *EUWA 2018, s 1*.

34 The Explanatory Notes to the European Union (Withdrawal) Act 2018, para 10 available at: www.legislation.gov.uk/ukpga/2018/16/pdfs/ukpgaen_20180016_en.pdf.

35 *EUWA 2018, s 2*.

36 *EUWA 2018, s 3*.

37 *EUWA 2018, s 4*.

38 *EUWA 2018, s 5* onwards.

law. The removal was effected by the *Taxation (Cross-border Trade) Act 2018 (TCBTA 2018), Sch 7.* The provisions of *paragraph 1(1)* state:

> 'Any direct EU legislation, so far as imposing or otherwise applying in relation to any EU customs duty, that forms part of the law of the United Kingdom as a result of section 3 of the European Union (Withdrawal) Act 2018 (incorporation of direct EU legislation) ceases to have effect.'

The meaning of 'in relation to' is not clear. Some EU legislation eg concerned with safety and security procedures is retained EU law. Other paragraphs of the Schedule provide that *Part 1* of the *TCBTA 2018* contains provisions replacing EU customs duties and is not EU retained law.[39] A significant body of secondary legislation is also essential for the new UK customs system. The UK Government has brought together in a single website, the customs, VAT and excise legislation which applies as from 1 January 2021.[40] The legislation is referred to as transition legislation, but that is not to be understood as legislation which operates during the transition period.

A full summary of the relevant legislation is beyond the scope of this chapter. Instead some of the main provisions are highlighted below together with other matters of general interest.

Before turning to the legislation, however, it may be noted that the UK's new customs regime has had to confront significant practical challenges commented on by, amongst others, the National Audit Office. One report delivered in November 2020 is entitled 'The UK Border: preparedness for the end of the transition period'.[41] It contains a number of warnings, for example, on the need to increase the market in customs intermediaries and the possible need for contingency plans to be made by ports and other third parties.[42] Key facts are highlighted including an expected increase in customs declarations to be handled by HMRC from 55 million to 270 million.[43]

The NAO also warned that: 'There is likely to be significant disruption at the border from 1 January 2021 as many traders and third parties will not be ready for new EU controls'.[44] In fact, during the first part of 2021 its worst fears were not fulfilled. At the time of writing, however, it seems that businesses are benefitting from having stockpiled goods prior to the end of 2020. Such statistics as are available are said to show a significant drop in trade between

---

39 See the *TCBTA, 2018, Sch 7, para 1(3)*. Note also *para 1(2)* and other legislation including *The Customs (Revocation of Retained Direct EU Legislation, etc.) (EU Exit) Regulations 2019, SI 2019/698.*

40 See www.gov.uk/government/collections/customs-vat-and-excise-uk-transition-legislation-from-1-january-2021.

41 HC 371 session 2019–2021 6 November 2020: www.nao.org.uk/wp-content/uploads/2020/11/The-UK-border-preparedness-for-the-end-of-the-transition-period.pdf.

42 See paras 14 and 16.

43 See p 4.

44 See para 15.

the UK and certain continental countries including Germany.[45] It may be some time before the practical position can be determined with certainty.

Customs regime: consultations

3.8 As may be expected there were consultations on the new UK customs regime and excise matters. A consultation on the UK's proposed general tariff closed on 5 March 2020.[46] The new tariff was published on 19 May 2020 and is noted further below.[47] Another consultation has taken place in respect of duty-free and tax-free goods in relation to excise duty and VAT.[48] Amongst other things, following this consultation, the government concluded that duty-free sales should be extended to those travelling to the EU and tax-free sales for airside products should cease except for alcohol and tobacco.[49]

A consultation on freeports closed on 20 July 2020.[50] A competitive bidding process was opened and in the Budget Report 2021 the creation of eight new freeports was announced. Subject to the satisfaction of governance criteria and other matters, they will be situated at East Midlands Airport, Felixstowe & Harwich, Humber, Liverpool City Region, Plymouth and South Devon, Solent, Teesside and Thames. [51] Discussions are to continue in relation to freeports in Northern Ireland, Scotland and Wales.[52] The establishment of freeports in Northern Ireland will have to take account of the application of EU law pursuant to the Ireland/Northern Ireland Protocol to the WA.

It is proposed that free ports will benefit from a 10% structures and buildings allowance, an enhanced capital allowance for a period in relation to plant and machinery, full relief from Stamp Duty Land Tax, full business rates relief up

45 See www.bbc.co.uk/news/56347096. Exports of goods from Germany were said to be down 29% in January 2021 compared with January 2020 and exports of goods from the UK to Germany were said to be down 52%.

46 See 'Approach to MFN Tariff Policy: Designing the UK Global Tariff for 1st January 2021' February 2020: Department for International Trade, available at: https://assets.publishing.service.gov.uk/government/uploads/system/uploads/attachment_data/file/864438/Approach_to_MFN_Tariff_Policy.pdf.

47 It was established by *The Customs Tariff (Establishment) (EU Exit) Regulations 2020, SI 2020/1430.*

48 'A consultation on the potential approach to duty- and tax-free goods arising from the UK's new relationship with the EU:' HM Treasury and HMRC's summary of responses September 2020: https://assets.publishing.service.gov.uk/government/uploads/system/uploads/attachment_data/file/917005/Passengers_Consultation_Response.pdf.

49 See the *Travellers' Allowances and Miscellaneous Provisions (EU Exit) Regulations 2020, SI 2020/1412.*

50 See 'Freeports: Response to the Consultation' CP 302 October 2020, at https://assets.publishing.service.gov.uk/government/uploads/system/uploads/attachment_data/file/924644/FINAL_-_200923_-_OFF_SEN_-_Freeports_Con_Res_-_FINAL.pdf.

51 'Budget 2021, Protecting the Jobs and Livelihoods of the British People': https://assets.publishing.service.gov.uk/government/uploads/system/uploads/attachment_data/file/966868/BUDGET_2021_-_web.pdf, paras 113–115.

52 Ibid para 114.

to 2026 and a relief in respect of employer's national insurance contributions.[53] The customs benefits have not yet been finally announced. Advantages which have been mentioned cover the suspension of duty and import VAT until goods enter the UK's domestic market, an exemption for exports, duty inversion so that the lower rate applicable to a finished product is applied instead of the higher rate applicable to its constituent parts, and simplified customs procedures.[54]

The new UK tariff

3.9 The UK's general tariff was published on 19 May 2020.[55] The legislative foundation for it is contained in the *TCBTA 2018, ss 7* and *8* considered below together with secondary legislation, in particular *The Customs Tariff (Establishment) (EU Exit) Regulations 2020.*[56]

The *TCBTA 2018, s 8* sets out the considerations which guide the rate of duty imposed. The first two considerations are: the interests of consumers and of producers of the goods concerned in the UK. Other considerations are the desirability of maintaining and promoting the external trade and productivity of the UK and the extent to which the goods concerned are subject to competition.[57] Any recommendation of the Secretary of State is also to be considered.[58]

The policy approaches underpinning the tariff have been enlarged on in response to the consultation on the tariff referred to above.[59] Tariffs of below 2% have been removed on the grounds that they were nuisance tariffs, the burden of which outweighed the benefit. The UK Government gives as examples, duty on certain pistachio nuts, refrigerators and fish-hooks. Other tariffs have been banded. Tariffs under 20% have been rounded down to the nearest multiple of 2. Tariffs between 20% and 50% have been rounded down to the nearest multiple of 5. Tariffs over 50% have been rounded down to the nearest multiple of 10.

---

53 Ibid para 115.

54 See 'Freeports Consultation: Boosting Trade, Jobs and Investment across the UK' CP 222, February 2020: https://assets.publishing.service.gov.uk/government/uploads/system/uploads/attachment_data/file/878352/Freeports_Consultation_Extension.pdf, Chapter 3, 'Customs' and 'Budget 2021, Protecting the Jobs and Livelihoods of the British People', para 2.115.

55 The tariff may be downloaded from www.gov.uk/guidance/uk-tariffs-from-1-january-2021. Rates for individual goods are available at www.check-future-uk-trade-tariffs.service.gov.uk/tariff?q=1604%2014%2028&n=25&p=1.

56 *SI 2020/1430.*

57 *TCBTA 2018, s 8(5).*

58 *TCBTA 2018, s 8(6).*

59 'Public Consultation: MFN Tariff Policy – The UK Global Tariff, Government response and policy' at https://assets.publishing.service.gov.uk/government/uploads/system/uploads/attachment_data/file/885943/Public_consultation_on_the_UK_Global_Tariff_government_response.pdf.

The way in which tariffs are calculated on agricultural goods has been simplified although compound tariffs have been retained. Some tariffs on key production inputs have been liberalised. The government has given as one example of this the duty on a particular category of cotton yarn in commodity code 5207 10 00 for which the duty falls from 5% to zero. Duty on wood, machinery and plastics is also affected. Duty has also been reduced to zero in respect of certain goods in respect of which the UK has zero or limited production so that consumers may benefit. This affects goods such as cotton bicycle parts and footwear. The tariff on goods such as trees and wind turbine parts has been reduced to zero in support of environmental policy.

While the areas in which duty rates have been reduced or duty has been removed are eye-catching, the products in respect of which duty has been retained are equally important. For example, the UK tariff on beef (16% compared with the EU rate of 16.6%) could have been of particular concern to Irish farmers had it not been for the provisions of the EU/UK TCA. Some duties, including some which have not been reduced when compared with the EU tariff, are subject to autonomous suspension and will be reviewed in due course.[60]

TCBTA 2018 and the new customs duty regime

3.10 The *TCBTA 2018* is a fundamental piece of legislation so far as concerns customs and excise after Brexit.[61] *Part 1* (*ss 1–38*) deals with import duty. *Part 2* (*ss 39–40*) deals with export duty. *Part 3* (*ss 41–43*) addresses VAT, *Part 4* (*ss 44–50*) concerns excise duty and *Parts 5* and *6* contain further and final provisions. So far as *Part 3* is concerned, it may be noted that one of the fundamental consequences of Brexit is that movements of goods between the UK and EU Member States become imports and exports for the purposes of VAT. The implications of this and of the changes to import VAT generally are considered in Chapter 2.

TCBTA 2018, s 1 establishes the basic principle that import duty is to be charged by reference to 'chargeable goods'. Goods are chargeable goods unless they are domestic goods. All goods in the UK are presumed to be domestic goods unless the contrary is shown.[62]

The important category of chargeable goods is defined in *s 33*. It provides that there are two groups of chargeable goods. The first group consists of goods

60 See, eg, the 6% duty in respect of aluminium engine brackets.

61 See generally the House of Commons Library Briefing Paper, Number 8126, 6 July 2018, The Taxation Cross-border Trade Bill: https://commonslibrary.parliament.uk/research-briefings/cbp-8126/.

The position in relation to Northern Ireland is considered below. The relevant domestic legislation affecting Northern Ireland includes the *Taxation (Post-transition Period) Act 2020*.

62 *TCBTA 2018, s 2* and *s 33(7)*. See also *The Customs (Import Duty) (EU Exit) Regulations 2018, SI 2018/1248, regs 102–106*.

wholly produced in the UK. The second group consists of those goods which have been subject to a chargeable customs procedure. This covers goods which have been declared for the free circulation procedure or an authorised use procedure and the procedure has been discharged.[63]

Goods cease to be chargeable goods if they are exported from the UK and the export is one which is required to be made in accordance with authorised export provisions.[64] That covers every export unless excepted.[65] There follow provisions fundamental to any customs system such as those containing the obligation to present goods to customs and identifying the person liable to duty.

The amount of duty payable is covered in *s 7* which tells one to have regard to the tariff amended to take account of such matters as preferential rates, quotas and so. *Section 8* sets out other essential provisions relating to the tariff. *Section 6* states the general principle that liability to customs duty rests on the person in whose name the customs declaration is made. Other persons may also be liable for the duty including customs agents.[66]

Two other fundamental features of any customs duty system concern the valuation and origin of goods. Although the UK may no longer have to have regard to EU law in relation to valuation it must consider WTO law and in particular the Agreement on Implementation of Article VII of the General Agreement on Tariffs and Trade 1994 (GATT 1994).

Valuation of goods

3.11 The basic rule is set out in the *TCBTA 2018, s 16*. This states that the value of goods is the transaction value of goods when sold for export to the UK. This covers the total amount payable for the goods or payable in connection with their transport to the UK.[67] Valuation is also dealt with in statutory instruments, in particular in *The Customs (Import Duty) (EU Exit) Regulations 2018*.[68]

These regulations specify that the transaction value of goods when sold for export is to be determined by means of up to six methods. The first three are to be applied, in the order set out, until a method is found by which the value of the relevant goods may be readily determined.[69]

Method 1 is the general method noted in the *TCBTA, 2018 s 16(2)*, namely, reference to the transaction value of goods when sold for export to the UK.

63 *TCBTA 2018, s 33(1)* and *(2)*.
64 *TCBTA 2018, s 33(3)*.
65 *TCBTA 2018, s 33(4)*.
66 *TCBTA 2018, s 6(2)* and *(3)* and *s 21(6)*.
67 *TCBTA 2018, s 16(2)* and *(3)*.
68 *SI 2018/1248*.
69 *SI 2018/1248, reg 108(2)*.

Method 2 is valuation by reference to identical goods. Method 3 is valuation by reference to similar goods. Method 4 is based on sales in the UK, while Method 5 gives rise to a constructed value based on relevant costs of matters like production and transport, with a sum included for profit. It is possible to elect that Methods 4 and 5 are applied in reverse order. Method 6 is a back-stop method which relies on the application of reasonable elements of the preceding methods and international principles.

Origin of goods

3.12 The origin of goods is of particular importance where a preferential rate of duty is sought. Relevant rules of origin will, often, be contained in a preferential trading agreement as they are in the UK/EU Trade and Cooperation Agreement. In some cases rules of origin will have a strong influence on the shape of a manufacturing chain and the identity of trading partners.

Where rules of origin in trade agreements are not applicable, non-preferential rules must be applied. Provision is made for them in the *TCBTA 2018*. They are in a traditional form and provide that goods originate from a country or territory if they are wholly obtained there. If the goods are obtained in more than one place then they originate in the country or territory where the last substantial processing of them which is economically justified has taken place.[70] Processing is 'substantial' if it results in the manufacture of a new product or represents an important stage of manufacture, and it takes place in an undertaking equipped for the purpose.[71] Importers should also note that it is for the person making a customs declaration to show that goods originate from a particular country or territory.[72]

TCBTA 2018, s 17(6) makes provision for regulations to be made and *The Customs (Origin of Chargeable Goods) (EU Exit) Regulations 2020* were made in December 2020. In addition to containing specific provisions in relation to the rules of origin, they bring into operation an important reference document entitled 'Rules of Origin: Special Rules for Determining Non-Preferential Origin, Version 1.0' dated 7 December 2020.[73]

Customs duty reliefs and other matters

3.13 The remainder of *Part 1* of the *TCBTA 2018* contains other essential elements of the UK customs system such as the definition of an export (*s 35*) and

70 *TCBTA 2018, s 17(2)* and *(3)*.

71 *TCBTA 2018, s 17(3)*.

72 *TCBTA 2018, s 17(5)*. Further provisions in relation to the UK/EU trade and Cooperation Agreement are dealt with below.

73 Available at www.gov.uk/government/publications/reference-document-for-the-customs-origin-of-chargeable-goods-eu-exit-regulations-2020.

the outward processing procedure (*s 36*). It also makes provision for customs duty reliefs in *s 19*, which gives power for statutory instruments to be made. Particular attention should be paid to *The Customs (Relief from a Liability to Import Duty and Miscellaneous Amendments) (EU Exit) Regulations 2020*.[74] Just as the statutory instrument dealing with non-preferential origin introduces a separate 'reference document', in this case it is the 'United Kingdom Customs Tariff: Reliefs from Import Duty', version 1.0 dated 8 December 2020.[75]

Statutory instruments and the new customs regime

3.14 Numerous statutory instruments, notices which have the force of law made under them and reference documents introduced by them, are relevant to the UK's new customs system. Many of them were made in late 2020 like those concerned with valuation, origin and reliefs, referred to above. Some other statutory instruments of significance are noted below. Inevitably, when considering any of them, one must consider whether or not they have been amended. There is not space here to consider all amending legislation.

As examples of statutory regulations in 2018 one may note those dealing with transit procedures;[76] and *The Customs (Import Duty) (EU Exit) Regulations 2018* mentioned above which deal with essential features of the customs system including customs declarations, payment and deferment of duty, repayment of duty, valuation and guarantees.[77] Deferment is possible for traders which are established in the UK.[78] Guarantees, which may be single or comprehensive in nature,[79] are required for various purposes under the UK customs system in particular in relation to customs procedures such as transit.[80] Repayment and remission is available in reduced liability cases, of which there are six kinds, and cases where there have been certain breaches or failures of customs requirements.[81] In some situations remission or repayment may be

74 *SI 2020/1431*.

75 Available at www.gov.uk/government/publications/reference-documents-for-the-customs-reliefs-from-a-liability-to-import-duty-and-miscellaneous-amendments-eu-exit-regulations-2020.

76 *The Customs Transit Procedures (EU Exit) Regulations 2018, SI 2018/1258*. These have been amended. *The Customs (Bulk Customs Declaration and Miscellaneous Amendments) (EU Exit) Regulations 2020, SI 2020/967* are of particular importance, see especially *reg 7* on the payment of duty and duty deferment. *Reg 7(10)* provides that a person is eligible for approval to defer payment of liability to import duty only if the person is established in the UK.

77 *The Customs (Import Duty) (EU Exit) Regulations 2018, SI 2018/1248* as amended.

78 Ibid, *reg 43(10)* and *reg 3*.

79 See *TCBTA 2018, Sch 6, para 6* and *The Customs (Import Duty) (EU Exit) Regulations 2018, SI 2018/1248* as amended, *reg 97*.

80 In relation to transit see *The Customs Transit Procedures (EU Exit) Regulations 2018, SI 2018/1258*.

81 *SI 2018/1248, regs 71–79*.

made without an application.[82] Other matters covered by statutory instruments include inward and outward processing.[83]

In 2018, amendments to statutory instruments which had already been passed began to be made[84] and that continued in 2019 during which statutory instruments concerned with customs duty continued to be passed.[85] Also in 2019, the statutory instruments were passed to which were attached the customs arrangements between the UK and the crown dependencies.[86]

The flow of statutory instruments continued in 2020 with, for example, *The Customs (Bulk Customs Declaration and Miscellaneous Amendments) (EU Exit) Regulations 2020*,[87] and *The Customs (Transitional Arrangements) (EU Exit) Regulations 2020*.[88] At the end of 2020 came many more statutory instruments including those dealing with customs valuation, origin and reliefs referred to in the previous section. Also passed in 2020 were *The Customs Tariff (Establishment) (EU Exit) Regulations*[89] referred to above[90] and *The Customs Tariff (Suspension of Import Duty Rates) (EU Exit) Regulations 2020* which brings into operation a reference document entitled 'The Tariff Suspension Document' Version 1.0 dated 10 December 2020.[91] Other instruments include cover travellers' allowances,[92] *The Customs Miscellaneous Non-fiscal Provisions and Amendments etc. (EU Exit) Regulations 2020*,[93] and *The Customs (Northern Ireland) (EU Exit) Regulations 2020*.[94]

Statutory instruments in respect of customs duty continue to appear in 2021, for example, see *The Customs Tariff (Establishment and Suspension of Import*

82 *Reg 70.*

83 *The Customs (Special Procedures and Outward Processing) (EU Exit) Regulations 2018, SI 2018/1249.*

84 *The Customs (Temporary Storage Facilities Approval Conditions and Miscellaneous Amendments) (EU Exit) Regulations 2018, SI 2018/1247*, later amended.

85 See eg *The Taxation (Cross-border Trade) (Miscellaneous Provisions) (EU Exit) Regulations 2019, SI 2019/486, The Taxation (Cross-border Trade) (Miscellaneous Provisions) (EU Exit) (No.2) Regulations 2019, SI 2019/1346* and *The Customs (Export) (EU Exit) Regulations 2019, SI 2019/108.*

86 See *The Crown Dependencies Customs Union (Jersey) (EU Exit) Order 2019, SI 2019/256, The Crown Dependencies Customs Union (Guernsey) (EU Exit) Order 2019, SI 2019/254* and *The Crown Dependencies Customs Union (Isle of Man) (EU Exit) Order 2019, SI 2019/257.*

87 *SI 2020/967.*

88 *SI 2020/1088.*

89 *SI 2020/1430.*

90 See **3.9** above.

91 Available at www.gov.uk/government/collections/customs-vat-and-excise-uk-transition-legislation-from-1-january-2021.

92 The position is necessarily different for travellers entering Great Britain and those entering Northern Ireland. See *The Travellers' Allowances and Miscellaneous Provisions (EU Exit) Regulations 2020, SI 2020/1412* and *The Travellers' Allowances and Miscellaneous Provisions (Northern Ireland) (EU Exit) Regulations 2020, SI 2020/1619.*

93 *SI 2020/1624.*

94 *SI 2020/1605.*

Duty) (EU Exit) (Amendment) Regulations 2021.[95] Amongst the amendments it makes are some relevant to the Crown dependencies.

The passage of so many statutory instruments is something of an achievement. Nevertheless, to those who were used to finding customs law in the UCC and a few pieces of implementing legislation the present array of statutory instruments is something of a contrast to the pre-Brexit state of affairs. Perhaps, once the UK has become used to its customs system, it can be persuaded to consolidate the law.

The UK/EU TCA

3.15 After 31 December 2020, the relationship between the UK and the EU had to be governed by a new agreement. The EU and the UK both published negotiating drafts.[96] The EU had sought a single new partnership agreement to govern the parties' relationship.[97] The UK on the other hand wanted a Comprehensive Free Trade Agreement and a range of other agreements covering matters including fisheries, air transport, social security coordination, law enforcement and judicial cooperation in criminal matters and the transfer of unaccompanied asylum-seeking children.[98]

The compromise was a Trade and Cooperation Agreement (TCA) which covers trade in goods, services, and a wide range of other matters including fisheries, air transport, judicial cooperation and social security coordination. A separate agreement was entered into in respect of the exchange of classified information.[99]

The TCA is now provisionally in force.[100] It has been brought into UK law by the *European Union (Future Relationship) Act 2020* (*EUFRA 2020*) the provisions of which create many potential problems of interpretation and implementation which cannot be reviewed here. It was originally expected that provisional application would last until February 2021.[101] That has been

95 *SI 2021/63.*

96 The UK published its draft on 19 May 2020, see www.gov.uk/government/publications/our-approach-to-the-future-relationship-with-the-eu. The EU published its draft on 18 March 2020, see https://ec.europa.eu/info/sites/info/files/200318-draft-agreement-gen.pdf.

97 The EU's draft agreement is available at: UKTF (2020) 14, 18 March 2020; https://ec.europa.eu/info/european-union-and-united-kingdom-forging-new-partnership/future-partnership/guide-negotiations_en.

98 The UK's drafts are available at: www.gov.uk/government/publications/our-approach-to-the-future-relationship-with-the-eu.

99 See the Agreement between the EU and the UK concerning security procedures for exchanging and protecting classified information [2020] OJ L 444/1463. The TCA is at [2020] OJ L 444/14.

100 See From the perspective of the EU the TCA is an association agreement established pursuant to the Treaty on the Functioning of the EU, Article 217 TFEU.

101 TCA, Article FINPROV.11: Entry into force and provisional application.

extended to 30 April 2021[102] when the European Parliament would ordinarily have finished its scrutiny of the agreement, although some doubt has been cast on that timetable.

The TCA: trade, goods and origin

3.16 The provisions in the TCA concerned specifically with customs are contained in Part Two,[103] headed 'Trade, Transport and Other Arrangements', Heading One (entitled 'Trade'), and Title I: 'Trade in Goods'.

The TCA makes clear that it creates a free trade area under GATT 1994, XXIV.[104] The agreement has been notified under the WTO's rules.[105] In pursuance of its aim of establishing a free trade area, the TCA provides in Article GOODS.5: Prohibition of customs duties, that: 'Except as otherwise provided for in this Agreement, customs duties on all goods originating in the other Party shall be prohibited.' The national treatment rule also applies and import/export restrictions are largely prohibited.[106] It is noteworthy that repaired and remanufactured goods are given favourable treatment.[107]

As Article GOODS.5 makes clear, and as is the case for any free trade area, one party gives benefits to 'goods originating in the other Party'. Consequently, the TCA's rules governing the origin of goods are fundamental to the operation of the agreement. There are three ways in which goods may acquire origin in a party. First, they may be wholly obtained there. Second, they may be produced exclusively from materials originating there. Third, they may be produced in a party but contain non-originating materials so long as other rules are satisfied.[108]

There are specific rules for certain products contained in the TCA's annexes,[109] Annexes ORIG-1, ORIG-2, ORIG-2A and ORIG-2B. There is a list of operations which are insufficient to ensure that goods acquire the origin of a party,[110] a set of tolerances which should be taken into account,[111] and

102 https://assets.publishing.service.gov.uk/government/uploads/system/uploads/attachment_data/file/963820/CDL_to_Maros_Sefcovic.pdf.
103 There are seven parts in total. Part Seven excludes Gibraltar (Article FINPROV.1.3) which is subject to a separate agreement made on 31 December 2020.
104 Article OTH.3: Establishment of a free trade area.
105 http://rtais.wto.org/UI/PublicShowRTAIDCard.aspx?rtaid=1137. Notification took place on 31 January 2021.
106 Article GOODS.4 and Article GOODS.10.
107 Article GOODS.8 and Article GOODS.9.
108 See TCA, Article ORIG.3: General requirements and Article ORIG.5: Wholly obtained products
109 See Annexes ORIG-1, ORIG-2, ORIG-2A and ORIG-2B.
110 Article ORIG.7: Insufficient Production.
111 Article ORIG.6: Tolerances.

origin quotas which treat as originating in a party products which would not otherwise do so.[112]

HMRC has also published guidance notes on the rules of origin[113] and the Department for Business, Energy and Industrial Strategy has answered some frequently asked questions.[114] Official information is essential reading both in relation to the substantive rules and the relevant procedures.

Modern manufacturing supply chains frequently cross national borders so that a good is produced in two or more countries. One way of adapting origin rules to this state of affairs is to implement cumulation of origin rules. These allow goods which would not otherwise be regarded as originating in a state or customs union, nevertheless, to originate there.

Cumulation rules can provide for full or unlimited cumulation, regional, diagonal or bilateral cumulation. Full cumulation allows a good from anywhere to be treated as originating in one of the parties if sufficient processing is carried on in the party in question. Regional or diagonal cumulation permits that treatment where the good comes from a specific geographical or economic region or specified trading partners. Bilateral cumulation permits the treatment where the good comes from one of the parties to the free trade agreement in question. The TCA provides for bilateral cumulation so that goods must originate in either the UK or the EU in order for cumulation to be available.[115]

The rules governing the procedural application of the rules of origin are as important as the rules of origin themselves. These cannot be reviewed here. Suffice it to say that importers may claim the benefit of the preferential rules of origin in two ways. The first is to rely on their knowledge that a product originates in the exporting Party. The second, more secure, way is to rely on an exporter's statement of origin containing the Exporter Reference Number.[116] If an importer is delaying the submission of a customs declaration, as is permitted under the Border Operating Model considered below, then proof of origin need be supplied only when the supplementary declaration is made.[117] In many situations, but not all, a supplier's declaration as to origin is necessary

112 Annex ORIG-2A.

113 See www.gov.uk/government/publications/rules-of-origin-for-goods-moving-between-the-uk-and-eu-from-1-january-2021.

114 'Tariffs and rules of origin (ROO) in the UK/EU Trade and Cooperation Agreement: Frequently Asked Questions (FAQs)' February 2021: www.bsif.co.uk/wp-content/uploads/2021/02/RoO-FAQ.pdf.

115 Article ORIG.4. The cumulation provisions originally sought by the UK were much more generous: see the negotiating draft at n 96 above.

116 Article ORIG.19 and ANNEX ORIG-4. The ERN number in the UK is the EORI number and in the EU the Registered Exporter Number (REX number).

117 See generally, the official guidance on claiming the preferential rates of duty between the UK and the EU at www.gov.uk/guidance/claiming-preferential-rates-of-duty-between-the-uk-and-eu and the guidance at n 113 above.

for each consignment. It may cover a period of up to two years.[118] There is, however, an important general easement contained in the official guidance. It states that:

> 'For UK-EU trade, until 31 December 2021, businesses do not need supplier's declarations from business suppliers in place when the goods are exported but they must be confident that the goods do meet the TCA preferential rules of origin. Businesses may be asked to retrospectively provide a supplier's declaration after this date.'[119]

The importer's customs authorities may verify the claim to preferential treatment so it is important that good records are kept.[120] Traders should also ensure their contracts are reviewed so that they are appropriately protected so far as possible.

Trade facilitation and other matters

3.17 The TCA's provisions on customs and trade facilitation are contained in Chapter 5 of Title I. The provisions on exchange of data have led to provisions in the *EUFRA 2020*.[121] Other provisions which may be briefly highlighted include those on advance rulings,[122] mutual recognition of authorised economic operator programmes,[123] compliance with the Common Transit Convention,[124] risk management and roll-on, roll-off traffic.[125] The provisions on mutual assistance between customs authorities are also likely to be of great importance.[126]

The TCA permits the parties to impose anti-dumping and countervailing duties as well as duties imposed under safeguard measures.[127] In this context it should be noted that the UK's Trade Remedies Authority will be established

118 See Annex ORIG-3: Supplier's Declaration, Article ORIG.4.4: Cumulation of origin and Article ORIG.18: Claim for preferential tariff treatment.

119 See www.gov.uk/government/publications/rules-of-origin-for-goods-moving-between-the-uk-and-eu/origin-procedures-proving-originating-status-and-claiming-preferential-treatment.

120 Article ORIG.22: Record-keeping requirements, Article ORIG.24: Verification and Article ORIG.26: Denial of preferential tariff treatment.

121 See *EUFRA 2020, ss 2, 3.*

122 Article CUSTMS.11: Advance rulings.

123 Article CUSTMS.9: Authorised economic operators and Annex CUSTMS-1.

124 Article CUSTMS.6: Transit and transhipment. See also Article GOODS.4A:Freedom of transit.

125 Article CUSTMS.18: Facilitation of roll-on, roll-off traffic.

126 Article CUSTMS.19: Administrative cooperation in VAT and mutual assistance for recovery of taxes and duties and the Protocols on administrative cooperation and combating fraud in the field of value added tax and on mutual assistance for the recovery of claims relating to taxes and duties and on Mutual administrative assistance in customs matters.

127 Article GOODS.17: Trade remedies

as an independent body pursuant to the Trade Bill which is in its final parliamentary stages.[128]

The TCA and governance

3.18 The governance structures established under the TCA are complex and cannot be reviewed here.[129] At the head of the structure is the Partnership Council to which may be added over 20 committees and a number of working groups. The Trade Partnership Committee, the Trade Specialised Committee on Goods, the Trade Specialised Committee on Customs Cooperation and Rules of Origin and the Trade Specialised Committee on Administrative Cooperation in VAT and Recovery of Taxes and Duties are particularly worthy of note.[130]

EU border controls, authorisations and rulings

3.19 As an EU Member State the UK had no customs, tax and regulatory borders with the EU. Once it ceased to be a Member State the border was reimposed. The UK/EU TCA facilitates trade in some respects between the parties but it does not remove the border. Border controls have, therefore, to be put in place. These may relate to customs duty matters but they may also relate to matters which are not concerned directly with duty, for example, export health certificates.

So far as customs matters are concerned, all goods entering the EU from the UK will need to fulfil EU customs formalities. From its perspective the EU has stated in its Communication 'Getting ready for changes' that:

> 'These controls are likely to lead to increased administrative burdens for business and longer delivery times in logistical supply chains.'[131]

The Communication deals with a number of matters but notes in particular, that the increased administrative burdens will include the need for UK businesses to acquire EU Economic Operator Registration and Identification (EORI) numbers and for EU businesses to acquire UK EORI numbers.[132]

128 HL Bill 128, clause 5 and Sch 4.

129 See in particular the TCA Part One: Common and Institutional Provisions and Title III: Institutional Framework.

130 Article INST.2: Committees.

131 The Communication at p 6.

132 Reference should be made to the Commission Guidance Note revised in July 2020: 'Guidance Note: Withdrawal of the United Kingdom and EU Rules in the Field of Customs Including Preferential Origin', Brussels 14 July REV2. The UK Government has also emphasised the need for EU businesses to obtain UK EORI numbers.

The reimposition of a border also has significance for other matters such as the certification or authorisation of products. For example, type approvals for motor cars or approvals for medical equipment issued by UK authorities are no longer valid in the EU. Marks or labels which refer to UK bodies or persons do not comply with EU legislation and representatives of manufacturers located in the UK do not satisfy requirements to be located in the EU.[133]

Many authorisations issued by UK customs will no longer be valid after the end of that period in relation to the EU,[134] although businesses established in the UK which were authorised economic operators before the end of the implementation period have had their registrations transferred automatically to the UK scheme. Other UK authorisations for some UK customs procedures have also be transferred for domestic use. For the future, as Northern Ireland is subject to EU customs law, separate authorisations will frequently be necessary in respect of Great Britain and Northern Ireland.[135] Binding origin rulings and binding tariff rulings issued by the UK authorities after 31 December 2020 will no longer be valid in the EU after the end of the transitional period.[136]

The UK Border Operating Model: GB/EU

3.20 The UK's border controls are the concern of the Border and Protocol Delivery Group (BPDG) which moved from HMRC to the Cabinet Office in June 2020. On 13 July 2020 the BPDG published its Border Operating Model: 'The Border with the European Union: Importing and Exporting Goods' (BOM).[137] It deals with movements of goods between Great Britain and the EU. The position in relation to Northern Ireland is subject to the Ireland/Northern Ireland Protocol which is considered below. The BOM was updated in December 2020. On 11 March 2020, the Rt, Hon. Michael Gove MP made a statement setting out some other amendments.[138] Further amendments are by no means unlikely so traders and their advisers should check carefully on the position when they come to consider specific transactions.

133 See further, Communication from the Commission to the European Parliament, the Council, the European Economic and Social Committee and the Committee of the Regions: 'Getting Ready for Changes Communication on Readiness at the end of the transition period between the European Union and the United Kingdom' COM (2020) 324 final, Brussels, 9.7.2020, p 9f. (The Communication).

134 European Commission, 'Guidance Note: Withdrawal of the United Kingdom and EU Rules in the Field of Customs Including Preferential Origin', Brussels 14 July REV2, p 32, Section 2.1.

135 See eg www.gov.uk/guidance/apply-to-import-goods-temporarily-to-the-uk-or-eu.

136 European Commission, 'Guidance Note Withdrawal of the United Kingdom and EU Rules in the Field of Customs Including Preferential Origin', Brussels 14 July REV2, p 32, Sections 2.3 and 22.

137 See www.gov.uk/government/publications/the-border-operating-model.

138 Border controls, statement made on 11 March 2021; https://questions-statements.parliament.uk/written-statements/detail/2021-03-11/hcws841.

A detailed consideration of the document of more than 250 pages is impossible in this chapter. In brief, in contrast to the introduction of full customs checks on goods coming from Great Britain as a third country, the UK Government initially decided to implement border controls, between the EU and Great Britain in three stages. The first was to start on 1 January 2021, the second on 1 April 2021 and the third on 1 July 2021.

As a result of these staged arrangements, goods originating in the EU are faced with less rigorous obligations than those originating from the rest of the world. That may be difficult to justify under the provisions of GATT 1994. To the extent that there is any infringement, however, it is likely to be said by the UK Government to be both unavoidable and very short-term. A detailed consideration of the impact of WTO law in relation to the issue is beyond the scope of this chapter. The staged process has now been altered but it is worth identifying the initial plan before considering how it has been amended.

As originally envisaged, during the first stage, traders importing standard goods would have to keep appropriate customs records and decide how to account and pay for VAT on imported goods. They would have six months to complete customs declarations. Payment of customs duty could be deferred until a declaration has been made. UK safety and security declarations would not be needed for six months. There would be physical checks on high-risk animals and plants. Export declarations and UK safety and security certificates will be required for all exports. All requirements of the Common Transit Convention will need to be followed.[139]

From the start of the second stage all products of animal origin (the document mentions eggs, milk, honey and meat) along with certain other plants and plant products would require health documentation and need to be pre-notified. Until July 2021, any necessary physical checks would be conducted at the destination.

The third stage was set for July 2021. From this time customs duty would need to be paid and declarations made at the point of entry. Safety and security declarations would be needed and checks on animals, plants and their products will be carried out at GB Border Control Posts. The goods vehicle movement service, which is to be introduced for goods vehicles, would be fully operational.

The Border Operating Model amended

3.21 That three-stage approach has now been amended somewhat. The latest statement in relation to it was made on 11 March 2020 as noted above.[140]

139 See the Convention on a Common Transit Procedure of 15 June 1987. The Members of the Convention are the UK, the EU, Iceland, Norway, Liechtenstein, Switzerland, Turkey, North Macedonia and Serbia. The UK was invited to join as from the date it was no longer an EU Member State or the end of the implementation period: OJ [2018] L317/56, 14.12.18.

140 https://questions-statements.parliament.uk/written-statements/detail/2021-03-11/hcws841.

In respect of all matters relating to the import and export of goods, it is essential to have regard to official guidance which is made available on the internet under 'Import, export and customs for businesses'.[141]

As a result of the amendments, the following are not required until October 2021: pre-notification requirements for products of animal origin, certain animal by-products and high-risk food not of animal origin along with export health certificate requirements, applicable for products of animal origin and certain animal by-products.

1 January 2022 is the relevant date for the submission of deferred customs declarations[142] and supplementary declarations submitted six months after goods have been imported, safety and security declarations for imports, certain physical sanitary and phytosanitary checks, including those on high-risk plants at border control posts. Also from 1 January 2022, pre-notification requirements come into operation along with documentary checks and the need for phytosanitary certificates in respect of low-risk plants and plant products.

The latest significant date is March 2022. From this time there will be checks on border control posts on live animals and low risk plants and plant products.

The Border Operating Model: general comments

3.22 So far as the completion of customs declarations is concerned, the BOM states bluntly: 'Customs declarations are complicated'.[143] Traders have been advised that in order to complete them they should obtain a GB Economic Operator Registration and Identification number (EORI number), decide if they have access to the appropriate IT systems to complete declarations or whether they will use a customs intermediary, ensure that they can obtain the customs value and commodity code for their goods, and check whether or not they will be using customs procedures such as transit, inward processing or warehousing.

There are other matters that traders need to consider. For example, they must assess whether or not they should use a duty deferment account.[144] Those who are moving goods in lorries must ensure that their lorry drivers have international

141 https://www.gov.uk/topic/business-tax/import-export.

142 Deferral is not available to traders moving controlled goods into Great Britain.

143 See the Border Operating Model at p 8, fn 49.

144 A duty deferment account may be used for VAT and customs duty. Import VAT may be payable along with other VAT liabilities, see *The Value Added Tax (Accounting Procedures for Import VAT for VAT Registered Persons and Amendment) (EU Exit) Regulations 2019, SI 2019/60.* See www.gov.uk/guidance/setting-up-an-account-to-defer-duty-payments-when-you-import-goods#apply-to-defer-import-vat.

driving licences.[145] A Goods Vehicle Management Service (GVMS) will be introduced as from 1 January 2021. This is an IT platform which will support a 'pre-lodgement model', that is that appropriate declarations are made for all goods before they board and that the person controlling goods knows by the time they arrive whether or not goods need to be checked before being allowed to proceed.

The GVMS will allow declaration references to be linked so that only one single goods movement reference needs to be presented at the frontier to prove that pre-lodged declarations have been made in respect of the goods. The movement of goods to declarations may be linked enabling declarations to be processed en route. The person controlling the goods will be informed whether or not goods have been cleared by the time they arrive and so will know where they need to proceed.[146]

Traffic management in Kent is to be controlled by initiatives including 'Operation Brock' which has been implemented pursuant to statutory instruments made under Acts relating to traffic management and regulation so that the arrangements are operational as from 1 January 2021. In particular, there is to be a new web service developed by the UK Government, known as 'Check an HGV is Ready to Cross the Border' for the Roll on Roll off Freight Industry.[147] In addition, all outbound HGV drivers who are taking goods from Great Britain to the EU using the Short Straits route will have to obtain a Kent Access Permit to access crucial roads in Kent, including the M20.[148] The M20 links Swanley in Kent to the Channel Tunnel and ports at Dover.

The Protocol on Ireland/Northern Ireland

3.23 The effect of the WA in relation to the border between Northern Ireland and Ireland is a well-known source of difficulty. In short it ensures, as is well known, that a substantial body of EU law relating to customs, VAT on goods, excise duty and other matters applies to Northern Ireland. The result is that the absence of a border on the island of Ireland is preserved but different laws must apply in Northern Ireland from those applying in Great Britain. The

145 See 'The Border with the European Union: Importing and Exporting Goods', Border and Protocol Delivery Group available at: https://assets.publishing.service.gov.uk/government/uploads/system/uploads/attachment_data/file/949579/December_BordersOPModel__2_.pdf.

146 Border Operating Model, para 3.1.3, p 106.

147 Border Operating Model, para 4.1.7, p 154.

148 Border Operating Model, para 4.1.7, p 155. For the Kent Access Permit see *The Heavy Commercial Vehicles in Kent (No.3) (Amendment) Order 2020, SI 2020/1146* which amends *The Heavy Commercial Vehicles in Kent (No. 3) Order 2019, SI 2019/1210* and introduces the definition of the Kent Access Permit at *art 1A(3)*. Note should also be taken of *The Heavy Commercial Vehicles in Kent (No. 1) Order 2019, SI 2019/1388*, *The Heavy Commercial Vehicles in Kent (No.2) Order 2019, SI 2019/1394* and *The Heavy Commercial Vehicles in Kent (No. 2) (Amendment) Order 2020, SI 2020/1155.*

difference in treatment was subject to an unsuccessful challenge in the Scots' courts.[149] The political constraints which governed the drafting, however, have resulted in a legal text which is opaque and which must be read in its totality if its implications are to be fully appreciated.[150]

The Protocol on Ireland/Northern Ireland mostly came into force from the end of the transition period on 31 December 2020.[151] Its provisions gave rise to concern amongst some politicians in the UK during 2020[152] and continue to do so. At one point there were introduced into the Internal Market Bill provisions which could have led to the Protocol being overridden.[153] More recently, the EU has threatened to bring legal proceedings against the UK because of certain easements which it has decided to implement.[154] According to Article 12.4 of the Protocol the CJEU has a powerful role in relation to certain provisions of the Protocol, including Article 5 on customs matters. The preliminary reference procedure is available. Furthermore, certain acts of the institutions, amongst other things, are to have the same effects in the UK as they have in the EU.[155]

The institutional framework established under the Protocol includes the Joint Committee[156] and specialised committees on issues related to the implementation of the Protocol on Ireland/Northern Ireland.[157] There is also a joint consultative working group on the implementation of the Protocol.[158] A number of important decisions and declarations were made by and in the context of the Joint Committee in late December 2020.

149 See *In the Petition of Jolyon Maugham for Suspension and Interdict* [2019] CSOH 80.

150 It has been said by Professor Weatherill that one should have regard to what the Protocol does rather than what it says: see the blog post on EU Law Analysis 'The Protocol on Ireland/Northern Ireland: What it says is not what it does' (17 March 2020): http://eulawanalysis.blogspot.com/2020/03/.

151 Article 185 WA. Article 18 Protocol contains provisions to ensure that the Protocol applies with the democratic consent of the people of Northern Ireland. Democratic consent must be sought, first, before the end of an initial period which ends four years after the end of the implementation period.

152 For example, on 5 November 2020 the First Minister and Deputy First Minister of Northern Ireland wrote to Maroš Šefčovič, Vice-President of the European Commission, stressing in particular the problems deriving from sanitary and phytosanitary controls in the context of Northern Ireland's food supply: www.rte.ie/documents/news/2020/11/letter-to-european-commission-05.11.2020.pdf.

153 See Part V of the Bill clauses 40–45. Bill 177 2019-21. The provisions were removed by the House of Lords on 9 November 2020 and do not appear in the *Internal Market Act 2020*.

154 See the statement by Vice President Maroš Šefčovič following the announcement by the UK Government regarding the Protocol on Ireland/Northern Ireland, 3 March 2021 at: https://ec.europa.eu/commission/presscorner/detail/en/STATEMENT_21_1018.

155 See Article 12.5 of the Protocol and other provisions of the WA such as Article 4 ('Methods and principles relating to the effect, the implementation and the application of this Agreement') and Article 5 ('Good faith').

156 Article 164 WA.

157 Article 165 WA. See also Article 14 Protocol, which sets out the functions of the committee.

158 See Article 15 Protocol.

A policy paper, last updated on 7 January 2021, 'Moving goods into, out of or through Northern Ireland' sets out some guidance on the Protocol[159] and traders may obtain some practical assistance from the Traders' Support Service.[160] This deals, for example, with customs declarations for businesses. They will need an Economic Operators and Identification Number starting with XI.[161] Some observers have noted that, at least in theory, if the problems which arise are solved, Northern Ireland may be an attractive place to do business having access to the EU market via the Republic of Ireland and to the UK market as a whole.[162]

Specific provisions of the Protocol

3.24 The Protocol was introduced into UK domestic law by the *Taxation (Post-transition Period) Act 2020* (*TPTPA 2020*). It allows for the implementation of the fiscal aspects of the Protocol including the imposition of customs duty on goods leaving Northern Ireland. It is noted further below in **3.26**.

The Protocol makes clear that it is without prejudice to the constitutional position of Northern Ireland and the principle of consent which provides that any change in that position can be made only with the consent of the majority of its people. It:

> '… sets out arrangements necessary to address the unique circumstances on the island of Ireland, to maintain the necessary conditions for continued North-South cooperation, to avoid a hard border and to protect the 1998 Agreement in all its dimensions.'[163]

As well as specific provisions dealing with customs and the movement of goods there are provisions on state aid,[164] unfettered market access for goods moving from Northern Ireland to the rest of the UK,[165] technical regulations, assessments, registrations, certificates, approvals and authorisations,[166] and VAT and excise.[167] In relation to excise duty, 11 excise duty directives are listed in Annex 3 as being applicable in Northern Ireland. These include

159 www.gov.uk/government/publications/moving-goods-under-the-northern-ireland-protocol and www.gov.uk/guidance/trading-and-moving-goods-in-and-out-of-northern-ireland. See also the comments in **3.26** below.

160 See www.gov.uk/guidance/trader-support-service.

161 See www.gov.uk/eori.

162 See the evidence of Aodhán Connolly, Director, Northern Ireland Retail Consortium to the Northern Ireland Affairs Committee, 30 April 2020 available at: www.parliamentlive.tv/Event/Index/667f5b0e-2e89-463c-a9ce-e71737c9c572#player-tabs.

163 Article 1.3 Protocol.

164 Article 10 Protocol.

165 Article 6 Protocol.

166 Article 7 Protocol.

167 Article 8 Protocol.

Council Directive 2008/118/EC referred to above, directives on administrative cooperation and assistance as well as directives concerning excise duty and alcohol, manufactured tobacco, energy products and electricity, travellers and imports.

Turning to the movement of goods and customs duty, Article 4 of the Protocol states that Northern Ireland is part of the customs territory of the UK. Accordingly, nothing is to exclude Northern Ireland from agreements made between the UK and third countries, provided that those agreements do not prejudice the application of the Protocol. It is made clear that nothing in the Protocol is to preclude the UK from making agreements with third countries which grant to goods produced in Northern Ireland the same preferential access to the third country's market as goods produced in the rest of the UK. Furthermore, nothing is to preclude the UK from including Northern Ireland in the territorial scope of its schedule of concessions under GATT 1994. On the other hand, the inclusion of Northern Ireland in the UK customs territory means that it will not be part of the EU's customs territory and, therefore, is unable to benefit from trade agreements which the EU has with third countries[168] and tariff rate quotas given to EU businesses under them.

The complications of the Protocol arise, in particular, by virtue of Article 5. Article 5.3 states that legislation as defined in Article 5.2 UCC, shall apply to and in the UK in respect of Northern Ireland, not including the territorial waters of the UK. The legislation includes the UCC and provisions supplementing it, or implementing it, adopted at Union or national level. Also within the definition are the common customs tariff, the legislation setting up a Union system of reliefs and international agreements containing customs provisions insofar as they are applicable in the Union.

Annex 2 to the Protocol, introduced by Article 5.4 contains a list of other legislation which applies under the prescribed conditions in relation to customs and the movement of goods. The list is divided into 47 different sections and covers over 22 pages. So far as customs is concerned, as well as substantive customs law, legislation on mutual assistance is referred to.

It is because the UCC applies that there will be a need for, for example, entry summary declarations[169] and customs declarations for customs procedures including for release for free circulation,[170] pre-departure declarations,[171] customs supervision and formalities on exit[172] and the application of rules concerning the work of involvement of the European Anti-fraud Office known

168 This is an inevitable result of NI not being a part of the EU customs territory: see the European Commission 'Guidance Note Withdrawal of the United Kingdom and EU Rules in the Field of Customs Including Preferential Origin', Brussels 14 July REV2, p 32.

169 Article 127 UCC.

170 Article 5(16) UCC and Title V, Chapter 2.

171 Article 263 UCC. Exit summary declarations are dealt with in Article 271 UCC.

172 Article 267 UCC.

as 'OLAF'.[1] Also included will be rules relating to animal health,[2] veterinary inspections,[3] sanitary and phytosanitary inspections[4] and the registration and approval of the establishments of food business operators.[5] Trade defence and anti-dumping legislation is included,[6] as is law on bilateral safeguards.[7] Other laws included concern motor vehicles, chemicals, pesticides, agriculture and fishing and intellectual property.

The Protocol also provides that Articles 30 and 110 TFEU are to apply to Northern Ireland. Both articles help to establish free movement of goods in the EU. Article 30 contains the prohibition of charges having equivalent effect to customs duty on which there is a considerable body of EU law. Article 110 deals with internal taxation. [8]

Article 5.1 of the Protocol states, in its first paragraph, that notwithstanding Article 5.3, there shall be no customs duty payable on goods brought into Northern Ireland from another part of the United Kingdom by direct transport. The second paragraph states that, notwithstanding Article 5.3, customs duties in respect of a good being moved by direct transport to Northern Ireland from outside the EU and the UK are to be UK duties. Both these provisions are, however, inapplicable where a good is 'at risk' of subsequently being moved into the Union, whether by itself or forming part of another good following processing.[9]

1 Regulation (EU, Euratom) No 883/2013 of the European Parliament and of the Council of 11 September 2013 concerning investigations conducted by the European Anti-Fraud Office (OLAF) and repealing Regulation (EC) No 1073/1999 of the European Parliament and of the Council and Council Regulation (Euratom) No 1074/1999 [2013] OJ L 248/1.

2 For example, Council Directive 2002/99/EC of 16 December 2002 laying down the animal health rules governing the production, processing, distribution and introduction of products of animal origin for human consumption [2003] OJ L18/11.

3 Regulation (EU) 2017/625 of the European Parliament and of the Council of 15 March 2017 on official controls and other official activities performed to ensure the application of food and feed law, rules on animal health and welfare, plant health and plant protection products, amending various Regulations [2017] OJ L95/1.

4 Council Directive 96/23/EC of 29 April 1996 on measures to monitor certain substances and residues thereof in live animals and animal products and repealing Directives 85/358/EEC and 86/469/EEC and Decisions 89/187/ EEC and 91/664/EEC [1996] OJ L125/10.

5 Regulation (EC) No 853/2004 of the European Parliament and of the Council of 29 April 2004 laying down specific hygiene rules for food of animal origin OJ [2004] L 139/55.

6 An example is Regulation (EU) 2016/1036 of the European Parliament and of the Council of 8 June 2016 on protection against dumped imports from countries not members of the European Union [2016] OJ L 176/21.

7 Including, for example, Regulation (EU) No 654/2014 of the European Parliament and of the Council of 15 May 2014 concerning the exercise of the Union's rights for the application and enforcement of international trade rules and amending Council Regulation (EC) No 3286/94 laying down Community procedures in the field of the common commercial policy in order to ensure the exercise of the Community's rights under international trade rules, in particular those established under the auspices of the World Trade Organization [2014] OJ L189/50.

8 *Ioan Tatu v Statul român prin Ministerul Finanţelor şi Economiei and ors* (Case C-402/09) [2011] ECR I-2711, para 34.

9 Article 5.2, first paragraph. In Article 5.1, third paragraph, there is an exemption for personal property brought into Northern Ireland by residents from elsewhere in the UK.

The terms of Article 5.2 deal with goods 'at risk'. They state that goods brought into Northern Ireland from outside the European Union (ie, including from Great Britain) are to be considered at risk of subsequently being moved into the European Union unless certain conditions are satisfied. That may not be consistent with the initial impression given by the opening words of the article in Article 5.1.

There are two conditions which goods must satisfy in order to avoid being goods 'at risk'. The first condition is that it is established that the good will not be subject to commercial processing in Northern Ireland. For these purposes, 'processing' means:

> 'any alteration of goods, any transformation of goods in any way or any subjecting of goods to operations other than for the purpose of preserving them in good condition or for adding or affixing marks, labels, seals or any other documentation to ensure compliance with any specific requirements.'[10]

The reference to operations other than for the purpose of preserving in good condition or fixing marks and so on results in the definition of processing being widely defined. A good deal may turn on what are 'operations'.

The second condition is that the good fulfils criteria established by the Joint Committee for considering that a good is not at risk of subsequently being moved into the Union. It must have had to make its decision taken before the end of the implementation period.

In making its decision the Joint Committee must take into account: (a) the final destination and use of the good; (b) the nature and value of the good; (c) the nature of the movement; and (d) the incentive for undeclared onward-movement into the Union, in particular incentives resulting from the duties payable pursuant to Article 5.1 considered above.

The Joint Committee: decisions and declarations

3.25 On 17 December 2020, the Joint Committee made decisions on agricultural subsidies,[11] on the determination of goods not at risk,[12]

10 Article 5.2, second paragraph.

11 Decision No 5/2020: https://assets.publishing.service.gov.uk/government/uploads/system/uploads/attachment_data/file/949845/Decision_of_the_Withdrawal_Agreement_Joint_Committee_on_agricultural_subsidies.pdf.

12 Decision No 4/2020: https://assets.publishing.service.gov.uk/government/uploads/system/uploads/attachment_data/file/949846/Decision_of_the_Withdrawal_Agreement_Joint_Committee_on_the_determination_of_goods_not_at_risk.pdf.

on errors and omissions amending the Protocol,[13] and on arrangements under Article 12(2) of the Protocol which concerned the presence of EU representatives when activities under the Protocol are carried out.[14] On the same day there were also various unilateral declarations by the UK in the Joint Committee on export declarations, meat products, official certification, human and veterinary medicines and state aid.[15] The declarations must be read in the light of the latest statements of the UK Government on implementation of the Protocol. They extend to 1 October 2021 the arrangements in respect of agrifood movements, of particular importance to supermarkets and their suppliers (see **3.26** below).

The unilateral declaration on export declarations states that the UK will consider that the relevant provisions requiring pre-departure and export declarations will be satisfied where equivalent information is provided and identifies the circumstances in which standard procedures will apply. The declaration on meat products is of particular importance for supermarkets and specifies the conditions under which meat products will be brought from Great Britain into Northern Ireland from 1 January 2021 to 1 July 2021, now extended to 1 October 2021.

The declaration on official certification is also of importance for supermarkets. It concerns products of animal origin, composite products, food and feed of non-animal origin and plant products which concerned products other than meat products. It is related to a limited number of supermarket suppliers bringing goods into Northern Ireland which required certification and was to last until 1 April 2021. The solution was said not to be renewable but the period in question has been extended to 1 October 2021. The declaration on medicines set out procedures for a period of up to 12 months after the end of the implementation period.

The Joint Committee's decision on goods not at risk significantly reduced the burden which the Protocol may otherwise have imposed on traders. It provided, in Article 2, that goods are not considered to be subject to commercial processing where the person lodging the relevant declaration had an annual turnover of less than £500,000 and in certain other situations, for example, where the processing in Northern Ireland is for the sole purpose of the sale of food to an end consumer in the UK. Other situations concern the activities of

---

13 Decision No 3/2020: https://assets.publishing.service.gov.uk/government/uploads/system/uploads/attachment_data/file/949847/Decision_of_the_Withdrawal_Agreement_Joint_Committee_on_errors_and_omissions.pdf.

14 Decision No 6/2020: https://assets.publishing.service.gov.uk/government/uploads/system/uploads/attachment_data/file/949848/Decision_of_the_Withdrawal_Agreement_Joint_Committee_on_arrangements_under_Article_12_2__of_the_Protocol.pdf.

15 www.gov.uk/government/publications/the-northern-ireland-protocol. The Joint Committee must also deal with matters concerned with fishing: see Article 5.3 Protocol.

the construction industry in Northern Ireland, the provision of health and care services there and animal feed.

Where goods are not considered to be subject to commercial processing under Article 2 and have been moved into Northern Ireland by direct transport from another part of the UK, they are not to be considered at risk of being subsequently moved into the EU where the EU duty is equal to zero or where the importer is appropriately authorised to bring the goods into Northern Ireland for sale to or final use by UK consumers.

According to Article 3, the goods are not 'at risk' where the goods have come from outside the EU or UK and the EU duty is equal to or less than the UK duty or where the importer is appropriately authorised to bring the goods into Northern Ireland for final use or consumption by end-consumers located in Northern Ireland, and the difference between the EU and the UK duties is lower than 3% of the customs value of the good.

Traders may apply to be authorised to declare their goods not at risk.[16]

The Protocol states that such duties as the UK imposes by virtue of the provisions of Article 5.3 are not to be remitted to the EU.[17] Furthermore, the UK may provide, in general, that customs duty which becomes chargeable in respect of goods brought into Northern Ireland may be remitted, the debt waived, reimbursement of duty may be made for goods which do not enter the Union and compensation may be provided to offset the impact of the charge under Article 5.3.[18]

The Protocol: UK implementation, guidance and domestic law

3.26 Inevitably, given its subject matter, the Protocol has been the subject of extensive political consideration. A significant command paper on the Protocol was issued by the Cabinet Office in December 2020.[19] Important guidance is also available.[20] There have been subsequent important statements in the House of Commons. One was made on 3 March 2021, by the Rt. Hon. Brandon Lewis MP. It concerns the implementation of the Protocol especially in relation to the position of supermarkets and their suppliers.[21] He indicated

16 See www.gov.uk/guidance/apply-for-authorisation-for-the-uk-trader-scheme-if-you-bring-goods-into-northern-ireland.

17 Article 5 Protocol at 5.5 and 5.6.

18 Article 5.6 Protocol.

19 The Northern Ireland Protocol CP 346 available at: https://assets.publishing.service.gov.uk/government/uploads/system/uploads/attachment_data/file/950601/Northern_Ireland_Protocol_-_Command_Paper.pdf.

20 The 'Moving goods under the Northern Ireland Protocol' sets out some guidance at www.gov.uk/government/publications/moving-goods-under-the-northern-ireland-protocol.

21 Hansard Vol 690, 3 March 2021: https://hansard.parliament.uk/Commons/2021-03-03/debates/21030327000007/NorthernIrelandProtocolImplementation.

that the current scheme for temporary agrifood movements to Northern Ireland (STAMNI) will continue until 1 October 2021. Certification requirements will then be introduced in phases alongside the rollout of the digital assistance scheme.

Further guidance on parcel movements from Great Britain to and from Northern Ireland has been provided.[22] It is too extensive to be reproduced here but, as an example of its provisions, business to business movements of goods from Great Britain to Northern Ireland will not require declarations unless the goods are greater than £135 and prohibited or restricted. The temporary arrangements for businesses will end on 1 October 2021. Other types of movements of goods will have six months to prepare for new arrangements rather than facing them on 1 April 2021.

The statement made on 3 March 2021 referred to practical problems of soil attached to the movement of plants, seeds, bulbs, vegetables and agricultural machinery and noted the absence of any charging regime in respect of agrifood goods under Official Controls Regulation 2017/625 was noted. The statement was followed by one from the Vice-President of the European Commission Maroš Šefčovič.[23] It indicates that the unilateral action of the UK is regarded by the EU as a violation of the provisions of the Protocol.

So far as concerns domestic law, reference should be made to the *TPTPA 2020*. *Section 1*, inserts into the *TCBTA 2018* a new *s 40A*. This allows customs duty to be charged on the removal of goods from Great Britain to Northern Ireland if the goods are not domestic goods or are at risk of subsequently being moved into the EU. *Section 2* makes provision for the removal of goods from Northern Ireland to Great Britain. It inserts *s 30A* into the *TCBTA 2018* and provides that Union goods imported into the UK as a result of their entry into Northern Ireland are to be treated for the purposes of this Part as if they were domestic goods not chargeable to UK customs duty. Other goods imported into the UK as a result of their entry into Northern Ireland are not chargeable to import duty, but are chargeable to duty under *s 30A*. Duty under *subs (3)* is chargeable in accordance with Union customs legislation as if the goods subject to the charge were brought into the customs territory of the European Union.[24] A charge to duty on the removal of goods from Northern Ireland to Great Britain is imposed pursuant to *TCBTA 2018, s 30C*.

The provisions of the *TPTPA 2020* are implemented by *The Customs (Northern Ireland) (EU Exit) Regulations 2020*.[25]

---

22 Guidance: 'Sending parcels to and from Northern Ireland': www.gov.uk/guidance/sending-parcels-between-great-britain-and-northern-ireland#history.

23 Statement by Vice-President Maroš Šefčovič following today's announcement by the UK Government regarding the Protocol on Ireland/Northern Ireland: https://ec.europa.eu/commission/presscorner/detail/en/STATEMENT_21_1018.

24 See *TCBTA 2018, s 30A(5)*.

25 *SI 2020/1605*.

UK and EU trade agreements

3.27 So far as the EU's trade agreements are concerned, UK content no longer originates in the EU. That may have implications for the treatment of the finished product under the applicable EU trade agreement. It will be important, of course, for the finished product to originate in the EU. According to the European Commission:

> '… this entails a need for EU exporters to reassess their supply chains. They may have to relocate production or change suppliers for certain inputs in order to continue to benefit from Union preferential trade agreements with current Union preferential partners.'[26]

The necessary reassessment will have to be carried out on a case by case basis.

So far as concerns the UK's own trade agreements with countries outside the EU, effective from 1 January 2021, the UK has made trade agreements which contain provisions on customs duties and rules of origin, with the following territories: Andean countries (Columbia, Ecuador, Peru), CARIFORUM, Central America (Cost Rica, El Salvador, Guatemala, Honduras, Nicaragua and Panama) Chile, Eastern and Southern Africa (ESA: Madagascar, Mauritius, Seychelles, Zimbabwe) Faroe Islands, Georgia, Israel, Jordan, Kosovo, Lebanon, Liechtenstein, Morocco, Pacific States (Fiji and Papua New Guinea), Palestinian Authority, South Africa Customs Union (Botswana, Eswatini, Lesotho, Namibia, South Africa) and Mozambique, South Korea, Switzerland and Tunisia.[27] The most recently agreed trade agreement is one between the UK and Japan.[28] Generally speaking, trade agreements are frequently applied on a provisional basis before they are formally ratified.

It is not proposed to consider these agreements in detail. Like the agreements that the EU has made with these countries, the UK's agreements are given different labels which reflect the different relationship between the parties. There are free trade or trade agreements (the Andean countries, Faroe Islands, South Korea), economic partnership agreements (CARIFORUM, ESA, Pacific States, South Africa Customs Union and Mozambique) and a comprehensive economic partnership agreement with Japan. There are association agreements (Chile, Central America, Jordan, Lebanon, Morocco and Tunisia). The agreement with Georgia is a strategic partnership and cooperation agreement. The one with Israel is a trade and partnership agreement. The agreement with Kosovo is referred to as one for partnership trade and cooperation, while the agreement with the Palestinian Authority is a political, trade and partnership agreement.

---

26 The Communication, pp 7–8.

27 See www.gov.uk/guidance/uk-trade-agreements-with-non-eu-countries.

28 See www.gov.uk/government/publications/ukjapan-agreement-for-a-comprehensive-economic-partnership-cs-japan-no12020.

More than half of the agreements made so far seek to preserve or build on the relationship established pursuant to EU agreements which covered the UK when it was a member of the EU. The agreement between the UK and Switzerland, for example, says in Article 2 that:

> 'The overriding objective of this Agreement is to preserve the existing trading relationship between the Parties under the Switzerland-EU Trade Agreements and to provide a platform for further trade liberalisation and development of the trade relations between them.'[29]

Agreements between the EU and Switzerland are incorporated into the UK's agreement.[30] The UK's agreement with Chile makes a similar point in Article 1.1:

> 'The overriding objective of this Agreement is to preserve the links between the Parties established by the association created in Article 2 of the EU-Chile Agreement.'[31]

Both agreements go on to set out the modifications which are to be made to the EU's agreement. In an Appendix to Annex 1 of the UK/Switzerland Agreement, for example, there is a new protocol 3 concerning the definition of the concept of 'originating products' and methods of administrative cooperation. The relevant protocol in relation to Chile is merely the protocol in the EU agreement amended.

Traders need to consider the terms of the new UK agreements carefully in relation to their particular business. Apparently small changes can have significant effects. As an example, the UK's agreement with the ESA provides that in respect of canned tuna and tuna loins derogations may be granted within an annual quota of 6,300 tonnes for canned tuna and 340 tonnes for tuna loins.[32] Under the EU/ESA agreement, the figures were 8,000 and 2,000.[33] That may be significant for specific participants in that particular trade.

As one would expect, the agreements do not fix the UK's trading relationships at a point in time immediately after the end of the implementation period. They

---

29 Trade Agreement between the United Kingdom of Great Britain and Northern Ireland and the Swiss Confederation, 11 February 2019, CP 55 (not yet ratified).

30 See Article 1 of the Agreement.

31 Agreement establishing an Association between the United Kingdom of Great Britain and Northern Ireland and the Republic of Chile 30 January 2019, CP 35 (not yet in force). See also Article 1 of the agreements with the Andean countries, Central America, the Faroe Islands, Israel, Jordan, Kosovo, Lebanon, Morocco, the Palestinian Authority and Tunisia. See also Article 2 of the agreement with the Pacific States.

32 See the Agreement establishing an economic partnership agreement between the Eastern and Southern Africa States and the United Kingdom of Great Britain and Northern Ireland, 31 January 2019, CP 31, Protocol 1, concerning the definition of the concept of 'originating products' and methods of administrative cooperation, Article 42.8.

33 See the Agreement between the EU and the ESA, Protocol 1 to the EU's Agreement concerning the definition of the concept of 'originating products' and methods of administrative cooperation, Article 42.8 [2012] L111/1023 at p. L111/1040.

allow for developments of trade policy in the future. The agreement with the ESA, for example, contains a list of matters for future negotiation. Article 52 specifies these under the heading 'Built in agenda'. The first of many items to be mentioned is customs and trade facilitation. The second includes rules of origin, related issues and trade defence issues.

There are other ways of ensuring that agreements are flexible. For example, the agreement between the UK and South Korea, Article 2.5.4, says that three years after the entry into force of the Agreement, at the request of either party, there shall be consultations to consider accelerating and broadening the scope of the elimination of customs duties on imports between them. Similar provisions, in Article 2.14, govern non-tariff measures. Another example is in the agreement with Switzerland. Article 8 says that within 24 months from entry into force of the agreement, the Parties are to conduct exploratory discussions with the aim of replacing, modernising or developing the agreement.

It will be apparent that the position which exists on 1 January 2021 in relation to trade and customs matters is merely the position from which the UK will develop its own trade policy. It is the starting point for a process of divergence which will continue for a long time. In due course, the policy can be expected to reflect, for example, the fact that in many areas of economic activity the interests of UK producers and consumers may be significantly different from those of the EU as a whole.

Excise duty

3.28 As well as being dealt with in the Protocol on Ireland/Northern Ireland, excise duty features also in the Withdrawal Agreement. Generally speaking, it has attracted much less attention than customs duty in relation to Brexit and there is space to deal with it only very briefly. For the assistance of stakeholders, the European Commission has produced a Notice which sets out briefly the consequences in relation to excise duty of the UK's withdrawal.[34]

It is impossible here to identify all the relevant EU excise duty legislation. There is some direct EU legislation[35] but most of it consists of directives requiring UK implementing legislation. It is worth noting briefly Directive 2008/118[36] so as to provide some approximate indication of the impact of EU legislation in this area.

34 See Notice to Stakeholders Withdrawal of the United Kingdom and EU rules in the field of excise, REV 1 which replaces the Notice of 11 March 2019.

35 See eg, Commission Regulation EC) No 684/2009 of 24 July 2009 implementing Council Directive 2008/118/EC as regards the computerised procedures for the movement of excise goods under suspension of excise duty of 24 July 2009 [2009] OJ L197/24 as amended.

36 This has been repealed as from 2023 see n 6 above. See also **3.6**.

Like the single market legislation in Directive 1992/12,[37] the directive of 2008 covers alcoholic products and manufactured tobacco. Whereas the earlier directive encompassed hydrocarbon oils, the directive of 2008 is expressed to cover energy products and electricity. It addresses, in Chapter II, the time and place of the chargeability of excise duty as well as exemptions, remission and reimbursement. Chapter III is concerned with the harmonisation of rules on the production, processing and holding of excise goods. Consequently, it contains rules concerned with tax warehouses. Chapters IV, V and VI address the movement of goods under duty suspension, the movement and taxation of excise goods after release for consumption and miscellaneous matters such as the marking of goods. After the UK leaves the EU, movement under duty suspension will not be possible. Goods moving between the UK and the EU will become imports and exports and UK warehouse registrations will cease to be valid.

Other EU legislation which has had to be implemented includes Council Directive 2003/96/EC restructuring the Community framework for the taxation of energy products and electricity.[38] Amongst other things, it imposes minimum levels of duty to various fuels and deals with exemptions. Also implemented were Council Directive 92/83/EEC which harmonised the structure of excise duties on alcohol and alcoholic beverages[39] and Council Directive 92/84/EEC[40] which set out certain minimum rates of duty in relation to them. In relation to the duty on manufactured tobacco Council Directive 2011/64/EU is important.[41]

A substantial amount of domestic legislation implements these directives both primary and secondary.[42] That domestic legislation stays in place after Brexit as so called 'retained EU law' and a number of statutory instruments have been passed.[43] In contrast to customs duty, therefore, the *TCBTA 2018* does not

37 See n 6 and **3.6** above.

38 Council Directive 2003/96/EEC of 27 October 2003 restructuring the Community framework for the taxation of energy products and electricity [2003] OJ L283/51.

39 Council Directive 92/83/EEC of 19 October 1992 on the harmonization of the structures of excise duties on alcohol and alcoholic beverages [1992] OJ L316/21.

40 Council Directive of 19 October 1992 on the approximation of the rates of excise duty on alcohol and alcoholic beverages [1992] OJ L316/29.

41 Council Directive 2011/64/EU of 21 June 2011 on the structure and rates of excise duty applied to manufactured tobacco [2011] OJ L176/24.

42 See eg, provisions of the *Alcoholic Liquor Duties Act 1979*, the *Hydrocarbon Oil Duties Act 1979*, the *Tobacco Products Duty Act 1979*, and *The Excise Goods (Holding, Movement and Duty Point) Regulations 2010, SI 2010/593* as amended. The well-known *Customs and Excise Management Act 1979* concerns the management and collection of revenues of customs and excise and intersects at many points with EU law.

43 See, eg *The Travellers' Allowances and Miscellaneous Provisions (EU Exit) Regulations 2020, SI 2020/1412*, *The Travellers' Allowances and Miscellaneous Provisions (Northern Ireland) (EU Exit) Regulations 2020, SI 2020/1619* and *The Excise Goods (Holding Movement and Duty Point)(Amendment etc.) (EU Exit) Regulations 2019, SI 2019/13* and other amending regulations. A full list is available at www.gov.uk/government/collections/customs-vat-and-excise-uk-transition-legislation-from-1-january-2021.

provide the foundations for the creation of a completely new system. *Sections 44–46* of the *2018 Act* give power for regulations to be made in relation to various aspects of excise duty.

Section 47 provides that EU direct legislation in relation to excise duty, in so far as it forms part of UK domestic law by virtue of the *EUWA 2018, s 3*, shall cease to have effect. *Section 47(4)* refers to other provisions of the *EUWA 2018* in particular *s 6*, which deals with the interpretation of 'EU retained law' as defined. Certain amendments to domestic law relating mostly to excise duty but also to customs are contained in *TCBTA 2018, Sch 9.*

The reference to the *EUWA 2018, s 6* above is an acknowledgement that, after Brexit, the UK's domestic law of excise duty is to be governed by the general principles set out in the *2018 Act.* As noted above, much excise duty law will be 'retained EU law'.[44] The interpretation of domestic excise duty law, its relationship to EU law generally and to the principle of supremacy of EU law will be governed by the provisions of the *EUWA 2018.* These will ensure that EU law and the case law of the CJEU will be relevant to UK excise duty for a long time to come. In that respect the position of excise duty law is comparable to that of VAT which is also governed by a great deal of primary and secondary UK law.

For a full consideration of the effects of the *EUWA 2018* and 'EU retained law' see Chapter 1, Part 1(V).[45]

CONCLUSION

3.29 The UK economy is well-known to be strong in the area of services of different kinds. Customs and excise law on the other hand is concerned with goods. Consequently, there is a large area of economic activity in the UK unaffected by the impact of Brexit on customs and excise matters. The movement of goods, however, is still crucial for important sectors of the economy of the UK. Many service industries have, of course, strong links to the provision of goods. Much more fundamentally, economic activity in relation to goods, their manufacture and assembly remain crucial for life across the UK, not least in sectors such as food production, processing and retail. Clearly, the effects of Brexit will be of profound importance in many areas and will be reflected in the nature of economic life in the UK and its trading partners for a long time to come.

44 *EUWA 2018, ss 2* and *6(7).*

45 Chapter 1, Part 1(V) The continued application of EU law in the United Kingdom post-31 December 2020 ('IP completion date'): 'retained EU law' at **1.22.**

Chapter 4

Brexit Implications for State Aid Legislation

Conor Quigley QC

STATE AID UNDER THE TFEU

4.1 State aid is a subject that was originally conceived as a means of controlling the amount of subsidies that public authorities might grant to national industries so as to prevent competition being distorted in the common market of the European Economic Community. The original provisions, Articles 92–93 EEC, were included in the section of the EEC Treaty headed common rules on competition. They were barely used in the 1960s, largely restricted to controlling regional investment aid in the 1970s, before flourishing in the 1980s, 1990s and 2000s to being applied to prohibit or control a wide range of state interventions across the economy, including in environmental policy, research and development and innovation, restructuring of undertakings in difficulty, and sectoral applications, such as agriculture, broadcasting, energy, financial services, shipbuilding and transport. Building on the two primary articles, now Articles 107–108 TFEU, there are now hundreds of pages of secondary EU legislation and European Commission notices and guidelines, which have given rise to well over a thousand judgments from the European Courts.[1] These have developed the scope of application of the state aid rules into every area of economic activity at every level of state intervention, whether national, regional, municipal or district. They apply to all types of state intervention, as long as this involves an effect on state finances, interpreted in a very wide sense. From the earliest times, they have applied in the field of taxation to prohibit the grant of state aid through fiscal measures, in particular through derogations or exemptions from normal tax liability.[2] In order to focus attention on fiscal-based state aid, the Commission in 1998 issued a notice on the application of the state aid rules to measures relating to

1 For a full exposition of the state aid rules, see Conor Quigley QC, *European State Aid Law and Policy*, 3rd edn (Bloomsbury/Hart Publishing, 2015).

2 *Italy v Commission* (Case 173/73).

direct business taxation.[3] Over the following 20 years, Commission decisions and court judgments on fiscal state aid mushroomed. In recent years, the Commission has turned its attention to specific tax rules and the application of those rules by national tax administrations, in particular through advance tax rulings, in order to tackle what it perceives as unwarranted deviation from an established norm. The Commission has certainly succeeded in broadening the scope of application of the prohibition on fiscal state aid. In this respect, however, the Commission has been only partially successful in the EU courts, with many of its arguments and decisions being overturned by both the Court of Justice and the General Court. The next few years will be pivotal in establishing definitively the full extent to which the state aid rules control or prevent the applicability of various national tax provisions.

In accordance with the Treaty on European Union, legal competence in matters of taxation is split between the EU and the Member States. Article 4(1) TEU provides that competences not conferred upon the EU remain with the Member States. Article 5(1) TEU provides that the limits of EU competences are governed by the principle of conferral, pursuant to which the EU shall act only within the limits of the competences conferred upon it by the Member States in the EU Treaties to attain the objectives set out in those treaties. Pursuant to Article 3(1)(b) TFEU, however, the EU has exclusive competence in establishing the competition rules necessary for the functioning of the internal market. It follows that, if a measure is properly classifiable as fiscal state aid, it falls within the scope of Articles 107–108 TFEU. That, however, necessarily begs the question of what fiscal measures are indeed properly classifiable as state aid. Moreover, as regards the adoption of harmonisation legislation, Article 115 TFEU requires, in relation to tax legislation, that directives can be adopted only by unanimity in the Council. Consequently, some tax measures will fall within the sole competence of the Member States, whilst others may come with the state aid jurisdiction of supervision by the Commission. Accordingly, the Commission cannot be accused of exceeding its powers under Article 108 TFEU by examining measures comprising an alleged aid scheme in order to determine whether it constitutes state aid within Article 107(1) TFEU,[4] and Member States must refrain from adopting any tax measure liable to constitute state aid incompatible with the internal market.[5] Otherwise, Member States remain competent to adopt tax legislation, subject to compliance with EU rules such as free movement, as they deem appropriate.

3 OJ 1998 C384/3. This Notice was superseded by the Notice on the notion of State aid, OJ 2016 C262/1.

4 *Belgium v Commission* (Joined Cases T-131/16 and T-263/16), para 67; *Luxembourg v Commission* (Joined Cases T-755/15 and T-759/15), para 107.

5 *Belgium v Commission* (Joined Cases T-131/16 and T-263/16), para 63; *Netherlands v Commission* (Joined Cases T-760/15 and T-636/16), para 143; *Luxembourg v Commission* (Joined Cases T-755/15 and T-759/15), para 135.

4.2 Application of EU law is without prejudice to the power of the Member States to decide on their economic policy and, therefore, on the tax system and the common or normal regime under it which they consider the most appropriate and, in particular, to spread the tax burden as they see fit across the different factors of production and economic sectors.[6] As EU law currently stands, with the exception of value added tax, certain aspects of excise duties and energy taxes, and specific issues in connection with direct taxation, which are the subject of EU directives, taxation, particularly direct taxation, generally falls within the exclusive competence of the Member States which are entitled to devise systems of taxation which they consider best suited to the needs of their economies.[7] Thus, in the absence of EU harmonising rules, it falls within the competence of the Member States to designate bases of assessment and to spread the tax across the various factors of production and economic sectors.[8] The Commission, thus, does not have competence to allow it to define in an autonomous manner the rules of normal taxation, disregarding national tax rules.[9] Moreover, although Article 107(1) TFEU prohibits unjustified discrimination in favour of certain undertakings, the assertion that there is a general principle of equal treatment in relation to tax in Article 107(1) TFEU would give that provision too broad a scope.[10] Consequently, for example, the application of progressive rates of taxation, including rates based on income or turnover, falls within the discretion of each Member State.[11] Equally, the Commission does not have the power autonomously to define the normal taxation of an undertaking, disregarding national tax rules.[12]

Article 107(1) TFEU provides that any aid granted by the state or through state resources in any form whatsoever, which distorts or threatens to distort competition by favouring certain undertakings or the production of certain goods, is, in so far as it affects trade between Member States, incompatible with the internal market. The CJEU has repeatedly summarised the constituent elements of Article 107(1) TFEU as follows: (i) there must be an intervention by the state or through state resources; (ii) the intervention must be liable to affect trade between Member States; (iii) it must confer an advantage on the recipient; (iv) it must distort or threaten to distort competition.[13] However, within these four criteria are a number of separate matters that must be considered, some of which give rise to complex issues especially in the context of fiscal state aid, which will be considered below. The criteria of effect on trade and distortion

6 Commission 2016 Notice on the notion of State aid, para 156.

7 *Bachmann v Belgium* (Case C204/90) [1992] ECR I249.

8 *Commission v Government of Gibraltar* (Joined Cases C-106/09P and C-107/09P), para 97; *ANGED v Generalitat de Catalunya* (Case C-233/16), para 50.

9 *Netherlands v Commission* (Joined Cases T-760/15 and T-636/16), para 159.

10 *Netherlands v Commission* (Joined Cases T-760/15 and T-636/16), para 168.

11 *Vodafone Maryarország Mobil Távközlési Zrt. v Nemzeti Adó- és Vámhivatal Fellebbviteli Igazgatósága* (Case C-75/18), paras 49–50; *Tesco-Global Áruházak Zrt. v Nemzeti Adó- és Vámhivatal Fellebbviteli Igazgatósága* (Case C-323/18), paras 69–70.

12 *Luxembourg v Commission* (Joined Cases T-755/15 and T-759/15), para 112.

13 *Commission v Deutsche Post* AG (Case C-399/08P), para 38.

of competition are generally considered to be easily fulfilled, without the need for substantial proof. Thus, when state aid strengthens the position of an undertaking compared with other undertakings competing in intra-EU trade, that trade must be regarded as affected by the aid.[14] Contrary to the position in EU anti-trust law, there is no threshold or percentage below which trade between Member States can be said not to be affected.[15] It is not necessary for there to be proof of an actual distortion of competition, since it is sufficient to show that the measure threatens to distort competition, and it is not necessary to demonstrate that the aid has an actual effect on trade between Member States, but only to examine whether that aid is liable to affect such trade.[16]

4.3 The notion of an intervention is not as such mentioned in Article 107(1) TFEU, which instead refers to aid granted by the state or through state resources. It may be assumed, however, that an intervention is a measure that grants aid. In one of its earliest state aid judgments, the CJEU held that Article 107(1) applies to interventions which, in various forms, mitigate the charges which are normally included in the budget of an undertaking and which, without, therefore, being subsidies in the strict meaning of the word, are similar in character and have the same effect.[17] Thus, the notion of aid requires the adoption of a measure that has the character of an intervention that deviates from the normal situation which would apply in the absence of that intervention. This must result in an innovation with regard to the previous legal position.[18] To put it another way, there must be a benefit that the undertaking in question would not have received in the normal course.[19] Thus there must be a normative liability in respect of which the state measure in question intervenes so as to create a benefit for certain undertakings or the production of certain goods. Clearly, legislation introducing a derogation or exemption from a general tax liability constitutes an intervention. In those circumstances, the generally applicable tax legislation imposes a liability to tax, whereas the derogating measure relieves the undertakings to which it applies from full liability. State aid may also be granted through a discretionary administrative measure, such as where a particular administrative tax measure reduces an existing tax liability of a specific undertaking.[20] In that event, the existing liability may be regarded as having arisen in the normal way, whereas the decision of the tax authority intervenes to reduce the liability. Tax administration involves various elements of interaction between the taxpayer and the tax authority. This may include correspondence, possibly by including a tax ruling, prior to a tax assessment being raised. The Commission's treatment of a tax ruling as a fiscal measure giving rise to an intervention has been accepted by the

14 *Philip Morris v Commission* (Case 730/79), para 11.
15 *Italy v Commission* (Case T-222/04), para 44.
16 *France* v *Commission* (Case C-301/87), para 33.
17 *De Gezamenlijke Steenkolenmijnen in Limburg v High Authority* (Case 30/59), p 19.
18 *Italy v Commission* (Case 173/73), para 6.
19 *Germany v Commission* (Case 84/82), *per* Advocate General Slynn, at p 1501.
20 *Commission v Slovakia* (Case C-507/08), paras 6–10.

General Court.[21] Although national authorities are bound to give full effect to EU law,[22] it is as yet undecided by the EU courts whether a decision of a tax authority taken in the normal course of assessing an individual liability must be regarded as granting state aid on the basis that the authority misapplied national tax legislation, through a mistake of fact or law, thereby giving rise to a lower tax liability than would have arisen through a correct assessment.

Usually, fiscal state aid is granted through a state aid scheme by which there is a derogation from the generally applicable legislation. Thus, state aid may arise, for example, through a measure which grants to certain undertakings a tax reduction or exemption or a deferral of liability that would otherwise be payable,[23] a tax credit[24] or a tax-free reserve out of profits,[25] or which substitutes a fixed rate levy for the taxes that would otherwise be payable.[26] Although aid must be granted through state resources, it is not necessary that there be a positive transfer of funds from the public authorities. Fiscal state aid generally involves negative expenditure constituting a financial burden borne by the state in that it entails an economic advantage in the form of exoneration from the obligation to pay the tax in question and, thus results in a loss of income to the state.[27] Aid may also be granted indirectly, for instance by way of a tax relief to a taxpayer on condition that the benefit of the relief is passed on to a third party. Thus, tax relief granted to taxpayers investing in specific companies may be classified as indirect state aid for those companies[28] and aid granted to employees through a tax exemption on their wages may be treated as passed on to their employers by means of a corresponding reduction in their wages.[29] In some circumstances, shareholders may be considered to have benefited indirectly from a recapitalisation measure which directly benefited the recipient undertaking.[30] Moreover, an advantage may be regarded as both direct and indirect, so that, for instance, a tax advantage granted through approval of a transfer pricing arrangement between a subsidiary and other group companies may constitute direct aid to the subsidiary and indirect aid to the group.[31]

Whereas Article 107(1) TFEU is concerned with aid granted by the state, the Court's classification set out above refers instead to the notion of an advantage

21 *Netherlands v Commission* (Joined Cases T-760/15 and T-636/16), para 151; *Luxembourg v Commission* (Joined Cases T-755/15 and T-759/15), para 143.

22 *Eesti Pagar AS v Ettevõtluse Arendamise Sihtasutus* (Case C-349/17), para 91.

23 *Italy v Commission* (Case C-66/02), para 78; *Ministerio de Defensa v Concello de Ferrol* (Case C-522/13), para 29.

24 *Territorio Histórico de Álava – Diputación Foral de Álava v Commission* (Case T-227/01 etc), para 126.

25 *Commission v Greece* (Case C-354/10), para 8.

26 *Italy v Commission* (Case C-66/02), para 80.

27 *Presidente del Consiglio dei Ministri v Regione Sardegna* (Case C-169/08), para 58.

28 *Germany v Commission* (Case C-156/98), para 26.

29 *3F v Commission* (Case C-319/07P), para 75.

30 *HSH Investment Holdings Coinvest-C sàrl v Commission* (Case T-499/12), para 68.

31 *Luxembourg v Commission* (Joined Cases T-755/15 and T-759/15), para 314.

conferred on the recipient. There are, however, different categorisations of advantage inherent in state aid law. First, there is the economic advantage inherent in aid being granted, whereby the recipient is in a better position than it would have been in the absence of the measure that granted the aid.[32] An aid measure gives rise to an economic advantage for a beneficiary where, as a result of the measure in question, its financial position is improved as compared to the position it would be in without the adoption of the measure.[33] Second, a selective advantage will arise where the economic advantage in question applies only to favour certain undertakings or the production of certain goods. In this regard, in the case of schemes of aid, it must be determined that the measure is such as to favour certain undertakings or the production of certain goods compared to others which, in the light of the objective pursued by the system in question, are in a comparable legal and factual situation.[34] In the case of grants of aid to individual beneficiaries of an ad hoc measure, however, the aid may be presumed to favour those beneficiaries selectively without there being a need to show a comparator non-beneficiary.[35] Third, the General Court has also stated that whether there is an advantage must be examined in the light of the anti-competitive effects caused by the measure in question.[36] Anti-competitive effects are, however, properly considered in the context of distortion of competition. As regards selectivity, the correct comparison is with undertakings that are in a comparable factual and legal situation in the light of the objective of the system, which is not limited to competitors of the recipient. For example, where a derogation from corporation tax favours certain undertakings, the comparison to be made is with the tax treatment of all other undertakings liable to corporation tax in the Member State, regardless of whether they are also competitors of the aid recipient. It follows that competitive advantage is not a proper criterion in the context of assessing whether there is an aid, as opposed to a distortion of competition caused by the aid. On the other hand, the criteria of economic advantage and selective advantage must be satisfied.

4.4 Occasionally, reference is made to a selective economic advantage or just to the bare notion of advantage. Indeed, especially in the case of aid schemes where some element of financial advantage is clear, the Commission and the Courts are happy to assume that there is an economic advantage and focus solely on whether the advantage is selective. As regards individual aid measures, the Commission has taken the view that whether a tax measure constituted a derogation from the reference system would generally coincide

32 *Italy v Commission* (Case 173/73), para 13.

33 *Greece v Commission* (Case T-314/15), para 47.

34 *Adria-Wien Pipeline and Wietersdorfer & Peggauer Zementwerke* (Case C-143/99), para 41.

35 *Orange v Commission* (Case C-211/15P), paras 53–54; *Commission v MOL* (Case C-15/14P), para 60.

36 *Ryanair Ltd v Commission* (Case T-500/12), para 65; *Aer Lingus Ltd v Commission* (Case T-473/12), para 43; *Luxembourg v Commission* (Joined Cases T-755/15 and T-759/15), para 182.

with the identification of the advantage granted to the beneficiary under that measure. In its view, where a tax measure results in an unjustified reduction of the tax liability of a beneficiary who would otherwise be subject to a higher level under the reference system, that reduction constitutes both the advantage granted by the tax measure and the derogation from the reference system. In that regard, the General Court held that the Commission's approach of examining the criteria of advantage and selectivity concurrently was not itself incorrect, given that both the advantage and the selective nature of that advantage were examined. Nevertheless, it held that it was appropriate to consider, first of all, whether the Commission was entitled to conclude that there was an advantage before going on, if necessary, to examine whether that advantage had to be considered as selective.[37] Normally, in any event, where a tax advantage is granted on an *ad hoc* individual basis, selectivity is presumed without it being necessary to determine that the measure introduces differential treatment between operators that are in a comparable factual and legal situation in light of the objective of the tax system.[38]

DIRECT TAXATION AND THE CRITERION OF SELECTIVITY

4.5 A measure is selective only if, within the context of a particular legal regime, it has the effect of conferring an advantage on certain undertakings over others which are, in the light of the objective pursued by that regime, in a comparable legal and factual situation.[39] In the context of taxation, a three-step test has been sanctioned by the European Courts for determining whether a measure gives rise to state aid within Article 107(1) TFEU. First, it is necessary to establish the relevant reference framework. Second, the measure must derogate from that reference framework, in which case there is a presumption of aid. Third, the measure will not be regarded as aid if the derogation is justified by the nature and general structure of the tax system of which it forms a part.

The notion of selectivity in tax matters was first developed in the context of regional taxation. Since state aid may be granted by any public authority, whether central, regional or local, it follows that aid may be granted through tax measures adopted by provincial authorities which mitigate the tax burden imposed on undertakings within their jurisdiction.[40] However, the question arose, given that state aid may be granted in any form whatsoever, as to whether state aid automatically followed where a regional authority exercising

37 *Netherlands v Commission* (Joined Cases T-760/15 and T-636/16), para 129; *Luxembourg v Commission* (Joined Cases T-755/15 and T-759/15), para 122.

38 *Greece v Commission* (Case T-314/15), para 81.

39 *Commission v Hansestadt Lübeck* (Case C-524/14P), para 58.

40 *Territorio Histórico de Álava – Disputación Foral de Álava v Commission* (Joined Cases T-127/99, T-129/99 and T-148/99), paras 162–70.

its own taxing powers legislated in a manner that imposed a lower burden of taxation than that applicable in other regions of the same Member State. Despite the Commission's argument that such legislation did constitute state aid, the CJEU held that the very existence of an advantage may be established only when compared with normal taxation, the normal tax rate being the rate in force in the geographical area constituting the reference framework. Since the reference framework need not necessarily be defined within the limits of the Member State concerned, a measure conferring an advantage in only one part of the national territory is not selective on that ground alone. On the contrary, an infra-state body may enjoy a legal and factual status which makes it sufficiently autonomous in relation to the central government of a Member State, with the result that, by the measures it adopts, it is that body and not the central government which plays a fundamental role in the definition of the political and economic environment in which undertakings operate. In such a case it is the area in which the infra-state body responsible for the measure exercises its powers, and not the territory of the Member State as a whole, that constitutes the relevant context for the assessment of whether a measure adopted by such a body favours certain undertakings in comparison with others in a comparable legal and factual situation, having regard to the objective pursued by the measure or the legal system concerned.[41] In consequence, regional tax measures which apply throughout the particular region will not amount to state aid by virtue of the fact that they result in a lower tax burden that applies in other regions of the Member State concerned, as long as the regional authority has sufficient institutional, procedural and economic autonomy.[42]

Selectivity based on criteria other than regional authority is collectively known as material selectivity. In order to ascertain whether a tax measure is materially selective, it is necessary to identify the relevant reference framework, the objective pursued by the measure, the extent to which other undertakings that are in comparable factual and legal situation, and whether the differentiation in tax treatment is justified by the nature of the general system.

4.6 In regard to the relevant reference framework, normal taxation is defined by the national tax rules so that tax rules of another Member State are not relevant.[43] In most cases, the parameters of the scheme in question are established by the relevant legislative provisions. However, having regard to the notion that state aid is defined by the effects of the measure and in order to ensure that the use of regulatory technique does not circumvent the state aid rules, it is not always necessary that the measure in question should

---

41 *Portugal v Commission* (Case C-88/03), paras 56–58.

42 *Portugal v Commission* (Case C-88/03), para 67; *Unión General de Trabajadores de la Rioja v Juntas Generales del Territorio Histórico de Vizcaya* (Joined Cases C-428/06 and C-434/06), para 51.

43 *Spain v Commission* (Case C-73/03), para 28.

derogate from a tax system considered to be an ordinary system.[44] The tax system in question may be a general tax, such as corporate income tax, or it may have a more specific scope, such as energy or environmental taxes. The reference system is based on such elements as the tax base, the taxable persons, the taxable event and the tax rates.[45] It constitutes the benchmark against which the selectivity of a measure is assessed.[46] Thus, for instance, in order to decide whether a special method of calculating taxable profits in Belgium for coordination centres of multinational groups constituted an advantage, it was necessary to compare that regime to the ordinary system of taxation of company profits.[47] In assessing an exemption from Spanish property tax, the relevant reference framework was established by the Spanish legislation which declared that any ownership or use of land entailed, in principle, liability to property tax.[48] A specific reference framework may be capable of being carved out within the scope of a wider tax regime, particularly in corporate income tax. Nevertheless, this does not allow for too narrow a definition to be applied. For example, the General Court rejected an argument that taxation of public infrastructure works was a reference system in itself, independent of general taxation, as this would result in favourable tax treatment being considered a distinct framework.[49] The reference framework in Spanish corporate income tax law for assessing tax deductibility on the acquisition of a shareholding was identified as the tax treatment of goodwill, which provided that goodwill could be amortised following a business combination.[50] The measure, which allowed for deductibility in the case of the acquisition of non-Spanish companies but not of Spanish companies, did not introduce a new general rule in its own right relating to amortisation of goodwill, but an exception to the general rule that only business combinations may lead to the amortisation of goodwill.[51] Similarly, concerning carry-forward of losses permitted under German corporate tax legislation, a restriction on the carry-forward rules applied in the case of certain specified acquisitions of shareholdings, whilst an exception to that restriction applied in the case of internal corporate restructuring satisfying certain conditions. The General Court upheld the Commission's finding that the rule governing the restriction of loss carry-forward constituted the general rule, with the exception to that restriction constituting the derogation.[52] On

44 *Commission v Government of Gibraltar* (Joined Cases C-106/09P and C-107/09P), paras 81–83; *Commission v World Duty Free Group SA* (Joined Cases C-20/15P and C-21/15P), para 77.

45 Commission Notice on the notion of State aid, para 134; *Poland v Commission* (Joined Cases T-836/16 and T-624/17), para 65; *Hungary v Commission* (Case T-20/17), para 80.

46 Commission 2016 Notice on the notion of State aid, para 132; *World Duty Free Group SA v Commission* (Case T-219/10 RENV), para 97.

47 *Belgium and Forum 187 ASBL v Commission* (Joined Cases C-182/03 and C-217/03), para 95.

48 *Ministerio de Defensa v Concello de Ferrol* (Case C-522/13), para 36.

49 *Greece v Commission* (Case T-314/15), paras 90–93.

50 *World Duty Free Group v Commission* (Case T-219/10 RENV), para 113.

51 *World Duty Free Group v Commission* (Case T-219/10 RENV), para 135.

52 *Heitkamp BauHolding GmbH v Commission* (Case T-287/11), para 107; *GFKL Financial Services AG v Commission* (Case T-620/11), para 115.

appeal, the CJEU held that the selectivity of a tax measure cannot be precisely assessed on the basis of a reference framework consisting of some provisions that have been artificially taken from a broader legislative framework. By excluding the general rule of loss carry-forward, the relevant reference framework had been defined too narrowly.[53] In two cases where turnover taxes were levied at progressive rates, the Commission, finding that these constituted state aid schemes in that some undertakings were taxed at a substantially lower rate compared to other undertakings that were in a comparable situation, held the reference system was the turnover tax itself but that the progressive structure of the tax did not form part of that reference system. However, the General Court held that whether tax is levied at a single rate or at a progressive rate, the tax rate forms part of the fundamental characteristics of a tax levy's legal regime.[54]

The next step in order to determine whether a measure is selective is to determine whether, within the context of a particular legal regime, it constitutes an advantage for certain undertakings as compared with others which are in a comparable legal and factual situation in light of the objective pursued by that measure. Account must be taken of the objective of the common regime as a whole.[55] Clearly, the objective of a tax measure is to raise public finance. However, that is an objective of all taxes and is generally insufficient of itself to identify the relevant objective of any tax, which must be more focussed. Thus, the objective of corporation tax is to tax company profits in the Member State in question.[56] When the Gibraltar authorities sought to introduce a new corporation tax with bases of assessment resulting in no tax liability for offshore companies, the CJEU still regarded those companies as falling within the scope of the tax, the objective of which was to introduce a general system of taxation for all companies established in Gibraltar.[57] A Spanish regional tax on large retail establishments was held to have as its purpose a contribution towards environmental protection and town and country planning, by having those establishments contribute toward the financing of environmental action plans and making improvements to infrastructure works.[58] Another Spanish tax, on the use of inland waters for the production of electricity, was aimed at the protection and improvement of public water resources, even though the tax also had an economic objective.[59] Having established the objective pursued by the tax measure, it is then necessary to prove that it introduces differential treatment between undertakings that are in a comparable legal and

53 *Andres v Commission* (Case C-203/16P), para 103; *Lowell Financial Services GmbH v Commission* (Case C-219/16P), para 106.

54 *Poland v Commission* (Joined Cases T-836/16 and T-624/17), para 65; *Hungary v Commission* (Case T-20/17), para 80.

55 *Finanzamt B v A-Brauerei* (Case C-374/17), para 41; *World Duty Free Group v Commission* (Case T-219/10 RENV), para 145.

56 *Ministero dell'Economia e delle Finanze v Paint Graphos* (Cases C-78/08–C-80/08), para 54.

57 *Commission v Government of Gibraltar* (Joined Cases C-106/09P and C-107/09P), para 101.

58 *ANGED v Generalitat de Catalunya* (Case C-233/16), paras 52–53.

59 *UNESA v Administración General del Estado* (Cases C-105/18–C-113/18), paras 66–69.

factual situation in light of that objective.[60] With regard to general taxation, undertakings subject to income or corporation tax are in a comparable legal and factual situation in light of the objective of that tax, which is to collect revenue on the basis of corporate profits. In a case concerning an exemption from property tax granted to an undertaking operating in the Spanish defence sector, it was held that not only undertakings which owned or used land for purposes partly related to national defence were in a comparable factual and legal situation in the light of the objective of taxing the ownership or use of land, but also those undertakings which owned or used land for exclusively civil purposes.[61] By contrast, where an environmental tax applied only to retail establishments with a sales area of a specified threshold, it was recognised that the environment impact of retail establishments is largely dependent on their size. Consequently, a condition relating to sales area thresholds was consistent with the objective pursued, such that retail establishments of a size lower than the threshold were not in a comparable situation to retail establishments subject to the tax in the light of the objectives pursued by the legislation. On the other hand, an exception to the tax applicable only to large retail establishments pursuing such business as, for example, a garden centre or selling vehicles or DIY stores, was held to be a selective advantage as it constituted a derogation as those establishments were in a comparable situation to other large establishments.[62] Nevertheless, the circumstances of categories of undertakings falling within the scope of a tax may differ so that they are not treated as being in a comparable legal and factual situation. For instance, cooperatives, which were characterised by various factors that distinguished them from other corporate entities, were held not to be in a comparable legal and factual situation to other undertakings for the purposes of Italian corporation tax.[63] By contrast, Spanish undertakings which acquired shareholdings in non-resident companies were, in the light of the objective pursued by the tax treatment of goodwill, in a comparable factual and legal situation to that of undertakings which acquire shareholdings in resident companies. Since there was no general provision that undertakings may benefit from the amortisation of goodwill in respect of the mere acquisition of shareholdings, the provision permitting amortisation in the case where a company acquired shares in a foreign company derogated from the normal regime.[64]

4.7 In recent years, the Commission has expended considerable effort in tackling fiscal state aid which it alleges arises out of certain tax rulings misapplying the arm's length principle in the context of transfer pricing arrangements between associated companies. The arm's length principle is based, in general, on comparing the conditions of a transaction between

60 *Commission v Netherlands* (Case C-279/08P), para 62.
61 *Ministerio de Defensa v Concello de Ferrol* (Case C-522/13), para 40.
62 *ANGED v Generalitat de Catalunya* (Case C-233/16), paras 53–58.
63 *Ministero dell'Economia e delle Finanze v Paint Graphos* (Cases C-78/08–C-80/08), para 61.
64 *World Duty Free Group v Commission* (Case T-219/10 RENV), paras 122–24.

affiliated companies with the conditions of a transaction between independent companies. In this context, the Commission held that the objective of the national corporate income tax system was to tax the profits of all companies, whether or not integrated, and that both types of company were in a similar factual and legal situation in the light of that objective.[65] However, in the context of determining the fiscal position of an integrated company which is part of a group of undertakings, the General Court noted at the outset that the pricing of intra-group transactions carried out by that company is not determined under market conditions. In so far as that pricing is agreed to by companies belonging to the same group, it is therefore not subject to market forces. Nevertheless, where national tax law does not make a distinction between integrated undertakings and stand-alone undertakings for the purposes of their tax liability, that law is intended to tax the profit arising from the economic activity of the integrated undertaking as though it had arisen from transactions carried out at market prices. In those circumstances, a comparison may be made of the fiscal burden resulting from the application by the tax authorities of a fiscal measure applied to the integrated undertaking with the fiscal burden resulting from the application of the normal rules of taxation applied to an undertaking, in a comparable factual situation, carrying on its activities under market conditions.[66] Thus, the General Court endorsed the Commission's position that the arm's length principle derived from the application of Article 107(1) TFEU and not, in this context, from national law.

A measure which creates an exception to the application of the general tax system may be justified by the nature and overall structure of the tax system only if the Member State concerned can show that that measure results directly from the basic or guiding principles of its tax system.[67] The General Court has stated that what is necessary is that the intended variation must not be arbitrary, that it must be applied in a non-discriminatory manner and must remain consistent with the objective of the tax concerned.[68] The burden lies on the Member State to justify the differentiation.[69] In order for tax exemptions to be justified by the nature or general scheme of the tax system of the Member State concerned, it is also necessary to ensure that those exemptions are consistent with the principle of proportionality and do not go beyond what is necessary, in that the legitimate objective being pursued could not be attained by less farreaching measures.[70] Tax exemptions which are the result of an objective that is unrelated to the tax system of which they form part cannot circumvent

---

65 *Netherlands v Commission* (Joined Cases T-760/15 and T-636/16), para 137; *Luxembourg v Commission* (Joined Cases T-755/15 and T-759/15), para 129.

66 *Netherlands v Commission* (Joined Cases T-760/15 and T-636/16), paras 148–49; *Luxembourg v Commission* (Joined Cases T-755/15 and T-759/15), paras 140–41.

67 *P Oy* (Case C-6/12), para 22.

68 *Poland v Commission* (Joined Cases T-836/16 and T-624/17), para 91; *Hungary v Commission* (Case T-20/17), para 103.

69 *Portugal v Commission* (Case C-88/03), para 80.

70 *Ministero dell'Economia e delle Finanze v Paint Graphos* (Cases C-78/08–C-80/08), para 75.

the requirements under Article 107(1) TFEU.[71] Accordingly, a distinction must be made between, on the one hand, the objectives attributed to a particular tax scheme which are extrinsic to it and, on the other, the mechanisms inherent in the tax system itself which are necessary for the achievement of such objectives.[72] Intrinsic basic or guiding principles of the tax system or inherent mechanisms necessary for the functioning and effectiveness of the system alone may justify a derogation.[73] Extrinsic or external matters include objectives of general economic policy.[74] It follows that social or regional objectives fall outside the scope of the justification, whereas objectives that are inherent in the tax system itself, such as efficiency in tax collection and progressive taxation, may come within it.[75] A tax exemption seeking to avoid double taxation may be regarded as intrinsic to the tax system and therefore stemming from the nature and general scheme of the system of which it forms a part.[76] By contrast, tax measures relating to the Italian banking sector were held not to be justified by the nature and general scheme of the Italian tax system, given that they did not represent an adaptation of the general system to meet particular characteristics of banking undertakings, but were intended as a means of improving the competitiveness of certain banking undertakings.[77] An exemption for certain categories of business, including garden centres, car dealers and DIY stores, from a Spanish environmental tax on large retail establishments was held to be capable of being justified as having fewer adverse effects on the environment since, by their very nature, they required large sales areas that were not intended to attract the greatest number of consumers who travelled there by private vehicle. On the other hand, the fact that collective large retail establishments were exempt from the tax was a selective advantage which was not justifiable.[78]

SPECIAL TAXES AND PARAFISCAL LEVIES

4.8 Subject to EU rules on harmonisation, Member States retain the power to adopt taxes or levies that apply in respect of particular goods or services. Accordingly, a tax imposed on certain undertakings does not normally constitute state aid to other undertakings which are not subject to the same tax. Nevertheless, any new tax imposed on a given category of economic operators may be viewed in theory as an advantage conferred upon all operators who

71 *British Aggregates Association v Commission* (Case T-210/02 RENV), para 48.

72 *Portugal v Commission* (C-88/03), para 81; *Finanzamt B v A-Brauerei* (Case C-374/17), para 48.

73 Commission 2016 Notice on the notion of State aid, para 138.

74 *Territorio Histórico de Álava – Diputación Foral de Álava v Commission* (Case T-227/01 etc.), para 183.

75 *P Oy* (Case C-6/12), para 29; *Greece v Commission* (Case T-314/15), para 103.

76 *Finanzamt B v A-Brauerei* (Case C-374/17), para 52.

77 *Italy v Commission* (Case C-66/02), para 101; *Unicredito Italiano SpA v Agenzia delle Entrate, Ufficio Genova 1* (Case C-148/04), para 51.

78 *ANGED v Generalitat de Catalunya* (Case C-233/16), paras 59–61.

are not subject to that tax but are in more or less close competition with the first category.[79] In order to determine whether or not a measure imposing a special levy is selective for the purposes of applying Article 107(1) TFEU, as with general taxation, it is necessary to examine whether, within the context of a particular legal system, that measure constitutes an advantage for certain undertakings by comparison with others which are in a comparable legal and factual situation in light of the objective of the measure in question.[80] This requires the determination of the proper reference framework for assessing which undertakings are in such a comparable situation.[81] However, whereas with general taxation the issue is whether or not a derogation may apply, with special taxes the additional question is whether certain persons or transactions have been excluded from the scope of the tax.[82] For example, with Spanish regional legislation establishing a tax on large retail establishments exceeding a specified sales area, although the tax criterion relating to the sales area did not appear to formally derogate from a given legal reference framework, its effect was nonetheless to exclude retail establishments whose sales area was less than that threshold from the scope of the tax. In that connection, it had therefore to be determined whether the retail establishments thus excluded from the scope of the tax were in a comparable situation to the establishments that came within its scope, bearing in mind the fact that it fell within the competence of the Member States to designate bases of assessment and to spread the tax across the various factors of production and economic sectors.[83]

This issue is of particular importance where the effect of levying a special tax on certain operators leads to a distortion of competition with other economic operators. Where, in circumstances where there existed only two directly competing distribution channels for a particular category of products, a special tax was imposed solely in respect of one channel with the objective of restoring the balance of competition, which had been distorted by the imposition of public service obligations on the other channel, this was equated to granting the latter a tax exemption whereby the authorities had, in practice, waived their right to receive tax payments, thus conferring upon them an economic advantage. The tax itself imposed on the single channel of distribution was held to constitute state aid inasmuch as it did not apply to the other channel in so far as the advantage exceeded the additional costs borne in discharging the public service obligations. Indeed, the CJEU held that the measure constituting the aid was the tax on itself and not some exemption from that tax.[84] However, a special excise duty imposed on the use of nuclear fuel which increased the costs of producing electricity from nuclear energy was held not to form

79 *Ferring SA v ACOSS* (Case C-53/00), *per* Advocate General Tizzano, at paras 36–39.

80 *Adria-Wien Pipeline GmbH v Finanzlandesdirektion für Kärnten* (Case C-143/99) [2001] ECR I-8365, para 41.

81 *Portugal v Commission* (Case C-88/03) [2006] ECR I-7115, para 56.

82 *British Aggregates Association v Commission* (Case C-487/06P) [2008] ECR I-10515, para 2.

83 *ANGED v Generalitat de Cattalunya* (Case C-233/16), paras 46–50.

84 *Laboratoires Boiron SA v URSSAF* (Case C-526/04), paras 36–39.

part of a regime for the taxation of energy sources used for the production of electricity. On the contrary, the tax was a special levy aimed at raising revenue to deal with the costs of storing radioactive waste which, in the context of electricity production, arose only in connection with electricity produced from nuclear energy.[85]

In principle, tax measures which serve to finance an aid do not themselves necessarily fall within the scope of application of the state aid provisions.[86] An aid measure cannot, however, be considered separately from the effects of its method of financing.[87] It must only be determined that the tax is hypothecated to the aid measure under the relevant national rules, in the sense that the revenue from the tax is necessarily allocated to the financing of the aid and has a direct impact on the amount of the aid and, consequently, on the assessment of the compatibility of that aid with the internal market.[88] For example, a charge imposed on advertising companies, which was levied specifically to finance aid for local radio stations, was to be regarded as forming an integral part of the aid scheme.[89] On the other hand, in the case of a tax on advertising that was intended to help finance an operational subsidy for French public television, the fact that the new tax was introduced to cover these costs was not sufficient, of itself, and without the existence of a regulatory act restricting the use of the tax to this effect, to show that there was a link between the new taxes and the financing of the aid in question.[90]

ENFORCEMENT OF FISCAL STATE AID RULES BY THE EUROPEAN COMMISSION

4.9 Whilst Article 107(1) TFEU provides that state aid is incompatible with the internal market, Article 107(2)–(3) TFEU provides that aid may, nevertheless, be declared compatible with the internal market. However, the power to declare aid compatible rests primarily with the European Commission, although in exceptional circumstances the Council may declare aid compatible. Enforcement of state aid rules is carried out pursuant to the supervisory powers set out in Article 108 TFEU and the Procedural Regulation.[91] In that connection, a distinction is drawn between new aid and existing aid, on the one hand, and between proposals to grant aid pending approval and aid that has been put into effect without approval, on the other. In principle, pursuant to Article 108(3) TFEU, all plans to grant aid must not be put into effect unless

85 *Kernkraftwerke Lippe-Ems GmbH v Hza Osnabrück* (Case C-5/14), paras 76–79.

86 *Telefónica de España SA v Commission* (Case T-151/11), para 99.

87 DTS Distribuidora de Televisión Digital SA v Commission (Case C-449/14P), para 67.

88 *Streekgewest Westelijk Noord-Brabant v Staatsecretaris van Financiën* (Case C-174/02), para 26.

89 *Régie Networks v Direction de Contrôle Fiscal Rhône-Alpes Bourgogne* (Case C-333/07), paras 100–112.

90 *TFI v Commission* (Case T-275/11), para 58.

91 Council Regulation (EU) No 2015/1589.

approved by the Commission. If the Commission grants approval, the aid may be implemented and, once implemented, becomes existing aid and is regarded as lawful. Aid is also deemed to be existing aid where it was already in effect at the time the Member State acceded to the EU. On the other hand, where aid is put into effect without waiting for approval, it is regarded as unlawful aid, is prohibited and must be repaid in full.

Article 107(2)–(3) TFEU establishes a number of categories of aid that may be deemed compatible with the internal market. The most important and wide-ranging of these is in Article 107(3)(c) TFEU which provides for approval of aid to facilitate the development of certain economic activities or of certain economic areas, as long as such aid does not adversely affect trading conditions to an extent contrary to the common interest. Other notable categories are aid to make good the damage caused by natural disasters or exceptional occurrences,[92] aid to promote economic development in poorer regions,[93] aid for the execution of an important project of common European interest or to remedy a serious disturbance in the economy of a Member State,[94] and aid to promote culture and heritage conservation.[95]

The Commission distinguishes between what is sometimes described as good aid, which is well-designed and targeted at identified market failures and objectives of common interest, and bad aid, which does not provide real incentives for companies, crowds out private investment and keeps inefficient and non-viable companies on life support.[96] The Commission has identified various categories of aid for which it has designed detailed guidelines or policies, including regional aid, aid for SMEs, training and education, R&D&I, environmental protection, agriculture, broadband, aviation, and aid for rescue and restructuring of firms in difficulty. Frameworks of specific rules were adopted to deal with the 2008 financial crisis, allowing aid for banks, in particular, and for the 2020 Covid-19 crisis, allowing state intervention on a much wider basis. The effect of the adoption of guidelines is equivalent to the effect of a limitation imposed by the Commission on itself in the exercise of its discretion so that, if a Member State notifies the Commission of proposed state aid which complies with those guidelines, the Commission must, as a general rule, authorise that proposed aid.[97] In addition to these guidelines, a number of Regulations have been adopted putting in place, for instance, a block exemption[98] covering a wide range of limited aid measures, typically allowing up to 10-15% of the investment costs of a project, and a *de minimis* rule,[99] whereby aid up to €200,000 over three years may be awarded to any undertaking. On the

92 Article 107(2)(b).
93 Article 107(3)(a).
94 Article 107(3)(b).
95 Article 107(3)(d).
96 *Report on Competition Policy* (2012), accompanying document, p 1.
97 *Kotnik v Slovenia* (Case C-526/14), para 43.
98 Commission Regulation (EU) No 651/2014.
99 Council Regulation (EC) No 994/98; Commission Regulation (EU) No 1407/2013.

other hand, an unpublished internal working document which is not intended to produce external effects does not bind the Commission.[100]

Normally, for aid to be permitted, it should be linked to investment. Aid must have an incentive effect, such that, in particular, a finding that an aid measure is not necessary can arise from the fact that the aid project has already been completed, or even started, by the undertaking concerned prior to the application for aid being submitted to the competent authorities. In such a case, the aid concerned cannot operate as an incentive.[101] Aid which is not linked to investment is treated as operating aid that merely reduces the operating expenses of a business and cannot be regarded as facilitating economic development. It follows that a mere reduction in tax which is not directly related to investment will normally not be approved. Operating aid includes aid granted indirectly in the form of tax relief granted to individuals in respect of investment in companies, where the companies are free to use the funds for any purpose.[102] Thus, a Spanish measure allowing for complete exemption from corporation tax for ten years on condition that the taxpayer invested a certain amount in fixed assets and created at least 10 jobs was held to be operating aid, as the tax relief was not specifically linked to either investment or job creation but depended on achieving taxable profits, subject to compliance with the relevant conditions.[103] Tax relief for costs of listing on a stock exchange was considered as operating aid since it was not concerned with a specific investment, but was an operation by which companies pursued financial objectives with a view to obtaining access to capital.[104] Operating aid is allowed, exceptionally, in certain cases relating, for example, to public service obligations, transport services and environmental protection, such as new energy taxes. A further essential condition for ensuring the assessment of aid is that it must be transparent. Transparency requires that opaque aid must not be introduced and that all aid must be capable of being measured as a percentage of the investment or expenditure incurred by the recipient.[105] As regards aid comprised in fiscal measures, transparency will be established where the measure provides for a cap ensuring that the applicable threshold is not exceeded.[106]

4.10 The procedure to be followed by the Commission, the Member States, aid recipients and other interested parties is set out in detail in the Procedural Regulation. The basic procedure for the Commission to assess new aid is straightforward. The Member State must first make a full notification, although

100 *Magic Mountain Kletterhallen GmbH v Commission* (Case T-162/13), para 56.

101 *Djebel-SGPS SA v Commission* (Case T-422/07), para 124.

102 *Germany v Commission* (Case C-156/98), para 30.

103 *Territorio Histórico de Álava – Diputación Foral de Álava v Commission* (Cases T-30/01 etc.), para 227.

104 *Italy v Commission* (Case C-458/09P), para 64.

105 Council Resolution of 20 October 1971, para 4.

106 Commission Regulation (EU) No 651/2014, Article 5(2)(d).

this may in fact be preceded by informal contacts in order to ensure that the notified measure will not present any particular problems. The Commission must then take a decision finding that the measure does in fact not constitute state aid or that it is aid that is clearly compatible with the internal market. Alternatively, if it cannot adopt either of those decisions, it must find that it is faced with serious doubts as to the compatibility of the measure and take a decision to open a formal investigation. During the formal investigation, it invites comments from the Member States and interested parties and conducts a detailed examination of the measure, following which it may, again, find that the measure is not state aid or that the aid is compatible with the internal market, possibly with conditions attached. If it cannot take either of those decision, it must find that the aid is incompatible with the internal market and decide that it must not be put into effect. Existing aid must be kept under constant review by the Commission. If it appears to the Commission that the aid has become incompatible with the internal market, it should propose to the Member State concerned that it amend or abolish the aid going forward, although this does not have any retroactive effect on the legality of the aid measure.

Where aid has been put effect without being notified to or approved by the Commission in accordance with Article 108(3) TFEU, it will be regarded as unlawful aid. The Commission, when it becomes aware of the measure, either of its own motion or following a complaint from an interested party, will investigate the matter and require the Member State to notify the measure in full. Largely the same decision-making process applies in determining whether the measure is aid, or aid that is compatible or aid that is not compatible. In the event that the Commission takes a final decision finding that the aid is incompatible with the internal market, it will, in addition to declaring the aid incompatible, require that the measure be retroactively abolished and that any aid already granted be recovered. The Commission, however, has no power to make a recovery order in the case of unnotified aid which is subsequently determined to be compatible with the internal market. A Member State to whom a decision is addressed obliging it to recover aid is obliged, pursuant to Article 288 TFEU, to take all the necessary measures to ensure the implementation of the decision. This must result in the actual recovery of the sums owed in order to eliminate the distortion of competition caused by the competitive advantage procured by the unlawful aid.[107]

The obligation on a Member State to abolish unlawful aid has as its main purpose the re-establishment of the previously existing situation by eliminating the distortion of competition caused by the competitive advantage afforded by the aid.[108] Recovery cannot, therefore, be challenged as entailing any element of unjust enrichment to the authority receiving the recovered amounts, since it is only recovering the amount that should not have been paid to the aid

107 *Commission v Poland* (Case C-331/09), para 55.

108 *Commission v Italy* (Case C-348/93), para 26.

recipient.[109] Moreover, the recipient of fiscal aid cannot claim that, in the absence of the aid measure, it would have organised its affairs differently so as to be subject to an alternative tax liability. Thus, where aid was granted through tax reductions to undertakings in the Italian banking sector, it was held that it would not be right to determine the amounts to be repaid in the light of various operations which could have been implemented by the undertakings if they had not opted for the type of operation which was coupled with the aid. Re-establishing the *status quo ante* means returning, as far as possible, to the situation which would have prevailed if the operations at issue had been carried out without the tax reduction. The CJEU held that this does not imply reconstructing past events differently on the basis of hypothetical elements such as the choices, often numerous, which could have been made by the operators concerned, since the choices actually made with the aid might prove to be irreversible. [110] Moreover, recovery of aid entails the restitution of the advantage procured by the aid for the recipient, not the restitution of any economic benefit the recipient may have enjoyed as a result of exploiting that advantage. That benefit may not be the same as the advantage constituting the aid and there may indeed be no such benefit.[111]

4.11 The recovery obligation is, however, subject to the qualification that recovery of aid may not be ordered by the Commission if this would be contrary to a general principle of EU law such as respect for the principles of legitimate expectations and legal certainty, proportionality and equal treatment. However, since recovery is the logical consequence of a finding that aid is unlawful, it cannot in principle be regarded as disproportionate,[112] nor does it constitute a penalty.[113] Where unlawful aid had been granted in the form of a tax exemption, that recovery of the aid does not require recovery in the form of a retroactive tax. Rather, recovery can be achieved merely by ordering the undertakings which had received the aid to pay sums corresponding to the amount of the tax exemption unlawfully granted to them.[114] Respect for the principle of equal treatment must be reconciled with the principle of legality, which means that no one may invoke in his favour an illegality committed in favour of others. Thus, where the Commission declared the non-taxation of certain ports in the Netherlands as giving rise to incompatible aid, the applicants could not rely on the fact that the Commission did not also require Belgium, Germany and France to abolish aid to their ports.[115] The right to rely on the principle of respect for legitimate expectations generally presupposes that three conditions are fulfilled. First, precise, unconditional and consistent

109 *SNCM v Commission* (Case T-454/13), para 269.

110 *Unicredito Italiano SpA v Agenzia delle Entrate, Ufficio Genova 1* (Case C-148/04), paras 114–18.

111 *Commission v Aer Lingus* (Joined Cases C-164/15P and C-165/16P), para 92.

112 *Belgium v Commission* (Case C-142/87), para 66.

113 *Commission v Aer Lingus* (Joined Cases C-164/15P and C-165/16P), para 114.

114 *Commission v Greece* (Case C-183/91), para 17.

115 *Groningen Seaports NV v Commission* (Case T-160/16), paras 116–18.

assurances originating from authorised and reliable sources must have been given by the EU institution concerned to the person concerned. Second, those assurances must be such as to give rise to an expectation that is legitimate on the part of the person to whom they are addressed. Third, the assurances given must be consistent with the applicable rules.[116] Thus, the Commission did not order recovery in its decision finding that Spanish legislation allowing for tax advantage on the acquisition of shares in foreign companies since it had previously given written answers to the European Parliament that the legislation did not give rise to state aid.[117] However, that applied only up to the date of the Commission's decision opening the formal investigation procedure since, once that procedure had been commenced, the persons concerned could no longer entertain the notion that the provision did not give rise to state aid.[118]

ENFORCEMENT OF FISCAL STATE AID RULES BY NATIONAL COURTS AND AUTHORITIES

4.12 Implementation of the system for supervision of state aid is a matter, on the one hand, for the Commission and, on the other, for the national courts. In that regard, the national courts and the Commission fulfil distinct but complementary roles, with differing powers and responsibilities. In particular, the Procedural Regulation does not contain any provisions relating to the powers and obligations of national courts, which continue to be governed by the provisions of the TFEU.[119] The Commission recognises that the principles for the application of state aid law by the national courts are complex and has issued a notice on enforcement of state aid law by national courts in order to clarify the issues involved. In accordance with the duty of cooperation under Article 4(3) TEU, the Commission must assist national courts when they apply state aid law. The Commission is committed to helping national courts where the latter find such assistance necessary for their decision on a pending case.[120] Equally, national courts must take all the necessary measures, whether general or specific, to ensure fulfilment of their obligations under EU law and refrain from those which might jeopardise the attainment of the objectives of the EU Treaties.[121] Given that assessment of the compatibility of aid measures falls within the exclusive competence of the Commission and the Council, it follows that national courts have no jurisdiction to declare aid compatible with the internal market pursuant to Article 107(3) TFEU.[122] On the other hand,

116 *Eesti Pagar AS v Ettevõtluse Arendamise Sihtasutus* (Case C-349/17), paras 97–98.
117 *World Duty Free Group v Commission* (Case T-219/10 RENV), para 282.
118 *World Duty Free Group v Commission* (Case T-219/10 RENV), para 292.
119 *Eesti Pagar AS v Ettevõtluse Arendamise Sihtasutus* (Case C-349/17), para 110.
120 Notice on the enforcement of State aid law by national courts, paras 77–78.
121 *Mediaset v Ministero dello Sviluppo Economico* (Case C-69/13), paras 29.
122 PGE Górnictwo I Energetyka Konwnecjonalna SA v Prezes Urzędu Regulacji Energetyki (Case C-574/14), para 32.

national courts are competent to interpret and apply Article 107(1) TFEU and Article 108(3) TFEU, as well as, for instance, the block exemption regulations.

Recovery of unlawful aid, which is the responsibility of the authorities of the Member State which granted the aid, must be effected without delay and in accordance with the procedures under the national law of the Member State concerned, provided, in accordance with the principle of effectiveness, that they allow the immediate and effective execution of the Commission's decision.[123] To this end, the Member State is obliged to take all the necessary steps that are available in its legal system, without prejudice to EU law.[124] A recovery decision is addressed to the Member State, not the recipient, and the decision itself imposes no direct obligation requiring payment on the recipient as such.[125] It follows that the decision cannot be considered in itself as requiring the recipient to repay the aid, so that the amount to be repaid by virtue of the decision alone does not constitute a debt due from the recipient.[126] Consequently, a Member State which is obliged to recover unlawful aid is free to choose the means of fulfilling the recovery obligation, provided that the measures chosen do not adversely affect the scope and effectiveness of EU law.[127] According to the Commission, this implies that the authorities responsible should carefully consider the full range of recovery instruments available under national law and select the procedure most likely to secure the immediate execution of the decision.[128] If national procedural rules do not enable the enforcement of recovery, the Member State must take steps to put the necessary mechanisms in place.[129]

In proceedings where a claimant has successfully invoked the direct effect of the prohibition on the implementation of unapproved aid in Article 108(3) TFEU, national courts must order the necessary remedial action and are not limited to measures suspending the aid or preventing further grants of aid. On the contrary, they are required, having decided that any measures already taken are unlawful, to provide all appropriate available remedies, including the repayment of aid already paid. In a recent case, the CJEU was asked for the first time whether national authorities must on their own initiative recover aid that it has unlawfully granted. It held that the immediate enforceability of the prohibition on implementation extended to all aid which had been implemented without being notified to the Commission pursuant to Article 108(3) TFEU. Directly effective obligations were binding on all the authorities of the Member States, i.e. not merely national courts but also all administrative bodies, including decentralised authorities. It followed that where a national authority finds that aid that it has granted is unlawful, it is bound to adopt all appropriate

123 Council Regulation (EC) No 1589/2015, Article 16(3).

124 *Commission v Germany* (Case C-527/12), para 38.

125 *France v Commission* (Case C-574/13P(R)), para 22.

126 *France v Commission* (Case T-366/13R), para 29.

127 *Commission v Germany* (Case C-527/12), para 40.

128 Notice on the recovery of unlawful aid, para 52.

129 *Commission v France* (Case C-214/07), *per* Advocate General Sharpston, at para 76.

measures, including recovery of the aid, on its own initiative. The legal basis for such recovery derives directly from Article 108(3) TFEU.[130]

The remedies that may be imposed are, in any event, limited to a declaration that a measure constitutes unlawful aid and ordering recovery of the aid from the recipient. Persons liable to pay an obligatory contribution cannot rely on the argument that an exemption enjoyed by other persons constituted state aid in order to avoid payment of that contribution,[131] except in the exceptional case where the tax and the aid measure constitute two inseparable elements of one and the same fiscal measure.[132] Similarly, in criminal proceedings, the illegality of an aid on the basis of a tax relief does not affect the legality of the tax itself, so that the taxpayer cannot evade penal sanctions for non-payment of the tax.[133]

BREXIT AND STATE AID IN THE UK

4.13 Following the decision of the UK to exit the European Union, which took effect on 31 January 2020, the future role of the state aid provision was in significant doubt. During the transition period, which ended on 31 December 2020, effectively all EU law remained in force. State aid law, including enforceability by both the European Commission and the national courts, remained in place in its entirety during the transition period.[134] From 1 January 2021, the EU-UK Trade and Cooperation Agreement provides for a new framework of state aid control which took place immediately and which will, in due course, be supplemented in the UK by a new state aid regime.

The Withdrawal Agreement[135] between the EU and the UK contains certain transitional provisions going forward as well as certain specific continuity in relation to Northern Ireland, which remains, to a large extent, within the internal market as regards goods. The CJEU continues to have jurisdiction in proceedings commenced before the end of the transitional period and to give preliminary rulings in cases referred by the UK courts before the end of the transitional period.[136] The Commission may, for a period of four years after the end of the transitional period, bring infringement proceedings against the UK in respect of infringements that occurred before the end of the transitional period.[137] The Commission remains competent for administrative procedures, including state aid investigations, which were initiated before the end of the

130 *Eesti Pagar AS v Ettevõtluse Arendamise Sihtasutus* (C-349/17), paras 89–95.
131 *HJ Banks & Co Ltd v Coal Authority* (Case C-390/98), para 80.
132 *Laboratoires Boiron SA v URSSAF* (Case C-526/04), para 45.
133 *A v B* (Case C-486/19), paras 26–27.
134 Article 127 Withdrawal Agreement.
135 OJ 2019 C384 I/1.
136 Article 86 Withdrawal Agreement.
137 Article 87 Withdrawal Agreement.

transitional period.[138] In respect of aid granted before the end of the transitional period, the Commission may commence new investigations during a further period of four years and shall continue to be competent in those investigations beyond that four year period.[139]

As regards Northern Ireland, a Protocol attached to the Withdrawal Agreement declares that the EU state aid provisions shall continue to apply to the UK in respect of measures which affect trade in goods between Northern Ireland and the EU.[140] These include not only the substantive state aid rules, including the Commission's block exemptions, notices and guidelines, but also procedural rules, in particular the Procedural Regulation. It follows that the European Commission may continue to exercise a supervisory role over state aid that falls within the scope of the Protocol. No mention is made of how to deal with UK legislation or administrative action that entails state aid throughout the UK, including in Northern Ireland. In particular, although Northern Ireland has a devolved administration with its own financial powers, tax legislation is generally controlled by the central UK government and applied throughout the UK. It remains to be seen how fiscal state aid granted through such UK-wide legislation will be regulated by the Commission on the basis of its supervisory powers in relation to Northern Ireland. Initially, the Internal Market Bill, brought before the UK Parliament, included proposed regulatory power for the total or partial inapplicability of these rules in the UK, contrary to the clear provisions of the Withdrawal Agreement. This proposal was withdrawn following negotiations with the EU in which, according to the UK account of the discussions, for an aid measure to have an effect on trade between Northern Ireland and the EU, and thus for the state aid provisions in the Protocol to apply, there must be a genuine and direct link to Northern Ireland, Northern Ireland's integral place in the UK must be taken into account, and the potential effects of an aid measure on trade between Northern Ireland and the EU must be real and foreseeable.[141]

As regards the future, a Political Declaration was agreed in November 2019, seeking to pave the way forward for a comprehensive agreement covering trade and security.[142] The future relationship was to be based on a balance of rights and obligations, taking into account the principles of each party. This balance had to ensure the autonomy of the EU's decision making and be consistent with the EU's principles, in particular with respect to the integrity of the single market and the customs union. It had also to ensure the sovereignty of the UK, including with regard to the development of its independent trade policy.[143] Given their geographical proximity and economic interdependence, the future relationship must ensure open and fair competition, encompassing robust

---

138 Article 92(1)Withdrawal Agreement.

139 Article 93(1) Withdrawal Agreement.

140 Withdrawal Agreement, Protocol on Ireland/Northern Ireland, Article 10 and Annex 5.

141 Report of the Cabinet Office on the Northern Ireland Protocol, December 2020.

142 OJ 2019 C384 I/178.

143 Political Declaration, para 4.

commitments to ensure a level playing field. The precise nature of commitments should be commensurate with the scope and depth of the future relationship and the economic connectedness of the parties. Those commitments should prevent distortions of trade and unfair competitive advantages. To that end, the parties should uphold the common high standards applicable in the EU and the UK at the end of the transition period in the area of, inter alia, state aid. The parties were in particular to maintain a robust and comprehensive framework for competition and state aid control that prevents undue distortion of trade and competition.[144]

In anticipation of a new UK state aid regime coming into force in 2021, the *State Aid (Revocations and Amendments)(EU Exit) Regulations 2020* provide for regulations that completely disapply the entire body of EU state aid rules in the UK from the end of the transition period. Part XI, Chapter 3 of the EU-UK Trade and Cooperation Agreement sets out the framework with which both the EU state aid regime and the new UK regime must comply. Since this framework applies equally to the EU, it is natural that it reflects and is consistent with the state aid rules already in force. Nevertheless, the TCA is designated as an international agreement governed by international law, including international law principles of interpretation, and is not necessarily to be interpreted according to pre-existing EU state aid law. The new UK regime, therefore, must comply with the TCA, but is not necessarily bound to adopt the same interpretation as EU state aid law.

4.14 The TCA requires conditions that ensure a level playing field for open and fair competition between the UK and the EU.[145] The intention is to prevent distortions of trade and investment, but not to harmonise standards.[146] Whereas Article 107(1) TFEU applies where state aid distorts competition and affects trade between Member States, the TCA applies where a subsidy has, or could have, an effect on trade or investment between the Parties.[147] A subsidy is defined as financial assistance which arises from the resources of the Parties, confers an economic advantage to one or more economic actors, and is specific insofar as it benefits certain economic actors.[148] Thus, whereas EU law applies to state aid, financed by state resources that favours certain undertakings, the TCA applies to subsidies financed from resources of one of the Parties which specifically benefits certain economic actors.

The notion of fiscal state aid is generally consistent with both EU and WTO law. A tax measure shall not be considered specific unless certain economic actors obtain a reduction in tax liability that they would otherwise have borne under the normal tax regime and those economic actors are treated

---

144 Political Declaration, para 77.
145 TCA, Title XI, Article 1.1(1).
146 TCA, Title XI, Article 1.1(4).
147 TCA, Title XI, Article 3.1(1)(b)(iv).
148 TCA, Title XI, Article 3.1(1)(b)(i)–(iii). There is no reference to imputability to the state.

more advantageously than others in a comparable position within the normal taxation regime. A normal tax regime is defined by its internal objective, its features (such as tax base, taxable person, taxable event and tax rate) and by an authority which is autonomous institutionally, procedurally, economically and financially and has the competence to design the features of the taxation regime.[149] This latter criterion reflects the notion of regional fiscal selectivity and is consistent with devolution within the UK. A subsidy shall not be regarded as specific if it is justified by principles inherent to the design of the general system. In the case of tax measures, examples of such inherent principles are the need to fight fraud or tax evasion, administrative manageability, the avoidance of double taxation, the principle of tax neutrality, the progressive nature of income tax and its redistributive purpose, or the need to respect taxpayer' ability to pay.[150] Special purpose levies shall not be regarded as specific if their design is required by non-economic public policy objectives, such as the need to limit the negative impacts of certain activities or products on the environment or human health, insofar as the public policy objectives are not discriminatory.[151]

Whereas Article 107(1) TFEU declares state aid incompatible with the internal market, subject to an assessment by the Commission under Article 107(2)–(3) TFEU declaring the measure compatible, and treats such aid as prohibited, the Trade and Cooperation Agreement (TCA) takes a rather more circuitous route. First, certain types of aid are effectively treated as not subject to the state aid control regime. These include: subsidies granted to compensate for damage caused by natural disasters or other exceptional non-economic occurrences;[152] subsidies of a social character targeted at final consumer;[153] subsidies granted on a temporary basis to respond to a national or global economic emergency;[154] and subsidies to agriculture, fisheries, and in the audio-visual sector.[155] *De minimis* aid is a subsidy of less than 325,000 SDRs.[156]

Secondly, with a view to ensuring that subsidies are not granted where they have or could have a material effect on trade and investment between the parties, the TCA requires that each Party has in place an effective system of subsidy control that ensures that the granting of a subsidy respects certain principles and that the legality of an individual subsidy is determined by the principles. These principles very much reflect EU practice as regards assessment of compatibility of aid with the internal market. Thus, for example, subsidies must: pursue a specific public policy objective to identify an identified market failure; be proportionate and limited to what is necessary; be designed to bring

149 TCA, Title XI, Article 3.1(2)(a)(i)–(ii).
150 TCA, Title XI, Article 3.1(2)(b).
151 TCA, Title XI, Article 3.1(2)(c).
152 TCA, Title XI, Article 3.2(1). Cf Article 107(2(b) TFEU.
153 TCA, Title XI, Article 3.2(2). Cf, Article 107(2(a) TFEU.
154 TCA, Title XI, Article 3.2(3). Cf Article 107(3)(b) TFEU.
155 TCA, Title XI, Article 3.2(5)–(6).
156 TCA, Title XI, Article 3.2(4).

about a change of economic behaviour of the beneficiary; be an appropriate policy instrument; entail positive effects that outweigh any negative effects on trade or investment between the Parties.[157] Certain categories of subsidies are identified as prohibited[158] including unlimited state guarantees,[159] rescue and restructuring that is not accompanied by a credible restructuring plan;[160] export subsidies;[161] and subsidies contingent upon the use of domestic content.[162]

Thirdly, supervisory mechanisms may differ as between EU and UK law. In particular, although the UK is required to establish an independent regulatory authority with an appropriate role in its subsidy control regime,[163] there is no requirement in the TCA that the UK establish ex ante control of subsidies similar to the obligation under EU law that all new aid must be notified to, and approved by, the Commission prior to being put into effect. There is a transparency requirement pursuant to which certain information on subsidies, including fiscal subsidies, that have been granted must be publicised on an official website.[164] Where the EU considers that a UK subsidy (and vice versa) has or could have a negative effect on trade or investment between them, it may request an explanation as to how the TCA principles have been respected. This might give rise to consultations in the Trade Specialised Commission on the Level Playing Field for Open and Fair Competition and Sustainable Development with a view to reaching a mutually satisfactory resolution of the matter.[165]

4.15 As regards enforcement, the TCA sets out requirements that are substantially the same as the applicable EU law rules. Courts or tribunals must be competent to review subsidy decisions taken by a granting authority or the independent regulatory authority, as well as any other decisions of the regulatory body and any relevant failure to act. They must be able to impose remedies that are effective, including suspension, prohibition or requirement of action by the granting authority, award of damages, and recovery of subsidy. Interested parties may also commence proceedings where they have standing.[166] It follows that, pending the designation of the UK regulatory body, the main remedy will be by way of judicial review of grants of subsidy by the relevant granting authority in the High Court or in disputes before the tax tribunals. Any interested party intending to commence such proceedings may request from the granting authority (or the regulatory body, once established) such information as allows the interested party to assess the application of the

157 TCA, Title XI, Article 3.4(1)–(3).
158 TCA, Title XI, Article 3.5.
159 TCA, Title XI, Article 3.5(2).
160 TCA, Title XI, Article 3.5(3)–(7).
161 TCA, Title XI, Article 3.5(8)–(11).
162 TCA, Title XI, Article 3.5(12).
163 TCA, Title XI, Article 3.9.
164 TCA, Title XI, Article 3.7.
165 TCA, Title XI, Article 3.8.
166 TCA, Title XI, Article 3.10(1).

TCA subsidy principles, subject to any proportionate restrictions which pursue a legitimate objective, such as commercial sensitivity, confidentiality of legal privilege.[167]

The UK must have in force an effective recovery mechanism where the court or tribunal makes a finding of a material error of law, in that: (a) a measure constituting a subsidy was not treated by the grantor as a subsidy; (b) the grantor failed to apply the TCA subsidy principle or applied them in a manner that falls below the requisite standard; or (c) the grantor acted outside the scope of its powers or misused its powers in relation to those principles.[168] Recovery is not required where a subsidy is granted on the basis of an Act of Parliament or an act of the and/or the Council of the EU.[169] The justification for this limitation on recovery is questionable. It is certainly the case that aid granted by a Member State on the basis of an EU directive is not considered state aid, since it is not imputable to the state but to the EU, and is therefore outside the scope of Article 107(1) TFEU.[170] There is no such logic in removing legislative-based subsidies from the obligation of recovery. Subsidies granted through an Act of Parliament still fall within the scope of the TCA and may be subject to other remedies, such as suspension, declaratory prohibition or damages. However, the preclusion of a requirement of recovery may lead to the effective emasculation of such proceedings. This is likely to be most remarkable in the case of fiscal subsidies, which are generally granted through Finance Acts or other Acts of Parliament.

In any event, either Party may deliver to the other Party a written request for information and consultations, with a view to finding a mutually acceptable solution, regarding any subsidy that is considers causes, or there is a serious risk that it will cause, a significant negative effect on trade or investment between the Parties. This may lead to the requesting Party unilaterally taking appropriate remedial measures, where it relies on reliable evidence relating to identifiable goods, service suppliers or other economic operators. The remedial measures must be strictly necessary and proportionate in order to remedy the alleged significant negative effects. The underlying dispute may be referred to an arbitration tribunal.[171]

---

167 TCA, Title XI, Article 3.7(5).
168 TCA, Title XI, Article 3.11(1)-(2).
169 TCA, Title XI, Article 3.11(5).
170 *Deutsche Bahn v Commission* (Case T-351/02).
171 TCA, Title XI, Article 3.12.

Part 2

Countries

Chapter 5

Austria

Manuela Wenger and Christian Wimpissinger

INTRODUCTION

5.1 The purpose of this chapter is to analyse the main consequences of the UK leaving the EU from an Austrian tax law perspective.

The analysis of this chapter is based on the assumption that the UK will not join the EEA.

On 23 October 2018 a new double taxation treaty between Austria and the UK (DTT AT-UK) was signed. While in the UK the agreement came into force in April 2019, in Austria the new agreement has been applicable only since 1 January 2020. The new agreement has been adapted with a view to the fact that with the expiry of the transition period on 31 December 2020 the provisions of the Parent-Subsidiary Directive[1] (PSD), the Interest and Royalties Directive[2] (IRD) and the Merger Directive[3] (MD) no longer apply.[4] Moreover, the new agreement also includes provisions on arbitration proceedings (Article 23(5) DTT AT-UK) as well as on the assistance in the collection of taxes (Article 25 DTT AT-UK), while a comprehensive administrate assistance arrangement including the latest standard of tax transparency was already comprised in the old DTT AT-UK. However, the provisions concerning arbitration proceedings will be applicable only from 1 March 2021. Regarding BEPS, the newly agreed DTT AT-UK meets the minimum standard.[5] For the sake of completeness, the methods for eliminating any double taxation provided in the DTT AT-UK should be mentioned. In order to eliminate double taxation, Austria applies the credit method. However, income that is exempt from taxation in Austria under the provisions of the double tax treaty is

1 Council Directive 2011/96/EU of 30 November 2011.
2 Council Directive 2003/49/EC of 3 June 2003.
3 Council Directive 2009/133/EC of 19 October 2009.
4 *BMF*, Taxes & Brexit, available at: www.bmf.gv.at/en/current-issues/brexit/brexit-taxes.html (accessed 1 May 2020).
5 *Jirousek* in ÖStZ 10/219, Neues Doppelbesteuerungsabkommen Österreich-UK, 267.

subject to progression (*Anrechnungsmethode unter Progressionsvorbehalt*).[6] The UK generally applies the credit method to eliminate double taxation, but with regard to dividends and permanent establishment profits originating from Austria, the exemption method applies.[7]

TAX RAMIFICATIONS FOR INBOUND INVESTMENTS

Outbound dividends

5.2 In general, dividends paid by an Austrian corporation to non-resident shareholders are subject to a 27.5% withholding tax deducted by the distributing corporation.[8] If the receiving entity is a corporation within the meaning of *§ 1* of the *Austrian Corporate Income Tax Act* (*CITA*, *Körperschaftsteuergesetz*, '*KStG*'), the reduced tax rate of 25% applies.[9]

However, *§ 94(2)* of the *Austrian Income Tax Act* (*ITA*, *Einkommensteuergesetz*, '*EStG*'), which is the provision implementing the outbound rules of the PSD, foresees an exemption from withholding tax on dividends if received by EU corporations[10] that own, directly or indirectly, at least 10% of the Austrian distributing corporation's capital for an uninterrupted period of at least one year. If a dividend is paid before the one-year period has lapsed, withholding tax will be imposed, but – in line with the *Denkavit* ruling of the CJEU[11] – refunded, once the period is up.[12]

Consequently, if the conditions of the PSD, as mentioned before, are met, dividends paid to companies in the UK do not trigger withholding tax until the end of the transition period on 31 December 2020. Since 1 January 2021 the PSD no longer applies. As under domestic law, a full exemption from withholding tax is no longer granted, except as foreseen under the double taxation treaty. The new DTT AT-UK provides an exemption from withholding taxation at source comparable to the provisions of the PSD. This should ensure that the taxation of dividends to 10% corporate shareholders, in particular, within corporate groups, remains the same as before Brexit.

According to Article 10 DTT AT-UK, the primary right of taxation is generally assigned to the state of residence of the recipient of the dividend. However, with regard to portfolio investments the source state is allowed to withhold a tax up to 10%, whereas intercompany dividends are exempt from

6 *Schmidjell-Dommes* in SWI 2/2019, Das neue Doppelbesteuerungsabkommen mit Großbritannien, 62; Article 21(1) DTT AT-UK.

7 *Jirousek* in ÖStZ 10/219, Neues DBA Österreich-UK, 270; Article 21(2) DTT AT-UK.

8 *§ 98(1)(5)(a)* in combination with *§ 93(2)(1) ITA*; *§ 27a(1)(2) ITA*.

9 *§ 93(1a) ITA*.

10 An EU corporation is a corporation according to the second annex to *ITA*.

11 CJEU 17 October 1996, *Denkavit I* (Case C-283/94).

12 *§ 94(2) ITA*.

withholding tax if the beneficial owner of the dividends is a company resident in the UK that controls, directly or indirectly, at least 10% of the voting power of the company paying the dividends.[13] This exemption of withholding tax also applies to dividends if the beneficial owner is a pension fund.[14] The definition of dividends in Article 10(3) DTT AT-UK differs from the definition of dividends in the OECD Model Tax Convention: for the purposes of the DTT AT-UK any other income that is subject to the same taxation treatment as income from shares by the laws of the state of which the company making the distribution is a resident has to be treated as dividends and consequently in accordance with Article 10 DTT AT-UK. Therefore, donations from Austrian private foundations are dividends according to the DTT AT-UK. Consequently, they must be treated in accordance with Article 10 DTT AT-UK instead of Article 20 DTT AT-UK that regulates other income.[15]

Dividends paid by a relevant investment vehicle, for example, distributions from real estate investment funds, may be subject to a withholding tax of 15%.[16]

According to Article 63(1) Treaty on the Functioning of the European Union (TFEU) all limitations on the free movement of capital between EU Member States as well as between EU Member States and third countries are prohibited. With regard to portfolio investments, dividends paid to foreign corporations that are not resident in the EU may trigger withholding tax up to a remaining tax rate of generally 10 or 15% in accordance with double tax treaties, while dividends paid to domestic corporations are not subject to withholding tax. *§ 21(1)(1a) CITA* provides a refund procedure for such withheld taxes, but only for corporations with limited tax liability resident in the EU or in the EEA. Regarding third countries, such an infringement of the free movement of capital is permitted, as long as the withholding tax will be credited in the parent company's country of residence under the double tax treaty.[17] In accordance with Article 21(2) DTT AT-UK, the UK exempts dividends from taxation. Consequently, if the UK does not grant a tax credit for any Austrian withholding tax and if *§ 21(2)(1a) CITA* is no longer applicable with the expiry of the transition period on 31 December 2020, an infringement of the free movement of capital may occur. Since the DTT AT-UK provides for an exchange of information in Article 24, there is no sufficient justification for not refunding the withholding tax.[18]

13 Article 10(2)(b)(i) DTT AT-UK.

14 Article 10(2)(b)(ii) DTT AT-UK.

15 *Jirousek* in ÖStZ 10/219, Neues DBA Österreich-UK, 268.

16 Article 10(2)(a)(ii) DTT AT-UK.

17 CJEU 14 December 2006, *Denkavit Internationaal BV* (Case C-170/05); Federal Fiscal Court 21 November 2019, RV/7102891/2012; *Knesl/Knesl/Zwick-Pevny* in BFGjournal 4/2020, KESt-Rückerstattung an eine Drittstaatsgesellschaft im Lichte der Kapitalverkehrsfreiheit, 169.

18 Austrian Administrative Court 25 October 2011, 2011/15/0070; Federal Fiscal Court 21 November 2019, RV/7102891/2012.

5.2 *Austria*

Another difference in the situation before and after Brexit could, in general, occur due to a practical application of the law by the Austrian tax authorities: relief from Austrian withholding tax on outbound dividends in accordance with either the rules implementing the PSD or in accordance with a double tax treaty is only possible if the recipient of the dividends provides a resident certificate to the distributing company in which, besides its tax residency, the recipient certifies that it is not a mere holding company and that it has its own employees and its own office space.[19] If such certification is not provided, Austrian withholding taxation is imposed, and the recipient has to file a refund application for the withheld amount. Such application can only be filed and processed in the year following the distribution.[20] This mechanism allows the authorities to look into the structure and determine whether a treaty shopping case is fulfilled.[21]

A decree published by the Austrian Federal Ministry of Finance on 15 September 2020 ensures clarity in this regard.[22] The decree announces the conclusion of the consultation agreement following a mutual agreement procedure pursuant to Article 23(3) DTT AT-UK between the competent authorities of Austria and UK. The consultation agreement came into force on 2 September 2020 and provides for administrative rules and procedures concerning the relief from Austrian withholding tax in connection with dividends paid to corporations that are resident in the UK. These rules and procedures are comparable to those foreseen in the PSD.

According to the decree, the Austrian resident certificate (ie form ZS-QU2) intended for withholding tax relief for legal entities has to be used in order to make a relief from Austrian withholding tax on outbound dividends. In addition to the general information about the dividends and its recipient that has to be included in the form, the recipient has to declare that its business activities go beyond the mere holding of participations and that the company has its own personnel and its own office space. Furthermore, the form has to include a resident certificate of Her Majesty's Revenue and Customs (*HMRC*).[23] If this information or the ZS-QU2 form cannot be provided the distributing company is obliged to withhold and pay the withholding tax to the competent tax authority. In order to accomplish the relief from Austrian withholding tax on outbound dividends in accordance with the DTT AT-UK, the recipient of the dividends may apply for a refund of the withheld amount.

19 *§§ 2* and *3(1) Double Taxation Treaty Implementing Regulation.*

20 § 240a Federal Fiscal Code; *Bendlinger* in SWI 4/2019, Die Rückzahlung österreichischer Abzugsteuer nach dem Jahressteuergesetz 2018, 199.

21 Austrian Administrative Court 26 June 2014, 2011/15/0080; *Marschner* in Jakom EStG, 13th edition (2020) *§ 94 Ann. 28.*

22 Austrian Federal Ministry of Finance (BMF) 15 September 2020, BMF-2020-0.588.377, AV-Nr 136/2020.

23 Austrian Federal Ministry of Finance (BMF) 15 September 2020, BMF-2020-0.588.377, AV-Nr 136/2020, para 2.

For this purpose, the recipient has to provide evidence that all prerequisites for the relief pursuant to the DTT AT-UK are fulfilled.[24]

However, in practice, the Austrian authorities have accepted that no withholding at source is required if the dividend is paid within the EU and the direct recipient is a mere holding, but its parent is not;[25] in investment structures this is often the case. It is critically discussed among Austrian practitioners, that is, that taking into account substance at a different level also in the context of third countries should be allowed for the purpose of avoiding Austrian withholding tax on dividends.

However, regarding the UK, the decree provides for such a practical procedure as well. If the criteria required cannot be fulfilled by the recipient itself, the relief of Austrian withholding tax may also apply if the recipient is directly and exclusively owned by a corporation other than a partnership that: (i) is resident in the UK, and (ii) is not a mere holding company and has its own employees and office space. Additionally, (iii) it has to be confirmed by HMRC that the conditions (i) and (ii) are fulfilled.[26] Consequently, this practical procedure, which generally applies in relation to EU Member States, even applies after Brexit due to the decree.

Outbound interest

5.3 Interest paid to non-resident companies is generally not subject to Austrian withholding tax under purely domestic Austrian tax law, irrespective of whether the Austrian debtor pays interest to a company resident in the EU or the EEA[27] or to a company in a third country.[28] In the absence of a link between the exemption from withholding tax and the creditor's state of residence, Brexit does not change anything with regard to the exemption from withholding tax granted for outbound interest.[29]

According to the DTT AT-UK the exclusive right of taxation is generally assigned to the state of residence of the recipient of the interest (Article 11 DTT AT-UK). In conformity with Article 11(3) OECD Model Tax Convention, Austria may only tax interest attributed to an Austrian permanent establishment. However,

24 Austrian Federal Ministry of Finance (BMF) 15 September 2020, BMF-2020-0.588.377, AV-Nr 136/2020, para 3.

25 Austrian Administrative Court 27 March 2019, Ro 2018/13/0004; Express Answer Service of the Ministry of Finance of Austria, 3234 (16 August 2011); *Mitterlehner/Panholzer* in ÖStZ 23/2019, Praxisfragen zur KESt bei EU-Holdingstrukturen, 627.

26 Austrian Federal Ministry of Finance (BMF) 15 September 2020, BMF-2020-0.588.377, AV-Nr 136/2020, para 4.

27 Tax exemption in accordance to *§ 99a ITA*.

28 Tax exemption in accordance to *§ 98(1)(5)* (last sentence) *ITA* in combination with *§ 94(13)* (first case) *ITA*.

29 *Leyrer/Petutschnig* in ÖStZ 23/2016, „Brexit" und die möglichen Auswirkungen auf das österreichische Steuerrecht, 656.

with regard to genuine silent partnership participations, profit-participating loans and participation bonds, item 2 of the Protocol on Article 11 DTT AT-UK grants an unrestricted right of taxation to the source country.[30] In this respect it is worth noting that Austria does impose 27.5% of withholding tax on debt bonds that are publicly issued. In that context, however, the tax law consequences do not change because of Brexit.

Outbound royalties

5.4 Outbound royalties paid to non-resident companies are generally subject to a withholding tax of 20%.[31]

While regarding outbound interest payments, in which case a purely domestic tax exemption applies to creditors irrespective of their residency, the applicable exemption for outbound royalties is limited to the concept of the Interest and Royalties Directive (IRD), meaning that only royalties paid to recipients who are resident in the EU and who are related through at least a 25% holding, either directly (parent-subsidiary) or through a common parent (sister companies), are not subject to withholding tax if the relation has been established at least one year before the royalty payment (see *§ 99a(6) ITA*).

Since 1 January 2021, the exemption available according to the Austrian provisions implementing the IRD no longer applies vis-à-vis the UK.

However, the non-applicability of the IRD brings into scope the provisions of double taxation treaties for determining if a withholding tax exemption for outbound royalties applies; needless to say this applies within the EU and outside the EU, since the IRD-provisions are rather limited (eg, they only apply regarding certain related parties, not regarding any related parties) and, therefore, double tax treaty provisions are highly relevant. In accordance with Article 12 of the DTT AT-UK, royalties are exclusively subject to the right of taxation of the recipient's resident state. This means that no tax is withheld if royalties are paid to a beneficial owner resident in the UK. The agreement also includes a permanent establishment reservation (Article 12(3) DTT AT-UK). Moreover, the term 'royalties' does not include rental fees for equipment (moveable asset leasing).

While in theory the taxation of royalties does not change before and after Brexit, since the double tax treaty rules are more beneficial than those of the IRD, in practice there will be a rather material change: in order to apply the IRD and, thereby, ensure relief from the Austrian withholding taxation on royalties at source, the only evidence to be provided is the uninterrupted affiliation by at least 25% for one year between parent and subsidiary or between sister companies through the same parent together with a resident

30 *Jirousek* in ÖStZ 10/219, Neues DBA Österreich-UK, 268.
31 *§ 99(1)(3) ITA* in combination with *§ 100(1) ITA*.

certificate;[32] in order to apply the relief from the Austrian withholding taxation under the double tax treaty, however, the UK recipient has to provide a resident certificate and it has to prove that it is not a mere holding company, because it pursues a business going beyond the mere holding of assets, and it has to prove that it has its own employees and its own office space.[33] If such evidence is missing, no relief from withholding tax at source is possible; instead a refund application for the Austrian withholding tax has to be filed.[34]

Capital gains on shareholdings in resident companies

5.5 Brexit should not have an impact on the taxation of capital gains.

Capital gains realised by non-resident shareholders of an Austrian corporation are, in general, subject to limited tax liability if the shareholder has held shares of at least 1% within the last five years before the realisation.[35] However, no withholding applies for capital gains (unless it concerns shares held through an Austrian securities account); rather such gains would have to be declared and assessed.[36] Apart from that, Austria can usually not tax these capital gains, as double taxation treaties normally assign the right of taxation to the shareholder's state of residence.[37] This also applies with respect to the DTT AT-UK.

Article 13 DTT AT-UK provides for the taxation of capital gains more or less in accordance with the OECD Model Tax Convention 2014.[38] Article 13(5) DTT AT-UK allocates the right to tax capital gains following the disposal of shares and other interests in corporations exclusively to the state of residency of the taxpayer (*Ansässigkeitsprinzip*).[39] Consequently, as before Brexit, capital gains on shareholdings in Austrian companies made by British shareholders are not subject to tax in Austria.

However, the new treaty provides a specific clause for real estate companies (*Immobiliengesellschaftenklausel*) that contradicts Austria's position within the Multilateral Instrument (MLI) and its usual agreement policy.[40] According to Article 13(2) DTT AT-UK, capital gains following the disposal of shareholdings obtaining more than 50% of their value directly or indirectly from immovable property are subject to tax in the state where the immovable

32 *§ 99a(6)* and *(7) ITA*.
33 *§§ 2* and *3(1) Double Taxation Treaty Implementing Regulation*.
34 § 240a Federal Fiscal Code.
35 *§ 98(1)(5)(e) ITA*.
36 *§ 94(13)* and *§ 102(1)(1) ITA*.
37 *Marschner* in Jakom EStG, 13th edition (2020) § 98 Ann. 97 et seq.
38 *Jirousek* in ÖStZ 10/219, Neues DBA Österreich-UK, 269 and 269.
39 *Loukota/Jirousek*, Internationales Steuerrecht I/1, 13. Veräußerungsgewinne (Stand 1.3.2015, rdb.at) Ann. 75.
40 *Wagner*, Neues DBA zwischen Österreich und Großbritannien, available at: www.tpa-group.at/de/news/neues-dba-zwischen-oesterreich-und-grossbritannien/ (accessed 3 March 2020).

property is situated (*Belegenheitsregel*). This provision only applies for shares not substantially and regularly traded on a Stock Exchange.[41]

Permanent establishments of non-residents in Austria

5.6 If a foreign company carries on a business through a permanent establishment in Austria or participates in such a business (eg, through a partnership stake), the foreign corporation has limited tax liability in Austria, also referred to as being subject to non-resident taxation or to source taxation.[42] In general, all income earned through the activities of a non-resident company's permanent establishment or derived from assets held by the permanent establishment as business property are taxable in Austria.[43] While the Austrian right to tax may be restricted through the allocation of taxation rights provided in double taxation treaties, an expansion of the domestic tax basis is not possible.[44] Further, for residents of an EU or EEA country and of a third country the participation exemption *(§ 10 CITA*) and the CFC regime (*Hinzurechnungsbesteuerung, § 10a CITA*; refer to **5.10** for more details) apply as well.[45]

With regard to the new DTT AT-UK, the provision concerning permanent establishments (Article 5 DTT AT-UK) has not changed compared to the old treaty and corresponds to the OECD Model Tax Convention 2014 before the Authorised OECD Approach (AOA) has been implemented.[46] For example, in order to constitute a construction permanent establishment, a construction activity of more than 12 months is required. Moreover, Article 5(4) DTT AT-UK includes the usual exceptions under OECD 2014 for certain fixed places of business that do not qualify as permanent establishments because of merely preparatory or ancillary activities.[47]

Compared to the old treaty the provision regarding business profits (Article 7 DTT AT-UK) has also not changed. The new provision corresponds to the OECD Model Tax Convention 2010.[48] In accordance with Article 7(1) DTT AT-UK, profits that an enterprise of a Contracting State receives from the other Contracting State may be taxed in the other Contracting State only to the extent such profits are attributable to a permanent establishment situated in that state. According to Article 7(2) DTT AT-UK the attribution of profits

41 *Jirousek* in ÖStZ 10/219, Neues DBA Österreich-UK, 269.

42 *§ 21(1)(1) CITA* in combination with *§ 98(1)(3) ITA*.

43 *Marschner* in *Bergmann/Renner/Wurm* (eds), Praxisbeispiele zur Körperschaftsteuer (2019), 307 et seq.

44 *Marschner* in *Bergmann/Renner/Wurm* (eds), Praxisbeispiele zur Körperschaftsteuer (2019), 307; *§ 21(1)(2) CITA*.

45 ErlRV 190 BlgNR XXVI. GP, 29.

46 *Jirousek* in ÖStZ 10/219, Neues DBA Österreich-UK, 268 and 271.

47 *Schmidjell-Dommes* in SWI 2/2019, Das neue DBA mit Großbritannien, 59 et seq.

48 *Schmidjell-Dommes* in SWI 2/2019, Das neue DBA mit Großbritannien, 60.

to a permanent establishment requires that those profits could have been made independently of the enterprise of which it is a permanent establishment (*arm's length principle*). Article 7(3)–(6) DTT AT-UK contain special provisions for determining profits of permanent establishments.[49]

Consequently, as before Brexit, income of a British company from a permanent establishment in Austria or attributable thereto is taxable in Austria. A change that could arise after Brexit is that anti-abuse rules may apply differently for residents outside the EU as compared to residents of the EU, since applying a stricter standard vis-à-vis EU residents might violate a fundamental freedom such as the freedom of establishment, but not the free movement of capital; usually the freedom of establishment applies when it comes to rules addressing permanent establishments and according to the CJEU's case law applying such freedom makes it impossible to apply the free movement of capital.

Regarding corporations with limited tax liability, for example foreign corporations' permanent establishments, the deduction of losses is restricted in two ways:[50] on the one hand, the loss deduction is limited to domestic permanent establishments, and on the other hand, the loss deduction has to be primarily offset against positive foreign income.[51] Moreover, a loss deduction is only allowed if the worldwide income is negative.[52] This should ensure that the utilisation of losses in Austria is only the fallback option. However, according to the Austrian Federal Ministry of Finance, this restriction to a negative worldwide income does not apply for residents of EU and EEA countries.[53] While this, generally, also applies to third countries if a double tax treaty with a non-discrimination clause for permanent establishments (*Betrieb sstättendiskriminierungsverbot*; Article 24(3) OECD Model Tax Convention) is in place,[54] additional requirements have to be fulfilled: namely, it has to be evidenced that a loss utilisation abroad is not possible or that if there is a loss utilisation abroad, a recapture rule is in place ensuring that losses are only utilised once. Generally, this is based on the principle that losses are not utilised twice.[55] As Article 22(2) DTT AT-UK provides a non-discrimination clause for permanent establishments, there should not be any changes due to Brexit regarding loss deduction as long as the impossibility of loss utilisation in the UK can be proven. However, after Brexit, in order to arrive at the same result, more administrative burdens have to be overcome.

---

49 *Schmidjell-Dommes* in SWI 2/2019, Das neue DBA mit Großbritannien, 60.

50 *§ 21(1)(1) CITA* in combination with *§ 8(4)(2) CITA* and *§ 102(2)(2) ITA*; *Corporate Income Tax Regulations, Ann. 381.*

51 *Marschner* in Jakom EStG, 13th edition (2020) § 102 Ann. 13.

52 *§ 102(2)(2)* (last sentence) *ITA*.

53 *Income Tax Regulations, Ann. 8059* (at the end) and *Corporate Income Tax Regulations, Ann. 383*; CJEU 6 September 2012, *Philips Electronics* (Case C-18/11).

54 *Corporate Income Tax Regulations, Ann. 383*; *Marschner* in Jakom EStG, 13th edition (2020) § 102 Ann. 14 et seq.

55 Express Answer Service of the Ministry of Finance of Austria, 3385 (18 July 2017).

TAX RAMIFICATIONS FOR OUTBOUND INVESTMENTS

Inbound dividends

5.7 If an Austrian company receives dividends from a foreign company, dividends from portfolio investments (*Portfoliobeteiligungen*) are treated differently than dividends from substantial participations (*Schachtelbeteiligungen*).

With regard to portfolio investments, dividends are tax exempt irrespective of the amount and duration of the investment provided that the following two conditions are met. First, if the distributing company is not resident in the EU or the EEA, a comprehensive agreement on mutual assistance regarding the exchange of information has to be in place between Austria and the third country to enjoy a tax exemption in Austria. Second, the foreign distributing company has to be comparable to a domestic corporation.[56]

Concerning substantial participations, dividends are generally tax exempt if the Austrian company holds at least 10% of the issued share capital for at least one year.[57] In such a case the international participation privilege, often also referred to as the participation exemption, applies, whereupon capital gains are tax exempt (and capital losses are, generally, disregarded for tax purposes). However, the Austrian shareholder may exercise an option against such tax exemption (and tax irrelevance) and thereby make dividends as well as capital gains and capital losses recognised for taxation purposes. This option is irrevocable and has to be exercised in the tax return of the year of acquisition.[58]

The tax exemption for international participation of at least 10% as well as for portfolio investments of at least 5% (qualified portfolio investment, *qualifizierte Portfoliobeteiligung*) does not apply if the foreign company predominantly generates passive income and is taxed at a low rate.[59] A low tax rate is considered any rate that does not exceed 12.5%. In this case a shift (switch over, *Methodenwechsel*) from tax exemption to taxation with crediting foreign taxes takes places.

Article 24 DTT AT-UK comprises the comprehensive agreement on mutual assistance regarding the exchange of information between Austria and the UK. Due to the fact that the tax exemptions for international investment income do not contain any other restrictions with regard to the residency of the distributing company, no tax liability arises in Austria if an Austrian company receives profit distributions from a British company, provided the foreign

56 *§ 10(1)(6) CITA.*
57 *§ 10(2) CITA.*
58 *§ 10(3)(1) CITA.*
59 *§ 10a(7) CITA.*

distributing company is comparable to a domestic corporation.[60] Moreover, there is no withholding tax on dividends in the UK in accordance with the current national determination.[61] Actually, the provisions of the DTT AT-UK do not have any scope of application. Therefore, there are no changes compared to the situation before Brexit.[62]

As mentioned above, in relation to foreign participations a shift from the tax exemption method (*Befreiungsmethode*) to the tax credit method (*Anrechnungsmethode*) may occur[63] if the low-taxed foreign corporation focuses on the generation of passive income and the passive income has not already been recorded as part of the CFC regime (see **5.10** below for more details concerning passive income determined under Austrian tax provisions).[64] With regard to portfolio dividends, this provision only applies to qualified portfolio investments.[65] Low taxation of a foreign company exists if the effective foreign level of corporate tax is not more than 12.5% (note: exactly 12.5% is already considered a low taxation for these purposes).[66] This also includes the situation if the nominal tax rate is higher than 12.5%, but the foreign corporate tax law provides extensive objective or subjective tax exemptions. This includes, for example, the case where the foreign corporate tax law provides an innovation box regime, or allows depreciations that are not allowed in Austria.[67]

As those provisions equally apply to companies that are resident in an EU/EEA Member State and in a third country, basically there is no change due to Brexit. Given the current corporation tax rate of 19% in the UK,[68] the change of method from exemption to taxation with crediting the foreign tax as foreseen by *§ 10a(9)(4) CITA* does not apply from today's perspective.

Capital gains on shareholdings in non-resident companies

5.8 Regarding capital gains on shareholdings in companies that are resident outside the EU or the EEA it has to be distinguished between portfolio investments and substantial participations, as already described regarding inbound dividends above (see **5.7**).

Contrary to dividends obtained from portfolio investments, in which case a tax exemption applies under certain circumstances (for more details see **5.7**),

60 *§ 10(1)(7) CITA* in combination with *§ 10(2)* or *10(1)(6) CITA*.

61 IBFD, UK/Corporate Taxation, 6.3.1. Dividends.

62 *Leyrer/Petutschnig* in ÖStZ 23/2016, „Brexit“ und die möglichen Auswirkungen auf das österreichische Steuerrecht, 655.

63 *§ 10a(9)(4) CITA*.

64 *§ 10a(7) CITA*.

65 *Bergmann/Wurm* in *Bergmann/Renner/Wurm* (eds), Praxisbeispiele zur Körperschaftsteuer (2019), 154.

66 *§ 10a(7) CITA* in combination with *§ 10a(3) CITA*.

67 *Raab* in SWI 19/2018, Die neue Hinzurechnungsbesteuerung, 844 et seq.

68 IBFD, UK/Corporate Taxation, 1.6.1. Income and capital gains.

capital gains on such shareholdings are subject to corporate income tax at the rate of 25%.[69] This also applies to capital gains on shareholdings a resident company holds in another resident company, since no participation exemption applies in the purely domestic context irrespective of any participation threshold.[70] On the contrary, capital gains on participations of at least 10% are tax exempt, unless the option for having capital gains treated as taxable income has been exercised in the tax return of the year of acquisition and unless the foreign company is low taxed and prevailingly generates passive income.[71] As these provisions equally apply to corporations resident in the EU or EEA or in a third country, there are no changes due to Brexit.[72]

Permanent establishments abroad

5.9 For the case of permanent establishments of Austrian taxpayers in the UK Brexit should, generally, bring no changes, as Austrian tax law allows the utilisation of foreign losses if they are not used abroad and provides for a recapture rule of such losses, once they are utilised abroad.

From a general perspective, according to the *Marks & Spencer* and the *Lidl Belgium* rulings of the CJEU,[73] losses of a permanent establishment have to be considered in the state of residence (or concerning *Marks & Spencer* in the resident state of a group parent) if these losses are unusable in the permanent establishment's country (or the subsidiary's country). Such rulings are based on the freedom of establishment which no longer applies to the UK after Brexit. According to the *Stahlwerk Ergste Westig* ruling of the CJEU,[74] no loss utilisation requirement exists regarding third countries. This, however, would only become relevant if Austria changes its domestic law (currently not anticipated).

CFC rules

5.10 If an Austrian corporate shareholder holds a controlling participation in a foreign entity that generates low taxed passive income, this low taxed passive income of the foreign subsidiary has to be included in the Austrian tax base as Austria chose version (a) of the two options provided by the EU Anti-Tax Avoidance Directive[75] (ATAD) for the concept of a CFC-regime.

---

69 *§ 10(1)(5)* and *(6) CITA* in combination with *§ 22(1) CITA*.

70 *§ 10(1)(1) CITA*.

71 *§ 10(3)(1) CITA*.

72 Regarding portfolio investments and the applicability of *§ 10(1)(6) CITA* with respect to the UK as a third country see **5.7** for further details.

73 CJEU 13 December 2005, *Marks & Spencer* (Case C-446/03); 15 May 2008, *Lidl Belgium* (Case C-414/06).

74 CJEU 6 November 2007, *Stahlwerk Ergste Westig* (Case C-415/06); *Achatz/Bieber* in *Achatz/ Kirchmayr* (eds), KStG (2011) § 7 Ann. 136.

75 Council Directive (EU) 2016/1164 of 12 July 2016.

While version (a) provides the CFC-inclusion rules for low taxed passive income, version (b) would have required a CFC-inclusion for non-genuine arrangements only.[76] A controlling participation is deemed to exist if an Austrian company owns directly or indirectly more than 50% of the shares or voting rights or is entitled to more than 50% of the profits. Low taxation is assumed if the effective tax rate in the foreign country does not exceed 12.5%. The CFC regime only applies if more than one third of the foreign entity's income originates from passive income. Passive income includes dividends, interest, royalties and capital gains from shares, finance lease income, income from banking and insurance activities and income from settlement companies. However, the CFC regime does not apply if the controlled foreign entity carries out a substantive economic activity supported by staff, equipment, assets and premises.[77] Contrary to ATAD's suggestion for allowing this proof of substance only to apply to controlled entities resident in the EU or in the EEA,[78] Austrian law implementing ATAD does not distinguish between foreign companies in this context, according to whether they are resident in the EU or EEA or of a third country.[79]

Since there is no difference in the application of the CFC regime between foreign companies resident in the EU or in the EEA, on the one hand, and foreign companies resident in third countries, on the other, there are no changes due to Brexit given the current corporation tax rate of 19% in the UK.[80]

IMPACT ON CROSS-BORDER GROUP TAX REGIMES

5.11 Under the Austrian group tax regime two or more companies may form a tax group, provided that the parent company holds, directly or indirectly, more than 50% of capital shares and voting rights (double majority) of the subsidiary throughout the entire fiscal year.[81] Foreign companies may only become tax group members if they are resident in an EU Member State or in a state having entered into a comprehensive administrate assistance arrangement with Austria.[82] However, with regard to group parents, corporations resident in a third country are generally excluded from being a group parent. The only possibility for foreign corporations to become group parent companies is having a branch office registered in the Austrian Companies' Register. The

76 Article 7(2) ATAD.

77 *§ 10a CITA*; *Wurm* in *Bergmann/Renner/Wurm* (eds), Praxisbeispiele zur Körperschaftsteuer (2019), 182 et seq.

78 Article 7(2)(a) (last sentence) ATAD.

79 ErlRV 190 BlgNR XXVI. GP, 23 et seq; *Klokar* in SWI 2/2020, Die österreichische Hinzurechnungsbesteuerung (CFC-Regime) und das Unionsrecht, 77.

80 IBFD, UK/Corporate Taxation, 1.6.1. Income and capital gains.

81 *§ 9(4)* and *(5) CITA*; *Maukner/Pinetz* in *Bergmann/Renner/Wurm* (eds), Praxisbeispiele zur Körperschaftsteuer (2019), 116 et seq.

82 *§ 9(2) CITA*.

exclusion from the ability to become a group parent even applies if a permanent establishment for tax purposes exists.[83]

Consequently, regarding group members, there are no changes due to Brexit as Austria and the UK have concluded a comprehensive agreement on mutual assistance regarding the exchange of information (Article 24 DTT AT-UK). This means that British corporations may be included as group members in an Austrian tax group, even after Brexit, if the aforementioned conditions are met. However, in terms of group parents there will be differences in the situation before and after Brexit. While before Brexit British corporations, as residents in an EU Member State, were able to function as group parents under certain circumstances, British corporations may not be a group parent with the expiry of the transition period on 31 December 2020.

This raises the question of what will happen to tax groups with a British group parent. In general, the group parent's leaving of the tax group leads to the dissolution of the tax group.[84] Moreover, in the opinion of the tax authorities the transfer of the position as group parent to a corporation outside the tax group by means of reorganisation leads to the resolution of the tax group as well, a position that has been criticised.[85]

Another question that has been raised is whether a tax group is possible between two domestic companies if a company, which is resident in another country, is interposed between such domestic companies, that is, the grandparent company wants to form a tax group with its sub-subsidiary, both being Austrian companies, even though the Austrian sub-subsidiary is indirectly held through a British subsidiary by the grandparent. While the CJEU decided that such a tax group has to be possible if the intermediary subsidiary is an EU company,[86] this may no longer apply after Brexit.

TAX RAMIFICATIONS FOR CROSS-BORDER MERGERS, OTHER REORGANISATIONS AND TRANSFERS OF RESIDENCE

Cross-border mergers and other reorganisations

5.12 The provisions implementing the EU Fiscal Merger Directive will no longer apply with respect to British companies after Brexit. The purpose

83 *§ 9(4) CITA*; *Pinetz/Stefaner* in *Lang/Rust/Schuch/Staringer* (eds), KStG, 2nd edition (2016) § 9 Ann. 42 et seq.

84 *Pinetz/Stefaner* in *Lang/Rust/Schuch/Staringer* (eds), KStG, 2nd edition (2016) § 9 Ann. 153a with further references; *Corporate Income Tax Regulations, Ann. 1591.*

85 *Pinetz/Stefaner* in *Lang/Rust/Schuch/Staringer* (eds), KStG, 2nd edition (2016) § 9 Ann. 153a with further references; *Reorganisation Tax Regulations, Ann. 354d* and *354e.*

86 CJEU 27 November 2008, *Papillon* (Case C-418/07); *Pinetz/Stefaner* in *Lang/Rust/Schuch/Staringer* (eds), KStG, 2nd edition (2016) § 9 Ann. 42.

of the Merger Directive is to ensure that hidden reserves (also referred to as unrealised gains) are not taxed until they are actually sold, that is, when income is realised. Consequently, Brexit leads to changes concerning the disclosure of hidden reserves and their immediate taxation.

In general, reorganisations are tax neutral procedures under the *Austrian Reorganisation Tax Act (Reorg Tax Act, Umgründungssteuergesetz, 'UmgrStG')*. However, if assets are transferred to a foreign country on the occasion of a reorganisation, an exit taxation in accordance with *§ 6(6) ITA* may be triggered (see **5.16** for further details).[87] If Austria loses the right of taxation in relation to another EU (or EEA) country, the payment of the relevant taxes in instalments spread over a period of five years can be requested. However, the tax liability is due immediately if the limitation of the taxation right occurs in relation to a third country. Consequently, if Austria's right of taxation will be limited in relation to the UK after Brexit, no payment by instalments will be possible, and taxes will be due immediately.[88]

Moreover, contributions according to *Article III Reorg Tax Act* are generally carried out at book-value rollover basis (*Buchwertfortführung*) and consequently, contributions are tax neutral, provided Austria's right of taxation is not limited.[89] This means that hidden reserves are generally not disclosed and taxed at the date of contribution, since contributed assets are valued at carrying amounts. If there occurs a limitation of taxation in relation to an EU/EEA Member State, exit taxation with the possibility of payment by instalments applies. However, if the right of taxation concerning shares of contributions is limited with regard to a third country, contributing assets may not be valued at carrying amounts but at fair market value (*gemeiner Wert*) pursuant to *§ 6(14)(b) ITA*.[90] This profit implementing exchange transaction causes immediate taxation at the effective date of contribution. Therefore, with the expiry of the transition period on 31 December 2020, contributions to a British corporation may lead to a tax liability that is due immediately. This applies even if the effective date of the contribution is within the transition period, due to the statutory retroactivity for tax law purposes.[91]

In this context concerns with regard to European Union Law may arise due to a possible infringement of the free movement of capital (to the extent this freedom applies),[92] because no deferral of immediate payment of the tax is provided in relation to third countries. Moreover, in consideration of the indications of the CJEU in the *DMC* case, it remains unclear if the justification

87 *§ 1(2) Reorg Tax Act.*

88 *BMF*, Taxes & Brexit, available at: www.bmf.gv.at/en/current-issues/brexit/brexit-taxes.html (accessed 1 May 2020); *Income Tax Regulations, Ann. 2518a.*

89 *§ 16(1) Reorg Tax Act.*

90 *§ 16(2)(2) Reorg Tax Act.*

91 *Titz/Wild* in SWK 13/2020, Ertragsteuerliche Auswirkungen des „Brexit" für Unternehmen, 735.

92 See for an argument in that direction: *Mair/Mayr* in *Wiesner/Hirschler/Mayr* (eds), Handbuch Umgründungen, 16th edition (2017) *§ 16 UmgrStG* Ann. 29.

of exit taxation requires Austria's actual prevention of taxation.[93] Contrary to *§ 16(2)(2) Reorg Tax Act*, a book-value roll-over should also be granted in relation to third countries as contributions are comprised within the free movement of capital.[94]

5.13 Regarding contributions of shares in corporations, *§ 16(1a) Reorg Tax Act* provides specific rules. However, this provision only applies if shares are contributed to a corporation resident in the EU or the EEA. Consequently, concerning contributions of shares to a British company, Austrian corporations can no longer make use of a contribution at carrying amounts (share swap, *Anteilstausch*) with the expiry of the transition period on 31 December 2020.[95] Consequently, taxes are due immediately since Austria's taxation right regarding the contributed shares is limited.

The law assumes that generally contributions are made in exchange for the issuance of new shares by the acquiring entity to the contributor.[96] However, if certain conditions are met, the granting of new shares is not mandatory for the purpose of benefiting from the rules of the *Reorg Tax Act*.[97] Due to European Union Law, *§ 19(2)(5)* (second half sentence) *Reorg Tax Act*, that refers to domestic shares of the acquiring entity taxable in Austria, does not apply, if shares taxable in Austria are contributed by an EU/EEA resident to an EU/EEA corporation. This means that the provisions of the *Reorg Tax Act* still apply, even though no consideration is granted.[98] With regard to the UK, contributions that will be resolved or contractually signed after the expiry of the transition period violate the conditions for the application of *Article III Reorg Tax Act* if no shares are granted, since the non-application of *§ 19(2)(5)* (second half sentence) *Reorg Tax Act* only applies to EU/EEA constellations. This means that after Brexit the *Reorg Tax Act* does not apply in such cases if no shares are granted.[99]

With regard to reorganisations that have been resolved or contractually signed within the transition period, that is, between 1 February 2020 and 31 December 2020, payment instalments can still be requested.[100] However, regarding contributions of shares by corporations with limited tax liability

93 CJEU 23 January 2014, *DMC* (Case C-164/12); *Mair/Mayr* in *Wiesner/Hirschler/Mayr* (eds), Handbuch Umgründungen, 16th edition (2017) *§ 16 UmgrStG* Ann. 29.

94 *Beiser* in ÖStZ 17/2014, Die Gleichbehandlung von In- und Auslandsansässigen bei Einbringungen, 433.

95 *BMF*, Taxes & Brexit, available at: www.bmf.gv.at/en/current-issues/brexit/brexit-taxes.html (accessed 1 May 2020).

96 *§ 19(1) Reorg Tax Act.*

97 *§ 19(2) Reorg Tax Act.*

98 *Titz/Wild/Schlager* in *Wiesner/Hirschler/Mayr* (eds), Handbuch Umgründungen, 17th edition (2018) *§ 19 UmgrStG*, 51 et seq; *Reorganisation Tax Regulations, Ann. 1087.*

99 *Titz/Wild* in SWK 13/2020, Ertragsteuerliche Auswirkungen des "Brexit" für Unternehmen, 735 et seq.

100 *Titz/Wild* in SWK 13/2020, Ertragsteuerliche Auswirkungen des „Brexit" für Unternehmen, 734.

to corporations resident in the EU or the EEA, applications for the tax not to be assessed (*Nichtfestsetzungsantrag*) can be filed.[101] Such share for share exchanges that have been resolved or contractually signed between 1 January 2020 and 31 December 2020[102] may be executed under the favourable share swap regime without tax assessment (*Anteilstauschregime mit Nichtfestsetzung*) involving British companies.[103] After the transition period is over, this will no longer be possible.

Within the scope of other reorganisations in relation to the UK that are not covered by the Reorg Tax Act, hidden reserves (= unrealised gains) have to be realised and taxed. An application for payment by instalments is not possible after 2020, since *§ 6(6)(c) ITA* is not applicable in relation to third countries (see **5.16** for further details).[104] In this respect it should be mentioned that Brexit may also lead to negative consequences for shareholders.[105] For example, the tax neutral share swap due to a merger only applies for shareholders resident in the EU or EEA.[106]

5.14 With regard to cross-border mergers some questions arise concerning mergers executed towards the end of the transition period on 31 December 2020, because of the retroactivity allowed under Austrian law: from an Austrian perspective, the effective date of the merger for tax purposes corresponds to the effective date of the merger under corporate law,[107] and that may not occur more than nine months prior to the registration of the merger in the companies' register.[108] Due to the statutory retroactivity for tax law purposes, the transfer of assets has to take place with the expiry of the effective merger date.[109] At the same time the tax liability in Austria generally ends for the transferring corporation, and consequently, its income has to be recorded at

101 *§ 16(1a) Reorg Tax Act* in combination with *§ 17(1a) Reorg Tax Act*; *Reorganisation Tax Regulations, Ann. 860b* in the version of the consultation draft of UmgrStR-Wartungserlass 2019/2020.

102 Since the share swap regime without tax assessment of *§ 17(1a) Reorg Tax Act* has been reintroduced through the *Tax Reform Act 2020* (*Steuerreformgesetz 2020*, *'StRefG 2020'*), this provision has been applicable only since 1 January 2020. The reintroduction of this provision is in line with the ruling of the CJEU (CJEU 22 March 2018, *Marc Jacob und Marc Lassus* (Case C-327/16)).

103 *Titz/Wild* in SWK 13/2020, Ertragsteuerliche Auswirkungen des „Brexit" für Unternehmen, 734 et seq.

104 *Marschner/Renner* in SWK 18/2019, Körperschaft-/Umgründungssteuer-Update Juni 2019: Aktuelles auf einen Blick 797.

105 *Titz/Wild* in SWK 13/2020, Ertragsteuerliche Auswirkungen des „Brexit" für Unternehmen, 735.

106 *§ 5(1)(3) Reorg Tax Act.*

107 *§ 2(5) Reorg Tax Act.*

108 *§ 220(3)* (third sentence) *Austrian Stock Corporation Act* (*Aktiengesetz*, „AktG") and *§ 202(2)(1) Austrian Commercial Code* (*Unternehmensgesetzbuch*, 'UGB'); *Hügel*, Grenzüberschreitende und nationale Verschmelzung im Steuerrecht (2009), § 2 Ann. 46.

109 *§ 2(3) Reorg Tax Act.*

the acquiring corporation.[110] In this context, a risk of double taxation or double non-taxation may arise if the transferring corporation's country of residence does not provide a retroactive effect comparable to Austrian law.[111] In practice, this issue may only occur if the assets are not attributable to a permanent establishment in the state of the transferring corporation's residence, as in such case the right of taxation is still assigned to the foreign country.[112]

If a British corporation merges into an Austrian corporation in March 2021, the British transferring corporation will exist until March 2021 even though the merger will be executed retrospectively to 31 December 2020 from an Austrian perspective. Subsequently, double taxation may occur as the transferring corporation's income is taxable in the UK as well as in Austria. It is questionable whether the taxes paid in the UK are allowed as a credit against any Austrian tax.

As the Merger Directive does not provide any legal basis for the elimination of the double taxation, no consequences arise due to Brexit. Moreover, double tax treaties do not prevent economical double taxation, as the same income is attributed to different persons, but rather legal double taxation.[113] The question of whether double tax treaties are applicable in the retroactive period has to be clarified through a mutual agreement procedure.[114] Unless a bilateral solution between the Contracting States is reached in the course of a mutual agreement procedure, the taxation conflict cannot be solved by means of double tax treaties.[115]

As the new agreement between Austria and the UK includes a provision concerning mutual agreement procedures (Article 23 DTT AT-UK) consistent with Article 25 OECD Model Tax Convention 2014, double taxation can be solved by such a procedure. However, it should be noted that there is no obligation to initiate such a mutual agreement procedure, leaving a broad discretion to the tax authorities. Another disadvantage is the very long duration of these proceedings.[116] As the UK is a third country since 1 January 2021, the procedure may be even more difficult.

5.15 For the sake of completeness, it should be mentioned that there might be Brexit-related consequences concerning mergers from a corporate law perspective. Since the Austrian *EU Merger Act* (*EU-Verschmelzungsgesetz*, '*EU-VerschG*') only applies for EU/EEA Member States,[117] cross-border mergers based on the *EU Merger Act* are generally no longer permitted for

110 *Staringer in Bertl et al*, Sonderbilanzen bei Umgründungen (2008), 221; *Zöchling/Pinetz* in *Kirchmayr-Schliesselberger/Mayr*, Umgründungen (2013), 126.
111 *Zöchling/Pinetz* in *Kirchmayr-Schliesselberger/Mayr*, Umgründungen (2013), 127.
112 Kirchmayr/Mayr/Hirschler/Wild, Importverschmelzungen (2018), 292 et seq.
113 *Zöchling/Pinetz* in *Kirchmayr-Schliesselberger/Mayr*, Umgründungen (2013), 129 et seq.
114 Express Answer Service of the Ministry of Finance of Austria, 3388 (20 July 2017).
115 *Zöchling/Pinetz* in *Kirchmayr-Schliesselberger/Mayr*, Umgründungen (2013), 130.
116 *Zöchling/Pinetz* in *Kirchmayr-Schliesselberger/Mayr*, Umgründungen (2013), 130.
117 *§ 3(1) EU Merger Act.*

British companies with the expiry of the transition period on 31 December 2020.[118] However, according to the prevailing view in literature, the *EU Merger Act* should be applicable analogously regarding third country related cross-border mergers.[119] If such a merger is accepted by the companies' register, the merger is also accepted for reorganisational tax law purposes due to the decisiveness of corporate law.[120] Consequently, cross-border mergers involving British companies based on the *EU Merger Act* might still be possible even after the end of the transition period; an uncertainty in that context exists nevertheless.

Transfer of residence abroad

5.16 Under Austrian tax law, the relocation of an Austrian branch to a foreign country or the fact that assets, functions and activities, which were in the past held or carried out by an Austrian branch, are transferred to a foreign branch (or the foreign head office or another group entity) may trigger exit taxation on the deemed capital gain realised on such relocation or transfer.[121] Moreover, further circumstances that lead to a limitation of Austria's right of taxation in relation to a foreign country are subject to exit taxation.[122] Decisive factors have to be valued in accordance with the arm's length principle. The difference between these values and the corresponding carrying amount provides the assessment basis for the exit tax at the regular corporate income tax rate of 25%. The resulting tax liability has to be paid equally by instalments within five years (two years concerning current assets).[123]

However, in terms of exit taxation, changes according to the *ITA* as well as to the *Reorg Tax Act* occur with the expiry of the transition period on 31 December 2020. In the event of an exit or if assets, functions or activities are considered to be transferred from Austria to the UK, Austrian exit taxation might be triggered at the regular corporate income tax rate of 25%. As distinguished from the situation before Brexit, taxation takes place immediately. Accordingly, an application for payment by instalments cannot be made any longer. This applies to all business relocations in accordance with *§ 6(6) ITA* that take place after the end of the transition period, as well as to reorganisations in the sense of the *Reorg Tax Act* that are decided or contractually signed after the end of the transition period.[124]

118 *Titz/Wild* in SWK 13/2020, Ertragsteuerliche Auswirkungen des „Brexit" für Unternehmen, 736.

119 *Schwarzinger/Wiesner*, Umgründungssteuer-Leitfaden I/1, 3rd edition (2013), 501.

120 *Reorganisation Tax Regulations, Ann. 23.*

121 *§ 6(6)(a) ITA.*

122 *§ 6(6)(b) ITA.*

123 *§ 6(6)(c), (d) and (e) ITA.*

124 *BMF*, Taxes & Brexit, available at: www.bmf.gv.at/en/current-issues/brexit/brexit-taxes.html (accessed 1 May 2020).

However, for companies that have already moved away before the end of the transition period and that have applied for the tax not to be assessed (before 2016) or for payment by instalments (from 2016 onwards), the expiry of the transition period does not lead to an immediate taxation or the immediate payment of outstanding instalments.[125] This also applies if the exit tax for reorganisations in accordance with the *Reorg Tax Act*, that have been resolved or contractually signed prior to this, has not been fixed or can be paid in instalments.[126]

Inbound transfer of residence

5.17 Assets or branches that are transferred from a foreign country to Austria have to be valued at the fair market value (ie, similar to transactions applying the arm's length principle).[127] This approach also applies if other circumstances lead to the new establishment of Austria's right of taxation in relation to other countries.[128]

Due to the fact that this regime does not distinguish between companies transferring to Austria from the EU or the EEA and those transferring to Austria from third countries,[129] there will be no changes due to Brexit. The aforementioned provisions are applicable in relation to the UK even after the transition period.

However, there are specific valuation rules concerning the inbound re-transfer of residency regarding assets that have been transferred to a foreign country prior to 1 January 2016, as those assets have to be valued at continued book values (*fortgeschriebene Buchwerte*), but not exceeding the fair market value meaning the book values are relevant, except if the fair market values are lower upon re-entry.[130] If, in such a specific scenario (ie, leaving Austria before 2016 and then re-transferring back) a sale or withdrawal takes place after the relocation of assets or branches back to Austria, an increase in value originating from the foreign EU or EEA area can be deducted from the sales revenue or withdrawal value (ie, if upon the transferring out of Austria the book value was €100 and, at such time, the fair market value was €120, while upon re-entry the fair market value was €150, when sold for €170, the taxable capital gain

125 *Marschner/Renner* in SWK 18/2019, Körperschaft-/Umgründungssteuer-Update Juni 2019: Aktuelles auf einen Blick, 797; *Income Tax Regulations, Ann. 2518a*; the explicit statement to the contrary in *Income Tax Regulations, Ann. 6157b* does not apply.

126 *BMF*, Taxes & Brexit, available at: www.bmf.gv.at/en/current-issues/brexit/brexit-taxes.html (accessed 1 May 2020); *Reorganisation Tax Regulations, Ann. 44a* in the version of the consultation draft of UmgrStR-Wartungserlass 2019/2020.

127 *§ 6(6)(f) ITA.*

128 *§ 6(6)(g) ITA.*

129 *Mayr* in *Doralt/Kirchmayr/Mayr/Zorn*, EStG, 19th edition § 6 (Stand 1.2.2017, rdb.at) Ann. 394f.

130 *§ 6(6)(h) ITA* in combination with *§ 27(6)(1)(e) ITA*; *Laudacher* in Jakom EStG, 13th edition (2020) § 6 Ann. 158.

in Austria is only €40 disregarding the value increase of €30 while abroad). This assumes the provision of a corresponding proof regarding the increase in value.[131] If assets that have been relocated from Austria to the UK prior to 1 January 2016 will re-enter the Austrian tax law system after the end of the transition period on 31 December 2020, the deduction of increases in value will be limited to increases until 31 December 2020. This is due to the wording of *§ 27(6)(1)(e) ITA* that explicitly refers to increases in value originating from the EU or EEA. However, from a more systematic perspective and in order to avoid double taxation, increases in value occurring from 1 January 2021 should be deductible as well, if these increases are subject to tax in the UK.[132]

OTHER

5.18 Foreign investment vehicles that fall within the definition of a foreign investment fund in the sense of the *Austrian Investment Funds Act* (*Investmentfondsgesetz*, *'InvFG'*) are subject to the same taxation as domestic investment funds.[133] Moreover, the provisions concerning the taxation of real estate investment funds also apply to foreign real estate funds.[134] As there is no distinction between EU/EEA Member States and third countries, there will not be any changes due to Brexit.[135]

131 *Income Tax Regulations, Ann. 2517i.*

132 *Titz/Wild* in SWK 13/2020, Ertragsteuerliche Auswirkungen des „Brexit" für Unternehmen, 733.

133 *Blum/Wimpissinger*, Austria – Investment Funds and Private Equity, IBFD Online Topical Analysis (2019).

134 § 40 Real Estate Investment Funds Act (*Immobilieninvestmentfondsgesetz*, 'ImmoInvFG').

135 § 42 Real Estate Investment Funds Act.

Chapter 6

Belgium

Henk Verstraete and Hannelore Niesten

INTRODUCTION

6.1 The purpose of this chapter is to analyse the main consequences of the United Kingdom of Great-Britain and Northern Ireland (United Kingdom/ UK) leaving the European Union (EU) from a Belgian income tax perspective (and thus becoming a third country).

The standstill of the Brexit Withdrawal Agreement[1] of 29 January 2020 until 31 December 2020 has direct effect in the Belgian legal order.[2] Nevertheless, the Belgian legislator similarly adopted a special fiscal Brexit law on various transitional regimes on 21 February 2020.[3] According to the Belgian Brexit Law, the UK will continue to be considered an EU Member State until 31 December 2020 for the application of certain provisions in the Belgian Income Tax Code/ITC (*Wetboek van de inkomstenbelastingen 1992/Code des impôts sur les revenus*).[4] Various technical nuances and exceptions have been made to the general equalisation rule. The

---

1 Agreement on the withdrawal of the United Kingdom of Great Britain and Northern Ireland from the European Union and the European Atomic Energy Community (*Pb.L.* 31 January 2020, ed. 29/7), available at: https://eur-lex.europa.eu/legal-content/EN/TXT/HTML/?uri=CELEX:12020W/TXT&from=NL.

2 Articles 126 and 127 Withdrawal Agreement. See also Article 7, para 1, and Article 127, para 6 Withdrawal Agreement.

3 Law of 21 February 2020 introducing various transitional regimes as regards the withdrawal of the United Kingdom of Great-Britain and Northern Ireland from the European Union, *Belgian Official gazette* of 12 March 2020 (*Wet van 21 February 2020 tot invoering van diverse fiscale overgangsbepalingen wat betreft de terugtrekking van het Verenigd Koninkrijk van Groot-Brittannië en Noord-Ierland uit de Europese Unie*).

4 Law of 3 April 2019 on the withdrawal of the United Kingdom from the European Union, *Belgian Official Gazette* of 10 April 2019 (*Wet van 3 april 2019 betreffende de terugtrekking van het Verenigd Koninkrijk uit de Europese Unie*, *Parl.St.* 2018-2019, nr. 54-3554/1, 5). The Law of 21 February 2020 changes the Law of 3 April 2019 on the Withdrawal of the United Kingdom from the European Union. The Law of 3 April 2019 was approved by Parliament but never entered into force. The intention was that this Law would only be implemented if no agreement was finally reached between the European Union and the United Kingdom.

arrangement was considered necessary to provide a more focused response to specific situations (see **6.3**).

This chapter highlights the key tax implications of Brexit for Belgian income tax law.[5] The analysis of this chapter assumes that the UK will be a third state in all respects for the application of ITC after 31 December 2020. EU law will not be applicable to the UK after the end of the transition period under the Withdrawal Agreement.

TAX RAMIFICATIONS FOR INBOUND INVESTMENTS

Outbound dividends

6.2 According to Belgian tax law, outbound dividends paid to non-resident corporate shareholders are generally subject to a final withholding tax (WHT) at a rate of 30% (27% before 2017).[6]

The EU Parent-Subsidiary Directive No. 2011/96/EU will no longer apply post-Brexit. The Parent-Subsidiary Directive provides a WHT exemption on dividends paid to a parent company that is resident in an EU Member State and that has held at least 10% of the capital of the subsidiary continuously for at least one year. Furthermore, the non-resident company must be subject to corporate income tax, or a similar tax levied at the rate of at least 10%.

The Belgian domestic provisions implementing the WHT exemption as provided for by the Parent-Subsidiary Directive will continue to apply after Brexit (subject to conditions). Therefore, Brexit does not have much impact on cross-border dividend distributions between Belgium and the UK. Indeed, Belgian law has extended the WHT exemption to include all states it has concluded a double tax agreement with, provided that the minimum holding period and minimum participation conditions have been met.[7]

As such, the WHT exemption applies to dividends paid by resident subsidiaries (Belgian company) to their parent companies resident in EU Member States or in a state with which Belgium has concluded a double tax treaty (DTT) or another treaty with a clause for the exchange of information, which is the case for the UK,[8] provided that the following conditions are met:[9]

---

5 For an analysis of the VAT-implications of Brexit, see T Lyons, 'VAT in the UK after Brexit' (2019) 571 *Tijdschrift voor fiscaal recht* 935–47.

6 Article 261,1° and 269, § 1, 1° ITC.

7 Article 266 ITC and Article 106, § 5 Royal Decree implementing the Income Tax Code (Royal Decree).

8 Article 26 Income Tax Treaty between Belgium and the United Kingdom of 1 June 1987, as amended by the protocol of 24 June 2009 (hereinafter 'UK-Belgian DTT').

9 Article 106, § 5 Royal Decree. See also Circular Ci. RH.233.437.131 of 16 July 1992.

- the subsidiary company and the parent company have one of the forms listed in the Directive No. 90/435/EEC, as amended by Directive No. 2003/123/EC;[10] and
- the subsidiary company and the parent company are subject to a corporate income tax or a similar tax without enjoying a tax system that deviates from regular law;[11] and
- the parent company holds at least 10% of the capital of the subsidiary;[12] and
- the parent company's minimum shareholding has been held continuously for at least one year.[13] A provisional exemption for WHT is granted when shares have not been held for at least one year when the dividends are distributed.[14]

Thus, when a Belgian subsidiary pays a dividend to its British parent company, the Belgian WHT exemption on dividend distributions will continue to apply post-Brexit (assuming the conditions have been met).

Outbound interest and royalties

6.3 According to Belgian tax law, outbound *interest* paid to non-resident persons (UK companies) is, in principle, subject to 30% final WHT.[15] Outbound *royalties* to non-resident persons (UK companies) are subject to a 30% final WHT.[16] In principle, a fixed deduction equal to 15% of the gross interest and royalties can be applied representing the expenses related to the interest and royalties.[17]

The EU Interest and Royalties Directive No. 2003/49/EC provides a WHT exemption on interest and royalties arising in an EU Member State if the participation (direct or indirect) equals at least 25% during a minimum period of two years. Belgian companies who participate in at least 25% of the debtor's capital may benefit from the exemption, as provided by the Interest

10 Article 106, § 5, s 3, a) Royal Decree. The circular Ci.RH.233/586.864 (AAFisc 33/2011) of 23 June 2011 provides that the exemption does not apply to entities which do not have one of the legal forms listed in the Annex to the directive, even if such entity is established in an EU Member State with which Belgium has signed a tax treaty providing for exchange of information.

11 Article 106, § 5, s 3, c) Royal Decree.

12 Article 106, § 6bis Royal Decree. *See* also A. Bax and L. Denys, *Dividenden zonder grenzen. De Moeder-Dochterrichtlijn en haar uitvoering in België en haar omringende landen* (Kalmthout, Biblom 1991), nr. 269.

13 Article 106, § 5, section 2, § 4 and § 14 Royal Decree.

14 Article 117, § 15 Royal Decree.

15 Articles 228, § 2, 2° ITC and 269, § 1, 1° ITC.

16 Articles 228, § 2, 2° ITC and 269, § 1, 1° ITC.

17 Article 22, § 3 ITC, and Article 3 Royal Decree.

and Royalties Directive. This exemption also applies when both companies have a common parent with a direct or indirect holding in both the paying and receiving company. Post-Brexit, interest and royalties might become subject to withholding tax at source. The Interest and Royalties Directive cannot be invoked from the moment the UK is no longer an EU Member State.

In general, under the Belgian domestic law provisions transposing the Interest and Royalties Directive, outbound interest and royalty payments are exempt from Belgian WHT if the recipient is an associated company of the paying company and is resident in another EU Member State or a company's permanent establishment situated in another EU Member State.[18] Two companies are 'associated companies' if, at the moment of attribution or payment, (i) one of them holds directly or indirectly at least 25% of the capital of the other, or (ii) both companies have a common shareholder established in the EU that has a direct or indirect holding of at least 25% of the capital of both companies for an uninterrupted period of at least one year. The relevant companies must have a legal form listed in the Annex of the Directive and be subject to corporate income tax. In principle, interest and royalties paid between associated companies are exempt from WHT. A law of 3 June 2004 provides that the exemption under this regime also applies to interest on bearer shares and zero bonds.

After Brexit, the WHT exemption for interest and royalties available according to the Belgian provisions implementing the Interest and Royalties Directive will no longer apply. As mentioned above, Belgium provides for an extension of the Parent-Subsidiary Directive to countries with which it has entered into a DTT (and an information exchange clause has been agreed between the tax authorities). However, Belgium has not implemented this for the Interest and Royalties Directive. The WHT exemption for interest and royalties in Belgian internal law is limited to companies established in an EU Member State (and not in relation to treaty countries). The WHT exemption can only be applied if the 'beneficial owner' of the interest or royalty payment is a qualifying EU company (or PE).

Post-Brexit it will be impossible to apply the exemption of Belgian WHT on interest and royalties that are paid by a Belgian subsidiary to a UK parent provided by Belgium. In other words, where a Belgian company pays interest or royalty to a recipient located in the UK, a 30% Belgian WHT will in principle be levied, subject however to other more specific exemptions that may apply. As a result, WHT may be payable on cross-border payments. To address the impossibility of applying the exemption provided by Belgium through the implementation of the Interest and Royalties Directive, a bilateral treaty could be concluded between the UK and the European Union.

18 Article 117, § 6bis Royal Decree.

In the absence of a new bilateral treaty, the provisions of the UK-Belgian DTT offer a useful solution:

- According to Article 11(2) of the UK-Belgian DTT, a reduced 10% WHT of the gross amount of the *interest* may apply if the beneficial owner of the interest payments is a person resident of the UK. No WHT is levied on interest payments in respect of a loan of any kind granted or a credit extended by an enterprise to another enterprise (Article 11(3) UK-Belgian DTT).[19]
- According to Article 12(1) of the UK-Belgian DTT, *royalties* arising in Belgium and beneficially owned by a UK resident shall be taxable only in the UK. Therefore, Belgian royalties are exempt in Belgium, and no WHT is due.

As a result, Brexit in many cases will not have any effect in terms of interest and royalty payments, given the broad exemptions in the double tax treaty between Belgium and the UK. However, the exemption based on the double tax treaty requires the specific formalities to be met and in particular forms 276 R. (for royalties) or 276 Int. (for interest) to be issued.[20] These formalities involve the intervention of the tax administration of both countries and increase the administrative burden. Therefore, this procedure is more time-consuming and complex than applying the exemption under the Interest and Royalties Directive.

Furthermore, Article 11(4) and Article 12(3) of the UK-Belgian DTT provide that if the interests and patent royalties are derived through a permanent establishment which the UK company maintains in Belgium, such income is included in the taxable profits of the permanent establishment and is subject to income tax on non-residents in the normal manner.

Besides, Belgian domestic law also provides a number of other specific exemptions, which may apply for payments to a resident of a UK, even after Brexit. These exemptions include, for example, interest paid on registered bonds.[21]

Recent and future developments relating to the Multilateral Convention to Implement Tax Treaty Related Measures to Prevent BEPS (MLI) which generally strengthen the conditions for treaty benefit entitlement, should also be considered since both the UK and Belgium have considered the double taxation agreement as a Covered Tax Agreement.

---

19 Many existing Belgian treaties do not provide for such an exemption. Important exceptions to this rule are found in the treaties with Germany, Luxembourg, the Netherlands, the UK and the US.

20 PJ Wouters and P Van Den Berghe, 'Brexit heeft grote impact op vennootschapsbelasting' (2019) 2 *Fiscale Actualiteit* 1–5.

21 Article 107, § 2, 5, a ITC and Article 110, 4° Royal Decree; Article 105, 6°, b) ITC and Article 107, § 6 Royal Decree.

Capital gains on shareholdings in resident companies

6.4 According to Belgian tax law, the income tax treatment of capital gains depends on the kind of assets realised and the person receiving the capital gains.[22] Capital gains derived from shares in Belgian companies are subject to income tax on non-residents in the same manner as resident companies.[23] Capital gains on shareholdings in resident companies realised by companies subject to Belgian non-resident corporate income tax are deemed to be taxable business profits. However, a capital gains exemption applies if the dividends relating to such shares qualify for the participation exemption (see **6.6**) at the moment the gains are realised.

Article 13(2) of the UK-Belgian DTT grants the taxing rights on the gains from the alienation of movable property forming part of a permanent establishment or a fixed base to the state in which the permanent establishment/fixed base is situated. Article 13(4) of the UK-Belgian DTT provides that the gains from the alienation of other movable property are usually taxable in the resident state. To the extent that the tax jurisdiction as source state is given to Belgium, Belgian tax may be due (on condition that Belgian domestic law provides for taxation).

Brexit does not impact the tax treatment of capital gains realised by UK residents on shareholdings in Belgian companies.[24] With effect from 2018, capital gains are exempt from taxation if the dividends relating to such shares meet the conditions of the participation exemption at the moment the gains are realised.[25] For the application of the participation exemption two sets of conditions must be met, that is, the quantitative conditions (dealing with the size and holding of the participation) and the qualitative conditions (dealing with the nature of the participation and the level of taxation that has been levied on the distributing company). The exemption only applies in so far as the capital gains exceed any previously deducted capital losses on the shares.

A specific taxation applies to capital gains realised on the sale of shares in a Belgian company to a legal entity resident outside the EEA, provided that the participation held by the transferor and his or her close family constituted at least 25% of the capital of that company at any time in the five years preceding the sale. In this case, the capital gain is taxed as miscellaneous income at a tax rate of 16.5%, increased by local taxes.[26] This tax is also triggered if the shares are initially sold to an EEA entity or an individual but are subsequently transferred by that purchaser to a non-EEA legal entity within a 12-month period of the initial sale.[27] Note that this tax can easily be avoided by using an

22 Article 24, section 1, 2° and 3° ITC juncto Article 183 ITC/Article 190 ITC.
23 Article 24, section 1, 2° and 27, section 3° ITC. Article 228, § 2 and § 9 ITC.
24 Articles 227–248(1) ITC.
25 Article 192 ITC juncto Articles 204–205 ITC.
26 Article 90, 9° and 171(4)(e) ITC.
27 Article 94 ITC.

EEA-resident acquisition vehicle and by including a covenant in the sale and purchase agreement that excludes the further transfer of the shares to a non-EEA entity for at least 12 months after the agreement.

As mentioned below (see **6.8**), the transitional regimes adopted under the Law of 21 February 2020 provide an exemption for capital gains realised before 31 December 2020 by private investment companies established in the UK.

Permanent establishments

6.5 Brexit does not result in differences regarding the permanent establishment definition. Belgium generally follows the OECD Income and Capital definition.[28] A permanent establishment includes a building site or construction project lasting continuously more than 30 days during any 12-month period, a storage room, and a stock of merchandise. Non-resident associates or members of foreign entities are deemed to have a permanent establishment in Belgium if the foreign entity has a permanent place of business in Belgium.[29] With respect to the 30-day rule, groups of companies may not avoid a permanent establishment by splitting a contract and dividing it over various group companies, because the duration of a project is determined at group level. The cumulative duration of the similar activities performed by associated companies in Belgium is taken into account to determine whether the duration of the activities in Belgium exceeds the aforementioned number of 30 days. An agent, other than an independent agent acting in the ordinary course of his business, is treated as a permanent representative of the non-resident for whose account he is acting, even if he has no authority to conclude contracts on behalf of the non-resident.[30] Non-resident associates or members of foreign entities are deemed to have a permanent establishment in Belgium if the foreign entity has a permanent place of business or registered office or management in Belgium.[31] Post-Brexit, Belgian establishments of UK companies will be regarded as permanent establishments of foreign companies governed by non-EU/EEA law. These permanent establishments will then be subject to the stricter disclosure requirements.

An investment firm and/or credit institution governed by UK law which has established (or wishes to establish) a permanent establishment in Belgium in order to provide or continue to provide investment services and/or perform investment activities will, according to the FSMA, be considered a third country company. Its permanent establishment will be allowed to perform or continue to perform the activities in Belgium provided that it complies with the conditions of the Act of 25 October 2016 concerning access to investment

28 Article 229, § 1–10 ITC.
29 Article 229, § 3 ITC.
30 Article 229, § 2 ITC.
31 Article 229, § 3 ITC.

services and the regime of and supervision on companies for asset management and investment advice.[32]

TAX RAMIFICATIONS FOR OUTBOUND INVESTMENTS

Inbound dividends

6.6 Current British tax legislation (as at March 2020) does not impose WHT on dividend distributions. Where the subsidiary is a UK company, the impact of Brexit on inbound dividends is non-existent for the treatment of dividends distributed by a UK company. As a result, when a British subsidiary pays a dividend to a Belgian parent company, this dividend remains exempt from British WHT. It remains to be seen whether the UK will adapt this legislation.

If the UK introduces a WHT on distributed dividends, the UK-Belgian DTT would offer relief. In accordance with Article 10(3) of the UK-Belgian DTT, a (UK) WHT exemption applies if the Belgian parent company holds (for an uninterrupted period of at least 12 months) shares directly representing at least 10% of the UK subsidiary's capital.

Only if a Belgian parent company does not hold 10% of the shares in the UK subsidiary for at least one year at the time of dividend declarations, would Brexit have consequences in any scenario where the UK introduces a WHT on dividends.[33]

According to Belgian tax law, dividends derived by the business activities of a Belgian permanent establishment are taxable as business income of the permanent establishment. The 100% participation exemption (DRD deduction) applies to dividends paid by a subsidiary established in the UK to its Belgian parent company, provided that certain formalities are complied with.[34] The participation exemption meets the requirement in the Parent-Subsidiary Directive to relieve the double taxation of qualifying dividends received from a subsidiary in another EU Member State. According to the DRD regime, the dividends can be 100% exempted for the Belgian parent company if the following cumulative conditions are met:

- The parent company has a minimum participation of 10% of a purchase value or the participation must have an acquisition value of at least 2,500,000 euros.[35]

---

32 *Belgian Official Gazette* 18 November 2016. See also FSMA_2019_06, The provision of investment services and the performance of investment activities in Belgium, after the entry into force of Brexit, by companies governed by UK law, 21 February 2019, 3–4.

33 K De Haen, 'An Englishman in the EU (post-Brexit)' (2019) 1 *Internationale Fiscale Actualiteit*.

34 Articles 202–205 ITC.

35 Article 202, § 2, 1° ITC.

- The shares must be held in full ownership for an uninterrupted period of at least one year.[36]
- Dividends come from companies subject to corporate income tax on the profits out of which the distribution is made ('subject to tax' requirement).[37]

  The distribution is not required to be from an EEA/EU company. In other words, if a UK subsidiary pays a dividend to a Belgian parent company, the latter can apply the DRD to the dividend received. However, it is important to note the following two issues:

  — First, when dividends are received from the UK (as a non-EEA country), the DRD regime can still be applied on the taxable profits, but not on so-called disallowed expenses listed exhaustively in Article 205, § 2 ITC (eg, restaurant costs, non-deductible gifts, fines, costs relating to capital losses on vehicles, reception costs, etc).[38] Article 205, § 2, section 2 ITC provides in this regard that the DRD is deductible from all items of disallowed expenses in the case of dividends from companies established in the EEA.[39] This provision is not applicable where the UK is a non-EEA country. Consequently, post-Brexit the DRD regime for dividends from a UK subsidiary will no longer be allocated to the 'disallowed expenses'.[40] The portion of the DRD that is subject to the deduction restriction can be added to the amount of the transferable DRD to subsequent tax periods.[41] This restrictive rule certainly comes into play post-Brexit, as the UK is no longer part of the EEA.

  — Second, the DRD regime cannot be applied if the distributing company is established in a country where the regular tax provisions are 'considerably more favourable than in Belgium'.[42] 'Considerably more favourable than in Belgium' means that the regular nominal rate is lower than 15%.[43] The subject-to-tax requirement is deemed to be met automatically for companies

36 Article 202, § 2, 2° ITC.
37 Article 203, § 1 ITC.
38 Article 205, § 2 ITC.
39 Article 205, § 2, section 2 ITC. Unless the dividends received, other than redemption or liquidation bonuses, are granted or allocated by a subsidiary established in an EEA Member State (and to the extent that the participation and holding period requirement of Article 202, § 2, first para. 1° and 2° ITC are met), the amount eligible for the DRD-deduction is limited to the total amount of the company's taxable residual profit remaining and reduced by the so-called disallowed expenses. *See* also: Circular Ci.RH.421.506.082.
40 PJ Wouters and P Van Den Berghe, 'Brexit heeft grote impact op vennootschapsbelasting' (2019) 2(1) *Fiscale Actualiteit*.
41 Article 205, § 3 ITC.
42 Article 203, § 1, section 1 ITC.
43 Article 203, § 1, section 2 ITC.

established in an EU Member State.[44] However, where the dividend comes from a company established in a non-EU country, its *nominal corporate income tax rate must be at least 15%* (if not, the WHT exemption does not apply).[45] For financial year 2020 (ie, from 1 April 2020 to 31 March 2021), the nominal rate in the UK is 19%.

Although the nominal tax rate in the UK stayed at 19% for financial year 2020, the corporate tax may decrease to less than 15%.[46] If the UK decides to reduce its nominal rate below 15%, the UK will be regarded by Belgium as a country with significantly more favourable tax law provisions, which will make it impossible to apply the DRD regime.

It is not clear whether the equal treatment clause in the UK-Belgian DTT is broad enough to cover the dividend exemption after the UK tax rate would decrease below 15%. The clause in the UK-Belgian DTT is limited,[47] making it currently unclear whether DRD will still be applicable if the UK rate falls below 15%.

Following the jurisprudence of the Court of Justice of the European Union (CJEU),[48] Belgian domestic law had been changed to the effect that the non-deductible part of foreign dividends may be carried forward indefinitely. The carry-forward system of the unused portion of the 100% DRD[49] also applies for dividends from EEA countries and from treaty countries (containing a non-discrimination clause implying that dividends paid by the foreign subsidiary are exempt under the condition that the exemption would apply if both companies were resident in Belgium).[50] This is the case for the UK-Belgian DTT.[51] Where the UK is no longer part of the EEA, the part that is subject to the above restrictions may, however, still qualify as 'transferable DRD deduction'. As a result, ultimately no DRD deduction will be lost, in the assumption that the company will make enough taxable profits in the future to

44 Article 203, § 1, section 3 ITC.

45 Article 203, § 1 ITC.

46 This is a change from the 2015 Budget announcement that the rate would be reduced to 18% from 1 April 2020, and the 2016 Budget announcement that the rate would be further reduced from 18% to 17% from 1 April 2020.

47 In certain DTT, an equal treatment clause has been included by Belgium. As a result, the DRD deduction will still be possible for the countries concerned (for instance, the DTT of Belgium with USA and Switzerland).

48 CJEU, *Belgische Staat v NV Cobelfret* (Case C-138/07); *Belgische Staat v KBC Bank NV and Beleggen, Risicokapitaal, Beheer NV v Belgische Staat* (Joined Cases C-439/07 and C-499/07).

49 Article 204 ITC.

50 Carry-forward is, however, not possible for dividends received from third countries. The Constitutional Court decided in *Agfa-Gevaert v Belgian State* on 11 October 2012 (No. 5259) that the non-application of the carry-forward to third countries is compatible with the equality principle of the Belgian Constitution.

51 Article 24 UK-Belgian DTT.

enjoy the DRD-regime. Consequently, only a temporary difference will exist. It is worth noting that it is incompatible with the Parent-Subsidiary Directive that the foreign dividends received must first be included in the taxable base of the parent company and, subsequently, the dividends are deducted before any other deduction that can be claimed even if other deductions can only be claimed during a limited period.[52]

Inbound interests and royalties

6.7 According to current UK tax law, outgoing interests and royalties are generally subject to WHT at the 20% savings rate of income tax.[53] However, the position in relation to WHT rates on interest and royalties depends on the nature of the double tax treaty in force between the UK and Belgium.

According to Article 11(2) of the UK-Belgian DTT, a reduced 10% WHT of the gross amount of the *interest* may apply if the beneficial owner of the interest payments is a resident of the other state. As such, interest paid by a UK company to a Belgian company is taxable in Belgium. The UK may also apply a WHT up to 10%, unless it concerns interest on a loan of any kind taken out between two companies. In the latter case, an exemption applies. The exemption will take place through the intermediary of the administration via the 276R (for royalties) or 276 Int. Aut. (for interest) form.[54]

According to Article 12 of the UK-Belgian DTT, *royalties* distributed by a UK company to a Belgian company may only be taxed in Belgium. In concrete terms, this means that even after Brexit, a WHT exemption can still be applied to royalty payments, even if there is a WHT in the UK under internal law.

Consequently, as the double tax treaty will continue to apply post-Brexit, there will be no change to the taxation of interest or royalties granted from the UK. Interest payments will be subject to a maximum WHT of 10% (followed by a Belgian final tax of 30%), while royalties will be exempt from withholding tax under treaty law and only the Belgian final tax of 30% will apply.

Moreover, Belgian tax law grants a credit for interest and royalties on which foreign tax has been levied.[55] For the application of the so-called fixed foreign tax credit (*forfaitair gedeelte van buitenlandse belasting*/FBB), different restrictive rules apply depending on whether the credit relates to foreign interest or royalties:

---

52 CJEU 19 December 2019, *Brussels Securities* (Case C-389/18).

53 K De Haen, 'An Englishman in the EU (post-Brexit)' (2019) 1 *Internationale Fiscale Actualiteit*.

54 PJ Wouters and P Van Den Berghe, 'Brexit heeft grote impact op vennootschapsbelasting' (2019) 2 *Fiscale Actualiteit* 1–5.

55 Articles 285–292 ITC.

- For *interest*, the credit is variable but subject to a maximum. The credit is not refundable. The credit is not granted in respect of interest originating from assets or capital used outside Belgium for business purposes[56] and interest paid to a person acting only as an intermediary on behalf of a third party who provided the funds and who bears all or part of the risks relating to the loan.[57] For foreign interest, a tax credit corresponding to the actual amount of foreign tax paid is granted, with a maximum of 15%.
- In the case of *royalties*, the foreign tax credit is granted in respect of royalties that are subject to a foreign tax similar to the Belgian tax. For royalties, not qualifying for the 80%[58] or 85%[59] deduction, the credit is equal to 15/85 of the royalties, net of foreign tax but before the deduction of the Belgian WHT which is levied in certain cases.

As a result, Brexit should not affect interest and royalty payments, as it is always possible to fall back to the UK-Belgian DTT.

Capital gains on shareholdings in non-resident companies

6.8 The exemption on capital gains from the sale of shares in UK resident companies made by Belgian resident companies should, in principle, continue as before (assuming that the UK does not become a low-tax jurisdiction).

The Belgian domestic provisions transposing the Parent-Subsidiary Directive into Belgian law include an exemption of capital gains on shares. Belgium has amended its internal law, so that the conditions for applying the exemption for capital gains now coincide with the conditions for the DRD-regime as provided by Articles 202 and 203 ITC, and not to the additional conditions in Article 205 ITC.[60] The exemption for capital gains depends on the following conditions: a minimum holding of 10% or with a purchase value of 2.5 million in the company from which it owns the shares,[61] full ownership for an uninterrupted period of at least one year,[62] and the taxation requirement of the DRD regime.[63] However, Article 205, § 2 of the ITC does not apply to any

56 Article 285 ITC.

57 Article 289 ITC.

58 This so-called patent income deduction was abolished with effect from 1 July 2016 and replaced by the innovation deduction regime. A transitional measure is applicable for patents requested or acquired before 1 July 2016 and allows taxpayers to benefit from the patent income deduction regime until 30 June 2021. See Articles 205/1–205/4 ITC.

59 The innovation deduction regime replaces the patent income deduction with effect from 1 July 2016. See Articles 205/1–205/4 ITC.

60 Article 192 ITC. See P Van Den Berghe and P-J Wouters, 'Regering zet in op versterking holdingregime' (2018) 4 *Fiscale Actualiteit* 6–10.

61 Article 202, § 2, section 1, 1° ITC.

62 Article 202, § 2, section 1, 2° ITC.

63 Article 203 ITC.

realised capital gain, so that a full exemption can be applied as soon as the relevant conditions have been met.[64]

The capital gains exemption only applies if the shares are held for a minimum holding period of 12 months (supplemented by the subject-to-tax test). The subject-to-tax condition will thus become a relevant assessment point for the exemption of capital gains realised by a Belgian company on shares in a UK company post-Brexit. If the holding period or the subject-to-tax test is not met, the gains are taxed at the general corporate income tax rate of 25%. As from fiscal year 2020, the capital gains realised with respect to short-term portfolio investments are also subject to a rate of 25%. These are shares sold within a period of 12 months after their acquisition (but where the minimum holding and the subject-to-tax test are met).

Capital losses on shares, except for liquidation losses, are not deductible.

Permanent establishments abroad

6.9 Brexit will have no impact on the operation of the optional foreign branch exemption.

Controlled Foreign Corporation rules

6.10 With effect from 1 January 2019, the Controlled Foreign Corporation (CFC) legislation has been introduced into Belgian tax law by implementing the mandatory rules provided for by the Anti-Tax Avoidance Directive (ATAD).[65] According to the CFC legislation, a Belgian company may be taxed on the 'non-distributed profits' derived by a foreign company or permanent establishment that qualifies as a CFC provided that the profits arise from an artificial structure which has been put in place for the essential purpose of obtaining a tax advantage.[66] For the determination whether a structure is artificial, a transactional approach applies. Accordingly, an artificial structure is deemed to exist, for example, when assets and risks are transferred outside Belgium to be owned by the CFC, but the main business decisions regarding the foreign company set-up are still made by the Belgian company or by its employees.

A foreign company is considered a CFC if the following two conditions are simultaneously met:[67]

---

64 A Lettens and S De Wachter, 'Welke impact heeft de Brexit op vennootschapsbelasting' (2019) 18 *Fiscale Wenken* available at: www.Monkey.be.

65 Article 185/2 ITC.

66 Article 185/2, § 1, section 1 ITC.

67 Article 185/2, § 2 ITC.

- *The control test*: the Belgian company owns (directly or indirectly) more than 50% of the voting rights, or holds directly or indirectly a participation of at least 50% of the capital, or is entitled to receive at least 50% of the profits of the foreign entity.
- *The taxation test*: the foreign company or permanent establishment is located in a country where it is either not subject to a corporate income tax or is subject to a corporate income tax rate that is less than half the rate that it would have been charged had it been located in Belgium.

If the conditions of the CFC are fulfilled, the non-distributed profits derived by such foreign company or permanent establishment immediately become subject to tax in the hands of the Belgian parent company. However, based on the application of the transactional approach, these profits will be limited to the profits attributable to the significant people functions carried out by the Belgian company or by its employees.

The CFC regime does not make a difference between third countries (such as the UK) or EU/EEA Member States. Post-Brexit, companies under the current UK national corporate tax regime (19% as regular nominal rate in the UK) are not considered a CFC. Where profits of these foreign establishments arise from 'non-genuine arrangements', they are attributed to (and taxed in the hands of) the head office. However, if the UK were to decide to reduce its nominal rate to half of the Belgian corporate income tax of 25%[68] (ie, below 12.5%), this would mean that the CFC regime applies. According to the preamble of the ATAD, it is then up to Belgium to determine 'a sufficiently high tax rate fractional threshold', be it by including the corporate tax rate level or by using white, grey or black lists.[69] Although currently not (yet) the case, if Belgium applied an effective tax rate test (as required under ATAD), a UK subsidiary could be caught by the CFC rule even if the nominal tax rate in the UK is higher than 12.5%.

Foreign losses

6.11 In general, foreign tax losses incurred by companies with activities abroad in a foreign permanent establishment (or losses of assets held abroad) may be deducted by the Belgian head office.[70] Losses from a treaty country are set off first against income which is exempt in Belgium under a tax treaty. The losses are only deductible if the Belgian company can demonstrate that these foreign losses were not already deducted elsewhere. Therefore, it must be proved that the losses were not set off against foreign profits of the same foreign activity or against other foreign profits.[71]

68 Article 215(1) ITC.
69
70 Article 185, § 3 ITC.
71 Article 185, § 3 ITC. *See* also Article 75 Royal Decree.

As from 1 January 2020 (tax assessment year 2021), the amount of professional losses incurred in foreign establishments or in relation to assets located abroad which the company has at its disposal and which are located in a state with which Belgium has concluded a DTT, is no longer automatically deductible from Belgian profits. The only exception is if it relates to definitive losses of earnings incurred within an EEA Member State.[72] As such, deduction of foreign losses will only be the case if the permanent establishment is located in an EEA Member State.

Consequently, post-Brexit, a Belgian company with a permanent establishment in the UK is no longer eligible to make the final offset of losses in Belgium.[73] Before Brexit, losses of the British permanent establishment could be offset in Belgium, regardless of whether the UK is still part of the EEA or not. However, from assessment year 2021 (and after the transition period), the new rule applies and the set-off will therefore disappear.

IMPACT ON CROSS-BORDER GROUP TAX REGIMES

6.12 Under the Belgian group contribution regime (effective from 1 January 2019; assessment year 2020), Belgian companies and Belgian permanent establishments of non-resident companies established in the EEA may transfer taxable profits to a loss-making group company or permanent establishment in a taxable period.[74] As such, Belgian group entity with profit (A) can provide a group contribution to a Belgian group entity with loss (B). With respect to A, the group contribution constitutes a tax deduction, while B must add the group contribution to its tax base. A group contribution may only be made to a company in which a 90% shareholding between the companies or via the EEA parent company is held for an uninterrupted period of at least five accounting years. Foreign companies established in an EEA country (ie, Belgian permanent establishments of companies resident in an EU/EEA Member State) may be included in a group.[75] Belgian subsidiary companies controlled by the same company resident in an EU/EEA Member State can opt to be included in the same fiscal unit. The group contribution regime allows the utilisation of tax losses from a qualifying foreign company, located in the EEA. The regime does not provide for a full consolidation. Each group company must file its own tax return.

The qualification of the UK as a non-EU/EEA Member State has the consequence that British parents with Belgian subsidiaries/permanent establishments can no longer make use of the group contribution regime

72 Article 185, § 3 ITC. *See* also Article 75 Royal Decree.

73 PJ Wouters and P Van Den Berghe, 'Brexit heeft grote impact op vennootschapsbelasting' (2019) 2 *Fiscale Actualiteit* 1–5.

74 Article 205/5 ITC.

75 Article 205/5, §2 ITC.

between its subsidiaries/permanent establishments because the parent (UK company) is not part of the EEA.[76] The group contribution regime will also not be applicable to Belgian resident sister companies controlled by a common parent company tax resident of the UK. Hence, in relation to existing fiscal units formed of sister companies controlled by a common UK resident parent company, in the absence of grandfathering rules, the qualification of the UK as a non-EU/EEA Member State might determine an interruption of the existing fiscal units with potential adverse consequences for the companies involved. For instance, the net losses of a foreign (UK) permanent establishments will no longer be deductible from the Belgian taxable basis if the losses are realized within a non-EU/EEA Member State.

In this regard, reference can be made, however, to the non-discrimination article in the UK-Belgian DTT.[77] For the purposes of granting the cross-border group tax regime, it should not make a difference whether the parent company is established in an EEA Member State or in another state. In this regard, the benefit should be extended to any common parent in a country with which Belgium has concluded a tax treaty determining a non-discrimination provision.[78]

TAX RAMIFICATIONS FOR CROSS-BORDER MERGERS, OTHER REORGANISATIONS AND TRANSFERS OF RESIDENCE

Tax neutral cross-border mergers and other reorganisations

6.13 In general, Merger Directive No. 2009/133/EC offers tax relief to cross-border reorganisations. The tax neutral treatment applies to reorganisations between intra-European companies (ie, every company of an EU Member State). Therefore, post-Brexit it will be impossible to invoke the Merger Directive where a UK company is involved in the reorganisation. However, the tax neutrality of the reorganisation covered by the Merger Directive will continue to apply during the transition period.

According to the Belgian domestic provisions implementing the Merger Directive, the exemption regime for cross-border reorganisations only applies if the receiving and transferring company is a domestic or intra-European company.[79] The law defines an intra-European company as a company resident in another EU Member State which qualifies for the benefits of the Merger

76 PJ Wouters and P Van Den Berghe, 'Brexit heeft grote impact op vennootschapsbelasting' (2019) 2 *Fiscale Actualiteit* 1–5.

77 Article 24(2) UK-Belgian DTT.

78 P Vancloosters, P Deré and D Verbeurgt, 'Invoering van de consolidatie in België: opportuniteiten en beperkingen?' (2018) 7 *AFT* 10.

79 Article 211 ITC.

Directive and is subject to a tax similar to the Belgian corporate income tax.[80] Because Brexit does not provide a specific provision that a UK company still qualifies for the Merger Directive, the Merger Directive will no longer apply. A merger of a Belgian company into a British company will no longer be exempted. As the conditions for tax neutrality are not met, the transferring company is deemed to be liquidated for tax purposes. All assets and liabilities of the company are deemed to be realised, implying that any built-in gains on the assets will become taxable and built-in losses will generally be tax deductible. The resulting net value will be deemed to be distributed to the shareholders. A taxable merger transaction will give rise to a step-up in tax basis in the hands of the receiving entity resulting in a significant reduction of the overall tax impact of a taxable merger transaction. Cross-border reorganisations that have occurred before Brexit remain exempt in principle. For this reason, several anticipatory mergers prior to Brexit have already taken place in order to still benefit from the exemption regime.

The Belgian Law of 21 February 2020 provides an arrangement which allows fiscal neutrality under certain conditions for the entire range of cross-border mergers, divisions, transfers and seat transfers with a UK component.[81] For the assimilation of the UK with an EU Member State, the relevant transaction must be published in the *Belgian Official Gazette* by 31 December 2020 at the latest.[82] The date on which the formal decision to restructure is taken, or the date on which the restructuring is implemented, is not relevant. Only the date of publication in the *Official Gazette* is important. Reorganisations where publication takes place after 31 December 2020 fall under the liquidation regime of Articles 208 and 209 ITC.

What will remain possible for foreign companies, including non-European companies, is the contribution of a Belgian establishment to a domestic company. Article 231, § 3 ITC provides that foreign companies (even if they are not tax residents in an EU Member State) can transfer the Belgian establishment to a domestic company without the creation of any latent capital gains on the contributed assets.[83] Depreciation, investment deductions, tax credits for research and development, deduction for patent and innovation income and so on will be taken over in the domestic company as if the transaction has not occurred.[84] This is the principle of fiscal continuity.[85]

Please also note that publication in the *Belgian Official Gazette* is not necessarily the final element of such cross-border reorganisations. For example, a special

80 Article 2, 5°, b) bis ITC.

81 *See* Article 184bis, § 4 and § 5, Article 184ter, section 8, Article 211, § 1, section 4 and 5, and § 2, section 6, Article 214bis, and Article 229, § 4, section 3 to 10, and Article 231, § 2 ITC.

82 Article 545, § 4 ITC.

83 PJ Wouters, 'Wat betekent het Brexit-akkoord voor de vennootschapsbelasting?' (2020) 9 *Fiscale Actualiteit* 4–8.

84 Article 231 § 3 ITC.

85 PJ Wouters and P Van Den Berghe, 'Brexit heeft grote impact op vennootschapsbelasting' (2019) 2 *Fiscale Actualiteit* 1–5.

general meeting of a Belgian company approves a merger in November 2020 whereby it is taken over by a British company. Suppose that the transaction is published in the *Belgian Official Gazette* before the end of 2020. Fiscal neutrality would then apparently apply even if this cross-border operation would not actually take place until sometime later – in 2021 – following the necessary procedural steps in the UK.

After the end of the transition period (31 December 2020), the UK will be a third country. As a result, reorganisations will no longer be carried out in a tax neutral manner.

Transfer of residence abroad

6.14 When a taxpayer takes assets or its tax residence outside the tax jurisdiction of a state (transfer of registered office), exit taxes may apply. These exit tax provisions apply to Belgian resident companies that cease to be tax resident in Belgium.[86] In accordance with these exit tax provisions, all latent capital gains of the company (ie, hidden reserves) are immediately subject to corporate income tax. However, the gains on assets which can be attributed to a Belgian permanent establishment of the migrated company are tax exempt. With effect from tax year 2019, the transfer of assets from a Belgian head office to a permanent establishment situated in another EU Member State or EEA country or a third state is subject to tax.[87] A step-up in value of the assets is applicable if the assets or tax residence of a company or permanent establishment is transferred abroad. Post-Brexit, the transfer to the UK will imply the immediate levy of exit tax. The same regime applies for other similar transactions (transfer of assets from branch to foreign head office, etc).

The exit tax on EEA outbound cross-border relocation of assets or business, migration or restructuring can be paid immediately or paid in instalments over a maximum period of five years.[88] The optional deferred payment regime is only available for several qualifying transactions, that is, a transfer by a Belgian company of its place of effective management (real seat) and/or its registered office to another EEA Member State. Moreover, to qualify for the outbound transfer of assets/business, the head office or the transferee permanent establishment must be established/located in another EEA Member State. For EEA Member States not being EU Member States, an additional condition is that there must be an agreement providing for mutual assistance for recovery. Consequently, transfer of a registered office from Belgium to the UK cancels the facility to defer taxation, and an immediate levy will occur.

86 Article 210, § 1, section 4 ITC.
87 Article 185, § 1 ITC.
88 Article 413/1 ITC.

Inbound transfer of residence

6.15 In relation to companies transferring their tax residence to Belgium, Belgian legislation provides that the tax basis of the assets of the company is stepped up to their actual value (*werkelijk waarde/valeur réelle*) as determined upon arrival.[89] An exception to this rule, however, applies for transfers of seat from tax havens or low tax jurisdiction.[90] For a definition, reference is made to the taxation condition for the application of the Belgian participation exemption as provided for by Article 203, § 1, al. 1, 1° ITC. An exception to the exception, however, applies for companies established in an EU Member State, which are subject to the general tax regime in that state. In the case of a transfer of seat from a tax haven or low tax jurisdiction to Belgium, Belgium still reserves the right to tax future value increases starting from the acquisition or investment value of the respective assets, as these value increases are deemed not to be subject to (sufficient) taxation in the state of transfer. Furthermore, future depreciations will only be recognised when they are founded on the acquisition or investment value and amortisations and capital losses will be determined on the basis of the acquisition or investment value minus the depreciations and amortisations that have occurred on the basis of the provisions of the ITC.[91] Since the UK is not considered a tax haven or low tax jurisdiction, even after the transition period, this provision should apply in relation to the UK.

The same regime applies to other similar transactions (transfer of assets, seat of management or administration from foreign branch to head office, etc).

OTHER

6.16 The non-EEA/EU membership of the UK is also important for other tax provisions, for instance, the deferred tax regime (Article 47 ITC), the conditions of applications of the tax shelter regime (Article 194ter and 194ter/1 ITC), etc. As discussed below, these benefits will cease upon the UK becoming a non-EEA member.

Deferred taxation

6.17 When a capital gain is realised on business assets, Belgian tax law provides an optional deferred taxation regime whereby the capital gain is not taxed immediately, but on a future pro rata basis over a number of years in proportion to the depreciation pertaining to the assets acquired.[92] If a company opts for deferred taxation, it needs to reinvest within the specified

89 Article 184ter, § 2, section 2 ITC.
90 Article 184ter, § 2, section 8 ITC.
91 Article 184ter, § 2, section 8 ITC.
92 Article 47 ITC.

reinvestment period. The reinvestment period is in principle three years, unless the reinvestment is made in buildings, aircraft or vessels, in which case the reinvestment period is extended to five years. The tax deferral applies to reinvestments made in assets located in EEA Member States. A reinvestment by a Belgian company in an asset located in the UK will therefore no longer qualify for the deferred taxation.

Tax shelter system

6.18 The tax shelter system can be opted for when certain conditions are met, including the need for qualifying expenditure in the EEA.[93] Expenditures incurred outside the EEA on the production and operation of eligible work cannot benefit from the tax shelter-regime.

Specific transitional provisions as provided for by the Belgian Brexit Law of 21 February 2020

6.19 The Belgian Law of 21 February 2020 contains various new and useful transitional provisions, but also a surprising flexibility in terms of future Brexit developments and agreements. It is worth noting that the Belgian Law of 3 April 2019 on the withdrawal of the UK from the EU previously provided a general transitional arrangement regarding all provisions included in the ITC until 31 December 2019, but never entered into force. The Law of 21 February 2020 now replaces this general transitional arrangement with 'specific' transitional arrangements until 31 December 2020.[94] This Law stipulates that the above-mentioned dates can be amended by Royal Decree until 31 December of the year in which the UK and Northern Ireland effectively leave the EU.

Specific transitional measures

6.20 The transitional regimes relevant from a corporate tax perspective include the following measures:

Deductibility of professional expenses of employer contributions

6.21 The Belgian Brexit Law provides the preservation of the deduction as a professional expense of employer contributions paid to an insurer or institution established in the UK related to supplementary pension, long-term savings and pension savings contracts concluded on or before December

93 Article 194ter, § 1, last sentence ITC.
94 *Parliamentary Senat,* Chamber 2019-2020, no. 55-0948.

2020.[95] The transition period is not limited to payments of contributions and premiums paid up to 31 December 2020, but will continue throughout the entire term of insurance contracts concluded no later than 31 December 2020. Consequently, taxpayers (during that transition period) can still make payments to institutions established in the UK and those taxpayers continue to be entitled to the associated Belgian tax benefits. During the term of such contracts, the Belgian regime remains applicable for payments made to funds and insurance companies established in the UK.[96]

This special transitional regime provides certainty regarding current contracts, in particular for companies that can only deduct certain employer contributions (within the meaning of Article 52,3°, b ITC) as business expenses if they are paid into an institution established in the EEA. The transitional arrangement is of course also crucial for natural persons, as only payments to an institution in the EEA are eligible for the tax reduction for pension and long-term savings that they can apply in personal income tax.

WHT reduction for research

6.22 A similar transition period applies to cooperation agreements between universities or colleges and companies, which may receive an exemption from payment of withholding tax on the wages of certain researchers.[97] These agreements entail typically long-term consequences. The exemption can continue to be applied to cooperation agreements that are concluded no later than 31 December 2020,[98] and not only to the wages of researchers who are paid until the end of 2020.

Exemption for capital gains by private investment companies

6.23 Capital gains realised before 31 December 2020 by private investment companies can be exempted if the 'more flexible' conditions of Article 192, §3 ITC are met. However, the private investment company must be established in the EU. If not, the conditions of Article 192, §1 ITC apply. The Belgian legislator provides that the UK is equated with a Member State of the EU for capital gains realised up to 31 December 2020.[99] However, it is not clear why a specific rule is required that provides for the same date as the general rule.[100]

95 New Article 545, § 1 ITC juncto Article 59, § 1, section 1, 1° ITC.
96 New Article 545, § 2 ITC.
97 New Article 275/3, §1 ITC.
98 Article 545, § 2 ITC.
99 New Article 545, § 3 ITC.
100 PJ Wouters, 'Wat betekent het Brexit-akkoord voor de vennootschapsbelasting?' (2020) 9 *Fiscale Actualiteit* 4–8.

Fiscal neutrality for cross-border reorganisations

6.24 As mentioned above, the Belgian Brexit Law provides that the UK is assimilated to a EU Member State for the relevant transactions and transfers that are published no later than 31 December 2020 in the *Belgian Official Gazette*.[101] Consequently, transactions and transfers involving a UK company migrating to Belgium, which are announced in the *Belgian Official Gazette* by 31 December 2020 at the latest, are tax exempt (see **6.13**).

Transition period of five years for real estate companies

6.25 Belgian law provides a reduced separate tax of 15% on dividends (both in WHT and personal income tax) paid by property investment funds and regulated real estate companies. This is the case if the real estate portfolio consists of at least 60% of real estate located in the EEA and that is exclusively or mainly used or intended for adapted residential units for residential care or healthcare.[102] To give property investment funds and regulated real estate companies sufficient time to adapt to that reality, the Belgian legislator stipulates that this arrangement also applies during a transition period of five years for real estate or legal rights on real estate located in the UK (until 31 December 2025). Until then, real estate in the UK can still be included in setting the 60% limit for being subject to a lower 15% WHT on dividends.

Note that the application of the arrangement is subject to the condition that the UK real estate (and in the case of indirect ownership also the participation in the company in which the real estate is held) has been continuously held since the end of the transition period, that is, since 31 December 2020, and this up to and including the payment or distribution of the dividend. The reference to 31 December 2020 seems unfortunate because the new Brexit law explicitly stipulates at the same time that the fiscal fiction (ie, that the UK is equated with an EU Member State until 31 December 2020) does not apply to the legal provisions providing for a reduced tax rate.[103] Therefore, a lack of clarity arises for dividends paid in 2020 regarding the application of the reduced tax rate (if UK real estate is required to reach the 60% threshold).

Tonnage tax regime

6.26 Upon request, Belgian companies (and private entrepreneurs) may opt to report taxable income for corporate income tax as a certain percentage of the volume transported if they operate sea vessels sailing under the flag of Belgium or another EU Member State or EEA country for the transport of goods or persons on (i) international sea routes, or (ii) routes from and to installations at sea used for the exploration for, or the exploitation of, natural

101 New Article 545, § 4 ITC.

102 Art. 171, 3°*quater* and 269, § 1, 3° ITC.

103 Articles 171, 3°quater and 269, § 1, 3° ITC. See Article 6 Belgian Brexit Law.

resources and certain related activities.[104] The fixed profit is determined on the basis of the tonnage of the seagoing vessels. The Belgian Brexit Law provides adjustments to the so-called 'tonnage tax regime' to obtain the same continuity in this context. The UK is deemed to be an EU Member State up to and including the tax year linked to the taxable period ending on 31 December 2020 at the latest. Since the general transition period only relates to ITC, and the tonnage tax is not regulated in the ITC, a separate equivalence fiction had to be inserted in the program law of 2 August 2020.[105] Note that the Regulation can only enter into force after a positive decision by the European Commission after notification.

Exclusions from the assimilation fiction

6.27 As mentioned, the equivalence provision applies to the entire ITC (considering the specific exceptions mentioned). However, the Belgian Brexit Law of 21 February 2020 excludes the general transitional arrangement for the application of three provisions (namely Articles 364bis, 364ter and 515septies ITC). These three provisions concern the situations in which a taxpayer (natural person) transfers (or has transferred) an insurance contract to another company within the EEA, or moved his tax residence within the EEA, without such transfers giving rise to taxation. The Belgian Brexit Law excludes these provisions from the scope of the general transitional arrangement without providing a specific transitional arrangement regarding these provisions. For these provisions, Brexit has all legal effects from the day it enters into force.

If such transfers take place outside the EEA, they are treated as payment or allocation of capital and thus lead to taxation in Belgium. If those provisions were also subject to a transition period, taxpayers could avoid tax due by moving their property or tax residence to the UK soon before the end of the transition period. For the application of those provisions, Brexit will therefore have all legal effects as of 31 January 2020 and no transition period applies. According to the Parliamentary preparation, the Belgian legislator wants to avoid abuse in this way.[106] However, not all transfers are primarily driven or exclusively for tax reasons, but the legislator does not make that distinction.[107]

---

104 Articles 115–119 Program Law of 2 August 2002.

105 New Article 208 Program Law of 2 August 2002.

106 Parliamentary Senate, 2019–2020, No. 55-0948/1, 13.

107 PJ Wouters, 'Wat betekent het Brexit-akkoord voor de vennootschapsbelasting?' (2020) 9 *Fiscale Actualiteit* 4–8.

Chapter 7

Czech Republic

Helena Navratilova

INTRODUCTION

7.1 The purpose of this chapter is to analyse the main consequences of the UK leaving the EU from a Czech corporate income tax perspective.

The analysis is based on the assumption that the UK, having reached no agreement with the EU in respect of taxation, will also not be part of the EEA. The outline of the rules below is relevant for the period following the transition period and starting from 1 January 2021. This analysis is further based on the *Czech Act no. 586/1992 Col On Income Taxes*, as amended (hereinafter the *ITA*), official guidelines thereto and the UK-Czechoslovakia Double Taxation Convention for the Avoidance of Double Taxation and the Prevention of Fiscal Evasion with Respect to Taxes on Income and Capital Gains (hereinafter the UK-Czech tax treaty).

For the purposes of this text, a Czech company is deemed to mean a company or a body of persons, other than a general partnership (*veřejná obchodní společnost*) or a limited partnership (commandite company, *komanditní společnost*), which is a tax resident of the Czech Republic and whose income is subject to corporate income tax. General partnerships are tax transparent and limited partnerships are semi-transparent in relation to the general partners. The activity of a transparent entity whose members are non-local persons gives rise to a permanent establishment of those members in the Czech Republic. Transparent entities are mainly used in international group structures that involve corporate entities as general partners. Due to the unlimited liability of the general partners and lack of any tax advantage, they are not very common in Czech domestic corporate structures.

Pursuant to the *ITA*, a company is deemed to be resident in the Czech Republic for corporate tax purposes if it has its registered office or place of (effective) management in the Czech Republic. The place of management is deemed to be the address of the place from which the entity is managed. For this purpose, management is considered to be the day-to-day management rather than only strategic decision making. Every case, however, needs to be assessed based on its own individual facts and circumstances.

TAX RAMIFICATIONS FOR INBOUND INVESTMENTS

Outbound dividends

7.2 In general, outbound dividends paid to non-resident corporate shareholders are subject to a 35% withholding tax, which applies to persons who are tax residents of any state which has no double taxation treaty with the Czech Republic or which does not take part in international exchange of tax information (*ITA, s 36, subs 1*).

In accordance with Article 10 of the UK-Czech tax treaty, if a recipient of dividends is a beneficial owner which is a tax resident of the UK, the withholding tax shall not exceed: (i) 5% of the gross amount of dividends paid to the UK company which controls at least 25% of the voting rights in the Czech company paying the dividends, or (ii) 15% of the gross amount of dividends in all other cases in which the beneficial owner is a UK tax resident.

The tax is withheld by the payer of the dividends as at the date on which the dividends are actually paid; however, this must be not later than by the end of the third month following the month in which the general assembly of shareholders approved relevant financial statements and decided on the dividend distribution. In the case of registered shares, the tax must be withheld by the end of the month following the month in which the dividend distribution was duly approved.

Dividends paid to a UK parent company will continue to be tax exempt in accordance with *ITA, s 19, subs 9* subject to underlying conditions similar to those set out in the EU Council Directive 2011/96/EU on Common Taxation of Parent Companies and Subsidiaries (Parent-Subsidiary Directive). In order to satisfy the conditions, any Czech subsidiary of a UK parent company must have the legal form of a limited liability company, joint-stock company or a cooperative, and the parent company needs to be a tax resident of the UK and have a legal form comparable with the stated legal forms of its Czech subsidiary. Furthermore, it must hold at least a 10% share in the registered capital of the subsidiary for at least an uninterrupted 12-month period as at the date of the decision on the dividend distribution and its profit must be subject to income tax charged at the rate of at least 12% in the given and immediately preceding tax period. (*ITA, s 19, subs 1, 3 and 9*). In the case of a company reorganisation, the entitlement to dividend income exemption is assessed cumulatively taking into account whether the underlying conditions have been satisfied at the legal predecessor of the recipient and at the recipient of the dividend income. A UK parent company exempt from tax or which can elect a tax exemption or similar relief does not qualify for the exemption of dividends from withholding tax (hereinafter the parent-subsidiary rules). The dividend exemption does not apply to dividends paid by a Czech subsidiary in liquidation.

The tax exemption of dividends outlined in above applies even before the 12-month holding period of at least a 10% share in the registered capital of the subsidiary is satisfied, provided that such time test is met subsequently. Any failure to meet the statutory requirement thereafter is treated in the same manner as a tax underpayment involving late interest charges and penalties.

In order to apply either a withholding tax rate on dividends reduced in accordance with the UK-Czech tax treaty or the exemption from withholding tax in accordance with the parent-subsidiary rules, the UK recipient of dividends must provide the Czech payer of dividends a certificate of tax residence in the UK and evidence that it is a beneficial owner of the dividends. The latter can be provided in the form of an affidavit.

The withholding tax on dividends at treaty rates or the tax exemption under the parent-subsidiary rules does not apply if the beneficial owner of the dividends, being a resident of the UK, carries on business in the Czech Republic through a permanent establishment situated therein and the company paying the dividends is also a resident of the Czech Republic, whilst the shareholding in respect of which the dividends are paid is effectively connected with such permanent establishment. In such a case, the provisions on taxation of business profits apply.

In summary, due to specific domestic provisions in the *ITA*, tax exemption available under the EU Parent-Subsidiary Directive as implemented in the Czech *ITA* will continue to apply to UK parent companies under the terms outlined above. If the conditions are not met, the reduced withholding tax rates will apply in accordance with the UK-Czech tax treaty.

Outbound interest

7.3 For the purpose of this text, interest means income from securities, bonds or debentures, loans and other debt-claims of any kind, as well as similar income in accordance with the *ITA*. Whether the principal is secured by mortgage and whether or not it carries a right to participate in profits is irrelevant.

In general, interest paid to non-tax residents is subject to a 35% withholding tax. However, in accordance with Article 11 of the UK-Czech tax treaty, interest paid by a Czech payer to a person who is a tax resident of the UK and beneficially owns the interest is only taxable in the UK. Both the tax residence status and the beneficial ownership need to be duly evidenced to the payer of the interest income before the interest is credited or actually paid by the payer.

In order to apply the exemption from withholding tax on interest income, the UK company as a recipient of interest income must provide the Czech payer of interest a certificate of tax residence in the UK and evidence that it is a beneficial owner of the interest. The latter can be provided in the form of an affidavit.

The exemption of interest from withholding tax does not apply if the beneficial owner of the interest, being a resident of the UK, carries on business in the Czech Republic, in which the interest arises, through a permanent establishment situated therein, or performs in the Czech Republic other state independent personal services from a permanent establishment situated therein, and the debt-claim in respect of which the interest is paid is effectively connected with such permanent establishment. In such a case, the provisions on taxation of business profits apply.

Interest arising in the Czech Republic and attributable to a permanent establishment of a UK company carrying on business in the Czech Republic is not subject to the treaty relief but is included in the corporate income tax base as it would be for Czech companies.

If, due to a special relationship between the payer and the beneficial owner of interest income, or between both of them and some other person, the amount of the interest paid exceeds the amount which would have been agreed upon by the payer and the beneficial owner in the absence of such relationship (arm's length amount of interest), the UK-Czech tax treaty provisions apply only to the arm's length amount. In such a case, the excess part of interest shall be treated as dividends. This means that it will be subject to withholding tax at the rate of 5% or 15%, as appropriate (see **7.2** above).

Prior to Brexit and until the end of 2020 interest on loans, bonds, debentures, notes and bills of exchange can be exempt from withholding tax in the Czech Republic provided that the following conditions are satisfied: the recipient of interest holds a share of at least 25% in the registered capital or 25% of the voting rights in the payer of the interest for at least 24 months and some further requirements, such as advance approval of the exemption issued upon request by a local tax administrator of the interest payer. Since this general relief provided pursuant to the statutory provisions implementing Council Directive 2003/49/EC on a Common System of Taxation Applicable to Interest and Royalty Payments Made between Associated Companies of Different Member States is less favourable than the UK-Czech tax treaty provisions, the tax treaty rules allocating the taxing rights to the UK prevail.

Outbound royalties

7.4 In accordance with Article 12 of the UK-Czech tax treaty royalties arising in the Czech Republic which are derived and beneficially owned by a UK company (or individual) are subject to a 10% withholding tax.

For the purpose of this text, royalties mean consideration of any kind paid for the use of, or the right to use, any patent, trademark, design or model, plan, secret formula or process, or for information concerning industrial, commercial, technical, technological or scientific experience. Contrary to many treaties on the prevention of double taxation, lease payments for the right to use any industrial, commercial or scientific equipment are also considered royalties. The Czech Republic made a reservation to Article 12 of the OECD Model Tax Convention on Income and Capital to the extent that it has the right to continue to levy withholding tax on lease payments arising in the Czech Republic. Furthermore, the 10% withholding tax applies also on royalties for the use of, or the right to use, any copyright of literary, artistic or scientific work (including cinematograph films or tapes for radio and television broadcasting). The royalties for using or the right to use software are also included in the scope of Article 12: Royalties of the UK-Czech tax treaty.

The tax must be withheld by the payer of the royalties, in most cases, as at the date on which the royalties are actually paid.

In order to apply the reduced rate of withholding tax on royalties in accordance with the UK-Czech tax treaty, the UK company as a recipient of royalties must provide the Czech payer of royalties a certificate of tax residence in the UK and evidence that it is a beneficial owner of the royalties. The latter can be provided in the form of an affidavit.

Royalties are deemed to arise in the Czech Republic if the payer is, inter alia, a resident of the Czech Republic. If, however, the person legally paying the royalties, whether he/she is a resident of the Czech Republic or not, has in the UK a permanent establishment in connection with which the obligation to pay the royalties arises and the royalties are borne by such permanent establishment, then the royalties shall be deemed to arise in the UK.

Similarly, withholding tax on royalties does not apply if the beneficial owner of the royalties, being a resident of the UK, carries on business in the Czech Republic, in which the royalties also arise, through a permanent establishment situated in the Czech Republic or performs independent personal services from a permanent establishment situated in the Czech Republic and the right or property in respect of which the royalties are paid is effectively connected with such permanent establishment. In such a case, the provisions on taxation of business profits or income from independent personal services apply.

Where, owing to a special relationship between the Czech payer and the UK beneficial owner or between both of them and some other person, the amount of the royalties paid exceeds, for whatever reason, the amount which would have been agreed upon by the payer and the beneficial owner in the absence of such relationship, withholding tax of 10% applies only to the last-mentioned amount. In such a case, the excess part of the royalties shall remain taxable at a 15% withholding tax rate.

Capital gains on shareholdings in resident companies

7.5 Assuming the withdrawal of the UK from the EU is made without an agreement concerning taxation of income and capital, the tax treatment of capital gains realised by UK resident companies or individuals in relation to Czech companies will not change.

In general, capital gains realised by Czech tax non-residents on alienation of shareholdings in companies having their registered office in the Czech Republic are subject to a 15% withholding tax.

This 15% tax is eliminated under Article 13: Capital gains of the UK-Czech tax treaty for tax residents of the UK since Article 13 allocates the taxing right over capital gains to the UK.

Permanent establishments

7.6 The membership of the UK in the EU had no impact on the tax treatment of a permanent establishment of a UK tax resident in the Czech Republic. Hence, Brexit has no impact on such tax assessment and tax treatment of a permanent establishment of a UK tax resident in the Czech Republic.

A transfer of assets from a permanent establishment of a UK tax resident located in the Czech Republic to the UK tax resident, ie with no change of the ownership of the assets, is subject to exit tax charged at 19% on the market value of the assets. The tax payment can be made in instalments spread over up to five years following the exit tax due date.

Other

7.7 Evidence of beneficial ownership and tax residence certification are the key requirements of the Czech tax administration for providing access to tax treaty benefits. The general and certain specific tax anti-avoidance rules enable the Czech tax authorities to deny treaty benefits to conduit entities and in other 'treaty shopping' situations.

The Czech Republic has not yet ratified the Multilateral Convention to Implement Tax Treaty Related Measures to Prevent BEPS. When it does so, the UK-Czech tax treaty will be amended so as to incorporate minimum standards to counter treaty abuse and to improve dispute resolution mechanisms. The interdiction of UK-Czech tax treaty abuse will be further supported by an anti-tax avoidance rule pursued as a legal principle by the Czech administrative courts as well as a more recent amendment to the Czech Tax Procedure Code. Moreover, some other specific provisions will impact inbound investments, such as thin capitalisation rules, principal purpose test for mergers and other company reorganisations concerning Czech subsidiaries of UK companies, limitation of excess borrowing costs etc.

TAX RAMIFICATIONS FOR OUTBOUND INVESTMENTS

Inbound dividends

7.8 In general, dividends paid by non-resident companies to Czech resident companies are included in a separate corporate tax base and are subject to 15% corporate income tax unless they are exempt under the parent-subsidiary rules (Please see **7.2** above). If the dividends are not exempt from corporate income tax at the Czech company, the tax withheld in the UK can be credited against the Czech tax charge on dividend income up to the amount based on the treaty withholding tax rate of 5% or 15%, as appropriate. This deduction of the tax credit shall not, however, exceed that part of the Czech corporate income tax, computed before the deduction, which is appropriate to the gross dividend which may be taxed in the UK.

The parent-subsidiary rules will continue to apply in the relationship between a Czech parent company and its UK subsidiary. In particular, a UK subsidiary of a Czech parent company needs to have a legal form comparable with a Czech limited liability company, joint-stock company or a co-operative and its profit must be subject to tax similar to Czech corporate income tax and be charged at the rate of at least 12% in the accounting/tax period in which it debited the dividend receivable and in the immediately preceding tax period. In the case of company reorganisation such as amalgamation, merger, de-merger or a spin-off, these conditions are assessed cumulatively for the legal predecessor and successor. A UK subsidiary company exempt from tax or which can elect a tax exemption or similar tax relief will not qualify for the exemption of dividends from withholding tax (*ITA, s 19, subs 1, 3 and 9*). The Czech parent company needs to be a tax resident of the Czech Republic, have the legal form of a limited liability company, a joint-stock company or a cooperative, and it must hold at least a 10% share in the registered capital of the UK subsidiary for at least an uninterrupted 12-month period as at the date of the decision on the dividend distribution (parent-subsidiary rules). The dividend (and similar shares in profit of a qualified subsidiary) exemption does not and will not apply to dividends paid to a Czech parent company by a UK subsidiary in liquidation.

The dividend exemption applies on the assumption that the Czech parent company beneficially owns the dividends and its UK subsidiary provides a tax residence certificate issued by a relevant UK tax authority.

Capital gains on shareholdings in non-resident companies

7.9 Article 13: Capital gains of the UK-Czech tax treaty grants the Czech Republic the right to tax capital gains on the alienation of a shareholding in UK resident companies made by Czech resident companies. These capital gains are included in the general corporate income tax base and are subject to corporate income tax at the rate of 19%, unless a tax exemption applies.

Capital gains generated on the sale of shares in UK subsidiaries may be exempt from corporate income tax under the same conditions as those which apply to the dividend income exemption. These conditions include a minimum 10% share of the parent company in the registered capital of the subsidiary which is held for at least 12 months, comparable legal form with a Czech limited liability company, joint-stock company or a cooperative, and its profit must be subject to tax similar to Czech corporate income tax. The exemption does not and will not apply to capital gains of a Czech parent company if its UK subsidiary is in liquidation.

Permanent establishments abroad

7.10 Tax charged in the UK on the profits of a permanent establishment of a Czech company located in the UK can be credited against the corporate income tax charged on the tax base of the Czech company in the Czech Republic. Such deduction must not, however, exceed that part of the Czech corporate income tax, computed before the deduction, which relates to the gross profits of the permanent establishment which may be taxed in the UK. After Brexit, this rule remains unchanged.

CFC rules

7.11 On 1 January 2020, the Czech Republic introduced specific CFC rules based on the EU Directive 2016/1164 laying down Rules against Tax Avoidance Practices that Directly Affect the Functioning of the Internal Market (Anti-Tax Avoidance Directive). The main function of these CFC rules is to deter Czech companies from shifting their profits to foreign (UK) low-taxed controlled entities or their permanent establishments. For a UK company to be considered as a CFC, the Czech company must hold, directly or indirectly, more than 50% of the voting rights or entitlement to profit on the capital of the UK company. Moreover, the effective tax rate on the profits of the UK company must be less than 50% of the Czech corporate income tax, that is, less than 9.5%, which it would have paid in the Czech Republic on its profits. The Czech CFC rules grant the Czech Republic the taxing rights on the Czech company's CFC's non-distributed income arising from a non-genuine arrangement which has been put in place for the essential purpose of obtaining a tax advantage.

Other

7.12 If a UK source income is exempt, the expenses attributable to the UK source (as much as to the local source) income exempt from tax, including in some cases future anticipated exempt income, are not deductible for Czech corporate income tax purposes. For the purpose of calculating the corporate income tax base, costs both directly and indirectly attributable to the exempt income must be taken into account. Interest expenses accruing in the period of six months preceding the date of a shareholding acquisition are deemed to be expenses directly connected with the acquisition of a shareholding unless the shareholder proves otherwise. Expenses attributable to divided income exempt from tax are deemed to amount to 5% of the gross dividend income, unless the Czech parent company provides evidence that the actual costs were lower. This rule applies to all parent companies.

As with dividends, gross liquidation proceeds, settlement shares etc which accrue from a UK subsidiary are included in a separate corporate income tax base that is subject to a 15% corporate income tax. The tax value of relevant acquisition costs can be deducted from the liquidation proceeds or settlement share received from that UK subsidiary.

IMPACT ON CROSS-BORDER GROUP TAX REGIMES

7.13 No group tax regime is available in the Czech Republic, as each entity is considered a separate taxpayer. There is no possibility of utilising any tax losses on a group level without prior steps (eg, merger of the companies). Brexit has no impact on this situation.

TAX RAMIFICATIONS FOR CROSS-BORDER MERGERS, OTHER REORGANISATIONS AND TRANSFERS OF RESIDENCE

Cross-border mergers and other reorganisations

7.14 The provisions implementing the Council Directive 2009/133/EC on the common system of taxation applicable to mergers, divisions, partial divisions, transfers of assets and exchanges of shares concerning companies of different Member States and to the transfer of the registered office of an Societas Europaea or European Cooperative Society between Member States will, following Brexit, no longer apply to company reorganisations involving Czech and UK companies.

The current Czech law on company transformations does not provide for cross-border mergers or another reorganisation between a Czech company and a UK company in the situation where the UK is not a member of the EU or EEA.

In terms of an incorporation of a UK branch in the Czech Republic, the rules remain unchanged and shall apply equally to branch incorporation of any foreign company in the Czech Republic.

Transfer of residence abroad

7.15 The transfer of a registered office implies a change of tax residence. A change of tax residence without the transfer of the registered office of a Czech company to the UK is considered a transfer of assets, which is subject to exit tax charged as corporate income tax at the rate of 19%. Exit taxation also occurs if the transfer entails a transfer of assets from a Czech head office to an existing branch/permanent establishment of the Czech company in the UK or the creation of a new branch/permanent establishment, whilst the gain on a subsequent sale of assets involved in the transfer would not be taxable in the Czech Republic due to the tax exemption of the income from the UK branch/permanent establishment in the Czech Republic. In such a situation, the transfer of assets is deemed to constitute a sale for an arm's length price of the assets to the Czech company transferring its registered office/tax residence to the UK. The income thus calculated must be included in the corporate income tax base. These rules are a result of the implementation of the Anti-tax avoidance Directive. These rules apply as from 1 January 2020 and shall continue to apply regardless of Brexit.

Similar rules apply in the case of a transfer of assets from a branch/permanent establishment of a UK company located in the Czech Republic to its head office in the UK.

The exit tax can be paid in instalments spread over up to five years following the exit tax due date: (i) on the assumption that a request for instalments is submitted in due course, and (ii) after Brexit, on the assumption that the UK enters into an agreement with the Czech Republic on mutual assistance in the enforcement of some financial claims. The decision allowing exit tax instalments is waived as of the date on which the UK company ceases to own the assets concerned or transfers the assets to a state which is not an EU Member State or a Member State of the EEA and the state did not conclude with the Czech Republic an agreement on mutual assistance in the enforcement of some financial claims.

Prior to Brexit, assets transferred from a UK company to a branch/permanent establishment in the Czech Republic can be depreciated/amortised from an input value equal to an arm's length price (potential step-up) provided that the transfer is subject to exit tax in the UK. After Brexit, depreciation, based on the relevant Czech rules, of assets transferred to a branch/permanent establishment of a UK company in the Czech Republic may continue based on the value from which the depreciation in the UK was calculated. The value of the assets shall be converted into Czech crowns based on the Czech National Bank's exchange rate applying on the date of transfer.

Inbound transfer of residence

7.16 In relation to companies transferring their tax residence to the Czech Republic from the UK after Brexit, there are no corresponding rules reflecting any potential exit taxation in the UK that allows for a potential step-up of the depreciation basis. However, tax depreciation/amortisation, based on the relevant Czech rules, of assets transferred in connection with the transfer of tax residence to the Czech Republic may continue based on the value from which the depreciation/amortisation in the UK or elsewhere (in the case of a permanent establishment of a UK company in a third state) was calculated whilst the depreciation/amortisation applied before the transfer to the Czech Republic must be duly recognised. The tax value of fixed assets shall be converted into Czech crowns based on the exchange rate published by the Czech National Bank for the day on which the transfer occurred.

OTHER

7.17 In the post-Brexit period, in the case of a transfer of assets from a UK company to a Czech company in the form of a capital contribution, and also a transfer of assets into a permanent establishment of a UK company in the Czech Republic, the value of the assets is converted into Czech crowns based on the Czech National Bank's exchange rate applying on the date of transfer. The value should be net of any revaluation based on the UK rules applied in connection with the transfer, if any. The same exchange rate applies to the conversion of depreciation and amortisation deducted in the UK, and the conversion of the reserves, provisions, correcting items, tax losses and similar items relating to assets and debts involved in the transfer. The Czech company may then apply, for example, tax depreciation in accordance with relevant provisions of the ITA. In general, no step-up for tax purposes is permissible.

A gratuitous transfer of assets to a UK company is considered income which is, in accordance with Article 21 of the UK-Czech tax treaty, subject to tax at the UK company.

Chapter 8

Denmark

Arne Møllin Ottosen and Jonas Lynghoj Madsen

INTRODUCTION

8.1 The purpose of this chapter is to analyse, from a Danish tax perspective, the main consequences for a UK company or similar entity when the UK leaves the EU. This chapter does not analyse the implications for UK individuals.

In the analysis in this chapter, it is assumed that the UK will be a third country and will not join the EEA.

TAX RAMIFICATIONS FOR INBOUND INVESTMENTS

Outbound dividends

8.2 In general, dividends distributed by a Danish company to its shareholders are subject to a 27% withholding tax (WHT). However, the dividend tax on outbound dividends paid to non-resident corporate shareholders is 22%. A 15% WHT rate applies if the relevant authority in the state of residence of the recipient must exchange information with the Danish authorities under a double tax treaty (DTT) or other international convention or agreement. It is a requirement that the non-resident corporate shareholder owns less than 10% of the share capital in the Danish company; also, if the non-resident shareholder is located outside the EU, it is an additional requirement that the collective holding of share capital for associated parties is less than 10%. As Denmark and the UK have entered into a DTT, this provision will still apply, but with the slight modification regarding the additional requirement applying to holdings by associated parties. Non-resident corporate shareholders may subsequently reclaim the 5%/12% difference, that is, the reclaim application must be submitted to the Danish Tax Authorities after the dividend distribution. The application must be filed using a specific application form provided by the Danish Tax Authorities. The application must document that: (i) the corporate shareholder is a resident for tax purposes in a country other than Denmark,

(ii) the dividends have been subject to WHT, (iii) the non-resident corporate shareholder was the beneficial owner of the shares when the distribution of dividends was approved, and (iv) the initial withheld taxes exceed the final WHT rate pursuant to national Danish tax law, a DTT, or EU Directive 2011/96.

A participation exemption provides for a 0% WHT rate if the non-resident company owns at least 10% of the share capital in the Danish company (Subsidiary shares) and the WHT is to be reduced or lowered according to EU Directive 2011/96 or a DTT. As Denmark and the UK have a DTT (UK-DK DTT), the UK resident corporate shareholder will be in the same position both before and after the UK has left the EU.

A participation exemption provides for a 0% WHT rate if the non-resident company controls the Danish company without the shares held being Subsidiary shares (Group shares) and the non-resident company is located within the EU/EEA. As this provision only applies to non-resident companies located within the EU/EEA, this participation exemption will not be available for a UK resident company after the UK has left the EU.

Furthermore, a reduction of the WHT rate may be available under the provisions of the UK-DK DTT. Particularly: (i) a 15% WHT rate applies if the beneficial owner of the dividends is a UK resident company; (ii) a 0% WHT rate applies if the beneficial owner is a UK resident company which holds directly at least 25% of the share capital of the Danish company paying the dividend.

Dividends distributed to a non-resident company by Danish investment companies and investment funds with minimum taxation may be lowered to 0% if the investment company or investment fund has paid a 15% Danish corporate income tax (CIT) on dividends from Danish companies.

Outbound interest

8.3 Interest paid to non-resident associated entities is subject to a 22% WHT. The WHT rate is lowered to 0% if EU Directive 2003/49/EC (IRD) or a DTT results in a lower or reduced WHT rate; thus, if the DTT results in for example 15%, the WHT rate will be lowered to 0%.

As Denmark and the UK have entered into a DTT reducing the rate, the WHT rate is lowered to 0%. As such, the interest payment is only taxable in the UK if the UK recipient is the beneficial owner, unless the interest payment relates to a debt claim which is effectively connected with a permanent establishment in Denmark.

Hence, a UK affiliated corporate lender should be in the same position before and after the UK has left the EU.

Outbound royalties

8.4 Outbound royalties are subject to a 22% WHT.

The exemption available according to the Danish provisions implementing the IRD will no longer be applicable.

However, an exemption from WHT applies in accordance with the UK-DK DTT whereby the royalty payment will only be taxable in the UK if the UK recipient is the beneficial owner of the payment.

Hence, a UK corporate person should be in the same position both before and after the UK has left the EU as it is also a requirement under EU law that the recipient is the beneficial owner of the payment.

Capital gains on shareholdings in resident companies

8.5 Brexit should not impact the tax treatment of capital gains realised by UK residents.

Capital gains and losses on shareholdings in Danish resident companies made by non-resident shareholders are not taxed in Denmark.

Permanent establishments

8.6 No difference due to Brexit.

TAX RAMIFICATIONS FOR OUTBOUND INVESTMENTS

Inbound dividends

8.7 No difference due to Brexit.

Dividends are subject to corporate income tax at the rate of 22%. However, only 70% of the dividend from unlisted shares is to be included in the corporate income tax base if the shareholder owns less than 10% of the share capital (portfolio shares).

Further, a participation exemption applies to dividend distributions from companies where the Danish company owns 10% or more of the share capital (Subsidiary shares) or where the Danish company controls the dividend paying company without the shares held being Subsidiary shares (Group shares), in which case dividends from said shares are exempt from Danish corporate income tax.

Capital gains on shareholdings in non-resident companies

8.8 No difference due to Brexit.

Capital gains from the sale of shares in UK resident companies made by Danish resident companies are subject to corporate income tax at the rate of 22%.

Capital gains and losses from portfolio shares, Subsidiary shares and Group shares are exempt from Danish corporate income tax.

Permanent establishments abroad

8.9 No difference due to Brexit.

Controlled Foreign Corporation (CFC) regime

8.10 As a result of the Danish CFC regime – if applicable – the positive net income of a foreign subsidiary is included in the taxable income of the Danish resident parent company, and credit is provided for paid foreign taxes on the income.

The Danish CFC regime applies if: (i) the Danish parent company controls the CFC subsidiary (generally this means that the parent company holds more than 50% of the voting rights in the subsidiary); (ii) the subsidiary's CFC income exceeds 50% of the subsidiary's total income in the relevant income year; (iii) the subsidiary's financial assets on average make up more than 10% of its total assets in the relevant income year; (iv) the parent company's shares in the subsidiary do not constitute shares in an 'investment company' (a UCITS pursuant to EU Directive 2009/65/EC or a company whose purpose is to trade in securities etc, and where the shareholders of the company may demand that the company buys back their shares using the capital of the company); and (v) the parent company's shares in the subsidiary are not held through a legal entity which is taxed as a life insurance company.

The CFC income includes different types of income which are considered mobile, for example interest income and expenses, gains/losses on receivables and other debt instruments, dividends, shares, IP etc.

A company's financial assets include assets the proceeds of which are considered to be CFC income.

There is currently a draft Bill in the Danish Parliament – concerning implementation of the Anti-Tax Avoidance Directive – which may result in changes to the CFC regime. As this is currently only a draft Bill, it is uncertain how the CFC regime will be affected. So far, the major changes are the removal of the 10% asset requirement *and* a decrease of the CFC income requirement from 50% to 33.3% of the relevant subsidiary total income. It is uncertain if or when the Bill will be passed.

The CFC regime does not apply if the group is part of the voluntary international joint taxation regime (see **8.11** below).

Certain financial services companies may be exempt from the Danish CFC regime. It is a requirement for exemption that the subsidiary is located in either Denmark, an EU/EEA Member State or a state with whom Denmark has concluded a DTT which provides for a reduced or lowered rate in case of dividends from Subsidiary shares.

Hence, there is no difference in the application of the CFC regime to third countries (such as the UK) or EU/EEA Member States where a DTT has been entered into and the DTT provides for a reduced or lowered rate on dividends from Subsidiary shares.

As the UK-DK DTT provides for a reduced WHT rate for dividends, the application of the Danish CFC regime will be the same before and after the UK has left the EU.

IMPACT ON CROSS-BORDER GROUP TAX REGIMES

Voluntary international joint taxation regime

8.11 The ultimate parent company of a group may opt to have the group subject to Danish taxation by opting for the voluntary international joint taxation regime. The regime results in total tax consolidation of the whole group in Denmark. The international joint taxation regime applies either to all group-related entities (group-related entities are entities which are subject to common control, which generally means that the same ultimate parent company (Danish or non-Danish) directly or indirectly controls more than 50% of the voting rights in a company) (Danish as well as foreign entities) or to none. The decision to opt for voluntary international joint taxation is binding for a period of 10 years. Generally, the requirements for opting for the regime are that the group must consist of separate taxable entities for Danish tax purposes, and the group must include a Danish company, which may serve as the administration company for Danish tax purposes. The administration company and the ultimate parent company of the group are then jointly liable for Danish corporate income taxes along with the other Danish entities in the group. The application of the voluntary international joint taxation regime does not distinguish between companies in EU/EEA Member States and states with whom Denmark has concluded a DTT (such as the UK). Hence, the application of the voluntary international joint taxation regime should not be affected by Brexit.

TAX RAMIFICATIONS FOR CROSS-BORDER MERGERS, OTHER REORGANISATIONS AND TRANSFERS OF RESIDENCE

Cross-border mergers and other reorganisations

8.12 The provisions implementing the Merger Directive (MD) will no longer be applicable.

However, tax-exempt cross-border mergers between UK and Danish companies with the UK company as the dissolving entity will still be possible after the UK has left the EU insofar as the UK company is dissolved by way of the merger and not by way of a liquidation.

A tax-exempt cross-border merger will follow the succession principle. Thus, the transfer of the UK company is not taxed in accordance with the normal Danish rules (but may have UK tax implications). Instead, the Danish company (the receiving company) assumes the tax position of the UK company, whereby the assets transferred are to be treated as if they had been acquired at the same time and at the same purchase price at which they were acquired by the UK company.

One important derogation from the succession principles applies to the transfer of losses. Only taxable losses from the period when the companies have been subject to joint taxation are transferable from the dissolving company to the receiving company.

The succession principle also applies at shareholder level. Hence, for shareholders of the UK company exchange of shares in the Danish company will be tax exempt. The new shares in the Danish company would then be considered acquired at the date and price at which the old shares in the UK company were acquired. Any cash consideration paid out for the old shares by the Danish company will be subject to either dividend tax or capital gains tax on shares according to the ordinary Danish rules.

As Denmark applies a territorial taxation principle, the rules may then only have limited practical importance as they would generally only be relevant to UK companies which have a permanent establishment in Denmark.

Further, the rules on succession for shareholders will still apply to mergers where a non-EU company (such as a UK company) merge with another company irrespective of where such other company is located. The application of the succession principle remains conditional upon the merger fulfilling the requirement of being a tax-exempt merger according to the Danish rules.

Transfer of residence abroad

8.13 Exit tax provisions apply to Danish resident companies that cease to be tax residents of Denmark. Accordingly, the latent gains of such a company are subject to corporate income tax unless they relate to assets attributable to a Danish permanent establishment of the company. Danish resident companies that transfer their residence to other EU/EEA Member States or to a permanent establishment of a company located in the EU are granted permission to suspend the payment of the exit tax. Following Brexit, a transfer to the UK will imply the immediate levy of exit tax. Moreover, since the transfer of residence to a third country triggers the termination of the suspension, when the UK becomes a third country, then companies that have transferred to the UK and opted for the suspension or instalment payment of the exit tax may be required to pay the full outstanding amount of the levy.

The same regime applies for other similar transactions (transfer of assets from branch to foreign head office etc.)

Inbound transfer of residence

8.14 Since 1995, Denmark has had provisions concerning the tax basis of assets and liabilities of a company transferring its tax residence to Denmark. As a main rule, the assets and liabilities are considered to have been acquired at the actual time of the company's acquisition, and the value is considered to be the market value at the time of the company transferring its tax residence to Denmark. The value of the assets may be impacted by the type of asset, for example different provisions on value apply to the value of goodwill, and other depreciable assets. The provisions will apply to any company transferring its tax residence to Denmark and will apply to assets and liabilities which have not previously been subject to Danish taxation. Furthermore, the provisions will also apply to companies that have a taxable presence in Denmark. As such, these provisions should apply in relation to companies in the UK even after the end of the transition period.

As a main rule, a company is considered to have transferred its tax residence to Denmark if it is registered in Denmark or has its headquarters in Denmark. A taxable presence may be established in numerous ways, for example through a permanent establishment in Denmark.

Chapter 9

France

Bruno Gibert

INTRODUCTION

9.1 The purpose of this chapter is to analyse the main consequences of the UK leaving the EU from a French tax perspective.

The analysis of this chapter is based on the assumption that: (i) the UK will be a third country and will not join the EEA, and (ii) UK will keep being listed among states providing for effective exchange of information due to the double tax treaty (DTT) between France and the UK.[1]

TAX RAMIFICATIONS FOR INBOUND INVESTMENTS

Outbound dividends

9.2 As a principle, outbound dividends distributed to non-resident corporate shareholders are subject to a withholding tax which rate is identical to the standard corporate income tax rate, that is, 28% in 2020, 26.5% in 2021 and expected 25% as from 2022 (Articles 119 *bis*, 187, 1 and 219, I of the French tax code). The withholding tax is applied to the gross amount distributed. The French Supreme Court recently stated that the withholding tax on dividends distributed to companies located in third countries falls within the scope of the Standstill Clause to the free movement of capital, where such capital movements involve direct investment (*Conseil d'Etat*, 30 September 2019, No. 418080, Société *Findim Investments*).

The withholding tax rate is increased to 75% for dividends paid to a company resident of a non-cooperative state or territory (Non-Cooperative Jurisdiction),

1 Convention between the government of the United Kingdom of Great Britain and Northern Ireland and the government of the French Republic for the avoidance of double taxation and the prevention of fiscal evasion with respect to taxes on income and on capital gains signed in London on 19 June 2008.

unless the payer can prove that the purpose and effect of the distributions in that state or territory are not, for the purpose of tax evasion, to locate such proceeds in that state or territory (Article 187, 2 of the French tax code). For the purpose of these provisions, the Non-Cooperative Jurisdictions targeted are both the states and territories registered on the French list set pursuant to Article 238-0 A of the French tax code, as updated, and the states and territories registered on the list provided by the European Union, as updated, which are considered as facilitating offshore structures or arrangements aimed at attracting profits which do not reflect real economic activity in the jurisdiction. The UK does not qualify as a Non-Cooperative Jurisdiction in either list.

The Parent-Subsidiary Directive exemption applies, as transposed into French law (Article 119 *ter* of the French tax code), to dividends distributed by a qualifying French subsidiary to its qualifying parent company which place of effective management is located in an EU Member State or in an EEA State that has entered into an administrative assistance agreement for combating tax fraud and tax evasion with France (ie, Norway, Iceland and Liechtenstein). French-source dividends distributed to a UK corporate resident will not benefit from the Parent-Subsidiary withholding tax exemption provided that the parent company's place of effective management will not be located in an EU Member State nor in an EEA State.

Similarly, following Brexit, UK non-profit organisations, assimilated to French non-profit organisations, as defined by the French tax code, in light of the disinterested nature of its management and the significantly preponderant nature of its not-for-profit activities, such as pension funds, will lose the benefit of the reduced 15% withholding tax rate for dividends distributed to certain non-profit organisations which head office is located in an EU Member State or in an EEA State that has entered into an administrative assistance agreement for combating tax fraud and tax evasion (Article 119 *bis*, 2 of the French tax code). The compatibility of these provisions with the free movements of capital, in the event where the third country has signed with France an administrative assistance agreement allowing for the exchange of information may be questioned.

As expressly specified by French guidelines (BOI-IS-CHAMP-10-50-10-40-20130325 n°580), UK non-profit organisations may still benefit from the withholding tax rate provided for by the double tax treaty between France and the UK, if more favourable than the domestic rate. In particular, Article 11(d) of said double tax treaty provides that the withholding tax on dividends distributed by French residents to pension funds created and approved for tax purposes in the UK shall not exceed 15%.

French-source dividends distributed to foreign Undertakings for Collective Investment in Transferable Securities (UCITS – *OPCVM*) located in another EU Member State or a state that has entered into an administrative assistance agreement for combating tax fraud and tax evasion with France may benefit from a withholding tax exemption, provided that the foreign entity: (i) meets the same definition as a French Collective Investment Vehicle (*organisme de placement collectif*), and (ii) raises capital from investors in order to make investments in their interest, given a predefined investment policy (Article 119 *bis*, 2 of the French tax code). Regarding the UK, this exemption should remain applicable since the double tax treaty between the UK and France contains mutual assistance provisions. French tax authorities are likely to proceed to the comparative analysis with reference to the criteria developed in their guidelines (see BOI-RPPM-RCM-30-30-20-70-20170607 n°90).

The double tax treaty between France and the UK allows reduced withholding tax rates to apply to distributions of dividends between treaty residents. In general, dividends distributed from France to the UK are subject to a withholding tax at the rate of 15% under the provisions of Article 11 of the double taxation treaty. However, there is no withholding tax applicable when the beneficial owner of the distribution is a company liable to corporate income tax that holds, directly or indirectly, at least 10% of the capital in the company paying the dividends. The benefit of these favourable provisions of the double tax treaty between France and the UK may be denied on the basis of the principal purpose test introduced by the anti-treaty abuse measure of the Multilateral Convention to Implement Tax Treaty Related Measures to Prevent Base Erosion and Profit Shifting (MLI) ratified by both France and the UK.

Due to the wording of the double tax treaty, the concept of dividends encompasses dividends regularly distributed by companies and deemed distributions such as hidden or disguised distributions (*Conseil d'Etat*, 13 October 1999, No. 190083, *min. c/ SA Banque française de l'Orient*).

Since 1 January 2020, a loss-making foreign company can claim a temporary refund of withholding tax incurred in France. Regarding withholding tax on dividends, companies resident in the EU, in the EEA or any another state can apply for such refund provided: (i) their country of residence has signed an administrative assistance agreement for combating tax fraud and tax evasion and an agreement on mutual assistance in recovery matters, and (ii) their interest in the French company distributing the dividends does not allow them to participate effectively in its management or control (Article 235 *quater* of the French tax code). This mechanism results from the decision in *Sofina* (EUCJ, 22 November 2018, (Case C-575/17), *Sofina SA e.a.*) and is based on the free movement of capital principle. There is no such assistance in recovery agreement between France and the UK; however, both countries are parties to the OECD Convention on Mutual Assistance in Tax Matters (as amended by Protocol in 2010) and, although there is no clear position on this, it could be considered as equivalent to such an agreement. Thus, following Brexit, the benefit of these provisions should not be compromised for qualifying loss-making UK resident companies.

Outbound interest

9.3 French-source interest paid to non-resident companies is generally exempt from withholding tax (Article 131 *quater* of the French tax code).

However, interest paid to a lender established or acting through an office to which the loan is effectively connected situated in a Non-Cooperative Jurisdiction or paid to an account opened in the name of or for the benefit of that lender in a financial institution situated in a Non-Cooperative Jurisdiction is subject to a 75% withholding tax (Article 135 A, III of the French tax code). In this case, the withholding is final and compulsory. It is applicable unless the taxpayer can prove that the purpose and effect of locating such payment or proceeds in that state or territory are not, for the purpose of tax evasion, to locate such proceeds in that state or territory. Certain categories of securities benefit from the safeguard provisions without the debtor having to prove the purpose and effect of the debt transaction, mainly securities offered as part of a public offer of financial securities or admitted to trading, provided the offer is not made on or the market is not located in a Non-Cooperative Jurisdiction. As a rule, the withholding applies without any consideration for the state of residence of the ultimate beneficiary, the sole payment of interests to a corporate entity located or on an account opened in a Non-Cooperative Jurisdiction triggers the tax liability. For the purpose of these provisions, the Non-Cooperative Jurisdictions targeted are both the states and territories registered on the French list, as updated, and those registered on the list provided by the European Union, as updated, which are considered as facilitating offshore structures or arrangements aimed at attracting profits which do not reflect real economic activity in the jurisdiction. The UK does not qualify as a Non-Cooperative Jurisdiction in either list.

In addition, no withholding tax is applicable to a UK resident, for the purpose of the double tax treaty, beneficiary of interest payments from a French resident under the provisions of the Article 12 of the double tax treaty between France and the UK, subject to the MLI principal purpose test, see **9.2** above. No change is expected following Brexit.

Outbound royalties

9.4 Outbound royalties paid by French resident companies to UK companies which do not have a permanent professional installation in France are subject to a withholding tax on their gross amount, at a rate identical to the standard corporate income tax rate: 28% in 2020, 26.5% in 2021 and expected 25% as from 2022 (Article 182 B of the French tax code). This withholding is non-final and can be credited against the corporate income tax liability. The scope of the withholding tax encompasses: (i) 'non-commercial' income (as targeted per Article 92 of the French tax code), (ii) non-commercial income earned by inventors or derived from copyright or income from industrial, commercial or similar property rights, (iii) sums paid as compensation for services of any kind provided or used in France, and (iv) sums, including wages, for sports services provided or used in France. Thus, the payments subject to the withholding tax are wider than those of the 'royalties' in the usual sense: they include not only income from the sale or licensing of patents, trademarks, manufacturing processes or techniques, but also income from the provision of services materially provided or actually used on French territory. Withholding tax rate on royalties paid to a resident of a Non-Cooperative Jurisdiction is increased to 75% unless the debtor can prove that the purpose and effect of locating such payment in that state or territory are not, for the purpose of tax evasion, to locate such proceeds in that state or territory (Article 182 B, III of the French tax code). The Non-Cooperative Jurisdictions targeted are identical to the ones mentioned above for dividends and interest.

Outbound royalties, as defined by the EU Interest and Royalties Directive, may benefit from the exemption of withholding tax provided by the domestic law implementing the provisions of said Directive, to the extent: (i) the beneficial owner of the payment is an associated company of the paying company and is a resident of another EU Member State, or (ii) the beneficial owner of the payment is a company's associated permanent establishment situated in an EU Member State (Article 182 B *bis* of the French tax code). Two entities are 'associated companies' when one of them holds a: (i) direct participation of at least 25% in the share capital of the other, or (ii) a third EU company holds a direct participation of at least 25% of the share capital of each company. In each case, the participation must have been held continuously for at least two years or must be subject to a commitment to do so and the relevant companies must have a legal form listed in the Annex of the Directive and be subject to corporate income tax. Following Brexit, this exemption will no longer be applicable to outbound royalties paid to UK corporate residents.

Moreover, a general anti-abuse clause provides that the exemption under the domestic law implementing the EU Interest and Royalties Directive does not apply when the royalties are paid to a company or a permanent establishment controlled directly or indirectly by non-EU residents and if the main purpose or one of the main purposes of the holding chain is to benefit from the withholding tax exemption (Article 119 *quater* of the French tax code). After Brexit, the anti-abuse provision will most likely be applicable to royalties paid to EU corporate residents when they are themselves controlled by UK residents provided the main purpose test is satisfied.

No material change is expected following Brexit in light of the provisions of the double tax treaty between France and UK: outbound royalties to the UK are exempt of withholding tax under the provisions of Article 13, subject to the MLI principal purpose test mentioned in **9.2** above. The conventional definition of royalties encompasses payments of any kind received as a consideration for the use of, or the right to use, any copyright of literary, artistic or scientific work, including cinematographs, films and software, any patent, trademark, design or model, plan, secret formula or process, or for information concerning industrial, commercial or scientific experience. There should be no effective impact as regards formalities: both the exemption under the double tax treaty between UK and France and under the EU Interest and Royalties Directive are conditional upon submission of forms 5000 and 5003.

Capital gains on shareholdings in resident companies

9.5 Under French law, and subject to the relevant double tax treaty, capital gains realised by a non-resident company (or an individual) on shares of a French company are exempt from taxes in France (Article 244 *bis* C of the French tax code), other than:

- capital gains realised by persons or entities domiciled, established or incorporated outside France in a Non-Cooperative Jurisdiction which are subject to a 75% withholding tax unless the taxpayer proves that the main purpose and effect of the profits do not consist in locating such profits in that state or territory;
- capital gains upon the sale of shares of French companies qualified as companies with a preponderance of real estate (*société à préponderance immobilière*) (Article 244 *bis* A of the French tax code), listed or not listed. A company is defined as having a preponderance of real estate if, at the end of the three financial years preceding the sale, more than 50% of its asset value may be attributed to immovable properties or rights in immovable properties located in France and not used for its own industrial, commercial or agricultural exploitation. Listed companies targeted are, in particular, listed real estate investment companies (*sociétés d'investissement immobilier cotées – SIIC*) and open-end predominantly real estate investment companies (*société de placement à prépondérance immobilière à capital variable – SPPICAV*), in each case provided the foreign shareholder holds more than 10% of its share capital.

  The withholding tax rate follows the corporate income tax rate: 28% in 2020, 26.5% in 2021 and expected 25% as from 2022, even if the foreign entity is located in a Non-Cooperative Jurisdiction. The withholding tax can be offset against the corporate income tax liability of the non-resident company. If the amount of withholding tax exceeds the corporate income tax liability, the non-resident entity can apply for a refund provided it is resident of an EU Member State or a state that has entered into an administrative assistance agreement for combating tax fraud and tax evasion with France. The chargeability of this domestic withholding tax and its refund mechanism if applicable should not be impacted by Brexit; however, the withholding tax will be levied according to tax base rules applicable to non-residents. The provisions of the double tax treaty between France and the UK do not prevent France from levying this withholding tax.

- capital gains derived from the sale by non-resident companies or individuals owning more than 25% of the shares or voting rights of a French company, which is not a company with a preponderance of real estate, at any time during the last five years (Article 244 *bis* B of the French tax code). Said capital gains are either:

  (i) exempt apart from a 12% recapture subject to corporate income tax at the standard rate if the selling entity is located in an EU Member State or in an EEA State that has entered into an administrative assistance agreement for combating tax fraud and tax evasion with France and the conditions to benefit from the French long-term regime over capital gains are met – however, the French Supreme Court recently ruled out that the provisions of Article 244 *bis* B of the French tax code are contrary to the EU freedom of establishment, and concluded that EU companies should not be subject to any withholding tax (*Conseil d'Etat*, 14 October 2020, No. 421524, *AVM International Holding)*; or

  (ii) subject to a final withholding tax which rate is identical to the corporate income tax rate (ie, 28% in 2020, 26.5% in 2021 and expected 25% as from 2022), or equal to 12.8% for individuals.

Under the provisions of Article 14, paragraphs 5 and 6 of the double tax treaty between France and the UK, capital gains over the sale of a substantial participation should only be taxable in the UK, except where the selling entity or person has been at any time during the previous six fiscal years a resident of France or is a resident of France at any time during the fiscal year in which the shares are alienated. In such a case, following Brexit, UK companies will not benefit from the exemption (apart from the 12% recapture) for participations satisfying the long-term regime criteria and could be subject to a 26.5% withholding tax (reduced to 25% as from 2020). However, and provided the French tax authorities do not appeal the case before the *Conseil d'Etat*, a recent decision of the French Administrative Court of Appeal has stated that this restriction to the benefit of the exemption (ie, to companies located in another EU Member State or in an EEA State that has signed an administrative assistance agreement for combating tax fraud and tax evasion with France) constitutes a breach of the free movement of capital which does not fall within the scope of the Standstill Clause, resulting in a capital gains tax exemption for resident of non-EU member states (*CAA Versailles*, 20 October 2020, No. 18VE3012, *Sté Runa Capital Fund I LP* – this judgment overturns that of the Lower French Administrative Court *TA Montreuil,* 26 June 2018, No. 1700014).

Permanent establishments

9.6 No difference due to Brexit.

Following Brexit, for the purposes of the French branch remittance tax, the net-of-tax income of French branches of UK companies will be deemed distributed each year. Due to Article 11, paragraph 4 of the double tax treaty between France and the UK, which eliminates the withholding tax applicable on the deemed distributions for the purpose of the branch tax, there will no impact of Brexit in this respect.

TAX RAMIFICATIONS FOR OUTBOUND INVESTMENTS

Inbound dividends

9.7 Brexit will not impact the tax regime in France affecting dividends distributed by UK subsidiaries, other than for certain French companies which are members of a tax consolidated group.

As a principle, dividends paid by UK subsidiaries to a French company are subject to corporate income tax in France at the standard rate (ie, 28% in 2020, 26.5% in 2021 and expected 25% as from 2022), unless the income is attributable to a foreign permanent establishment (Article 209 of the French tax code).

French companies may opt for certain exemption regimes:

- the domestic participation exemption regime (Articles 145 and 216 of the French tax code), under which dividends are exempt, apart from a 5% recapture (*quote-part de frais et charges*) which is subject to corporate income tax at the standard rate, provided the parent company: (i) is liable to corporate income tax at the standard rate, and (ii) owns at least 5% of the share capital of the distributed company for at least two years (or undertakes to keep such holding for at least two years); the permanent establishment of a foreign company may opt for this participation exemption regime provided the shares are booked as assets of the permanent establishment and said permanent establishment is effectively subject to corporate income tax. There is no specific requirement as regards the taxable regime of the UK subsidiary; the benefit of the participation exemption regime is not conditional upon effective taxation at the level of the subsidiary (*Conseil d'Etat*, 12 April 2019, No. 410315, *Sté Compagnie de Saint-Gobain*). In addition, the 5% recapture is calculated on the gross amount of the dividends, without any deduction of foreign withholding tax (the *Conseil d'Etat* ruled that this is compliant with the EU law, drawing the consequences of case law of the Court of justice of the EU – *Conseil d'Etat*, 6 October 2008, No. 262967, *Banque fédérative du Crédit mutuel*. The *Conseil d'Etat* also admitted this principle outside the EU – *Conseil d'Etat*, 17 January 2007 No. 262967, *Banque fédérative du Crédit mutuel*). Finally, due to the exemption from corporate income tax, any tax credit on foreign withholding tax may not be offset against corporate income tax; said tax credit may neither be offset against corporate income tax on the 5% recapture (*Conseil d'Etat*, 23 April 1997, No. 145611, *SA Fournier Industrie et Santé*). In practice, a tax credit on foreign withholding tax may be offset against withholding tax due by the French parent company distributing the received dividends to its foreign shareholders.

- the specific participation exemption regime, under which the recapture, subject to corporate income tax at the standard rate, may be reduced to 1%. This regime requires that the parent company holds at least 95% of the share capital and the voting rights of the subsidiary and that:
  - dividends are received by a company belonging to a French tax consolidated group from a subsidiary within the same tax consolidated group;
  - dividends are received by a company belonging to a French tax consolidated group from a foreign subsidiary located in another EU Member State or an EEA State that has entered into an administrative assistance agreement for combating tax fraud and tax evasion with France, which, if it were located in France, would meet the conditions for being part of the tax consolidated group;
  - dividends are received by a company not belonging to a tax consolidated group from a foreign subsidiary located in another EU Member State or an EEA State that has entered into an administrative assistance agreement for combating tax fraud and tax evasion with France which, if it were located in France, would have met the conditions, along with its parent company, to form a tax consolidated group.

  Dividend distributions, that do not satisfy the conditions for the participation exemption regime, paid to a French-resident company member of a tax consolidated group by a subsidiary located in another EU Member State or an EEA State that has entered into an administrative assistance agreement for combating tax fraud and tax evasion with France, which, if it were located in France, would meet the conditions for being part of the tax consolidated group are neutralised for 99% of their amount (Article 223 B of the French tax code).

9.8 Following Brexit, the participation exemption regime will still be applicable to UK-source dividends received by French companies, other than the benefit of the reduced 1% recapture and the specific 99% neutralisation.

French tax authorities set a transitional tax measure for dividends distributed by a UK-resident to its French-based parent until the end of the fiscal year during which the withdrawal of the UK occurs: pursuant to a published ruling (BOI-RES-000035-20200415) dividends received from UK-resident companies are deemed to be received from European companies until the end of the fiscal year during which Brexit has occurred, that is, 31 December 2020 or pending on 31 December 2020. As a result, the reduced 1% recapture under the specific participation exemption regime and the 99% neutralisation under the tax consolidated group regime would still be temporarily applicable for qualifying inbound dividends from the UK.

As an exception, dividends sourced in a Non-Cooperative Jurisdiction are excluded from the benefit of the participation exemption regime unless the parent company proves that the activities of the foreign company reflect genuine transactions which purpose and effect do not consist in locating the benefits in that state or territory for the purpose of tax evasion. The UK does not qualify as a Non-Cooperative Jurisdiction for the purposes of the abovementioned two lists (Articles 145, 6(d) and 238-0 A of the French tax code).

A general anti-abuse rule, implementing the Anti-Tax Avoidance Directive (ATAD), also applies to the participation exemption regime (Article 205-A of the French tax code). Any arrangement or series of arrangements which, having been put in place for the main purpose or one of the main purposes of obtaining a tax advantage that defeats the object or purpose of the applicable tax law, is not genuine having regard to all relevant facts and circumstances. An arrangement may comprise more than one step. A structure or series of structures is deemed not to be genuine if it is not set up for sound commercial reasons. The general anti-abuse provision is applicable regardless of the country in which the subsidiary is located (ie, France, EU or third countries) and irrespective of the date on which the arrangement was implemented.

Capital gains on shareholdings in non-resident companies

9.9 In general, capital gains derived by French corporate residents from the sale of participations in UK resident companies are subject to corporate income tax at the standard rate: 28% in 2020, 26.5% in 2021 and expected 25% as from 2022 (Article 219, I-a *quater* of the French tax code).

However, under the long-term capital gains regime, gains realised upon the sale of qualifying equity securities (*titres de participation*) are exempt, other than a 12% recapture subject to corporate income tax at the standard rate, resulting in an effective tax rate of circa 3.5% for fiscal year 2020 and 3.3% for fiscal year 2021 (Article 219, I-a *quinquies* of the French tax code). Broadly, eligible shares are 'equity securities' qualified as such from an accounting point of view, that is, shares whose long-term holding is deemed useful for the company's business activity in particular because it enables the company holding the shares to exercise influence or control over the subsidiary – shares representing at least 10% of the share capital of the subsidiary are deemed to qualify as such. Shares acquired in the context of a public offer and shares qualifying for the participation exemption regime (as outlined above) can also benefit from the long-term regime provided they represent at least 5% of the share capital of the subsidiary.

Capital gains over certain qualifying equity securities are excluded from the benefit of the long-term regime:

- capital gains derived from the disposal of shares in companies established in Non-Cooperative Jurisdictions, unless the company holding the shares proves that the activities of the foreign company reflect genuine transactions which purpose and effect do not consist in locating the benefits in that state or territory for the purpose of tax evasion (Article 219, I-a *sexies* 0 *ter* of the French tax code);
- capital gains derived from the sale of companies with a preponderance of real estate (*société à prépondérance immobilière*) – shares of listed companies with a preponderance of real estate are subject to a reduced 19% rate (Article 219, I-a of the French tax code).

These rules apply equally to sales of shares in French or foreign companies, whether they are located in the European Union, in the EEA or in third countries. As a result, Brexit would not have an impact on the taxation of such gains in France.

Assuming the gains from the sale are subject to tax in the UK, French tax authorities consider that, under the long-term regime, foreign tax cannot be deducted from the tax liability in France (BOI-IS-BASE-20-20-10-20-20160203 No. 180). Yet the amount of tax paid abroad may be deducted from the gross capital gains realised as costs incurred in collection with the disposal and thus reduces the base for the 12% recapture.

Permanent establishments abroad

9.10 No difference due to Brexit.

CFC rules

9.11 Brexit will substantially change the application of the CFC regime to UK entities.

Article 209 B of the French tax code provides for a CFC regime under which the profits of an entity: (i) controlled by a French company, and (ii) located in a jurisdiction where it benefits from a tax-privileged regime (a 'Controlled Foreign Corporation' or 'CFC') qualify as deemed dividends and, as such, are subject to corporate income tax in France.

For the purposes of this regime:

- A French company is considered as controlling a CFC if it directly or indirectly holds 50% or more of the shares, financial rights or voting rights of such CFC.
- A CFC benefits from a tax-privileged regime if it is tax exempt or if it is subject to tax on its profits for an amount representing less than 40% of the corporate income tax which would have been due on these profits had the CFC been a French tax resident. *Nota bene*: based on administrative guidelines – BOI-IS-BASE-60-10-20-20-20140627 No. 120 – it is generally accepted that exemption on capital gains does not qualify as a tax-privileged regime when the shares sold by the CFC would have been eligible to the French participation exemption on capital gains had the CFC been a French tax resident; in the view of the authors, the same should apply to exemption on dividends, if the shares giving right to dividends would have been eligible for the French participation exemption had the CFC been a French tax resident.
- The French CFC regime may apply at any level of the legal structure of a group, that is, may apply even if non-CFC entities are interposed between the CFC and the French company.

The French CFC regime provides for two safe harbours (Article 209 B, paragraphs II and III):

- EU safe harbour: the French CFC regime does not apply to profits derived from a CFC established in an EU jurisdiction, unless the French tax authorities prove that the CFC is an artificial scheme that is purely tax driven.
- Non-EU safe harbour: the French CFC regime does not apply if the French company proves that the main purpose and the main effect of the CFC's activities do not consist in allowing the location of profits in a jurisdiction where this CFC benefits from a tax-privileged regime. This condition is deemed fulfilled when the CFC mainly carries out an actual industrial or commercial activity in the jurisdiction where it is established.

Following Brexit, a French company holding a UK-CFC will have to prove the following:

- *main purpose and main effect test*, both conditions being cumulative:
  - *Main purpose*: the French company shall prove that it did not principally aim at locating profits in a tax-privileged jurisdiction, that is, the French company should prove that the setting-up of the CFC in the tax-privileged jurisdiction was not mainly tax driven. According to case law (for instance, *Conseil d'Etat* QPC, 2 February 2012, No. 351600, *Sté Sonepar* or *Conseil d'Etat*,

30 December 2015, No. 372522, *Sté Paribas International* and the related conclusions of the Public Rapporteurs), the main purpose shall not be to avoid French tax, that is, only French tax evasion shall be challenged under the French CFC regime.

— *Main effect*: according to French administrative guidelines (BOI-INT-DG-20-50-20140211, No. 260), the French company shall provide the French tax authorities with any factual and quantitative proof allowing an objective comparison between the amount of the tax gain resulting from the location in the tax-privileged jurisdiction and the amount of the other non-tax advantages of such location.

- These conditions are deemed to be met where the CFC entity is carrying out an actual industrial or commercial activity in a tax-privileged jurisdiction: the CFC shall have adequate substance in the tax-privileged jurisdiction and its activity shall be effective.

The non-EU safe harbour regime is thus less favourable to taxpayers than the EU-safe harbour regime.

If the UK corporate income tax rate were to decrease in the future, we find it useful to note that the application of the French CFC regime regarding UK should be monitored closely.

Other

9.12 Taxable profits realised by a company incorporated in a foreign country could be taxed in France where the French tax authorities consider that the tax residency of the company is in fact in France (or that such company holds a permanent establishment in France).

Pursuant to Article 209 of the French Tax Code and corresponding guidelines, profits realised: (i) by a company whose 'head office' is located in France (other than profits realised in the context of a business carried on abroad), or (ii) by a company whose 'head office' is located outside of France (as long as, notably, a business is carried on in France), irrespective of its nationality, are taxable in France (BOI-IS-CHAMP-60-10-10-20140627 No. 50 and BOI-IS-CHAMP-60-10-30-20180801 No. 1). The 'head office' may not necessarily correspond to the registered head office (BOI-IS-CHAMP-60-10-2020120912 No. 1).

The French tax authorities may therefore argue that the 'real head office' of a foreign company is in fact in France, so as to consider that the company is resident in France for tax purposes and attract all of its profits (other than the ones carried out abroad) within the French tax base. Although there is no legal definition of 'real head office' or place of effective management in French tax law, French tax authorities traditionally tend to consider the place of effective management as corresponding to the place where the people holding the most senior management positions in the company officially take decisions. Such traditional interpretation is however evolving and case law tends to focus increasingly on the place where the decisions are actually made.

No change is expected due to Brexit.

As a principle, securities held by a company in a resident or foreign UCITS are revaluated at the end of each tax year. Any unrealised capital gain resulting is subject to tax under the provisions of Article 209-0 A of the French tax code. This revaluation does not apply however to French UCITS and UCITS domiciled in another EU Member State, that is, where at least 90% of their asset value is represented by stocks of companies domiciled in an EU Member State subject to corporate income tax.

After Brexit, this exclusion from revaluation may be challenged in respect of both UCITS established in the UK and UCITS whose assets are composed of stocks of UK resident companies.

IMPACT ON CROSS-BORDER GROUP TAX REGIMES

9.13 Separate companies can be treated as a single taxpayer for corporate income tax purposes under the French tax consolidated group regime (*intégration fiscale*) provided certain conditions are met. The scope of the group is determined by the head company when exercising the option: companies, subject to corporate income tax, for which the 95% voting and financial rights threshold is satisfied and that have the same opening and closing dates for their fiscal years may be encompassed (Article 223 A of the French tax code).

Initially, both the head company and every subsidiary along the holding chain had to be subject to corporate income tax in France in order to form a tax consolidated group. Then the domestic regime had to evolve on two levels to comply with the EU freedom of establishment:

- the freedom of establishment precludes legislation that allows a French head company to form a tax consolidated group with a French sub-subsidiary detained through a French subsidiary but cannot where it holds that sub-subsidiary through companies which are resident of another EU Member State (ECJ, 27 November 2008, *Papillon* (Case C-418/07)).
- the freedom of establishment also precludes legislation under which two resident sister companies held by a common foreign parent company resident of another EU Member State cannot form a tax consolidated group (ECJ, 12 June 2014, Joined Cases C-39/13, C-40/13, C-40/13 and C-41/13 *SCA Group Holding BV, X AG, MSA international Holdings BV* and *MSA Nederland BV*).

As a result, the French tax consolidated groups may be constituted as follows, provided the 95% of voting and financial rights threshold is satisfied at each level:

- a so-called 'vertical' tax consolidated group is constituted with subsidiaries held directly by the head company, indirectly through French companies that are members of the tax consolidated group or indirectly through 'intermediate companies' (*sociétés intermédiaires*) resident of another EU Member State or an EEA State that has entered into an administrative assistance agreement for combating tax fraud and tax evasion with France (Article 223 A, I – §1 of the French tax code).
- a so-called 'horizontal' tax consolidated group is constituted by two or more French sister or cousin companies held directly, or indirectly through qualifying EU or EEA companies ('foreign companies' *sociétés étrangères*), by a common head company established in another EU Member State or in an EEA State that has entered into an administrative assistance agreement for combating tax fraud and tax evasion with France, a 'foreign parent company' (*entité mère non résidente*) (Article 223 A, I – §2 of the French tax code).

After Brexit, intermediate companies based in the UK will no longer allow their French subsidiaries to be part of a vertical French tax consolidated group and UK-based parent companies – as well as UK-based foreign companies – will no longer allow their French subsidiaries to maintain such a tax consolidated group. This will result in the traditional consequences of an exit of a tax consolidated group (eg, potential deneutralisation of certain intra-group transactions, and allocation of losses to the head company).

Budget Law for 2019 has set up a transitional measure to mitigate the effects of the exit of a Member State from the EU on French tax consolidated groups (Article 223 L, § k and l of the French tax code). As a result, when the state of residency of a foreign parent company or an intermediate company withdraws from the EU or the EEA, the foreign parent company or the intermediate company is deemed to meet the residency conditions until the end of the pending exercise at the exit date. French tax authorities' guidelines (BOI-IS-GPE-50-60-40-20200415) comment on the transitional measures and specify that, as regards Brexit, the eligibility conditions are deemed to be met until the end of the financial year ending on 31 December 2020 or pending on 31 December 2020. This would allow both: (i) horizontal tax consolidated groups constituted under a UK-resident parent company, and (ii) French subsidiaries detained by a French parent through foreign intermediate companies to continue to form a valid tax consolidated group until the end of their fiscal year.

In addition, the transitional measures, as supplemented by the French tax authorities' guidelines, provide that the UK parent company may be substituted by another qualifying foreign company, held by the UK parent company, without termination of the tax consolidated group, to the extent the substitution is notified within three months of the end of the fiscal year ending on 31 December 2020 or pending on 31 December 2020. The perimeter of the tax consolidated group may also be preserved by way of a reclassification of the shares held by a UK intermediate company or UK parent company to another qualifying intermediate company or qualifying foreign parent company until the end of the fiscal year ending on 31 December 2020 or pending on 31 December 2020 and fulfilment of the relevant formalities (ie, letters of option, notification of amendment to the perimeters) within the statutory period.

TAX RAMIFICATIONS FOR CROSS-BORDER MERGERS, OTHER REORGANISATIONS AND TRANSFERS OF RESIDENCE

Cross-border mergers and other reorganisations

9.14 As a principle, mergers and assimilated operations (ie, divisions and transfer of assets) are considered as a cessation of business leading to the immediate taxation of all non-taxed income, provisions and capital gains resulting from the operation carried out (Articles 221, 2 and 201 of the French tax code).

Both domestic and European law provide for preferential regimes allowing companies to carry out reorganisations under a principle of tax neutrality. The European regime results from the EU Merger Directive (Directive 2009/133/CE of 23 November 2009) which aims at: (i) avoiding tax costs becoming an obstacle to the realisation of European restructuring operations, and (ii) safeguarding the rights of the states of the transferring companies in respect of future taxation of capital gains. Regarding its geographical scope, the EU Merger Directive only applies to reorganisations involving companies resident in EU Member States. As a result, the preferential regime would not be applicable to reorganisations involving UK resident companies after Brexit.

Conversely, the domestic regime, as amended following the decision in *Euro park* (ECJ, 8 March 2017, *Euro Park Service* (Case C-14/16)), under Article 210-0 A of the French tax code has a broader geographical scope: both domestic mergers and cross-border mergers are concerned to the extent the companies involved are located in a country or territory which has signed a double tax treaty with France including an administrative assistance clause. Provided all conditions are met, UK resident companies would thus still qualify for the domestic tax neutrality regime even after Brexit as Article 27 of the double tax treaty between the UK and France provides for a mutual assistance clause.

French law covers both domestic and cross-border mergers (*fusions*), divisions (*scissions*) and transfers of assets (*apports partiel d'actifs*):

- provided that for cross-border operations the foreign entity is resident in a jurisdiction that has signed an administrative assistance agreement for combating tax fraud and tax evasion with France (Article 210 0-A of the French tax code); and
- to the extent that the assets of the transferring company are connected to a permanent establishment of the foreign company receiving the assets in France (Article 210 C of the French tax code), unless the elements contributed consist exclusively of equity securities (for mergers) or involve the contribution of equity securities assimilated to a complete branch of activity (for transfers of assets) (BOI-IS-FUS-10-20-20-20190410 No. 100).

If the conditions to benefit from the automatic tax neutrality regime are not satisfied, the entity may seek the prior approval of the French tax authorities (eg, where a division of the assets does not represent at least two full branches of activity, if the assets transferred do not represent a full branch of activity) (Article 210 B of the French tax code).

French law provides general anti-abuse provisions applicable to reorganisations. The domestic tax neutrality regime may be denied where mergers, divisions or transfers of assets have as their principal purpose or as one of their principal purposes tax evasion or tax avoidance. A reorganisation operation is deemed to have such a purpose when it is not carried out for valid commercial reasons, such as the restructuring or rationalisation of the companies involved in the operation (Article 210-0 A, III of the French tax code – BOI-IS-FUS-10-20-20-20190410 No. 193 and 195).

To the extent all the conditions are met and considering its broader geographical scope compared to the EU regime, each eligible reorganisation involving a UK resident will continue to benefit from the domestic tax neutrality regime after Brexit.

At shareholder level, they may opt for a specific tax neutrality regime which provides for a tax deferral on the capital gain resulting from the exchange of shares upon a merger or a division. As set forth by Article 38, 7 *bis* of the French tax code, this optional tax deferral can apply if the following conditions are cumulatively met: (i) the merger satisfies the definition provided for by Article 210-0 A of the French tax code; (ii) in the event of a foreign restructuring resulting in the allocation of shares to a French tax-resident shareholder, the companies involved must be located in a state or territory which has signed a tax treaty with France including an administrative assistance clause; (iii) the restructuring does not have as its principal objective or as one of its principal objectives tax evasion or tax avoidance; and (iv) the French shareholder is a company subject to corporate income tax.

Brexit will not have any impact on the benefit of this tax neutrality regime.

From a French tax standpoint, in principle, the attribution of shares resulting from a spin-off (ie, which has the same effect as a partial division) is a taxable event which is treated as a deemed distribution at the level of the shareholder (distribution which can however benefit from the French participation exemption regime – see **9.7** above). A specific tax neutrality regime is provided for by Article 115, 2 of the French tax code, which may apply to both French shareholders of French or foreign entities or foreign shareholders of French entities.

The benefit of the tax neutrality regime is dependent upon the following conditions being met: (i) the transfer of assets benefits from the tax neutrality regime provided for by Article 210 A of the French tax code (ie, it is not taxed); (ii) the transferring entity holds at least one complete branch of activity after completion of the contribution; (iii) the attribution of shares, which must be proportional to the financial rights of each shareholder in the share capital, takes place within a maximum one-year delay; and (iv) where it implies foreign restructuring operations, the companies involved are located in a state or territory state or territory which has signed a tax treaty with France including an administrative assistance clause (BOI-IS-FUS-20-40-40-20190109).

Thus, following Brexit, subject to the general anti-abuse provisions and to the relevant conditions being satisfied, UK shareholders will remain exempt from withholding tax on the attribution of shares as a result of a qualifying spin-off.

Transfer of residence abroad

9.15 In general, the transfer of a registered seat is treated as a cessation of business and leads to the immediate taxation of all non-taxed income, provisions and capital gains resulting from the operation realised (Articles 221, 2 and 201 of the French tax code).

However, a resident company may transfer its registered seat to another EU Member State or EEA State that has signed with France a mutual assistance agreement on recovery with a scope similar to that provided for in Council Directive 2010/24/EU of 16 March 2010 (ie, Iceland and Norway) without necessarily having to sustain the consequences of a cessation of business. In that case, the tax consequences of the transfer of a registered seat depend on whether or not assets are transferred outside of France (Article 221, 2 of the French tax code – BOI-IS-CESS-30-20-20130903):

(i) where the operation is limited to the transfer of a registered seat in another EU Member State or in a mentioned EEA State, the remaining assets and liabilities are considered as forming a permanent establishment in France, subject to corporate income tax under general rules. In that case, the transfer is tax neutral;

(ii) adversely, where the transfer of a registered seat to another EU Member State or in a mentioned EEA State results in a transfer of assets abroad, capital gains related to such assets become immediately taxable in France. In that case, the company can request the payment of the exit tax to be divided over five yearly instalments.

Following Brexit, transfer of registered seats from France to the UK will no longer benefit from the favourable provisions, regardless of any transfer of assets abroad. Consequently, a transfer of seat to the UK will be treated as a cessation of business (resulting in taxation of pending capital gains, loss of all carry-forward losses and taxation of the reserves as deemed distribution). In addition, all pending instalments of exit tax will become immediately payable on the ground of a transfer of residence to a third country (Article 221, 2(b) §2 of the French tax code).

Inbound transfer of residence

9.16 There is no specific provision in domestic law relating to inbound transfers of residence from a foreign country.

However, binding guidelines from the French tax authorities give useful insight for transfers realised from an EU Member State (or Iceland and Norway) to France. In that case, for consistency purposes, and in order to avoid taxing a foreign capital gain already realised, the French tax authorities allow the booking value for tax purposes of the assets of the company to be stepped up to the arm's length value of such assets as determined upon arrival (which is consistent with the EU Council Resolution of 2 December 2008 on exit tax coordination – 2008/C-323/0 – and the principles set out in Article 5 of the ATAD Directive – (EU)2016/1164 dated 12 July 2016). This arm's length value must be retained for the amortisation of the transferred assets and for the computation of later capital gains derived from the sale of such assets. To that end, companies may provide the French tax authorities with an opening balance justifying the values retained. As they encompass only transfers from other EU Member State, these guidelines would not be applicable to transfers of residence from the UK following Brexit.

In the case of a UK company holding a permanent establishment in France, absent any specific provisions under French law, the transfer of its residence to France should entail the following consequences: if the transfer is possible from the UK without loss of the legal personality, there should be no tax consequences in France (ie, no cessation of business regarding the permanent establishment in France); if it is not the case, then the provisions applicable to the cessation of business in France would be applicable to the French branch of the company transferred, leading to the immediate taxation of profits and unrealised capital gains.

OTHER

Convention considerations

9.17 The application of tax treaties concluded between France and countries outside the European Union could be challenged after Brexit regarding the application of domestic withholding taxes. Some of these treaties, such as the double tax treaty between France and the US, contain 'Limitation on Benefits' (LOB) provisions that exclude from their scope companies owned by non-EU residents.

Following the exit of the UK from the EU, French companies may therefore no longer benefit from the advantages provided for in these tax treaties, particularly in the event of the payment or receipt of dividends, interest and royalties.

Following Brexit, French provisions implementing Council Directive (EU) 2017/1852 of 10 October 2017 on tax dispute resolution mechanism in the European Union should no longer be applicable to disputes arising from the interpretation and application of the double tax treaty between France and the UK (Articles L. 251 B to L. 251 ZH of the French tax procedure book).

Affected persons will still be able to initiate a mutual agreement procedure on the basis of the provisions of Article 26 of the double tax treaty, as amended by the MLI, which set a mandatory arbitration on demand upon expiration of a two-year period following the mutual agreement request. The scope of the dispute targeted by the double tax treaty between France and the UK is more restricted than the scope set by the EU Directive and Article 26 does not provide for appeal mechanisms against the decision taken by the competent authorities of the contracting state.

Corporate considerations

9.18 A tax credit for research and development (R&D) expenses is available under the provisions of Article 244 *quater B* of the French tax code. This amounts to 30% of the qualifying expenses in relation to R & D up to a maximum of EUR 100 million, and 5% for expenses above that. It is creditable against corporate income tax for the year during which the qualifying expenditures are incurred; any excess of credit may be carried forward for three years and then refunded. In order to be eligible, the R&D expenses must: (i) be included among the expenses exhaustively listed by law, (ii) be deductible from the tax base of the French company; and (iii) relate to R&D activities carried out within the EU or in an EEA State that has signed an administrative assistance agreement for combating tax fraud and tax evasion with France; however, the last condition does not apply to expenditures related to patents and those for technology monitoring and defence costs.

As a result, expenditures in connection with R&D activities carried out in the UK by French resident companies (or subcontracted to public or private providers located in the UK) will no longer be eligible for the tax credit after Brexit; only patents-related costs, technology monitoring and defence costs will remain eligible.

In line with OECD's nexus approach, France has recently introduced a tax regime applicable to income from industrial property (Article 238 of the French tax code). Said income is taxed at a reduced 10% rate upon option of the taxpayer. The regime encompasses the income derived from the licensing, sublicensing or sale of patents, plant variety rights, industrial manufacturing processes, copyrighted software or certain qualifying patentable but not patented inventions. Guidelines issued by the French tax authorities specifically provide that patents granted in the context of the European patent procedure or issued by a foreign industrial property office are to be treated in the same way as French patents for the application of the regime (BOI-BIC-BASE-110-20190717 No. 20 and 60).[2]

According to an analysis published in November 2019 by the European Parliament's Policy Department for Citizens' Rights and Constitutional affairs,[3] there is no doubt that the UK remains a signatory state of the European Patent Convention[4] defining the European patent procedure. Therefore, Brexit should have no impact on this regime.

Donations made by French companies to non-profit organisations where head office is located within an EU Member State or an EEA State that has signed an administrative assistance agreement for combating tax fraud and tax evasion with France are eligible for the patronage tax rebate. The patronage tax rebate amounts to 60% of the amount paid for donations up to EUR 2 M and 40% above, within the limit of the higher of EUR 20,000 or 5% of the turnover (Article 238 *bis* of the French tax code). Donations to UK non-profit organisations will no longer qualify for the patronage tax rebate.

Considerations for individuals

9.19 The French exit tax regime affects taxpayers upon the transfer of their tax residence outside France. Unrealised capital gains recorded on corporate rights and securities which account for at least 50% of a company's corporate profits or which total value exceeds EUR 800K are subject to tax (Article 167

2 The guidelines also require that the plant variety rights may be granted either by a French (ie, INOV) or foreign qualifying entity (BOI-BIC-BASE-110-20190717 No. 90).

3 Available at: https://www.europarl.europa.eu/RegData/etudes/IDAN/2019/596800/IPOL_IDA(2019)596800_EN.pdf.

4 Convention on the Grant of European Patents (European Patent Convention) of 5 October 1973 as revised by the Act revising Article 63 EPC of 17 December 1991 and the Act revising the EPC of 29 November 2000.

bis of the French tax code). However, taxpayers can benefit from a payment deferral upon express request and having satisfied the obligation to report the amount of capital gains concerned, appoint a tax representative in France and provide guarantees to ensure recovery. This deferral is automatically granted to taxpayers transferring their tax residence outside France to an EU Member State or any state or territory that has signed with France an administrative assistance agreement for combating tax fraud and tax evasion and a mutual assistance agreement on recovery having a scope similar to that provided for in Council Directive 2010/24/EU of 16 March 2010.

There is no such assistance in recovery agreement between France and the UK; however, both countries are parties to the OECD Convention on Mutual Assistance in Tax Matters (as amended by Protocol in 2010) and, although there is no clear position on this, it could be considered as equivalent to such an agreement.[5] Therefore, the automatic payment deferral (ie, without reporting obligation, designation of a tax representative and recovery guarantees) should continue to apply to transfers of tax residence outside France to the UK to the extent that the UK would meet the abovementioned condition after leaving the EU.

French legislation provides for tax efficient investments through share savings plan (PEA) and PEA for small and medium-sized enterprises (PEA-PME). In order to be eligible, securities must be issued by companies resident in an EU Member State or in another EEA State that has signed an administrative assistance agreement for combating tax fraud and tax evasion with France (Article L. 221-31 of the French monetary and financial code).

This condition would no longer be fulfilled following Brexit, as the UK is not a party to the EEA Agreement, and securities issued by UK resident companies would no longer be eligible for PEA and PEA-PME. The holding of such shares would constitute a breach of the operating rules of the PEA and lead to its immediate closure under Article 1765 of the French tax code.

However, the French tax authorities introduced an amnesty through their binding guidelines (BOI-RPPM-RCM-40-50-50-20170925 No. 40, 45 and 65) allowing PEAs not to be closed in the event of a company's head office transfer to a state that is neither an EU Member State nor an EEA State. In that case, the taxpayer can benefit from a regularisation procedure for a maximum period of two months from the occurrence of the event rendering the securities ineligible. This procedure allows for either: (i) the withdrawal from the plan of the ineligible securities, or (ii) their sale.

Ordinance No. 2020-1595 adopted on 16 December 2020, specified by Order dated 22 December 2020 (published at the OJ No. 0313 dated 27 December 2020), has introduced specific temporary measures maintaining the eligibility

5 The French tax authorities seem to share this point of view as expressed in its Brexit Q&A for individuals, although not binding: 'the United-Kingdom has legal instruments for assistance in recovery and for combating fraud similar to those existing between EU Member States'.

for PEA and PEA-PME of securities issued by UK companies and of units in UK Collective Investment Vehicles (*organisme de placement collectif*) until 30 September 2021 (Article 3 of Ordinance No. 2020-1595 and Article 1 of the Order). The benefit of this nine-month transition period maintaining the eligibility to PEA and PEA-PME applies to:

- securities issued by UK companies that have been regularly subscribed or acquired before 31 December 2020;
- securities issued by UK companies within the quota of 75% of Collective Investment Vehicles, provided that these Collective Investment Vehicles were eligible as at 31 December 2020; and
- units or shares of UK UCITS (Undertakings for Collective Investment in Transferable Securities – *OPCVM*) regularly subscribed or acquired before 31 December 2020.The Ordinance and the Order also provide for certain mandatory disclosure obligations by the account keepers and/or the management companies to the benefit of the persons whose PEA and PEA-PME are affected.

Regarding social security contributions:

- in principle, French residents, subject to a compulsory French social security system, are liable to said contributions on their income (Article L. 136-1 of the French social security code);
- as regards income from assets and investment income, persons, domiciled in France, who are not covered by a compulsory French social security system but who are covered by social legislation subject to the provisions of European regulation (EC) No. 883/2004 on the coordination of social security systems (ie, social legislation of another EU Member State, EEA State or Switzerland) are exempt from French generalised social contribution (*CSG*) and the contribution for the reimbursement of the social debt (*CRDS*) (Article L. 136-6 of the French social security code – as adapted to comply with ECJ case law *de Ruyter*; 26 February 2015 (Case C-623/13)).

The 7.5% solidarity surcharge on income from assets (*Prélèvement de solidarité*) under the provisions of Article 235 *ter* of the French tax code will be maintained after the UK leaves the EU for all taxpayers, whether or not they are covered by a compulsory social security scheme in the UK.

French residents covered by a UK social legislation will no longer benefit from the exemption of CSG-CRDS as the UK social legislation would no longer be covered by the EU regulation mentioned above – CSG-CRDS on investment income currently amounts to 17.2%.

Employees and senior officers of foreign companies seconded to France are entitled to a partial income tax exemption under the provisions of Article 155 B of the French tax code provided they have not been tax resident in France during the previous five years (the 'inpatriate regime' which aims at granting a favourable tax regime to individuals moving to France for work). Inpatriates who took up their duties after 6 July 2016 may benefit from the favourable regime for eight years. The exemption notably covers, under certain conditions:

- income tax and salary tax as regards the inpatriation premium (which corresponds to the additional compensation directly related to the exercise of a professional activity in France);
- income tax on the portion of the remuneration related to work carried out abroad;
- income tax on 50% of the passive income (dividends, interest, life insurance, capital gains, income from IP rights) derived from a country which has signed an administrative assistance agreement for combating tax fraud and tax evasion with France; and
- French wealth tax on immovable properties located outside of France.

Regarding the UK, the partial exemption on passive income should remain applicable after Brexit since the double tax treaty between the UK and France contains administrative assistance provisions.

Article 150-0 B of the French tax code provides for a deferment of taxation on capital gains taxable in France upon transfer by individuals of qualifying shares to a company subject to corporate income tax in France or an equivalent tax and established in an EU Member State or in a state or territory that has signed an administrative assistance agreement for combating tax fraud and tax evasion with France, provided the company receiving the contribution is not controlled by the transferor. Following Brexit, this favourable regime should remain applicable since the double tax treaty between the UK and France contains mutual assistance provisions.

Where the company receiving the contribution is controlled by the transferor, Article 150-0 B *ter* of the French tax code provides for a tax deferral on capital gains taxable in France upon transfer by individuals of qualifying shares to a company subject to corporate income tax in France or an equivalent tax and established in an EU Member State or in a state or territory that has signed an administrative assistance agreement for combating tax fraud and tax evasion with France. In general, the tax deferral expires upon: (i) disposal, repurchase, reimbursement or cancellation of the shares received as consideration for the contribution, or (ii) disposal, repurchase, reimbursement or cancellation of the shares contributed. In both cases, the transfer capital gains immediately become taxable.

As an exception, the tax deferral does not end after the disposal of the shares contributed provided the beneficiary company reinvests the proceeds of the sale in an eligible economic activity. Broadly, are the following considered eligible reinvestments: (i) the financing of permanent resources allocated to a qualified economic activity, (ii) the acquisition of a fraction of the share capital of a company pursuing such activity provided it has its registered seat in an EU Member State or an EEA State that has entered into an administrative assistance agreement for combating tax fraud and tax evasion with France, or (iii) the investment in the subscription of shares of certain funds or private equity vehicles or similar organisations of another EU Member State or of another EEA State that has entered into an administrative assistance agreement for combating tax fraud and tax evasion with France. Eligible assets must be kept for a period of one year in order to qualify for the continuation of the tax deferral.

Following Brexit, UK-based companies, funds or private equity vehicles resident of the UK would no longer qualify as eligible reinvestments for the purpose of the tax deferral under Article 150-0 B *ter* of the French Tax code as the UK will not be a party to the EEA agreement, nor the EU. Furthermore, it cannot be guaranteed that ongoing reinvestments involving UK assets will not result in the forfeiture of the deferral, as they will no longer meet the requirements mentioned above (BOI-RPPM-PVBMI-30-10-60-20-20191220 No. 270).

It can be noted that under EU case law (ECJ, 22 March 2018, No. 327/16 and 421/16), a state is entitled to tax a capital gain which benefits from a tax deferral, realised by a non-resident taxpayer or a taxpayer that has transferred his residence outside France before the expiration of the tax deferral; any capital loss should be taken into account if it would be taken into account in a domestic situation. Regarding the UK, taxpayers resident in the UK at the time of the transfer of shares, or taxpayers who transfer their tax residence to the UK afterwards, remain subject to capital gains tax in France in the event that the tax deferral expires. The *Conseil d'Etat* has already ruled along these lines in the case of a UK resident, drawing the consequences of the case law of the Court of Justice of the EU (*Conseil d'Etat*, 25 June 2018, No. 360352).

Other expected consequences of Brexit:

(i) donations to UK non-profit organisations and subscriptions to the share capital of SMEs may cease to qualify for tax credit which may be offset against individual income tax;

(ii) capital gains realised by French residents on the sale of shares in UK companies may no longer qualify for the enhanced holding period allowance (Article 150-0 D of the French tax code) and the fixed allowance for retiring executives (Article 150-0 D *ter* French tax code).

Chapter 10

Germany

Marcus Mick and Christoph Klein

INTRODUCTION

10.1 On 29 January 2020, the EU Parliament approved the Brexit Withdrawal Agreement, which came into force on 1 February 2020. Since then, the United Kingdom (UK) has no longer been a member of the European Union (EU). At the same time, a transition period began which ran until 31 December 2020.[1]

Although the UK was no longer a member of the EU during the transition period, EU law continued to apply. Both the tax laws and the corresponding administrative instructions were applicable to matters relating to the UK. During the transition period, the EU and the UK have negotiated the EU-UK Trade and Cooperation Agreement of 24 December 2020 which entered into force at the end of the transition period and (instead of EU law) governs the future relations between the EU and the UK. Despite the agreement, the UK will be treated as a third country in relation to the EU as of 1 January 2021, with all (negative) consequences this entails.

With the '*Brexit Tax Accompanying Act*' of 25 March 2019,[2] the German legislature has already reacted to some disadvantageous tax consequences which can be triggered by a hard Brexit, ie UK leaving the EU and the European Economic Area (EEA). This was important since in many cases German tax law distinguishes between EU/EEA cases and non-EU/EEA cases.

The purpose of this chapter is to analyse the main consequences of Brexit from a German tax perspective.

1 The transition period could have been extended by a maximum of two years by mutual agreement. However, the extension deadline ended on 30 June 2020 without any action being taken by the UK or the EU.

2 *Gesetz über steuerliche und weitere Begleitregelungen zum Austritt des Vereinigten Königreichs Großbritannien und Nordirland aus der Europäischen Union (Brexit-Steuerbegleitgesetz – Brexit-StBG)* of 25 March 2019, BGBl I 2019, 357.

TAX RAMIFICATIONS FOR INBOUND INVESTMENTS

Outbound dividends

Direct investments

10.2 In general, outbound dividends paid by a German corporation to non-resident shareholders are subject to a 26.375% withholding tax (WHT).[3] Under domestic law it is possible for corporate shareholders to get a refund of two fifths of that tax.[4] In this case, the effective tax burden amounts to only 15.825% of the dividend. Non-resident (corporate) shareholders are in general not eligible for an assessment procedure for dividends which means that they are not entitled to file a German tax return. As a result, non-resident shareholders cannot deduct expenses related to such dividends and they do not benefit from the participation exemption enshrined in the *German Corporate Income Tax Act (CITA), s 8b* which may provide for a 95% exemption of the received dividends. WHT on dividends (15.825% for corporate shareholders) has compensatory effect.[5]

Prior to Brexit, UK corporations could also benefit from the WHT exemption according to the *German Income Tax Act (ITA), s 43b* which implements Article 5 of the EU Parent-Subsidiary Directive (PSD). Where profit distributions are made to a parent company which is tax resident in another EU country with a shareholding of at least 10%, a full WHT exemption on dividends can apply. However, gross dividends can only be paid out after an exemption certificate has been issued by the Federal Tax Office (*Bundeszentralamt für Steuern – BZSt*), *ITA, s 50d, para 2*. If such certificate has not been issued, WHT must be withheld but a refund of the withheld tax is granted provided that the conditions of the PSD are met (*ITA, s 50d, para 1 sent 3*).[6]

After Brexit, UK shareholders can no longer rely on the PSD. However, a reduction of the WHT rate is available under the Double Tax Treaty (DTT) between Germany and the UK. According to Article 10 para 2 lit. a DTT-UK, a 5% WHT rate will be granted if the beneficial owner is a company (other than a partnership) which directly holds at least 10% of the shares in the distributing company. A 10% WHT rate is granted where there is a pension scheme as shareholder (Article 10 para 2 lit. b DTT-UK); a reduction to 15% WHT is granted in any other case (Article 10 para 2 lit. c DTT-UK).[7] The

3 cf *ITA, s 43, para 1 sent 1 no 1, s 43a, para 1 sent 1 no 1*: 25% plus 5.5% solidarity surcharge on top.

4 cf *ITA, s 44a, para 9.*

5 *cf ITA, s 50 para 2 sent 1, CITA, s 32 para 1 no 2*. For a possible infringement of the EU free movement of capital see below, at the end of **10.2**.

6 The requirements of the German anti-treaty/directive-shopping-rule (*ITA, s 50d para 3*) must be fulfilled.

7 The requirements of the German anti-treaty/directive-shopping-rule (*ITA, s 50d para 3*) must be fulfilled.

dividend-paying company must have an exemption certificate by *BZSt* in order to pay a dividend under a lower WHT rate. If such certificate has not been issued, WHT must be withheld at a rate of 26.375%, which can partly be refunded, see above.

Illustration: profit distribution from a German corporation to a UK parent company

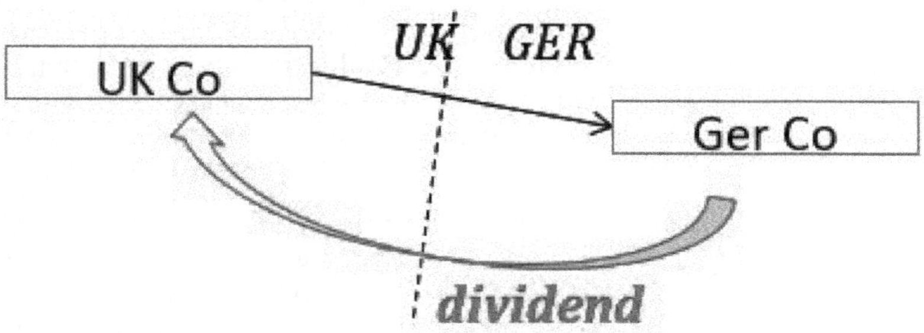

- Prior to Brexit, application of PSD (*ITA, s 43*), if shareholding ≥ 10%
  - **exemption from WHT**
- After Brexit, application of DTT between Germany and UK
  - Article 10 para 2 lit. a DTT-UK: **5% WHT** on gross dividend if shareholding ≥ 10%
  - Article 10 para 2 lit. b DTT-UK: **10% WHT** on gross dividend if shareholder is pension scheme
  - Article 10 para 2 lit. c DTT-UK: **15% WHT** on gross dividend in any other case

It is questionable whether the application of 5% (or more) WHT on dividends distributed to non-resident corporate shareholders constitutes an infringement of the free movement of capital. German resident corporate shareholders in general benefit from the participation exemption which provides for a 95% exemption of received dividends if the shareholding is 10% or more. With an effective tax rate of approx. 30% (15.825% CIT and solidarity surcharge and approximately 15% additional trade tax), the dividends are effectively taxed at a rate of approximately 1.5%. In addition, German resident corporate shareholders are permitted to deduct expenses related to dividend income whereas non-resident corporate shareholders are not entitled to do so, regardless of the respective shareholding quota. This makes it very likely that a 5% (or more) WHT on dividends constitutes an infringement of the free movement of capital.[8]

Indirect investments

Impact of Germany's anti-treaty/directive-shopping rule

10.3 The absence of PSD exemption has consequences for WHT on outbound dividends not only in the case of a direct shareholding by a UK parent company. As a result of Germany's anti-treaty/directive-shopping rule (*ITA, s 50d para 3*), Brexit also affects group company arrangements (constellations) where a UK company holds a German participation via another EU company (see **10.4**) and where a UK company itself is a holding company (see **10.5**).

According to Germany's anti-treaty/directive-shopping provision WHT relief under a DTT or PSD is only applicable to a foreign company if: (a) the shareholders in the foreign company would be entitled to the same WHT relief if they directly held the German subsidiary, or (b) certain substance requirements are met at the level of the foreign company. Such substance requirements are fulfilled if the gross earnings of the foreign company result from its own business activity or if there are economic or other substantial reasons for the involvement of the foreign company and the foreign company participates in general economic transactions *(allgemeiner wirtschaftlicher Verkehr)* with an appropriately established business *(angemessen eingerichteten Geschäftsbetrieb).*

Unfortunately, there are no clear guidelines with regard to the exact content of the substance requirements. For practical reasons, it is always recommended to provide for the following:

- The foreign company must have an appropriately established business in its country of residence, that is, qualified personnel capable of managing the day-to-day business, business premises, technical means of communication, etc.
- The foreign company should constantly employ management and other personnel for the performance of its activities. Such personnel must perform their activities in the company's premises.

---

8 In the past, the Federal Tax Court has held the view that the threshold at which the free movement of capital is replaced by the freedom of establishment is a statutory participation rate of 10% (I R 7/12). However, because of recent CJEU decisions (i.a. *Itelcar* (Case C-282/12) and *Kronos International* (Case C-47/12)), the Federal Tax Court has meanwhile changed its view. Accordingly, a shareholding of at least 10% does not necessarily give its holder 'definite influence' over the company's decisions (I R 75/16). The distinction between the free movement of capital and freedom of establishment is relevant as only the free movement of capital provides protection for third country taxpayers.

In the past, German tax authorities held the view that a mere asset management activity is not sufficient in order to fulfil the requirements of a foreign company's 'substance'. However, in a CJEU ruling of 20 December 2017 (*Deister Holding and Juhler Holding* (Cases C-504/16 and C-613/16), which was in line with *Eqiom and Enka* (Case C-6/16)), the court held the view that Germany's anti-avoidance rule constitutes an infringement of both freedom of establishment and PSD.[9] As a first reaction, the German Ministry of Finance amended its previous view by issuing an updated decree dated 4 April 2018 according to which a foreign company participates in general economic transactions if its gross earnings result from mere asset management activities. The foreign company must actually exercise its rights as a shareholder.

New legislation for Germany's anti-treaty/directive-shopping rule which is in line with the EU fundamental freedoms and PSD is currently pending. The Federal Ministry of Finance published a draft legislation on 19 November 2020 containing a proposal for a compliant regulation.

EU company as holding company

10.4 If a UK company held a German participation indirectly via for example a Dutch or Luxembourg holding company, it was not necessary to provide evidence for such intermediate holding company's substance according to Germany's anti-treaty/directive-shopping rule prior to Brexit, provided the UK parent company itself was entitled to PSD benefits (see **10.3**). After Brexit, substance requirements (see **10.3**) have to be fulfilled at the level of the EU holding company to benefit from the 0% WHT treatment.

UK company as holding company

10.5 The UK will become less attractive as a location for holding companies because of the increased WHT obligation on dividends received by the UK holding company. If, for example, a US company which may claim a zero rate under the DTT between Germany and the US (Article 10 para 3, Article 28 DTT-US) holds an indirect participation in a German corporation via an EU holding company, it was not necessary for the EU holding company to provide evidence of the company's substance as the US company is also entitled to a zero WHT rate. After Brexit, a 5% WHT on dividends is levied in such case as the entitlement of a (full) relief of an indirect shareholder is not taken into account for the purpose of the German anti-treaty/directive-

9 CJEU ruling of 20 December 2017 (*Deister Holding and Juhler Holding* (Cases C-504/16, C-613/16)) dealt with the 2007 version of *ITA, s 50d, para 3*. The ECJ ruling of 14 June 2018 (Case C-440/17, *GS*) constituted an infringement of freedom of establishment and PSD for the current version of *ITA, s 50d, para 3*.

shopping rule.[10] The same result is given for an EU company as the parent of the UK company.

Outbound interest

10.6 According to German domestic law, interest paid to non-resident lenders triggers German WHT of 26.375% only in very rare cases, for example interest from specific hybrid finance instruments. Non-residents are, however, subject to limited (corporate) income tax liability on interest, for example if the loan in question is secured with domestic real estate or similar collateral (cf *ITA, s 49, para 1, no 5, lit c*) or if the interest is attributable to a domestic permanent establishment (cf *ITA, s 49, para 1, no 2, lit a*). In such a case, the taxpayer must file a tax return, and taxes on interest payments are levied by way of an assessment. Financing within a group, between related parties or between third parties, however, typically does not give rise to German taxes if the interest is based on a straightforward loan with at arm's length interest payments and without domestic real estate as collateral.

Should the interest payment be subject to German tax or WHT the exemption available according to *ITA, s 50g* that implements the EU Interest and Royalties Directive (IRD) will no longer apply after Brexit if the recipient is a UK person. However, according to Article 11 para 1 DTT-UK, a full tax exemption of German (withholding) taxes on interest payments to UK lenders will apply.

Illustration: interest paid by German entity to UK entity

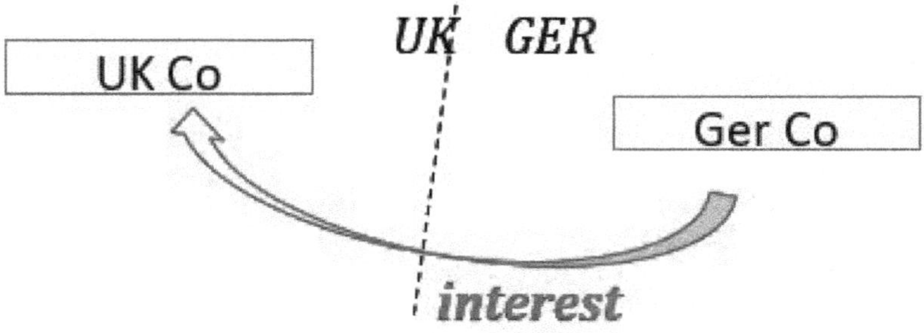

10 cf Letter of the Federal Ministry of Finance dated 24 January 2012, B 3-S 2411/07/10016, BStBl I 2012, 171, mn. 4.3.

- Prior to Brexit, application of IRD (*ITA, s 50g*), if shareholding of UK Co in Ger Co is ≥ 25%
- After Brexit, (only) application of DTT between Germany and UK
  - Article 11 DTT-UK: **exemption from WHT on interest**

Brexit should therefore not lead to any changes if debtor and creditor are respectively German and UK persons. However, additional tax burdens may arise in constellations in relation to Eastern and Southern European countries, as numerous DTTs with these countries do not fully restrict Germany's right to tax. If, for example, a German subsidiary of a UK parent company pays interest to an Italian affiliate and the loan is secured by German real estate, such interest payment should be taxable in Germany and Germany has a right to levy a tax of 10% on the gross amount of the interest (cf Article 11 para 2 DTT-Italy). Such taxation would have been avoided under IRD but *ITA, s 50g* is only applicable if all shareholdings are between companies resident in the EU (cf *ITA, s 50g, para 5, no 5, lit b, sent 2*). However, such taxation can also be easily avoided by not using German real estate as security.

Outbound royalties

10.7 Royalties paid by a German licensee to a non-resident licensor are in general subject to a 15.825% WHT (cf *ITA, s 50a*). In general, the WHT on royalties has compensatory effect and the non-resident licensor is not eligible to deduct any related expenses.

For licensors that are domiciled within the EU/EEA, it is possible to deduct expenses that are directly related to the royalties (*ITA, s 50a, para 3*). The WHT rate then amounts to 31.65% for individuals and 15.825% for corporations.[11] The tax base for WHT in such cases is therefore the 'net' licence payment. In addition, German implementation of IRD (*ITA, s 50g*) is applicable and may provide for a full exemption from WHT on royalties.

After Brexit, the German implementation of IRD and net taxation pursuant to *s 50a, para 3* will not be applicable. However, according to Article 12 para 1 DTT-UK, royalties arising in Germany and beneficially owned by a resident of the UK shall be taxable only in the UK. The DTT provision provides for a full exemption of German (withholding) taxes on the royalties.

11 Including solidarity surcharge. According to the Federal Tax Court (I R 32/10), net taxation is also permissible for royalties – contrary to the wording of the provision, cf Letter of the Federal Ministry of Finance dated 17 June 2014, 2014-06-17 IV C 3-S 2303/10/10002:001, BStBl I 2014, 887.

Illustration: royalties paid by German entity to UK entity

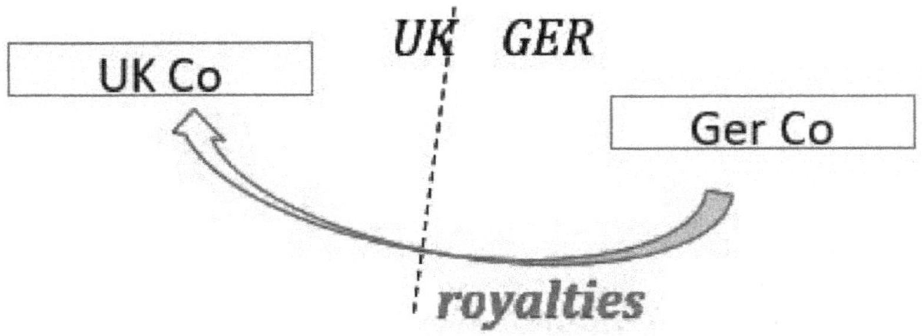

- <u>Prior to Brexit,</u> application of IRD (*ITA, s 50g*), if shareholding of UK Co in Ger Co is ≥ 25%
- <u>After Brexit,</u> (only) application of DTT between Germany and UK
  - Article 12 DTT-UK: **exemption from WHT on royalties**

Brexit should therefore not lead to any changes if the licensee and licensor are respectively German and UK persons. But, as with outbound interest, additional tax burdens may arise in constellations in relation to Eastern and Southern European countries, as numerous DTTs with these countries do not fully restrict Germany's right to tax. If, for example, a German subsidiary of a UK parent company pays royalties to a Polish affiliate, such royalties are in general subject to a 5% German WHT (cf Article 12 para 2 DTT-Poland). Such taxation could have been avoided under IRD.[12]

Capital gains on shareholdings in resident companies

10.8 Capital gains deriving from the disposal of shares are subject to German limited (corporate) income tax liability if the corporation has its seat or place of management in Germany and the shareholding amounts to or exceeds 1%. In addition, any capital gain deriving from the disposal of shares (regardless of the company's seat or place of management) is subject to German taxation if more than 50% of the share value at any time during 365 days prior to the disposal was directly or indirectly based on domestic real estate and the shares were attributable to the seller at that time (cf *ITA, s 49,*

12 *ITA, s 50g* is only applicable if all shareholdings are between companies resident in the EU, cf *ITA, s 50g, para 5, no 5, lit b, sent 2.*

para 1, no 2, lit e).[13] In the latter case, the capital gains are taxable only on appreciation in value since 1 January 2019.

Where the seller is a foreign individual, such capital gain is 40% tax exempt (*ITA, s 3, no 40; 3c, para 2*). Where the seller is a foreign corporation, such capital gain is generally fully tax exempt (*CITA, s 8b, para 2*; exemption applies to credit and insurance companies) unless the shares are attributable to a German permanent establishment.[14] If the shares are attributable to a German permanent establishment of the foreign corporation, the capital gain is 95% tax exempt.

Germany's right to tax capital gains of a foreign person – which is only relevant if the 100% tax exemption does not apply – is usually restricted under an applicable DTT. For example, according to Article 13 para 2 DTT-UK, Germany only has the right to tax capital gains derived from the alienation of shares by a UK resident if more than 50% of the share value is directly or indirectly based on German immovable property.[15] Germany also has the right to tax capital gains if the shares are attributable to a German permanent establishment (Article 13 para 3 DTT-UK). In any other case, the UK as the resident country has the sole right to tax capital gains derived by a UK resident (Article 13 para 5 DTT-UK) and, hence, Germany's right to tax is fully excluded.

Brexit does not have an impact on the tax treatment of capital gains realised by UK residents.

Permanent establishments

10.9 According to *ITA, s 49, para 1, no 2 lit a*, business income that is attributable to a permanent establishment located in Germany is subject to limited German income tax liability. Germany also has the right to tax such income according to Article 7 paras 1 and 2 DTT-UK.

Brexit does not lead to any changes with regard to German permanent establishments of UK companies.

13 In order to determine the ratio, the asset's book values according to German tax law are decisive.

14 In general, capital gains on the disposal of shares by corporations are only 95% tax exempt because 5% of the capital gain is deemed to be non-deductible expenses (cf *CITA, s 8b, para 3*). However, according to a recent decision by the Federal Tax Court (I R 37/15), the imputed 5% non-deductible expenses do not apply in the case of a non-resident seller, which leads to a 100% tax exemption for corporate shareholders if the shares are not attributable to a German permanent establishment.

15 However, such capital gain is fully tax exempt if the seller is a foreign corporation (see above).

Other – capital repayments

10.10 From a German tax perspective, distributions by corporations to their shareholders may qualify either as (taxable) dividends or as a (tax-neutral) **repayment of capital** (other than a repayment of the nominal/share capital that is always free of German tax). Repayments of capital are taxable as a sale of the underlying shares only to the extent that the repayments of capital exceed the shareholder's acquisition costs. Such capital repayments are not subject to German WHT.

According to the explicit wording of the law, only corporations subject to unlimited tax liability in Germany are eligible to maintain a capital contribution account for tax purposes (*steuerliches Einlagekonto,* cf *CITA, s 27*) and thus can make capital repayments. Upon request, corporations which are subject to unlimited tax liability in other EU or EEA[16] countries can make a corresponding capital repayment as well (*CITA, s 27, para 8*). Under current legislation, however, it is not possible for third country corporations to make such a request. Therefore, the German tax authorities hold the view that third country corporations are not entitled to make tax-neutral capital repayments to their shareholders and in general will qualify any distribution made by a third country corporation as a taxable profit distribution.

However, in a recent ruling (I R 15/16), the Federal Tax Court identified this treatment to constitute a violation of the free movement of capital. A third country corporation must be permitted to pay out capital contributions to its German shareholders in some manner. It is expected that a tax decree will be issued which will govern the treatment of capital repayments by third country corporations and the respective prerequisites. An amendment to German tax law in this regard is also expected.

As a result, it is expected that UK corporations should still be entitled to make tax free capital repayments to German shareholders even after Brexit.

TAX RAMIFICATIONS FOR OUTBOUND INVESTMENTS

Inbound dividends

10.11 Dividends paid to resident corporate shareholders are in general 95% CIT exempt if the shareholding is 10% or more. The German unilateral participation exemption provided by *CITA, s 8b* applies to domestic dividends,

16 The wording of the law only covers EU corporations. However, the Letter of the Federal Ministry of Finance dated 4 April 2016 also treats EEA corporations as within the scope of the regulation.

EU/EEA dividends as well as dividends originating from third countries. Foreign WHT on inbound dividends cannot be credited against German CIT due to the tax exemption (*CITA, s 26*). If the shareholding interest is less than 10%, the dividend is fully taxable for CIT purposes (15.825% CIT including solidarity surcharge). In such a case, foreign WHT on the dividend can be credited against the German CIT burden.

For trade tax purposes,[17] the treatment of received dividends also does not depend on whether the distributing corporation is German, EU/EEA or third-country resident. The dividend is 95% trade tax exempt if the participation is 15% or more at the beginning of the collecting period (ie, typically the beginning of the calendar year, cf *German Trade Tax Act, s 9, no 2a and no 7*). However, Article 23 para 1 lit a sent 2 DTT-UK provides for a participation exemption if the shareholding of the German parent in the UK corporation is directly 10% or more at the time the dividend is received. Further, the dividend must be 'effectively taxed' in the UK and the UK subsidiary must realise its gross income for which the dividends were paid exclusively or almost exclusively from activities within the meaning of the *German Foreign Tax Act (FTA), s 8, para 1*, that is, 'active income' as defined in the German Controlled Foreign Corporation (CFC) regime.

Pursuant to a tax decree issued by the Federal Ministry of Finance, foreign dividends are deemed to be 'effectively taxed' in the source country even if there is no taxation as a result of Article 4 para 1 or Article 5 of EU PSD.[18] Accordingly, the lower participation quota of 10% for trade tax purposes was applicable prior to Brexit even when no WHT in UK was levied. After Brexit, however, dividends must be 'effectively taxed' in the UK, that is, the UK must levy a WHT of 5% on such dividends according to Article 10 para 2 lit a DTT-UK in order to qualify for the participation exception under Article 23 para 1 lit a sent 2 DTT-UK. As the UK currently does not levy any WHT on dividends, the participation exemption provided by Article 23 DTT-UK is de facto not available for German shareholders after Brexit.

The trade tax rate on dividends depends on the municipality in which the German corporation is located. Typically, the trade tax rate amounts to approximately 15%. Trade tax cannot be credited nor deducted against CIT.

17 Trade tax is an additional 'business tax' levied by the municipalities.

18 cf Letter of the Federal Ministry of Finance dated 20 June 2013, IV B 2-S 1300/09/10006, BStBl I 2013, 980, mn. 2.3.

Illustration: profit distribution from a UK corporation to a German parent company

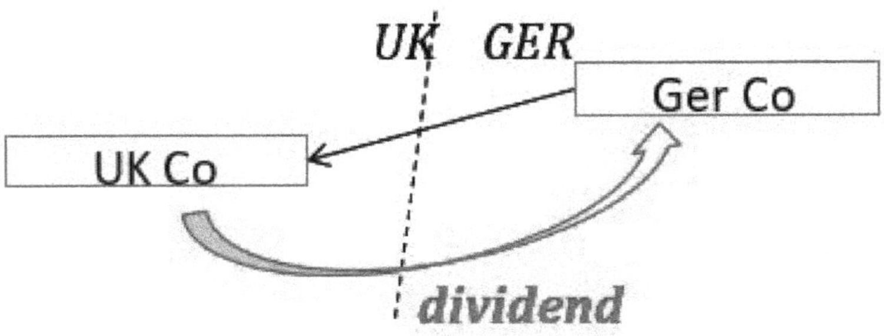

- Prior to Brexit, CIT and trade tax exemption for dividends if shareholding ≥ 10%: **95% CIT and TT-exempt → effective tax rate approx. 1.5%**
- After Brexit, stricter rules apply for trade tax-exemption
    - o if shareholding ≥ 15%: **95% CIT and TT-exempt → effective tax rate approx. 1.5%**
    - o if shareholding ≥ 10% but < 15%: **95% CIT-exempt but subject to TT → effective tax rate approx. 15.75%**
- Prior to/after Brexit
    - o if shareholding < 10%: **dividend is subject to CIT and TT → effective tax rate approx. 30%**

Inbound dividends paid to German resident individuals are in general taxable at a rate of 26.375% (income tax including solidarity surcharge, cf *ITA, s 32d*). Foreign WHT on such dividend can be credited against the German income tax burden. Brexit will not lead to a different treatment with regards to inbound dividends paid to individuals.

Capital gains on shareholdings in non-resident companies

10.12 Capital gains from the disposal of shares in a UK resident corporation realised by a German resident corporation are in general subject to corporate income tax plus solidarity surcharge (15.875%) and additional trade tax (approximately 15%). However, such capital gain is 95% CIT and trade tax exempt according to the participation exemption which leads to an effective tax rate of approximately 1.5% on the gain (5% on CIT plus Solidarity Surcharge and trade tax). The tax exemption does neither depend on the company's seat or place of management nor on the participation quota in that company.

In general, Germany has the right to tax such capital gains according to Article 13 para 5 DTT-UK unless the shares are attributable to a foreign permanent establishment. However, Germany's right to tax may be restricted according to Article 13 para 2 DTT-UK where more than 50% of the shares' value directly or indirectly derives from immovable property situated in the UK. Other DTTs may also restrict Germany's right to tax where the UK company holds immovable property situated in other countries.

Brexit does not lead to any changes with regards to capital gains on shareholdings in UK resident companies.

Permanent establishments abroad

10.13 According to Article 7 paras 1 and 2 DTT-UK the UK has the right to tax business income that is attributable to a permanent establishment located in the UK. Such income is tax exempt in Germany if it is effectively taxed in the UK (Article 23 para 1 lit a DTT-UK).

Under German tax law, the transfer of a business asset from a German permanent establishment to a foreign permanent establishment triggers income tax on the built-in gain (ie, hidden reserves) of the transferred business asset (exit taxation, cf *ITA, s 4, para 1, sent 3 and 4*; *CITA, s 12, para 1*). However, the taxpayer is able to account for a balance sheet item *(Ausgleichsposten)* in the amount of the hidden reserves. The balance sheet item has to be dissolved by one-fifth in the financial year in which it is formed and in each of the following four financial years (*ITA, s 4g*). The exit tax triggered can thus be apportioned over five years in equal instalments. However, such deferral is only available where the business asset is transferred to a permanent establishment within the EU.

After Brexit, the deferral option according to *ITA, s 4g* will no longer be applicable for business assets which are transferred to a UK permanent establishment.

In the past, it was questionable whether Brexit would lead to a mandatory dissolution of an already formed balance sheet item, as a balance sheet item must be dissolved where the transferred asset ceases to be taxable in a Member State of the EU. Now the *Brexit Tax Accompanying Act*[19] provides a clarification: the withdrawal of the UK from the EU alone shall not lead to a mandatory dissolution of an already existing balance sheet item (*ITA, s 4g,*

19 *Gesetz über steuerliche und weitere Begleitregelungen zum Austritt des Vereinigten Königreichs Großbritannien und Nordirland aus der Europäischen Union (Brexit-Steuerbegleitgesetz – Brexit-StBG)* of 25 March 2019, BGBl I 2019, 357.

para 6). Thus, a tax deferral shall not cease but continues until the end of the five-year period, even after Brexit.

CFC rules

10.14 According to current German CFC rules (*FTA, ss 7–14*) 'passive income' (ie, in general interest, royalties, etc) of a foreign company is added to the tax base of the shareholder(s) if German tax residents own more than 50% of the foreign company's shares (controlled company) and the income of the controlled company is taxed at a rate of less than 25%. Specific 'passive investment income' is added even in case the participation is below 50%. After the CJEU ruling *Cadbury Schweppes* in 2006 (Case C-196/04), German legislature implemented an exception: passive income and passive investment income will not be added if the statutory seat or place of management of the controlled company is located in an EU or EEA Member State and the controlled company carries out 'genuine economic activities' in that state. After Brexit, a UK controlled company can no longer rely on such exculpation.

On 10 December 2019, the draft Bill for the implementation of the Anti-Tax Avoidance Directive (ATAD) was published by the German Ministry of Finance which will revise German CFC rules so as to align them with the ATAD.[20] It is not yet clear when the law will be implemented or whether there will be any additional amendments in the draft law. But the draft CFC rules also provide for an exculpation only for controlled companies that have their statutory seat or place of management in an EU or EEA Member State.[21] Exculpation for third country companies is, however, possible for 'passive investment income' as no control of the respective company is required. This takes into account the recent CJEU decision *X-GmbH* of 26 February 2019 (Case C-135/17) in which the court identified a restriction of the free movement of capital in relation to the current German CFC rules with regard to 'passive investment income'. Accordingly, a UK company will remain eligible for exculpation under the draft Bill if CFC rules stipulate the addition of 'passive investment income' and the participation is less than 50%.

IMPACT ON CROSS-BORDER GROUP TAX REGIMES

10.15 The German tax group regime in general allows the consolidation of profits and losses of controlled entities (*Organgesellschaften*) with profits and losses of the controlling entity (*Organträger*) at the level of the controlling

20 Originally, the draft Bill was to be passed on 18 December 2019; however, voting on the Bill was postponed and it is expected that the legislative procedure will be completed in the course of 2020.

21 In addition – and in contrast to current law – the controlled company must be engaged in a 'significant economic activity' in that state which means that more substance is required.

entity (cf *CITA, ss 14–17*). A German tax group requires the financial integration of the controlled entity, that is, the controlling company must have the majority of the voting rights from the shares in the controlled entity from the beginning of its financial year. Further, it is required that a specific profit and loss transfer agreement is concluded between the group companies.

Foreign companies are also eligible as controlling companies. However, the shares in the controlled entities must be functionally attributable to a German permanent establishment of the controlling company during the entire term of the tax group. The income of the respective domestic permanent establishment must be subject to German tax liability and Germany must also have the right to tax such income under an applicable DTT. Due to these restrictive requirements, a controlling company is typically set up as a German legal entity without any foreign permanent establishments. The set-up of a German corporation typically ensures that the shares of the controlled company will be attributed to a German permanent establishment of the controlling entity which gives Germany the unrestricted right to tax such income.

In order to qualify as a controlled entity, the respective company must be a corporation from a German tax perspective, that is, a *Gesellschaft mit beschränkter Haftung* (GmbH), an *Aktiengesellschaft* (AG) or a comparable foreign incorporated entity (eg, a British limited company). The controlled entity must have its place of management in Germany and must have its statutory seat within a Member State of the EU (including Germany) or the EEA.

Due to the restrictive requirements, 'foreign' controlled entities, that is, corporations with a statutory seat in another EU/EEA Member State, are rare. Therefore, it is expected that Brexit should have minimal impact on German tax group relationships. In any event, a British limited company could no longer qualify as a controlled entity within a German tax group. An existing corporate group with a UK controlled company should cease to exist at the time of Brexit.

TAX RAMIFICATIONS FOR CROSS-BORDER MERGERS, OTHER REORGANISATIONS AND TRANSFERS OF RESIDENCE

Cross-border mergers and other reorganisations

General

10.16 In general, any merger, division, conversion, contribution of business and contribution/exchange of shares qualifies as taxable sale of assets at the level of the transferring entity and as acquisition of such assets at the level of the receiving entity. The same applies for the shareholders of a converted, divided or merged entity, that is, the shares are deemed to be sold and purchased at fair market value.

Tax-neutral reorganisations (both shareholder and company level) are, however, possible under the *German Reorganization Tax Act* (*RTA*). The material scope of application does not only cover domestic reorganisations according to the *German Reorganization Act*. The *RTA* is also applicable to foreign reorganisations that are comparable to domestic reorganisations (*RTA, s 1, paras 1 and 3*).

The personal scope of the *RTA*, on the other hand, is limited to reorganisations involving only 'European' parties. European parties in this context are legal entities that are established under the laws of Member States of the EU or EEA and must have their statutory seat and place of management within a Member State of the EU or EEA (*RTA, s 1, paras 2 and 4*).[22] There are exceptions to this general rule:

- Share for share exchange (*RTA, s 21*): Only the acquiring legal entity must be tax resident within a Member State of the EU or EEA.
- Contribution into a partnership (*RTA, s 24*): There are no restrictions with regard to the tax residency of involved parties in the case of contribution of a business, branch or co-entrepreneurial share *(Mitunternehmeranteil)* into a partnership.

Apart from the *RTA*, *CITA, s 12, para 2, sent 1* provides for a tax-neutral merger of third country companies. If the total assets of a third country corporation with limited corporate income tax liability in Germany (eg, German permanent establishment) are transferred to another corporation of the same country by a transaction comparable to a German (legal) merger within the meaning of the *German Reorganization Act*, the transferred assets are generally transferred at fair market value, that is, the transferor realises a taxable gain on the transferred assets. However, the merger must be recognised at book value (without realising a gain), provided:

(1) it is ensured that the assets will later be subject to corporate income tax at the level of the receiving entity;

(2) Germany's right to tax with regard to the transferred assets at the level of the receiving corporation is not restricted;

(3) a consideration is not granted or consists in company rights only; and

(4) the receiving and the transferring legal entity do not meet the personal requirements of *RTA, s 1, para 2* (see above).

Under the abovementioned conditions, a merger of third country companies does not result in a taxable realisation of hidden reserves (eg, of hidden

22 In the case of individuals, they must be tax resident within the EU or EEA.

reserves in assets that are allocated to a German permanent establishment of the merged company).

CITA, s 12, para 2, sent 2 provides for a tax-neutral treatment of the shareholders of the merged third country company: in the event of a third-country merger in the meaning of the abovementioned conditions, it is possible for the shareholders of the entities to apply for a roll-over of the book value of their shares (instead of a deemed sale and purchase of new shares at fair market value). An application for a roll-over of the value of the shares is also possible if the merged company is not subject to limited corporate income tax liability in Germany.

Already carried out reorganisations involving UK entities or UK shareholders

10.17 The personal scope of the *RTA* (ie, 'European' parties according to *RTA, s 1, paras 2 and 4*) must be given at the time of the reorganisation.[23] Subsequent status changes, for example due to a transfer of residence, do not invalidate the carried-out tax-neutral reorganisation. As a result, Brexit should in general not have an effect on already carried out reorganisations.

A transitional regulation has been introduced for cross-border mergers under German civil law. Pursuant to the *German Reorganization Act, s 122m*, the merger of a British company into a German company is still subject to the *Reorganization Act* if the merger plan (*Reorganization Act, s 122c, para 4*) has been notarised prior to the expiration of the transition period of Brexit and the merger is filed for entry in the commercial register immediately, but no later than two years after the notarisation of the merger plan. According to *RTA, s 1, para 2, sent 3*, such cases are also covered by the *RTA* and a tax-neutral merger is possible.

Tainted shares

10.18 The general rule that a subsequent change in status of an EU/EEA company into a third country company and vice versa does not affect the carried-out reorganisation is not true in the case of so-called 'tainted shares' (*sperrfristbehaftete Anteile, RTA, s 22*). Tainted shares are shares issued in exchange for a tax-neutral contribution of a business, branch or co-entrepreneurial interest into a corporation (*RTA, s 20 para 2, sent 2*). Within a period of seven years after the contribution, a (partial) disposal of the shares

23 According to the prevailing opinion, the 'time of the reorganisation' is the time when the conversion takes effect under civil law. In contrast, the German tax authorities hold the view that the tax transfer date should be decisive. The tax transfer date can be agreed retroactively and is thus in general prior to the effective date under civil law.

(or a comparable event) results in a retroactive taxation of the capital gain at the time of the contribution (so-called 'contribution profit I', *Einbringungsgewinn I*). According to *RTA, s 22, para 1, sent 1 no 6* a 'comparable event' to a disposal of shares is given if the personal requirements for applying the *RTA* (ie, 'European' parties) are no longer fulfilled. An event such as Brexit would therefore trigger the contribution profit I where the tainted shares are held by a British company or a British individual (but see below).

Tainted shares are also given in case of a tax-neutral share for share exchange where the contributor is not a corporation (*RTA, s 22, para 2*). In such a case, a disposal of the contributed shares (or a comparable event) by the acquiring entity within a period of seven years after the share for share exchange results in a retroactive taxation of the capital gain in the contributed shares at the time of the exchange (so-called 'contribution profit II', *Einbringungsgewinn II*). According to *RTA, s 22, para 2, sent 6* a 'comparable event' to a disposal of the contributed shares (= tainted shares) is given if the personal requirements for applying the *RTA* are no longer fulfilled regarding the acquiring entity. An event such as Brexit would therefore trigger the contribution profit II where the acquiring entity is a British company (but see below).

The German legislator became aware of the disadvantageous and retroactive tax consequences of the involved parties and provided under the *Brexit Tax Accompanying Act*[24] that the withdrawal of the UK from the EU shall not qualify as an event comparable to a disposal of tainted shares (*RTA, s 22, para 8*). Thus, Brexit itself does not trigger a contribution profit I or a contribution profit II.

Reorganisations after Brexit

10.19 After Brexit (ie, after the expiry of the transition period), any reorganisation involving UK entities (ie, UK resident companies and double resident companies) in general qualifies as taxable sale of assets at the level of the transferring entity as well as acquisition at the level of the receiving entity. So, for instance, a British corporation that decides to incorporate its existing German permanent establishment will not be entitled to a tax-neutral contribution of the business into a corporation under the *RTA, s 20* as the personal requirements would not be fulfilled. Such contribution leads to a taxable realisation of hidden reserves in the assets associated with the German permanent establishment.

Exceptions are available for share for share exchanges (*RTA, s 21*) and a contribution of a business, branch or co-entrepreneurial interest into a partnership (*RTA, s 24*), see **10.16** above.

24 *Gesetz über steuerliche und weitere Begleitregelungen zum Austritt des Vereinigten Königreichs Großbritannien und Nordirland aus der Europäischen Union (Brexit-Steuerbegleitgesetz – Brexit-StBG)* of 25 March 2019, BGBl I 2019, 357.

For mergers of UK corporations, the provision of *CITA, s 12* must be applied at the level of the merged entities and at the level of the shareholders. For details, see **10.16** above.

TRANSFER OF RESIDENCE ABROAD

Outbound transfer of residence – corporations

10.20 German corporate tax law provides for different legal consequences relating to the relocation of a corporation's place of management depending on the company's statutory seat. If, on the one hand, a corporation relocates its place of management from Germany to another country but retains its statutory seat within the EU/EEA, exit taxation only applies to those business assets for which Germany's right to tax is restricted or excluded (cf *CITA, s 12, para 1*). Should the relocated company maintain a German permanent establishment and provided all business assets of the company can be allocated to this German permanent establishment the relocation will not attract taxable capital gains in Germany. However, the German tax authorities apply a 'rebuttable presumption' for participations in subsidiaries or intangible assets that are deemed to be functionally allocated to the new management permanent establishment abroad after relocation. Such assets are then deemed to have been sold at fair market value. Taxes on such capital gains may be apportioned over a period of five years with annual equal instalments if the destination country is another EU or EEA Member State (*ITA, s 4g*, see **10.13** above).

If, on the other hand, a corporation relocates its place of management as well as its statutory seat to a country outside the EU/EEA and the corporation thereby ceases to be subject to unlimited tax liability in an EU or EEA Member State (or if the corporation is deemed to be tax resident in a country outside the EU/EEA under an applicable DTT), the company is deemed to be dissolved from a German tax perspective (cf *CITA, s 12, para 3*). In this case, exit taxation would even affect business assets that remain taxable in German permanent establishments of the corporation. A tax deferral is not applicable.

It was debatable whether an event such as Brexit would trigger an exit taxation. In the meantime, the *Brexit Tax Accompanying Act*[25] guarantees that Brexit itself should not result in an exit taxation according to *CITA, s 12, para 3* (cf *CITA, s 12, para 3, sent 4*). But it is undisputed that an exit tax according to *CITA, s 12, para 3* will affect a British corporation (eg, limited company) that relocates its place of management from Germany 'back' to the UK subsequent to the expiry of Brexit's transition period.

25 *Gesetz über steuerliche und weitere Begleitregelungen zum Austritt des Vereinigten Königreichs Großbritannien und Nordirland aus der Europäischen Union (Brexit-Steuerbegleitgesetz – Brexit-StBG)* of 25 March 2019, BGBl I 2019, 357.

Illustration: UK Ltd. with permanent establishment in Germany

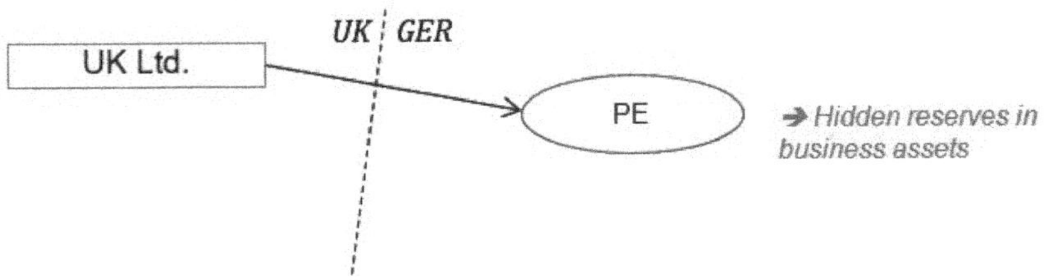

- UK Ltd. has its statutory seat in UK
  - (1) Place of management in Germany
  - (2) Place of management in UK
- After Brexit
  - (1) Relocation of place of management to UK triggers exit taxation on PE's hidden reserves (*CITA, s 12, para 3*)
  - (2) Brexit itself does not trigger exit taxation (*CITA, s 12, para 3, sent 4*).

Inbound transfer of residence

10.21 If a taxpayer (individual or corporation) moves his tax residency to Germany and Germany hereby assumes the right to tax business assets, *ITA, s 4, para 1, sent 8* provides for a tax-free step-up in basis of the business assets to the fair value of such assets.

Individuals holding shares in a corporation (at least 1% in the corporation's nominal capital) as a private asset also receive a tax-free step-up of acquisition costs to the value of which the respective taxpayer was subject to an exit taxation in the country of departure (but limited to the respective fair value of the shares, *ITA, s 17, para 2, sent 3*).

The law does not distinguish between the countries from which the taxpayer migrates. Thus, Brexit does not affect the step-up in basis regulations.

OTHER

British companies in Germany

10.22 Due to the jurisdiction of the CJEU, many British entities with different legal forms (eg, Ltd or LLP) have moved their place of management to Germany. Prior to Brexit, their legal recognition was granted according to the EU freedom of establishment. The CJEU has made it clear that companies with a statutory seat within the EU must be recognised and treated as such in the host countries, that is, in the countries in which they have their place of management (cf CJEU ruling *Centros* of 9 March 1999 (Case C-212/97) and CJEU ruling *Überseering* of 5 November 2002 (Case C-208/00)).

From a German corporate law perspective, a legal recognition of British entities located in Germany is no longer guaranteed after Brexit. A compulsory change of legal form into a German partnership (GbR or OHG) is possible which leads to an unlimited liability for the shareholders.

From a German income tax perspective, however, no immediate change of the tax regime (opaque vs. transparent entity) is expected due to a comparison-of-legal-forms test (*Typenvergleich*). From a German tax perspective, a British limited company is comparable to a German corporation (GmbH or AG) and thus is treated as such for tax purposes even after Brexit.

Limitation on benefits clause according to Article 28 DTT-US

10.23 Brexit will also have an impact on companies with UK shareholders that wish to rely on a DTT concluded with the US. DTTs concluded with the US are often based on the US model income tax convention, in which the treaty eligibility is restricted by the so-called Limitation on Benefits (LoB) clause.

As an example, Article 28 of the DTT between Germany and the US provides for a requirement of 'substance' in order to receive treaty benefits. Only 'qualified persons' are entitled to all benefits under the DTT-US. Companies must fulfil specific requirements, or tests, such as the:

- public ownership test;
- active trade or business test; or
- derivative benefits test (Article 28 para 3 DTT-US).

According to Article 28 para 3 and para 8 DTT-US a corporation generally satisfies the derivative benefits provision if 95% or more of its shares are owned by seven or fewer 'equivalent beneficiaries' and less than 50% of the company's gross income is paid or accrued to persons who are not 'equivalent beneficiaries'. Equivalent beneficiaries in the meaning of this provision are ultimate owners who are entitled to identical benefits under their own DTT with the US and are resident in a NAFTA, EU or EEA country.

After Brexit, UK residents no longer qualify as 'equivalent beneficiaries' under US tax treaties which could preclude treaty benefits.

Exit taxation for individuals

10.24 Individuals holding shares in corporations are also affected by an exit taxation when migrating from Germany to another country.

If an individual has held at least 1% in a corporation's nominal capital within the last five years and he or she has been subject to German unlimited income tax liability for a total of at least ten years, *FTA, s 6* provides for a taxation of the increase in value of such shares if his or her income tax liability ends by giving up domicile or habitual abode in Germany. Certain comparable events also lead to such exit taxation, for example if tax residency is established in another country under an applicable DTT or if Germany's right to tax capital gains on the disposal of the shares is restricted or excluded. The fictitious capital gains tax according to *FTA, s 6* is applicable regardless of the corporation's statutory seat or place of management. The capital gain is 40% tax exempt (*ITA, s 3, no 40*). The 60% taxable part is taxed at the personal rate of the taxpayer which can be up to 47.475%.

In reaction to the CJEU decision *Lasteyrie du Saillant* (Case C-9/02), a deferral system was introduced in 2004. *FTA, s 6, para 5* allows EU/EEA citizens to defer the triggered exit tax (without charging interest and without the provision of collateral), provided that the taxpayer will become subject to an unlimited income tax liability that is comparable to German unlimited income tax liability in an EU/EEA Member State.[26] As a result, exit tax according to *FTA, s 6* does not immediately have to be paid when migrating into a different EU or EEA country. The deferral is revoked in certain cases, for example if the shares are sold or if the unlimited income tax liability in the EU/EEA Member State is terminated (*FTA, s 6, para 5, sent 4*).

It is undisputed that the deferral rule no longer applies where a relocation of tax residency to the UK takes place after Brexit. It was questionable whether an already granted deferral is revoked by Brexit as the individual's unlimited tax liability within the EU/EEA ceases. However, the *Brexit Tax Accompanying Act*[27] guarantees that Brexit itself shall not lead to a revocation of an already granted deferral (*FTA, s 6, para 8*).

On 10 December 2019, a draft Bill for the implementation of ATAD was published by the German Ministry of Finance which will revise German exit taxation rules according to *FTA, s 6*.[28] Among other things, the draft

26 In this context, it has always been questionable whether special tax regimes, such as UK remittance-base taxation, Italian lump sum taxation for HNWI or Portuguese NHR for newcomers, meet this requirement.

27 *Gesetz über steuerliche und weitere Begleitregelungen zum Austritt des Vereinigten Königreichs Großbritannien und Nordirland aus der Europäischen Union (Brexit-Steuerbegleitgesetz – Brexit-StBG)* of 25 March 2019, BGBl I 2019, 357.

28 Originally, the draft Bill was to be passed on 18 December 2019; however, voting on the Bill was postponed and it is expected that the legislative procedure will be completed during the course of 2020.

legislation shall abolish the ability to 'perpetual defer' within the EU/EEA. Draft law provides for a 'one-fits-all solution', regardless whether the country of migration is an EU/EEA Member State or a third country. Upon request, the taxpayer may pay the exit tax triggered in seven equal annual instalments. A collateral deposit is generally required but interest will not be levied. In certain events, immediate payment of the outstanding tax amount is due, for example failure to pay the annual instalment on time, sale of the underlying shares or breach of the taxpayer's obligation to cooperate.

The abolition of the perpetual deferral is criticised in German tax literature and is considered not to be compliant with EU law, in particular with the CJEU ruling *Wächtler* of 26 February 2019 (Case C-581/17), in which the court considered a temporary deferral of the exit tax to be disproportionate. The German legislator, however, considers a perpetual deferral within the EU/EEA to be no longer necessary with reference to CJEU rulings (*DMC* of 23 January 2014 (Case C-167/12) and *Verder LabTec* of 21 May 2015, (Case C-657/13), in which the court has held that a temporary deferral of exit taxation, that is, over five years with annual equal instalments is proportionate. It is arguable that there are some inconsistencies within the CJEU jurisdiction and it is uncertain how the CJEU will judge on the new regulation if it is implemented.

According to the latest draft, the regulation should have been applied as of 1 January 2021. However, the law was not passed in 2020 and it is questionable if a new draft will still refer to 1 January 2021 as the applicable date. Besides, the latest draft provided for a grandfathering rule for EU/EEA deferrals that are already running as at 31 December 2020. Such deferrals are not affected by the change in law. Thus, if a perpetual EU/EEA deferral has already been granted when an individual has migrated to the UK prior to 31 December 2020, the deferral will continue regardless of Brexit or the change in law.

Real estate transfer tax

10.25 The *Brexit Tax Accompanying Act*[29] has also amended the *German Real Estate Transfer Tax Act* (*RETTA*) in order to mitigate the effects of Brexit as regards Real Estate Transfer Tax (RETT) matters.

RETT is in general levied if real estate located in Germany is transferred to another (legal) owner. In addition, there are certain triggering events in case of share deals. For example, RETT is triggered if at least 95% of the shares in a company (corporation or partnership) holding German real estate are directly or indirectly unified in the hands of one acquirer or in the hands of controlling and/or controlled companies (*RETTA, s 1, para 3*). For partnerships, RETT is also triggered if at least 95% of the partnership interest is directly or

29 *Gesetz über steuerliche und weitere Begleitregelungen zum Austritt des Vereinigten Königreichs Großbritannien und Nordirland aus der Europäischen Union (Brexit-Steuerbegleitgesetz – Brexit-StBG)* of 25 March 2019, BGBl I 2019, 357.

indirectly transferred to new partners within a period of five years (*RETTA, s 1, para 2a*).[30] The RETT burden depends on the value of the real estate (tax base) and the federal country in which the real estate is located (tax rate). The tax rate amounts to 3.5%–6.5% depending on the federal country.

As described in **10.22**, a legal recognition of British entities located in Germany is no longer guaranteed after Brexit and a compulsory change of legal form is possible. Such change of legal form may be decisive for RETT purposes. For example in case of a single-shareholder British limited company with its place of management in Germany, Brexit may lead to a RETT-able change of legal ownership of the real estate from the limited company to its sole shareholder. In order to avoid this result, a new tax exemption provision was introduced: Transfers that are solely based on the withdrawal of UK from the EU are exempt from RETT (*RETTA, s 4, no. 6*). Other tax exemptions governing such compulsory change of legal form were implemented with the *Annual Tax Act 2020*[31] in *RETTA, s 5, para 3 and s 6 para 3.*

10.26 Another amendment affects the group restructuring exemption clause of *RETTA, s 6a*.[32] The provision can in general only be applied if a group restructuring (in which real estate and/or shares are transferred) involves exclusively one controlling company and one or more dependent companies or several dependent companies. A company is a dependent company if the controlling company has held an uninterrupted participation of at least 95% directly or indirectly in the capital or corporate assets of the depending company for five years before and for five years after the legal transaction.

Brexit could lead to a change of legal ownership of a shareholding participation that is held by a British company and thus could affect the holding period of *RETTA, s 6a*. The *Brexit Tax Accompanying Act*,[33] however, has made it clear that the withdrawal of UK from the EU alone does not result in a violation of the stipulated five-year holding period (*RETTA s 6a, sent 5*).

30 Draft legislation provides for several amendments with regard to share deals.

31 *Jahressteuergesetz 2020 (JStG 2020)* of 21 December 2020, BGBl I 2020, 3096.

32 In previous years, *RETTA, s 6a* was not applied in practice because proceedings were pending at CJEU whether the regulation could qualify as unlawful state aid. With the CJEU ruling of 19 December 2018 (Case C-374/17) the court, however, decided that the regulation does not qualify as unlawful state aid and does therefore not infringe European law.

33 *Gesetz über steuerliche und weitere Begleitregelungen zum Austritt des Vereinigten Königreichs Großbritannien und Nordirland aus der Europäischen Union (Brexit-Steuerbegleitgesetz – Brexit-StBG)* of 25 March 2019, BGBl I 2019, 357.

Chapter 11

Hungary

Pál Jalsovszky

INTRODUCTION

11.1 The purpose of the chapter is to analyse the main consequences of the UK leaving the EU from a Hungarian tax perspective.

The analysis of this chapter is based on the assumption that after the transition period, the UK will be a third country and will not join the EEA.

TAX RAMIFICATIONS FOR INBOUND INVESTMENTS

Outbound dividends

11.2 No difference due to Brexit.

Hungary does not levy any withholding tax (WHT) on dividends paid to foreign companies or entities treated as body corporates for tax purposes based on its domestic law. Further, according to the double taxation treaty concluded between Hungary and the UK (DTT), Hungary does not levy WHT on dividends paid to pension schemes, even if they were not treated as body corporates for tax purposes under Hungarian law.

In general, dividends paid to private individuals are subject to 15% personal income tax. However, according to the DTT, if the beneficial owner of the dividends is tax resident in the UK, the WHT is limited to: (i) 10% of the gross amount of dividends; or (ii) 15% of the gross amount of the dividends where those dividends are paid out of income derived directly or indirectly from immovable property by a real estate investment trust (or similar investment vehicle).

Outbound interest

11.3 No difference due to Brexit.

Hungary does not levy any withholding tax on interest paid to foreign companies or entities treated as body corporates for tax purposes under its domestic law.

Interest paid to private individuals is subject to 15% personal income tax. However, if the beneficial owner of the interest is a UK tax resident, no WHT will be levied under the DTT.

Outbound royalties

11.4 No difference due to Brexit.

Hungary does not levy any withholding tax on royalties paid to foreign companies or entities treated as body corporates for tax purposes under domestic law.

Royalties paid to private individuals are subject to 15% personal income tax. However, if the beneficial owner of the interest is a UK tax resident, no WHT will be levied under the DTT.

Capital gains on shareholdings in resident companies

11.5 Capital gains realised by non-residents on the transfer of shares (or business quotas) in a Hungarian resident company are, in principle, not taxable in Hungary.

However, if the company is a real estate company, the capital gains realised by the alienation of its shares by a non-resident could be taxable in Hungary at 9%, if the tax treaty allows Hungary to tax such capital gains.

The DTT allows taxation of the capital gains realised by the alienation of the company's shares or comparable interests deriving more than 50% of their value directly or indirectly from immovable property.

Under Hungarian law a company qualifies as a real estate company if:

- the value of Hungarian real estate exceeds 75% of the aggregate book value of the total assets shown in its financial statement either individually or on a group level (including the taxpayer, its Hungarian tax resident related companies and the foreign related companies having a Hungarian permanent establishment either with or without Hungarian real estate); and
- any of the shareholders of the taxpayer or of a group member is resident for at least one day in the tax year in a non-treaty foreign country, or in a treaty country where the tax treaty allows Hungarian taxation on such capital gains.

These rules do not apply if the real estate company is listed on a recognised stock exchange.

Alienation for the purposes of this rule includes under Hungarian law: sale, in-kind contribution, transfer without consideration or the withdrawal of shares through a capital decrease. The DTT does not provide specific provision on what should be considered as alienation.

Brexit should not have an impact on the above rules.

Permanent establishments

11.6 No difference due to Brexit.

TAX RAMIFICATIONS FOR OUTBOUND INVESTMENTS

Inbound dividends

11.7 No difference due to Brexit.

Dividends paid by UK resident companies to Hungarian resident companies are generally exempt from corporate income tax (unless the payer is classified as a controlled foreign company). No minimum holding or holding period requirements apply.

Dividends received by private individuals tax resident in Hungary are subject to 15% personal income tax.

Capital gains on shareholdings in non-resident companies

11.8 No difference due to Brexit.

Capital gains from the sale of shares in UK resident companies derived by Hungarian resident companies are subject to corporate income tax at the rate of 9%. However, under the Hungarian participation exemption regime, the sale or in-kind contribution of participations are exempt from corporate income tax, if: (i) the shares are kept for at least one year, and (ii) such holding is reported to the tax authority within 75 days following the acquisition of the shares or incorporation of the subsidiary.

Permanent establishments abroad

11.9 No difference in the tax treatment of foreign permanent establishments and branches.

CFC rules

11.10 Hungary decided to adopt the so-called transactional or non-genuine transactions approach (Article 7(2)(b) ATAD) as opposed to the other so-called entity/categorical approach (Article 7(2)(a) ATAD) in terms of CFC regulation.

Under Hungarian law, a foreign company or permanent establishment constitutes a CFC if:

- the Hungarian tax resident company holds (directly or indirectly) more than 50% of its shares or holds the majority of its voting rights or is entitled to more than 50% of its profits ('control test'); and
- the effective tax rate on the foreign company's profits is less than 50% of the hypothetical tax that it would have paid, had it been a Hungarian taxpayer in a similar situation ('effective tax test'). In simple terms, the effective tax test means that the effective foreign tax burden should at least reach 4.5% of the tax base calculated under Hungarian rules or that the given type of income should be tax exempt under the Hungarian rules.

However, a foreign entity or permanent establishment is not considered as a CFC in the given tax year if:

- its accounting profits do not exceed HUF 243,952,500 (approx. EUR 700,000), while its non-trading income does not exceed HUF 24,395,250 (approx. EUR 70,000) ('profit and non-trading income test'); or
- its accounting profits do not represent more than 10% of its operating costs for the tax year in question ('profit level on opex test'); or
- its income arises only from genuine arrangements ('genuine activity test').

A transaction: (i) is non-genuine if it is put in place for the essential purpose of obtaining a tax advantage, and (ii) the foreign entity/PE 'would not own the assets or would not have undertaken the risks which generate its income if it were not controlled by a company where the significant people functions, which are relevant to those assets and risks are carried out and are instrumental in generating the controlled company's income'.

The exemption related to the 'profit and non-trading income test' does not apply, if the foreign entity (or PE) resides in a non-cooperating jurisdiction. The list of non-cooperating jurisdictions is stated and updated in ministerial decrees.

A permanent establishment is exempted from CFC status, if it is located in a country outside the EU or the EEA zone with whom Hungary has concluded a tax treaty that provides for exemption from corporate income tax on the income attributable to such a permanent establishment. This means that after the transition period, permanent establishments situated in the UK would not qualify as CFCs under Hungarian regulation by virtue of the law.

Brexit should not have an impact on the application of the above rules, except for the one mentioned in the previous paragraph.

TAX RAMIFICATIONS FOR CROSS-BORDER MERGERS, OTHER REORGANISATIONS AND TRANSFERS OF RESIDENCE

Cross-border mergers and other reorganisations

11.11 The provisions implementing the Merger Directive will no longer be applicable.

The consequences of the above are twofold:

(i) From a corporate law perspective, there is no settled practice whether mergers, divisions etc are even possible in respect of third country companies.

(ii) Brexit will also have an impact on the application of preferential taxation rules regarding mergers, divisions, transfer of assets or exchange of shares, as these preferential rules cannot be applied in relation to third country companies (including UK companies). Without the application of such rules, certain items are subject to immediate taxation, the payment of which could otherwise be deferred under the preferential regime.

Transfer of residence abroad

11.12 Hungary has recently implemented exit tax provisions that apply to Hungarian resident companies that cease to be a tax resident of Hungary. In accordance with such provisions, the difference between the book value and the market value of the companies' assets at the time of the transfer of the residence is subject to corporate income tax at a rate of 9%.

The same tax regime applies to assets transferred: (i) from a Hungarian head office to a permanent establishment in another state, or (ii) from a permanent establishment in Hungary to a head office or a permanent establishment in another state, including cases where an entire line of business activity is moved abroad, in so far as the assets transferred are not subject to corporate taxation in Hungary following the transfer.

Where the transfer is made to an EU/EEA Member State, the taxpayer is permitted the possibility to pay the exit tax in five even, annual instalments.

This allowance will not be available for companies moving their tax residence to the UK after Brexit. Under the conservative approach, if the transfer is made to the UK during the transition period, the outstanding instalments will be due upon the end of the transition period, that is, once the UK qualifies as third country.

Inbound transfer of residence

11.13 The DTT will remain in effect after Brexit, continuing to provide the option for UK tax resident companies to "migrate" and move their tax residence to Hungary. In the case of such transfers, the UK exit tax regime has to be applied first. Unlike many countries, Hungary does not assess a value step-up obligation for migrating companies, meaning that the company's assets and liabilities keep their current recognised book value.

The reported share and intellectual property regulation of the Hungarian corporate income tax system provides a tax exemption on the sale and – in some cases – on the income generated by qualifying assets. The qualification requirements include a reporting obligation towards the tax authority after the company's first legal statement as a tax resident, as well as a minimum holding period in both cases. The nexus rules also have to be taken into consideration when applying the exemption for IPs.

Chapter 12

Republic of Ireland

James Somerville and Darragh Noone

INTRODUCTION

12.1 The purpose of the chapter is to analyse the main consequences of the UK leaving the EU from an Irish tax perspective.

The analysis in this chapter is based on the assumption that the UK will be a third country and will not join the EEA.

TAX RAMIFICATIONS FOR INBOUND INVESTMENTS

Outbound dividends

12.2 In general, outbound dividends paid to non-resident corporate shareholders are subject to Irish dividend withholding tax at the rate of 25% (DWT). DWT applies to all dividends and 'distributions' paid by Irish companies. DWT is due and payable within 14 days from the end of the month in which the dividend or distribution is paid and must be paid to Irish Revenue by the Irish paying company when filing the DWT return online.

'Distribution' is broadly defined for the purposes of Irish tax law and includes, for example, certain types of interest payments, including interest paid to a 75% non-Irish parent company. This recategorisation of interest as a distribution, and the resulting DWT treatment, will not apply where the parent company is resident for the purposes of corporation tax in an EU Member State, or where the recipient company is resident in a country with which Ireland has concluded a double taxation agreement (DTA) and it had made the appropriate election. From 1 January 2021 UK-resident companies have to make this election if they do not want interest payments received from their 75% Irish subsidiaries to be regarded as a distribution under Irish tax law.

There are a number of exemptions available from Irish DWT. These include: (i) where dividends are paid to a related 5% EU-tax resident company under the EU Parent Subsidiary Directive (EU PSD) (as transposed into Irish law under the *Taxes Consolidation Act 1997, s 831* (as amended) (*TCA 1997*)), and (ii) where dividends are paid to a company tax resident in a country with which Ireland has concluded a DTA, provided that the company is not ultimately under the control of an Irish tax resident (the DWT DTA Country Exemption) (as provided for under *TCA 1997, s 172D*). Unlike under the EU PSD, to avail of the DWT DTA Country Exemption, the recipient of the dividend/distribution must provide a declaration to the payer confirming the conditions of the exemption are met before the dividend/distribution is paid. The paying company must still file a nil DWT return online by the 14th day of the month following the end of the month in which the dividend/distribution is paid.

From 1 January 2021 UK tax resident companies are no longer able to avail of the EU PSD exemption. However, they may continue to be able to avail of the DWT DTA Country Exemption by virtue of being resident in a country with which Ireland has concluded a DTA, provided that they are not ultimately under the control of an Irish tax resident. To avail of the DWT DTA Country Exemption, the UK related company must complete the appropriate declaration (Non-Resident Form V2B) before receiving the dividend/distribution. Once completed, the Non-Resident Form V2B is valid for the year in which it is issued plus a further five calendar years.

A reduced rate of DWT may also be available under the terms of Article 11 of the Ireland/UK DTA. Where the beneficial owner of the dividends is a UK-resident company which controls, directly or indirectly, at least 10% of the voting power in the Irish company paying the dividends, a 5% rate of DWT will apply. In all other cases where the recipient company is UK tax resident, a 15% DWT rate will apply (subject to the possible exemptions outlined above).

Outbound interest

12.3 At the outset, it is worth bearing in mind that, as outlined at **12.2**, interest paid to a 75% non-resident parent company may be recategorised as a distribution and subject to DWT treatment instead of the interest withholding tax (WHT) treatment discussed here, unless the parent company is tax resident in the EU or is tax resident in a DTA country and has made the appropriate election.

Where interest is not recategorised as a distribution, the paying company must operate Irish WHT at the standard rate of income tax (currently 20%) on the gross amount of any yearly interest and include this amount in its corporation tax return, unless one of the exemptions apply.

There are a number of exceptions to the obligation to deduct WHT on interest payments, including where:

(i) interest is paid by one member of a payments group to another member of the same group or by a company owned by a consortium to one of the members of the consortium (the 'Group Payments Exemption'). Companies are members of a payments group where the paying company is a 51% subsidiary of the recipient, or both are 51% subsidiaries of a third company, or where the recipient company is a 51% subsidiary of the paying company. The Group Payments Exemption only applies where the interest payment is treated as a charge on income for the purposes of Irish corporation tax and, where the recipient is not resident in Ireland, the interest payment is taken into account in computing the taxable profits of the recipient. Both the recipient and paying companies must be resident in the EU or a DTA country;

(ii) interest is paid by a company or an investment undertaking, in the ordinary course of its trade or business, to a company resident in an EU Member State or a country with which Ireland has concluded a DTA, and that country imposes a tax that generally applies to interest receivable in that territory by companies from sources outside that territory (the 'Domestic Exemption');

(iii) interest is paid by a company or an investment undertaking, in the ordinary course of its trade or business, to a company where the interest is exempted from the charge to income tax under a DTA which Ireland has concluded with the relevant territory (the 'Treaty Exemption') (as provided for under *TCA 1997, s 246*). Under the terms of Article 12 of the Ireland/UK DTA, if the beneficial owner of the interest is UK tax resident, a 0% rate of WHT will apply. To avail of the Treaty Exemption, the recipient company must complete a Form IC6. The Form IC6 may be completed before the payment of interest to prevent tax being withheld or the recipient can complete the Form IC6 within four years following the end of the calendar year in which the tax was deducted in order to claim a refund of interest withheld; or

(iv) interest is paid to a related EU-tax resident company under the EU Interest and Royalties Directive (as transposed into Irish domestic law under *TCA 1997, ss 267G–267K*) (the EU IRD Exemption).

While the EU IRD Exemption no longer applies to UK-resident companies following Brexit, the Domestic Exemption, the Treaty Exemption and, where applicable, the Group Payments Exemption may continue to offer relief such that Irish WHT will not apply on interest payments to UK companies.

The ability of the Irish company to claim a corporation tax deduction for the interest paid (either as a corporation tax trading deduction, a trade charge or a rental expense, depending on the circumstances) is not affected by Brexit and remains available, subject to the usual qualifying criteria.

Outbound royalties

12.4 Under Irish law, companies are obliged to operate WHT on patent royalty payments and deduct income tax at the standard rate (currently 20%), unless one of the exemptions applies. In respect of non-patent royalties, the obligation to operate WHT will depend on whether the royalties are considered an 'annual payment'. The term 'annual payment' is not defined in Irish legislation and is the subject of a body of case law. A detailed analysis of the term is beyond the scope of this chapter, but there is a specific Irish Revenue precedent confirming that copyright royalties will not constitute such an annual payment.

The main exemptions from the WHT obligation in respect of patent royalties are broadly the same as those outlined in respect of outbound interest (ie the Group Payment Exemption, the Domestic Exemption and the EU IRD Exemption). It is important to note that in order to avail of the Domestic Exemption for royalty WHT, the paying company must satisfy an additional test. *TCA 1997, 242A(2)(c)* requires that the payment of royalties must be made for bona fide commercial reasons and must not form part of any arrangement or scheme of which the main purpose or one of the main purposes is the avoidance of liability to tax. Unlike the Domestic Exemption in respect of interest payments, the company receiving the patent royalties does not need to complete a declaration or form of confirmation to avail of the exemption and receive the royalties free of WHT.

As noted in respect of Interest WHT, from 1 January 2021, the EU IRD Exemption is no longer applicable to UK tax resident companies. However, the Domestic Exemption and, where applicable, the Group Payment will still be relevant.

In any event, WHT at the lower of the domestic rate or the rate provided for under the Ireland/UK DTA will apply to payments in respect of patent royalties. Under Article 13 of the Ireland/UK DTA, if the beneficial owner of the payment is UK tax resident, a 0% rate of WHT will apply.

Capital gains on shareholdings in Irish-resident companies

12.5 Brexit does not impact on the Irish capital gains tax implications for UK residents on the disposals of Irish shareholdings.

Non-Irish tax residents (whether individuals or corporates not holding shares through an Irish branch or agency) are only subject to Irish capital gains tax on the disposal of shares (which can include debt instruments and other securities) which are: (i) unquoted shares, and (ii) derive the greater part of their value, directly or indirectly, from Irish land and buildings, minerals or mineral rights in the state, or exploration rights within the Irish Continental Shelf. Where the disposal of shares is within scope of Irish capital gains tax, the gain is subject to tax at the rate of 33%, subject to any reliefs being available.

Irish legislation also contains a specific anti-avoidance provision in the case of chargeable gains accruing to non-resident companies which would be considered a 'close company' if they were Irish tax resident. In this case, the gains will be attributed to the participators (broadly speaking, the shareholders or loan creditors) in the company. A 'close company' means a company which is under the control of five or fewer participators, or participators who are directors, but it does not include a company which is controlled by a company which is not a close company or where 35% or more of the shares of the company are held by the public and such shares are listed on a recognised stock exchange and have been the subject of dealings on such stock exchange within the preceding 12 months. This anti-avoidance section does not apply to the sale by a company of certain types of assets such as tangible assets or specified intangible assets (eg patents, registered designs, trademarks, copyrights and computer software) which have been used for the purposes of the trade of the company or of another group company.

Permanent establishments

12.6 Brexit should have no impact on permanent establishments from an Irish tax perspective.

TAX RAMIFICATIONS FOR OUTBOUND INVESTMENTS

Inbound dividends

12.7 The rules on dividends received from UK-resident companies are not affected by Brexit. However, the amount of credit relief available in respect of UK dividends may be restricted in certain circumstances.

Foreign dividends are taxable in Ireland at either 12.5% or 25%. Where an Irish-resident company can prove that dividends received from subsidiaries resident in the EU or a country with which Ireland has concluded a DTA satisfy certain conditions, it can elect (through its corporation tax return) to have the dividends taxed at the lower rate of 12.5%. Those conditions are:

(i) the dividend must be paid out of the 'trading profits' of the foreign subsidiary; and

(ii) throughout the period out of the profits from which the dividend is paid, the paying subsidiary must have been resident in an EU or DTA country, or the principal class of the shares of the paying subsidiary (or its 75% parent) must have been substantially and regularly traded on a recognised stock exchange in Ireland, the EU or a DTA country.

A special rule applies to dividends received by portfolio investors. A portfolio investor is an investor that holds no more than 5% of the dividend paying company. Such investors can treat a dividend received as being paid out of trading profits of the dividend paying company in order to avail of the 12.5% rate in Ireland. Where the dividends form part of the trading income of the portfolio investor company, they are exempt from Irish corporation tax.

Under the Ireland/UK DTA, the Irish recipient company may also avail of credit relief in respect of underlying UK tax suffered on the profits out of which the dividend is paid where it controls, directly or indirectly, at least 10% of the voting power in the UK company.

Brexit, however, has an impact in relation to the availability of the 'additional foreign tax credit' (AFTC) under Irish law. The AFTC was introduced following the CJEU's decision in *Test Claimants in the FII Group Litigation* (Case C-446/04) due to the fact that the tax credit entitlement in Ireland for tax suffered on foreign sourced dividends is based on the amount of foreign tax actually paid on underlying profits. The AFTC is only available where the effective level of company profits in a 'relevant Member State' (ie EU plus Norway and Iceland) is generally lower than the prescribed nominal rate of tax. It would apply, for example, where no tax was paid on the underlying profits out of which a dividend was paid in the UK due to the operation of group relief.

The AFTC operates by topping-up the existing tax credit to the 12.5% rate where a dividend from a company resident in a 'relevant Member State' is liable to Irish corporation tax at that rate. The AFTC is similarly available for dividends liable to tax at the 25% rate. The AFTC is not available in respect of 'excluded' dividends (ie dividends received from a company resident in a relevant Member State paid out from source profits that have not been subject to tax and which in turn had been received directly or indirectly from a third connected company, not resident in a relevant Member State and those profits had not been subject to tax) or exempt dividends (eg portfolio dividends received by certain companies, such as insurance companies).

Inbound interest

12.8 Brexit does not impact inbound interest payments from UK-resident companies to Irish-resident companies. Interest payments received by Irish-resident companies will be subject to tax at 12.5% or 25% depending on whether such payment is regarded as trading or non-trading (passive) income. The outbound payment may be subject to withholding tax in the UK but, as outlined at **12.3** above, relief should be available under the Ireland/UK DTA such that a 0% rate of WHT should apply.

Inbound royalties

12.9 Similar to inbound interest payments from UK-resident companies, Brexit does not impact inbound royalty payments from UK-resident companies. Depending on whether the royalty income is regarded as trading or non-trading income, a corporation tax rate of 12.5% or 25% will apply. As is currently the case, pursuant to the Ireland/UK DTA, the royalty income will be taxable only in Ireland unless the property in respect of which the royalties arise is connected with a permanent establishment maintained in the UK. If WHT arises in the UK, the 0% rate provided for under the Ireland/UK DTA should apply.

Capital gains on shareholdings in non-resident companies

12.10 Brexit does not impact the Irish tax consequences of capital gains on shareholdings in non-resident companies.

Irish-resident companies are subject to corporation tax on their worldwide profits or gains. Generally speaking, on disposing of shares in a foreign company, Irish-resident companies will be subject to corporation tax on any chargeable gains arising from the disposal at an effective rate of 33%. However, there is a 'substantial shareholding' participation exemption available for disposals of qualifying shares such that any gain is exempt from Irish corporation tax. The participation exemption applies where, for a consecutive 12-month period in the two years preceding the date of disposal, the disposing company has held at least 5% of the ordinary share capital in the subsidiary and either the subsidiary is a trading company, or the parent company and all companies which meet the holding period test, when taken together, are considered trading companies. The participation exemption applies in respect of disposals of shares in 5% subsidiary companies that are tax resident in the EU or a DTA country. The exemption also applies on the disposal of certain assets related to shares (ie options and convertible debt). Brexit does not impact the availability of the participation exemption.

Permanent establishments abroad

12.11 Brexit does not impact the Irish tax treatment of permanent establishments abroad.

CFC rules

12.12 Following the issuing, at EU level, of Council Directive 2016/1164 of 12 July 2016 laying down rules against tax avoidance practices that directly affect the functioning of the internal market (EU Anti-Tax Avoidance Directive, ATAD), and pursuant to the *Finance Act 2018*, Ireland introduced CFC rules. The rules apply for accounting periods beginning on or after 1 January 2019. CFC rules are an anti-abuse measure targeted at the diversion of profits to offshore entities in low or no tax jurisdictions. The basic premise of CFC rules is to attribute certain undistributed income of the offshore entity to its controlling parent and taxing same. Broadly an entity will be a CFC where it is: (i) subject to more than 50% control by a parent company and its associated enterprises, and (ii) taxed on its profits account for less than half the tax that would have been paid had the income been taxed in the parent company's country of tax residence.

The CFC regime applies to Irish tax on income of foreign resident companies where certain activities are performed in Ireland by a company that controls the CFC.

ATAD allows Member States to determine whether the income of a CFC should be attributed to its parent using one of two options. Ireland has opted for option B. Option B attributes undistributed income arising from non-genuine arrangements put in place for the essential purpose of obtaining a tax advantage. It focuses on bringing the income that is artificially diverted from Ireland to a low tax jurisdiction back into the Irish tax net. There are a number of exclusions from the scope of the CFC charge. For example, the CFC charge does not apply where securing a tax advantage was not the essential purpose of the arrangement giving rise to the CFC's income or where the CFC has profits of less than EUR 75,000 or low value activities.

Brexit does not have any impact on the operation of Irish CFC rules.

IMPACT ON CROSS-BORDER GROUP TAX REGIMES

12.13 Irish legislation provides that transfers between capital gains group (CGT group) companies where both the transferor and transferee are Irish tax resident are treated as being made for such consideration as would give rise to neither a gain nor a loss for the disposing company. The transferee inherits the original base cost and acquisition date from the transferor. A CGT group comprises a principal company and all of its effective 75% subsidiaries, together with their effective 75% subsidiaries. Previously, a CGT group only included companies resident in the EU or an EEA country with which Ireland had concluded a DTA. However, it is now deemed to also include companies resident in the UK. Therefore, Brexit does not have any impact on CGT groups for Irish tax purposes and UK-resident companies can be included in the regime.

Irish law also recognises the concept of corporation tax groups (both loss groups and payments groups, as well as consortia). Loss groups comprise a parent company and its 75% subsidiaries (or where both companies are 75%

subsidiaries of a third company). Loss groups only include group members that are tax resident in either the EU or a DTA country, or 'quoted' companies where the principal class of shares are substantially and regularly traded on a recognised stock exchange. Similar to CGT groups, Brexit does not impact loss groups.

Payments groups comprise a parent company and its 51% subsidiaries (or where both companies are 51% subsidiaries of a third company). However, payments groups only include companies that are resident in the EU or an EEA country with which Ireland has concluded a DTA. Assuming that the UK does not join the EEA following Brexit, UK companies will no longer form part of payments groups for Irish corporation tax purposes. The main relief available to payments groups is an exemption from WHT on certain relevant payments (ie annual payments, certain interest payments and payments of patent royalties). The effect of Brexit on breaking payments groups should have minimal impact in practice as UK companies can still receive such payments free of WHT pursuant to the Group Payments Exemption described at **12.3** and **12.4** above. In addition, the Ireland/UK DTA provides for a 0% rate of WHT on such payments where the beneficial owner is UK tax resident.

Stamp duty groups, which comprise companies that are 90% associated, are not restricted by any conditions as to the tax residence or place of incorporation of companies. Instead, the relief focuses on 'body corporates', meaning that only companies that correspond, under their domestic law, to a body corporate with ordinary share capital, will qualify. Brexit has no impact on the operation of stamp duty groups from an Irish tax perspective.

Relief from stamp duty exists in the case of certain reconstructions or reorganisations. The relief is available subject to certain conditions being satisfied including that the acquiring company was incorporated in the EU or the EEA. This condition has been broadened, with Brexit in mind, to include a company incorporated in the UK.

TAX RAMIFICATIONS FOR CROSS-BORDER MERGERS, OTHER REORGANISATIONS AND TRANSFERS OF RESIDENCE

Cross-border mergers and other reorganisations

12.14 Following Brexit, the provisions of Council Directive 2009/133/EC (the Merger Directive) (as transposed into Irish domestic legislation under *the European Communities (Cross-Border Merger) Regulations 2008* and *TCA 1997, Part 21*)) no longer apply to UK-resident companies. The Merger Directive, as implemented under Irish law, only permits cross-border mergers (CBMs) between EU/EEA companies. As there is no comparable procedure permitting a CBM between an Irish company and a non-EU/EEA company, any such merger with a UK company post-Brexit would need to be structured by way of a contractual arrangement, thereby losing the tax reliefs offered under the Merger Directive.

The Merger Directive serves to defer capital gains tax which would otherwise accrue to mergers, divisions, transfers of assets and exchanges of shares between companies from different Member States of the EU/EEA. It also ensures tax neutrality where a company of a Member State converts its branch in another Member State into a subsidiary company there.

Transfer of residence abroad

12.15 Pursuant to the ATAD, Ireland introduced exit tax provisions in the *Finance Act 2018* (which were subsequently broadened pursuant to the *Finance Act 2019*). The measures provide that where a company migrates its tax residence from Ireland or where a company transfers assets from its Irish permanent establishment to its head office or to a permanent establishment in another territory or transfers a business (including the assets of a business) carried on by an Irish permanent establishment to another territory, it will be deemed to have disposed of and immediately reacquired the assets at market value. The deemed disposal and reacquisition will be regarded as a chargeable event giving rise to a chargeable gain (or loss), subject to tax at a rate of 12.5%. The charge will not apply where Ireland retains taxing rights on a subsequent disposal of the assets (ie where they remain within the charge to Irish tax).

Where the assets are transferred to an EU/EEA country, the company can elect to defer payment of the exit tax when filing its corporation tax return. The exit tax is then payable in six equal instalments, with the first instalment being due nine months after the event triggering the exit charge. As a result of Brexit, this option is no longer available to companies who migrate their residence or transfer assets from an Irish permanent establishment to the UK.

Inbound transfer of residence

12.16 From an Irish tax perspective, Brexit has no impact on companies transferring their residence to Ireland from the UK.

Other

Ireland/US DTA

12.17 The ability of Irish tax resident companies that are controlled, directly or indirectly, by UK residents, to benefit from the Ireland/US DTA may be restricted. The Ireland/US DTA contains a derivative benefits test in its Limitation of Benefits provision which (in broad terms) enables Irish tax resident companies to avail of benefits under the DTA where such companies are 95% controlled, directly or indirectly, by seven or fewer residents of an EU or North American Free Trade Agreement Member State. Unless the US issues a protocol, following Brexit Irish-resident but UK-owned companies will not, for example, qualify for zero withholding from the US on interest payments under the DTA so the normal 30% rate would apply.

Commercial Mortgage-Backed Securities/Residential Mortgage-Backed Securities transaction

12.18 Where a company is treated as a 'qualifying company' for the purposes of *TCA 1997, s 110* there are a number of tax consequences. For example, while the profits of a qualifying company are taxable at 25% the benefit of operating as such is that it is possible to reduce the qualifying company's taxable profits to a minimal amount (through the deductibility of profit dependent and/or excessive interest) thereby making the company, in effect, tax neutral.

Under *Finance Acts 2016* and *2017*, provisions were introduced to amend the tax treatment applicable to a qualifying company investing in Irish real estate related assets. These amendments deny a tax deduction for: (i) profit dependent interest, or (ii) interest to the extent it exceeds a reasonable commercial return, in each case to the extent it exceeds a reasonable commercial return (the Affected Interest) where such interest is attributed to a 'specified property business' being the holding and/or managing by a qualifying company of 'specified mortgages', units in an IREF (an Irish Real Estate fund within the meaning of *TCA 1997, Chapter 1B of Part 27*) or shares that derive their value or the greater part of their value directly or indirectly from Irish real estate. A 'specified mortgage' for this purpose includes a loan which is secured on, and which derives its value, or the greater part of its value, directly or indirectly from Irish land.

Where Affected Interest arises by reason of being associated with a 'specified property business', and an exemption is not available, it is treated as interest which is not deductible for tax purposes and will thus form part of the taxable profits of the issuer.

A 'specified property business' does not include, among other things, a CMBS/RMBS transaction. In other words the above mentioned restrictions on the tax deductibility of Affected Interest do not extend to a CMBS/RMBS transaction as defined in *TCA 1997, s 110(5A)*. *TCA 1997, s 110(5A)* defines a 'CMBS/RMBS transaction' as a securitisation transaction entered into by a 'qualifying company' where:

(a) the originator (within the meaning of paragraph (a) of the definition of 'originator' in Article 4 of Regulation (EU) No 575/2013 of the European Parliament and of the Council of 26 June 2013 on prudential requirements for credit institutions and investment firms and amending Regulation (EU) No 648/2012 (the CRR)) retains a net economic interest in the credit risk of the securitisation position in accordance with Article 405 CRR; or

(b) an originator (within the meaning of paragraph (b) of the definition of 'originator' in Article 4 of the CRR) retains a net economic interest in the credit risk of the securitisation position in accordance with Article 405 CRR and is a financial institution (within the meaning of the CRR) or credit institution (within the meaning of the CRR) regulated by a competent authority in a relevant Member State or the state or is authorised by a third country authority, recognised by the European Commission as having supervisory and regulatory arrangements at least equivalent to those applied in a relevant Member State or the state, to carry out similar activities;

Brexit may impact transactions where the relevant originator for the purposes of *TCA 1997, s 110(5A)* is a UK financial institution or credit institution. Prior to Brexit, such institutions may have qualified as an originator within the meaning of the CRR. Following Brexit however, there is a risk that transactions involving such institutions would fail to satisfy the definition of 'CMBS/RMBS transaction'. While it is anticipated that it is likely there will be mutual recognition by the EU Commission of UK regulatory authorisations, there is currently no certainty on this. Accordingly, unless and until mutual recognition procedures are put in place, following Brexit, CMBS/RMBS transactions involving UK originators may fall outside the scope of the carve out from the Affected Interest deductibility restriction.

Chapter 13

Italy

Nicola Saccardo, Paolo Arginelli, Mario Tenore, Gabriele Colombaioni

INTRODUCTION

13.1 This chapter aims at highlighting the main consequences of Brexit from an Italian tax perspective. It focuses on corporate tax consequences after the transition period, that is as from 1 January 2021, and is based on the assumption that the UK will be regarded as a state that ensures an effective exchange of information with Italy regardless of the application of the Directive on Administrative Corporation.[1]

TAX RAMIFICATIONS FOR INBOUND INVESTMENTS

Outbound dividends

13.2 Under Italian tax law, dividends are regarded as sourced in Italy where paid by Italian resident companies (Article 23(1)(b) of Presidential Decree n. 917 of 22 December 1986, hereafter the 'Decree 917/1986').

After the transition period, dividends paid by an Italian resident company to a UK company, which does not have a permanent establishment to which the participation in the Italian company is attributable, will be subject to a final withholding tax at the rate of 26% (Article 27(3) of Presidential Decree 29 September 1973, no. 600, hereafter 'Decree 600/1973'). The withholding tax applies on the gross amount of the dividends.

1 This is because of the application of the provisions on the exchange of information of: (i) the convention between the UK and Northern Ireland and the Italian Republic for the avoidance of double taxation and the prevention of fiscal evasion with respect to taxes on income, signed on 21 October 1988 (UK-IT tax treaty); and (ii) of the Convention on Mutual Administrative Assistance in Tax Matters of the OECD and of the Council of Europe of 1988 (of which both Italy and the UK are parties).

The 26% withholding tax will apply also to dividends paid by Italian resident companies to UK investment funds and UK pension funds, subject to the comments below.

For distributions subject to the 26% withholding tax, UK shareholders that are subject to UK corporate tax on the dividends sourced in Italy and can prove the payment of such tax (by means of a certificate issued by UK tax authorities) are entitled to claim the refund up to an amount of 11/26 of the withholding tax levied in Italy (Article 27(3) of Decree 600/1973). As clarified by Circular letter 26 June 1998, no 165, the refund regime is an alternative to (ie, it may not be combined with) the application of tax treaty benefits (see below).

Brexit will affect the tax regime of dividends paid to UK resident companies. After the transition period, in fact, the following regimes will no longer be applicable to distributions made by Italian resident companies to UK corporate shareholders:

- the reduced withholding tax regime (1.2% tax rate) applicable to dividends paid to entities resident in EU or EEA Member States that are liable to corporate tax in those states (Article 27(3-ter) of Decree 600/1973);[2]
- the withholding tax exemption regime provided for in Article 27-*bis* of Decree 600/1973, which implements Council Directive 2011/96/EU of 30 November 2011 (the Parent-Subsidiary Directive).

Brexit will also impact the tax treatment of dividends paid by Italian resident companies to UK pension funds. In particular, the following regimes will no longer apply after the transition period:

- the reduced 11% withholding tax applicable to pension funds established in EU/EEA Member States (Article 27(3) of Decree 600/1973);
- the withholding tax exemption applicable to dividends paid to EU/EEA pension funds with regard to shareholdings held in Italian resident companies for at least five years and that represent no more than 10% of the gross asset value of the pension fund of the previous year.[3]

A reduced withholding tax rate may be available under the provisions of the UK-IT tax treaty. In particular, under Article 10(2) of the treaty, dividends paid by Italian resident and attributable to UK resident beneficial owners are subject to a:

- 5% maximum withholding tax, if the beneficial owner of the dividends is a UK resident company that holds, directly or indirectly, at least 10% of the voting rights in the company paying the dividends; or

2 Circular letter no. 32/E of 8 July 2011 clarified that the requirement of the 'liability to tax' is fulfilled if the recipient is an entity falling into the subjective scope of the corporate tax applied in the EU/EEA Member State of residence.

3 Article 1(95) of Law No. 232 of 11 December 2016 (as subsequently amended).

- 15% maximum withholding tax in all other cases.

Additionally, as the Italian legislation applicable to dividends paid by Italian companies to its shareholders does not generally differentiate on the basis of the size of the investment, it appears that the free movement of capital may apply to Italian-source dividends paid to UK corporate shareholders (and funds). In particular, the protection granted by Article 63 TFEU should apply regardless of whether, in the specific circumstances, the UK shareholder holds a minority shareholding or a shareholding that enables it to exercise a decisive influence over the Italian company paying the dividends (CJEU, 10 April 2014, *Emerging Markets* (Case C-190/12), § 32).

In this respect, it could be argued that Italian tax legislation infringes Article 63 TFEU in the following instances:

- the application of domestic 26% withholding tax to dividends paid to UK corporate shareholders (reduced to 15% or 5% under the treaty), while comparable dividends paid to Italian corporate shareholders are exempt for 95% of their amount and taxed on the remainder 5% at a 24% tax rate;

- the application of domestic 26% withholding tax to dividends paid to UK investment funds (potentially reduced to 15% or 5% under the treaty), while comparable dividends paid to Italian investment funds benefit from a full tax exemption. The CJEU has already found the existence of a breach of EU law in similar circumstances, where a Member State exempted dividends paid to domestic investment funds, while dividends paid to foreign investment funds were subject to withholding tax. The CJEU has acknowledged the existence of a breach of EU law irrespective of whether foreign investment funds were established in the EU (see, for example, CJEU, 10 May 2012, *Santander Asset Management SGIIC SA and others* (C-338/11 to C-347/11)) or outside (CJEU, 10 April 2014, *Emerging Markets Series of DFA Investment Trust Company v Dyrektor Izby Skarbowej w Bydgoszczy* (Case C-190/12)). This discrimination is not triggered by Brexit since the 26% withholding tax already applies to distributions made by Italian companies to UK investment funds;

- the application of domestic 26% withholding tax to dividends paid to UK pension funds, where the 15% – 5% treaty rates were deemed not to apply[4] as comparable dividends paid to Italian pension funds, are subject to a 20% flat tax on the pension fund's net yearly accrued yield.

---

4 In order for the tax treaty regime to apply, the UK pension fund must qualify as a 'resident person'. This should not be the case, for example, for an Authorised Contractual Scheme (ACS) that is a UK-authorised fund structure, and tax transparent in the UK. With regard to the latter, Italian tax authorities recently confirmed however that the participants to ACS can benefit from the treaty based on the clarifications entailed in the Commentary to Article 1, § 5 (see Ruling No. 156 of 28 May 2020 concerning dividend payments made to an ACS that was holding and managing investments for a UK pension fund).

This discrimination is triggered by Brexit, which will lead to the non-application, to dividends paid to UK pension funds, of the aforementioned 11% withholding tax or exemption regimes available to distribution to EU/EEA pension funds (see above). The CJEU has recently found the existence of a breach of EU law in similar circumstances in the case *College Pension Plan* (Case C-641/17), concerning the source taxation applicable in Germany to dividends paid to Canadian pension funds. The CJEU held that the application of the withholding tax to foreign pension funds entailed a discriminatory treatment and therefore violated the free movement of capital, insofar as the foreign pension funds could be found in a comparable situation to a domestic pension fund. The existence of a discrimination is subject to an assessment *in concreto* of the comparability between the funds.

Finally, it appears the standstill clause of Article 64 TFEU would not apply in the above cases. On the one hand, it expressly does not apply to portfolio investments (unless they are connected to the provision of financial services). On the other hand, with regard to direct investments (as well as in the case of the provision of financial services), it applies only insofar as the relevant restrictions have been in place – without interruption – since 31 December 1993. This is not the case for all the above restrictions.

Outbound interest

13.3 Under Italian tax law, interest income is regarded as sourced in Italy where it is paid by the government, by an Italian resident person or by an Italian permanent establishment of a non-resident person (Article 23(1)(b) of Decree 917/1986).

Subject to the exemptions discussed below and to the application of treaty provisions, Italian-sourced interest paid to UK corporate recipients is subject to a final withholding tax at the rate of 26%, applicable on the gross amount of the payment (Article 26(5) of Decree 600/1973).

There are certain domestic exemptions applicable to outbound interest, in particular:

- interest and other proceeds paid to non-resident persons and accruing on bank deposits, bank accounts or postal savings deposits are not subject to tax (see Article 23(b) of Decree 917/1986);
- interest paid to: (i) foreign central banks, or bodies investing the public reserves of foreign countries, (ii) residents of countries that allow an adequate exchange of information with Italy and that are currently listed in the Ministerial Decree issued on 4 September 1996 ('White List' and 'White List State' – this includes the UK and is expected to continue to include the UK despite Brexit, given the existence of a fully-fledged

exchange of information provision in the UK-Italy tax treaty); or (iii) institutional investors, whether or not subject to tax, established in a White List State, insofar as the interest (or similar proceeds) accrues on:

(a) bonds issued by Italian banks, as well as companies whose shares are traded on regulated markets or multilateral trading facilities of EU/EEA States;

(b) bonds traded on regulated markets or multilateral trading facilities of EU/EEA States issued by Italian unlisted companies (other than banks);

(c) unlisted bonds issued by Italian unlisted companies (other than banks) that are held only by, and that can only be transferred to, 'qualified investors';[5] and

(d) notes issued by Italian securitisation SPVs.

After the transition period, for items listed under (a) and (b), where the bonds are traded or regulated on the UK market, the exemption thereof will no longer be applicable.

Brexit will also trigger other changes to the tax regime applicable to Italian-source interest paid to UK recipients. From 1 January 2021, the latter will no longer benefit of the following exemption regimes:

- the exemption from withholding tax applicable to interest on medium long-term financings paid to certain EU recipients, such as banks established under the laws of an EU Member State; entities listed in Article 2(5), no. 23 of Directive 2013/36/EU; insurance companies established and licensed under the laws of an EU Member State (Article 26(5-bis) of Decree 600/1973). After the transition period, this exemption will apply to UK entities only where the latter qualify as white-listed 'institutional investors' subject to regulatory supervisions (whether or not subject to tax in the UK);
- the withholding tax exemption provided for in Article 26-quater of Decree 600/1973, which implements Council Directive 2003/49/EC of 3 June 2003 (Interest and Royalties Directive).

5 According to the clarifications provided by Circular Letter No. 23/2002 and Circular Letter No. 20/2003 of the Italian tax authorities, 'Institutional Investors' include entities that, regardless of their legal or tax status in their state of residence, have as their principal activity that of managing investments on their own account or on behalf of third parties, such as insurance companies, investment funds, SICAV (open-end investment companies) and pension funds. Institutional investors may be entities that are subject to regulatory supervision (*vigilanza*) in their country of incorporation. Entities that are not subject to any regulatory supervision in their country of establishment must satisfy additional conditions, as they are required to have specific skills and expertise in transactions on financial instruments and they may not have been created to manage investments made by a limited number of investors.

In addition, from 1 January 2021, interest paid by Italian resident companies to UK companies that meet all the requirements for the application of the Interest and Royalties Directive except for not being the beneficial owner of the payment, will no longer benefit from the reduced 5% withholding tax provided for in Article 26-quarter(8-bis) of Decree 600/1973. Such reduced rate applies if the additional following conditions are cumulatively met: (i) the relevant financings are granted to a resident company by a non-resident company (lender) which issues bonds that are listed on a regulated market of a EU/EAA jurisdiction; (ii) the interest paid to the non-resident lender is used by the latter to pay the interest due to the bondholders; (iii) the bonds issued by the non-resident company are guaranteed by either the resident company or another company of the group.

Article 11(2) of the IT-UK tax treaty provides for the application of maximum withholding tax rate of 10% on interest payments sourced in Italy and beneficially owned by UK resident persons.

Outbound royalties

13.4 Payments for the use of intellectual property, patents and trademarks, as well as processes, formulas and information relating to knowledge acquired in the industrial, commercial or scientific field, are regarded as sourced in Italy where paid by the Italian State, an Italian resident person, or an Italian permanent establishment of a non-resident person (Article 23(2)(c) of Decree 917/1986).

As a rule, royalties sourced in Italy and paid to non-resident companies are subject to a 30% final withholding tax, which generally applies to 75% of the gross amount of the payment, resulting in a 22.5% effective tax rate (Article 25(4) of Decree 600/1973).

After the transition period, UK corporate recipients will no longer be entitled to the exemption provided for in Article 26-quater of Decree 600/1973, implementing the Interest and Royalties Directive (see, in this respect, § 2.2.4, let. b).

A reduced withholding tax rate is available under the UK-IT tax treaty. In particular, under Article 12(2) of that treaty, royalties arising in Italy and beneficially owned by a resident of the UK are subject to a maximum 8% withholding tax.

Capital gains on shareholdings in resident companies

13.5 Capital gains derived by non-resident companies from the sale of participations in Italian companies are subject to a final 26% substitute tax, subject to certain exceptions.

In particular, capital gains realised by non-resident companies from the sale of non-substantial shareholdings in Italian resident companies are exempt in Italy under the following circumstances:

- if the shares are traded in a regulated market (Article 23(1)(f)(1) of Decree 917/1986);
- if the taxpayer is tax resident in a state that ensures an adequate exchange of information with Italy (such as the UK), or qualifies as an 'institutional investor', whether or not subject to tax, established in a state that ensures an adequate exchange of information with Italy (Article 5(5) of Legislative Decree 461/1997).

A substantial participation exists if it: (a) represents more than 20% (or 2% if the shares are listed in a regulated capital market) of the voting rights in the stakeholders' meeting of the issuing entity; or if it (b) represents more than 25% (or 5% if shares are listed in a regulated capital market) of the capital of the issuing entity. In order to establish whether a substantial participation is sold, all sales occurred in any 12-month period must be grouped together.

The 26% substitute tax cannot apply under Article 13 of the UK-IT tax treaty, the state of residence of the seller having the exclusive right to tax such capital gains.

It is also worth mentioning that the 26% substitute tax applicable to capital gains derived from the alienation of participations in Italian resident companies, which is generally prevented by the UK-Italy tax treaty, could entail a breach of Article 63 TFEU (see **13.2** above), due to the fact that capital gains derived by resident companies are generally subject to a lower tax burden (equal to 1.2%) (see, in this respect, CJEU, 19 January 2006, *Margaretha Bouanich v Skatteverket* (Case C-265/04)).

Permanent establishments

13.6 Brexit will not have any impact on the taxation of the Italian permanent establishment UK entities.

TAX RAMIFICATIONS FOR OUTBOUND INVESTMENTS

Inbound dividends

13.7 Under Article 89(3) of Decree 917/1986, inbound dividends received by resident companies and Italian permanent establishments of non-resident companies generally benefit from a 95% exemption.

This rule is subject to the 'low-tax regime exception', according to which the 95% exemption does not apply if the company paying the dividends is subject to a tax rate lower than 50% of the relevant Italian corporate tax rate (currently set at 24%). The tax regimes in force in EU Member States and EEA Member States are never regarded as low-tax regimes.

It follows that, after the transition period, UK companies might qualify as subject to a low-tax regime. In particular, under Article 47-bis(1) of Decree 917/1986 this might occur in the following two cases:

(a) If the recipient of the dividends controls a UK company (the prerequisite of control is the same that applies for Controlled Foreign Corporation (CFC) purposes – see below), the latter is regarded as subject to a low-tax regime if the effective tax rate applied in the UK (gross of any foreign tax credit) is lower that 50% of the effective tax rate that would have applied to that company if it had been resident in Italy.

(b) On the contrary, if the recipient of the dividends does not control the UK company, the latter is regarded as subject to a low-tax regime if the nominal tax rate in the UK is lower than 50% of the nominal tax rate applicable to similar companies in Italy. In order to establish the nominal tax rate in the UK, the effects of UK special tax regimes are taken into account; for the purposes of Article 47-bis(1)(b) of Decree 917/1986, special tax regimes are those that apply due to the specific characteristics of the beneficiary and, although not directly impacting on the tax nominal tax rate, provide for exemptions or other reductions in the tax base suitable for effectively reducing that tax rate below 50% of the Italian nominal tax rate. In addition, where the special tax regimes apply solely in respect of some of the economic activities carried out by the UK company, their effects should be taken into account only insofar as those activities are predominant, in terms of the revenues they generate, as compared to the remainder activities of the UK company.

Where the tax regime applicable to the UK company paying the dividends is regarded as a low-tax regime, the dividends are included – as a general rule – in the Italian tax base for their entire amount and are subject to the standard 24% corporate tax rate. However, the following special provisions apply:

- Dividends paid by UK companies that qualify as CFCs, are fully exempt in Italy if they represent distributions of profits that have already been taxed in Italy under the CFC rule.
- The 95% exemption regime applies if the taxpayer can prove that the investment in the UK company did not achieve the result of shifting income to low-tax jurisdictions. This burden of proof may be satisfied, in particular, by giving evidence that the profits of the UK company have been subject to an effective taxation not lower that 50% of the Italian corporate tax rate, taking into account also the taxes levied by other countries (both on the profits as they arose, and on the profits distribution).

- If none of the above exceptions applies, and the UK company carries on a substantive economic activity supported by staff, equipment, assets and premises:
  - only 50% of the dividends is included in the corporate tax base; and
  - an indirect tax credit for the taxes levied on the profits of the UK company (both on accrual and on distribution) is granted, if the recipient of the dividends controls the UK company (once again, the prerequisite of control is the same that applies for CFC purposes). Where corporate taxpayers may combine the 50% exemption and the indirect tax credit, the latter is reduced accordingly (thus only 50% of the foreign taxes may be credited against the Italian tax levied on the dividends).

The tax regime applicable after the transition period to dividends paid by UK companies to Italian companies could be found in breach of the EU free movement of capital provided in Article 63 TFEU.

First, as the Italian legislation applicable to dividends paid to Italian companies does not differentiate on the basis of the size of the investment, it appears that the free movement of capital applies. In particular, the protection granted by Article 63 TFEU may apply both in cases of minority shareholdings and in cases where the Italian parent company exercises a decisive influence over the UK company paying the dividends (CJEU, 10 April 2014, *Emerging Markets* (Case C-190/12), § 32).

Second, a discriminatory tax treatment of the UK-source dividends appears to be at stake, as compared to Italian-source dividends which benefit from the 95% exemption irrespective of the tax rate applied to the company distributing the dividends. The indirect tax credit (which is, in any case, applicable only in the case of controlling shareholdings) and the 50% exemption are not sufficient to eliminate the difference in treatment.

Third, the standstill clause provided for in Article 64 TFEU would not apply in this situation. On the one hand, it expressly does not apply to portfolio investments (unless they are connected to the provision of financial services). On the other hand, with regard to direct investments and the provision of financial services, it applies only insofar as the relevant restriction has been in place – without interruption – since 31 December 1993. This is not the case in relation to the legislation at stake.

Capital gains on shareholdings in non-resident companies

13.8 Capital gains accrued to Italian resident companies (and permanent establishments) from the sale of interests in UK companies are subject to corporate income tax at the rate of 24%.

Under Article 87 of Decree 917/1986, a 95% exemption of the capital gain is granted if four conditions are cumulatively met:

(a) the participation sold has been held without interruption since the beginning of the 12th month preceding the sale;

(b) the participation sold has been classified amongst the fixed financial assets in the first statutory financial statements closed after its purchase;

(c) the UK company is not subject to a 'low-tax regime'. As previously stated with regard to dividends, the tax regimes in force in EU Member States and EEA Member States are never regarded as low-tax regimes. After the transition period, however, UK companies might qualify as subject to a low-tax regime. The rules applicable for the purpose of establishing whether the UK company is subject to a low-tax regime are the same as those described in respect to the taxation of inbound dividends. As a general rule, this requirement (sub (c) requirement) must have been satisfied without interruption for the entire holding period; however, where the participation is sold to a third party, it is sufficient that the sub (c) requirement has been satisfied without interruption for the last five tax years preceding the sale; and

(d) the UK company carries on an effective business activity (holding real estate for investment purposes is generally not regarded as an effective business activity). This requirement must have been met for the last three tax years preceding the sale.

Where the tax regime applicable to the UK company is regarded as a low-tax regime, as a general rule the capital gain stemming from the sale of the interest held in that company is included in the Italian tax base for its entire amount and is subject to the standard 24% corporate tax rate. However, the following special provisions apply:

(i) If the profits of the UK company are taxed in Italy under the CFC rule, the amount of those profits increase the cost for tax purposes of the interest held in the UK company. As a result, insofar as the capital gain only reflects the accumulated profits that have been taxed in Italy under the CFC rule, no gain will be taxed in the hands of the Italian participating company; otherwise just the part of the capital gain exceeding those CFC accumulated profits is taxed.

(ii) The 95% exemption regime applies if the taxpayer can prove that the investment in the UK company did not achieve the result of shifting income to low-tax jurisdictions. This burden of proof may be satisfied, in particular, by giving evidence that the profits of the UK company have been subject to an effective taxation not lower that 50% of the Italian corporate tax rate, taking into account also the taxes levied by other countries (both on the profits as they arose, and on the capital gain).

(iii) If the 95% exemption does not apply under (ii) above and the UK company carries on a substantive economic activity supported by staff, equipment, assets and premises, under Article 86(4-bis) of Decree 917/1986 an indirect tax credit for the taxes levied on the profits of the UK company is granted, under the condition that the Italian resident company (or permanent establishment) controls the UK company (once again, the prerequisite of control is the same that applies for CFC purposes).

The tax regime applicable after the transition period to capital gains stemming from the sale of participations in UK companies could be found to infringe the EU free movement of capital provided in Article 63 TFEU.

First, as the Italian legislation applicable to capital gains on shares and other interests in companies does not differentiate on the basis of the size of the investment, it appears that the free movement of capital applies. In particular, the protection granted by Article 63 TFEU may apply both in cases of minority shareholdings and in cases where the Italian parent company exercises a decisive influence over the UK company (CJEU, 10 April 2014, *Emerging Markets* (Case C-190/12), § 32).

Second, a discriminatory tax treatment of the capital gains on the sale of interests held in UK companies appears to be at stake, as compared to capital gains on Italian shares (or quotas) which benefit from the 95% exemption where conditions (a), (b) and (d) listed above are satisfied, irrespective of the tax rate applied to the participated company. The indirect tax credit (which is, in any case, applicable only in the case of controlling shareholdings) is not sufficient to eliminate the difference in treatment.

Third, the standstill clause provided for in Article 64 TFEU would not apply in this situation. On the one hand, it expressly does not apply to portfolio investments (unless they are connected to the provision of financial services). On the other hand, with regard to direct investments and the provision of financial services, it applies only insofar as the relevant restriction has been in place – without interruption – since 31 December 1993. This is not the case in relation to the legislation at stake.

Permanent establishments abroad

13.9 As a general rule, the profits of UK permanent establishments are subject to tax in Italy in the hands of the resident enterprises. International double taxation on those profits is avoided by means of the credit method provided for by Article 165 of Decree 917/1986 and the ITA-UK tax treaty. In this respect, no difference arises as a consequence of Brexit.

Alternatively, under Article 168-ter of Decree 917/1986, resident enterprises may also opt to exempt the profits of UK permanent establishments.

That option, if exercised, is irrevocable and covers all foreign permanent establishments of the resident enterprise. In addition, it requires that the losses of the foreign permanent establishments cannot be used to offset the Italian profits of the resident enterprises. Where a foreign permanent establishment satisfies the conditions for the application of the CFC rule, the profits of that permanent establishment are not exempt, unless it is proved that the permanent establishment carries on a substantive economic activity supported by staff, equipment, assets and premises.

CFC rules

13.10 The Italian CFC rule does not distinguish between EU/EEA Member States and third countries. Therefore, no difference emerges as a consequence of Brexit.

The CFC regime is set out in Article 167 of Decree 917/1986 and applies to both resident persons and Italian permanent establishments of non-resident persons controlling foreign entities that qualify as CFCs.

For CFC purposes, an Italian resident person (or permanent establishment) is deemed to control the foreign entity: (i) if the former may exercise a definite influence, via voting rights or even contractual relationships, over the latter, or (ii) if the former holds, directly or indirectly, more than 50% of the profit participation rights in the latter.

A foreign entity qualifies as a CFC if two conditions are cumulatively met:

(i) The foreign entity's effective tax rate is lower than 50% of the effective tax rate that would apply if that entity were a tax resident of Italy; and

(ii) More than one third of the revenues realised by the foreign entity are 'tainted', that is, interest; dividends; royalties; capital gains on shares; revenues from financial leasing; revenues from insurance, banking and other financial activities; revenues from trading goods that are purchased from or sold to associated enterprises, with the addition of no or little economic value; and revenues from supplying services that are purchased from or provided to associated enterprises, with the addition of no or little economic value. Whether or not the foreign entity sells goods or supplies services with little or no added value is established on the basis of transfer pricing regulations.

As a general rule, if the controlled foreign entity qualifies as a CFC, the whole profits of the CFC (not just the tainted income) are attributed for tax purposes, based on profits participation, to the Italian controlling person and subject to the ordinary Italian income tax rate (24% in the case of companies). The CFC's profits are computed by applying the Italian corporate tax rules and are ring-fenced from the other profits of the Italian controlling person, so that they may be offset neither by current, nor by previous tax losses of that person.

The profits of the CFC, however, are not taxed in the hands of the controlling Italian person if the CFC carries on a substantive economic activity supported by staff, equipment, assets and premises.

TAX CONSOLIDATION

13.11 Italian tax legislation provides for both a worldwide and a domestic tax consolidation regime.

Brexit does not trigger any relevant change in the application of the worldwide tax consolidation regime.

With regard to the domestic tax consolidation regime, the following should be noted. Before 2015, a non-resident company could opt for such regime only if it: (i) was resident in a country that had a tax treaty in force with Italy that allowed for an adequate exchange of information, and (ii) had a permanent establishment in Italy. Moreover, non-resident companies could opt for the regime only as parent companies and not as subsidiary companies.[6]

In order to make the group consolidation regime compliant with the freedom of establishment, as interpreted by the CJEU,[7] Legislative Decree 147/2015 widened the scope of the domestic tax consolidation regime so that:

(a) resident sister companies could opt for the application of the domestic tax consolidation regime if they were under the common control of a non-resident company not having a permanent establishment in Italy (horizontal consolidation);

(b) non-resident companies with Italian permanent establishments could join a domestic tax consolidation as subsidiary companies.

The application of the regime in cases (a) and (b) above is subject to the condition that the foreign company is resident in an EU/EEA Member State and has a legal form similar to those of the Italian companies admitted to the domestic tax consolidation regime.

The domestic tax consolidation regime is optional and applies if both the parent company and the subsidiaries make an election for its application. Once the election has been made, the regime is irrevocable for a period of three

6 For the purposes of the group consolidation regime, a company qualifies as a parent company if it: (i) holds, directly or indirectly, the majority of the voting rights that can be exercised at the shareholders' meeting of the subsidiary, (ii) holds, directly or indirectly, more than 50% of the subsidiary's stated capital, and (iii) is entitled, directly or indirectly, to more than 50% of the profits of the subsidiary.

7 See the Circular Letter No. 40/E of 2016, where the Revenue Agency mentions that the 2015 changes had been introduced to comply with the principles laid down in the judgment of the CJEU in *SCA Holding* (Cases C-39/13–C-41/13) (judgment 12 June 2014). In this respect, it is worth pointing out that the changes seem also to make the Italian regime compatible with the ruling of the CJEU in *Philips Electronics* (Case C-18/11) (judgment 6 September 2012).

tax years. Where one of the requirements for the domestic tax consolidation ceases to be fulfilled in the course of the compulsory three-year period, the tax consolidation is discontinued (either entirely, or solely with regard to the subsidiary in respect of which the requirement has ceased to be fulfilled).

After the transition period

13.12

(a) Resident sister companies under the common control of a UK resident company will no longer be entitled to participate in a horizontal tax consolidation.

(b) Italian permanent establishments of UK resident companies will no longer be eligible for the application of the domestic tax consolidation regime as subsidiary companies.

At the end of the transition period, domestic tax consolidations including UK resident companies acting under (a) and (b) above are likely to be discontinued, as residence in an EU/EEA Member State is one of the requirements for the application of the domestic tax consolidation regime in those cases.[8] In particular, in (a) above the whole tax consolidation is likely to be discontinued, while in (b) the risk is limited to the tax consolidation of the UK subsidiary.

On the other hand, Brexit should not remove the right for UK resident companies with an Italian permanent establishment to opt for the domestic tax consolidation regime as parent companies. This option, in fact, is not subject to the requirement that the parent company is resident in an EU/EEA Member State, but just to the condition that it is resident in a state that has concluded a tax treaty (in force) providing for an effective mechanism for exchange of information. For the same reason, those domestic tax consolidations should not be discontinued as a result of Brexit.

TAX RAMIFICATIONS FOR CROSS-BORDER MERGERS, OTHER REORGANISATIONS AND TRANSFERS OF RESIDENCE

Cross-border mergers and divisions

13.13 The provisions implementing the Merger Directive apply to cross-border mergers and divisions involving companies resident in EU Member

8 This conclusion is supported by the fact that Article 13, paragraph 1, letter e) explicitly stipulates that if a company that is a member of a horizontal consolidation transfers its residence from Italy to a third country, the consolidation is discontinued.

States. Therefore, after the end of the transition period, such provisions will no longer be applicable to mergers and divisions involving companies resident in the UK.

In the Ruling No. 470/E of 3 December 2008, the Revenue Agency held that the tax provisions concerning domestic mergers[9] should apply also to cross-border mergers and divisions that are outside the scope of the Merger Directive, if the following conditions are met:

(a) The merger (or division) must be carried out pursuant to company law provisions similar to those governing Italian mergers (or divisions), that is, that the transferring company should transfer all its assets and liabilities to the recipient company and, upon such transfer, should be dissolved without being liquidated. Regarding this condition, in the Ruling No. 42/E of 12 February 2008, the Revenue Agency addressed the reorganisation of one insurance company, the assets and liabilities of which were transferred to another insurance company; both such companies were tax resident in the UK and had an Italian permanent establishment. The Revenue Agency concluded that the reorganisation at stake could not be regarded as a merger because the applicable (English) law: (i) did not provide that the entirety of the assets and liabilities of the first company was transferred to the other one, and (ii) did not determine the dissolution without liquidation of the first company. Indeed, the dissolution without liquidation was only one of the potential effects of the reorganisation and not one that was mandatorily applicable.

(b) The companies involved must be incorporated in a legal form similar to any of the legal forms provided under Italian company law.

(c) The reorganisation must have Italian tax ramifications (this is the case, for example, if one of the companies is resident in Italy or has an Italian permanent establishment).

If the tax rules concerning domestic mergers (and divisions) are applicable, cross-border mergers (and divisions) involving companies resident in the UK should not give rise to taxable gains or to deductible losses with regard to the assets and liabilities of the merging companies to the extent that such assets and liabilities are attributed either to a company resident in Italy or to an Italian permanent establishment. The assets and liabilities benefiting from the tax neutrality regime keep the same tax basis that they had before the merger. Moreover, the attribution to the shareholders of the shares of the companies participating in the merger (or division) do not generally give rise to capital gains or losses. As mentioned, similar considerations apply also to divisions.

9 Particularly, Article 172 of Decree 917/1986.

Contributions of businesses

13.14 Under Italian income tax legislation, contributions to companies are regarded as tantamount to sales and give rise to a taxable gain or a deductible loss in the hands of the contributing company for a value equal to the difference between the arm's length value of the assets and liabilities contributed and their tax basis.

The provisions implementing the Merger Directive apply to the contributions of business ('transfers of assets' according to Article 2(d) of the Directive) arising between a company resident in Italy and a company resident in another EU Member State,[10] as well as to contributions of Italian permanent establishments arising between companies resident in different foreign EU Member States.[11] Therefore, after the end of the transition period, such provisions will no longer be applicable to contributions of businesses involving UK resident companies.

A special tax neutrality regime[12] applies if the contribution concerns an Italian business, regardless of the residence of the companies involved in the contribution. Thus, even after the transition period, such regime should continue to apply to contributions involving UK resident companies. Under this regime, the contribution does not give rise in Italy to any taxable gain or a deductible loss for the contributing company and the participation received by such company as a consideration for the contribution will take the same tax basis attributed to the business prior to the contribution. With reference to the beneficiary of the contribution, the assets and liabilities benefiting from the tax neutrality regime will take the same tax basis that they had in the hands of the contributing company before the contribution. This tax neutrality regime will continue to apply, for example, to the contribution of an Italian business by a UK company into an Italian company.[13]

Contributions and exchanges of shares

13.15 Contributions and exchanges of shares are considered as tantamount to sales and, therefore, they generally give rise to taxable gains or deductible

10 Article 178(1)(c) of Decree 917/1986.

11 Article 178(1)(d) of Decree 917/1986.

12 Article 176 of Decree 917/1986.

13 In Ruling No. 63/E of 2018, the Revenue Agency took the view that the shareholding obtained by the non-resident company upon contribution of the Italian business should be attributed to the Italian permanent establishment of the contributing company. In the absence of such attribution (because, for example, the permanent establishment is extinguished upon contribution), or if later on the permanent establishment is extinguished, or the shareholding is attributed to the head office, a capital gain arises as a result of the deemed disposal of the shareholding for a price equal to the fair market value of the shareholding as determined pursuant to Italian income tax provisions. Such capital gain may benefit from the participation exemption regime described at **13.8** above.

losses. If the transferring company is resident in Italy and/or the transfer is made through an Italian permanent establishment, the participation exemption could apply (see **13.8** above).

The provisions implementing the Merger Directive apply to exchanges and contributions of shares through which a company resident in an EU Member State acquires a controlling participation in a company resident in another EU Member State (or acquires an additional shareholding in a controlled company resident in another EU Member State) on the further condition that at least one of the parties making the contribution or exchange is resident i Italy, or the shareholding is attributable to an Italian permanent establishment of a company resident in another EU Member State.[14] Therefore, after the end of the transition period, the neutrality regime provided by such provisions will no longer apply to exchanges and contributions of shares involving UK resident companies. In particular it will not apply to exchanges and contributions of shares:

(a) through which a company resident in the UK acquires a controlling shareholding in a company resident in an EU Member State (or acquires an additional shareholding in a controlled company resident in an EU Member State) from one or more companies resident in Italy and/or Italian permanent establishments;

(b) through which a company resident in an EU Member State acquires a controlling shareholding in a company resident in another EU Member State (or acquires an additional shareholding in a controlled company resident in another EU Member State) from the Italian permanent establishment of a company resident in the UK;

(c) through which a company resident in Italy, or an Italian permanent establishment of a company resident in an EU Member State, acquires a controlling shareholding in a company resident in the UK (or acquires an additional shareholding in a controlled company resident in the UK).

A special regime[15] applies to contributions of shares made by Italian resident companies to other Italian resident companies when, through the contribution, the acquiring company obtains the controlling shareholding in another company. As the regime applies regardless of the tax residence of the participated company, it should continue to apply to contributions of shares in companies resident in the UK after Brexit. Under this regime, the gain stemming from the contribution is computed as the difference between:

(a) the higher between: (i) the book value attributed by the contributing company to the shares in the acquiring company received by the former as a consideration for the contribution, and (ii) the book value

14 Article 178(1)(e) of Decree 917/1986.

15 Article 175 of Decree 917/1986.

attributed by the acquiring company to the shareholding received from the contributing company; and

(b) the tax basis of the shares in the hands of the contributing company.

If the contribution gives rise to a loss, such loss is computed under the ordinary rules (fair market value less tax basis) unless the participation exemption regime applies.

With regard to the special regime described above, a specific anti-abuse provision applies where the contributing company contributes a shareholding that does not qualify for the participation exemption regime[16] (without taking into account the minimum holding period requirement) and receives as a consideration a shareholding that does qualify for the participation exemption (again, without taking into account the minimum holding period requirement). In this case, the special regime described above does not apply.

There are three other special tax regimes applicable to contributions and exchanges of shares where the transferring company is resident in the UK and the transferred company is resident in Italy. As these regimes apply regardless of the residence of the transferring company, they should not be affected by Brexit.

The first regime[17] concerns exchanges of shares through which an Italian resident company obtains a controlling shareholding in another company that is resident in Italy and settles such an exchange by giving treasury shares to the UK transferring company. The regime provides that the exchange does not give rise to a taxable gain and that the shares received by the transferring company take the same tax basis of the shares that were given in exchange.

The second regime[18] also applies to contributions of shares through which an Italian resident company obtains a controlling shareholding in another company that is resident in Italy. Under this regime, the contribution gives rise to a taxable gain equal to the difference between the book value of the increase in the net assets of the acquiring company due to the contribution and the tax basis of the shares. Based on Ruling No. 38/E of 20 April 2012, if the contribution gives rise to a loss, such loss is computed under the ordinary rules (tax basis less fair market value of the shares).

The third regime[19] provides for an extension of the regime described in the previous paragraph to contributions of shares through which the acquiring company does not obtain a controlling shareholding, if the following conditions are met: (i) the contributed shares represent more than 20% of the voting rights of the issuing company (or more than 2% if the company is listed), or more than 25% of the capital of the issuing company (or more than 5% if the

16 On the participation exemption regime see **13.8** above.
17 Article 177(1) Decree 917/1986.
18 Article 177(2) Decree 917/1986.
19 Article 177(2-bis) Decree 917/1986.

company is listed), and (ii) the contributing company is the sole shareholder of the acquiring company.

Under a specific anti-abuse provision,[20] the regimes described in the previous paragraphs do not apply if the transferring company transfers a shareholding that does not qualify for the participation exemption regime[21] (without taking into account the minimum holding period requirement) and receives as a consideration a shareholding that does qualify for the participation exemption (again, without taking into account the minimum holding period requirement).

Outbound transfers of residence

13.16 Under Italian tax law, an exit tax applies to Italian companies that transfer their tax residence abroad.[22] The exit tax is computed by applying the corporate tax rate to a tax basis equal to the difference between the arm's length value of the assets and liabilities transferred (at the end of the tax year when the transferring company loses its status as tax resident person) and their respective tax values. The exit tax does not apply to the gains related to the assets and liabilities that remain connected to an Italian permanent establishment of the company after the transfer.

Under the current rule, companies transferring their tax residence to other EU/EEA Member States[23] have the option to pay the exit tax in five yearly instalments. Before the implementation of the ATAD, those companies might also opt to defer the payment of the exit tax.

The legislation provides that the benefits of those options are discontinued if the company further transfers its residence to a third country. In such an event, the company will pay all the outstanding exit tax within the deadline for its closest tax payment.

20 Article 177(3) Decree 917/1986.

21 On the participation exemption regime see **13.8** above.

22 Article 166 Decree 917/1986. Similar provisions apply also in the following cases: Italian resident company that transfers assets to its foreign permanent establishment that benefits from the branch exemption regime for Italian tax purposes; non-resident company that transfers assets from the Italian permanent establishment to its headquarters or to another non-Italian permanent establishment; Italian resident company merged into a non-resident company; Italian resident company that transferred part of its assets to a non-resident company through a division; Italian resident company that contributed a foreign permanent establishment or part of it to a non-resident company. The contribution will focus on the application of exit tax provisions to the transfer of residence but, given the similarity of the rules, similar considerations are also valid in relation to such other cases.

23 In relation to transfers to an EEA Member State, the option for payment in instalments is subject to the further condition that such a state is included in a white list of countries that exchange information with Italy and that signed an agreement for assistance in the collection of taxes, having provisions comparable to those of Directive 2010/24/EU.

After the transition period, Italian resident companies transferring their tax residence to the UK will no longer be able to opt for the payment of the exit tax in five annual instalments.

In addition, Brexit might trigger a discontinuation of the benefits of the tax deferral or payment in instalments for companies that transferred their tax residence from Italy to the UK in the past. Indeed, the circumstance that such companies will be resident in the UK when the UK will not be regarded as an EU Member State could be considered as tantamount to a transfer of residence to a third country. Such companies might, therefore, be required to pay all the outstanding amount of the exit tax.

Inbound transfers of residence

13.17 Specific provisions[24] apply for establishing the tax basis of the assets and liabilities of non-resident companies that transfer their tax residence to Italy.[25] Pursuant to these provisions, the tax basis of the assets and liabilities is their respective arm's length value regardless of the application of an exit tax in the country of departure. The application of such rule is subject to the condition that the state of origin (before the transfer) is an EU Member State or a state included in the list of countries that exchange information with Italy provided for in the Ministerial Decree of 4 September 1996.

Since the UK is currently included in the abovementioned list and will probably continue to be included therein after Brexit, companies transferring their tax residence from the UK to Italy will be able to rely on the above provision even after the transition period.

OTHER

The transition period

13.18 Under Article 126(1) of the Withdrawal Agreement (WA), 'Union law shall be applicable to and in the United Kingdom during the transition period'. Pursuant to Article 3 WA, the provisions concerning the fundamental

24 Article 177-bis, Decree 917/1986.

25 Similar provisions apply also in the following cases: non-resident company that transfers assets to its Italian permanent establishment; non-resident company that transfers to Italy a going concern; company resident in Italy that transfers to Italy assets of its foreign permanent establishment that benefits from the branch exemption regime; non-resident company that is merged into an Italian resident company; a non-resident company attributes assets and/ or liabilities to a resident company through a division; a non-resident company contributes a non-Italian permanent establishment to a resident company. The contribution will focus on the application of the provisions in relation to transfers of residence to Italy but, given the similarity of the rules, similar considerations are valid also in relation to such other cases.

freedoms laid down by the TFEU and the European Directives are considered as Union law for the purposes of the WA.

Pursuant to Article 127(6) WA, 'during the transition period, any reference to Member States in the Union law applicable pursuant to paragraph 1, including as implemented and applied by Member States, will be understood as including the United Kingdom'. For the purposes of such provision, it seems possible to group Italian provisions on non-harmonised taxes in three categories:

(i) Provisions implementing European Directives, such as the provisions implementing the Parent-Subsidiary Directive (see **13.2** above), the Interest and Royalties Directive (see **13.3** above); the Merger Directive (see **13.13**; **13.14** and **13.15** above) and the ATAD (see **13.16** above).

(ii) Provisions that ensure that the Italian tax system is compliant with the fundamental freedoms (see the provisions described at **13.2**, **13.3**, **13.7**, **13.11**, and **13.16** above and **13.20**–**13.22** below).

(iii) Provisions that make reference to the notion of EU Member State, but that cannot be included in any of the categories of (i) and (ii). These are, for example, the regimes that grant a more favourable treatment to certain entities resident in EU Member States as compared to the treatment applicable to comparable entities resident in Italy (see, for example, the regime described at **13.3** above concerning the withholding tax exemption in relation to outbound interest payments made to certain companies established in other EU Member States in relation to long-term loans).

Under Article 127(6) WA, Italy should be required to regard the UK as an EU Member State until the end of the transition period for the purposes of the application of the provisions of both (i) and (ii) above. This obligation, in theory, does not apply in respect of the provisions of (iii). This is because such provisions implement neither EU fundamental freedoms, nor EU Directives. However, it is worth pointing out that, if such provisions were to be applied during the transition period as if the UK were not an EU Member State, such application could give rise to an infringement of the fundamental freedoms (see the judgment of the CJEU in the case *Sopora* (Case C-512/13)). If this were the case, during the transition period Italy would be required to treat the UK as a Member State of the EU also for the purpose of the specific provision in (iii).

Substitute tax on long-term loan granted by EU banks, funds and insurance companies

13.19 Under Italian tax law, indirect taxes (stamp taxes, registration tax, mortgage and cadastral taxes) generally apply on loans executed in Italy and on their securities (for example, if Italian real estate property is given as a collateral, a 2% mortgage tax applies; if there is a guarantee given by a person other than the debtor, a 0.5% registration tax should apply).

An optional substitute tax[26] is available in relation to medium/long-term loans (ie, loans having a contractual duration of more than 18 months) granted by certain qualifying lenders. If the option for the substitute tax is exercised, the loan is subject to a 0.25% tax on the amount lent (other rates apply in certain specific cases), but no indirect taxes are due on the security package. Non-resident lenders qualify for this regime if they are: banks operating in Italy through a permanent establishment; banks of EU Member States operating in Italy without a permanent establishment under the provisions implementing the freedom to provide services; insurance companies established and authorised to operate in EU Member States (this should include Italian permanent establishment of insurance companies authorised to operate in the EU); collective investment vehicles established in EU Member States or EEA Member States. After the transition period, UK lenders will qualify for the option for the substitute tax only if they are either banks or insurance companies and if they operate through an Italian permanent establishment.

Exemption from financial transaction tax for pension funds

13.20 The legislation on the Italian financial transaction tax provides that Italian pension funds are exempt from such tax. In order to render the legislation compliant with the fundamental freedoms, this exemption had been extended to pension funds established in EU Member States and subject to surveillance pursuant to Directive 2003/41/EC. Such exemption will no longer apply to pension funds established in the UK after the transition period. The levy of the financial transaction tax on pension funds established in the UK could nonetheless determine an infringement of the free movement of capital to the extent that such funds should be regarded as comparable to funds established in Italy that benefit from the exemption (see above).

Tax exemption for Italian pension funds

13.21 Pension funds established in Italy are subject to a special annual tax of 20% on their net profits. Every year, they are allowed to invest a value equal to up to 10% of their net assets as reported in the financial statements relevant to the previous financial year in certain qualifying investments. The income and gains from such qualifying investments, other than gains from substantial participations, are exempt from the 20% tax. Qualifying investments are

26 Article 15 and the following of the Presidential Decree 601/1973.

holdings in companies and certain collective investment vehicles and loans issued by entities that are either resident, or established in Italy or in EU and EEA Member States. After the transition period, Italian pension funds will no longer be able to benefit from this exemption in relation to UK investments. Also in this case, the non-application of the exemption could determine an infringement of the free movement of capital (see above).

Favourable regimes for individuals

13.22 Brexit will affect a number of favourable regimes currently available for individuals.

Individuals resident in Italy are subject to wealth tax on their foreign real estate. The taxable base is generally equal to the purchase price of the real estate. However, if the real estate is located in an EU or EEA Member State, the taxable basis is set at the value resulting from the foreign cadastral registers, or any other value that is relevant for the purpose of the foreign income, wealth or transfer taxes. This rule is meant to render the Italian legislation compliant with the free movement of capital as wealth tax on Italian real estate applies on the cadastral value of the real estate (which is the value determined on the basis of the deemed income attributed to the real estate and recorded in the Italian land registry), which is generally lower than the market price. In relation to properties located in the UK, the Revenue Agency clarified that the taxable value should be established based on the Council tax bands. After the transition period, however, wealth tax will apply to UK properties held by individuals resident in Italy based on the relevant purchase price. This new regime might be said to infringe the free movement of capital, for the very same reasons pointed out in previous sections of this chapter.

Income from holdings in qualifying collective investment vehicles established in EU and EEA Member States derived by resident individuals are subject to a 26% flat tax, in lieu of the ordinary progressive tax rates (up to 43% plus regional and municipal surcharges). After the transition period, this 26% flat tax will no longer apply to the income from holdings in UK collective investment vehicles, which will be subject, instead, to progressive tax rates. This new regime might be said to infringe the free movement of capital, for the very same reasons pointed out in previous sections of this chapter.

As far as Italian inheritance and gift taxes are concerned:

(i) Transfers of government bonds issued by Italy and other EU or EEA Member States are exempt from inheritance tax. After the transition period, this exemption will no longer apply to bonds issued by the UK.

(ii) Transfers to qualifying charitable entities resident in Italy or other EU and EEA Member States are exempt from both inheritance and gift taxes. For entities resident in third countries the exemption is subject to a reciprocity condition. After the transition period, this exemption will apply to charities resident in the UK subject to the reciprocity condition.

The non-application of the above exemptions in relation to transfers of UK government bonds and transfers to charities resident in the UK might be said to violate the free movement of capital.

Chapter 14

Luxembourg

Peter Adriaansen and Pierre-Antoine Klethi

INTRODUCTION

14.1 The purpose of the chapter is to analyse the main consequences of the UK leaving the EU from a Luxembourg tax perspective. As with other chapters, the hypothesis taken is that the UK and its residents will, after the end of the transition period, no longer benefit from any EU law instrument, nor will it be a member of the EEA. This chapter furthermore assumes that the UK will maintain to a large extent continuity with its current tax policy and will not make significant changes to the tax base of corporate taxpayers in the UK. 'Brexit' in this chapter is used to designate the date on which the transition period ends and the UK fully exits the EU.

TAX RAMIFICATIONS FOR INBOUND INVESTMENTS

Outbound dividends

14.2 In general, dividends paid by a Luxembourg company to non-resident shareholders are subject to a 15% withholding tax (WHT). Qualifying shareholders may, however, be eligible for the domestic WHT exemption or a WHT reduction under the double tax treaty concluded between Luxembourg and the UK (the tax treaty).

Domestic withholding tax exemption

14.3 A domestic exemption from WHT is available for dividends paid by Luxembourg resident companies under the following conditions:

- the recipient of the payment is, in particular:
  - — a Luxembourg regularly taxable resident company; or
  - — an entity which is covered by Article 2 of the Parent-Subsidiary Directive (PSD); or

- an entity that is resident in a tax treaty country and is a capital company that is subject to a comparable foreign tax (ie, a tax at an effective rate of at least 8.5% when the tax is computed on a base comparable to the Luxembourg corporate income tax base) (the 'Comparable Tax Test'); and

- at the time of the distribution, the recipient must have held (or commit to hold) for an uninterrupted period of at least 12 months:
  - a participation of at least 10% of the nominal paid-up capital of the Luxembourg subsidiary; or
  - a participation in the Luxembourg subsidiary with an acquisition cost of at least EUR 1.2 million.

Following Brexit, UK resident companies will not be covered by the PSD. Nonetheless, in most cases the domestic WHT exemption should still be available in relation to the UK, since it is a treaty country, subject to meeting all the other requirements, and in particular the Comparable Tax Test.

Treaty withholding tax reduction

14.4 A reduction of the WHT rate may be available under the provisions of the tax treaty:[1] a 5% WHT rate applies if the beneficial owner of the dividends is a company resident in the UK which controls, directly or indirectly, at least 25% of the voting rights in the company paying the dividends. The application of the tax treaty is, of course, subject to not being caught by the principal purpose test introduced by the OECD Multilateral Instrument ratified both by the UK and Luxembourg.

Outbound interest

14.5 As a general rule, Luxembourg does not levy WHT on interest.

In the following situations a WHT would apply:

(i) A 20% WHT (in discharge of personal income tax) on interest paid by a Luxembourg paying agent to a Luxembourg resident beneficial owner of such interest.

(ii) (In principle) a 15% WHT on interest paid to a related party which exceeds an arm's length amount. The excess amount of interest is treated as a hidden profit distribution and assimilated to a dividend for WHT purposes.

1 Article 10 of the tax treaty.

(iii) (In principle) a 15% WHT on profit-participating bonds and assimilated securities, when the bond-holder, on top of the fixed interest, is entitled to a variable interest depending on the amount of profits distributed to the shareholders.

These exceptions (other than the first one, specific to internal situations in Luxembourg) do not depend on the geographic location of the recipient. Therefore, Brexit should have no impact.

Outbound royalties

14.6 There is no WHT on outbound royalties in Luxembourg (provided they are at arm's length). Therefore, Brexit should have no impact.

Capital gains on shareholdings in Luxembourg resident companies

14.7 Brexit should not have an impact on the rules applicable to the taxation of non-residents on capital gains on shareholdings in Luxembourg resident companies.

Under domestic law, capital gains derived by a UK shareholder on the shares of a Luxembourg resident company are in principle tax exempt unless:[2]

(i) the shareholding qualifies as substantial participation, that is, the UK shareholder holds or has held (for an individual, together with his spouse and underage children), directly or indirectly, more than 10% of the corporate capital of the Luxembourg company at any time in the five years prior to the date the shares are disposed of; and

(ii) (a) the disposal takes place less than six months after the date of the acquisition; or

(b) the shareholder became a non-resident within the five years preceding the disposal of the participation and prior to that had been a resident of Luxembourg for more than 15 years.

Even if the capital gain does not benefit from an exemption under domestic law, the tax treaty provides that the right to tax capital gains derived by a UK shareholder on the shares of a Luxembourg resident company is generally allocated to the UK, unless the Luxembourg company is held by a Luxembourg permanent establishment or permanent representative of the UK company (or constitutes a permanent establishment of the UK company), in which case

2 Article 156(8) of the Luxembourg income tax law (*loi modifiée du 4 décembre 1967 concernant l'impôt le revenu*; 'LIR').

the Luxembourg domestic rules apply.[3] The same applies if a UK individual shareholder holds the shares in the context of a professional or business undertaking and in that context has a permanent establishment or permanent representative to whom the shares are allocable.

Permanent establishments

14.8 Brexit should not impact the Luxembourg rules applicable to Luxembourg permanent establishments of UK companies.

According to the tax treaty, profits realised by a Luxembourg permanent establishment of a UK company would be taxable in Luxembourg on the amount of profits allocable at arm's length to that permanent establishment.

TAX RAMIFICATIONS FOR OUTBOUND INVESTMENTS

Inbound dividends

14.9 Dividends paid by a UK resident company to Luxembourg resident companies are in principle regarded as part of the taxable profit of the Luxembourg company and subject to corporate income tax (CIT) and municipal business tax (MBT) at a standard combined rate of 24.94% (tax rate applicable in 2020 for companies resident in Luxembourg-City, including surcharges).

Dividends received from qualifying subsidiaries, however, may be exempt under the participation exemption regime. Dividends received from non-qualifying subsidiaries may still be eligible for a partial exemption.

The question arises whether Brexit affects the application of these domestic provisions.

Domestic participation exemption regime

14.10 In order to qualify for the domestic participation exemption regime, the following conditions must be met:

- The Luxembourg parent company must, at the time of the distribution, have held (or commit to hold) for an uninterrupted period of at least 12 months:[4]

3 Article 13 of the tax treaty.

4 During the 12-month period, the percentage of the participation should not fall below the threshold of 10% or of the EUR 1.2 million threshold.

- a participation of at least 10% of the nominal paid-up capital of the subsidiary; or
- a participation in the subsidiary having an acquisition cost of at least EUR 1.2 million.

- The subsidiary must be:
  - an entity covered by Article 2 of the PSD; or
  - a capital company that is fully subject to Luxembourg CIT; or
  - a capital company that meets the Comparable Tax Test.

Following Brexit, UK resident companies will no longer be covered by Article 2 PSD. However, the participation exemption regime may still be applicable if the subsidiary is a capital company subject in the UK to a tax comparable to the Luxembourg CIT.

This criterion has therefore become particularly relevant. While the statutory tax rate in the UK does not appear to raise issues – the current CIT rate in the UK for the fiscal year starting from 1 April 2020 is 19%,[5] which is more than half of the current CIT rate in Luxembourg – the comparability of the tax base must be analysed more carefully in the future. At present, it is generally expected that a UK company subject to the ordinary UK tax regime would meet the Comparable Tax Test, but a case by case analysis would be needed

Finally, as a result of Brexit, the anti-abuse rule specific to the PSD will no longer apply in relation to dividends derived by a Luxembourg company from a qualifying UK subsidiary. However, the domestic general anti-abuse rule remains applicable.

Partial exemption for non-qualifying participations

14.11 In case not all participation exemption requirements are met, a more general exemption amounting to 50% of the dividends received is available for dividends received from:[6]

- A fully taxable Luxembourg resident company.
- A company covered by Article 2 PSD.
- A capital company that is located in a treaty country and that satisfies the Comparable Tax Test.

5 Available at: https://www.gov.uk/government/publications/rates-and-allowances-corporation-tax/rates-and-allowances-corporation-tax.

6 Article 115 (15a) LIR.

Based on the existence of the tax treaty and to the extent the Comparable Tax Test is met, the provision may still apply to dividends received by taxpayers in Luxembourg from UK companies.

Capital gains on shareholdings in UK companies

14.12 Capital gains from the sale of shares in UK resident companies derived by Luxembourg resident companies are in principle subject to corporate income tax and MBT at a standard combined rate of 24.94% (tax rate applicable in 2020 for companies resident in Luxembourg City, including surcharges).

The participation exemption is, however, also available for capital gains realised by Luxembourg companies under the same conditions as the dividend exemption. The sole difference is that if the 10% participation in the share capital of the UK subsidiary is not met, the minimum acquisition cost of the shareholding must amount to EUR 6 million rather than EUR 1.2 million.

To the extent the participation exemption requirements are met by the UK subsidiary, in particular the Comparable Tax Test, Brexit should not affect the tax treatment of these capital gains.

Permanent establishments abroad

14.13 Brexit should not impact the rules applicable to UK permanent establishments of Luxembourg companies.

According to the tax treaty, profits realised by a UK permanent establishment of a Luxembourg company would only be taxable in the UK subject to a profit breakdown between the Luxembourg company and the permanent establishment. Luxembourg rules governing the recognition of a foreign permanent establishment and the allocation of profits to it are of general application and do not differentiate between the country where the permanent establishment is located.

There may be one difference with respect to the anti-hybrid rules on disregarded foreign permanent establishments, which require Luxembourg to tax the (otherwise exempt) profits of a foreign permanent establishment located in a treaty jurisdiction: the anti-tax avoidance directive[7] ('ATAD') foresees that these rules prevail over tax treaties with other EU countries but not over tax treaties with third countries.

7 Council Directive (EU) 2016/1164 of 12 July 2016 laying down rules against tax avoidance practices that directly affect the functioning of the internal market, as amended by Council Directive (EU) 2917/952 of 29 May 2017 amending Directive (EU) 2016/1164 as regards hybrid mismatches with third countries.

CFC rules

14.14 Luxembourg introduced CFC rules with effect from 1 January 2019. These rules do not contain a safeguard clause for EU/EEA Member States, so that there is no difference in the applicable rules for EU/EEA Member States or third countries.

Brexit should therefore not impact the application of CFC rules to UK companies.

IMPACT ON CROSS-BORDER GROUP TAX REGIMES

14.15 Luxembourg allows so-called 'horizontal' fiscal unities, that is, the set-off of the standalone taxable results of several Luxembourg companies of the same group owned directly or indirectly by a common parent, without that common parent forming part of the fiscal unity. This possibility was introduced following the Court of Justice of the European Union's judgment in case *X AG*.[8]

One of the conditions for a horizontal fiscal unity is that the non-integrating common parent (hereafter, 'Non-integrating Parent'; in original French, *société mère non-intégrante*) is either a Luxembourg resident fully taxable company, or a company resident in the EEA that meets the Comparable Tax Test,[9] or a Luxembourg permanent establishment of a non-Luxembourg company that meets the comparable tax test, or an EEA permanent establishment (that meets the Comparable Tax Test) of a non-Luxembourg company that meets the Comparable Tax Test.

Prima facie, Brexit would thus make fiscal unities with a UK Non-integrating Parent no longer possible. In addition, existing fiscal unities with a UK Non-integrating Parent would no longer meet one of the criteria laid down in the law and would thus be terminated as of 1 January 2021, when the Brexit transition period has ended. This could have a significant adverse effect for fiscal unities that have been in place for less than five years at that date: if a fiscal unity is broken up prior to the end of the mandatory minimum duration of five years, members of the fiscal unity are taxed on a retroactive basis as if the fiscal unity had never existed.

Notwithstanding the fact that a UK company could no longer qualify as Non-integrating Parent based on the text of the law, Luxembourg direct and indirect subsidiaries of a UK company that meet all other criteria to form a horizontal

8 *X AG* (Case C-40/13) (joined with Cases C-39/13 and C-41/13).

9 There is no definition of comparable tax in the law. Based on certain parliamentary documents, the comparable tax test requires the foreign company to be mandatorily subject to tax on its profits at an effective rate of at least half the Luxembourg corporate income tax rate (50% × 17% = 8.5%, based on the 2020 rate) computed on a tax base similar to the Luxembourg corporate income tax base.

fiscal unity should nevertheless consider claiming the benefit of the fiscal unity regime on the basis of the non-discrimination clause of the tax treaty.[10]

The relevant clause (Article XXVI(4) of the tax treaty, which is worded very similarly to Article 24(5) of the OECD Model Tax Convention) reads as follows:

> 'Enterprises of a Contracting State, the capital of which is wholly or partly owned or controlled, directly or indirectly, by one or more residents of the other Contracting State, shall not be subjected in the first-mentioned Contracting State to any taxation or any requirement connected therewith which is other or more burdensome than the taxation and connected requirements to which other similar enterprises of that first-mentioned State are or may be subjected.'

This provision prohibits Luxembourg from discriminating against Luxembourg companies controlled by a common UK parent company (compared to Luxembourg companies controlled by a common Luxembourg parent company) on the basis that their capital is owned or controlled by one or more residents of the UK.

Luxembourg companies that wish to be fiscally integrated should qualify as 'resident' of a contracting state for the purposes of the tax treaty, as they need to be fully taxable resident companies in order to be an integrating, respectively integrated subsidiary in the first place. Moreover, the tax treaty prevails over the domestic rules on fiscal unity, since treaties rank higher than domestic law in the hierarchy of norms in Luxembourg. In addition, the tax treaty covers corporate income tax and MBT, which are the corporate taxes for which it is possible to be taxed in a fiscal unity. Furthermore, a UK parent company should normally meet the comparable tax test.

While a cross-border fiscal unity is not possible,[11] the discrimination would arise between Luxembourg companies owned by a UK company (which could not form a horizontal fiscal unity) and Luxembourg companies owned by a Luxembourg company (which could form a horizontal fiscal unity). To the extent all the other conditions to form a fiscal unity are met *pari passu* in both situations, the jurisdiction of residence of the parent company would be the sole difference.

The impossibility of forming a horizontal fiscal unity between Luxembourg companies owned by a UK parent company would amount to subjecting them in Luxembourg to a 'taxation or […] requirement connected therewith which is other or more burdensome than the taxation and connected requirements

10 The argument is developed in more detail in KLETHI P-A., MARTEL D., *Le principe de non-discrimination comme source d'extension du régime d'intégration fiscal*, Revue Générale de Fiscalité Luxembourgeoise, No 1/2019, pp 9–16.

11 See paragraph 77 of the commentary to Article 24 of the OECD Model Tax Convention (2017).

to which other similar enterprises of [Luxembourg] are or may be subjected.' This would amount to a violation of Article XXVI(4) of the tax treaty.

Because of the superiority of tax treaties over domestic law, the requirement that the Non-integrating Parent company be an EEA company should be disapplied by the Luxembourg tax authorities, and horizontal fiscal unities with a UK Non-integrating Parent should be permitted, to the extent all other criteria for forming a horizontal fiscal unity are met.

TAX RAMIFICATIONS FOR CROSS-BORDER MERGERS, OTHER REORGANISATIONS AND TRANSFERS OF RESIDENCE

Cross-border mergers and other reorganisations

14.16 The UK no longer being an EU Member State, a tax neutral merger of a Luxembourg company into a UK company (so far subject to certain conditions) will no longer be possible. Hence, such merger would amount from a tax perspective to a liquidation of the Luxembourg company. The company would be taxed on the difference between the fair market value of its net assets at the time of the merger and the book value of its net assets at that same point in time. The applicable tax would be the ordinary CIT and MBT.

The same will apply to demergers whereby a Luxembourg company transfers part of its net assets to a UK company.

Similarly, upon a merger of a UK company into a Luxembourg company or the division of a UK company involving the transfer of part of the net assets to a Luxembourg entity, it will no longer be possible to value the assets at a value other than the fair market value. For inbound mergers/divisions involving companies resident in an EEA country, it is possible subject to certain conditions to value the assets at the book value reported by the foreign company, in which case the acquisition date by the Luxembourg company is deemed to be the original acquisition date of the assets by the absorbed company.

The transfer of a Luxembourg permanent establishment of a UK company to an EU-resident company or of an EU-resident company to a UK company could also no longer be tax neutral (by occurring at book value).

Transfer of residence abroad

14.17 Under Luxembourg domestic law, the transfer of residence of a Luxembourg company abroad triggers the same effects as a liquidation,[12] that

12 Article 172 referring to Article 169 LIR.

is, the immediate taxation of its latent capital gains, as at the moment of the migration. The taxable gain corresponds to the difference between the fair market value of the net assets of the company and the book value of these net assets prior to the migration. An exception is made for cases where assets and liabilities can be allocated to a permanent establishment in Luxembourg of the migrating company, in which case the book value of the assets and liabilities can be maintained for Luxembourg tax purposes. Gains on participations qualifying for the participation exemption regime (see **14.12** above) benefit from the exemption provided by that regime.

If the country towards which the transfer is made does not take into account capital losses realised after the transfer, a corrective taxation can take place in Luxembourg for the tax year of the transfer, but only if the transfer is made towards an EU/EEA country.[13] Therefore, following Brexit, no corrective taxation would be possible for migrations towards the UK, should the UK fail to take into account capital losses after the transfer.

For the exit tax, Luxembourg law used to provide for a payment deferral without limitation in time where the transfer occurred to an EU/EEA country or to a country with which Luxembourg had concluded a tax treaty containing a clause on exchange of information that is in line with Article 26(1) of the OECD model tax convention, subject to certain conditions (in particular the annual documentation of the continued ownership of the transferred assets). Further to the implementation of ATAD, as from 1 January 2020 this deferral regime has been replaced so that it is now possible to pay the exit tax in instalments over five years. The right to pay exit tax in instalments is limited to cases where the migration is to EU countries and EEA countries with which Luxembourg has concluded a tax treaty. Payment deferrals granted with respect to migrations having taken place prior to 1 January 2020 benefit from a grandfathering and are not affected by the change in law.

Since the UK would no longer be a member of the EU or EEA after Brexit, deferrals or payments in instalments would no longer be possible. Ongoing payments in instalments would be terminated and exit tax would become immediately due. The grandfathered exit tax payment deferrals should not be affected: although the UK would no longer be a member of the EEA, the tax treaty contains a clause on exchange of information in line with Article 26(1) of the OECD model tax convention.

Inbound transfer of residence

14.18 Companies transferring their tax residence to Luxembourg do not benefit from particular tax incentives. The transfer is treated in the same manner as a regular incorporation of a Luxembourg company. Assets and

13 Article 38(2) LIR.

liabilities are recorded at their going concern value, that is, the fair market value at the time of the migration to Luxembourg. This rule is of general application, and Brexit would not impact this.

OTHER

Roll-over provision in case of exchange of assets

14.19 As a general rule, in Luxembourg, an exchange of an asset against another asset is seen as a disposal of the first one and a subsequent acquisition of the second one. Article 22*bis* LIR provides, however, for the possibility to perform tax neutral exchanges (ie, exchanges without realising gains embedded in the asset given) in the following situations, and provided the related cash consideration does not represent more than 10% of the nominal or par value of shares issued:

- Transformation of a collective undertaking (*organisme à caractère collectif*) into another collective undertaking: the shareholder can on a tax-neutral basis get securities representing the share capital of the post-transformation collective undertaking in exchange for the securities in the pre-transformation collective undertaking.
- Merger or division between Luxembourg and/or EU capital companies: the shareholder of the absorbed or divided company can on a tax-neutral basis receive shares in the absorbing or recipient company in exchange for the shares it held in the absorbed or divided company.
- Acquisition by an EU company or a capital company fully subject to a tax comparable to the Luxembourg CIT in the share capital of another such company of a participation resulting in the former obtaining or increasing its majority of voting rights in the acquired company: the shareholder of the acquired company can on a tax-neutral basis receive shares in the acquiring company in exchange for the shares in the acquired company.

The first and the third of these situations do not require the relevant foreign company to be an EU or EEA company. As such, they should not be affected by Brexit. The second situation addresses situations covered by the EU Merger Directive, which will no longer apply to the UK after Brexit. Hence, a roll-over would no longer be possible after Brexit where a Luxembourg company merges with a UK company or there is a cross-border division involving both Luxembourg and UK companies.

Investment tax credits

14.20 Luxembourg tax law provides for two types of investment tax credits, mainly for tangible amortisable assets. These credits amongst other conditions require that the investment is 'physically used on the territory of Luxembourg or of another State member of the European Economic Area (EEA).' The extension to EEA countries was implemented after the European Court of Justice's judgment in *Tankreederei I S.A.* (Case C-287/10) [2010].

As the UK would no longer be party to the EEA after Brexit, investments physically used in the UK (by a Luxembourg undertaking) would no longer qualify.

The probability of successfully invoking the tax treaty's non-discrimination clause in relation to these credits *prima facie* appears rather low, because the provision does not discriminate based on the nationality or residence of the Luxembourg undertaking or its owners, but solely on the basis of where the investment is put to use.

CONCLUSION

14.21 Brexit will generally have a limited impact from a Luxembourg tax perspective, as far as the interaction between Luxembourg and the UK are concerned. This is notably due to the fact that Luxembourg has (as a general rule) no WHT on interest and royalties, as well as a domestic participation exemption regime (and related dividend WHT exemption regime) that is broader in scope than the corresponding EU rules. Where the domestic rules do not suffice, the tax treaty may help maintain existing regimes, such as a horizontal fiscal unity between Luxembourg companies owned by a non-integrating UK parent company.

Chapter 15

The Netherlands

Marc Klerks, Stephan Kraan, Amit Havenaar and Erik Kastrop

INTRODUCTION

15.1 In this chapter, we set out the main consequences of the United Kingdom (UK) leaving the European Union (EU) from a Dutch corporate income tax and dividend withholding tax (DWT) perspective, based on Dutch law and tax treaty provisions as applicable on 1 January 2021 (unless specified otherwise).

The analysis of this chapter is based on the assumption that the UK is a third country and not part of the European Economic Area (EEA). The Brexit consequences as described below only apply after the end of the transition period that was agreed upon in the Agreement on the withdrawal of the UK from the EU (dated 17 October 2019), taking into account the EU-UK Trade and Cooperation Agreement (the TCA) concluded between the EU and the UK (which has become provisionally applicable after having been agreed between the EU and UK negotiators on 24 December 2020).

TAX RAMIFICATIONS FOR INBOUND INVESTMENTS

Outbound dividends

Domestic DWT exemption

15.2 Distributions of profits (in whatever name or form) made by Dutch resident companies are in principle subject to 15% DWT. Subject to defined conditions, though, a Dutch domestic withholding tax exemption (DWT exemption) may apply.

The DWT exemption may apply to distributions by Dutch resident companies if the dividend payment is made to shareholders that:

- are resident in a state with which the Netherlands has concluded a tax treaty with a dividend article or are resident in an EU/EEA Member State;

- at the moment of the profit distribution, hold an interest in the distributing entity that would entitle the shareholder to application of the participation exemption (at least 5%) if the shareholder would have been a Dutch resident;
- are not, according to a tax treaty concluded by their state of residence with another state, considered residents of a state outside of the EU/EEA, or of a state with which the Netherlands has not concluded a tax treaty containing a dividend article; and
- are considered the beneficial owner of the dividends received.

The application of the DWT exemption is denied where abuse is found. If the shareholder receiving the dividend meets the so-called relevant substance requirements in its jurisdiction (reference is made to Annex A), then it is in principle deemed that no abuse is present, unless the Dutch Tax Administration provides counterevidence to demonstrate that the structure is abusive.

If the relevant substance requirements are not met, still no abuse is deemed to be present if either one (or both) of the below tests are met:

- the shares or membership rights in the Dutch resident company are not held with the main purpose, or one of the main purposes, to avoid DWT due by another individual or entity (Avoidance Test);
- the holding of the shares or membership rights in the Dutch resident company is not part of an artificial arrangement or transaction (or a series of artificial arrangements or composite of transactions), which will be the case if there are valid business reasons reflecting economic reality (Artificial Arrangement Test).

For the Avoidance Test it must be determined whether DWT would be due, without the interposition of the non-resident shareholder(s). For this purpose, one needs to disregard all intermediate companies between the ultimate shareholders and the Dutch resident company. However, this look-through approach is applied differently where an (in)direct shareholder (not necessarily the ultimate shareholder) is engaged in an active trade or business, in which case, the Avoidance Test is applied at that entity level.

For the purposes of the Artificial Arrangement Test, an arrangement should (eg) not be regarded as artificial where one of the following requirements is met:

- the foreign corporate shareholder has real business activities and the shares in the Dutch resident company are allocable to these business activities; or
- the foreign corporate shareholder functions as a top holding company with substantial functions (eg, managerial, policy making and financial functions) for the business activities of the group.

Impact of Brexit

15.3 The DWT exemption may also apply to shareholders that are resident in non-EU Member States with which the Netherlands has concluded a tax treaty with a dividend article. Since the tax treaty between the Netherlands and the UK includes a dividend article, Brexit as such should not impact the application of the DWT exemption for dividends distributed by Dutch companies to UK shareholders.

Refund of DWT

15.4 For shareholders of Dutch resident companies that are resident in EU/EEA Member States and exempt from corporate income tax in their own jurisdiction, and would be exempt from Dutch corporate income tax if they had been a Dutch resident, the Netherlands provides for a possibility to claim a refund of DWT.[1] Exempt shareholders that are a resident in non-EU/EEA Member States can only apply for such a refund if: (i) their shareholding in the Dutch resident company qualifies as a portfolio investment, which is an investment that falls under the free movement of capital as meant in the Treaty on the Functioning of the European Union, and (ii) the respective state of which the shareholder is resident has concluded a tax information exchange agreement with the Netherlands. A refund of DWT is not available to entities which are comparable to regulated investment institutions subject to the investment institution regime in the *Dutch Corporate Income Tax Act*.

Impact of Brexit

15.5 As a result of Brexit, in general, UK shareholders can no longer request a refund of DWT on non-portfolio investments, but can only apply for a refund in respect of their portfolio investments. However, qualifying pension funds holding non-portfolio investments may rely on the tax treaty between the Netherlands and the UK which provides for an exemption of DWT for pension funds (subject to the principal purpose test and other limitations). The impact for qualifying pension funds may therefore be limited.

Outbound interest and royalties

15.6 The Netherlands has introduced a withholding tax on intragroup interest and royalty payments to countries with a statutory profit tax rate of less than 9% or to jurisdictions that are included in the European list of non-

1 This refund procedure is also available for Dutch shareholders that are exempt from corporate income tax.

cooperative jurisdictions, which has come into force on 1 January 2021. The withholding tax on interest and royalty payments will apply to payments (and under circumstances on an accrual basis) by Dutch resident entities (entities incorporated under Dutch law are always deemed to be a Dutch resident for corporate income tax purposes), but also to payments by permanent establishments in the Netherlands of non-resident entities. The withholding tax rate will be equal to the main corporate income tax rate, which is 25% in 2021.

The withholding tax only targets interest and royalty payments to related entities whereby control, that is, 50% or greater voting control, is the relevant criterion.

The withholding tax will also apply in certain abusive situations and certain situations involving hybrid entities or permanent establishments. The artificial interposition of a non-low taxed intermediate conduit company between the low taxed jurisdiction and the Dutch paying entity may be considered as an abusive situation (for instance if that conduit company is not the beneficial owner of the interest and royalty payments). In principle no withholding tax applies if such an intermediate conduit company meets the relevant substance requirements (see Annex A) or if such an intermediate conduit company can demonstrate valid economic reasons. However, meeting the substance requirements will not be a safe harbour as the Dutch Tax Administration may provide counterevidence to demonstrate that a structure is abusive, even if these substance requirements are satisfied.

Transitional rules are proposed where a tax treaty with a low-tax jurisdiction or EU blacklisted country restricts the withholding tax from being levied. The Netherlands has announced plans to approach such treaty partner to amend the tax treaty.

Impact of Brexit

15.7 The withholding tax applies to intragroup interest and royalty payments to jurisdictions with a statutory profit tax rate of less than 9% or EU blacklisted jurisdictions. Since this currently excludes the UK (save from certain abusive situations), Brexit as such should have no impact on these rules.

Capital gains on shareholdings in resident companies

15.8 A non-Dutch resident company with a 5% or greater shareholding in a Dutch resident company may under certain circumstances be subject to Dutch non-resident corporate income tax (NRCT) with respect to the income (eg, dividends, capital gains and interest) derived from this shareholding.

However, such income is only subject to NRCT where the following cumulative conditions are met:

- the main purpose or one of the main purposes of the non-resident corporate entity for holding the substantial interest in the Dutch resident company is to avoid Dutch personal income tax (PIT) of another person, that is, an ultimate individual shareholder (NRCT Avoidance Test); and
- there is an artificial arrangement or a series of artificial arrangements (which can consist of different steps or parts). An arrangement or a series of arrangements will be regarded as artificial where it was not put into place for valid business reasons reflecting economic reality (similar to the Artificial Arrangement Test of the DWT exemption as referred to in **15.2** above).

The NRCT Avoidance Test differs from the Avoidance Test for Dutch DWT purposes. For the purposes of the Avoidance Test for Dutch NRCT purposes, it should be determined whether Dutch PIT would be due, without the interposition of the non-resident corporate shareholder. Generally, such avoidance motive is only present when there are one or more ultimate individual shareholders who indirectly own an interest of 5% or more. In this scenario, when the individual would have held the shares in the Dutch resident company directly, he or she would have been subject to Dutch PIT on the income derived therefrom.

Impact of Brexit

15.9 The NRCT rules as described above apply regardless of the geographical location of a non-Dutch resident company with a 5% or greater shareholding in a Dutch resident company. Therefore, Brexit should not change the NRCT position of UK resident corporate shareholders of Dutch resident companies.

Permanent establishments

15.10 Non-Dutch resident entities are subject to corporate income tax in the Netherlands if they derive income from a business enterprise carried on through a permanent establishment or a permanent representative in the Netherlands. The same applies to income derived from real estate situated in the Netherlands.

Impact of Brexit

15.11 These rules apply regardless of the geographical location of a non-Dutch resident company. Therefore, Brexit should not change the position of UK resident companies that derive income from a business enterprise carried on through a permanent establishment or a permanent representative and/or real estate in the Netherlands.

TAX RAMIFICATIONS FOR OUTBOUND INVESTMENTS

Inbound dividends

15.12 Dutch resident companies that receive dividends from resident and non-resident companies may benefit from the Dutch participation exemption, which provides for a full exemption for dividend and capital gains income derived from shareholdings in qualifying participations. The Dutch participation exemption applies, in summary, if the following three conditions are met:

- the Dutch resident company itself or a related party holds a participation of at least 5% of, as a general rule, the nominal paid-up share capital of a company with a capital divided into shares (Minimum Threshold Test); and
- one of the following three tests is met:
  - the holding company's objective with respect to its participation is to obtain a return that is higher than a return that may be expected from portfolio investment management (Motive Test); or
  - the direct and indirect assets of the subsidiary generally consist of less than 50% of 'low-taxed free passive assets' (Asset Test); or
  - the subsidiary is subject to an adequate levy according to Dutch tax standards (Subject-To-Tax Test); and
- the payment received from the subsidiary is not deductible for corporate income tax purposes in the country of the subsidiary.

Minimum Threshold Test

15.13 Where the Dutch resident company does not hold at least 5% of the nominal paid-up share capital of the subsidiary, the Minimum Threshold Test may still be met if: (i) the Dutch resident company holds at least 5% of the voting rights over the subsidiary; (ii) the subsidiary is established in an EU Member State; (iii) the Netherlands has concluded a bilateral tax treaty with that Member State; and (iv) that tax treaty provides for a reduction of withholding taxes on dividends based on the voting rights that can be effectuated by the Dutch resident company.

Motive Test

15.14 The Motive Test is a facts and circumstances test that will be met if the shareholding is not considered a passive investment, that is, if the size and nature of the investment (and the return expected on the investment) exceeds that of a regular portfolio investment.

Asset Test

15.15 An asset is a 'low-taxed free passive asset' if: (i) it is a passive asset that is not reasonably required in the enterprise carried out by its owner; and (ii) the income from such asset is effectively taxed at a rate of less than 10%. Real estate is considered to be a 'good' asset for the purposes of the Asset Test by operation of law.

Subject-To-Tax Test

15.16 As a general rule, a participation is considered to be subject to an adequate levy if it is subject to a tax on profits levied at an effective rate of at least 10%, according to Dutch tax accounting principles. However, certain tax base differences, such as the absence of any limitations on interest deduction, a too broad participation exemption, deferral of taxation until distribution of profits, or deductible dividends, may cause a profit tax to disqualify as an adequate levy.

Impact of Brexit

15.17 Brexit should not substantially impact application of the Dutch participation exemption to income derived from shareholdings in UK subsidiaries, as the rules should not deviate between subsidiaries established within or outside the EU. Only for the Minimum Threshold Test, in cases where the Dutch resident company does not hold a participation of at least 5% of the nominal paid-up share capital, then it can no longer rely on meeting this test through holding at least 5% of voting rights.

Capital gains on shareholdings in non-resident companies

15.18 The Dutch participation exemption does not differentiate between dividend income and capital gains income derived from (qualifying) participations. Therefore, reference is made to **15.12** above albeit that the condition under sub paragraph (c) should not be relevant for capital gains.

Foreign permanent establishments of Dutch resident companies

15.19 Dutch resident companies are granted an exemption (the so-called 'object exemption') for (in short) positive and negative amounts of profit attributable to another state. The 'profit attributable to another state' is defined as the following net benefits:

- profits attributable to a foreign enterprise carried on through a permanent establishment or permanent representative situated in the other state;
- proceeds, less allocable expenses, from immovable property situated in the other state; and
- other benefits which are subject to tax in the other state pursuant to rules for the avoidance of double taxation.

However, if a foreign enterprise is a low-taxed foreign passive investment, the object exemption is substituted for a credit system unless an applicable tax treaty provides otherwise. A foreign enterprise is a low-taxed foreign passive investment if:

- the activities of the foreign enterprise, together with the entities in which at least a 5% (direct or indirect) interest can be attributed to the foreign enterprise, for the greater part consist of 'passive activities'; and
- the profit from the foreign enterprise is not subject to a profit tax that results in a 'realistic levy' according to Dutch tax standards (see the Subject-To-Tax Test as outlined in **15.12** above).

'Passive activities' are defined as portfolio investing, intragroup financing and putting assets at the disposal of group companies. Activities related to holding immovable property and rights relating thereto do not qualify as 'passive activities' if the immovable property (rights) are not owned by an (exempt) investment institution.

Impact of Brexit

15.20 Brexit should not impact the application of the Dutch object exemption, as the rules should not distinguish between intra-EU and extra-EU situations.

CFC rules

15.21 As of 1 January 2019, the Netherlands has introduced 'controlled foreign corporation' (CFC) rules on the basis of the EU Anti-Tax Avoidance Directive. Under the CFC rules, certain undistributed items of passive income of a direct or indirect subsidiary or a permanent establishment are included in the tax base of the Dutch taxpayer if the subsidiary or permanent establishment is established in a jurisdiction that is included on: (i) a yearly published Dutch blacklist (of jurisdictions that have no corporate income tax regime or a corporate income tax regime with a statutory rate of less than 9%); or (ii) the European list of non-cooperative jurisdictions.

The CFC rules only apply to direct permanent establishments of a Dutch resident company, and direct or indirect subsidiaries if the Dutch shareholder, alone or together with an associated enterprise or person, holds an equity interest of more than 50% in the subsidiary. Certain exceptions apply, including if the subsidiary or permanent establishment has 'real economic activities', which is deemed to be the case in relation to subsidiaries if that subsidiary meets the relevant substance requirements as included in Annex A.

Impact of Brexit

15.22 The Dutch CFC rules do not differentiate between subsidiaries and permanent establishments within or outside the EU. Assuming that the UK is not added to the Dutch blacklist or the European list of non-cooperative jurisdictions (which is not expected), Brexit should not impact application of the Dutch CFC rules.

IMPACT ON CROSS-BORDER GROUP TAX REGIMES

Fiscal unity

15.23 Profits and losses of a Dutch resident parent company can for Dutch corporate income tax purposes be consolidated with the profits and losses of one or more of its Dutch resident subsidiaries if these companies form a so-called 'fiscal unity'. Under circumstances, a fiscal unity can – broadly speaking – also be formed between Dutch taxpayers if they are both held by a foreign parent company based in the EU or EEA (a so-called 'sister fiscal unity') or between a Dutch parent company and Dutch second-tier subsidiaries when the intermediate EU or EEA subsidiaries are not established in the Netherlands (a so-called 'Papillon fiscal unity').

Papillon fiscal unity

15.24 At its simplest, a Papillon fiscal unity is a consolidation of a Netherlands-based parent company and sub-subsidiary, where a qualifying intermediate holding company based in the EU or EEA, but outside the Netherlands, holds the shares in the sub-subsidiary.

To qualify as an intermediate holding company, such company must meet certain requirements in respect of its legal form and country of incorporation. It is also required that such non-Dutch intermediate holding company would be subject to Dutch corporate income tax if it were a resident in the Netherlands and it may not carry out a business enterprise through a permanent establishment in the Netherlands.

Most importantly in the context of Brexit, however, is that the intermediate holding company must be resident in an EU/EEA Member State (not the Netherlands) in accordance with the tax legislation of that EU/EEA Member State; and on the basis of a tax treaty concluded by that state it must not be resident of a state outside of the EU/EEA ('establishment requirement').

Not only the formation of a Papillon fiscal unity, but also its continued existence, depends both on the intermediate holding company status of one entity, and on the parent's qualifying shareholding in that company. If any of these conditions ceases to be met, the fiscal unity is automatically terminated.

Sister fiscal unity

15.25 At its simplest, a sister fiscal unity is a consolidation of two subsidiaries resident in the Netherlands whose shares are held by a parent company resident in the EU/EEA, but not in the Netherlands (referred to below as the 'top holding company').

To qualify as a top holding company, similar requirements apply as set out above in respect of intermediate holding companies. Top holding companies also have to meet the establishment requirement as defined above.

Note, again, that not only the formation of a sister fiscal unity, but also its continued existence, depends on whether an entity is a qualifying top holding company.

Impact of Brexit

15.26 It will no longer be possible to form a Papillon and/or sister fiscal unity through one or more UK tax resident top and / or intermediary holding companies.

Furthermore, existing Papillon and sister fiscal unities which depend on the presence of one or more UK tax resident top and/or intermediary holding companies will automatically be terminated after the transition period. The termination of a fiscal unity may have adverse Dutch corporate income tax consequences, by virtue of certain statutory anti-abuse measures.

Fiscal unity including UK company with a permanent establishment in the Netherlands

15.27 In certain circumstances, it is possible to form a fiscal unity including a foreign taxpayer that carries out a business enterprise through a permanent establishment in the Netherlands. In general, there are two distinct fiscal unity variants in this respect:

- A fiscal unity including a subsidiary that can be considered a foreign taxpayer for Dutch corporate income tax purposes: that is, a Dutch resident parent company and a non-resident subsidiary subject to corporate income tax in the Netherlands because of a Dutch permanent establishment have formed a fiscal unity.
- A fiscal unity including a parent company that can be considered a foreign taxpayer for Dutch corporate income tax purposes: that is, a non-resident parent company subject to corporate income tax in the Netherlands because of a permanent establishment in the Netherlands, and one or more Dutch resident subsidiaries have formed a fiscal unity.

Unlike the Papillon and sister fiscal unity, in principle any company resident in a country with which the Netherlands has concluded a treaty can form part of a fiscal unity, provided it has a Dutch permanent establishment. A prescribed condition for a fiscal unity with a non-resident parent company is that the shares in the Dutch subsidiary (or subsidiaries) are attributable to the non-resident parent company's permanent establishment in the Netherlands. However, the requirement that the shares in the subsidiary are attributable to the permanent establishment does not apply in EU/EEA situations.

Impact of Brexit

15.28 It will no longer be possible to form a fiscal unity between a UK resident parent company that carries on a business enterprise through a permanent establishment in the Netherlands and a Dutch resident subsidiary if the shares in the Dutch subsidiary are not attributable to the UK parent's permanent establishment in the Netherlands.

Along the same lines, currently existing fiscal unities where the shares in the Dutch subsidiary are not attributable to the UK parent's permanent establishment in the Netherlands will automatically be terminated. The termination of a fiscal unity may have adverse Dutch corporate income tax consequences, by virtue of certain statutory anti-abuse measures.

TAX RAMIFICATIONS FOR CROSS-BORDER MERGERS, OTHER REORGANISATIONS AND TRANSFERS OF RESIDENCE

Cross-border mergers and other reorganisations

15.29 Following Brexit, a cross-border legal merger between a Dutch and UK entity will no longer be possible on the basis of Dutch corporate law as it only allows cross-border mergers between companies resident in an EU Member State.

Under Dutch tax principles a company that ceases to exist as a result of a merger must recognise any accrued unrealised gains (and losses), that is, the company will have to mark to market all its assets and liabilities. However, in the case of a Dutch domestic merger or a cross-border merger within the EU/EEA, a roll over relief may apply, that is, the recognition of accrued unrealised gains may be deferred. For cross-border mergers within the EU/EEA roll-over relief only applies if and to the extent assets and liabilities remain within the scope of Dutch corporate income taxation, for example if the assets and liabilities are attributable to a Dutch permanent establishment resulting from the merger.

If and to the extent assets and liabilities are transferred to outside the scope of Dutch corporate income taxation as a consequence of an EU/EEA cross-border merger, deferral of payment of the resulting corporate income tax liability may be available, along the lines set out in **15.33** below.

Impact of Brexit

15.30 As a matter of Dutch corporate law, cross-border mergers will no longer be possible in relation to the UK. Roll over relief under Dutch corporate income tax principles will no longer be available and neither will there be a possibility of deferring tax payments in relation to a cross-border merger with the UK following Brexit.

Inbound transfer of residence

15.31 When a foreign entity transfers its residence to the Netherlands, with or without a conversion of its legal form into a Dutch legal form, it must mark to market all its assets and liabilities on its opening balance sheet for Dutch corporate income tax purposes. In other words, a step-up to fair market value is obtained for Dutch corporate income tax purposes upon becoming a Dutch resident taxpayer.

There is no step up for Dutch DWT, though, so any pre-existing profit reserves will be brought within the scope of Dutch DWT and any future distributions will be subject to Dutch DWT. It is noted that a legislative proposal is currently pending to introduce such a step-up, which would have the effect that pre-existing profit reserves are treated as paid in capital for Dutch DWT purposes.

Impact of Brexit

15.32 The above principles are applied in the Netherlands regardless of whether the entity migrates to the Netherlands from within the EU, or from outside of the EU. As such, these principles should not be impacted by Brexit.

Transfer of residence abroad

15.33 In general, exit taxation for corporate income tax purposes applies if a Dutch company ceases to be a Dutch resident for corporate income tax purposes. Immediately prior to it ceasing to be a tax resident, the entity must recognise any accrued unrealised gains and losses (ie, the entity is deemed to alienate these assets and liabilities against fair market value, whereby the difference between that fair market value and the tax book value constitutes income), unless such assets are attributable to a permanent establishment in the Netherlands and remain within the scope of Dutch corporate income taxation.

Under the exit tax rules, where a transfer of the tax residence is to an EU/EEA Member State, the taxpayer can pay the tax due upon migration in five annual and equal instalments, unless the hidden reserves that resulted in the tax due are in the meantime actually realised, for example through a disposal of the asset(s). The deferral carries interest and may be conditional on the taxpayer providing sufficient security, for instance by means of a bank guarantee. Aside from the disposal of the asset, the Dutch corporate income tax liability also becomes recoverable upon a (further) transfer of the tax residency to a third (that is, non-EU/EEA) country, or in the event the taxpayer ceases to provide sufficient security.

Impact of Brexit

15.34 As a result of Brexit, Dutch resident entities would no longer be able to apply for a deferral of the Dutch corporate income tax liability upon a transfer of the place of effective management or statutory seat to the UK. For Dutch resident entities that entered into a deferral arrangement before the end of the transition period, there is a risk that all outstanding deferral arrangements with taxpayers that have transferred their residence to the UK could be cancelled. If so, any amounts still outstanding would become immediately collectable. The Dutch government may decide unilaterally to grandfather deferrals that were already accepted prior to Brexit. The foregoing may depend on whether the UK continues to provide (mutual) assistance to the Netherlands in the recovery of tax claims (as is currently arranged under Council Directive 2010/24/EU).

OTHER

Other aspects for Dutch resident companies

Innovation box

15.35 The Dutch innovation box regime provides for the possibility that income and gains from qualifying intangible assets are effectively taxed at a reduced rate of 9% (instead of the regular corporate income tax rate of 15%–25%).

The innovation box regime can only be applied with respect to intangible assets that result from research and development (R&D) activities for which the Dutch resident company has obtained one or more R&D certificates (in essence a self-developed intangible asset). Depending on the relative size of the taxpayer[2] it is possible that, in addition to the R&D certificates, one or more so-called legal entry tickets are required to have an intangible asset qualify for the innovation box. One of these listed legal entry tickets is that the asset must be a self-developed intangible asset for which an EU marketing authorisation for medicinal products is granted.

Impact of Brexit

15.36 An asset for which only the UK has granted authorisation to market a medicinal product to the Dutch taxpayer (and which currently is a qualifying intangible asset) will no longer be considered a qualifying intangible asset. Therefore, income related to this asset would no longer qualify for the innovation box. Otherwise, the application of the innovation box in the Netherlands should not be impacted by Brexit.

Country-by-Country Reporting

15.37 A multinational enterprise (MNE) with a consolidated group revenue of at least EUR 750 million in the year preceding the reporting year of the MNE group has the obligation to provide certain information items per country in which the MNE group is active (eg, the amount of revenues, realised profit, taxes paid, number of employees).

In principle, Dutch resident companies belonging to such MNE group must file a Country-by-Country (CbC) report with the Dutch Tax Administration within

2 In this regard, a distinction is made between 'small and medium sized enterprises' and 'other taxpayers'. Small and medium sized enterprises are defined as taxpayers that: (i) derive benefits from qualifying intangible assets of less than EUR 37,500,000 in the financial year and the four preceding financial years combined; and (ii) have a net turnover of less than EUR 250,000,000 in the financial year and the four preceding financial years combined.

twelve months of the end of the reporting year of the ultimate parent entity of the MNE group (that is, a local filing obligation). A local filing obligation does not apply if a qualifying foreign ultimate parent entity or surrogate parent entity exists that files the CbC report and the foreign authorities actually exchange this CbC report (within the appropriate timescale) with the Dutch Tax Administration.

A Dutch resident company doesn't have the local filing obligation if an EU based company within the same MNE group is appointed to meet the Dutch resident company's local filing obligation (provided that the EU based company actually files the CbC report and the authorities of that EU Member State actually exchange this CbC report in time with the Dutch Tax Administration).

Impact of Brexit

15.38 It will no longer be possible to appoint a UK company to meet the local filing obligations for Dutch resident companies after the transition period.

Furthermore, it is currently unclear whether there will be an agreement between the UK and the Netherlands for the exchange of CbC reports and, if so, when. A local filing obligation in the Netherlands may therefore still exist, even if the UK ultimate parent entity files the MNE's CbC report in the UK. In the current absence of such agreement, it is also unclear whether a UK entity may qualify as surrogate parent entity for Dutch corporate income tax purposes. A local filing obligation in the Netherlands may therefore still exist where a UK company is appointed as surrogate parent entity.

Limitation on benefits provisions in tax treaties concluded by the Netherlands

15.39 A number of tax treaties concluded by the Netherlands include 'limitation on benefits' (LOB) provisions. In short, such LOB provisions prevent so-called 'treaty shopping' by denying treaty benefits unless one or more specific tests are met. Tests that are regularly included in LOB provisions are, amongst others, the so-called 'derivative benefits test' and the 'stock exchange test'.

The derivate benefits test provides that a treaty resident can benefit from the treaty if its non-resident owners are granted the same benefits if they had a direct relationship with the other treaty country resident. These non-resident owners are commonly referred to as 'equivalent beneficiaries'. In the tax treaties concluded with the US and Barbados, only companies resident in an EU/EEA Member State and/or a limited number of other countries can qualify as equivalent beneficiaries. The tax treaty with Japan also contains a derivative benefits test, but does not explicitly limit the definition of equivalent beneficiary to, for example, only EU Member States.

In brief, the stock exchange test provides that treaty benefits are granted to a treaty resident if its shares are traded on a specifically listed recognised stock exchange. If the treaty resident itself is not listed, but its shareholder is, treaty benefits may under certain treaties – subject to other requirements – still be available for the treaty resident that is not listed on a recognised stock exchange itself. Some of the LOB provisions in treaties concluded by the Netherlands provide that any of the stock exchanges in the Member States of the EU is considered a recognised stock exchange.[3]

The tax treaties with Barbados, Ethiopia, Hong Kong, Panama and the US currently include an LOB provision (or similar kind of provision for certain income items) with one or more references to EU Member States in this provision.[4] Furthermore, the Netherlands has special tax arrangements with Curacao and St. Maarten (both constituent countries within the Kingdom of the Netherlands) which also include LOB-like provisions with references to EU Member States.

The references to EU Member States have mostly been included as part of the stock exchange test and/or the derivative benefits test. However, in the case of the tax treaty with the US, certain references to EU Member States have also been included for (parts of) other tests within the LOB provision.

Impact of Brexit

15.40 Because of the references to EU Member States, it is for example possible for Dutch resident companies to pass LOB tests because a UK stock exchange is considered a recognised stock exchange, or because a UK (in) direct shareholder is considered an equivalent beneficiary for purposes of the LOB provision (particularly in the tax treaties concluded with Japan and the US).

It should be reviewed whether the treaty resident (only) relies on tests where references to EU Member States have been made (eg, the stock exchange test or the derivative benefits test). A treaty resident that only meets the LOB provision because of the fact that its (in)direct shareholder is listed on a UK stock exchange may no longer be able to obtain the benefits of the tax treaty between the Netherlands and the relevant treaty country. UK stock exchanges may be recognised if the competent authorities of the Netherlands and the relevant treaty partner agree on doing so.

Furthermore, specifically in the case of the tax treaty with the US, if a Dutch resident company currently only relies on the application of the derivate

3 In the tax treaties between the Netherlands and: (i) the US, and (ii) Japan, certain stock exchanges – including the stock exchange of London – have explicitly been listed as recognised stock exchanges.

4 It should be noted that eg the tax treaty between the Netherlands and Japan contains an LOB provision, but this treaty does not include specific references to the EU.

benefits test through one or more UK equivalent beneficiaries it may no longer be able to obtain the benefits of the tax treaty between the Netherlands and that treaty country.

Main consequences for individuals

Social security

15.41 Cross-border employees and regular business visitors within the EU currently often have a so-called 'A1-statement' (certificate of coverage) in place, supporting that they can remain covered by their 'home country' social security system and that they and their employer pay home country social security contributions in respect of their duties in their host country for up to five years.

As the European Social Security Regulation (883/2004) will no longer apply, the A1-statement in principle becomes invalid which might trigger a liability for social security contributions for employees working in the Netherlands and/or the UK in both the Netherlands and the UK (although the Agreement on the withdrawal of the UK from the EU did provide for some grandfathering rules in relation to A1-statements issued before the end of the transition period).

As part of the TCA, a protocol on social security coordination has been concluded. The principles agreed on in this protocol are generally in line with the European Social Security Regulation. This means that apart from some deviations, the TCA should to a large extent result into a continuance of the status quo.

Pensions – tax deductibility of pension contributions

15.42 Based on a unilateral decree issued by the Dutch State Secretary of Finance on the international aspects of pensions (Pensions Decree), as a general rule, pension contributions made into a Dutch/EU pension plan are tax deductible for Dutch PIT purposes. Non-EU pension plans may also qualify for Dutch PIT purposes by virtue of non-discrimination provisions in tax treaties between the Netherlands and non-EU countries, or under the Pensions Decree (but as the Pensions Decree imposes stringent requirements for non-EU pension plans, approval under the Pensions Decree is in practice not often obtained).

Impact of Brexit

15.43 Given that the UK will be considered a non-EU country, the Pensions Decree no longer provides for (full) deductibility of contributions into a UK pension plan, if no corresponding approval for such pension plan has been obtained. The tax treaty between the Netherlands and the UK does provide protection: contributions made by or on behalf of a UK individual who exercises (self-)employment in the Netherlands to a pension scheme that is recognised for tax purposes in the UK will have to be treated in the same way as contributions made to a pension scheme that is recognised for tax purposes in the Netherlands. Depending on the actual facts and circumstances applicable to an individual, for example on the scope of the allowable deduction in the Netherlands, the deductibility of pensions contributions may be limited compared to the pre-Brexit deductibility.

Migration of individuals from the Netherlands

15.44 Reference is made to **15.46** below for a high-level description of the tax ramifications of the migration of an individual from the Netherlands, which also includes aspects related to pensions built up by an individual resident in the Netherlands.

Qualifying non-resident taxpayer status

15.45 Within the framework of Dutch PIT, 'qualifying non-resident taxpayers' may take into account negative income of owner-occupied property, expenses for income schemes, and personal deductible items to the extent these allowable deductions cannot be effectuated in their country of residence. Furthermore, qualifying non-resident taxpayers qualify for certain tax credits for PIT purposes.

To be considered a qualifying non-resident taxpayer, certain requirements have to be met, including that such taxpayer has to be a resident of the EU, the EEA, Switzerland or the Dutch Caribbean Islands (Bonaire, St. Eustatius and Saba).

Because of Brexit, UK resident individuals will no longer be considered – nor be able to qualify as – qualifying non-resident taxpayers for Dutch PIT purposes.

Migration of individuals from the Netherlands

15.46 Upon migration by an individual from the Netherlands, PIT may be triggered in respect of certain Dutch source assets (eg, an old age retirement scheme or pension, a substantial shareholding). The *Dutch Tax Collection Act* allows for the relevant PIT liability to be deferred for a maximum of ten years subject to the individual taxpayer posting collateral. However, where there is emigration to an EU Member State, no collateral is required and payment deferral is in principle applied automatically.

As a result of Brexit, individuals migrating from the Netherlands to the UK can no longer benefit from automatic deferral of the Dutch PIT liability. If deferral of this liability is desired, such individual will furthermore have to post collateral with the Dutch Tax Administration. For individuals who migrated before the end of the transition period and who currently make use of a deferral arrangement, there is a risk that such arrangement could be cancelled. If so, any amounts still outstanding would in principle become immediately collectable, unless the taxpayer is able to request new deferral and to post collateral. Alternatively, the Dutch government may decide unilaterally to grandfather deferrals that were already accepted prior to Brexit. The foregoing may perhaps depend on whether the UK continues to provide (mutual) assistance to the Netherlands in the recovery of tax claims (as is currently arranged under Council Directive 2010/24/EU).

Dutch PIT aspects of cross-border reorganisations

15.47 Dutch resident individuals may be subject to Dutch PIT where they hold shares in a company involved in a (cross-border) reorganisation. For example, for Dutch PIT purposes, an individual is deemed to dispose of his shares in a company that is involved in a merger (as entity ceasing to exist) or de-merger (as de-merging entity). However, where the companies involved in the reorganisation are resident in the Netherlands, or the EU/EEA, a roll-over is available for Dutch PIT purposes, provided the other conditions are met. This roll-over allows the individual to postpone realisation of a hidden reserve present on the shares. Following Brexit, this facility will no longer be available insofar as a UK resident company is involved in the reorganisation.

ANNEX A – DUTCH RELEVANT SUBSTANCE REQUIREMENTS

15.48 The following requirements are referred to as the Dutch relevant substance requirements:

(1) at least half of the total number of statutory board members of the company with decision making powers resides or is actually established in the Netherlands;

(2) the board members residing or established in the Netherlands have the required professional knowledge to properly perform their duties;

(3) the company has qualified employees for proper implementation and registration of the transactions to be entered into by it;

(4) the management decisions are taken in the Netherlands;

(5) the main bank accounts of the company are held in the Netherlands;

(6) the books of the company are kept in the Netherlands;

(7) the company meets the Office Space Requirement (as outlined below); and

(8) the company meets the Salary requirements (as outlined below).

With respect to the Office Space Requirement, it is noted that the company will need to avail of its own office space (owned or rented), located in its jurisdiction of establishment, for the duration of at least 24 months. To meet the Salary Requirement the company needs to incur salary costs of at least EUR 100,000 per year (which amount may, in accordance with a Dutch regulation, be lower based on local living and income standards).

Chapter 16

Poland

Piotr Augustyniak

INTRODUCTION

16.1 The purpose of this chapter is to analyse the main consequences of the UK leaving the EU from the Polish tax perspective.

Due to the transition period the consequences of Brexit are not fully in place yet. Until 31 December 2020, the UK is obliged to apply EU tax law as before, and therefore the internal market freedoms will remain in force. After this date the UK will not be obliged to apply EU law.

During the transition period the UK and EU shall negotiate the conditions for future cooperation. As of today, it is not certain whether the UK will be a member of the European Economic Area (EEA).

The analysis of this chapter is, however, based on the assumption that: (i) the UK will be a third country and will not join the EEA, and (ii) the UK will remain listed as a state providing for effective exchange of information due to the double taxation treaty between Poland and the UK.

TAX RAMIFICATIONS FOR INBOUND INVESTMENTS

Outbound dividends

16.2 Generally, according to the *Polish Corporate Income Tax Act* (Journal of Laws 2019, item 865 with amendments), dividends payable to non-resident corporate shareholders are subject to withholding tax at 19%. The withholding tax is applicable to the gross amount of dividend and a Polish subsidiary is the tax remitter responsible for proper calculation and collection of tax.

After the end of the transition period, the Parent Subsidiary Directive regime will not apply. The Parent-Subsidiary Directive regime is applicable to dividends distributed by a qualifying Polish subsidiary to its qualifying parent company which place of effective management is located in EU Member State and/or in European Economic Area State that has entered into an administrative assistance agreement for combating tax fraud and tax evasion with Poland. As a consequence, under the given circumstances, Poland sourced dividends distributed to a UK company will not benefit from the Parent-Subsidiary Directive regime after Brexit.

The exemption with respect to dividends may be applied based on the provisions of the double taxation treaty concluded between Poland and UK. Article 10 of the double taxation treaty stipulates the same conditions for the dividend exemption. According to that Treaty, dividends paid by a company which is a resident of a Contracting State may be taxed in that other state. However, such dividends shall be exempt from tax in the Contracting state of which the company is a resident, if the beneficial owner of the dividends is a company which is a resident of the Other Contracting State and holds at least 10% of the capital of the Company paying the dividends on the date the dividends are paid and has done so or will have done so for an uninterrupted 24-month period in which that date falls. In order to benefit from the reduced tax rates stipulated by the double taxation treaty the taxpayer needs to be provided with the tax residency certificate.

Outbound interest

16.3 Polish-sourced interest paid to non-resident companies is generally subject to withholding tax at the rate of 20% (*Article 21.1.1* of the *Polish Corporate Income Tax Act*).

Outbound interest, as defined by the EU Interest and Royalties Directive, may benefit from the exemption of withholding tax provided by the domestic law implementing the provisions of said Directive, to the extent: (i) the beneficial owner of the payment is a tax resident of another EU Member State or EEA State (*Article 21.3.2* of the *Polish Corporate Income Tax Act*). Moreover, a Polish payer or foreign beneficiary (one of them) holds a direct participation of at least 25% in the share capital of the other The participation must have been held continuously for at least two years or must be subject to a commitment to do so and the relevant companies must have a legal form listed in the Annex of the Directive and be subject to corporate income tax. Following Brexit, this exemption will no longer be applicable to outbound interests paid to UK corporate residents.

Taxpayers will be able to benefit from the reduced tax rate stipulated by the double taxation treaty (Article 11), provided that they can present a tax residency certificate. For interests the reduced rate stipulated by the double taxation treaty was set at a rate of 5%. The term 'interest' as used in the treaty means income from debt claims of every kind, whether or not secured by mortgage and whether or not carrying a right to participate in the debtor's profits and, in particular, income from government securities and income from bonds or debentures.

It should be noted, however, that under *Article 26.1* of the *Polish Corporate Income Tax Act* which covers the special anti-avoidance rules (source income tax), a domestic entity that makes cross-border payments in excess of PLN 2 million to a foreign entity during a single tax year is required to withhold tax at the time of payment at the standard domestic rate (ie, 20%, except for dividends, which are taxed at 19%) on the amount exceeding PLN 2 million. A Polish payer company may apply a reduced rate or withholding tax exemption under an applicable tax treaty or an EU directive but only if: (i) the company's management board provides a signed statement to the tax authorities confirming, under penalty of perjury, that the recipient of the payment qualifies for the tax relief; or (ii) a withholding tax clearance opinion is obtained from the tax authorities.

In addition, Poland has made the requirements to qualify as the beneficial owner of a payment under a tax treaty more stringent. As from 1 January 2019, beneficial owners must: (i) receive payments for their own benefit and bear the economic risk of loss for the payments, (ii) not be obligated to transfer any part of the payment to another person, and (iii) carry out actual economic activities in their country of residence if the payments received are related to these economic activities (a requirement that also applies to holding companies). This may also make payments to the UK more difficult or at least more complicated.

Outbound royalties

16.4 Outbound royalties paid to non-resident companies are generally subject to withholding tax at the rate of 20% (*Article 21.1.1* of the *Polish Corporate Income Tax Act*).

Outbound royalties, as defined by the EU Interest and Royalties Directive, may benefit from the exemption of withholding tax provided by the domestic law implementing the provisions of said Directive, to the extent the beneficial owner of the payment is a tax resident of another EU Member State or EEA State (*Article 21.3.2* of the *Polish Corporate Income Tax Act*). Moreover, Polish payer or foreign beneficiary (one of them) holds a direct participation of at least 25% in the share capital of the other The participation must have been held continuously for at least two years or must be subject to a commitment to do so and the relevant companies must have a legal form listed in the Annex of the Directive and be subject to corporate income tax. Following Brexit, this exemption will no longer be applicable to outbound interests paid to UK corporate residents.

Taxpayers will be able to benefit from the reduced tax rate stipulated by the double taxation treaty (Article 12), provided that they can present a tax residency certificate. For royalties the reduced rate stipulated by the double taxation treaty was set at a rate of 5%. The term 'royalties' means payments of any kind received as a consideration for the use of, or the right to use, any copyright of literary, artistic or scientific work (including cinematograph films, and films or tapes for radio or television broadcasting), any patent, trademark, design or model, plan, secret formula or process, or for the use of, or the right to use any industrial, commercial, or scientific equipment or for information (know-how) concerning industrial, commercial or scientific experience.

Capital gains on shareholdings in resident companies

16.5 Under Polish law, and subject to the relevant double taxation treaty, capital gains realised by a non-resident company on shares in a Polish company are taxed in Poland in the following circumstances:

- Where capital gains are realised on publicly traded equities.
- Where capital gains are realised on shares in a company where at least 50% of its asset value is derived from real estate situated within the territory of the Republic of Poland (*Article 3.3* of the *Polish Corporate Income Tax Act*).

According to Article 13 of the PL-UK double taxation treaty, gains derived by a UK resident from the alienation of shares, other than shares in which there is substantial and regular trading on a Stock Exchange and other than shares deriving their value or the greater part of their value directly or indirectly from immovable property situated in Poland, are taxed in Poland. Generally, other capital gains (sales of shares in Polish entities) realised by a UK resident will be taxable only in the UK. However, this exemption does not include the situation when gains are being realised on alienation of any property on a person who is, and has been at any time during the previous six fiscal years, a resident of Poland.

Capital gains taxable in Poland are subject to the regular 19% tax.

Permanent establishments

16.6 No difference due to Brexit

TAX RAMIFICATIONS FOR OUTBOUND INVESTMENTS

Inbound dividends

16.7 Brexit shall impact the regime in Poland of dividends distributed by UK subsidiaries.

Currently, dividends received from foreign sources may be exempt from corporate income tax in Poland where:

- They are distributed by companies resident in an EU Member State or EEA State or in Switzerland.
- The Polish company has held at least 10 % (or 25% for companies with their registered office in Switzerland) of the shares in the company distributing the dividend for at least two years.

In general, dividends received by a Polish taxpayer from sources located abroad are subject to 19% corporate income tax. Amounts of dividends increase the taxable income from Polish sources unless the tax treaty states otherwise.

Tax paid abroad may be deducted from Polish corporate income tax; however the deduction cannot exceed the amount of corporate income tax due under Polish law for the part classified as foreign income.

Dividends received by the Polish shareholder from its UK subsidiary might be subject to 19% corporate income tax. However the Polish shareholder will be able to take advantage of the indirect tax credit in accordance with *Article 20.2* of the *Polish Corporate Income Tax Act*, provided that he holds at least 75% shares in the UK company's share capital.

Capital gains on shareholdings in non-resident companies

16.8 In general, capital gains realised by Polish corporate residents from the sale of participations in UK resident companies are subject to corporate income tax at the standard 19% rate.

A capital loss can offset capital gains of the same type and can be carried forward in the subsequent five tax years.

Permanent establishments abroad

16.9 No difference due to Brexit.

CFC rules

16.10 No difference in application of the CFC regime to third countries (such as the UK) or EU/EEA Member States.

Under the controlled foreign corporation (CFC) rules, Polish taxpayers are taxed at 19% on the income of their CFCs. A subsidiary is characterised as a CFC if:

- the entity is located in a country that engages in 'harmful tax practices';
- the country of the entity's seat or place of management, registration or location does not engage in the exchange of information with Poland or the EU; or
- the Polish company effectively controls or holds (either on its own or jointly with its related entities) over 50% of a foreign entity that derives at least 33% of its revenue from passive income and the amount of tax actually paid by the foreign entity is lower than the difference between the tax that would have been payable had the entity been a Polish resident and the tax the foreign entity actually paid.

The rules do not apply if a CFC carries out relevant genuine economic activities. The tax base (taxable income) under the CFC regime may be reduced by the amounts already included in the Polish taxpayer's tax base in respect of dividends received from a CFC and income from the sale of shares in a CFC.

Following Brexit, a Polish company holding a UK-CFC will have to prove that the main purpose of the subsidiary is not tax driven. In other words, Polish tax authorities will seek to verify that the main purpose of the UK subsidiary is not to avoid Polish tax and the arrangement is not artificial.

Furthermore, the UK company should be able to provide proof of its economic activity, substance (office, employees) relevant to the volume of its business. Polish authorities also check if the profits received by the foreign company will not be immediately distributed to the same jurisdiction under a different title (ie, business profits received by the beneficial owner in Poland from the foreign source on the basis of dividends received from Poland by the foreign holding, in circular structures).

IMPACT ON CROSS-BORDER GROUP TAX REGIMES

16.11 Polish tax law does not allow the creation of cross-border tax groups; therefore Brexit will not affect the regime.

TAX RAMIFICATIONS FOR CROSS-BORDER MERGERS, OTHER REORGANISATIONS AND TRANSFERS OF RESIDENCE

16.12 As a general rule, mergers, divisions and transfers of assets are considered as taxable events, and as a consequence are subject to corporate income tax at the standard rate (19%).

Polish and European law provide for preferential regimes allowing companies to carry out reorganisations in a tax neutral way. The European regime results from the EU Merger Directive (Directive 2009/133/CE of 23 November 2009). The EU Merger Directive applies to reorganisations involving companies resident in EU Member States. Therefore, this regime will not be applicable to reorganisations involving UK resident companies after Brexit.

Polish tax legislation does not provide for tax neutrality for cross-border mergers other than within the EU or EEA.

Hence, after Brexit, such reorganisations may trigger a tax liability in Poland.

Transfer of residence abroad

16.13 As of 1 January 2019, exit tax (ie, taxation of unrealised capital gains in the case of transfer of assets, change of tax residence, or taxpayer's PE outside the territory of Poland) has been introduced.

The exit tax rate has been set at 19%. The tax base is the surplus of the market value of assets, with respect to which Poland would lose taxing rights, over their tax value. Under certain conditions, taxpayers may be able to apply for payment in instalments for a period not exceeding five years.

The exit tax applies in the same way to both transfers to EU and non-EU States, so its application should not be affected by Brexit.

Inbound transfer of residence

16.14 There is no specific provision in domestic law taxing inbound transfer of residence from a foreign country.

OTHER

16.15 Poland introduced stricter General Anti-Avoidance Rules. The most important feature of GAAR is the right given to the authorities to disregard, in tax computations, an artificial arrangement (or series of arrangements) with tax savings as its principal purpose if the tax savings are not compliant, under the circumstances of the case, with the provisions and purpose of tax laws.

Arrangements investigated under GAAR will be compared to arrangements that could be made by a reasonable taxpayer following fair market goals. These comparative arrangements will form the basis of assessment. Some of the arrangements which may be considered as artificial include:

- operations unreasonably divided;
- intermediaries unreasonably involved;

- transactions resulting in a situation similar to the one prior to the arrangement (looping);
- transactions consisting of mutually nullifying or compensating elements;
- arrangements connected with a business risk exceeding the expected benefits (other than tax savings) to the extent that one must consider a reasonable person not to have chosen this course of action.

Generally speaking, the situation after Brexit will be more complicated, however lot of both treaty as well as directives benefits in Poland have been limited. Last reforms of the Polish tax system have been focused on elimination of tax optimisation structures. Therefore, tax audits concluded on multinational corporations as well as international investors are currently complex. International tax planning in Poland became much more complicated and costs of compliance increased dramatically.

What has to be underlined, today, is that the benefits of being a member of the European Union for multinational corporations are not practically significant from income tax perspectives. The borders between tax evasion, tax avoidance and tax optimisation somehow disappeared in Poland and it may be taken for granted that any tax benefit will be carefully examined by the authorities during the tax audit.

Chapter 17

Portugal

Nuno Cunha Barnabé and Maria Inês Assis

INTRODUCTION

17.1 Portuguese law is founded on the principle of non-discrimination when considering the nationality of the investment,[1] as, in general, investment requirements apply indistinctively to national and foreign investors.

As such, Portuguese investors are under no restrictions regarding investment in other countries (outbound investment) and foreign investors face no constraints when deciding to invest in Portugal (inbound investments).

Portugal does not also discourage, from a tax point of view, companies resident in Portugal from investing capital in companies established abroad or in Portugal. The country adopts a capital export neutrality (CEN) approach, whereby, as a rule, the same tax burden should apply to resident companies investing in Portugal and those investing abroad.

Nevertheless, the tax treatment applicable to a specific investment may slightly differ depending on whether the investment is made, in the case of an outbound investment, and where the investor is resident for tax purposes, that is, in an EU Member State, in an EEA country or in a third country, in the case of an inbound investment.

Clarity on the tax treatment applicable is key, however, on any investor's – whether inbound or outbound – decision-making process.

As such, the purpose of this chapter is to analyse, from a Portuguese tax perspective, the tax regime applicable to investors on cross-border

1 In Portugal, investment is limited only in regard to certain economic activities (both to foreign and domestic investors). These include the harnessing, treatment and distribution of water for public consumption, postal services, rail transport as a public service and the running of maritime ports. Private sector companies (either foreign or domestic) can operate in these areas only through the concession of a management contract.
At the same time, most areas of investment in Portugal are unregulated – authorisation is required just for investment (carried out either by foreign or domestic investors) in sensitive areas (such as defence) and regulated areas (such as banking, media and financial services).

investments made to and from the UK with respect to Portugal and following Brexit.

The analysis in this chapter is based on the following assumptions:

- the term UK means Great and Northern Ireland, including any area outside the territorial sea of the UK which, in accordance with international law, has been or may hereafter be designated, under the laws of the UK concerning the Continental Shelf, as an area within which the rights of the UK with respect to the sea bed and sub-soil and their natural resources may be exercised. The term UK does not include UK overseas territories and Crown dependencies;
- the UK will be a third country and will not join the EEA space;
- the UK will provide for effective exchange of information due to the double tax treaty between Portugal and the UK;[2]
- the double tax treaty between Portugal and the UK, as it presently reads, will remain in force;
- the UK will not be included in the Portuguese list of jurisdictions having a privileged tax regime (hereinafter the 'tax havens list');[3] and
- the items of income considered are not attributable to (registered or deemed) permanent establishment in Portugal of the UK investor (either as payer or payee of such income).

TAX RAMIFICATIONS FOR INBOUND INVESTMENTS

17.2 Non-resident companies without a permanent establishment in Portugal to which the income is attributed are only subject to Portuguese Corporate Income Tax (hereinafter 'CIT') on income deemed to be obtained in Portugal, that is, Portuguese sourced income.[4]

2 The Convention between the government of the United Kingdom of Great Britain and Northern Ireland and the government of the Portuguese Republic for the avoidance of double taxation and the prevention of fiscal evasion with respect to taxes on income and on capital gains signed in Lisbon on 27 March 1968. This double tax treaty is covered by the Multilateral Convention to Implement Tax Treaty related measures to prevent base erosion and profit shifting (MLI).

3 As per the list approved by Order in Council of the member of the Government responsible for the area of finances (Ministerial Order no. 150/2004, of 13 February 2004, as amended from time to time). In this respect, please note that the UK overseas territories and Crown dependencies are included in the Portuguese tax havens list (eg, Anguilla, Ascension Islands, Bermuda, British Virgins Islands, Cayman Islands, Falkland Islands, Gibraltar, Montserrat, Pitcairn Island, Saint Helena, Ascension, Tristan da Cunha and Turks and Caicos Islands, Channel Islands – Isle of Man, Jersey and Guernsey).

4 Investment income derived from and/or capital gains from the sale of shares and other corporate rights or securities in a resident company or a non-resident company, provided in the latter case that the related income is attributable to a permanent establishment in Portugal.

Outbound dividends

17.3 Dividends paid by a Portuguese resident company to a non-resident corporate shareholder are deemed Portuguese sourced income and are, as such, liable to tax in Portugal.

In broad terms, under Portuguese tax law, outbound dividends distributed by Portuguese resident companies to non-resident corporate shareholders (without a permanent establishment in Portugal to which the dividend payment is made or allocated) are subject to a withholding tax of 25%.[5]

Whenever dividends are paid to a company located in a tax havens listed territory, a 35% withholding tax will apply instead (anti-abuse rule). The UK is not included in the Portuguese Tax havens list (and this should not change after Brexit) but UK overseas territories[6] and Crown dependencies[7] are.

Notwithstanding, dividend payments made by Portuguese resident companies are exempt from withholding tax in Portugal whenever the requirements set out by the EU Parent-Subsidiary directive are met.

The Parent-Subsidiary directive exemption, as transposed into Portuguese tax law, applies to dividends distributed by a qualifying Portuguese subsidiary to its qualifying parent company resident in an EU Member State or in an EEA State that has entered into an administrative assistance agreement for combating tax fraud and tax evasion with Portugal. As such, once the Brexit transition period agreed upon in the Withdrawal Agreement has elapsed, Portuguese-source dividends distributed to a UK tax resident corporate shareholder will no longer benefit from the withholding tax exemption provided for by the EU Parent-Subsidiary directive.

Nonetheless, a UK corporate shareholder may still benefit from a withholding tax exemption on dividends distributed by Portuguese resident companies[8] under the Portuguese domestic participation exemption regime.

5 If the non-resident company has a permanent establishment in Portugal to which the dividend payment is made or allocated, the withholding tax suffered is a mere payment on account of the CIT liability of such permanent establishment in Portugal in respect of a specific fiscal year.

6 Anguilla, Ascension Islands, Bermuda, British Virgins Islands, Cayman Islands, Falkland Islands, Gibraltar, Montserrat, Pitcairn Island, Saint Helena, Tristan da Cunha and Turks and Caicos Islands, etc.

7 The Isle of Man, Jersey and Guernsey.

8 Under Portuguese tax law, the participation exemption regime on outbound dividends is extended, under certain conditions, to dividends distributed by a Portuguese resident company to a permanent establishment situated in an EU or EEA country of a company resident in another EU or EEA country or a country with which Portugal has concluded a double tax treaty. So, following Brexit, this CIT withholding tax exemption shall continue to apply to dividends paid to a permanent establishment located in another EU or EEA country from a compliant UK company. But it will no longer be applicable to dividends paid by a Portuguese company to a UK permanent establishment, even if its head office is located in an EU or EEA country. Although, in principle, permanent establishments are not 'persons' for treaty purposes and are

17.3 *Portugal*

The Portuguese domestic participation exemption regime provides for an exemption applicable to dividends paid by a Portuguese resident company to a non-EU or EEA resident corporate shareholder, provided the following criteria are jointly met:

- the non-resident company is resident of a state with which Portugal has concluded a double tax treaty which provides for the exchange of information;
- the non-resident company is subject and not exempt from a tax similar to the Portuguese CIT which tax rate may not be less than 60% of the Portuguese CIT rate in force (currently 21%, thus a 12.6% minimum);
- the non-resident company holds (directly or indirectly) a minimum of 10% of the share capital or voting rights of the Portuguese company making the dividend distribution;
- such participation has been held continuously during the period of one year before the date of the dividend distribution;
- the dividend payment does not take place in the context of an arrangement which was not put into place for valid commercial reasons and does not reflect economic reality (specific anti-abuse clause); and
- the Portuguese resident company complied with its reporting obligations under the legal regime of the Central Register of Beneficial Ownership of Companies and none of its beneficial owners is deemed resident for tax purposes of a territory included in the Portuguese tax havens list.

Portugal has concluded a double tax treaty with the UK[9] which provides for the exchange of information. As such, based on a literal interpretation of the law, the aforementioned exemption should apply to dividends distributed by a Portuguese resident company to its UK corporate shareholder after Brexit, provided all the remaining requirements are met.[10]

---

thus not entitled to treaty benefits, in a triangular case involving a permanent establishment, Portugal's taxing rights over Portuguese-sourced dividends, interest and royalties may, nonetheless, be bound by the conditions imposed by the double tax treaty concluded between Portugal and the country where the 'head office' of the UK permanent establishment is located (if any), in which case Portugal would only be entitled to impose a withholding taxation on such investment income at a limited rate (usually, 10% or 15%).

9 See fn 2.

10 To benefit from this exemption, the non-resident corporate shareholder entitled to receive the dividends has to prove that the requirements for its application are met and to present to the Portuguese subsidiary, before the dividends being paid or becoming available for payment, a declaration confirmed and certified by the UK tax authorities stating that: (i) it is tax resident in the UK as per Article 4 of the double tax treaty concluded between Portugal and the UK, (ii) it is subject to and not exempt in the UK from a tax similar to the Portuguese CIT; and (iii) the tax rate applicable to it in the UK is not less than 60% of the Portuguese CIT rate (ie, currently 12.6%). If such proof is not made on time by the non-resident corporate shareholder, the Portuguese resident company is obliged to withhold tax on the dividends to be distributed (at a 25% or reduced tax rate provided a double tax treaty is applicable). Within

However, the wording of the Portugal-UK treaty exchange of information provision has not yet been amended in accordance with the 2010 update to the OECD Model Tax Convention. Up till now there has been no administrative guidance or case law on whether the aforementioned exemption applies to all cases where a double tax treaty has been concluded by Portugal which provides for the exchange of information, regardless of its wording (with or without the 2010 update to the OECD Model Tax Convention).

Therefore, following Brexit, although the Portugal-UK double tax treaty provides for the exchange of information, it is possible that Portuguese tax authorities may try to deny the application of the exemption arguing that it should only apply where the 2010 update has been adopted.

Where the Portuguese domestic participation exemption regime applies to dividends distributed to a UK resident corporate shareholder and the only requirement not met is the minimum one-year holding period at the time the distribution of dividends take place, the tax withheld (at a 25% rate or at a reduced rate under the double tax treaty, if applicable) can be refunded later on completion of the said minimum holding period.[11]

In the event that one or more of the aforementioned requirements (besides or despite the one-year minimum holding period) are not met (or while the one-year minimum holding period requirement is not met), the CIT withholding tax rate applicable in Portugal to dividends distributed by Portuguese resident companies to a UK resident corporate shareholder may, nevertheless, be reduced under the double tax treaty concluded between Portugal and the UK, provided both entities involved (Portuguese paying company and UK beneficial owner) comply with the requirements to trigger its application.[12]

---

two years counting from the end of the tax year in which the withholding taxation took place, the non-resident corporate shareholder may file a request for the total reimbursement of the tax withheld in excess using tax form Mod 22 RFI; the reimbursement procedure must be concluded by the Portuguese tax authorities within one year counting from the date in which the corresponding request and all supporting documentation has been filed; otherwise on top of the tax to be reimbursed, indemnity interest (at a rate of 4% per annum) will also be due by the Portuguese tax authorities.

11 A request for the reimbursement of the tax withheld in excess may be filed within two years counting from the date in which the one year minimum holding period is completed; the reimbursement procedure must be concluded by the Portuguese tax authorities until the end of the third month following the one in which the corresponding request and all supporting documentation has been filed; otherwise on top of the tax to be reimbursed, interest (currently at a rate of 4% per annum) will also be due by the Portuguese tax authorities.

12 For this double tax treaty to apply, both the UK corporate shareholders and the Portuguese resident companies must be entitled to treaty protection, meaning the UK corporate shareholder and the Portuguese resident company must qualify as a body corporate or as an entity treated as a body corporate for UK and Portuguese tax purposes, respectively, and must be deemed resident for tax purposes 'liable to tax' in its country of incorporation.
To benefit from this reduction on the withholding tax rate applicable, the non-resident corporate shareholder entitled to receive the dividends has to provide evidence that the requirements for its application are met and has to present to the Portuguese subsidiary, prior to the dividends being paid or becoming available for payment, a tax form (Mod. 21 RFI) duly

17.3 *Portugal*

Under Article 10 of the double tax treaty at stake, reduced withholding tax rates apply to distributions of dividends, as follows:

- 10% CIT withholding tax rate, provided the UK beneficial owner holds directly at least 25% of the share capital of the Portuguese resident company making the distribution of dividends; and
- in all other cases, a 15% CIT withholding tax rate will apply.

Presently, no amendment to the Portugal-UK tax treaty is expected following Brexit. However, the benefit of these favourable provisions of the double tax treaty concluded between Portugal and the UK may be denied on the basis of the principal purpose test[13] introduced (as a mandatory minimum standard) by the anti-treaty abuse provision of the multilateral convention to implement tax treaty related measures to prevent base erosion and profit shifting (MLI) ratified by both Portugal and the UK.[14]

---

filed in and certified by the UK tax authorities or the same tax form Mod. 21 RFI just filed not certified by the UK tax authorities accompanied by a tax residence certificate issued by the UK tax authorities attesting the tax residency of the corporate shareholder in the UK for the purposes of Article 4 of the double tax treaty at stake.

As a rule, the tax form Mod. 21-RFI is valid for one year regarding the claim of benefits provided for under double tax treaties (however, if the recipient of the income is a bank or a governmental agency resident in a country that has a tax treaty with Portugal, there is no period of validity for the form, ie, it is only necessary to issue it once and then no renewal is necessary).

If such proof is not made on time by the non-resident corporate shareholder, the Portuguese resident company is obliged to withhold tax on the dividends to be distributed (at a 25% tax rate). Within two years counting from the end of the tax year in which the withholding taxation took place, the non-resident corporate shareholder may file a request for the total reimbursement of the tax withheld in excess (through the tax form Mod 22 RFI); the reimbursement procedure must be concluded by the Portuguese tax authorities within one year counting from the date in which the corresponding request and all supporting documentation has been filed; otherwise on top of the tax to be reimbursed, indemnity interest (currently at a rate of 4% per annum) will also be due by the Portuguese tax authorities.

13 Please note that the original – and still in force – wording of Article 10 of the double tax treaty concluded between Portugal and the UK already includes an anti-abuse treaty provision under which the benefits granted under such favourable provision may be denied. As such no treaty limitations will be imposed on Portugal's taxing rights over dividends distributed by a Portuguese resident company, whenever the UK treaty resident corporate shareholder (owning 10% or more of the class of shares in respect of which the dividends are paid) does not bear tax in the UK at a rate exceeding 20% in respect of the dividends received, to the extent that those dividends have been paid only out of profits which the Portuguese company paying the dividends earned or other income which it received in a period ending 12 months or more before the date on which the UK treaty resident corporate shareholder became the owner of the class of shares in question. This anti-abuse rule shall not apply if the shares in question were acquired for bona fide commercial reasons and not primarily for the purpose of securing the treaty benefits.

14 In Portugal, the deposit of instrument of ratification took place on 28 February 2020. In the UK, the deposit of instrument of ratification took place on 29 June 2018. MLI shall have effect in Portugal and in the UK, with respect to taxes withheld at source on amounts paid to non-residents, where the event giving rise to such taxes occurs on or after 1 January 2021.

Whenever withholding tax is due, such tax is final and levied on the gross amount of dividends distributed by the Portuguese resident company. The Portuguese resident company, as the latter, must remit the tax amount to the Portuguese tax authorities by the 20th day of the month following that in which the dividend payment is due.

Moreover, the Portuguese resident company paying the dividends is obliged to prepare a list of those dividends' beneficiaries and to keep appropriate records of the benefits granted (elimination or reduction of the withholding tax) and the supporting documentation, as well as to provide the Portuguese tax authorities with such information by the end of July of the year following that in which the tax has been withheld.

Non-resident companies without a permanent establishment in Portugal, which have Portuguese sourced income liable to withholding taxes, for example dividends, are exempt from any tax reporting obligation to the Portuguese tax authorities.[15]

Outbound interest

17.4 Interest payments made by a Portuguese resident company to a non-resident corporate creditor are deemed to be Portuguese-sourced income and, as such, subject to tax in Portugal.

As with outbound dividends, Portuguese-sourced interest paid (or accrued [16]) to non-resident companies (without a permanent establishment in Portugal to which the interest payment is made or allocated) is subject to withholding tax at a rate of 25% due on its maturity date or its payment date, whichever occurs first. However, that rate is increased to 35% where the interest is due to or paid to a company located in a tax haven listed territory[17]).

However, the EU Interest and Royalties Directive precludes any withholding tax on interest payments to associated EU companies. This exemption, as

15 Whenever the non-resident company derives income from Portuguese sources not subject to final withholding tax (as is the case of income derived from real estate located in Portuguese territory or capital gains derived from the sale of shares in a Portuguese company), such entities are obliged to comply with income and reporting obligations in Portugal to assess and proceed with the payment of the tax due. In this case, the non-resident company must appoint an individual or a company, resident for tax purposes in Portugal, to represent it before the Portuguese tax authorities and file the competent tax forms (including commencement of activities tax form, CIT tax return and Annual Return of the Accounting and Tax Information and, later on, a cessation of activities tax form).

16 Please note that, according to the Portuguese tax law, in the case of sale of a bond, the part of the sales price that corresponds to the payment of accrued interest will be regarded, for tax purposes, as interest and not capital gains.

17 See fn 5. The UK overseas territories and Crown dependencies are included in the Portuguese list of tax havens (see fns 6 and 7).

transposed into Portuguese tax law, applies provided the following conditions are jointly met:

- the non-resident corporate recipient takes one of the forms listed in the Annex of the EU Interest and Royalties Directive and is subject, and not exempt, to a corporate income tax also listed in the Annex;
- the non-resident corporate recipient is considered to be resident for tax purposes in one of the EU Member States and under the terms of a double tax treaty concluded by Portugal not considered resident for tax purposes outside the EU;
- the non-resident corporate recipient is considered to be an associated company of the Portuguese paying company;[18]
- the participation is held continuously during two years prior to the interest due or payment date;[19] and
- the non-resident corporate recipient to which the payments are made is considered to be the beneficial owner of those payments (which can be verified if the company receives the income on its behalf and not as an intermediary).

As such, once the Brexit transition period agreed upon in the Withdrawal Agreement has elapsed, payment of interest by a Portuguese company to a UK company, even if these are associated companies, will no longer benefit from the withholding tax exemption provided for under the EU Interest and Royalties Directive.[20]

Portugal has introduced a special anti-abuse provision that denies the EU Interest and Royalties Directive withholding tax exemption, when the majority of the share capital or of the voting rights in the associated enterprise, which is the interest beneficial owner is held, directly or indirectly, by one or more residents of third countries, such as the UK after the transition period (except if it is possible to prove that the shareholding chain does not have the main purpose of benefit from the withholding tax exemption).

---

18 Two companies are 'associated companies' if: (a) one of them holds directly at least 25% of the capital of the other, or (b) a third EU company holds directly at least 25% of the capital of the two companies.

19 This condition can also be met after the payments are made.

20 Also, once the transition period has elapsed and Brexit becomes effective, the CIT withholding tax exemption on outbound interest will cease to apply: (a) to payments made by a Portuguese permanent establishment of a UK company; (b) whenever the beneficial owner of such payments is an EU permanent establishment from a UK company; or (c) whenever the beneficial owner of such payments is a UK permanent establishment from an EU company. Only interest payments made by a Portuguese paying entity (either a company or a permanent establishment of an EU company) to an EU permanent establishment of a qualifying company in another EU country will be exempt from withholding tax in Portugal. Please see fn 8 above for comments with the necessary adjustments, where applicable.

Nonetheless, following Brexit the UK recipient company may still benefit from a reduction to 10% of the withholding tax rate due in Portugal on interest payments, through the application of the double tax treaty concluded between Portugal and the UK, provided all the conditions for its application are met[21] and subject to the MLI principal purpose test.

Regardless of the above, under Portuguese domestic law no withholding tax will be levied in Portugal on outbound interest in the following cases:

- interest paid by a Portuguese resident credit institution to a non-resident financial or credit institution in respect of loans or fixed-term deposits, respectively. This exemption applies to all non-Portuguese tax resident financial or credit institutions, provided the interest paid cannot be allocated to a Portuguese permanent establishment of those non-Portuguese tax resident financial or credit institutions. This exemption will not apply where: (a) the beneficiaries of the income at stake are deemed resident for tax purposes in a jurisdiction included in the tax havens list, or (b) when the non-Portuguese tax resident financial or credit institutions are held, in more than 25% of its share capital, directly or indirectly, by Portuguese tax resident entities;
- interest paid to a non-resident financial institution in connection with swap, forwards and any operations connected with the latter carried out with the Portuguese State, acting through the Portuguese Treasury and Government Debt Agency (*Instituto de Gestão da Tesouraria e da Dívida Pública*, IGCP, E.P.E.) or through the Portuguese Institute for the Management of Social Security Capitalization Funds (*Instituto de Gestão de Fundos de Capitalização da Segurança Social*, I.P.). This exemption applies to all non-Portuguese tax resident financial or credit institutions provided the interest paid cannot be allocated to a Portuguese permanent establishment of those non-Portuguese tax resident financial institutions. This exemption will not apply where: (a) the beneficiaries of the income at stake are deemed resident for tax purposes in a jurisdiction included in the tax havens list, or (b) when the non-Portuguese tax resident financial or credit institutions are held, in more than 25% of its share capital, directly or indirectly, by Portuguese tax resident entities;
- interest paid by the state, autonomous regions, local authorities and their associations, or any of its departments, institutions and organisations, even a public service or company that provides public services to

21 In order to benefit from such reduction, both the UK recipient company and the Portuguese paying company must comply with certain requirements established by the Portuguese tax authorities, aimed at verifying the non-resident status and entitlement to the respective tax treaty benefits. Please see fn 12 for comments with the necessary adjustments, where applicable.

non-resident companies[22] in respect of foreign capital loans[23] under authorisation of the Minister of Finance;[24]

- interest paid in respect of foreign capital borrowed under a '*Schuldscheindarlehen*' loan contract entered into by the Portuguese Treasury and Government Debt Agency (*Instituto de Gestão da Tesouraria e do Crédito Público*), in name and in representation of the Portuguese State, provided the creditor is a non-Portuguese resident entity;[25] and
- interest paid to non-resident corporate noteholders[26] from Portuguese debt securities (either public or private), including perpetual and convertible bonds, registered: (i) with a centralised system recognised by the Portuguese Securities' Code and complementary legislation (such as the Euronext Lisbon, whose clearing system is managed by Interbolsa),[27] or (ii) with an entity managing an international clearing system with its head office or place of effective management in an EU Member State or EEA Country with which Portugal has signed a double tax treaty.[28] In order for this exemption to apply the noteholders must be deemed resident in a country with which Portugal has concluded a double tax treaty or exchange of information on tax matters and cannot be resident in a listed tax haven (with the exception of central banks and government agencies or international organisations recognised as such by Portugal located in those listed tax haven jurisdictions).[29] Thus, from

22 This exemption is also available to non-resident individual creditors.

23 Representing loans and leasing payments for imported equipment.

24 A full or partial CIT exemption may be granted.

25 This exemption is also available to non-resident individual creditors. The non-resident company or individual receiving the investment income from a given Portuguese debt security must receive it in its own name and not as a (paying) agent or (authorised or not) representative of a third party.

26 This special debt securities tax regime also applies to non-resident individual noteholders.

27 Where non-resident noteholders hold Portuguese debt securities through a domestic cleared account registered for the purposes of the PSTRDS (ie, Interbolsa), the exemption from Portuguese withholding tax may be applied 'upfront'. To qualify for such 'upfront' exemption, such non-resident noteholders must provide evidence of their non-resident status to the direct registering entity (entity affiliated on the centralised system where the securities are integrated) prior to the investment income payment date.

28 Where non-resident noteholders hold Portuguese debt securities registered with an entity managing an international clearing system, the evidence provided by the noteholder (the same required for domestic cleared notes) to the direct registering entity must be forwarded to the participants (ie, the entities that operate in the international clearing system), through the international clearing system managing entity, prior to each payment date, and must take into account the total accounts under their management relating to each noteholder that are tax exempt or benefits from the waiver of Portuguese withholding tax (the certificate does not need to be periodically renewed in the case of credit or financial institution, a pension fund or an insurance company).

29 Pursuant to Decree-Law no. 193/2005, of 7 November, as amended by Law no. 93/2013, 9 December (the PSTRDS).

the corporate noteholder point of view, following Brexit, this exemption should continue to be applicable to UK corporate noteholders. However, this exemption will no longer apply, regardless of where the corporate noteholder is considered to be resident for tax purposes, whenever the Portuguese debt security is registered with an entity managing an international clearing system with its head office or place of effective management in the UK.

Lastly, please note that Portuguese tax law grants an exemption of CIT withholding tax on interest payments to financial institutions resident in Portugal, meaning that they are taxed on their net income. As this exemption does not apply to non-resident financial institutions (and Portuguese withholding tax on interest paid to them is imposed on the gross amount of the income received), on 13 July 2016 the Court of Justice of the European Union (CJEU) judged that provision to be against European Union Law.[30] Portuguese tax law is expected to be amended in line with the CJEU jurisprudence, although arguably not to EU third states. Therefore after the transition period the UK should not benefit from such eventual amendment.[31]

Whenever withholding tax is due, such tax is final and levied on the gross amount of interest due by the Portuguese debtor. The Portuguese resident company, as the latter, is obliged to remit the tax amount to the Portuguese tax authorities by the 20th day of the month following that in which the withholding took place.

Moreover, the Portuguese paying company is also obliged to prepare a list of those income streams' beneficiaries and to keep appropriate records of the benefits granted (elimination or reduction of the withholding tax) and its supporting documentation as well as to provide the Portuguese tax authorities with such information by the end of July of the year following that in which the tax has been withheld.

Non-resident companies without a permanent establishment in Portugal, which have Portuguese sourced income liable to withholding taxes, for example interest, are exempt from any tax reporting obligation to the Portuguese tax authorities.

30 In *Brisal* (Case C-18/15), the CJEU held that levying withholding tax on interest paid to non-resident financial institutions constitutes a restriction of the freedom to provide services, which is not justified. The CJEU ruled that Portuguese law discriminates between residents and non-residents since, with regard to the latter, it does not permit the deduction of business expenses directly related to the financial activity carried out (in other words, withholding tax is levied on the gross and not on the net income). As such, in addition, the CJEU ruled that financing costs should, in principle, be deducted for non-resident financial institutions, under the same conditions as for resident financial institutions.

31 It is debatable if such discrimination can be sustained under EU law even if just for EU third states, but to date the issue has not been raised before the CJEU, unlike with respect to EU Member States.

Outbound royalties

17.5 Royalties paid by a Portuguese resident company to a non-resident company are deemed to be Portuguese-sourced income and, as such, subject to tax in Portugal.

Under Portuguese domestic tax rules, royalties paid by Portuguese resident companies to non-resident companies are subject to withholding tax at a rate of 25%. The tax must be withheld at the earliest of the date of payment or the date in which the royalty amount can be determined.

Whenever outbound royalty payments are made to entities resident in a tax haven listed territory, an aggravated tax rate of 35% shall apply.

As with outbound interest payments, outbound royalties, as defined by the EU Interest and Royalties Directive, may benefit from the exemption of CIT withholding tax, to the extent: (i) the beneficial owner of the payment is an associated company of the paying company and is a resident of another EU Member State, or (ii) the beneficial owner of the payment is a company's associated permanent establishment situated in an EU Member State. Two entities are 'associated companies' when one of them holds a: (i) direct participation of at least 25% in the share capital of the other, or (ii) a third EU company holds a direct participation of at least 25% of the share capital of each company. In each case, the participation must have been held continuously for at least two years or must be subject to a commitment to do so and the relevant companies must have a legal form and be subject to one of the corporate income taxes listed in the Annex to the Directive.

Following Brexit's transition period, this exemption will no longer be applicable to outbound royalties paid to UK corporate residents.[32]

Moreover, a general anti-abuse clause provides that the exemption under the domestic law implementing the EU Interest and Royalties Directive does not apply when the royalties are paid to an EU company or a permanent establishment controlled directly or indirectly by non-EU residents where the main purpose or one of the main purposes of the holding chain is to benefit from the withholding tax exemption. Following the transition period, the anti-abuse provision will be applicable to royalties paid to EU corporate residents controlled by UK residents provided the main purpose test is satisfied.

32 Also, once the transition period has elapsed and Brexit becomes effective, the CIT withholding tax exemption on outbound royalties will cease to apply in the following cases: (i) to payments made by a Portuguese permanent establishment of a UK company; and (ii) whenever the beneficial owner of such payments is an EU permanent establishment from a UK company or a UK permanent establishment from an EU company. Only royalty payments made by a Portuguese paying entity (either a company or a permanent establishment of an EU company) to an EU permanent establishment of a qualifying company in another EU country will be precluded from CIT withholding taxation in Portugal. Please see fn 8 above for comments with the necessary adjustments, where applicable.

After Brexit, UK resident companies bound to receive Portuguese-source royalties may still rely on the double tax treaty concluded between Portugal and the UK to reduce their tax exposure in Portugal.

Under Article 12 of the double tax treaty, a reduced 5% withholding tax rate applies to royalties paid to UK resident companies, subject to the MLI principal purpose test.

Please note that, contrary to the wording adopted in the majority of the double tax treaties signed by Portugal and even the OECD Model Tax Convention, the conventional definition of royalties adopted under the double tax treaty concluded between Portugal and the UK encompasses not only payments of any kind for the use of, or the entitlement to use, any copyright of literary, artistic or scientific work (including cinematograph films and films or tapes for radio or television broadcasting), any patent, trademark, design or model, plan, secret formula or process, or for the use of, or the right to use, industrial, commercial, or scientific equipment, or for information concerning industrial, commercial, or scientific experience, but also (capital) gains derived from the sale or exchange of any right or property giving rise to such royalties.

In terms of formalities, the application of the reduced CIT withholding tax rate provided for outbound royalties under the double tax treaty concluded between Portugal and the UK is conditional upon submission of the same forms and procedure described above for outbound interest payments.

Whenever withholding tax is due in Portugal, such tax is final and levied on the gross amount of royalties due by the Portuguese debtor. The Portuguese resident company is obliged to remit the tax amount to the Portuguese tax authorities by the 20th day of the month following that in which the withholding took place.

Moreover, the Portuguese paying company is also obliged to prepare a list of those income streams' beneficiaries and to keep appropriate records of the benefits granted (elimination or reduction of the withholding tax rate levied) and its supporting documentation as well as to provide the Portuguese tax authorities with such information by the end of July of the year following that in which the tax on the royalties has been withheld.

Non-resident companies without a permanent establishment in Portugal, which have Portuguese sourced income liable to withholding taxes, for example interest, are exempt from any tax reporting obligation to the Portuguese tax authorities.

Capital gains on shareholdings in resident companies

17.6 Capital gains derived from the sale of shareholdings and equity instruments in Portuguese resident companies are deemed Portuguese sourced income and, as such, subject to tax in Portugal in the hands of the non-resident company realising such capital gains.

Moreover, the sale of shareholdings and equity instruments in non-resident companies may also give rise to a taxable capital gain in Portugal when, in any of the 365 days preceding the transaction, more than 50% of the company's value derives, directly or indirectly, from owning or holding any rights *in rem* over real estate located in Portugal, which is not being used for agricultural, industrial or commercial purposes (other than buying for resale).[33]

Under Portuguese domestic tax rules, capital gains realised by non-resident companies in Portugal are subject to CIT at the rate of 25%.

However, capital gains derived by a non-resident company directly from the disposal of shares, equity instruments and securities in Portuguese resident companies are exempt from CIT in Portugal,[34] unless:

- more than 25% of the non-resident company is owned, directly or indirectly, by a Portuguese tax resident (except if additional conditions are cumulatively met); or
- the non-resident company is domiciled or incorporated in a tax havens listed territory; or
- the shares from which the capital gains derive relate to a Portuguese real estate company (ie, a company in which more than 50% of its assets consists of Portuguese-situs real estate) or to a Portuguese resident holding company that controls such a Portuguese real estate company; or
- the shares from which the capital gains derive pertain to a non-resident company that, in any of the 365 days preceding the transaction, derived more than 50% of its value, directly or indirectly, from owning or holding any rights *in rem* over real estate located in Portugal that are not used for agricultural, industrial or commercial purposes (other than buying for resale).

The application of this domestic capital gains tax exemption regime will continue to apply to qualifying UK corporate shareholders after Brexit.

However, even when the conditions for the application of the aforementioned domestic tax exemption regime are not met, Portugal's taxing rights over capital gains realised by non-resident companies from the disposal of Portuguese companies' shares may still be overridden by a double tax treaty.

---

33 Before 2018, no Portuguese taxation would apply on capital gains derived from the sale of a non-Portuguese holding company (even if the latter would own stock in a Portuguese company), unless the beneficiary of the income was a Portuguese resident company or individual (in which case the general taxation rules would apply).

34 This exemption is also available to non-resident individual shareholders, except if they are deemed resident for tax purposes in a listed tax haven.

In fact, the majority of the double tax treaties signed by Portugal provide for the waiver of taxation in Portugal regarding capital gains obtained by a non-Portuguese tax resident from the sale of shares or interest in a Portuguese company,[35] unless the companies' assets are mainly composed of real estate located in Portugal.

Under the provision of Article 13 of the double tax treaty concluded between Portugal and the UK, capital gains derived by a UK company over the sale of a Portuguese participation should only be taxable in the UK so Portugal has no taxing rights over this type of income when realised by a UK resident company.

It should be noted that under the MLI, Portugal has opted to apply Article 9(4) 'Capital Gains from Alienation of Shares or Interests of Entities Deriving their Value Principally from Immovable Property' to its Covered Tax Agreements but the UK has declined to do so. Therefore there will be no automatic update of the double tax treaty granting taxing rights also to Portugal on this type of income.

Where the UK resident company does not meet the requirements to benefit from the domestic tax exemption nor is entitled to treaty protection, as previously mentioned, it will be liable to tax in Portugal on the capital gains realised at a CIT rate of 25%.

Since capital gains are not subject to withholding tax but rather to CIT, the non-resident company realising the capital gains is obliged to comply with income and reporting obligations in Portugal to assess and proceed with the payment of the tax due (a local representative must be appointed to that effect).[36]

Under Portuguese tax law, the taxable income of non-Portuguese resident companies is ascertained in accordance with the rules applicable to individuals.

In the case of securities (unless exempt under the regime described in the previous list):

- capital gains can result from the sale, redemption, remission, liquidation or extinction of any form of security, such as shares;
- the capital gain is given by the sale price subtracted of the acquisition price and costs incurred with the acquisition and sale (the acquisition price is adjusted according to inflation provided the sale takes place at least two years after the acquisition date – every year a ministerial order is approved containing the relevant coefficients);

---

35 The exception to this rule is the double tax treaty concluded between Portugal and Brazil that grants taxing rights to both the transferor's residence state and the source state in the case of a company's shares regardless of the nature of its underlying assets.

36 The non-resident company must file, at least, a commencement of activities tax form, CIT tax return and Annual Return of the Accounting and Tax Information and later on a cessation of activities tax form.

- capital gains are taxed on an annual basis and not per transaction and shall take into account all gains and losses realised by the non-resident company in Portugal in any given tax-year from the sale of any form of securities (meaning it will be possible to offset capital losses within the same tax-year);
- securities transactions occurring in the same calendar year will be reported by the non-resident company in its annual CIT return, to be filed by the end of May of the year following the one in which the operations took place.

In the case of real estate or any rights *in rem* over real estate:

- capital gains can result from the sale of real estate or any rights *in rem* over real estate;
- the capital gain is given by the sale price subtracted of the acquisition price and costs incurred with the acquisition and sale (the acquisition price is adjusted according to inflation provided the sale takes place at least two years after the acquisition date – every year a ministerial order is approved containing the relevant coefficients);
- each sale will be reported by the non-resident company in a CIT return, to be filed within 30 days of the date of sale.

Permanent establishments

17.7 Under Portuguese tax law, the participation exemption regime on inbound dividends is extended to dividends distributed to a (Portuguese) permanent establishment by a company resident in a country where it is subject to (and not exempt from) an income tax similar to the Portuguese CIT and with which Portugal has concluded a double tax treaty that foresees a mechanism for exchange of information (provided such country is not listed as a tax haven).

Therefore, following Brexit, this exemption should continue to apply to dividends paid by a compliant UK company to a Portuguese permanent establishment.

The participation exemption is also applicable to dividends distributed by and attributable to a (Portuguese) permanent establishment of companies resident in an EU Member State or an EEA country subject to a legal regime similar to the one applicable in Portugal to regional development companies,[37] investment companies or broker-dealers, regardless of the percentage held in the share capital or the voting rights of the subsidiary making the distribution

37 Financial companies which promote productive investment in their region so as to support economic and social development.

of the dividends and the holding period of such participation. Following Brexit, only the 'standard' Portuguese participation exemption regime will apply in these circumstances, that is, a minimum percentage of shareholding or voting rights as well as a minimum holding period must be met to allow the beneficial owner to be entitled to CIT exemption in Portugal on dividends received from its subsidiary.

The Portuguese participation exemption regime on capital gains on the disposal of shareholdings in non-resident companies also applies to capital gains obtained by an inbound (Portuguese) permanent establishment from a subsidiary resident in a country where it is subject to (and not exempt from) an income tax similar to the Portuguese CIT and with which Portugal has concluded a double tax treaty that foresees a mechanism for exchange of information (provided such country is not listed as a tax haven). Following Brexit, this exemption should continue to apply to capital gains obtained by a Portuguese permanent establishment from the sale of a shareholding in a compliant UK subsidiary.

Following Brexit, the Portuguese head office company may also continue to opt to exclude from its taxable income the profits and losses attributable to a UK (outbound) permanent establishment.[38]

Other

17.8 A domestic exemption from withholding tax applies to investment income derived by pension funds established and operating in accordance with the law applicable in an EU Member State or in an EEA State that has entered into an administrative assistance agreement for combating tax fraud and tax evasion with Portugal provided certain conditions are met.[39] Brexit will result in this tax exemption ceasing to apply to UK pension funds.

Income distributed and gains arising from the redemption of units/participations of Real Estate Collective Investment Undertakings (hereinafter 'CIUs') by non-resident corporate investors[40] are subject to withholding tax in Portugal,

---

38 Assuming that, after Brexit, the double tax treaty concluded between Portugal and the UK will remain in force and the UK will not be included in the Portuguese tax haven's list of jurisdiction. In addition, the UK permanent establishment must continue to be subject to (and not exempt from) an income tax similar to the Portuguese CIT.

39 The pension fund must be the beneficial owner of the Portuguese-sourced income; where the income at stake is Portuguese-source dividends the corresponding shares from which dividends are being distributed must be held for an uninterrupted minimum period of one year. Moreover, the pension fund must guarantee exclusively the payment of retirement due to old age or invalidity, survivor's pension, pre-retirement or early retirement and that of their dependants in the event of death and must be managed by institutions for occupational retirement provision compliant with the EU Directive 2003/41/C.

40 These rules are also applicable to non-resident individual investors.

at a definitive rate of 10%.[41] Any capital gain arising from the disposal of such units/participations to a third party is subject in Portugal to an autonomous taxation of 10% in the hands of the non-resident corporate investors. By contrast, income distributed and gains arising from the redemption of units/participations in Securities CIUs are tax exempt in Portugal for non-resident corporate investors.[42] [43] Brexit shall not prevent the continuing application of those exemptions to qualifying UK corporate investors.

Income distributed or gains arising from the redemption of units held by a non-resident corporate investor[44] in: (i) a venture capital fund, established and operating under Portuguese legislation, and (ii) a CIU dedicated to forestry resources projects,[45] also established and operating under Portuguese legislation, are tax exempt in Portugal.[46] Capital gains derived from the sale of participating units in such investment vehicles are taxed in Portugal at a 10% CIT rate in the hands of the non-resident corporate investor (provided none of the Portuguese tax exemptions on capital gains provision apply).[47] After Brexit, UK resident companies will continue to be entitled to those exemptions.

Lastly, as per Portuguese tax law, no CIT will be due in Portugal on:

- capital gains realised by non-resident corporate noteholders[48] from Portuguese debt securities (either public or private), including perpetual and convertible bonds, registered: (i) with a centralised system recognised by the Portuguese Securities' Code and complementary legislation (such as the Euronext Lisbon, whose clearing system is managed by Interbolsa), or (ii) with an entity managing an international clearing system with its

41 Note that income paid by Real Estate CIUs (and subject to the flat tax rate of 10%) is qualified as property income for domestic and double tax treaty purposes. As a consequence, the provisions of the double tax treaty regarding the distribution of dividends and capital gains derived from the sale of securities will not be applicable. Additionally, the Portuguese participation exemption regime that might have been applicable in such a way as to exempt outbound dividend distributions and capital gains from the sale of Portuguese participations (if the Real Estate CIUs were a corporate entity) will not apply.

42 These rules are also applicable to non-resident individual investors.

43 In both cases – Real Estate or Securities CIUSs – the low tax regimes will not apply only if the non-resident corporate investor is domiciled or incorporated in a listed tax haven (as established by the Portuguese Government) or if more than 25% of the non-resident corporate investor is owned, directly or indirectly, by a Portuguese tax resident (except if additional conditions are cumulatively met).

44 This regime also applies to non-resident individual investors.

45 Real estate investment fund (FII) or a special regulated Portuguese property investment company ('Sociedade de Investimento Imobiliário' or SIIMO) where more than 75% of their assets are dedicated to the (certified) exploitation of forestry resources.

46 Except if more than 25% of such non-resident corporate investor is owned, directly or indirectly, by a Portuguese tax resident or the non-resident company is domiciled or incorporated in a listed tax haven (as established by the Portuguese Government), in which case the income distributed or the gain realised is subject to withholding tax at the rate of 10%.

47 This exemption also applies to non-resident individual investors.

48 This special debt securities tax regime also applies to non-resident individual noteholders.

head office or place of effective management in an EU Member State or EEA country with which Portugal has signed a double tax treaty. In order for this exemption to apply the noteholders must be deemed resident in a country with which Portugal has concluded a double tax treaty or exchange of information on tax matters treaty and cannot be resident in a listed tax haven (with the exception of central banks and government agencies or international organisations recognised as such by Portugal). Following Brexit, this exemption will continue to be applicable to UK corporate noteholders;

(ii) gains realised by a non-resident financial institution in connection with swap, forwards and any operations connected with the latter carried out with the Portuguese State. This exemption applies to all non-Portuguese tax resident financial institutions, with the exception of those deemed resident for tax purposes in a listed tax haven or those held in more than 25% of its share capital, directly or indirectly, by Portuguese tax resident companies. Following Brexit, this exemption will continue to be applicable to qualifying UK financial institutions; and

(iii) gains obtained by non-resident financial institutions as a result of repurchase transactions with resident credit institutions. After Brexit, this exemption will continue to be applicable to UK financial institutions.

TAX RAMIFICATIONS FOR OUTBOUND INVESTMENTS

17.9 Portuguese resident companies are taxed on their worldwide income. The Portuguese CIT Code adopts a wide definition of taxable income, and both dividends and capital gains, regardless of where they are obtained or realised, are treated as ordinary business profits and taxed accordingly.

Inbound dividends

17.10 The net accounting profit (as disclosed in the financial statements according to the Portuguese GAAP or IFRS where applicable, adjusted in accordance with the tax rules) of a Portuguese resident company is taxed in Portugal at the standard CIT rate (currently 21%), plus municipal surcharge (at variable rates according to the decision of the municipal bodies, up to 1.5% of the taxable profits) and state surcharge, if applicable,[49] but tax exemption regimes are available.

49 Portuguese tax resident companies may also be subject to a state surcharge of 3%, for a taxable income from EUR 1,500,000.00 to EUR 7,500,000.00, 5% for the taxable income from EUR 7,500,000.00 to EUR 35,000,000.00, and 9% for taxable income exceeding EUR 35,000,000.00.

Dividends distributed by a UK subsidiary to its Portuguese corporate shareholder are treated as ordinary business profits of the latter.

Following Brexit, even though dividends distributed by a UK subsidiary will no longer qualify for the application of the CIT exemption provided for under the EU Parent-Subsidiary Directive, the Portuguese corporate shareholder may still rely on the Portuguese domestic participation exemption regime to benefit from a CIT exemption on inbound dividends from the UK, provided the following criteria are met:[50]

- the Portuguese company holds (directly or indirectly) a minimum of 10% of the share capital or the voting rights of the UK subsidiary;
- such participation is held continuously during the year preceding the distribution of dividends or, if held for less time, there is a commitment to maintain that participation for the necessary time to complete that one-year period;
- the Portuguese tax transparency special regime is not applicable to the Portuguese company; and
- the UK subsidiary is subject to, and not exempt from, a tax similar to the Portuguese CIT which CIT tax rate is not less than 12.6% (ie, 60% of the Portuguese CIT rate currently of 21%).[51]

As such, Brexit shall not impact the domestic participation tax exemption regime applicable in Portugal to dividends distributed by a UK subsidiary to a Portuguese company whose main activity is of a commercial, industrial or agricultural nature.

Nonetheless, Portuguese tax law comprises a special anti-abuse clause which excludes from the scope of application of the Portuguese domestic participation exemption regime any arrangement or series of arrangements which, having been put in place for the main purpose or one of the main purposes of eliminating economic double taxation, are considered not genuine having regard to the relevant facts and circumstances.

Whenever inbound dividends paid by non-resident subsidiaries do not satisfy the conditions for the application of the domestic participation exemption regime, Portugal grants:

---

50 The Portuguese corporate shareholder shall gather (before the submission of its annual CIT return) the documentation that proves that the requirements for the application of this exemption are met (namely a declaration confirmed and certified by the UK tax authorities stating that the subsidiary: (i) is tax resident in the UK as per Article 4 of the double tax treaty concluded between Portugal and the UK, (ii) is subject to and not exempt in the UK from a tax similar to the Portuguese CIT, and (ii) the tax rate applicable to it in the UK is not less than 60% of the Portuguese CIT rate) and keeps such documentation in its records together with other relevant accounting documentation for a ten-year period.

51 It is assumed also that, after Brexit, the UK will not be included in the Portuguese tax havens list and that the double tax treaty concluded between Portugal and the UK will remain in force.

- an ordinary tax credit to eliminate international double taxation, equal to the lower of the foreign tax paid[52] or the Portuguese tax payable on such income. This tax credit is available to both income derived from treaty and non-treaty countries, although, for treaty countries, the credit that may be granted is limited to the amount of tax payable in the source country under the provisions of the treaty in force; and
- an indirect tax credit to eliminate economic international double taxation.

Lastly, Portuguese tax resident entities whose main activity is neither commercial, industrial or agricultural, following Brexit, will no longer be able to exclude from their tax basis 50% of the amount of dividends distributed by a UK subsidiary, as this possibility is only available for dividends distributed by EU subsidiaries (provided the additional requirements set forth in the EU Parent-Subsidiary directive are met).

Capital gains on shareholdings in non-resident companies

17.11 As a rule, capital gains derived by a Portuguese resident company from the sale of a participation (or equity instruments) in a UK resident company are included in its taxable profit. As previously mentioned, the taxable profit of a Portuguese resident company will be taxed in Portugal at the standard CIT rate (currently 21%), plus municipal surcharge (up to 1.5%) and state surcharge, if applicable.

However, Portugal offers a competitive participation exemption regime for capital gains (but also capital losses realised by Portuguese resident companies with the sale of shareholdings and equity instruments in non-resident companies). Provided the same conditions imposed for the application of the participation exemption regime on dividends are verified (as per **17.10** above), these capital gains and losses are not taken into account in determining the taxable profit of the Portuguese corporate shareholder. This exclusion from CIT is not available, though, whenever; (i) the non-resident company is domiciled or incorporated in a listed tax haven, or (ii) when the shares of the non-resident company derive more than 50% of its value, directly or indirectly, from real estate (or partial rights over real estate) located in Portugal that are not used for agricultural, industrial or commercial purposes (other than buying for resale).

Besides these exceptions, the Portuguese participation exemption regime at stake applies equally to capital gains derived from the sale of shares and equity instruments in Portuguese companies as well as in foreign companies (whether

52 The original (or a certified copy) of a document issued by the foreign tax authorities confirming the amount of foreign tax paid may be requested as proof by the Portuguese tax authorities.

they are located in an EU, EEA or third country). As a result, Brexit should have no impact on the tax regime applicable in Portugal to those capital gains.

Note that this regime is also applicable to capital gains on the transfer of shares derived from a non-tax-neutral merger, division, transfer of assets or exchange of shares.

Where the Portuguese corporate shareholder does not meet the requirements to benefit from the participation exemption regime, as previously mentioned, the positive net difference between capital gains and capital losses arising from the transfer of shares in a specific tax year will be taxed as part of ordinary business profit for CIT purposes in the hands of the Portuguese corporate shareholder.

In this respect, we note that under Article 13 of the double tax treaty concluded between Portugal and the UK, the UK has no tax rights over capital gains realised by Portuguese resident companies from the disposal of UK companies' shares (even if those companies' assets are mainly composed of real estate located in the UK) and this distribution of tax rights will not change with the MLI. So even if the UK was to levy a tax over these realised capital gains, Portugal would not grant any foreign tax credit, as such tax would not be in line with the provisions of the double tax treaty concluded between Portugal and the UK.

Permanent establishments

17.12 Following Brexit, the Portuguese head office may continue to opt to exclude from its taxable income the profits and losses attributable to its UK (outbound) permanent establishment.[53]

Nonetheless, the Portuguese head office must immediately pay the CIT due in Portugal upon allocation of (part or all of) its assets to such UK permanent establishment. Such allocation will be deemed as a sale and, after Brexit, it may no longer benefit from a deferral of CIT payment in terms similar to the ones applicable in the case of transfer of residence abroad of a Portuguese company (better explained under **17.16** below). Currently, whenever a Portuguese head office, which has opted to exclude from its taxable income the profits and losses attributable to a permanent establishment, decides to allocate (all or part of) its assets to a permanent establishment located in another EU Member State or in an EEA country bound to administrative cooperation on tax matters (both in terms of exchange of information and collection of taxes) equivalent to the

53 Assuming that, after Brexit, the double tax treaty concluded between Portugal and the UK will remain in force and the UK will not be included in the Portuguese tax havens list. In addition, a UK permanent establishment must continue to be subject to (and not exempt from) an income tax similar to the Portuguese CIT and the effective income tax paid in the UK cannot be lower than 50% of the tax that would be due if the Portuguese corporate income tax rules were to apply.

cooperation established within the EU, the CIT due in Portugal as a result of such allocation can be settled in five annual instalments. Each instalment must amount to one-fifth of the CIT assessed (as in the case of a transfer of residence abroad of a Portuguese company, explained under **17.16** below).

CFC rules

17.13 Brexit will impose additional requirements to avoid the application of the Portuguese CFC regime to UK subsidiaries controlled by Portuguese shareholders.

As an overview, the Portuguese CFC regime[54] establishes that the undistributed profits of a non-resident entity subject to a more favourable tax regime are to be attributed to the Portuguese company having a substantial interest in such entity. In such a case the Portuguese company shall be taxed on the proportionate share of its interest in the non-resident entity. For the purposes of this regime:

- 'Substantial interest' occurs where a Portuguese company holds, directly or indirectly, even if through a proxy, a fiduciary or another interposed person,[55] 25% or more of the share capital, voting rights or rights to income or assets of a non-resident entity (or a 10% stake where more than 50% of the share capital, voting rights or rights to income or assets are owned by a Portuguese resident company); and
- an entity is deemed to be a low-tax entity:
  - if it is resident in a listed tax haven; or
  - if the effective income tax paid is lower than 50% of the tax that would be due if the Portuguese corporate income tax rules were to apply.

The Portuguese CFC regime provides for two safe harbours. As such, even when one of the conditions referred to above is met, the CFC rules on profit attribution will not apply in the following circumstances (not cumulative):

- the sum of income arising from one or more of the following categories of income does not exceed 25% of its total income:
  - royalties or other income derived from intellectual property rights, image rights or similar rights;
  - dividends and income from the sale of shares of capital;

54 It is important to note that CFC rules have recently been amended following the transposition of the EU Anti-Tax Avoidance Directive (ATAD) provisions.

55 The Portuguese CFC regime may apply at any level of the legal structure of a group, ie, it will remain applicable even if non-CFC entities are interposed between the CFC and the Portuguese company having a substantial interest.

- income from financial leasing, income from banking activity, even if not exercised by credit institutions, insurance business or other financial activities carried out with entities with which there are special relations;
- income from billing entities that earn income from commerce and from goods and services purchased and sold to entities with which they have special relations, and that add little or no economic value; and
- interest or other income from capital.

- it is resident in another EU Member State or in an EEA country bound to administrative cooperation on tax matters equivalent to the cooperation established within the EU, provided the Portuguese resident entity proves that the incorporation and functioning of the non-resident entity are based on: (a) valid commercial reasons, and (b) that the entity carries out a business activity (either commercial – including the rendering of services industrial or agricultural activities) using adequate personnel, equipment, assets and facilities.

Whenever CFC rules apply, the undistributed profits of the UK CFC subsidiary will be taxed in the hands of the Portuguese shareholder, together with its remaining taxable income.[56]

Once the CFC profits are distributed up the chain a deduction is granted in order to prevent said income from being taxed twice. In other words, each time the Portuguese shareholder receives an actual dividend distribution from the UK CFC subsidiary, it will deduct from its taxable profits and up to that limit the undistributed dividends imputed in previous years. This corresponds to a 'de-attribution' or a 'reversal of attribution' mechanism, and the law makes it clear that the attribution is merely anticipatory taxation of the final tax due on the profits when they are distributed.

In the wake of Brexit, a Portuguese company holding, directly or indirectly, a substantial interest in a UK-CFC can no longer rely on the EU safe harbour rule to set aside the application of the Portuguese CFC regime; instead, in that particular case, the Portuguese company can only rely on the CFC's type of income safe harbour, where the level of 'protection' is narrower and, as a result, less favourable.

Although it does not seem likely that the UK will be included in the Portuguese tax havens list, Portuguese companies holding a substantial interest in a UK company should confirm whether this remains outside the scope of the Portuguese CFC regime. Also, following Brexit, the UK will no longer be bound by EU rules on state aid. Thus, in aiming to attract foreign investment

56 To note that the allocation/imputation at stake shall be made in the respective tax year and in proportion with the rights over assets held by the Portuguese company in the CFC entity.

as well as strengthen the competitiveness of its economy, the UK may consider the reduction of its CIT rate, something that would not come as a surprise considering that this measure has been discussed in the context of the Brexit referendum.

IMPACT ON CROSS-BORDER GROUP TAX REGIMES

17.14 As per the Portuguese CIT code, Portuguese resident companies which are members of an economic group may opt to be taxed under the special tax regime of group or tax unit taxation (RETGS – '*Regime Especial de Tributação de Grupos de Sociedades*'). RETGS applies when a Portuguese resident company (parent) holds, directly or indirectly (including through a company resident for tax purposes in an EU Member State or in an EEA country,[57] provided those companies are, in turn, held, directly or indirectly, at least in 75% by the Portuguese dominant company), at least 75% of the share capital of other Portuguese resident companies (controlled entities) and as long as such participation grants more than 50% of the voting rights. Besides the fact that controlled Portuguese companies may still be part of economic group taxed in Portugal under the RETGS when held by an EU or EEA resident company (provided some conditions are met in respect to the latter), the Portuguese CIT code also allows a parent (dominant) company resident for tax purposes in an EU Member State or in an EEA country (again, provided some conditions are met in respect to the latter) to apply for the Portuguese RETGS. However, as the RETGS does not allow the tax consolidation to include non-Portuguese resident entities, in such a case, the tax group regime will only apply to the Portuguese resident companies of the group.[58]

The application of the RETGS allows the taxable profits of an economic group to be computed by the dominant company (or by the Portuguese reporting company, where the dominant company is resident in an EU or EEA country) in which case it will correspond to the algebraic sum of the taxable profits and tax losses individually reported by all the Portuguese entities that comprise the corporate group.

Brexit will have a major impact on the application of RETGS to those economic groups in Portugal where the dominant company is resident in the UK or where the Portuguese dominant company holds (some or all) of its participation in the Portuguese controlled companies that are part of a corporate group through

57 An EEA resident company can only be considered for this purpose provided such EEA country is bound to administrative cooperation on tax matters equivalent to the cooperation established within the EU.

58 For that to happen, the group must appoint one of the Portuguese controlled companies that are part of the economic group as the reporting company, being such company responsible for complying in a timely manner with all the tax reporting and payment obligations imposed by this tax regime for its application.

a UK resident company. Considering the RETGS regime as it now stands, following Brexit:

- The shareholdings in Portuguese controlled companies held by a Portuguese dominant company through a UK resident company will no longer be covered by the CIT group taxation regime. This change in the tax group circumstances must be communicated to the Portuguese tax authorities by the end of the third month after the end of the fiscal year in which Brexit takes place. Failure to report in time cancels the application of RETGS to the remaining group companies.
- The group taxation regime ceases to apply to all Portuguese controlled companies where the dominant company is a UK resident company, unless the latter becomes also a controlled company of a new Portuguese dominant company. Again, this situation must be communicated to the Portuguese tax authorities within the same timescale. If the new dominant company fails to report in time, the application of the RETGS to the remaining group companies will cease.

As a result, in the wake of Brexit, the RETGS regime will not only cease to apply for the future to the cases described above but most likely will imply significant changes to economic groups that already exist and are currently covered by RETGS. As such, it is of utmost importance to closely monitor how the Portuguese CIT provisions in this respect will evolve and whether the Portuguese legislator introduces some additional or transitory measures to safeguard the tax decisions already taken by Portuguese economic groups of which UK resident companies are also part (in particular where they are the dominant companies).

TAX RAMIFICATIONS FOR CROSS-BORDER MERGERS, OTHER REORGANISATIONS AND TRANSFERS OF RESIDENCE

Cross-border mergers and other reorganisations

17.15 Certain corporate restructuring operations may be carried out under a principle of tax neutrality for both the companies involved in those operations as well as their shareholders, provided the conditions set out in the EU Merger Directive and transposed to the Portuguese CIT code, are met. However, this principle of tax neutrality is only available to mergers, divisions, partial divisions, transfers of assets and exchange of shares involving companies (and respective partners) resident in the Portuguese territory or in other EU Member States.

As such, following Brexit, it will no longer be possible to carry out tax neutral corporate restructuring operations involving UK resident companies.

Transfer of residence abroad

17.16 The transfer of a Portuguese company's tax residence abroad will trigger exit tax (CIT) in Portugal.[59] The Portuguese exit tax regime was introduced originally in 2006, but it was amended with the Portuguese CIT Reform in 2014 to make it compliant with the CJEU's decisions on this matter. Currently, under Portuguese tax law, the transfer of a company's residence abroad is treated and assimilated to a liquidation procedure (ie, it leads to the termination of activity for CIT purposes) and, thus, is subject to CIT on the positive balance between the market value, at the time of the transfer, and the tax acquisition cost of all the assets as a whole transferred.[60] However, the deemed capital gain realised upon such transfer may be exempt from CIT in Portugal provided the conditions for the application of the Portuguese participation exemption regime are met (see **17.11** above). However, where the Portuguese company decides to transfer its residence to an EU Member State or to a qualifying third country (that is, one with which Portugal has signed a mutual assistance agreement on the recovery of taxes with a scope similar to that provided for in EU Directive 2010/24/EU of 16 March 2010), the CIT due as result of such transfer may be settled in five annual instalment payments, each one of them corresponding to one-fifth of the exit tax assessed.[61]

The temporary transfer of residence to an EU Member State or to a qualifying third country followed (immediately or not) by an exit to the UK, will force the migrating Portuguese company to immediately proceed at once with the payment of the whole amount of exit tax due, as Portuguese tax law has implemented a special anti-abuse provision to tackle this situation.[62]

As a result if, after Brexit, the UK does not conclude with Portugal a mutual assistance agreement on recovery of taxes (or enters into a treaty with the EU that foresees the application of EU Directive 2010/24/EU of 16 March 2010) with a scope similar to that provided for in the applicable EU directive, neither the CIT exemption on the deemed capital gains realised, provided for in the Portuguese participation exemption regime, nor the option of payment by instalments of the exit tax due will be available to:

59 The Portuguese CIT code also sets other cases that will trigger immediate taxation, such as the actual sale of the assets liable to exit tax in Portugal.

60 No taxation shall apply to assets and liabilities that remain allocated to a permanent establishment of the Portuguese migrating company in Portugal upon the envisaged relocation, provided certain conditions and requirements are met.

61 Should the qualifying migrating company opt for the payment by instalments of the exit tax due, interest will be charged at an annual rate of 4.786% (currently), counting from the day following the one in which the deadline to file the company's CIT tax return ends until the moment the tax due is totally paid.

62 The Portuguese CIT code also sets other cases that will trigger immediate taxation, such as the actual sale of the assets liable to exit tax in Portugal.

(i) Portuguese companies migrating their head office to the UK;

(ii) Portuguese permanent establishments on the transfer of all or part of their assets and liabilities to their UK head offices or to UK permanent establishments, as a direct result or not of the termination of their activities in Portugal, respectively;

(iii) Portuguese resident companies when allocating assets and liabilities to their UK permanent establishments, provided the Portuguese head offices have elected the option to exclude from their taxable income the profits and losses attributable to the UK permanent establishments.

After Brexit, the deemed capital gain realised upon transfer of the tax residence is included in the CIT return of the tax year in which such transfer takes place and the CIT due, if any, must be paid immediately for the whole amount.

Inbound transfer of residence

17.17 Law no 32/2019 of 3 May 2019 (which amended the Portuguese CIT code in line with the EU ATAD provisions) has introduced specific provisions dealing with the tax base of the assets held by a foreign company transferring its legal seat and/or place of effective management to Portuguese territory. Under the Portuguese CIT code, in an inbound transfer of residence, the tax cost of the assets held by the foreign company,[63] which will be considered for the computation of taxable capital gains in the case of their future sale or in the case of (re)transfer of residence abroad, will equal their book value at the departing state, provided this does not exceed the assets' market value at the date of transfer. Current and non-current liabilities of a foreign company that transfers its residence to Portugal will be accounted also according to their respective book value.[64]

Whenever the foreign company making the move originally had its legal seat and/or place of effective management in an EU Member State, it may consider as tax cost in Portugal of its current and non-current assets and liabilities the deemed sales price considered by the departing EU State for the purposes of calculating the eventual exit tax due there. Following Brexit, a UK company can no longer take advantage of this step-up regime. As a result, the inbound transfer of residence of an originally UK company to Portugal may entail double taxation whenever the tax base under the general CIT regime of its assets and liabilities is lower than the exit tax base in the UK.

63 The assets at stake may not, at the date of inbound transfer of residence of a foreign company, be attributable to a permanent establishment located in Portugal of such foreign company.

64 This regime also applies in the case of a transfer of a current or non-current asset and/or liability attributable to a foreign permanent establishment of a Portuguese company to its head office in Portugal.

OTHER

Convention considerations

17.18 No relevant impact is expected following Brexit. None of the double tax treaties concluded between Portugal and non-EU Member States has a limitation of benefits (LoB) clause safeguarding the application of the treaty benefits whenever the Ultimate Beneficial Owner (hereinafter the UBO) is resident for tax purposes in another EU Member State (as it has been agreed in double tax treaties signed by other EU Member States). In fact, the scope of all LoB clauses included in the double tax treaties signed by Portugal is quite narrow and exclude from treaty benefits all companies ultimately owned by non-Portuguese tax residents: either they are EU or non-EU residents so, in this context, Brexit should have no impact.

Corporate considerations

17.19 As a general rule, corporate expenses are deductible for CIT purposes only to the extent they are necessary to generate taxable income and are properly documented. However, special rules apply that further limit the deductibility of certain expenses. In this respect, the Portuguese CIT code sets out that contributions to pension funds made by the employer on behalf of its employees are, provided certain conditions are met and up to a certain annual limit, regarded as deductible costs for CIT purposes. If, at some point in time, the conditions for the application of this regime are no longer met, the employer must add to the CIT due in that fiscal year the CIT that otherwise would have been due had the costs related to the contributions made to a pension fund not been considered as a cost deductible for CIT purposes (inflated by 10% for each year that has passed since the fiscal year in which the contributions at stake were claimed as a tax deductible cost). This CIT 'recap' penalty rule does not apply, however, whenever the employer transfers the contributions originally made, on behalf of its employees, to a specific pension fund managed by an institution for occupational retirement provision compliant with the EU Directive 2003/41/C. In the wake of Brexit, UK institutions for occupational retirement provision may no longer qualify for this exclusion.

After Brexit, a UK entity which is part in a multinational enterprise group required to file a Country-by-Country (CbC) Report for each fiscal year, containing financial and tax information for each of its entities by country or jurisdiction, may no longer be designated as the reporting entity, within the EU group of entities and in their representation. Moreover, after Brexit, a UK entity may no longer automatically act as a substitute ultimate parent entity in such a group of which a Portuguese resident company is part. Only if certain requirements are met may the UK company act as such and, as a result, will the Portuguese resident company be exempt from the CbC report filing obligation.

After Brexit, a Portuguese company may adopt (or continue to adopt) a tax year different from the calendar year (ie, the standard tax year in Portugal) in order to be in line with the tax year of its UK corporate shareholder.

Lastly, following Brexit, those UK resident entities (either companies or permanent establishments) that continue to hold a Portuguese-situs asset (either real estate or a participation in a Portuguese resident company) and/or continue to obtain Portuguese-sourced income must appoint a tax representative in Portugal (a company or an individual resident for tax purposes in Portugal).[65] The same obligation will fall on UK resident companies appointed as board members of Portuguese resident companies.

Considerations for individuals

17.20 Portugal, as an EU country, has implemented the EU Merger Directive and, in the case of Portuguese individual shareholders, grants, provided certain conditions are met, a deferral from taxation of the capital gains realised upon a share-for-share tax neutral transaction. As such, taxation of the capital gains realised at the level of individual shareholders with the transfer of the shares in the acquired company to the acquiring company is deferred until they dispose of the new shares received in the acquiring company or until they transfer their tax residence abroad (see the following paragraph), whichever occurs first. For this regime to apply two prerequisites must be jointly met: (i) both the acquired company and the acquiring company must be considered resident for tax purposes in Portugal or in another EU Member State; and (ii) the shareholders of the acquiring company must be resident in Portugal or in an EU or third country, but in the latter cases provided the acquiring company is resident for tax purposes in Portugal. In addition, the Portuguese tax authorities have issued a tax ruling confirming that an exchange of shares can only be tax neutral from a Portuguese point of view provided a link with Portugal is maintained once the exchange is concluded, as only such a link will safeguard the taxing rights of Portugal over the capital gains deferred. An appropriate link may be either the acquiring company, where it is resident for tax purposes in Portugal, or, if that is not the case, the Portuguese tax resident individual shareholders. Thus, the Portuguese tax authorities only grant tax neutrality in the following exchanges of shares: (a) between a Portuguese or EU acquired company and a Portuguese acquiring company, in both cases regardless of where the individual shareholders are considered to be resident for tax purposes (Portugal, EU Member State or third country); or (b) between a Portuguese acquired company and an EU acquiring company, provided the individual shareholders are considered to be resident for tax purposes in Portugal. Either way, following Brexit, capital gains realised by Portuguese

65 Duties of the Portuguese tax representative entail being the official link between the represented taxpayer and the Portuguese tax authorities, as well as receiving official communications from the authorities regarding the represented taxpayer's tax issues.

individual shareholders upon the exchange of shares involving UK resident companies (either as acquired company or acquiring company) will be subject to tax in Portugal and no tax deferral will be allowed.

The Personal Income Tax (PIT) code also sets out a principle of tax neutrality for mergers and divisions carried out by Portuguese tax resident individuals involving companies resident in the Portuguese territory and/or in other EU Member States. As such, following Brexit, it will no longer be possible for Portuguese tax resident individuals to benefit from a tax deferral on capital gains realised on mergers and divisions involving UK resident companies.

There is no exit tax for individuals abandoning Portuguese tax residence, except for shareholders who have been involved in tax neutral corporate reorganisations where the respective capital gains taxation has been deferred. Current Portuguese exit tax rules for individuals are in line with the CJEU case law so those individual shareholders involved in tax neutral corporate reorganisations transferring their tax residence outside of Portugal to an EU Member State or to an EEA country (that has entered into an administrative assistance agreement for tax matters with Portugal) may benefit (upon express request) from a payment deferral of the tax due on the deemed capital gains realised upon exit.[66]

There is no payment deferral option available to individual shareholders involved in tax neutral corporate reorganisations transferring their tax residence outside of Portugal to a third country. As such, after Brexit, those individual shareholders transferring their tax residence outside of Portugal to the UK will be immediately liable to PIT in Portugal on their deferred taxation capital gains. The temporary transfer of residence to an EU Member State or to a qualifying EEA country followed (immediately or not) by an exit to the UK will also trigger exit tax in Portugal, as Portuguese tax law has implemented a special anti-abuse provision to tackle this type of arrangement.

Portuguese legislation provides, under certain conditions, for a (total or partial) exclusion from PIT in Portugal on Portuguese-situs real estate capital gains realised by Portuguese tax resident individuals. In general terms, this total or partial PIT exemption applies if the real estate being sold is the individual's primary residence and the sale's proceeds are reinvested (within 36 months counting from or 24 months prior to the moment of sale) in the acquisition, improvement or construction of another primary residence in Portugal or in an EU Member State or in an EEA country that has entered into an administrative assistance agreement for tax matters with Portugal.

After Brexit, a reinvestment in the acquisition, improvement or construction of a residence in the UK will no longer be eligible for the application of the total or partial PIT exemption regime in Portugal on Portuguese-sourced real estate capital gains.

66 Provided specific tax reporting obligations are complied with.

Other expected PIT consequences of Brexit for individuals are:

- individual UK tax residents may no longer opt (provided the income obtained in Portugal in a specific year corresponds to at least 90% of their total income obtained worldwide) to be taxed in Portugal as if they were resident for Portuguese tax purposes, as this option is only available to individual tax residents of an EU Member State or an EEA country that has entered into an exchange of information agreement with Portugal concerning tax matters;
- even when Portuguese-situs real estate capital gains do not correspond to 90% or more of the worldwide income obtained, individual tax residents of an EU Member State or an EEA country that has entered into an exchange of information agreement with Portugal concerning tax matters may, nonetheless, opt for such income to be taxed in Portugal in accordance with the rules applicable to the individuals resident for tax purposes in Portugal (meaning taxed on 50% of the capital gain realised at PIT progressive tax rates plus surcharge, if applicable[67]) instead of being taxed on such capital gains realised at a 28% flat tax rate.[68] Once again, following Brexit, this option should no longer be available to UK tax resident individuals; and
- regarding Portuguese-sourced employment income, non-Portuguese tax resident individuals are liable to tax in Portugal at a final withholding tax rate of 25%, provided Portugal's taxing rights over such income are not overridden by the applicable double tax treaty. Individual tax residents of an EU Member State or an EEA country that has entered into an exchange of information agreement with Portugal concerning tax matters may, however, request a (total or partial) reimbursement of the tax withheld in Portugal (25% of the gross income) on the amount that exceeds the tax bill that would otherwise be levied had the Portuguese PIT progressive tax rates applied to the individual's worldwide income.[69] After Brexit, this option will no longer be available to UK tax resident individuals.

Regarding social security contributions, as a general rule they are due in the country where the employment activity is carried out. However, according to the European regulation (EC) No. 883/2004 (as amended by the EC No. 465/2012) on the coordination of social security systems, within the EU, EEA State or Switzerland, expatriates may continue to make social security

---

67 The general PIT rates vary from 14.5% to 48%. The maximum tax rate applies to taxable income exceeding EUR 80,882. An additional solidarity surcharge of 2.5% applies to income between EUR 80,000 and EUR 250,000. The part of income that exceeds EUR 250,000 will, in turn, be taxed at the rate of 5%.

68 This election only makes sense where the taxable capital gain realised with the sale of Portuguese-situs real estate falls below EUR 24,000.

69 This election only makes sense where the individual's worldwide income falls below EUR 15,000.

contributions to the social security system of their home (departure) country, being, as a result, excused from making contributions to the host-country social security system (ie, the country where the employment activity is actually carried out).

This special regime applies whenever an individual is working in one Member State for a company upon which he usually depends for employment and is assigned by that company to work in another Member State. In such a case, the individual will still be subject to the social security law of the first Member State, provided the assignment period does not exceed 24 months (although this deadline may be extended for up to five years) and where the assignment is not conceived for the replacement of another employer that has ended his own assignment period. Nevertheless, the application of this regime requires that the assigned employee is still subject to the authority and direction of the employing company.

In the wake of Brexit, former UK tax resident individuals moving to Portugal, as well as former Portuguese tax resident individuals moving to the UK, in both cases as a result of an employment assignment agreement, may no longer rely on the EU regulation mentioned above as the UK social security legislation will no longer be covered by it. Portugal might sign in the future a bilateral agreement on social security matters with the UK, to become effective after the Brexit transition period ends. However, until then, expats moving between Portugal and the UK may be covered concurrently by the social security legislation of the host country (where they are carrying out their activity) as well as of the home/departure country (where the employer is located). This situation may potentially lead to an overlapping of social security base/coverage and, as a result, end up in the duplication of mandatory payments of social security contributions. However, Portugal has unilaterally adopted in its domestic legislation a regime for coordinating its own social security system with the social security system of non-EU or EEA countries with which Portugal has not yet concluded a bilateral agreement on social security matters. Therefore, during a 12-month period, no social security contributions will be levied in Portugal to: (a) UK tax resident employees working from Portugal, provided they prove they remain subject to social security contributions in the UK, and (b) Portuguese tax resident employees working from the UK, if they become subject to social security contributions in the UK.

Portugal also offers a special PIT regime for those individuals who wish to establish either permanent residence (eg, High-Net-Worth Individuals or retired people) or temporary residence in Portugal (eg, expats) and, as a result, become Portuguese tax residents:[70] the so-called non-habitual tax resident regime (NHR). Under this special PIT regime, expats may benefit from:

70 Under the Portuguese PIT code as well as under the applicable double tax treaty. In addition, individuals that wish to benefit from the NHR regime must not have been taxed in Portugal as residents in the five preceding tax years.

- a 20% flat PIT rate on Portuguese sourced employment or self-employment income, if derived from high value-added activities performed in Portugal as defined by law[71];
- PIT exemption on employment income obtained outside of Portugal provided such income is effectively taxed in the source state, as per the provisions of the applicable double tax treaty; and
- PIT exemption on self-employment income obtained outside of Portugal if such income is attributable to a permanent establishment existing in the source state and may be taxed in that country.

The NHR regime also includes a set of rules dealing with foreign sourced passive income (such as interest, dividends, rents, etc), which, provided some conditions are met, is exempt from PIT in Portugal.

An individual who is granted NHR status in Portugal acquires the right to be taxed as such for a period of 10 consecutive years, provided that in each year of application of the regime the individual is considered tax resident in Portugal.

This special PIT regime applies irrespective of the nationality of the individual, as well as regardless of the origin country. As such, the NHR regime will remain applicable to those UK nationals or former UK tax residents wishing to redomicile to Portugal.

It should be noted that the NHR regime is a tax regime and not an immigration permit. Therefore, after the Brexit transition period, UK nationals wishing to reside in Portugal and take advantage of the NHR tax regime must get an appropriate immigration visa that permits them to live and/or work in Portugal (the EU nationals' visa exemption will cease to apply as the freedom of movement of individuals is restricted to EU nationals).

Lastly, UK tax-resident individuals after Brexit who continue to keep a Portuguese-situs asset and/or continue to obtain Portuguese-sourced income must appoint a tax representative in Portugal (a company or an individual resident for tax purposes in Portugal)[72]. The same obligation will fall on UK resident individuals appointed as board members of Portuguese resident companies. The exemption from appointing a tax representative in those circumstances is exclusively granted to tax residents of EU Member States.

---

71 The list of 'high added value activities' includes, eg, architects, engineers, artists, actors, musicians, auditors, medical doctors, computer technology and data processing activities, Portuguese branch legal representatives and directors, provided it can be proved they are able to legally bind the Portuguese company.

72 See fn 65.

Chapter 18

Spain

Ramón Tejada Fernandez

INTRODUCTION

18.1 The purpose of this chapter is to analyse the main consequences, from a Spanish tax perspective (and mainly from a Spanish corporate income tax perspective), of the UK's withdrawal from the European Union (EU).

The analysis of this chapter is based on the following facts and assumptions:

- After Brexit, the UK will be a third country and will not join the European Economic Area (hereinafter, EEA).
- During the transition period (in theory comprising the period extending from 1 February 2020 until 31 December 2020, with a possible extension of up to two years to be agreed upon before 1 July 2020) EU law remains to be fully applicable to and in the UK. Therefore, the EU will treat the UK as if it were a Member State (which mainly entails that the UK remains in the European Customs Union and in the Single Market with all four freedoms and EU policies temporarily still in force). However, the UK ceases to participate in the institutions, agencies and bodies of the EU as well as in the EU decision-making process and governance structures.
- The UK will keep being white listed (ie, listed among the states providing for the effective exchange of information) due to the fact that, even if it is eventually agreed that the provisions of the pre-existing Directive on Administrative Cooperation (DAC) cease to be applicable after the transition period, the UK will still be bound by the provision for the exchange of tax information incorporated into the UK-Spain double tax treaty (hereinafter, DTT).

TAX RAMIFICATIONS FOR INBOUND INVESTMENTS

Outbound dividends

18.2 In general, according to Article 25, section 1, paragraph f) of Royal Legislative Decree 5/2004, outbound dividends paid to non-resident corporate shareholders are subject to a 19% WHT.

Nonetheless, according to the Spanish provisions implementing the Parent Subsidiary Directive, a WHT exemption is applicable in relation to dividend payments made to a company or entity (including pension plans and collective investment institutions) liable to corporate income tax in another EU or EEA Member State, as long as certain requirements are met (among others, a minimum participation of 5% or an acquisition value exceeding 20 million euros, and a minimum one-year holding period). This exemption will no longer be applicable in relation to dividend payments made to UK companies.

Notwithstanding the above, under the provisions of the UK-Spain DTT, dividend payments made by a Spanish subsidiary to its UK corporate shareholders will remain exempt from Spanish WHT after Brexit, insofar as a minimum participation of 10% is held and the Spanish company distributing the dividends is not a real estate investment vehicle. This exemption is also applicable to repatriation of profits from a Spanish Branch into the UK headquarters as long as the branch profit tax is not allowed by the UK-Spain DTT as detailed in **18.6** below.

Dividend payments made by a Spanish subsidiary to its UK corporate shareholders, whenever the aforementioned corporate shareholder holds a participation smaller than 10% in the Spanish company, will be subject to a 10% WHT, as long as the beneficial owner of the dividends is indeed a resident of the UK (if that was not the case, taxation at source would not be limited according to the UK-Spain DTT). However, where the Spanish company distributing the dividends is a real estate investment vehicle (ie, the Spanish REITs known as *Sociedades Cotizadas Anónimas de Inversión en el Mercado Inmobiliario* or SOCIMI under Spanish legislation), WHT amounts to 15% of the gross amount of the dividends.

The domestic WHT exemption that applies in relation to dividend payments made to pension funds set up in another EU or EEA Member State (Article 14, section 1, paragraph k) of Royal Legislative Decree 5/2004) will no longer apply to pension funds set up in the UK. However, under the UK-Spain DTT provisions, UK pension plans are, in any case (ie, regardless of minimum participation percentage and minimum holding period), exempt from WHT on dividend payments arising from Spain.

A similar partial exemption (only 1% of the outbound dividends would be taxed in Spain) is applicable to dividends collected by UCITS resident in the EEA, which will no longer be applicable to UK mutual funds or similar investment vehicles. However, it should be noted that there have been some jurisprudential precedents confirming the application of the Freedom of capital movements to sustain the application of equal treatment to non-EU funds as long as they may be considered 'similar' to EU investment funds.

To sum up, only the following UK taxpayers will be impacted by Brexit: (i) a UK company (including a collective investment institution) receiving dividends from a Spanish company in which the former company participates in a percentage lower than 10% but higher than 5%, which will be subject to a 10% WHT instead of being exempt; and (ii) UK companies receiving dividends from a Spanish SOCIMI (regardless of participation percentage), which will be subject to a 15% WHT.

Outbound interest

18.3 Interest paid to non-resident companies is subject to a 19% WHT.

Nonetheless, under domestic law, interest paid to UK companies or to UK permanent establishments (PE) of residents in other EU States, as residents in a EU Member State, is currently exempt from taxation (WHT) in Spain. As a consequence of Brexit, the domestic exemption will no longer be applicable to interest payments made to UK residents.

Notwithstanding the above, the UK-Spain DTT provides for exclusive taxation, in the UK, of interest payments made from Spain to UK residents (either individuals or companies), as long as the UK residents are the beneficial owners of the interest payments (that is, as long as the UK residents economically benefit from the interest payments and are able to freely determine their use).

As regards permanent establishments, the current widespread interpretation is that, instead of the DTT corresponding to the permanent establishment, the DTT between Spain and the country of residence of the parent company is applicable. Therefore, Spanish-source interest payments to UK permanent establishments of residents in other EU States would not be covered by either the UK-Spain DTT or by the domestic exemption (given that they would be deemed payments to a non-EU Member State), which after Brexit could lead to effective taxation of those interest payments under the corresponding DTT.

Interest payments encompass income arising from public values, bonds and debentures. On the other hand, interest on arrears is not deemed to be interest payment for UK-Spain DTT purposes.

Therefore, the UK's withdrawal from the EU will not alter the taxation of interest payments made from Spain to UK residents, insofar as the UK-Spain DTT provisions will continue to be fully applicable. However, taxation of interest payments made from Spain to UK permanent establishments of residents in other EU States may indeed vary, although it cannot be dismissed that the UK and the EU may eventually reach an agreement in order to avoid deviation from the current tax treatment.

Outbound royalties

18.4 In general, according to Article 25, section 1, paragraph a) of Royal Legislative Decree 5/2004, outbound royalties paid to non-resident corporations are subject to 24% WHT. However, reduced WHT rates (19%) are applicable whenever the beneficiary is resident in another EU or EEA Member State. Brexit would automatically entail the application of the general 24% WHT to royalties paid by Spanish residents to residents in the UK.

Nevertheless, up till now, royalties received by UK residents and originating in Spanish territory have been exempt under domestic legislation (Article 14, section 1, paragraph m) of Royal Legislative Decree 5/2004), insofar as the Spanish company paying the royalties and the UK company receiving them could be considered related parties (25% holding between them or a third company holding a 25% stake in both of them) and a minimum one-year holding period is fulfilled.

The exemption available according to the Spanish domestic provisions will no longer be applicable.

Nevertheless, UK-Spain DTT provisions (in particular, Article 12) currently ensure that royalties arising from Spain and being collected by UK residents, as long as those residents are indeed the beneficial owners of the royalties, can only be taxed in the UK, even in cases where the intervening parties are not actually related. The exception to this general rule is whenever related parties agree on higher-than-market-value remuneration, in which case the excess over the previously mentioned market value can be taxed in Spain as well.

Therefore, Spanish-origin royalties obtained by UK residents are currently not taxed in Spain (unless, as previously mentioned, there is excessive remuneration among related parties) and, even after Brexit, would continue to be exempt under the UK-Spain DTT.

Capital gains on shareholdings in resident companies

18.5 Under the current domestic legislation, capital gains obtained by residents in another EU or EEA Member State would be taxed in Spain (at a 19% WHT) exclusively in the following instances:

(i) Capital gains derived from the transfer of shareholdings in Spanish resident companies whose main assets are immovable property located within Spanish territory.

(ii) Capital gains obtained by non-resident individuals who, in any given moment within the previous year, held a stake of 25% or higher in the resident company whose shares are being transferred.

(iii) Capital gains obtained by non-resident companies in cases where the shareholding did not fulfil the requirements set out by *Article 21* of the *Corporate Income Tax Law* in order to be exempt (minimum participation of 5% or an acquisition value exceeding 20 million euros, minimum one-year holding period, minimum taxation)

However, the UK-Spain DTT stipulates (Article 13) that, in cases of UK transferors, only the gains previously mentioned in section (i) can be taxed in Spain.

For their part, capital gains arising from the transfer of immovable property located in Spanish territory are taxed at a 19% rate, with a previous 3% WHT being retained by the acquirer.

Therefore, Brexit should not impact taxation of capital gains in the following sense:

- Capital gains arising from the transfer either of immovable property located within Spanish territory or of shareholdings in resident companies whose main assets are immovable property located within Spanish territory will continue to be taxed at a 19% WHT.
- Capital gains arising from the transfer of movable property (including shareholdings other than the ones mentioned in the paragraph above) will still be exempt under the UK–Spain DTT provisions.

Permanent establishments

18.6 No significant differences arise as a consequence of Brexit. However, the possibility of requesting the deferral (until a subsequent transfer to a third party) of tax payment due as a result of the relocation to another EU or EEA Member State of assets attached to a Spanish PE will no longer be available in respect of relocation to the UK.

Currently, given that the UK is a Member State of the EU, repatriation of income obtained by a PE in Spain to its UK parent company is not subject to the supplementary 19% taxation (branch profit tax) foreseen by Article 19, section 2 of Royal Legislative Decree 5/2004. After Brexit, the supplementary 19% taxation will still not be applicable due to the fact that Spain and the UK have a DTT in force which does not foresee the taxation of income repatriation by a PE.

Other

18.7 As a general rule, and notwithstanding the particular treaty provisions previously referred to regarding dividends, interest payments, royalties and capital gains, income obtained by a resident in the UK will no longer be taxed at a 19% rate after Brexit (reduced rate only applicable to residents in another EU Member State), but instead a 24% rate will be applicable. However, as long as the UK-Spain DTT remains in force, more beneficial rates may apply in respect of certain categories of income.

Post-Brexit, the taxable base in cases of residents in the UK (without a PE in Spanish territory) will not include those expenses envisioned by Article 24, section 6 of Royal Legislative Decree 5/2004 (basically, expenses directly related to the income obtained by the non-resident in Spain, an inextricable economic link between those expenses and the economic activity carried out in Spanish territory being necessary).

According to the *Spanish Corporate Income Tax Law*, contributions made by promoters of pension plans to labour retirement institutions authorised or registered in another Member State are deductible expenses. After Brexit, contributions made to UK institutions will no longer be considered deductible expenses.

Regarding individuals, the following two additional effects emanate from the withdrawal of the UK from the EU:

- Individuals resident in the UK will no longer be able to opt to be taxed under the domestic personal income tax legislation applicable to resident individuals. Instead, taxation will mandatorily be under the non-residents income tax legislation. Formerly, UK tax residents were allowed to apply personal income tax rules (in theory, only applicable to individuals who are deemed to be tax residents in Spain) to assess their non-residents income tax liability, as long as any of the following requisites were duly met:
    - At least 75% of the total income (ie, within Spain and abroad) obtained by the UK tax resident corresponds to employment income and earnings from economic activities carried out in Spain and such income has been effectively taxed under non-residents income tax.
    - Income obtained in Spain during the fiscal year is lower than 90% of the personal and family allowance that would have been applicable if the individual had been subject to personal income tax in Spain and such income has been effectively taxed under non-residents income tax. Additionally, income obtained outside of Spain during the same fiscal year must also be lower than 90% of the aforementioned personal and family allowance.
- Capital gains realised by individuals resident in the UK from the sale of their habitual abode in Spain will no longer be exempt even where there is reinvestment in order to acquire a new habitual residence.

TAX RAMIFICATIONS FOR OUTBOUND INVESTMENTS

Inbound dividends

18.8 No differences effectively arise from the implementation of Brexit in connection with corporate income tax and personal income tax.

Dividends paid by UK resident companies to Spanish resident companies are subject to Spanish corporate income tax at the hands of the payee (a 25% rate is applicable in fiscal year 2020). Nevertheless, the proportion of dividends that are subject to tax in Spain may be reduced by the following exemptions:

- Full exemption (100%) if all the following conditions are met:
  - — The Spanish parent company has at least a 5% shareholding in the UK resident subsidiary distributing the dividends (or, by default, an acquisition price that exceeds EUR 20 million). This 5% shareholding requirement must be satisfied in respect of indirect subsidiaries in instances where the UK direct subsidiary derives a percentage higher than 70% of its income from dividends and capital gains from the transfer of shareholdings (ie, when the direct subsidiary is a holding company), unless the indirect subsidiaries prepare consolidated accounting statements alongside the direct UK subsidiary.

    Notwithstanding the above, the minimum shareholding in the indirect subsidiary will not be required if it can be duly proven that the dividends and capital gains obtained by the UK direct subsidiary have in fact been included in the latter's taxable base, without the possibility of applying any type of exemption regime or double taxation tax credit;
  - — The shareholding has been kept for a minimum period of one year (although, if this condition has not been fulfilled at the time of dividend distribution, it can be satisfied later). Whenever the shares were previously owned by companies within the same group of corporations (not necessarily a tax group), the holding period will include the previous owner/-s as well;
  - — The UK resident subsidiary has been taxed, and not exempted, from taxation under a corporate income tax similar to Spanish corporate income tax at a minimum nominal tax rate of 10% in the year to which the dividend distribution corresponds, regardless of the application of any kind of exemption, allowance, reduction or tax credit. Even disregarding that the UK tax rate is currently 19% and therefore above 10%, since the UK has signed a DTT with Spain, this requirement is in any case considered to be fulfilled. As in the case of the minimum holding percentage, when the direct subsidiary is a holding company, the sufficient taxation condition

must also be satisfied at the level of the indirect or second-level subsidiaries.

- If any of these conditions are not duly met, dividends are fully subject to corporate income tax in Spain. However, when the sufficient taxation requisite is the one requisite not being fulfilled, tax credits are available (with limitations) under Spanish domestic corporate income tax legislation in order to avoid taxation at the level of the subsidiary distributing the dividends and at the level of the Spanish parent company receiving those same dividends.
- Any WHT borne at source by a Spanish-resident company can be credited as long as the Spanish tax corresponding to the foreign income is equal or higher than the foreign WHT to be credited.
- The aforementioned exemption and tax credits are not dependent upon the UK being a member of the EU. Therefore, as previously mentioned, the impact of Brexit on inbound dividends is non-existent.

Capital gains on shareholdings in non-resident companies

18.9 No differences arise directly due to Brexit for corporate investors, although there might be some minor differences for individual investors as described below.

Capital gains from the sale of shares in UK resident companies made by Spanish resident companies are also subject to Spanish corporate income tax at the hands of the transferor (a 25% rate is applicable in fiscal year 2020). Nevertheless, the proportion of capital gains that is subject to tax in Spain may be reduced by the following exemptions:

- Full exemption (100%) if all the following conditions are met:
  - — The Spanish parent company has at least a 5% shareholding in the UK resident subsidiary whose shares are being transferred (or, by default, an acquisition price that exceeds EUR 20 million). This 5% shareholding requisite must be satisfied in respect of indirect subsidiaries in instances where the UK direct subsidiary derives a percentage higher than 70% of its income from dividends and capital gains from the transfer of shareholdings (ie, when the direct subsidiary is a holding company), unless the indirect subsidiaries prepare consolidated accounting statements alongside the direct UK subsidiary.

    In cases where only some of the indirect subsidiaries met the percentage, holding period and taxation requirements, the exemption is only applicable: (i) to the part of the capital gain arising from the net increase of benefits not distributed by those indirect subsidiaries meeting the taxation requirement, and (ii) to the part of the capital gain not arising from the net increase of non-distributed benefits that can be allocated to those indirect subsidiaries meeting the taxation requirement.

Notwithstanding the above, the minimum shareholding in the indirect subsidiary will not be required if it can be duly proven that the dividends and capital gains obtained by the UK direct subsidiary have in fact been included in the latter's taxable base, without the possibility of applying any type of exemption regime or double taxation tax credit;

- The shareholding has been kept for a minimum period of one year (unlike the position regarding dividends, this period must have been fulfilled at the time of the transfer of the shares). Whenever the shares were previously owned by companies within the same group of corporations (not necessarily a tax group), the holding period will include the previous owner/-s as well;

- The UK resident subsidiary has been taxed, and not exempted, from taxation under a corporate income tax similar to Spanish corporate income tax at a minimum nominal tax rate of 10% in the year to which the transfer of shares corresponds, regardless of the application of any kind of exemption, allowance, reduction or tax credit. This requirement must be met not only in the year when the transfer takes places, but every year the shares were owned by the transferor prior to the transfer.

  Even disregarding that the UK tax rate is currently 19% and therefore above 10%, since the UK has signed a DTT with Spain, this requirement can in any case considered to be fulfilled. As in the case of the minimum holding percentage, when the direct subsidiary is a holding company, the sufficient taxation condition must also be satisfied at the level of the indirect or second-level subsidiaries.

For the determination of capital gains derived from the sale by a Spanish resident individual of shares in the capital of a UK company, the following special rules would be no longer applicable after Brexit:

- The period under which the acquisition of the same securities will prevent the computation of any capital loss derived from homogenous securities will be one year even if the shares are listed in the UK, since the two-month period is only applicable to securities traded in EU exchanges.

- The special rules for the determination of the taxable income of non-listed securities will be applicable to shares traded in the UK stock markets.

- The distribution of share premium or capital reductions will not reduce the tax basis of the investment into UK listed shares since the 'deemed dividend' rule applies to shares that are not traded in EU exchanges.
- Investments into UK mutual funds would no longer be considered as EU UCITS and consequently the general rule applicable to EU funds (deferral of income) will not be applicable. A case by case analysis will be needed to conclude if the UK fund is subject to transparency/flow-through/attribution of income.

Permanent establishments abroad

18.10 There will be no difference in the post-Brexit taxation of Spanish permanent establishments located in the UK.

CFC rules

18.11 The *Spanish Corporate Income Tax Law* incorporates, in *Article 100*, CFC rules in order to ensure taxation in Spain (at the level of the Spanish tax resident shareholders who hold, by themselves or alongside related parties, at least 50% of the stake in the non-resident company) of income (mainly, certain categories of passive income such as income arising from immovable property, dividends, interest payments, and royalties) obtained within Spanish territory by companies who are tax resident in low taxation jurisdictions.

In this regard, jurisdictions are deemed to be of low taxation in cases where taxation is lower than 75% of the tax rate that would have been implemented under the Spanish corporate income tax legislation (ie, jurisdictions with nominal tax rates lower than 18.75%).

Whenever the non-resident entity lacks the corresponding personal and material resources structure, the Spanish CFC rules enable the taxation, at the level of the Spanish tax resident shareholders, of the entirety of the income obtained in Spain by the non-resident company.

On the other hand, when the non-resident entity residing in a low taxation jurisdiction does have the necessary personal and material resources, only the following categories of income are assigned to the shareholders:

- Income from immovable property (either urban or rural), unless the assets are employed for the performance of an economic activity or the rights to use have been transferred to a non-resident company.
- Income arising from stake held in any category of entity or from financing granted (ie, dividends and interest payments).
- Income resulting from capitalisation and insurance transactions.

- Income derived from intellectual and industrial property, technical assistance and image rights.
- Income from derivative financial instruments.

However, Spanish CFC rules do not apply in respect of income obtained in Spain by non-resident entities that are in turn tax resident in another EU Member State, as long as the non-resident entity has been incorporated and operates under valid economic reasons. Before the withdrawal finally takes place, companies resident in the UK (unless they have not been incorporated or do not operate under valid economic reasons) can benefit from this exception to the application of the CFC rules foreseen in *Article 100* of the *Spanish Corporate Income Tax Law.*

After Brexit, companies resident in the UK will no longer be exempt from the application of the aforementioned CFC rules. Therefore, the pertinent income (either the entirety of the income obtained in Spanish territory by the company resident in the UK or only the passive income) would be correspondingly allocated to the shareholders resident in Spain if the rest of the conditions are satisfied.

The mandatory application of CFC rules to companies resident in the UK increases in relevance if the UK nominal tax rate were to be reduced below 18.75% in future fiscal years.

Other

18.12 The *Spanish Corporate Income Tax Law* permits a reduction of taxes (*patent box* incentive) due in respect of income obtained by a Spanish company from the granting of licences to use patents, designs, patterns, plans, formulae, secret procedures and information regarding industrial, commercial and scientific developments (ie, royalties).

To qualify, one of the prerequisites is that the transferee resides in a jurisdiction not deemed a tax haven for Spanish corporate income tax purposes. However, where it is considered a tax haven and it is located within the EU, the reduction can nevertheless be applied (subject to the fulfilment of the other conditions). This is currently the situation for Gibraltar, territory considered a tax haven by the Spanish Tax Authorities.

The withdrawal of the UK (and, hence, Gibraltar) from the EU thus negates this concession for any transferee who is tax resident in Gibraltar. Notwithstanding the foregoing, it should be monitored whether the International Tax Agreement regarding Gibraltar signed between Spain and the UK on 4 March 2019, which includes a provision for the exchange of tax information, is considered sufficient for the removal of Gibraltar from the Spanish tax haven list.

Additionally, the *Spanish Corporate Income Tax Law* foresees the application of a tax credit with respect to research, development and technological innovation activities. This tax credit consists of: (i) 25% of the expenses incurred during the corresponding fiscal year (12% for technological innovation expenses), and (ii) 8% of the investment made in tangible fixed assets and in intangible assets employed for research, development and technological innovation activities.

In this regard, only research and development expenses related to activities carried out in Spanish territory or in the territory of another EU or EEA Member State are taken into consideration to calculate the amount of the tax credit available.

Thus, the classification of the UK as a third country after Brexit implies that expenses related to research and development activities carried out in the UK by Spanish taxpayers will not generate the aforementioned tax credit.

Regarding those tax credits related to investment in and production of motion pictures and fiction, animated or documentary audiovisual series, there are two effects deriving from Brexit:

- The current general limit applicable to the tax credit for investing in Spanish motion pictures and audiovisual series (25% of the first 1 million euros and 20% of the remaining investment) is 50% of the production cost. However, an increased limit of 60% is available in cases of Spanish motion pictures and audiovisual series financed by more than one EU Member State and co-produced by producers from more than one EU Member State. The exit of the UK from the EU means that co-productions involving UK producers and financed by the UK would not benefit from the increased limit.
- As for the tax credit enabling Spanish producers to credit against their tax liability an amount equal to 20% of the production expenses incurred within Spanish territory (with a minimum expense of 1 million euros required), one of the expenses currently permitted by Spanish legislation is personnel expenses for employees who are tax resident in another EU or EEA Member State. With the removal of the UK from the EU and the EEA, such personnel expenses will no longer be included in the calculation of the tax credit.

IMPACT ON CROSS-BORDER GROUP TAX REGIMES

18.13 Spanish sister companies controlled by the same company resident outside of Spain can opt to be included in the same fiscal unit (ie, consolidated tax regime). This special tax regime can be applied regardless of the residence of the controlling company inside or outside the EU or the EEA. Therefore, the withdrawal of the UK from the EU does not have any impact on Spanish cross-border tax groups with a UK-resident controlling company.

Spanish permanent establishments of non-resident companies (inside or outside the EU or the EEA) may be included in Spanish consolidated tax groups. Therefore, after Brexit, such tax regimes will still be permissible.

TAX RAMIFICATIONS FOR CROSS-BORDER MERGERS, OTHER REORGANISATIONS AND TRANSFERS OF RESIDENCE. NO APPLICATION OF THE MERGER DIRECTIVE

Cross-border mergers and other reorganisations

18.14 *Chapter VII* of *Title VII* of the *Spanish Corporate Income Tax Law* envisions the application to corporate reorganisations of a special tax regime known as the tax neutrality regime. Accordingly, taxation is deferred until unrealised gains made as a consequence of corporate reorganisation are effectively realised upon a subsequent transfer to third parties.

The application of the tax neutrality regime requires the existence of valid economic reasons, other than tax reasons, for the intended reorganisation. The Spanish General Directorate of Taxation has issued a binding ruling[1] stating that reorganisation of a corporate group in order to minimise the risks posed by Brexit and procure the necessary flexibility to ensure that the corporate group will be able to provide post-Brexit services to its clients in a cohesive way constitutes a valid economic reason for the application of the tax neutrality regime.

The tax neutrality regime can be applied to exchange of securities by shareholders that can be tax residents in Spain, in another EU Member State or even in a third country. The securities received in exchange can in theory be either those of a Spanish company or of an EU company.

However, where shareholders are resident in a third country, the securities received in exchange must be those corresponding to an entity resident in Spain.

Therefore, after Brexit, if the tax neutrality regime is intended to be applied, the securities received by the shareholders (ie, securities of the acquiring company) cannot be those of a UK company. Additionally, where the shareholders receiving the securities are tax residents in the UK, the securities received in exchange can only be from a Spanish corporation.

The tax neutrality regime is also applicable to mergers and spin-offs, regardless in principle of the tax residence of the shareholders receiving shares in the acquiring company (in Spain, in another EU Member State or even in a third

1 See binding ruling V2253-18, of 26 July 2018.

country). Nevertheless, the tax residence of the shareholders in a third country forces the acquiring company to be resident in Spain in order to qualify.

Therefore, after Brexit, if the tax neutrality regime is intended to be applied, the acquiring company must be resident in Spain whenever the shareholders are tax resident in the UK.

Transfer of residence abroad

18.15 Unrealised gains deferred as a consequence of the application of the tax neutrality regime must be subject to corporate income tax when the resident shareholder relocates outside of Spain. The exception to this general rule is whenever the shares remain attached to a Spanish PE or relocation takes place within the EU. In those cases, payment of taxes can be deferred. The withdrawal of the UK from the EU will lead, in cases of relocation of Spanish shareholders to the UK, to the mandatory inclusion in the taxable base of gains previously deferred under the tax neutrality regime.

Changes of registered address, from Spain to the UK, by European Companies or by European Cooperatives will no longer be sheltered under the tax neutrality regime.

Moreover, there are exit tax provisions that apply to Spanish resident companies that cease to be tax resident of Spain. In accordance with such provisions, unrealised gains are subject to corporate income tax (ie, exit tax or tax over unrealised gains) upon relocation outside of Spain. Nonetheless, deferral until a subsequent transfer of assets being relocated is available for relocations within the EU. Furthermore, the forthcoming transposition of the Anti-Tax Avoidance Directive into Spanish legislation will allow the payment of the tax liability arising as a result of the difference between the market value and the tax value of the assets being transferred to another EU Member State to be paid up over five years. Following Brexit, the UK will fall outside this scheme.

Individuals who have been resident in Spain for at least ten of the last 15 fiscal years are subject to exit tax provisions as well.

- Relocation to another EU Member State: exit taxes only arise in one of the following three instances:
  - In the ten years following the relocation, the shares owned by the former Spanish tax resident are transferred *inter vivos*.
  - In the ten years following the relocation, the former Spanish tax resident loses this status within the EU.
  - The tax resident fails to properly inform the Spanish tax authorities about any capital gain generated, the Member State to which he is relocating, further changes of address or the maintenance of the shares.

- Relocation outside of the EU: exit taxes arise in respect of the capital gain resulting from the positive difference between the market value of the shares owned by the taxpayer (market value equal to EU list value or, in the case of non-listed entities or entities listed outside of the EU, to the highest of the following: (i) net equity corresponding to the shares according to the last balance sheet available; or (ii) the amount that results from capitalising at 20% the average of the accounting profits corresponding to the previous three fiscal years) and their acquisition cost.

  However, in order for exit taxes to arise, the market value of the corresponding shares must be at least EUR 4 million (jointly) or, whenever the shares amount to more than 25% of the equity of the entity, EUR 1 million (individually).

  Withdrawal of the UK from the EU would then mean:

- In cases of relocation outside of the EU by taxpayers holding shares in UK companies, the capital gain subject to exit tax would always be assessed taking into account the highest of the net equity corresponding to the shares according to the last balance sheet available and the amount that results from capitalising at 20% the average of the accounting profits corresponding to the previous three fiscal years, regardless of listing in the UK.
- Taxation of capital gains realised as a consequence of relocation to the UK could not be deferred until a subsequent *inter vivos* transfer or until relocation outside of the EU.

Inbound transfer of residence

18.16 Brexit will have no effect on the inbound transfers of residence.

OTHER

18.17

- Please bear in mind that the *Budget Law* for fiscal year 2021 (currently under parliamentary progress) foresees the reduction of the full exemption available for inbound dividends (see **18.8** above) and capital gains on shareholdings in non-resident companies (see **18.9** above) to a partial exemption of 95%. Furthermore, the Draft envisions the removal of the default condition of an acquisition price exceeding EUR 20 million (ie, shareholdings below 5% but with an acquisition price exceeding EUR 20 million would no longer be covered by the exemption after 1 January 2021. However, shareholdings of this type acquired before 1 January 2021 would be covered by the exemption until 2025).

Removal of the default condition of an acquisition price exceeding EUR 20 million would also be implemented as regards the WHT exemption applicable to outbound dividends (see **18.2** above).

Additionally, the *Budget Law* foresees the extension to EEA residents of the domestic law exemption applicable to interest paid to residents in an EU Member State (see **18.3** above).

- The *Spanish Corporate Income Tax Law* foresees that insurance companies domiciled in another EEA Member State and operating in Spain under the freedom to provide services shall be obliged to make withholdings or payments on account in relation to operations carried out in Spain. Thus, as a consequence of Brexit, UK entities will not be subject to the withholding obligation, unless they operate in Spain through a permanent establishment).

- Currently, European economic interest groups (therefore, including UK economic interest groups) can apply the same beneficial tax regime applicable in respect of Spanish economic interest groups: basically, allocation to Spanish resident shareholders (or to non-resident shareholders who have a PE within Spanish territory) of non-deducted financial expenses, capitalisation reserves, taxable bases, net operating losses (NOLs), tax credits and allowances and withholding taxes. Therefore, the economic interest group is only taxed on income not allocated to its Spanish shareholders. Furthermore, dividends distributed to resident shareholders who have been allocated taxable bases from the economic interest group are not subject to corporate income tax or to personal income tax, nor do they increase the acquisition cost of the shares of the economic interest group.

  After Brexit, however, UK economic interest groups will be subject to the general corporate income tax regime.

- Under the current Spanish corporate income tax legislation, shipping entities devoted to the exploitation of vessels commercially and strategically managed from the UK (including Gibraltar) can benefit from the application of the Spanish tonnage tax regime, under which corporate income tax liability is assessed taking into account the weight (in tons) of the vessel, instead of the income obtained.

  Disengagement of the UK from the EU ends this arrangement. Consequently, shipping entities exploiting vessels that are being commercially and strategically managed from the UK will assess their corporate income tax liability post-Brexit taking into account income obtained (instead of weight of the vessels).

Furthermore, owning or leasing vessels devoted to towing and dredging activities will not allow shipping entities to be taxed under the Spanish tonnage tax regime whenever those vessels are registered in the UK.

- Individuals who are shareholders of collective investment institutions and who obtain capital gains as a result of the transfer of the stake in the aforementioned institutions are not taxed on such income as long as the amount obtained is reinvested in the acquisition of further stake in other collective investment institutions. Taxation is thus deferred up until the subsequent transfer of the new shares (via frozen acquisition value and acquisition date). However, the application of this reinvestment deferral is subject to the residence within the EU of the collective investment institution. Accordingly, after Brexit, transfer of the shares in a collective investment institution that is tax resident in the UK will be fully taxable at the moment of sale, regardless of the reinvestment of the capital gain obtained in the acquisition of new shares in collective investment institutions.

- As regards tax on inheritance and gifts, the withdrawal of the UK from the EU would in theory hinder the application of tax allowances approved by the Spanish autonomous regions. These allowances, although initially foreseen exclusively in respect of residents in Spanish territory, were extended to residents in the EU after the judgment of the Court of Justice of the EU of 3 September 2014 (Case C-127/12). However, the application of the aforementioned allowances has not yet been legislated for in regard to residents outside of the EU (although there are already rulings by the Spanish courts confirming the application of these regional allowances to residents outside of the EU). As a consequence, if the recent jurisprudence issued by the Spanish courts is approved, residents in the UK (who after Brexit would be residents outside of the EU) could also enjoy the tax allowances approved by autonomous regions in respect of tax on inheritance and gifts, in direct implementation of the free movement of capital.

- As is the case with tax on inheritance and gifts, legislation approved by the different autonomous regions regarding wealth tax permits taxpayers resident in their corresponding territory certain tax allowances. Notwithstanding the above, taxpayers who are resident in another EU or EEA Member State can apply the regional tax allowances as well. Therefore, Brexit may lead to the impossibility of applying the aforementioned tax allowances. However, Brexit could have no effect whatsoever on taxation of Spanish wealth owned by residents in the UK inasmuch as the doctrine set out by the Spanish courts regarding tax on inheritance and gifts is applied to wealth tax as well.

- Exit from the EU also implies that residents in the UK will not be safeguarded any longer by the freedom of establishment and by the freedom to provide services, both of them exclusively foreseen by the

Treaty of the EU in respect of residents within the EU. Nonetheless, the free movement of capital and payments will continue to be in force, since it is fully applicable to countries outside of the EU.

- Any impact on EU state aid legislation should also be carefully monitored, especially taking into account that discontinuance of its former application enables the UK to potentially foster tax incentives or benefits that may affect the functioning of the EU internal market.

Chapter 19

Sweden

Martin Segerström and Lawrence Williams

INTRODUCTION

The purpose of this chapter

19.1 The purpose of this chapter is to analyse the post-transition period[1] implications of the UK leaving the EU from a Swedish corporate income tax perspective.[2] We have conducted our analysis based upon the assumption that the UK will be a third country and will not join the European Economic Area (EEA) after the transition period ends on 31 December 2020. Based on this assumption, the general Swedish rules on third country companies will determine: (1) what are the corporate income tax implications for a company in the UK, which either conducts business in Sweden or targets the Swedish market; and (2) the corporate income tax implications for a Swedish company, which either conducts business in the UK or targets the UK market.

From a systematic point of view, any Swedish tax liability at first instance is determined based on domestic tax rules.[3] The tax liability under domestic rules may in a second step be restricted by a tax treaty.[4] In addition to tax treaties, the Swedish claim to tax may be impacted by the requirements of the Treaty on the Functioning of the European Union (TFEU) where Article 63 on the free movement of capital is applicable in relation to third countries.[5]

1 The UK left the EU at 23:00 GMT on 31 January 2020; however, during the period of writing this chapter, the UK was in a 'transition period', which kept the UK bound to the EU rules until 31 December 2020. Thus, this analysis looks at the potential implications from a Swedish corporate income tax perspective during the post-transition period of Brexit, ie from 1 January 2021.

2 This chapter does not include an analysis on VAT, customs duties, state aid legislation or the Withdrawal Agreement from a Swedish tax perspective. Therefore, please refer to the applicable chapters in this book, which cover these topics from a holistic perspective.

3 The corporate income tax rate in Sweden for 2020 is 21.4%, which will be reduced to 20.6% in 2021.

4 For the purposes of this chapter, the applicable tax treaty is the double tax treaty entered into by Sweden and the UK, which was signed on 26 March 2015 (the 'UK-Sweden Tax Treaty').

5 The authors have not a conducted a comprehensive analysis of the free movement of capital in this chapter. Rather, specific areas where the Swedish claim to tax may be impacted by the requirements of Article 63 TFEU have been discussed.

TAX RAMIFICATIONS FOR INBOUND INVESTMENTS

Introduction

19.2 The purpose of this section is to examine the potential implications on inbound investments from a Swedish corporate income tax perspective during the post-transition period of Brexit.

Outbound dividends[6]

19.3 The general rule for outbound dividends outlined in the *Swedish Withholding Tax Act* is that an individual or legal entity which receives dividends, to which it is entitled,[7] from a Swedish limited liability company (AB), from a European Company (SE) registered in Sweden, or from a Swedish investment fund,[8] and who is not subject to unlimited tax liability in Sweden, is liable to Swedish withholding tax on the dividend. This assumes that the dividend is not taxable in Sweden on the basis that it is effectively connected to a Swedish permanent establishment (PE).[9] The Swedish withholding tax amounts to 30% of the dividend amount.[10]

Domestic law contains several exemptions from withholding tax, one of which is a 'direct' implementation of the Parent-Subsidiary Directive which would be unavailable to UK companies once the transition period has ended. In order to understand the potential effects of that, we outline the various exemptions in the following sub-sections below:

Exemption 1: direct implementation of the Parent-Subsidiary Directive

19.4 The first exemption is contained in the *Swedish Withholding Tax Act, s 4(5)*, which provides for a direct implementation of the Parent-Subsidiary

6 While this chapter discusses the tax effects of Brexit based on where the law stands today, we do note that the Swedish Government has presented a proposal for a new withholding tax act (Ds 2020:10). Noteworthy changes include broadening the scope of the Swedish General Anti-Abuse Rule to cover withholding tax and abolishing the present act's anti-abuse rule; as well as limiting the scope of the 'foreign company' exemption to entities resident within the EEA (see Exemption 2 below for a discussion of this exemption under existing law). The proposal, however, represents an early step in the legislative process and it remains to be seen what a potential final proposal will look like.

7 This concept denotes, somewhat simplified, formal (legal) rather than beneficial ownership.

8 There are two forms of Swedish investment funds: UCITS funds (*värdepappersfonder*) regulated by legislation, which is largely based on the UCITS IV Directive, and 'special funds'. Both types of fund are contractual funds.

9 Dividends which are attributable to a Swedish PE are generally taxed in Sweden in line with the tax rules applicable for the investor in question. Therefore, the corporate income tax rate of 21.4% (2020) and 20.6% (2021) for a limited liability company is applicable.

10 *Swedish Withholding Tax Act, s 5.*

Directive. Post-transition period, this exemption will no longer be applicable, due to the UK no longer being an EU Member State.

Exemption 2: participation exemption available to 'foreign companies'

19.5 The second exemption is contained in the *Swedish Withholding Tax Act, s 4(6)* and applies to recipients which qualify as 'foreign companies'. This term implies that the entity must be subject to taxation in its state of residence, which is similar to the taxation of Swedish companies; or alternatively, be eligible for benefits under a complete tax treaty entered into by Sweden and the state of residence.

This exemption further mirrors the main features of the Swedish participation exemption regime by requiring, first, that the recipient must be comparable to Swedish entities which may hold participation shares.[11] The comparability test performed is outlined in the next paragraph. Second, this exemption also mirrors some of the main grounds upon which holdings of such entities may qualify for the participation shares. In this regard, holdings of unquoted shares which are not held as inventory usually qualify as participation shares. Quoted shares, not held as inventory, normally qualify if they have been held for at least one year and represent at least 10% of the voting rights. Notably, shares in an EU resident company can qualify as tax exempt even if the shares are held as inventory, provided the holding represents at least 10% of the capital. Once the transition period ends, this exemption on shares being held as inventory, provided the holding represents at least 10% of the capital, will no longer be applicable to UK companies.

In relation to determining whether a UK company, after the transition period ends, would qualify as comparable to a Swedish AB, it is important to consider that Swedish case law looks at a comparison from a legal perspective as well as from a tax perspective. Whether a UK recipient would qualify would be decided on a case-by-case basis taking all facts into account. There is a wide range of case law concerning these comparability aspects. Some illustrative examples are highlighted in the following paragraphs.

The Swedish Supreme Administrative Court has held that a Russian limited liability company in the form of an OOO (Obchtchestvo s Ogranitschennoy Otvetstvennostuy) was sufficiently similar to a Swedish AB. Despite differences being identified from a legal perspective, such as the co-owners of a Russian OOO owning interests in the company, as opposed to shares and the ability to exclude co-owners, the Swedish Supreme Administrative Court concluded

11 Such entities include: (1) a Swedish AB or Swedish economic association that is not an investment company; (2) a Swedish foundation or Swedish non-profit association; (3) a Swedish savings bank; or (4) a Swedish mutual insurance company.

that a Russian OOO may be considered to correspond to a Swedish AB.[12] While this case indicates that the comparison is not overly strict, it should be required that the owners of the foreign entity have limited liability and that the share capital is not variable.[13]

As to the comparison from a tax perspective, case law indicates that the foreign company cannot be tax transparent and must be regarded as a tax subject where it is resident. There is no requirement, however, that the tax rate must be at a certain minimum level.

In 2019, the Swedish Supreme Administrative Court considered the comparability between a Swedish AB and a United States Domestic International Sales Corporation (DISC) from a tax perspective.[14] The court concluded that the DISC did not correspond to a Swedish AB because it was not considered to be subject to tax 'in fact' given certain elections made which meant that it did not pay tax in practice.[15]

In conclusion, whether a UK recipient would qualify as comparable to a Swedish AB under the *Swedish Withholding Tax Act, s 4(6)* would be decided on a case-by-case basis taking all facts into account. However, Swedish case law indicates that the comparison is not overly strict both from a legal and tax perspective. Furthermore, an identified difference once the transition period ends is that the participation exemption regime to shares being held as inventory, provided that the holding represents at least 10% of the capital, will no longer be applicable due to the UK no longer being a member of the EU.

Exemption 3: Swedish partnerships, European economic interest groups and foreign partnerships

19.6 The *Swedish Withholding Tax Act, s 4(8)* provides an exemption to tax transparent entities of the following forms: Swedish partnerships,

12 The Swedish Supreme Administrative Court in case HFD 2009, ref 100.

13 Concerning variable capital, see also the Swedish Supreme Administrative Court's judgment in case RÅ 1992 ref. 5, whereby a Luxembourg SICAV in the form of a limited liability company was not considered to correspond to a Swedish AB. As to the limited liability of the owners, it may be noted that there is strictly speaking no case law indicating that *all* owners must have limited liability; however, the STA considers this to be a requirement (see opinion no. 8-154412 dated 27 May 2020), and a company with one shareholder with liability for the entity's debts would indeed, in this regard, be more similar to a Swedish limited partnership (Swedish: *kommanditbolag*) than a Swedish AB.

14 Swedish Supreme Administrative Court's judgment in case HFD 2019 ref. 49.

15 See also the Swedish Supreme Administrative Court in case HFD 2017 ref. 29, whereby the court considered whether a company limited by shares, which has been formed and registered in the British Virgin Islands, corresponds to a Swedish AB in relation to participation shares. The court held that due to the *British Virgin Islands Business Companies Act* stating that all companies enjoy a general and complete exemption from income tax, this meant that the company in this case was not an income tax subject in its home country and, thus, not comparable to a Swedish AB.

European economic interest groups, and foreign partnerships which are legal entities.[16] The exemption is applicable provided that a corresponding dividend would have been tax exempt for the partner under one of the aforementioned exemptions from withholding tax.

In determining whether the dividend had been tax-free had the partner received it directly, the shareholding shall be determined based on the size of the indirect owner's interest in the transparent entity. This exemption was introduced in connection with the expansion of the participation exemption regime to include indirect holdings through the same categories of transparent entities. In summary, the exemption means that dividends which would have been exempt from withholding tax in the case of a direct holding would also benefit from the exemption in the case of an indirect holding through one of the defined transparent entities.

By contrast, foreign partnerships which are not legal entities from a Swedish tax perspective are not covered by this exemption. As a starting point, such entities should simply be 'looked through' as the partners are considered to hold the investment directly.[17]

In sum, due to the Parent-Subsidiary Directive no longer being applicable once the transition period ends, only the exception provided under the *Swedish Withholding Tax Act, s 4(6)* concerning participation exemption would be relevant under the look-through approach required in relation to the *Swedish Withholding Tax Act, s 4(8)*.

Exemption 4: investment funds

19.7 There is an explicit exemption from withholding tax liability for foreign security funds and special funds contained in the *Swedish Withholding Tax Act, s 4(9)*.

Under the *Swedish Withholding Tax Act, s 4(9)*, dividends to foreign funds which fulfil requirements corresponding to those of the UCITS Directive[18]

16 Whether a foreign partnership is a legal entity is determined from the perspective of Swedish tax law, under which a foreign legal entity should meet the following three criteria, all of which must be tested according to the legislation of the state where the association belongs: (1) the association may acquire rights and assume obligations; (2) the association may bring proceedings before courts and other authorities; and (3) individual partners cannot freely dispose of the assets of the association.

17 A look-through approach is apparently not always straightforward. An example is a case where a General Partner of a Jersey Limited Partner (LP) has been considered as the owner of all shares held by the LP, which does not constitute a legal entity from a Swedish tax perspective. The case is currently pending before the Swedish Supreme Administrative Court.

18 Directive 2009/65/EC of the European Parliament and of the Council of 13 July 2009 on the coordination of laws, regulations and administrative provisions relating to undertakings for collective investment in transferable securities (UCITS). Article 2(1) of the Directive defines a UCITS as an undertaking: (a) with the sole object of collective investment in transferable

(the 'UCITS exemption'), as well as foreign equivalents to Swedish 'special funds' are exempt from withholding tax. The application of the exemption requires that the foreign fund is established within an EEA Member State, or a state with which Sweden has entered into an agreement regarding exchange of information. In order to understand these exemptions, it is helpful to understand Swedish funds from a tax and regulatory perspective.

Very briefly, the Swedish fund legislation contains two main types of funds: UCITS funds (*värdepappersfonder*) and special funds (*specialfonder*). Both Swedish UCITS funds and special funds are contractual funds. The special funds are regulated in a manner similar to Swedish UCITS funds but may deviate in certain respects from those rules (eg, by being allowed to invest in other categories of assets or by targeting narrower categories of investors).

The Swedish fund legislation also contains the concept of alternative investment funds (AIFs) following the implementation of the AIFM Directive.[19] Swedish contractual special funds are a type of AIF. However, Swedish AIFs may also be organised in the form of legal entities such as a Swedish AB or partnerships, in which case they cannot be special funds. By contrast to Swedish UCITS and special funds, such AIFs are not regulated in detail by the fund legislation but function under the general rules applicable to the entity in question, such as the *Swedish Companies Act* for an AIF in the form of a Swedish AB.[20] That means, *inter alia*, that there are no restrictions regarding which investments are allowed but also that investors do not have any special rights to have their units repurchased or redeemed.

As to the tax treatment, Swedish UCITS funds and special funds are tax subjects even though they are not legal entities. They are, however, exempt from taxation on income from assets which are part of the fund. Investors in such funds are taxed for capital gains and dividends based on the general tax rules applicable to each investor.[21] By contrast, AIFs which are not special funds are simply taxed based on the general tax rules applicable to the entity used for the AIF (ie, an AIF 'built' on a Swedish AB is taxed under the normal

---

securities or in other liquid financial assets referred to in Article 50(1) of capital raised from the public and which operate on the principle of risk-spreading; and (b) with units which are, at the request of holders, repurchased or redeemed, directly or indirectly, out of those undertakings' assets.

19 Directive 2011/61/EU of the European Parliament and of the Council of 8 June 2011 on Alternative Investment Fund Managers and amending Directives 2003/41/EC and 2009/65/EC and Regulations (EC) No 1060/2009 and (EU) No 1095/2010. The Swedish legislation define AIFs, in line with the Directive, as collective investment undertakings which raise capital from a number of investors, with a view to investing it in accordance with a defined investment policy for the benefit of those investors, and do not require authorisation pursuant to the UCITS Directive.

20 Generally speaking, the AIFM Directive and Swedish implementing legislation regulate the managers of the AIFs rather than the funds as such.

21 Most investors are also liable to tax on a standardised income which is intended to correspond to the tax credit which arises because the income generated by the funds is not taxed until it is distributed to the investors.

tax rules applicable to Swedish ABs). To conclude, Swedish UCITS and special funds are subject to tax rules which recognise that they function as collective investment vehicles by exempting the funds' income from tax, while AIFs which are not special funds must make do with 'normal' tax rules.

The exemption for UCITS funds is drafted in a way which causes some uncertainty regarding whether or not the exemption may apply to funds which meet the definition of a UCITS but are not established within the EEA and therefore not covered by the UCITS Directive.[22] It is the Swedish Tax Agency's (STA) position that the UCITS exemption is only applicable to UCITS funds established within the EEA leaving non-EEA funds with the exemption for foreign equivalents of Swedish special funds.

Interestingly, the Swedish Supreme Administrative Court held that a US mutual fund in the form of a legal entity (a US Regulated Investment Company, RIC) was not precluded from being in a comparable situation, in relation to the free movement of capital under Article 63 TFEU, merely on the basis of being a legal entity.[23] Up until this judgment, the STA had taken a previous Swedish case,[24] which did not concern the free movement of capital, to mean that only foreign funds which are not legal entities could qualify as equivalents of a Swedish special fund throughout almost all relevant domestic rules, including the *Swedish Withholding Tax Act*, and that being a legal entity also prevented such funds from being in a situation comparable to that of a Swedish special fund under the free movement of capital.[25]

The judgment should be of significance to non-EEA funds in the form of legal entities such as a UK open-ended investment company (OEIC). While the judgment concerned a previous version of the legislation, it may be possible to interpret the present wording of the exemptions in a way which is

---

22 The exemption simply refers to the definition of UCITS funds in the Swedish *UCITS Act* (see Ch. 1 Sec 1 first paragraph 9), ie the act which governs UCITS funds from a regulatory perspective. However, that definition simply corresponds to the definition of a UCITS fund in the UCITS Directive and does not as such require the fund to be established within the EEA. Nevertheless, the act as a whole only governs Swedish UCITS funds and the Swedish activities of management companies of UCITS funds established within the EEA. For other funds, the act refers to the provisions of the *Swedish Alternative Investment Funds Managers Act* which is the implementation of the AIFM Directive.

23 Swedish Supreme Administrative Court's judgment in case HFD 2020 ref. 3.

24 See Swedish Supreme Administrative Court's judgment in case HFD 2016 ref. 22. The question in that case was whether Swedish investors in a Luxemburg SICAV (an AIF) corresponded to a Swedish special fund for the purposes of the rules regarding the levying of a tax on a standardised income of the investors. The fund in question was essentially similar to a Swedish special fund except for being a legal entity. The Swedish Supreme Administrative Court held that the fund did not correspond to a Swedish special fund for this reason and referred to the fact that Swedish AIFs that are not special funds are simply taxed based on the general rules applicable to the entity in question, ie without any tax exemption for the income of the fund and without any levying of a tax on a standardised income of the investors. As this was beneficial for the taxpayer in the case at hand, there was no need to consider comparability aspects from the perspective of the free movement of capital.

25 See opinion of the STA dated 22 March 2017, ref no 131 103422-17/111.

consistent with the Swedish Supreme Administrative Court's judgment and the requirements of the free movement of capital.[26]

The judgment does not mean that all foreign funds will automatically be exempt from withholding tax. In the specific case concerning the US RIC, it can be simply stated that the Court of Appeal – after the case had been referred back to the lower court by the Swedish Supreme Administrative Court – held that the fund in question was in a situation comparable to that of a Swedish special fund based on the similarity with Swedish special funds from a regulatory perspective. The authors agree with that approach which was also that of the STA and lower courts before 2016.[27] It should, however, be noted that any assessment of a situation under the free movement of capital requires, as clearly discussed by the Swedish Supreme Administrative Court, that the comparability aspect is understood in light of the purpose of the domestic legislation and in particular the criteria for distinguishing between different situations in domestic law.[28] Such an assessment needs to account for the fact that no general tax exemption applies to Swedish AIFs which are not special funds.

Apart from the discussion regarding the importance of a fund's status as a legal entity, another notable case[29] concerned an Irish unit trust fund. The Swedish Supreme Administrative Court held that such a fund should be considered 'entitled to'[30] dividends received under the *Swedish Withholding Tax Act* even though a unit trust is not, as such, a legal entity which can own shares, but rather an agreement (trust deed) between a manager and a trustee who is the formal owner of the assets. The STA and the lower Swedish courts dismissed the fund's reclaim, which was filed on the basis that withholding tax was incorrectly withheld, due to the fund not being entitled to the dividends and, hence, not being the right person to file for a reclaim.

In reaching its conclusion, the Swedish Supreme Administrative Court noted that the withholding tax legislation seems to rest upon the assumption that funds, or at least UCITS funds, may indeed be entitled to dividends regardless of how they are organised, and also stated that Swedish contractual UCITS funds should be considered entitled to dividends received. For these reasons, so could a unit trust fund.

There may be good reasons for considering the same to apply also in relation to at least some non-UCITS funds organised as unit trusts. However, there is no clear equivalent to such funds (or trusts in general) in Sweden and therefore unit trusts may pose challenges when it comes to applying Swedish tax rules.

26 cf the special addendum to the Swedish Supreme Administrative Court in case HFD 2020 ref. 3 of Justices Ståhl and Saldén Enérus suggesting such an interpretation.
27 See opinion of the STA dated 23 May 2012, ref no 131 128777-12/111.
28 See Swedish Supreme Administrative Court's judgment in case HFD 2020 ref. 3.
29 See Swedish Supreme Administrative Court's judgment in case HFD 2020 ref. 31.
30 As noted in fn 6, this concept denotes formal rather than beneficial ownership.

Exemption 5: applicability of the UK-Sweden Tax Treaty

19.8 Article 10 of the UK-Sweden Tax Treaty provides for the following reductions to the general Swedish domestic tax rule of 30% withholding tax on outbound dividends:

- 0% if the beneficial owner is a company directly or indirectly controlling at least 10% of the voting power in the Swedish company;
- 15% if paid out of income (including gains) derived directly or directly from immovable property within the meaning of Article 6 (income from immovable property) by an investment vehicle that distributes most of this income annually and whose income from such immovable property is exempted from tax; or
- otherwise 5%.

It should be noted that Article 10(6) of the UK-Sweden Tax Treaty also contains an anti-abuse rule which provides that '[n]o relief shall be available under this Article if it was the main purpose or one of the main purposes of any person concerned with the creation or assignment of the shares or other rights in respect of which the dividend is paid to take advantage of this Article by means of that creation or assignment'. Therefore, the benefits of Article 10 will not be available where an arrangement is deemed to be abusive under this provision.

The applicability of the anti-abuse rule of the Swedish Withholding Tax Act

19.9 Withholding tax could, notwithstanding the domestic and treaty-based exemptions, potentially still be charged under an anti-abuse rule contained in the *Swedish Withholding Tax Act, s 4(3)*. The *Swedish Withholding Tax Act, s 4(3)* provides that withholding tax shall be charged if 'the shares of the distributing company are held with the purpose of someone else receiving an undue tax benefit or an exemption from withholding tax'. Historically, this rule has been applied rarely and never in relation to holding structures. Rather, a narrow interpretation has been favoured whereby the rule has been considered to apply only to abusive securities lending transactions.[31] At the date of writing, there are no precedents from the Swedish Supreme Administrative Court with respect to the anti-abuse rule.

However, due to an amendment to the Parent-Subsidiary Directive in 2015, it became mandatory for EU Member States to implement a 'minimum anti-abuse rule' in their domestic legislation with respect to situations covered

31 Judgment on 15 June 2007 of the Administrative Court of Appeal in *Sundsvall* (case no 575-05).

by the Parent-Subsidiary Directive ('PSD General Anti-Avoidance Rule ('GAAR')'). The PSD GAAR must reasonably be construed so as to apply to artificial holding structures and not only to securities lending.

Following the introduction of the PSD GAAR, Sweden inserted *s 4a* into the *Swedish Withholding Tax Act*, which provides that a requirement for applying the exemptions of the *Swedish Withholding Tax Act* is that the recipient of the dividend does not hold the shares under such circumstances, which are referred to in the anti-abuse rule. It was stated in the preparatory works to the legislation that this was in order to clarify (leaving it open whether this actually entailed any change) that the anti-abuse rule shall be possible to apply to situations covered by the exemptions.[32]

Upon amending the *Swedish Withholding Tax Act*, the Swedish Government also stated that the wording of the anti-avoidance rule covers all situations covered by the PSD GAAR. Accordingly, the PSD GAAR did not require any other legislative changes in the view of the Swedish Government. It has, nevertheless, been debated whether the anti-abuse rule should be possible to apply to holding structures going forward considering inter alia that the wording of the rule has not changed.

In the views of the authors, the principle of consistent interpretation requires that the anti-abuse rule of the *Swedish Withholding Tax Act* is read in a manner consistent with the PSD GAAR.[33] [34] Although the exact scope of the PSD GAAR is not entirely clear, that should entail that the Swedish rule – as an implementation of the principle of prohibition of abuse of law and the PSD GAAR – will going forward be possible to apply to abusive holding structures. The whole body of CJEU case law relating to abuse of law should in principle be relevant to the interpretation of the rule, but the 'Danish beneficial owner'

32 Government Bill 2015/16-14.

33 In a Swedish context, the Supreme Administrative Court has quashed an advance tax ruling issued by the National Board for Advance Tax Rulings on the application of the anti-abuse rule. While the ruling was quashed on formal grounds, the court's reasoning gives some guidance as to the interpretation of the anti-abuse rule following the introduction of the PSD GAAR (although the decision is not a formal precedent). The ruling concerned an individual who had transferred two Swedish groups, directly held by the individual, under a common parent company incorporated in Malta. Dividends distributed from the two groups to the Maltese parent were to be either distributed to the individual or invested and managed by the Maltese parent (alternatively a Maltese subsidiary). In its reasons for its decision, the Supreme Swedish Administrative Court stated, referring to the preparatory works to the changes to the *Swedish Withholding Tax Act*, that those changes were intended to implement the PSD GAAR and, therefore, that the anti-abuse rule should be interpreted in light of the PSD GAAR. The court furthermore stated that the facts were such that it could not be excluded that there was a situation at hand to which the PSD GAAR was intended to apply. The court, however, proceeded to state that the factual circumstances were not sufficiently clear for it to be appropriate to issue a ruling.

34 This position was further strengthened by the 'Danish beneficial owner' cases where the benefits of the Directive were denied based only on the principle of prohibition of abuse of law (as the cases concerned years before the introduction of the PSD GAAR) and without any clear basis in Danish internal law for applying anti-abuse principles.

cases are of particular importance as they represent the first attempt to provide concrete guidance regarding when a holding company may be part of an abusive arrangement.

The fact that the anti-abuse rule of the *Swedish Withholding Tax Act* has historically not been applied to holding structures, taken together with the fact that the domestic exemptions of the act are not combined with a beneficial ownership-test, has meant that the abuse perspective has in practice not been a significant concern for most taxpayers. In this regard, there has been a clear shift following the introduction of the PSD GAAR and the judgments in the Danish beneficial owner cases.

Against this background, it is interesting to consider the role of the anti-abuse rule of the *Swedish Withholding Tax Act* in relation to potentially abusive holding structures using holding companies in third countries (ie, 'treaty shopping' rather than 'Directive shopping'). On the one hand, the Parent-Subsidiary Directive – and consequently the PSD GAAR – is only applicable in an EU context and can presumably not require Sweden to set aside domestic exemptions in a non-EU context. On the other hand, the anti-abuse rule of the *Swedish Withholding Tax Act* is, according to its wording, applicable regardless of where the foreign owner is resident and applying it only to holding companies within the EU would arguably represent a strained interpretation of the rule. As there is still no case law regarding the interpretation of the anti-abuse rule, neither in relation to EU Member States or third countries, it remains to be seen how the rule will be interpreted and applied.

Outbound interest

19.10 Sweden does not levy withholding tax on interest.

Outbound royalties

19.11 Sweden does not levy withholding tax on outbound royalty payments. It should be noted, however, that there may nevertheless be Swedish source-state taxation on the basis that royalty income is attributed to a 'deemed' Swedish PE due to a special rule of the *Swedish Income Tax Act*. This rule may apply even where the standard requirements of the domestic PE definition, which largely corresponds to the OECD Model Tax Convention, are not fulfilled, see in this regard **19.13**.

Capital gains on shareholdings in resident companies

19.12 As Sweden does not levy any source-state taxation of capital gains on shares, the capital gains taxation will only be relevant in relation to shares which are attributable to a Swedish PE.

In the view of the authors, Sweden should nevertheless be required to extend the benefits of the regime to UK companies, which are eligible for treaty benefits and which are similar to Swedish ABs or such other Swedish entities which may own participation shares. This follows from the non-discrimination clause (Article 22) of the UK-Sweden Tax Treaty.

In summary, there appears to be no significant corporate income tax implications from a Swedish perspective relating to capital gains on shareholdings in resident companies once the transition period ends, subject to the non-discrimination clause of the UK-Sweden Tax Treaty being applicable.

Permanent establishments

19.13 The Swedish definition of a PE largely corresponds to that of the OECD Model Tax Convention. As the PE definition is not regulated by EU law, but rather domestic law and tax treaties, there should not be an impact, once the transition period ends, with respect to when a foreign enterprise may have a taxable presence in Sweden.

There are, however, two notable differences compared to the PE definition of the OECD Model Tax Convention in relation to: (1) royalties, and (2) periodical payments for the use of tangible or intangible assets, which are worth highlighting.

A foreign company which receives such payments from a Swedish company[35] will be deemed to have a PE (a 'deemed PE') to which the income is considered to be attributable.[36] Therefore, the recipient is taxed in Sweden on the net income[37] at the ordinary corporate income tax rate. It should be noted that the principles for calculating the net income of a deemed PE and for attributing costs to the deemed PE do not correspond to the principles for attributing profits to an 'ordinary' PE under the main rule.

The Swedish tax levied on income attributable to a deemed PE is limited to the lower of 21.4% of the net income (the tax claim under domestic law) or the amount which Sweden is allowed to tax under the UK-Sweden Tax Treaty, which is discussed below.

35 This provision is technically also applicable to payments made from a Swedish PE of a foreign enterprise to a foreign recipient.

36 *Swedish Income Tax Act, ch 6 s 11(2).*

37 Taxation of the net income implies that deductions for costs attributable to the deemed PE will be allowed. However, the wording of the law provides no guidance on how the net income should be computed and what costs should be attributed to the deemed PE and, consequently, be deductible for tax purposes. It is not entirely clear how to determine the net income, but preparatory works to the legislation indicate eg that direct as well as indirect costs that have arisen in relation to the income may be deductible regardless of whether they have been incurred in Sweden or abroad, and that annual depreciation/amortisation, financial and administrative costs may also be deductible (see SOU 1999:79, government bill 2003/04:126 and the court case RÅ 1940 ref. 45).

In this regard, it is first necessary to determine which article of the UK-Sweden Tax Treaty is applicable. If the payment in question falls under the definition of royalties contained in Article 12 of the UK-Sweden Tax Treaty,[38] then the withholding tax rate should be 0% subject to a beneficial owner test.

Other payments may fall under Article 7 (business profits) of the UK-Sweden Tax Treaty. In such cases, Sweden should not be allowed to tax the income as the treaty does not contain any rule corresponding to the 'deeming fiction' applicable under domestic law and, consequently, there is not a PE under the UK-Sweden Tax Treaty.

Notably, Sweden has implemented the EU Interest and Royalty Directive which may in certain situations provide for exemptions. The fact that the Directive will no longer be applicable to the UK once the transition period ends should generally not entail any adverse effects for taxpayers given the protection offered by the UK-Sweden Tax Treaty.

In situations where the limited tax liability in Sweden terminates because the business of a PE in Sweden is transferred to another EU or EEA Member State a deferral of exit tax is permitted. However, the deferment of exit taxation is only applicable if the business of a PE in Sweden is transferred to another EU or EEA Member State. Thus, post-transition period, such a deferral will no longer be applicable due to the UK no longer being within the EU/EEA.[39]

In sum, once the transition period ends a transfer of the business of a PE in Sweden to the UK will imply the immediate levy of exit taxation. Moreover, since the transfer of residence to a third country triggers the termination of the suspension of the payment by instalments, after the UK becomes a third country, in situations where a company has transferred the business of a PE in Sweden to the UK and opted for the suspension or instalment payment of the exit tax, it might thus be required to pay the full outstanding amount of the levy.

Other

19.14 With effect from 1 January 2017, resident shipping companies in Sweden may opt for a tonnage tax regime. The tonnage tax regime is an alternative to the normal Swedish corporate income tax regime and constitutes a form of state aid. The tonnage tax regime has been approved by the European Commission. In this regard, the European Commission approved

38 Article 12(2) UK-Sweden Tax Treaty states that the term 'royalties' as used in this Article means payments of any kind received as a consideration for the use of, or the right to use, any copyright of literacy, artistic or scientific work including cinematograph films and films or tapes for radio or television broadcasting, any patent, trademark, design or model, plan, secret formula or process, or for information (know-how) concerning industrial commercial or scientific experience.

39 Please refer to **19.26** for further information in this regard.

a prolongation of the tonnage tax regime in December 2016 for a duration of three years (1 January 2020 to 31 December 2022). The tonnage tax regime is available for renewable periods of ten years.

In order to be deemed a 'qualified ship', the ships need to meet the following requirements: (i) gross tonnage of at least 100 tonnes; (ii) having their strategic and financial management in Sweden; and (iii) mainly used for international transport or domestic transport in another country during the tax year. Furthermore, at least 20% of the vessels in a fleet must be registered in Sweden or in another EU or EEA Member State.

In the event that a shipping company has a number of vessels in the UK for instance, which will no longer be within the EU/EEA then the incentive ceases to be applicable to those companies, should the 20% threshold not be met.

TAX RAMIFICATIONS FOR OUTBOUND INVESTMENTS

Introduction

19.15 The purpose of this section is to examine the potential implications on outbound investments from a Swedish corporate income tax perspective during the post-transition period of Brexit.

Inbound dividends

19.16 The general rule under Swedish domestic tax law is that dividends received from abroad are included in the taxable income. However, there is a participation exemption on inbound dividends.[40]

In addition, Sweden applies a hybrid mismatch rule in respect of foreign dividends received by resident companies. This hybrid mismatch rule applies to both EU Member States and third countries.

In summary, there appear to be no additional Swedish corporate income tax implications relating to inbound dividends, once the transition period ends.

Capital gains on shareholdings in non-resident companies

19.17 The general rule under Swedish domestic tax law is that capital gains on shareholdings in non-resident companies are taxed at the standard corporate

40 Please refer to **19.5** on outbound dividends for further information on the participation exemption rules in Sweden.

income tax rate. However, the Swedish participation exception regime may be applicable to the sale of shares held in a non-resident company.[41]

From 1 January 2010, the participation regime was expanded to cover interests in partnerships which qualify as legal entities from a Swedish tax perspective,[42] and to cover shares held by such partnerships with gains being tax-exempt and corresponding losses consequently being non-deductible. With that said, capital gains on interests in partnerships established outside the EEA do not qualify for the participation exemption regime, while losses on such interests are nevertheless still non-deductible.[43]

Therefore, once the transition period ends, in a situation whereby a Swedish AB disposes of a UK partnership qualifying as a legal entity then such a situation falls outside of the Swedish participation exemption rules with a negative difference in treatment regarding potential gains as consequence. Having said this, UK partnerships would according to our understanding generally not qualify as legal entities.

Permanent establishments abroad

19.18 Under Swedish domestic tax law and the UK-Sweden Tax Treaty, profits and losses of PEs in the UK are immediately available through the inclusion of the worldwide profits of the Swedish resident company in its Swedish tax return. This means that the CJEU's case law regarding final losses (see in particular Lidl Belgium) is not relevant in this context.

However, there has been a Swedish case whereby a Swedish company with a UK branch did not initially receive a deduction of pension costs attributable to the branch. The company's operations were conducted exclusively in the UK and all its employees were employed there. In order to secure the employees' retirement, the company had made provisions in accordance with a UK pension scheme by transferring funds to a trust. The provisions were eligible for deductions in the UK. The question in the case was whether the company was entitled to deductions for the insurance costs also in Sweden. The STA concluded that payments made to the UK pension scheme did not qualify as a pension cost and were not deductible from a Swedish tax perspective. However, the Swedish Supreme Administrative Court stated that such an assessment can be made less strict with regard to an institution that is not active in Sweden. The Supreme Administrative Court proceeded to state that an example of such

41 Ibid.

42 As noted in **19.6**, whether a foreign partnership qualifying as a legal entity should fulfil certain criteria, according to the legislation of the state where the association belongs, such as being able to acquire rights and assume obligations. See fn 16 for further details. See also **19.6** regarding the 'look-through' approach applicable to partnerships which do not qualify as legal entities.

43 *Swedish Income Tax Act, ch 25a s 3.*

a situation is where the activities of the company are carried out through a PE within the EEA. The Swedish Supreme Administrative Court found that the trust could be equated with a Swedish pension foundation and found that the company was entitled to a deduction.

The judgment seems to leave room for continuing to apply the flexible approach once the transition period ends, and the reasoning of the Swedish Supreme Administrative Court provides an interesting precedent in relation to the more lenient requirement of comparability between a Swedish pension foundation and a UK trust. However, it cannot be excluded that the assessment could be affected by whether or not the other jurisdiction is a EU/EEA Member State.[44]

CFC rules

19.19 Under the Swedish CFC rules, the general rule is that a Swedish shareholder with a direct or indirect interest equal to at least 25% of the capital or voting rights in certain low taxed foreign legal entities is subject to current taxation on its proportionate share of the foreign legal entity's profits.

Under the general rule the income of a CFC is deemed to be subject to low taxation if it is not taxed at all or is subject to tax at a rate that is less than 11.77% (55% of the Swedish tax rate of 21.4%).

In addition, the *Swedish Income Tax Act* contains a 'White list' of countries, whereby shareholders in companies, which are resident in countries contained in this 'White list' may be exempt from CFC taxation. Under the White list contained in the *Swedish Income Tax Act*, jurisdictions are categorised into three separate groups, according to how their corporate income tax systems correspond with regular tax systems. The first category covers those jurisdictions with regular tax systems and income from such jurisdictions is not subject to current taxation in Sweden. The second category details partially included jurisdictions, which are those with regular corporate income tax but where beneficial tax regulations apply to certain activities. The second category, like the first category, is listed as 'White'. However, the second category is listed 'White' with an exception or a number of exceptions for a certain activity. The third category contains completely excluded states, which are not subject to the White list exemption.

The UK belongs to the second category of partially included jurisdictions due to the beneficial tax regulations, which are applied to certain banking and finance operations and other financial and insurance activities, which are not taxed at the normal income tax rate in the UK. It is our understanding that the UK will remain in the second category of White listed countries, once the transition period ends.

44 Swedish Supreme Administrative Court's judgment in case HFD 2019 ref. 53.

There is also an exemption applicable to income from a CFC that is resident within the EEA, which was introduced following the decision of the CJEU in *Cadbury Schweppes*,[45] and is only applicable if the shareholder can show that the foreign entity is established in the other country for business reasons and is engaged in real economic activities, and is moreover only applicable in relation to CFCs in EU or EEA Member States. Due to the UK no longer being an EU or EEA Member State, this exemption will no longer be applicable once the transition period ends.

In summary, apart from the non-applicability of the exemption contained in the *Swedish Income Tax Act* based upon the decision by the CJEU in *Cadbury Schweppes*, other implications for the Swedish CFC rules once the transition period ends have not been identified.

IMPACT ON CROSS-BORDER GROUP TAX REGIMES

19.20 Swedish companies are not taxed on a consolidated basis. Nevertheless, it is possible for qualifying groups (ie, a holding greater than 90% of the capital, which must have been upheld during the whole fiscal year) to effectively offset operating losses of one company against profits of another company by way of group contributions.[46]

Only Swedish companies or foreign companies established within the EEA may give or receive group contributions. A fundamental requirement is that the recipient is liable to tax in Sweden on income to which the contribution relates, meaning that group contributions to non-Swedish companies established within the EEA need to be attributed to a Swedish PE of the recipient.[47] A further requirement is that the recipient – whether it be a Swedish company or a foreign company – is not tax resident in a state outside the EEA under a tax treaty.

Additionally, for a group contribution between two Swedish or EEA companies to be deductible, the group contribution regime requires that any intermediate companies in the ownership structure are also established in Sweden or the EEA, and not resident outside of the EEA under a tax treaty.

45 *Cadbury Schweppes plc and Cadbury Schweppes Overseas Ltd v Commissioners of Inland Revenue* (Case C-196/04).

46 A group contribution is essentially a value transfer from one company to another, which both companies elect to treat as deductible/taxable in their tax returns. A group contribution does not have to be paid out in cash; however, there must be a real transfer of value. For this purpose, it is generally sufficient that a debt is booked in the company making the group contribution and that a corresponding receivable arises in the recipient company.

47 This entails that the recipient must recognise the group contribution as taxable income in its Swedish tax return; however, no special connection between the group contribution and the business activities is required.

The aforementioned requirements of Swedish domestic law entail the following potential issues once the transition period ends: First, a group contribution from a Swedish AB to a Swedish PE of a UK company, or vice versa, is not possible under domestic law. Second, two Swedish companies held by a common UK parent would not be able to exchange group contributions once the transition period ends under domestic law. Similarly, any structure with an intermediate UK company would preclude group contributions.

An interesting question is whether group contributions could still be exchanged by reference to Article 22 (non-discrimination) of the UK-Sweden Tax Treaty in these situations. The potential applicability of this article is discussed in the following sections in light of Swedish case law.

Group contributions where there is an intermediate UK company

19.21 In situations, where there is no support in Swedish domestic law for allowing deductions for group contributions, a group contribution can still be allowed in certain cases when there is a tax treaty between Sweden and the other state, and the tax treaty contains an Article on non-discrimination. For example, the ownership rule contained in the non-discrimination Article of a tax treaty has been considered to be of relevance to situations where there is an intermediary foreign entity. The Swedish Supreme Administrative Court held that a Swedish AB could give a group contribution to a Swedish subsidiary, which was indirectly held through a US company.[48]

In addition, it is worth noting that it was not possible to exchange group contributions in a similar case where there were two intermediary companies resident in Germany and Switzerland. In that case, the Swedish Supreme Administrative Court reasoned that it would be required to apply the non-discrimination articles of two separate tax treaties in parallel, and the court found that such application of the treaties was not possible.[49]

In summary, due to the UK-Sweden Tax Treaty including an Article on non-discrimination and based on the reasoning of the Swedish Supreme Administrative Court it should be possible for a Swedish AB to provide a group contribution to a Swedish subsidiary, which is indirectly held through a UK company. However, a group contribution would not be permitted in a situation whether there are two intermediary companies one being located in the UK and the other being located in another country, which is not resident in the EEA, which would require the application of the non-discrimination Articles of two separate tax treaties in parallel.

48 RÅ 1993 ref. 91 I.
49 RÅ 1993 ref. 91 II.

Group contributions from a Swedish PE of a UK company to a Swedish AB

19.22 In a 2011 case, the Swedish branch of a US company received an advance tax ruling from the National Board for Advance Tax Rulings regarding when a group contribution could be made under the Swedish group contribution rules. However, the Swedish Supreme Administrative Court quashed the ruling on appeal, by stating that it was not clear that a branch of a company established outside of the EEA could exchange group contributions, because the applicability of the non-discrimination Article was not clear.[50] The court stated that the application of the rule prohibiting discrimination based on nationality requires that the foreign company is 'in the same circumstances' as a Swedish company, and that a non-resident generally is not in the same circumstances as a Swedish company (being a resident of Sweden based on registration). Furthermore, the court noted that the rule requiring the taxation of PEs not to be less favourable than the taxation of enterprises of the source state carrying on the same activities only applies, according to the commentary to the OECD model, to the taxation of the PE's own activities. For these reasons, it was not appropriate to issue a ruling, which assumed that there was, in principle, a right to exchange group contributions as that question should have been answered first.

Notably, the decision to quash the tax ruling does not constitute a precedent regarding the matter of discrimination as the Swedish Supreme Administrative Court never tried the case on merits. Nevertheless, in explaining why it would not do so, the court provided reasons which led the STA to issue an opinion clarifying its view that the non-discrimination articles of tax treaties generally do not apply to Swedish PE of foreign companies.

Following the decision of the Swedish Supreme Administrative Court, the STA has considered, in a 2012 opinion, the issue of group contributions to or from a Swedish PE of a non-EEA company.[51]

First, the STA takes the position that the PE rule of the non-discrimination clause of tax treaties based on the OECD model is not applicable for the reasons alluded to by the Swedish Supreme Administrative Court, that is, that the PE rule does not extend to domestic rules that take account of the relationship between an enterprise and other enterprises such as rules that allow consolidation.

It should be noted that the reach of the PE rule of the non-discrimination clause has been subject to debate, and it is in the view of the authors by

50 Tax rulings by the National Board for Advance Tax Rulings may be appealed directly to the Swedish Supreme Administrative Court.

51 See opinion of the STA dated 28 June 2012, ref. no. 131 461482-12/111.

no means obvious that the provision could not apply to Swedish group contributions.[52]

Second, as an exception, the STA has taken the position that in certain situations the nationality rule contained in the non-discrimination Article of tax treaties based on the OECD Model Tax Convention, in its wording at the time of the opinion, may entail a right to deduct group contributions provided from the foreign company's PE in Sweden to a Swedish AB, which is elaborated upon further in the following sections.

Sweden does not apply the place of effective management as a criterion for tax residency (unlimited tax liability), but merely considers legal entities registered in Sweden to be Swedish tax residents. A foreign company can therefore never be tax resident in Sweden under a tax treaty. It is always resident in the other contracting state. Another country may, on the other hand, consider a Swedish company to be resident in that country because the Swedish company has its place of effective management (or similar criterion) there.

With that said, the STA has stated that a group contribution may be provided from the foreign company's PE in Sweden to a Swedish AB, if the other country applies the principle of effective management as a basis for tax residency and the tax treaty with the other country corresponds to Article 4(3) of the OECD Model Tax Convention (according to its wording at the time). According to that wording of Article 4(3) of the OECD Model Tax Convention, a company which is a resident of both contracting states under their respective domestic laws, is considered to be resident in the state in which it has its place of effective management. In such a case, the STA has reasoned that group contributions are permissible on the basis of the nationality rule in Article 24 of the OECD Model Tax Convention.[53]

Turning to the UK-Sweden Tax Treaty, it can be seen that Article 4(3) of the UK-Sweden Tax Treaty requires residency to be agreed by the Competent Authorities where a taxpayer has dual residency.[54] The comparison potentially

52 See eg JF Avery Jones, et al, Article 24(5) of the OECD Model in Relation to Intra-Group of Transfers of Assets and Profits and Losses, 3 World Tax J. (2011) Journals IBFD (accessed 25 June 2020).

53 In this regard, the STA based its analysis on a judgment by the Swedish Supreme Administrative Court (RÅ 1999 ref. 58) case, where the court held that a Norwegian non-life insurance company that would conduct business from a PE in Sweden had the right to request taxation in accordance with the rules that applied to Swedish non-life insurance companies on the basis of the nationality rule in the Nordic tax agreement. In this case, the court made a comparison between, on the one hand, a Swedish company conducting business in Sweden but having its place of effective management in Norway, and consequently tax residency in Norway under the Nordic tax treaty, and on the other hand, a Norwegian company resident in Norway and conducting business in Sweden. These two companies were considered to be in the same circumstances. See, the Swedish Supreme Administrative Court's judgement in case RÅ 1999 ref. 58.

54 In the absence of a mutual agreement by the competent authorities of the UK and Sweden, the person shall not be considered a resident of either Sweden or the UK for the purposes

becomes less obvious with such a version of the tie-breaker clause, as a hypothetical Swedish company with its place of effective management in the UK would not 'automatically' be a UK resident under the treaty. To our knowledge, the STA has not so far had the opportunity to consider whether the reasoning from its 2012 opinion is applicable also to treaties with this type of tie-breaker rule.

Group contributions from a Swedish AB to a Swedish PE of a UK company

19.23 First, in line with the approach to group contribution from a Swedish PE of a non-EEA company, the STA takes the position that the PE rule of the non-discrimination clause of tax treaties based on the OECD model is not applicable (see **19.22**).

Second, the STA does not consider the nationality rule to be applicable in relation to group contributions from a Swedish AB to a Swedish PE of a non-EEA company (cf the argument accounted for in **19.22**). The reason being that the *Swedish Income Tax Act, ch 35, s 3(4)* states that Swedish ABs that are resident in a state outside of the EEA, due to a tax treaty, cannot receive group contributions. Therefore, there is no discrimination when a Swedish PE of a non-EEA company cannot receive group contributions either.

In summary, group contributions from a Swedish AB to a Swedish PE of a UK company may not be permissible once the transition period ends.

Group contributions under the 'Marks and Spencer' doctrine

19.24 It is also worth noting briefly that Sweden has introduced a special chapter of the *Swedish Income Tax Act* (*ch 35a*), intended as an implementation of the Marks and Spencer doctrine, whereby final losses of a foreign group company can be deducted in the Member State of the resident company within the same group. However, this has only been implemented in relation to EEA Member States and once the transition period ends it will no longer be applicable to the UK as a third country.

In summary, the Marks and Spencer doctrine, implemented in the *Swedish Income Tax Act, ch 35a* will no longer be applicable to the UK as a third country.

---

of claiming any benefits provided by the tax treaty, except those provided by Article 21 (Elimination of double taxation), Article 22 (Non-discrimination), and Article 23 (Mutual Agreement Procedure).

TAX RAMIFICATIONS FOR CROSS-BORDER MERGERS, OTHER REORGANISATIONS AND TRANSFERS OF RESIDENCE

Cross-border mergers and other reorganisations

19.25 The EU Merger Directive has been implemented in its entirety into Swedish domestic tax law. The *Swedish Income Tax Act* covers business transfers of shares, assets, mergers, and partial (de-merger) divisions. These tax rules regarding these types of reorganisation are applied to situations covered by the Directive, as well as domestic reorganisations and reorganisations where one or both participating entities fall under the definition of a foreign company as outlined in **19.2**.

In summary, the Merger Directive will no longer be applicable when the UK leaves the EU. However, under the *Swedish Income Tax Act*, UK companies who are taxed in the same manner as a Swedish AB will continue to be a party to a merger or other reorganisation. Furthermore, UK companies which fall under the scope of the UK-Sweden Tax Treaty are also able to be a party to a merger or other reorganisation under the *Swedish Income Tax Act.*

Transfer of residence abroad

19.26 According to the exit taxation rule of the *Swedish Income Tax Act*, assets and services that are removed from the business are taxed as if they had been disposed of at market value.

It is possible to apply for a deferral of the payment of exit tax triggered by a migration under a tax treaty entered into with another EEA Member State, provided that the assets of the migrating entity are part of a business, which is continued to be carried on within the EEA after the migration (the *Swedish Tax Procedure Act, ch 63 s 2* and *(14)*). The deferral is granted upon application by the taxpayer and only when the final notice of assessment for the fiscal year in question has been issued. The deferral is granted for one year from the day when the tax is due at the latest, with a possibility of extension for one year at a time if the requirements for obtaining the deferral are still met, (the *Swedish Tax Procedure Act, ch 63 s 14 (2)*).

The above described general rule is, however, subject to an exception which provides for a gradual reversal of the deferral with respect to equipment (five years) and intangible assets (ten years). This is achieved through a mechanism which stipulates that the allowed deferral shall be decreased with one fifth (for equipment) or one tenth (for intangible assets) annually, (the *Swedish Tax Procedure Act, ch 63 s 21 (2)*).

From 1 January 2020, the possibility to defer the payment of the exit tax was extended to cover cases where the limited tax liability of a non-resident in Sweden terminates because the business of a PE in Sweden is transferred to another EU or EEA Member State. In such situations, a deferral of one year is available with the option for renewal should the requirements still be satisfied. However, the maximum amount of deferral, which is allowed will be reduced by one fifth each year when a new deferral is granted. The deferred amount may be subject to interest.

In summary, once the transition period ends transfers to the UK will imply the immediate levy of exit taxation. Moreover, since the transfer of residence to a third country triggers the termination of the suspension of the payment by instalments, after the UK becomes a third country, companies that transferred to the UK and opted for the suspension or instalment payment of the exit tax might be required to pay the full outstanding amount of the levy.

Inbound transfer of residence

19.27 Inbound transfers of residence to Sweden are not possible as only companies registered in Sweden are considered Swedish tax residents under domestic law.

Therefore, even if a UK company has all its activities in Sweden, it would only be a non-resident with a large PE in Sweden. Thus, a UK company cannot transfer its tax residency to Sweden before or after the transition period ends.

However, if a UK company transfers a number of assets to its Swedish PE, then it is nevertheless necessary to determine the tax base in the assets (acquisition value) under the *Swedish Income Tax Act, ch 20a*. Under this chapter, the Swedish tax base in various categories of assets are regulated in more or less standardised ways. For example, the Swedish tax base of equipment shall be determined based on the foreign company's original acquisition cost increased with the costs of improvement and decreased on a straight-line basis with 20% per annum from the original acquisition, and the tax base of inventory shall be set at the lowest of the acquisition cost and the fair value.

While the preparatory works to the legislation recognise that it would be correct from a theoretical perspective to apply the fair market value as acquisition value throughout, this approach was not opted for. There are exceptions, however, which include financial instruments classified as inventory (ie, generally instruments held for trading purposes) and the situation where the transfer of an asset to a Swedish PE has triggered exit taxation in the other state. Both of these exceptions are contingent upon the other state being an EEA Member State, or a jurisdiction with which Sweden has entered into a tax treaty, which includes an exchange of information article.

In summary, Sweden has rules in relation to acquisition values for assets, such as equipment, inventory etc that may not be as beneficial as they should be from a systematic point of view. To the extent that the rules have been made more beneficial in certain situations, UK companies should generally qualify prior to Brexit, during the transition period and after the transition period due to the UK-Sweden Tax Treaty.

OTHER

Interest limitations

19.28 From 1 January 2019, the interest limitation rule was amended in Sweden in order to comply with the EU ATAD Directive. Accordingly, taxpayer's deductions for net interest expense is limited to a maximum of 30% of earnings before interest, taxes, depreciation and amortisation.

In this regard, it is also worth noting that there is a safe harbour rule, whereby interest expense up to SEK 5 million is deductible. Interest deductions which are not utilised can be carried forward up to six years. However, if there is a change of ownership the unused interest deductions are lost.

In the case of loans between affiliated parties, the *Swedish Income Tax Act, ch 24, s 18(1)* states that interest is deductible only if: (i) the lender is established in an EEA country; (ii) in a country which has a tax treaty with Sweden covering the income in question; or (iii) the interest income would have been taxed at a minimum rate of 10% in the residence state of the recipient, assuming that such income was its only income.

Due to Article 11(1) of the UK-Sweden Tax Treaty covering interest income, the UK should be covered by the *Swedish Income Tax Act, ch 24, s 18(1)*.

However, it is also worth mentioning that the *Swedish Income Tax Act, ch 24, s 18(1)* is not applicable if the debt relationship was established exclusively or virtually exclusively, in order for the group to obtain a substantial tax benefit as stated in the *Swedish Income Tax Act, ch 24, s 18(2)*. A case regarding the compatibility of a previous version of this rule with the EU freedom of establishment is currently pending before the CJEU, and that case, or arguments in general pertaining to the freedom of establishment, may not be relevant in relation to the UK once the transition period ends.

EU Arbitration Convention

19.29 The EU Arbitration Convention[55] establishes a procedure to resolve disputes where double taxation occurs between enterprises of different EU Member States as a result of an upward adjustment of profits of an enterprise of one EU Member State. It is hoped that disputes involving Sweden

55 Convention on the elimination of double taxation in connection with the adjustment of profits of associated enterprises (90/463/EEC).

and the UK, which have arisen prior to Brexit and during the transition period, would be dealt with pursuant to the terms of the Arbitration Convention. In December 2020, HM Revenue & Customs announced that from the end of the transition period, it will no longer accept applications to resolve double tax treaty disputes under either the EU Arbitration Convention or the Arbitration Directive.[56] Nevertheless, recourse to the tax dispute mechanism contained in Article 23 of the UK-Sweden Tax Treaty would still be available. Interestingly, the UK-Sweden Tax Treaty is one of the few tax treaties currently entered into by Sweden which contains an arbitration clause.

Article 23 of the UK-Sweden Tax Treaty enables taxpayers to undertake a mutual agreement procedure in cases when the actions of Sweden and/or the UK result or will result in a taxpayer being taxed not in accordance with the provisions of the UK-Sweden Tax Treaty. In such a case, Article 23 of the UK-Sweden Tax Treaty states that the case must be presented within three years from the first notification of the action resulting in taxation not in accordance with the provisions of the Convention. The competent authorities of the UK and Sweden will communicate with each other directly in order to reach an agreement; if no agreement is reached then any unresolved issues shall be submitted to arbitration, if the taxpayer requests. Under the UK-Sweden Tax Treaty, such unresolved issues shall not, however, be submitted to arbitration if a decision on these issues has already been rendered by a court of administrative tribunal of either state.

56 *Double Taxation Dispute Resolution (EU) (Revocation) (EU Exit) Regulations 2020.*

Chapter 20

United Kingdom

Kelly Stricklin-Coutinho

20.1 This chapter is the country chapter for the UK. During the transitional period, the UK made no substantive changes to its tax laws which were directly related to the UK's departure from the EU. Following the end of the transitional period, in a Spring Budget delivered on 3 March 2021, announcements were made which included tax, although few gave an indication as to the UK's direction in tax matters after Brexit. A further Budget is expected in Autumn 2021. Tax Day was on 23 March 2021, when a number of consultations and calls for evidence in relation to tax matters were published.

For this edition of this book, therefore, the topics set out in the other country chapters will be outlined here as they arise in the UK, although there are few changes (if any) of a substantive nature to report which arise specifically from the UK's departure from the EU. It is anticipated that this is, however, an area likely to change in the months and years after the end of the transition period, as the UK repositions itself globally. Inevitably, tax measures at present focus more on the impact of the pandemic, since that is the most urgent situation for the Exchequer. Looking further ahead, it is highly likely that the UK's tax landscape will feature in international discussions as to trade, and may be a key feature of its attractiveness as a jurisdiction. Future editions of this chapter will contain those changes that are made to UK tax law under the topics outlined here. This version of the chapter therefore gives a flavour of the law as it currently stands and highlights some potential issues in relation to the UK's departure from the EU.

However, while there are few substantive changes to tax legislation to report at the date of writing, there are other changes which give rise to differences in how tax matters are to be dealt with in the UK, and those topics are considered here. This chapter also considers some topic areas where divergence is particularly likely with regard to how the courts deal with tax law and EU law, taking into account national court practice in the UK to date.

SPRING BUDGET 2021

20.2 As explained above, few measures announced in Spring Budget 2021 directly relate to the end of the transitional period, although some will be of general interest from the perspective of tax competition.

One such measure is the announcement that from 1 April 2023, the corporation tax rate will be increased to 25% for companies with profits over £50,000, and there will be a small profits rate of 19% for companies with profits not exceeding £50,000. There will be a tapered rate for profits between £50,000 and £250,000.

The rate of Diverted Profits Tax will also be increased to 31% from the same date, although the rates in relation to ring-fenced profits are unchanged.

In respect of trading losses, a period of three years' carry back for trading losses in the current and next financial or tax years will be permitted. The losses will be carried back against later years first and there are limits as to the amount and timing of carry back. Loss carry back may produce a repayment of tax and there are detailed rules as to how the carry back of losses fits with other rules on loss relief.

There will be a super-deduction for companies investing in qualifying new plant and machinery between 1 April 2021 and 31 March 2023. Qualifying expenditure on main rate assets will be subject to a super-deduction of 130%, and there are other rules for qualifying special rate assets.

Eight freeports have been announced in England. In addition to the customs and tax rules that will apply to those freeports, there will also be relief for SDLT on purchases of land or property used for a qualifying commercial purpose in the Freeport, as well as allowances for structures and buildings, capital allowances, business rates relief for five years and relief from secondary NICs. Freeports will also benefit from non-tax related measures involving planning, infrastructure and innovation, as well as a share of £175 million of seed capital funding. HM Treasury's Freeports: Bidding Prospectus of November 2020 stated that the policy will comply with subsidy control rules including the UK's domestic subsidy control regime, WTO obligations, State aid obligations under the Northern Ireland Protocol and under the subsidy control provisions in the Trade and Cooperation Agreement (TCA).

Finally, as set out below, changes have been made to reflect the removal of effect of certain Directives. Those changes include the application of DAC 6 and the exemption for payments of interest and royalties.

This chapter is in four main parts, and will take the following structure.

Section I contains the topics addressed by the country chapters in this book. This section states in brief terms the law as it currently is, and, if any indication has been given as to the likely future of those laws, it will be addressed here.

Section II sets out some brief comments as to the UK's position as a third country.

Section III concerns tax disputes in the UK. It covers both the status of current disputes and principles where national court practice has already shown divergence from EU law principles.

Section IV considers EU level tax dispute mechanisms, specifically the impact of their absence on taxpayers and tax authorities.

Section V contains a short conclusion.

I THE UK'S TAX LEGISLATION

Introduction

20.3 Much of the legal and political focus in respect of tax in relation to the UK departing from the EU has concerned customs and excise duties, and VAT, which has given rise to legislation such as the *Taxation (Cross-border Trade) Act 2018*. That legislation provides powers to impose and regulate a UK customs duty regime on the import and export of goods after the end of the transition period. It replaces the Union Customs Code in the UK and amends domestically implemented VAT and excise duty laws. That legislation is dealt with elsewhere in this book.[1]

A similar approach has been taken by the European Commission, for example, the European Commission's notices for readiness[2] in respect of customs and tax focus on excise duties, VAT on goods, VAT on services and customs, including preferential origin. Much of the political discussion on specific measures has concerned those topics, which are discussed elsewhere in this book.[3]

However, the key issue of international tax competition, which has been a feature of political discourse and of recent legal developments, has not yet made its way into legislative changes in the UK, or indeed any announced policy direction which directly arises from Brexit. That is perhaps not surprising given the pandemic, and given that much of the focus of potential legislative changes in the UK has been on the measures which had to be put in place before the end of the transition period, rather than on policy changes which the government wishes to make as it navigates its future relationship with the EU and other trading partners. Those changes were not required in order for there to be an orderly transition. That focus will, no doubt, shift, in the years after the end of the transition period.

1 See Chapter 3.
2 See https://ec.europa.eu/taxation_customs/uk_withdrawal_en.
3 See Chapters 2 and 3.

Tax ramifications for inbound investments

20.4 This section considers the law as it applies to a situation in which an EU resident company (EU Company) wholly owns a UK resident company (UK Company). Dividend or distribution payments will therefore be made by the UK Company to the EU Company. In respect of interest, the EU Company will lend money, and the UK Company will pay interest. Payments of royalties will be made to the EU Company by the UK Company.

Outbound dividends

20.5 Where a UK Company pays a dividend to another UK Company, the dividend is income in the hands of the recipient company, but that distribution is exempt from tax. Where a UK Company pays a dividend to a non-resident UK company, the UK does not impose income tax on non-UK residents.[4] In ordinary circumstances, therefore, there is no withholding tax on dividends or distributions paid by UK Companies to its non-UK investors, or indeed to its UK based investors.

Withholding tax

20.6 There are some, limited, circumstances in which the UK does require UK tax resident companies to withhold, or deduct income tax from payments of dividends or other distributions of profit.

Two of these concern property investment, and are applicable both domestically and cross-border.

The first of those circumstances concerns property income on dividends paid by real estate investment trusts (REITs). A REIT is a company which qualifies as such under the *Corporation Tax Act 2010* (*CTA 2010*) and which notifies HMRC that it elects to join the REIT regime. The qualifying conditions have several elements, including that it is a property rental business, and the business must involve at least three properties, none of which may be more than 40% of the total value of the property business. A property rental business may be UK based[5] or 'overseas' based (defined as income generated from land outside the UK).[6] In the briefest of terms, a REIT is exempt from tax on the profits (and capital gains) of its qualifying property rental business, and distributions of the profits (and capital gains) (known as property income distributions, or 'PIDs') are treated as UK property income in the hands of the shareholders.

4 *Income Tax Act 2007 (ITA 2007), ss 815 and 816.*
5 *CTA 2009, s 205.*
6 *CTA 2009, s 206.*

Withholding tax of 20% is imposed on these distributions, subject to some exceptions.

The second circumstance also concerns property, specifically property income distributions made by property authorised investment funds (PAIFs). A PAIF is an open-ended investment company (OEIC), which is a collective investment scheme that invests in property.

PAIFs may be any one of three types of distributions, being property income distributions (PIDs), dividend distributions or interest distributions. PAIFs are required to withhold income tax from PIDs at a rate of 20% (subject to certain exemptions).

Under both of these schemes, there is the possibility of a payment of a dividend or distribution to an EU Company, which is subject to withholding tax.

Another type of distribution which is potentially subject to withholding tax is non-dividend distributions of tax-elected funds (TEFs). TEFs are authorised investment funds (AIFs), (which may be either an authorised unit trust (AUT) or an OEIC), which choose to join the TEF regime. The TEF regime exempts TEFs themselves for certain types of income, and the investors in the TEF are taxed as if they owned directly the underlying assets of the TEF.

A TEF must divide its income into four streams, being dividend income, property investment income, property business income and other income. Amounts to be distributed to investors are allocated to one of those four categories and are then distributed as a dividend or a non-dividend. Investors are subject to tax on non-dividend distributions, and up until 6 April 2017, they were subject to withholding tax obligations.[7] Distributions paid on or after 6 April 2017 are not subject to withholding tax.[8] As to dividend distributions, corporate investors receiving such a dividend must split the dividend into its component parts of exempt dividends, non-exempt dividends, property investment income and property business income.

Outbound interest

20.7 The UK's regime on taxation of interest is complex, and no attempt is made here to summarise it in full. Instead, the salient features which will be relevant to EU Companies as to the tax treatment of interest paid to it by a UK Company are set out at a high level here.

UK income tax (at the basic rate of 20%) must be withheld from any payment of yearly interest with a UK source,[9] unless certain exemptions apply. 'Interest' is a broad term and may include certain payments of premium and guarantee

7 *AIF Regulations 2006, reg 69Z63.*
8 *ITA 2007, ss 888C and 888D.*
9 *ITA 2007, s 874.*

payments. Payments which are treated as distributions within *CTA 2010, s 1000* but which otherwise would have constituted interest are not treated as interest for withholding tax purposes. Yearly interest includes interest where it is possible for the loan to be extended beyond a period of a year (or more).

Whether interest is paid from a UK source is a question which is decided based on a number of factors. Interest paid by a UK resident borrower will usually be regarded by HMRC has having a UK source,[10] although following recent case law[11] HMRC's guidance states that the factors to be considered include residence, asset location, the place of performance of the contract constituting the debt and method of payment, the jurisdiction for legal action, the law of contract applicable to the debt and the residence of any guarantor and location of any security for the debt. In addition, certain other UK sourced interest payments may be regarded as ones from which income tax should be withheld. Those include the situation of a UK branch of a non-UK resident company.

If a UK borrower has withheld tax from its interest payments, it must account to HMRC for it, and it is chargeable to tax as if it were the borrower's own liability.[12]

Set out further below, the Spring Budget 2021 announced the repeal of the withholding exemption for interest and royalty payments to EU companies.

Outbound royalties

20.8 In one of the few measures to directly arise from the end of the transitional period, Spring Budget 2021 announced that the UK's withholding exemption for interest and royalties payments to UK companies would be repealed. Specifically, the Finance Bill 2021 repeals *ITTOIA 2005, ss 757–767* and *ITA 2007, ss 914–917* which exempt royalties payments from the UK. The draft legislation also includes a number of consequential amendments which remove the effect of the exemption in respect of a range of other legislation including, for example, the interaction of the exemption with diverted profits tax and intangible property tax avoidance provisions. The Bill also repeals *The Exemption from Tax for Certain Interest Payments Regulations 2004, SI 2004/2622*. The changes will take effect for payments made on or after 1 June 2021, or in certain circumstances payments made on or after 3 March 2021 (ie, the day of the announcement). The circumstances in which the changes take effect for payments made on or after 3 March 2021 are where the payment is made in consequence of, or in connection with, any arrangements having as one of its main purposes securing that the repealed provisions continue to apply to it.

---

10 See eg, HMRC's manual at SAIM9095, and *Westminster Bank Executor and Trustee Co and Channel Islands Ltd v National Bank of Greece SA* [1970] 46 TC 471 at p 493.

11 *Ardmore Construction Ltd v HMRC* [2018] EWCA Civ 1438.

12 *ITA 2007, Pt 15, Chs 15* and *16*.

There are three types of royalty payments which are subject to withholding tax in the UK, at a rate of 20%. They concern royalties paid to persons outside the UK,[13] patent royalties or sums for the use of a patent, and qualifying annual payments. Royalties paid to persons outside the UK are those with a UK source, which includes a payment made in connection with a trade carried on by a non-UK resident through its UK permanent establishment.[14] If a royalty payment falls within one of these categories, exemptions may be available.

The UK's intangibles regime may give relief from tax for payments of royalties by a company that is subject to corporation tax.[15] A feature of the regime is that expenditure on intellectual property that meets certain criteria is tax deductible for corporation tax purposes.[16] There are limits on what is deductible under the intangibles regime, including transfer pricing rules.[17] The diverted profits tax regime may also apply where cross-border payments are made in relation to IP to a low or no tax jurisdiction.[18] The UK's Controlled Foreign Corporation (CFC) regime may also apply.

Capital gains on shareholdings in resident companies

20.9 There are no changes to the UK's regimes for taxing capital gains on shareholdings in resident companies which arise specifically from the UK's departure from the EU.

A non-resident company that does not carry on a trade in the UK through a UK permanent establishment is not chargeable to UK corporation tax or capital gains tax, except for specific circumstances. Those circumstances include where a corporation tax charge is due for non-resident property traders or developers.[19] Non-UK residents are liable[20] to capital gains tax on the disposal of:

(a) assets situated in the UK with a relevant connection to the person's UK branch or agency and are disposed of at a time when the person has that branch or agency;

(b) assets not within the previous paragraph that are interests in UK land; and

(c) assets, wherever situated, that derive at least 75% of their value from UK land where the person has a substantial indirect interest in that land.

13 *ITA 2007, s 907.*
14 *Income Tax (Trading and Other Income) Act 2005 (ITTOIA 2005), s 577A.*
15 *CTA 2009, Pt 8.*
16 *CTA 2009, s 728.*
17 *Taxation (International and Other Provision) Act 2010 (TIOPA 2010), Pt 4.*
18 *Finance Act 2015, Pt 3* and *Sch 16.*
19 *Finance Act 2016, ss 76–82.*
20 *Taxation of Chargeable Gains Act 1992 (TCGA 1992), s 1A.*

An asset has a relevant connection to a person's UK branch or agency if it is used for the purposes of the trade, profession or vocation

Permanent establishments

20.10 There are no changes to the UK's applicable regimes in respect of permanent establishments which arise specifically from the UK's departure from the EU.

Corporation tax is generally chargeable if a company is either resident in the UK for tax purposes (in respect of its worldwide profits),[21] or carries on a trade in the UK through a permanent establishment (in respect of profits attributable to that permanent establishment).[22] Where permanent establishments are referred to in the legislation in the above sections, they have been set out.

Other

20.11 One immediate consequence of the deal brokered at the end of 2020 was that on 29 December 2020, *The International Tax Enforcement (Disclosable Arrangements) (Amendment) (No. 2) (EU Exit) Regulations 2020, SI 2020/1649* were made. These regulations amend the previous regulations which implemented Council Directive (EU) 2018/822 of 25 May 2019 amending Directive 2011/16/EU as regards mandatory automatic exchange of information in the field of taxation (DAC 6).

The change made in the new regulations results in only hallmark category D of DAC 6 (which concerns specific hallmarks concerning automatic exchange of information and beneficial ownership) remains applicable in the UK, and hallmark categories A, B, C and E in Part 2 of Annex IV of DAC 6 are omitted. The measure had effect from 11pm on 31 December 2020.

The government has announced that it will consult on draft regulations to implement the OECD's mandatory disclosure rules (MDR).

There are changes as regards the impact of how EU law will be taken into account which will impact the management of cross-border tax issues. These are addressed below.

Tax ramifications for outbound investments

20.12 This section considers the law as it applies to a situation in which a UK Company wholly owns an EU Company. Dividend or distribution

21 *CTA 2009, s 5.*

22 *CTA 2009, ss 5(3)* and *19.*

payments will therefore be made by the EU Company to the UK Company. In respect of interest, the UK Company will lend money, and the EU Company will pay interest. Payments of royalties will be made to the UK Company by the EU Company.

In respect of outbound investments the UK has made no substantive changes to the law as a result of the UK's departure from the EU.

Inbound dividends

20.13 There are no changes to the UK's applicable regimes in respect of inbound dividends which arise specifically from the UK's departure from the EU.

In principle, UK and non-UK sourced dividends or distributions paid to a UK company on or after 1 July 2009 are subject to corporation tax, unless the dividend or distribution falls within an exemption.[23] In practice, the available exemptions are broad ranging and broadly drafted, such that in general terms, all dividends are exempt from corporation tax, unless they fall within anti-avoidance rules.

Small companies exemption

20.14 If a company is a small company, and meets certain criteria, then a dividend received by that company will be exempt. A small company is one with fewer than 50 employees and whose annual turnover and/or annual balance sheet total does not exceed EUR 10 million, and is not an OEIC, AUT, insurance company or friendly society.[24] The criteria[25] for a dividend received by a small company to be exempt are:

(a) The dividend payer is resident in the UK or in a qualifying territory (which is one with which the UK has a DTC with a non-discrimination provision).

(b) The distribution is not made under *CTA 2010, s 1000(1)* (non-dividend distributions).

(c) No tax deduction is permitted for a resident of a territory outside the UK in respect of the dividend.

23 *CTA 2009, s 931A.*
24 *CTA 2009, s 931S.*
25 *CTA 2009, s 931B.*

(d) The dividend is not paid as part of a tax advantage scheme, which means a scheme the main purpose, or one of the main purposes of which is to obtain a tax advantage[26] (other than one that is negligible).

Dividends received by other companies

20.15 A dividend received from a company which is not a small company is also exempt from corporation tax where certain conditions are met. Those conditions[27] are:

(a) Where the payment is a type of distribution other than a dividend, the payment does not fall within *CTA 2010, ss 1000(1)E* or *(1)F.*

(b) The dividend falls into an exempt class, and is not taken out of the exempt class by virtue of anti-avoidance rules.

(c) No tax deduction is allowed to a resident of a territory outside the UK in respect of the dividend.

The exempt classes of dividend are:

(a) Dividends or distributions paid to a company that controls the company making the distribution.[28] Control is defined as both *de facto* control and greater than 50% control. Where the dividend is paid as part of a scheme the purpose, or main purpose of which is to obtain an exemption, the exemption will not apply.[29]

(b) Dividends or distributions paid in respect of non-redeemable ordinary shares.[30] Where the dividend is paid as part of a scheme the purpose, or main purpose of which is to obtain an exemption, the exemption will not apply.[31]

(c) Dividends or distributions paid in respect of portfolio shareholdings.[32] In this provision, the exemption applies where the dividend recipient holds less than 10% of the issued share capital of the paying company, is entitled to less than 10% of the profits available for distribution and it would be entitled to less than 10% of the assets of the paying company

26 A tax advantage is, in turn, defined as any of a relief or increased relief from tax, a repayment or increased repayment of tax, the avoidance or reduction of a tax charge or possible tax charge, the avoidance or reduction of a charge or assessment to a charge under the *TIOPA, Pt 9A*, the avoidance or reduction of a charge or assessment to the bank levy under the *Finance Act 2011, Sch 19* or the avoidance or reduction of a charge to diverted profits tax (see *CTA 2009, s 931V*, applying *CTA 2010, s 1139*).

27 *CTA 2009, s 931D.*

28 *CTA 2009, s 931E.*

29 *CTA 2009, s 931J.*

30 *CTA 2009, s 931F.*

31 *CTA 2009, s 931K.*

32 *CTA 2009, s 931G.*

available for distribution on a winding up.[33] The exemption will not apply where the dividends are paid as part of a scheme involving shareholdings between connected persons, with the main purpose of ensuring the dividend qualifies for exemption.[34]

(d) Dividends or distributions paid in respect of shares accounted for as liabilities, and which would be taxed as loan relationships, except that they are not held for an unallowable purpose.

(e) Dividends or distributions paid in respect of relevant profits, which are profits available for distribution at the time the dividend is paid, other than profits which derive from a transaction (or series of them) which have as their effect and main purpose to achieve more than a negligible reduction in tax.[35]

A dividend will also not be exempt if it is paid under certain schemes. Those schemes include situations in which:

(a) A shareholder pays for an otherwise exempt dividend, or gives up a right to income in return for it, where that distribution is part of a scheme the main purpose, or one of the main purposes of which is to obtain a more than negligible tax advantage (and the payment meets other conditions).[36]

(b) There are excessive claims to deductions where transfer pricing rules do not apply, which are paid for by otherwise exempt distributions, and the distribution is part of a scheme the main purpose, or one of the main purposes of which is to obtain a more than negligible tax advantage.[37]

(c) The dividend exemption is used to produce a return equivalent to interest, whether the payer and recipient are connected, and the main purpose, or one of the main purposes of which is to obtain a more than negligible tax advantage.[38]

(d) An overseas tax deduction is given in respect of an amount determined by reference to the distribution, where the distribution is paid as part of a scheme the main purpose, or one of the main purposes of which is to obtain a more than negligible tax advantage.

For the sake of completeness, it should be noted that it is possible to elect that a distribution which would otherwise be exempt is not exempt.[39] The counter-intuitive nature of this provision can be explained by virtue of the fact that the UK's CFC rules contain an acceptable distribution policy, and a taxpayer may

---

33 *CTA 2009, s 931G.*
34 *CTA 2009, s 931L.*
35 *CTA 2009, s 931H.*
36 *CTA 2009, s 931O.*
37 *CTA 2009, s 931P.*
38 *CTA 2009, s 931E.*
39 *CTA 2009, s 931R.*

wish to elect that the dividend is not exempt in order to assist compliance with the CFC rules.

Non-exempt foreign dividends

20.16 To the extent that there are foreign dividends that do not fit the criteria for an exemption, those dividends may be subject to a claim a credit for double tax in respect of any withholding or underlying tax attributable to the dividend, provided that the recipient is UK resident, and no relief is given against overseas tax.[40] Relief is given for foreign tax paid on the relevant profits attributable to the dividend,[41] and is capped to prevent the mixing of underlying dividends from low and high tax resident subsidiaries, in order to obtain a low mixed rate.[42] Where the tax relevant foreign tax is repaid to the recipient of the credits, or to any person connected with the recipient, the tax credits for foreign tax are denied or withdrawn.[43] There are also rules which restrict credit for foreign tax where that credit is derived from certain arrangements, the main purpose, or one of the main purposes of which is obtaining the credits.[44]

Historically, a more complex system was in place, which was the subject of much litigation in the domestic and European courts. That system is no longer in place, having changed in 2009, and will therefore only be impacted by the UK's departure from the EU to the extent that any claims for repayment have not yet been finally determined by the courts. Issues arising on dealing with those claims are set out in more detail below at Section III.

For the present purposes, therefore, a brief summary only is necessary here. Prior to its abolition for distributions paid on or after 6 April 1999, advance corporation tax (ACT) was payable by a company whenever it made a qualifying distribution.[45] As it was an advance payment, ACT could be set off against the corporation tax liability. Where set off was not possible (for example, because there was no liability in that year), ACT could be carried back or carried forward. Carry forward of ACT was permitted indefinitely. As a result of restrictions on the amount of ACT that could be set off against the corporation tax liability, and the fact that ACT had to be paid whenever there was a qualifying distribution regardless of whether there was a corporation tax liability to pay in the year of the distribution, ACT often accrued a surplus.

Under that historic system, qualifying distributions received by a UK resident company were exempt from corporation tax. Further, where onward distributions were to UK resident group companies, only one charge to ACT

40 *TIOPA 2010, s 57.*
41 *TIOPA 2010, s 59.*
42 *TIOPA 2010, s 58.*
43 *TIOPA 2010, s 34.*
44 *TIOPA 2010, ss 81–88.*
45 *Taxes Act 1988, s 14(1)*, now repealed

was made. The recipient company would receive franked investment income, which meant that when it made qualifying distributions it could use the credit on what it had received to 'frank' the distribution, so that it no longer had to pay ACT.

There are regulations as to how any unrelieved surplus ACT should be dealt with.[46]

Litigation on the issues arising from these systems is ongoing.

Capital gains on shareholdings in non-resident companies

20.17 There are no changes to the UK's applicable regime in respect of capital gains which arise specifically from the UK's departure from the EU.

Generally speaking, a company is subject to corporation tax on its chargeable gains if it is resident in the UK, or is carrying on a trade through a UK permanent establishment. There are specific rules as to share identification, which also apply to other fungible assets, which deal with a situation where a company acquires shares through multiple purchases and then disposes of some but not all of the shares.[47] There is no change to these rules.

CFC rules

20.18 Although they have been the subject of multiple changes as a result of the impact of EU law, the UK's CFC rules have not changed as a result of the UK's departure from the EU.

The UK's CFC rules are, of course, subject to the ongoing appeal and recovery process in respect of the European Commission's decision that the rules concerning the group financing exemption breached state aid law.

The impact of Brexit on state aid law in the UK is dealt with elsewhere in this book.[48] This chapter simply notes, therefore, that the interaction of the litigation, the recovery process, and the UK's departure from the EU is one which has a number of moving parts which may affect taxpayers' strategy in dealing with the issues.

Impact on cross-border group tax regimes

20.19 Despite the extensive litigation in relation to the UK's cross-border group and consortium relief rules, there are no changes to the UK's applicable

46 *Corporate Tax (Treatment of Unrelieved Surplus ACT) Regulations 1999, SI 1999/573.*

47 *TCGA 1992, s 104.*

48 See Chapter 4.

regimes in respect of cross-border group relief (or consortium relief) which arise specifically from the UK's departure from the EU.

There is, however, much ongoing litigation in respect of the application of the fundamental freedoms, which will be affected by the UK's legislation as to the impact of EU law after the end of the transition period. That litigation includes *Gallaher Limited v HMRC* [2020] UKUT 0354 (TCC) (which has been referred to the CJEU for a preliminary ruling) and *VolkerRail Ltd & Ors v HMRC* [2020] UKFTT 476 (TC).

Tax ramifications for cross-border mergers and transfers of residence

20.20 There are no changes to the UK's applicable regime in respect of cross-border mergers and transfers of residence which arise specifically from the UK's departure from the EU.

Other

20.21 It is this area where the UK is most likely to see some potential for diversion from the EU's position in future. At present, all measures remain the same, but since the referendum the UK government has indicated an interest in ensuring the UK is a tax competitive jurisdiction, to varying degrees, as leadership has changed. That said, while the UK may not have to comply with Directives, for example, on anti-tax avoidance, the UK's involvement in the OECD's action points on BEPS means that it unlikely to deviate from BEPS outcomes. In practice, therefore, the ability of the UK to deviate very far from the EU's position may be limited. This is highly dependent on the policy of the government of the day.

Anti-tax avoidance

20.22 While the UK has made no changes to the UK's applicable regime in respect of anti-tax avoidance measures which arise specifically from the UK's departure from the EU, future EU law measures agreed in respect of anti-tax avoidance will not bind the UK.

The UK is highly likely to continue to comply with OECD measures. Initial concerns that the UK intended to position itself as a low tax jurisdiction have not yet been borne out by changes in announced tax policy. Article 5.2 of the Second Part, Title XI, Chapter 5 of the TCA provides for Taxation Standards, specifically that a party shall not weaken or reduce the level of protection provided for in its legislation below the level provided for by the standards and rules which have been agreed in the OECD at the end of the transition period in relation to exchange of information concerning financial accounts, cross-border tax rulings, country by country reports between tax administrations and potential cross-border tax planning arrangements, as well as in relation to the rules on interest limitation, CFCs and hybrid mismatches. It also provides that a party shall not weaken or reduce the level of protection provided for in its legislation at the end of the transition period in respect of public country by country reporting by credit institutions and investment firms, other than small and non-interconnected investment firms.

Tax incentives to attract businesses

20.23 Spring Budget 2021 contains some measures which might be thought of as tax incentives intended to attract business after the end of the transitional period (such as the super-deduction) but it remains to be seen whether the economic result of those changes is in practice of incentive effect.

Recent focus has, of course, been on stimulus measures following the impact of COVID-19 on the UK's economy, and the measures have been of largely domestic impact.

II THE UK AS A THIRD COUNTRY

Free movement of capital

20.24 To the extent that a taxpayer is impacted by measures in its member state of the EU which breach Article 63 TFEU in relation to capital movements to the UK, that taxpayer may be able to rely on Article 63 TFEU. There will, however, be practical difficulties in doing so, not least as to the issue of which fundamental freedom prevails when, on the face of it, more than one may be applicable.[49]

Article 63 TFEU is, of course, subject also to Article 65, which provides that the provisions of Article 63 shall be without prejudice to the right of Member States to apply the relevant provisions of their tax law which distinguish between taxpayers who are not in the same situation with regard to their place of residence or with regard to the place where their capital is invested. That is in turn subject to the caveat that Article 65(1) shall nonetheless not constitute a means of 'arbitrary discrimination' or a disguised restriction on the free movement of capital and payments. Based on the interpretation of Article 63 by the CJEU, the free movement of capital shall be applied, in substance, like the other fundamental freedoms in respect of non-discrimination between residents and non-residents.

49 See, eg, *Fidium Finanz* (Case C-452/04).

The nomenclature at Annex 1 of Directive 88/361/EEC provides a definition of a movement of capital, as held by the CJEU.[50]

III TAX DISPUTES IN THE UK

Procedure

20.25 The law as it is to be applied by English courts and tribunals has been set out elsewhere in this book.[51] This section considers the impact of those principles on current tax disputes, and sets out some areas in which there is already a difference in approach between the implementation of EU law between courts and tribunals in the UK and the European Courts.

The effect of the statutory regime relating to EU law after UK's departure from the EU[52] is that the CJEU will hear and determine proceedings brought before 31 December 2020,[53] and its decisions will be binding whenever they are decided. Proceedings which are pending before a UK court or tribunal can therefore proceed to finality, and references could be made to the CJEU before the end of the transition period,[54] whose rulings will be binding in these circumstances even after 31 December 2020. Other than in cases where the proceedings have been initiated before 31 December 2020, decisions of the CJEU will generally not be binding, as set out in more detail elsewhere in this book.[55]

The position is similar in respect of state aid proceedings. Pending state aid administrative proceedings may run their course, during which the European Commission retains its powers, including those to ensure proper recovery of the aid.[56] In addition, the European Commission can still institute proceedings in respect of aid received before 31 December 2020, up until 31 December 2024, through the European courts.[57]

In practical terms, for tax disputes before the UK courts and tribunals, matters in respect of which a reference may be needed had to be before the courts before 31 December 2020, and a reference sought before then also. As a further practical note, a request for a preliminary ruling will be considered to have been made when the document initiating the proceedings has been registered by the registry of the Court of Justice (or General Court, as appropriate). Domestically in the UK, this required the court to order a request

50 *Commission v Germany* (Case C-112/05).

51 [Cross reference Julian Ghosh's chapter].

52 *European Union (Withdrawal Agreement) Act 2020* (*EUWAA 2020*) and *European Union (Withdrawal) Act 2018* (*EUWA 2018*).

53 Article 86(1) Withdrawal Agreement.

54 Article 86(2) Withdrawal Agreement.

55 [Cross reference to the paragraphs in Julian's chapter].

56 Article 92 Withdrawal Agreement.

57 [Cross refer to Conor Quigley's chapter] Article 87(1) Withdrawal Agreement.

for a preliminary ruling, and for that order to be transmitted to the Court of Justice, all of which required a number of administrative steps to be taken.

It should also be noted that the English courts chose not to approve an early request for a preliminary ruling from the CJEU simply because of the timing of the end of the transition period. In *Coal Staff Superannuation Scheme Trustees Limited v The Commissioners for Her Majesty's Revenue and Customs* [2017] UKUT 137 (TCC), Mrs Justice Rose (as she then was) considered an application to the Upper Tribunal for an immediate reference to the CJEU in respect of questions which it was argued had to be answered before the Tribunal could dispose of an appeal from the decision of the First-tier Tribunal (Tax Chamber). The appeal to the Upper Tribunal had not yet been heard. It was argued for the appellant that the sole issue concerned the compatibility of domestic law with EU law. It was accepted that it would be unusual for the Tribunal to make a reference to the CJEU without first hearing the appeal, but it was argued that 'we live in unusual times'. Specifically, shortly after the hearing of the application, the government served its notice under Article 50(2) TEU. It was argued that in the circumstances arising from the service of the Article 50 notice, the Upper Tribunal was in effect a tribunal of a Member State against whose decision there is no judicial remedy under national law, and if that is the case, the Upper Tribunal must make a reference of a question if a decision is necessary to enable it to give a judgment on the appeal. In the alternative, it was submitted that even if the Upper Tribunal was not required to make a reference, the UK's departure from the EU meant that the Tribunal should exercise the discretion in Article 267(2) in favour of referring the question.

HMRC submitted that there was no justification for the Tribunal to depart from its usual practice. It is noted that with the benefit of hindsight, assisted by the subsequent Withdrawal Agreement, there was in fact some time before the UK courts would become unable to seek a preliminary ruling from the CJEU. However, at the time the application was made, that was not clear.

In the event the court rejected the application on the basis that it was difficult to decide at that stage how many questions would need to be referred and on what issues, that the Tribunal would be assisted by having a full grasp of both parties' contentions before deciding whether a reference was necessary, and thirdly the likelihood of the case having repercussions beyond the facts of the case itself was limited. It was also held that there was a body of case law from the CJEU which was applicable and that the lower courts had considered cases and concluded that it was the application of those principles which was the issue between the parties. On that basis, the court held that a preliminary ruling could not be said to be necessary at that stage.

Another practical matter to consider is what the wording of Article 86 means in the context of a tax dispute. Article 86 states that the CJEU '*shall continue to have jurisdiction in any proceedings brought by or against the United Kingdom before the end of the transition period*'. In domestic tax disputes there are a number of ways a taxpayer can start a dispute. There is a statutory dispute mechanism which requires notification to HMRC of an appeal, and permits a review of a decision by HMRC, before that decision is appealed to the FTT. The appeal itself is a formal process before the First-tier Tax Tribunal which commences proceedings there. Other methods of challenging tax decisions include judicial review, where a decision may be challenged on public law grounds. There, a letter before action is good practice, but 'proceedings' may not be initiated until a claim has been issued. One view as to what is required in order to fall in the scope of Article 86(1) is that if the matter is within the procedure for appealing a tax liability, then an appeal notice must be filed with the Tax Tribunal before the end of the transition period. Others consider that a taxpayer dispute may fall within those circumstances prior to a notice of appeal being issued.

Substantive divergences

20.26 Domestic courts' implementation of EU law often diverges across the EU. The UK's courts are not alone in that regard. There are some areas of divergence which may be particularly relevant in this context. This section gives a flavour of some divergences which already exist and which, while they are currently relatively minor, may result in domestic law in the UK developing along a different line to the EU's case law.

For example, one might consider a situation in which an arm's length principle is applied in relation to a transaction in order to identify whether conditions of free competition (and therefore no selective advantage) exists.[58] In the context of that judgment an arm's length principle was considered to be a suitable benchmark to verify that there was no advantage.

In a different context, namely a case concerning whether an arm's length principle breached the freedom of establishment, the CJEU considered[59] a situation in which the taxpayer's arrangements were not on arm's length terms, but there was nonetheless a commercial reason for the arrangements. The German tax authority in that case argued that the concept of a 'commercial justification' in that context must be interpreted

> 'in the light of the principle of free competition, which, by its nature, rules out acceptance of economic reasons resulting from the position of the shareholder.'

The Court then noted that it was clear that the group companies had negative equity capital and the financing bank made the granting of loans required for the continuation and expansion of business operations contingent on the

58 *Ireland, Apple v Commission* (Cases T-778/16 and T-892/16), para 194.
59 *Hornbach-Baumarkt* (Case C-382/16).

provision of comfort letters by the parent company. The court then went on to hold:

> '54. In a situation where the expansion of the business operations of a subsidiary requires additional capital due to the fact that it lacks sufficient equity capital, there may be commercial reasons for a parent company to agree to provide capital on non-arm's-length terms.'

The Court then proceeded to conclude that:

> '56. Accordingly, there may be a commercial justification by virtue of the fact that Hornbach-Baumarkt AG is a shareholder in the foreign group companies, which would justify the conclusion of the transaction at issue in the main proceedings under terms that deviated from arm's length terms. Since the continuation and expansion of the business operations of those foreign companies was contingent, due to a lack of sufficient equity capital, upon a provision of capital, the gratuitous granting of comfort letters containing a guarantee statement, even though companies independent from one another would have agreed on remuneration for such guarantees, could be explained by the economic interest of Hornbach-Baumarkt AG itself in the financial success of the foreign group companies, in which it participates through the distribution of profits, as well as by a certain responsibility of the applicant in the main proceedings, as a shareholder, in the financing of those companies.'

In this example, the CJEU concludes that when considering the arm's length principle (in the context of a challenge based on the fundamental freedoms), in order for the tax law under consideration to be considered proportionate, it must take account of the characteristic of the parent company which is its interest in the financial success in its subsidiary. That reads like a caveat to the arm's length principle to take account of the characteristics of the investor.

One reason this is pertinent to the UK in the context of Brexit is that the English courts rejected[60] this very argument (by majority, with Arden LJ (as she then was) dissenting, and taking a similar view to the CJEU in *Hornbach-Baumarkt).* The Court of Appeal held that the arm's length test is what would have been agreed under fully competitive conditions. It rejected the taxpayers' argument that where the transaction was not on arm's length terms, EU law required the UK to allow taxpayers to prove that it was nonetheless done for a commercial purpose.

In response to the taxpayers' argument that, when applying the arm's length test to a subsidiary within a group of companies, it was necessary to take account of the fact the subsidiary is within the group, the Court of Appeal held that there was nothing in the *Thin Cap GLO* judgment in the CJEU (Case C-524/04) to suggest that UK legislation might be incompatible because of its

60 *Thin Cap GLO* [2011] EWCA Civ 127.

failure to take into account a subsidiary's membership of a non-UK group of companies.

Dissenting, Arden LJ held that: 'While it might be tempting to think that, if a transaction fails to meet a test of arm's length, it cannot be commercial, it is necessary to recall the jurisprudence of the court prior to Thin Cap [i.e. Lankhorst-Hohorst] and the context in which the question of what is commercial arises' (underline emphasis added).

There would appear then, to be a potential disparity between how the English courts and the European courts have dealt with the arm's length principle, and specifically whether a commercial purpose and context justifies a departure from it.

Since the TCA contains a different regime than the EU state aid regime, and of course, the UK will also be subject to subsidy control in other regimes (the domestic regime, WTO subsidy rules and any future FTA subsidy rules), the application of those rules to tax will be important. Subtle differences of approach could have substantial effects.

Further potential for substantive divergence arises from the TCA's subsidy rules and the current consultation on 'Subsidy Control: designing a new approach for the UK'. The consultation is very broad ranging and includes questions on objectives the Government should consider for its subsidy control regime. Other topics which are the subject of consultation are transparency, who should enforce state aid law, the publication of competition impact reviews, and the implementation of the recovery power. Any of those could be relevant to how subsidy control of tax measures works in practice in future.

One key point of practical importance in relation to the application of state aid law to tax is that it is only in rare circumstances that taxpayers are able to mount a challenge on the basis their competitor has received a subsidy, as information as to a taxpayer's tax treatment is not usually in the public domain. As such, in practice state aid challenges in relation to tax were usually brought by the European Commission. However, the TCA makes specific provision for transparency in relation to tax measures, specifying that certain listed information 'shall be made public within one year from the date the tax declaration is due'. As the consultation picks up what transparency measures should apply in the UK's domestic regime, the practical effect of the TCA and the UK's domestic subsidy control regime could lead to an increase in competitor challenges to tax subsidies.

IV EU LEVEL TAX DISPUTE AND INFORMATION MECHANISMS

20.27 To the extent that the UK's implementation of EU law mechanisms are also based on following BEPS, it is unlikely that the UK's departure from the EU will lead to changes. Council Directive 2011/16/EU on administrative cooperation in the field of taxation and its consequential amendments which provide for exchange of information between Member States' tax authorities, and the UK's implementing legislation on this and other international measures to improve tax transparency is unlikely to change to any significant extent.

The UK has made regulations (the *Taxes (Amendments) (EU Exit) Regulations 2019, SI 2019/689* which include provisions permitting disclosure of information to authorised officers of authorities in jurisdictions where there are arrangements for international tax enforcement.

Similarly, Council Directive (EU) 2018/822 on mandatory automatic exchange of information in the field of taxation, which introduces mandatory disclosure rules for intermediaries where there are cross border arrangements with specific hallmarks has been implemented in the UK in *International Tax Enforcement (Disclosable Arrangements) Regulations 2020, SI 2020/25.*

The *Double Taxation Dispute Resolution (EU) Regulations 2020, SI 2020/51* were made on 22 January 2020 to implement Council Directive (EU) 2017/1852 on tax dispute resolution mechanisms in the EU (and a Tax Information and Impact Note was published at the same time, making reference to the measure building on the UK's network of bilateral tax treaties with other Member States and the Arbitration Convention (90/463/EEC)).

As to the use of the Arbitration Convention, the UK has updated its guidance to note that 'No new MAP claims will be accepted under the Convention from 1 January 2021'.[61] It has also published elsewhere[62] that 'No new MAP claims will be accepted under either the Arbitration Directive or the Union Arbitration Convention from 1 January 2021' and notes that the measure will be monitored and assessed by the European Commission (with the Arbitration Directive requiring evaluation by 30 June 2025).

In practical terms, taxpayers sometimes have cross border tax issues where there is no challenge available based on freedom of movement or where there is no applicable legislation which would resolve their cross-border tax issue. One such example is where there is a technical fault in the system for cross border refunds of VAT, which falls outside the scope of the rules on reasons for refusal and the consequent appeals. In circumstances like those, one available option was to complain to the European Commission to request it to start infraction proceedings. The availability of that mechanism after the transition period is dealt with elsewhere in this book,[63] but it is sufficient to say here that in circumstances where a taxpayer may previously have chosen to try to resolve their issue in this way, the opportunity to do so is now curtailed.

---

61 www.gov.uk/guidance/double-taxation-objecting-if-your-company-isnt-being-taxed-correctly.

62 www.gov.uk/government/publications/legislating-the-double-taxation-dispute-resolution-eu-regulations-2020/legislating-the-double-taxation-dispute-resolution-eu-regulations-2020.

63 See Chapter 1.

V CONCLUSION

20.28 In conclusion then, at present the UK's tax laws remain largely unchanged, although changes to substantive tax laws are anticipated in future. That will particularly be the case once the UK has time to make tax policy beyond the current impact of COVID-19, and once there is more clarity as to the UK's future relationship with the EU. Tax competition is a highly political and highly disputed area between the UK and the EU, as is the impact of state aid law generally. Further change can be expected.

Index

[All references are to paragraph number.]